Family Law, Sex and Sc

Comparative in both approach and framework, *Family Law, Sex and Society* provides a critical exposition of key areas in family law, exploring their evolution and development within their historical, cultural, political and legal context.

Cross-referencing to English law throughout, this comparative textbook pays particular attention to the transformation of marriage; the development of divorce laws; matrimonial property; the legal recognition of unmarried heterosexual and same-sex cohabitants; the universal adoption of the best interests standard for children in domestic and international legislation; and the impact of the Human Rights Act 1998 on family law in a variety of jurisdictions.

Family Law, Sex and Society covers:

- A jurisdictional and historical survey of some of the main themes in family law, as well as consideration of the evolution of the Western family.
- The English law relating to divorce, marital property and children, and a comparison with the equivalent law in the civil law jurisdictions of France and Germany.
- Family law developments in other common law countries such as Australia and New Zealand, selected American jurisdictions, parts of Africa and some Far Eastern countries, and hybrid jurisdictions such as Japan and Russia.
- An analysis of the law relating to unmarried cohabitation and domestic partnerships in civil law jurisdictions such as France, Germany and Sweden in comparison with Anglo-American law.
- A comparative analysis of the laws relating to domestic violence.

Family Law, Sex and Society offers valuable socio-legal and socio-cultural insights into the practice of family law, and is the only textbook that provides a unified, coherent and comparative approach to the study of family law as it operates in these particular jurisdictions.

Peter de Cruz, LLB. LLM. PhD, is Professor of Law at Liverpool John Moores University.

Family Law, Sex and Society

A Comparative Study of Family Law

Peter de Cruz

Taylor & Francis Group

LONDON AND NEW YORK

Published 2010 by Routledge
2 Park Square, Milton Park, Abingdon, Oxon, OX14 4RN

Simultaneously published in the USA and Canada
by Routledge
270 Madison Avenue, New York, NY 10016

Routledge is an imprint of the Taylor & Francis Group, an informa business

© 2010 Peter de Cruz

Typeset in Times New Roman by
Pindar NZ, Auckland, New Zealand

Printed and bound in Great Britain by
CPI Antony Rowe, Chippenham, Wiltshire

British Library Cataloguing in Publication Data
A catalogue record for this book is available from the British Library

Library of Congress Cataloging-in-Publication Data
De Cruz, Peter.
Family law, sex, and society : a comparative study of family law /
Peter de Cruz.
    p. cm.
1. Domestic relations. I. Title.
K670.D3 2009
346.01'5—dc22   2009032319

ISBN-13: 978-1-85941-638-9 (pbk)
ISBN-10: 1-85941-638-1 (pbk)

ISBN-13: 978-0-415-48430-5 (hbk)
ISBN-10: 0-415-48430-8 (hbk)

eISBN-13: 978-0-203-85862-2 (ebook)
eISBN-10: 0-203-85862-X (ebook)

Contents

Preface   vii
Table of cases   x

PART I
Introductory overview   1

PART II
Jurisdictional survey   39

1   Family law in Europe   41
2   Family law in the United States   75
3   Family law in Australia and New Zealand   114
4   Family law in Africa and Asia   148
5   Family law in the Russian Federation   202
6   Family law in Japan: the Japanese family – between
    tradition and modernity   223

PART III
**Cohabitation, informal unions and civil
partnerships in comparative perspective**   237

PART IV
Domestic violence – a comparative survey   285

PART V
The impact of human rights law on family law   319

PART VI
**Common themes, key debates and
comparative overview**   357

Index   403

Preface

This book is a comparative and historical study of the development of family law in a range of jurisdictions, and examines the common themes which emerge from their responses to the central questions in family law, namely, their approach to the 'family', matrimonial property, divorce and the legal position of children in these jurisdictions, usually in the context of post-divorce arrangements.

This highly selective study looks at certain common law and civil law jurisdictions, which is typical of comparativist ventures, and also includes jurisdictions such as Japan, Russia and South Africa, which is not. This book may be regarded as the first phase in an ongoing research enterprise. The first stage, which forms the content of this book, attempts to present a brief conspectus of the family law in these regions, informed, as far as possible, by a brief look at their history, sources of law, legal style, distinctive or characteristic institutions and a brief overview of the ways in which they have dealt with common problems related to family law. The objective is to identify common themes and common responses and also to seek to discover, at least in some measure, how and why the particular jurisdiction has reached its current stage of development in its family law. The second stage will attempt to explore the socio-legal environment of these jurisdictions in greater detail and the final stage will delve more deeply into non-Western jurisdictions whose particular development merits individual attention by exploring broader questions such as the impact of culture, religion and the political backdrop within which the family law in these regions has evolved. Of course, all three of these stages are examined to some extent in this book but an analysis of all the developments that have taken place in all these jurisdictions would require a book at least twice the size of this one. At this stage, this book simply hopes to stimulate interest in comparative study in family law and to lay down a marker on how such study might be undertaken.

Consequently, the book does not claim to offer definitive findings but seeks to paint a broad canvas on which an historical, cultural and legal landscape can be configured. It offers some pointers as to how communities divided by oceans, language and culture have responded to similar or common problems and how similar challenges and sometimes solutions have arisen and been selected across the world. It also considers, albeit briefly, the viability of legal transplants in family law, a subject which has exercised comparatists for many years and will doubtless continue to do so.

No doubt the jurisdictions selected, the features highlighted and the conclusions drawn are open to debate. There are certainly other topics which I would have liked to include such as adoption, child abduction and child support. Throughout the book, comparative observations will be made, usually at the end of a chapter or a section. The final chapter seeks to bring together the various common themes which have arisen through the study and reviews the last few decades of family law in a range of jurisdictions.

Part I is an *Introductory Overview* of the basic elements in our study, examining terminological questions, then tracing the development of marriage, sex and the evolution of the Western family, divorce, the property aspects of family law and the relevance that fault still plays in various aspects of family law. It also considers the convergence/divergence debate and discusses the various methodological approaches to our present comparative enterprise.

Part II contains the *Jurisdictional Survey*. It commences with *Chapter One*, dealing with family law in Europe, which is an historical and contemporary survey of divorce and its consequences in terms of property distribution, marital property and the legal approach to children. The chapter focuses on the common law jurisdiction of England in comparison with two examples of civil law countries, France and Germany.

Chapter Two examines family law in the United States, briefly tracing the evolution of the family, divorce, property distribution and the American legal approach to children in the context of relationship breakdown. It also considers child protection in the United States.

Chapter Three deals with aspects of family law in Australia and New Zealand which are Western jurisdictions situated in non-Western localities.

Chapter Four considers family law in countries in non-Western post-colonial regions.

Africa, and South Africa in particular, is a mixture of legal systems and various foreign influences. India, Hong Kong and Singapore may be classified as common law countries as they have a strong British heritage, with case law as their main source of law, supplemented by statutes. All continue to recognise customary law from time to time.

Chapter Five examines the development of family law in the Russian Federation, which was predominantly a civil law country before it adopted a socialist system. It is closest to a civil law system with traces of its socialist history in its style of legislation.

Chapter Six explores the historical development of family law in Japan, which is also selected because of its unique mixed heritage.

Part III is a comparative study of *Cohabitation, Informal Unions and Civil Partnerships*, and includes same-sex and opposite sex unions and civil partnerships in both common law and civil law jurisdictions.

Part IV presents a comparative conspectus of *Domestic Violence* in various common law and civil law jurisdictions.

Part V is a study of the *Impact of Human Rights Law on Family Law*. The main focus is on European family law and the European Convention on Human Rights.

Part VI reviews the *Common Themes and Key Debates*, past and present, in the family law of various jurisdictions and seeks to evaluate and develop some of the ideas and issues raised in the preceding chapters.

This book has been a long time in gestation and I would like to acknowledge the assistance of Newcastle University Law Library and various law librarians who were kind enough to allow me access to materials over many years, Joanne Beswick (Staffordshire University Law School) for her help in procuring online materials, and Anne Sanders (formerly English Law Commission) for supplying me with information on recent changes in German maintenance law. I also wish to thank Jo Reddy and Sonny Leong who were the original supporters of this book and who constantly offered encouragement over the years when they were at the forefront of commissioning new works from relatively unknown authors. Thanks are also due to the staff at Routledge, for being so patient with the submission of the book, especially Lloyd Langman. I would also like to thank Frank Murphy for permission to use two lines from his poem, and for his intellectual stimulation, insights and moral support over many years. As usual, all errors and inaccuracies remain the writer's sole responsibility.

Finally, I would like to dedicate this book to my wife, Lois, for her constant love and support over three decades, and to my late parents, who first sparked my interest in comparative study, and who would have been amazed at the speed and scope of the developments in family law over the past few decades.

Peter de Cruz
Liverpool John Moores University
August 2009

Table of cases

Abdulaziz, Cabales and Balkandali (A/94) (1985) 7 EHRR 471 (EU) 330
Ahmut v The Netherlands (1997) 24 EHRR 62 (EU)...331
Airey v Ireland (A/32) (1979) 2 EHRR 305 (EU) 326
Anon 55 Ala 433 (1876) (US) 97
Anufrijeva v Southwark London Borough Council [2004] 1 AC 604 (UK) 354
Application No. 12513 v United Kingdom (1989) 11 EHRR 46 (EU) 328
Ashingdane v United Kingdom (A/93) (1985) 7 EHRR 528 (EU) 324
Attorney-General of Nova Scotia v Walsh (2002) 4 SCR 325 (Canada) 264

B v B [1997] 1 FLR 139 (UK)..56
B v B [1998] 2 FLR 490 (UK)..30
B v B [2002] 1 FLR 555 (UK)..96
B v S (1995) (3) SA 571 (South Africa)..168
Baiai v Secretary of State for the Home Department [2007] 2 FLR 627 (Court of Appeal)
    (UK)...324–6
Baker Vermont 744 A 2d 864 (1999) (US) 8
Baxter v Baxter [1948] AC 27 (UK)..7
Beckman v Mayhew 49 Cal App 3d 529 (1975) (US)...252
Bellinger v Bellinger [2002] 1 FLR 1043 (UK) 335–6
Bergen v Wood 14 Cal App 4th 854 (1993) (US) 254
Berrehab v The Netherlands (A/138) (1988) 11 EHRR 322 (EU) 330–1, 347
Best v Best (1993) FLC 92–418 (Aus) 127–8
BGH NJW 1979 (Germany) 67
Blackwell v Blackwell [1943] 2 All ER 579 (UK)..323
Booysen v Minister of Home Affairs [2001] 7 BCLR 654 (CC) (South Africa)...........167
Boyle v United Kingdom (1995) 19 EHRR 179 (EU)...331
Buchberger v Austria, Application No. 32899/96 (EU) 344
Burden v United Kingdom [2008] STC 252 (EU)..247
Burns v Burns [1984] Ch 317 (UK)..242–3, 254
Bury Metropolitan Borough Council v D [2009] EWHC 446 (UK) 350
Byrne v Laura 52 Cal App 4th 1054 (1997) (US) 255

C v C [1980] Fam 23 (UK)..191
C v C [1988] 2 FLR 291 (UK)...56
C v C [1990] 2 HKLR 183 (Hong Kong) 180–1

Carhart v Stenberg 530 US 914 (2000) (US)..365
Chan Chiu Lam v Yau Yee Ping [1998] 2 HKC 569 (Hong Kong)..............................178
Chan Yong Keay v Yeo Mei Ling [1994] 2 SLR 541 (Singapore) 195
Choa Choon Neoh v Spottiswoode (1869) 1 Ky 216 (Singapore)..................................187
Choo Eng Neo v Neo Chan-Neo (1908) 12 SSLR 120 (Singapore)...............................188
CIR v Van Doorme [1983] NZLR 495 (NZ)..137
Clark v Clark [1999] 2 FLR 498 (UK) 96
Clauson v Clauson (1995) FLC 92–595 (Aus) 128
Cleary v Cleary [1974] 1 All ER 501 (UK)..45
Cooke v Head [1972] 2 All ER 38 (UK) 244
Corbett v Corbett [1971] P 83 (UK) 332, 335
Cour d'Appel de Douai, 27 Fevrier 2003, AJ Famille 2003 p. 313 (France).................272

D- E v A- G (1845) 1 Rob Eccl 279 (UK)..7
D v H [2000] NZLR 242 (NZ)..145
Davut and Raif (1994) FLC 92–503 (Aus)..127
Devine v Devine 398 So 2d 686 (1981) (US)...98
Dodds v Dodds (1974) (UK)..44
Dravitzki v Methven (2006) FAM 2004–043–000714, 18 January 2006 (NZ) 263
du Toit v Minister of Welfare and Population Development (2003) (2) SA 198 (CC)
    (South Africa)...168
Durga Prasanna v Arunhati (2005) (7) SC 596 (India)..184–5
Durham v Durham (1885) 10 PD 80 (UK) 370

Evans v Evans [1989] 1 FLR 351 (UK)...29, 96
Eves v Eves [1975] 3 All ER 768 (UK)..243–4

F v M [2004] EWHC 727 (UK)..341
Fay v Fay [1982] AC 835 (UK)..191
Fei Tai-chung v Gloria Fei (1995) Court of Appeal Action No 170 of 1994 (HONG
    KONG) 181
Ferraro v Ferraro (1993) FLC 92–335 (Aus)..126
Fisher v Fisher 535 A 2d 1163 (1988) (US) 100, 110
Fitzpatrick v Sterling [2000] 1 FLR 271 (UK)...8, 333
Fletcher v Fletcher (1948) 1 SA 130 (A) (South Africa)..387
Fletcher v People 52 Ill. 395 (1869) (US)..104
Fowler v Barron [2008] EWCA Civ 377 (Court of Appeal) (UK)............................246–7
Friedman v Friedman 29 Cal App 4th 876 (1993 (UK)...254

Gaskin v United Kingdom (1990) 12 EHRR 36 (EU)...331
Ghaidan v Godin-Mendoza [2004] 2 FLR 600 (UK) 333–4, 336, 371
Gillick v West Norfolk and Wisbech Area Health Authority [1985] 3 All ER 402 (HL)
    (UK)...144, 196–7, 220, 389
Gissing v Gissing [1971] AC 886 (UK) 50, 324
Glaser v United Kingdom [2001] 1 FLR 153 (EU) 340–1
Golder v United Kingdom (A/18) (1975) 1 EHRR 524 (EU) 323
Goodrich v Department of Public Health 798 NE 2d 941 (Mass. 2003) (US)................362
Goodwin v United Kingdom [2002] 2 FLR 487 (UK) 332, 334, 336–7

Grant v South West Trains Ltd [1998] All ER 193 (UK)...270

Haase v Germany [2004] 2 FLR 39 (EU)..349–51
Hammond v Mitchell [1992] 2 All ER 109 (UK)..243–4
Hansen v Turkey [2004] 1 FLR 142 (EU)...341
Heysteck (2002) (2) SA 754 (T) (South Africa)..169
Hickey (2003) FLC 93–143 (Aus)..127
Hill v Estate of Westbrook 95 Cal App 599 (1950) (US)..252
Hinton v Hinton 321 SE 2d 161 (1984) (US) 95
Hokkanen v Finland (1994) 19 EHRR 139 (EU)..340, 348
Hopes v Hopes [1948] 2 All ER 920 (UK)...66
Hoppe v Germany [2003] 1 FLR 384 (UK)..340
Hornsby v Greece (1997) 24 EHRR 250 (EU) 340
Hui I-mei v Cheng Yau-shing (1996) Court of Appeal, Civil Appeal Action No 157 of
    1996 (HONG KONG) 181
Hussain v Hussain [1986] 2 FLR 271 (UK) 289
Hyde v Hyde (1866) LR 1 P&D 130 (UK)...7, 153, 370

I v United Kingdom [2002] 2 FLR 518 (UK)..332, 334–5
Ignaccolo-Zenide v Romania (2000) 31 EHRR 212 (EU)..340–1
In Marriage of Jaeger (1994) 122 Fam LR 209 (Aus)...133
In Marriage of JG and BG (1994) 18 Fam LR 255 (Aus) 133
In Marriage of Patsalou (1995) 18 Fam LR 426 (Aus)...133

J v C [1969] 1 All ER 788 (UK)..181
J v C [1970] AC 668 (UK)...345
Jackson (2002) (2) SA 303 (South Africa) 168
Jacob v Schulz-Jacob 923 A 2d 473 (2007) (US)..82
Johansen v Norway (1996) 23 EHRR 33 (EU)..............................331, 344–5, 351–2, 387
Johnson v Calvert 851 P 2d 776 (1993) (US)...83–5, 213
Johnson v Walton [1990] 1 FLR 350 (UK) 289
Johnston v Ireland (A/112) (1986) 9 EHRR 203 (EU) 326, 328, 347
Jones v Jones [1975] 2 All ER 12 (UK) 96

K and T v Finland [2001] 2 FLR 707 (EU) 331
K v K [1988] 1 FLR 469 (UK) 30
K v United Kingdom (No. 11468/85, Commission decision of 15 October 1986) (EU)
   329
Kakali Dass v Dr Asish Kumar (2004) Hindu Law Reporter (1) 448 (India) 184
Keegan v Ireland (A/290) (1994) 18 EHRR 342 (EU).....................................328, 330, 347
Kehoe [2005] 2 FLR 1249 (UK) see R (Kehoe) v Secretary of State for Work and
    Pensions...134
Khabbaz v Commissioner 930 A 2d 1180 (2007) (US)...82
Kinniburgh v Williams [2004] NZFLR 469 (NZ) 138
Kokosinski v Kokosinski [1980] Fam 72 (UK)...30
Kosmopolou v Greece [2004] 1 FCR 427 (EU) 340
Kroon v The Netherlands (A/297-C) (1994) 19 EHRR 263 (EU).............................329–30
Kroopf v Guffey 183 Cal App 3d 1351 (1986) (US)..253

Krugel v Krugel (2003) (6) SA 220 (T) (South Africa)...169

Laerskool Middelburg v Departementshoof Mpumalanga Departement van Inderwys
    (2003) (4) SA 160 (T) (South Africa) 168
Lai Lai-hing v Lai Kwai-ping [1995] 1 HKC 654 (Hong Kong) 181
Lambert v Lambert [2003] 1 FLR 139 (UK)...282
Lambert v Lambert [2003] 2 WLR 63 (UK) 51–2, 379
Lancashire County Council v B [2000] 2 WLR 590 (UK)..31
Laura G v Peter G NYS 2d 496 (App. Div 2007) (US)..82
Lawrence v Texas 123 S Ct 1472 (2003) (US)..250, 362
Leadbeater v Leadbeater [1985] 1 FLR 789 (UK)............................30, 53, 96, 381
Lebbink v The Netherlands (Application No. 45582/99) [2004] 2 FLR 463 (EU).........329
Lehr v Robertson 463 US 248 (1983) (US)...102
Lines v Lines (1963) The Times, 16 July (UK)...46
Loizidou v Turkey (1995) 20 EHRR 99 (EU) 323
Loving v Virginia 388 US 1 (1967) (US)..77
LS v ZJ [2005] NZFLR 932 (NZ)...261
Lynskey v Walsh (No. 2) (1999) Auckland, FP975/95 (NZ) 145

M v H (1999) 2 SCR 3 (Canada) 8
M v H, Tauranga Family Court, FP 070/210/03, 19 May 2004 (NZ).............................261
M v R [1991] NZLR 382 (NZ) 145
McLay v McLay (1996) FLC 92–667 (Aus) 126
McMichael v United Kingdom (A/308) (1995) 20 EHRR (EU) 346
Marckx v Belgium (A/31) (1979) 2 EHRR 330 (EU) 328–9, 331, 346, 393
Martin v Martin [1976] 3 All ER 625 (UK) 96
Marvin v Marvin 134 Cal Reptr 815 (1976) (US)...251–5
Mason v Mason (1980) 11 Fam Law 143 (UK) 45
Michael H v Gerald D 491 US 110 (1989) (US) 76
Midland Bank v Cooke [1995] 2 FLR 915 (UK)...243
Milian v De Leon 181 Cal App 3d 1185 (1986) (US) 254
Miller v Miller [2006] UKHL 24 (UK) 30, 53, 381
Mitchell v Mitchell (1995) FLC 92–601 (Aus) 128
Moore v City of East Cleveland 431 US 494 (1977) (US)..76
Mr X v Hospital Z (1999) All India Report SC 495 (India)...184
Mthembu v Letsela (1997) (2) SA 936 (T) (South Africa)...168
Murphy v Murphy (1992) Court of Appeal, Civil Appeal Action of 1992 (Hong Kong)
   181

National Coalition for Gay and Lesbian Equality v Minister of Home Affairs (2000) (2)
    SA 1 (CC) (South Africa)..164
Naveen Kohli v Neelu Kohli (2006) Judgements Today (3) SC 491 (India) 184
Ng Hwee Keng v Chia Soon Hin William [1995] 2 SLR 231 (Singapore)....................195
Ng Kuk Mui v Yu Big Fong Rebecca (1997) HCAP 2/97 (Hong Kong)....................177–8
Nuutinen v Finland (2000) 34 EHRR 358 (EU) 340

Odievre v France (2003) ECHR No. 42326/98 (EU) 390
Okonkwo v Okagbue (1994) 9 NWLR 301 (Nigeria) 171–2

Olsson v Sweden (No. 1) (1988) 11 EHRR 259 (EU)..326
Om Prakash Bharuka v Shakuntala Modi (1993) All India Reporter 38 (India)............186
O'Neill v O'Neill [1975] 3 All ER 289 (UK)...46
Orr v Orr 440 US 269 (1979) (US)...102
Oxley v Hiscock [2004] EWCA Civ 546 (UK)...243
Oyelowo v Oyelowo (1987) 2 NWLR 239 (Nigeria) 173

P v D (1996) 14 PRNZ 470 (NZ)...144–5
Padilla v Padilla 38 Cal App 2d 319 (1940) (US) 252
Pastrikos (1980) FLC 90–897 (Aus)..127
Paton v United Kingdom (1981) 3 EHRR 408 (EU) 365
Payne v Payne [2001] 1 FLR 1052 (UK)..344–5
Pennings v Pennings 786 A 2d 622 (2001) (US)...87
Perry v West [2004] NZFLR 515 (NZ) 140–1
Pettit v Pettit [1970] AC 777 (UK)..50–1, 324
Planned Parenthood of Central Missouri v Danform 428 US 52 (1976) (US) 365
Planned Parenthood of Southeastern Pennsylvania v Casey 505 US 833 (1992) (US)
....365
Powelson v Powelson (1863) 22 Cal. 358 (US) 79
Prather v Prather 4 Des. 33 (S. C. 1809) (US)..97
Price v United Kingdom (1998) No. 12402/86 (EU)...331
Public Trust v Whyman [2005] 2 NZLR 696 (NZ) 138–9
PZ v JC [2006] NZFLR 97 (NZ) 263

R (Greenfield) v Secretary of State for the Home Department [2005] UKHL 14 (UK)
....354
R (Kehoe) v Secretary of State for Work and Pensions [2005] 2 FLR 1249 (UK).........134
R (Mambakasa) v Secretary of State for the Home Office [2004] QB 1124 (UK).........354
R v Hills [2001] 1 FLR 580 (UK)..293
R v R (Rape: Marital Exemption) [1991] 4 All ER 181 (UK)..........................289–90, 299
Rasmussen v Denmark (A/87) (1985) 7 EHRR 377 (EU)..342
Re A (Children: 1959 UN Declaration) [1998] 1 FLR 354 (UK)...........................56, 143
Re B (Adoption: Sole Natural Parent) [2002] 1 FLR 196 (UK)....................................344
Re B (Care: Interference with Family Life) [2003] 2 FLR 813 (UK) 349
Re Baby M 537 A 2d 1227 (1988) (US)..82–3, 85
Re C (A Minor) (Adoption: Parental Agreement) [1993] 2 FLR 260 (UK).....................31
Re C (Detention: Medical Treatment) [1997] 1 FLR 180 (UK)....................................220
Re Certification of the Republic of South Africa (1996) (4) SA 744 (CC) (South Africa)
....167
Re D [1987] 1 All ER 20 (UK)..350
Re G (Care: Challenge to Local Authority's Decision) [2003] 2 FLR 42 (UK) 327, 340
Re G [2006] UKHL 43 (UK)..55–6
Re H [1991] 3 All ER 185 (UK)..169
Re H [1993] 2 FLR 552 (UK)..389
Re H [1996] 2 FLR 65 (UK)..217
Re H and A (Children) (Paternity: Blood Tests) [2002] 1 FLR 1145 (UK)....................217
Re J (An Infant) [1996] 2 NZLR 134 (NZ) 144
Re L (Care: Assessment: Fair Trial) [2002] 2 FLR 730 (UK)...............................327, 339

Re L [1962] 1 WLR 886 (UK)..54
Re Lao Leong An (1893) 1 SSLR 1 (Singapore)..188
Re M (Contact: Violent Parent) [1999] 2 FLR 321 (UK).......................................31
Re M [1999] 2 FLR 1097 (UK) 389
Re M [2001] 2 FLR 1300...327
Re Marriage of Buzzanca 72 Cal Rptr 2d 280 (1998) (US) 84
Re Moschetta 30 Cal Rptr 2d 893 (1994) (US) 84
Re P [2007] EWCA Civ. 2 (UK) 352–4
Re S (A Minor) (Custody) [1991] 2 FLR 388 (NZ) 143
Re S [1993] 2 FLR 437 (UK) 389
Re S [1993] 3 All ER 36 (UK)..220
Re S [2005] 1 AC 593 (UK)..332
Re T (Paternity: Ordering Blood Tests) [2001] 2 FLR 1190 (UK) 217
Re W (A Minor: Medical Treatment) [1992] 4 All ER 627 (UK).....................220, 389
Re W (A Minor) (Residence Order) [1992] 2 FLR 332 (NZ) 143
Reed v Reed 404 US 71 (1971) (US)...98, 102
Reynolds v United States 98 US 165 (1878) (US) 75
Richards v Richards [1972] 3 All ER 695 (UK)...192
Roberts v Roberts [1994] NZLR 200 (NZ)...137
Rodrigues Da Silva and Hoogkamer v The Netherlands, 2006, 31 January (s. III.C) (EU)
....338
Roper v Roper [1972] 1 WLR 1314 (UK); 3 All ER 668 (UK) 45
RR v MH 689 NE 2d (1998) (US)..85
Ruka v Department of Social Welfare [1997] NZLR 154 (NZ)..............................262

S v S [1982] Fam Law 183 (UK)..96
S v W [2006] NZFLR 699 (NZ) 262
S(BD) v S(D) [1977] 1 All ER 656 (UK)...54
Saffi v Italy (1999) 30 EHRR 756 (EU) 340
Sahin v Germany [2002] 1 FLR 119 (EU)..344
Satchwell v President of the Republic of South Africa (2001) (12) BCLR 1284 (South
    Africa)...164–5
Schafer v Superior Court 180 Cal App 3d 305 (1986) (US)...................................253
Schimdt v Jawad [2006] NZFLR 410 (NZ)..261
Scragg v Scott [2006] NZFLR 1076 (NZ)...262–4
Seddon v Seddon (1862) 2 Sw & Tr 640 (UK) 370
Selmouni v France (2000) 29 EHRR 403 (EU)...328
Sham Sunder v Shushma (2004) (8) SC 166 (India) 184
Shirley Khoo v Kenneth Mok Kong Chua [1989] 2 MLJ 264 (Singapore)............195
Silver v Silver [1958] 1 WLR 259 (UK) 323
Simey v Simey (1881) 1 SC 171 (South Africa) 167
Singh v Entry Clearance Officer, New Delhi [2005] 1 FLR 308 (EU) 330
Sisojeva v Latvia, 2007, 15 January (s. III.B) (EU)..338
Slivenko v Latvia [GC] No. 48321/99, ECHR 2003-X (EU)..............................338–9
Soering v United Kingdom (A/161) (1989) 11 EHRR 439 (EU) 324
Sparks v Sparks 485 NW 2d 893 (1992) (US)...94
Spindlow v Spindlow [1979] 1 All ER 169 (UK)...288
Stack v Dowden [2007] 1 FLR 1858 (UK)..245–6

Stanley v Illinois 405 US 645 (1972) (US)..102
Stringfellow v Stringfellow [1976] 2 All ER 539 (UK)......................................192
Surrogate Parenting Associates, Inc v Commonwealth ex rel. Armstrong 704 SW 2d 209
   (1986) (US)..84
Sylvester v Austria [2003] 2 FLR 210 (EU)..340–1

T v AG (1999) 18 FRNZ 48 (NZ)..144–5
T v M (1988) 5 NZFLR 252 (NZ)..145
T v M (1997) (1) SA 54 (South Africa)..168
Tan Bee Giok v Loh Kum Yong [1997] 1 SLR 155 (Singapore)....................196
Tavoulareas v Tavoulareas [1998] 2 FLR 418 (UK)...30
Taylor v Fields 178 Cal App 3d 653 (1986) (US).......................................253–4
Thomas v Fuller-Brown [1988] 1 FLR 237 (UK)...245
Troxel v Granville 530 US 57 (2000) (US)...75, 388
Trutalli v Meraviglia 215 Cal 698 (1932) (US)...252
Tyler [2004] 4 All SA 115 (South Africa)..169
Tyrer v United Kingdom (A/26) (1978) 2 EHRR 175 (EU)..............................323

Updeck v Samuel 123 Cal App 2d 264 (1954) (US)..252

V v V (1998) (4) SA 169 (C) (South Africa)..167, 169–70
Van Rooyen (1999) (4) SA 435 (C) (South Africa)..168
Van Zijl v Hoogenhout [2004] 4 All SA 427 (SCA) (South Africa)................168
Venema v The Netherlands [2003] 1 FLR 552 (EU)...........................350–1, 353
Village of Belle Terre v Boraas 416 US 1 (1974) (US).......................................76

W and W v H (Child Abduction: Surrogacy) [2002] 1 FLR 1008 (UK).........85–6
W v United Kingdom (1987) 10 EHRR 29 (UK)..353
Wachtel v Wachtel [1973] Fam 72 (UK)..29
White v White [2000] 2 FLR 981 (UK)..181, 282
White v White [2001] 1 AC 596 (UK)...51–3, 379–80
Wilkinson v Kitzinger (No. 2) [2007] 1 FLR 295 (UK).............7, 266–7, 273, 281, 337–8

X, Y and Z v United Kingdom [1997] 3 FCR 341 (EU).....................................329

Yah Cheng Huat v Ong Bee Lan (1995, Div Pet. 1147/1995) (Singapore).....196
Yip Mei Ling Agnes v Tan Thiam Chye [2003] SGDC 99 (Singapore).........196
Yousef v The Netherlands [2004] 1 FLR 210 (EU)...349
Yudhister Singh v Sarita (2004) Hindu Law Reporter (1) 228 (India).............184

Zablocki v Redhail 434 US 374 (1978) (US)..77–8

Part I

Introductory overview

Introduction

This chapter provides a preliminary overview of the fundamental terminology and historical background to some of the key topics that underlie our study of selected aspects of family law – such as the classification of sources of family law, the legal relevance of sex in family law, the evolution of the Western family, trends in marriage, changes in the marital dyad and an overview of the property aspects of marriage – before presenting a global survey of divorce laws, exploring in particular the relevance of the 'fault/no-fault divide' in the divorce grounds of various jurisdictions. This introduction provides a comparative historical backdrop to our subsequent study of individual jurisdictions and explores the central concepts underpinning the multi-faceted prism that is family law. The chapter concludes with a review of the possible methodological approaches that are available to a comparatist looking at the development of family law in different jurisdictions and clarifies the approach adopted for this book.

Terminology

Defining 'Family Law'

According to the *International Encyclopaedia of Comparative Law*, family law may be defined as 'the private aspects of marriage, the parent-child relationship, guardianship ... and those ... matters as to which kinship is relevant, ie such duties of support as are established in modern laws among kindred other than parent and child' (Rheinstein, 1974, p. 3). The custom of grouping these topics under the heading of family law was developed by the German Pandectists of the nineteenth century.

In Anglo-American jurisdictions, the older term was the Law of Domestic Relations.

In the last three decades, 'one of the major developments in family law has been an increase in challenges to legal definitions of marriage and the family by individuals and interest groups seeking legal validation of non-traditional lifestyles' (Glendon, 2006, p. 3).

Another definition of family law has been suggested by Krause, one of the doyens of comparative family law, who says: 'Family Law involves the rules by which men and women establish intimate relationships that have legal consequences' (Krause, 2008, p. 1111). In a similarly broad vein, Herring states: 'Family Law is usually seen as the law governing the relationships between children and parents, and between adults in close emotional relationships' (Herring, 2007, p. 13).

Writing towards the end of the last century, Willekens stated that family law has been concerned with the organization of three types of relationships, namely, between cohabiting sexual partners, between parents and children and between members of the nuclear family and those of the more extended family.

Significantly, he points out that these three types of relations are, to a certain extent, regulated independently of each other (Willekens, 1998, p. 48), since, for instance, the status of a child cannot be simply inferred from the legal relations between its parents. As Willekens expresses it, legitimacy was the focal point of family law (Willekens, 1998, p. 49).

The current editors of a leading family law textbook, Masson, Bailey-Harris and Probert, argue that the many complicated changes concerning the law, families and family life make a straightforward definition virtually impossible. This is because a definition would have to encompass a wide variety of family forms and functions, and although much of family law deals with issues of *status* such as determining who may marry or enter into a civil partnership, it is also concerned with 'setting out the *rights and responsibilities flowing from the status of being a spouse, civil partner or parent* (Masson, Bailey-Harris, Probert, 2008, p. 3) (emphasis added). Moreover, they highlight a third key element in family law, which is the protection of the weaker members of the family, in providing legal remedies for adults who suffer violence from other family members and 'in allowing state intervention to protect children who suffer at the hands of their parents or other family members' (Masson, Bailey-Harris, Probert, 2008, p. 3).

The immutability of family norms

The family has always existed in various forms and, as Konig has pointed out, no known society has had only one family type. Konig also points out that kinship relations are less subject to fluctuation than ideas about the relations between men and women: 'Ideas concerning the topic of love and marriage are much more diverse and flexible than the structure of the family. While notions of marriage often change with fashion, the family as a universal human institution is not so easily changed' (Konig, 2003, Ch 1 and s. 39).

Diduck and Kaganas also make the important point that although the law's attempts to define the family adopt a functional approach (although the functions may nowadays be more open to debate than previously), they 'remain within an ideal in which conjugality and the privatization of care and dependency are central' and 'law's model is still the "private, heterosexual, traditional family"' (Diduck and Kaganas, 2006, p. 23). Hence while the range of people who may be allowed into it may have increased, the norms by which they live remain the same (Diduck, 2001).

Family law has a long history

Cretney reminds us that going back 2000 years, the people of Israel with whom Christ lived and worked, had a sophisticated and developed system of family law (Cretney, 2000, p. 1). However, despite the Gospels proclaiming the indissolubility of marriage, Cretney points out that there was very little in the Mosaic laws about family obligations. The Canonists, drawing upon Roman law, developed a 'huge body of doctrine concerning marriage and the family' (Cretney, 2000, p. 1). As is well known and documented, the church had in Europe 'exclusive jurisdiction over marriage and its consequences' for hundreds of years (Cretney, 2000, p. 1). This has meant that with the virtual disappearance of such control, family law has had to adapt to modern conditions while grappling with its heritage of a set of established beliefs and value systems.

Classification and sources of family law in various jurisdictions

The English legal tradition, the so-called 'common law tradition', relied on case law as its main source of law for many centuries. This was gradually supplemented by statute law, the volume of which reached its height in the 1980s during the Thatcher government's era when a mountain of legislation, primary and subordinate, was passed. This was exemplified in a series of statutory instruments seeking to clarify the main child support law. Family law has therefore been contained primarily in case law, supplemented by a few major statutes such as the Children Act 1989 and the Matrimonial Causes Act 1973, which has been amended several times. English family law remains primarily derived from case law, supplemented by statutory codes, which themselves require judicial interpretation and whose meaning has to be ascertained through a study of the case law.

In civil law countries (countries which inherited a history of Roman law) such as France, however, the French Civil Code of 1804 and those codes which followed its pattern, deal in some detail with the formation, incidents and dissolution of marriage, relationships of parent and child and other kindred and guardianship. These are found in the First Book (*On Persons*), whereas the title on marital property, called *On the Marital Contract and on Matrimonial Regimes* is the fifth title of the Third Book, which is entitled *On the Different Ways of Acquiring Property* (Rheinstein, 1974, p. 3).

In countries such as the former Soviet Russia, which may be classified as a hybrid jurisdiction (as it began with civil law traditions then adopted Socialist/ Marxist/Leninist laws before becoming a federation of states, with 'democratic' and capitalist laws) special legislative treatment was given to family law, contained in codes or authoritative statutory collections. This trend has continued beyond the disintegration of the former Soviet Union in the Russian Federation. Codes and edicts continue to be the predominant source of law in the Russian Federation (see Part II, Chapter 5 on Russian law for its family law history and more recent legislative developments).

Law and the nature of family law

The nature of family law has been the subject of much discussion in civil law countries (generally based on Roman law) and socialist countries. The question has been whether it is a branch of private law or does it belong to the realm of public law or to the field called 'social law', or is it an autonomous branch of the law sui generis? Rheinstein poses these questions and points out that this classificatory problem has not attracted attention in Anglo-American countries, which do not usually concern themselves with classifications of branches of law per se (Rheinstein, 1972, p. 3). 'Law' has been defined in many ways, but in the modern world, as used by modern lawyers, it appears to refer to 'that set of norms of human conduct which is sanctioned by the state' (Rheinstein, 1972, p. 3). Definitions of 'law' do not usually include norm systems such as canon law and other religious systems yet these are particularly relevant in the regulation of certain aspects of marriage in countries such as Spain, Pakistan, Israel or Burma.

The social purposes of marriage

Krause argues that marriage and the family served – and in many parts of the world still serve – as the 'sole legally and morally permissible harbour for sexual activity and child-rearing' (Krause, 2008, p. 1112). Krause identifies four purposes which were served by this paradigm of marriage and the family: 'This (i) assured the birth of children into two-parent families as the natural and then (pre-Pill, pre-abortion) unavoidable consequence of sexual activity, (ii) provided the structure for socializing children by means of role division between the marriage partners, (iii) made parental role division possible by providing economic security for the stay-at-home partner through legal support obligations as well as through moral, social, and harsh legal strictures against divorce, and (iv) assured old-age provision for parents through their children's reciprocal moral and legal support obligation' (Krause, 2008, p. 1112).

Sex and marriage

Sex within marriage

As Konig puts it: 'The family is not only a group whose members are bound by strong feelings but also a group in which the younger members are usually the biological offspring of the elders' (Konig, 1974, p. 51). Consequently, sex and marriage are inextricably linked, certainly as far as history and sociology are concerned. As early as 1927, it was recognized by Soviet law makers that it is possible to analyse the institution of the family whenever a man and a woman live together in a lasting sexual relationship and jointly rear their progeny, 'even if the economic, social and political bases are to be found in a broader body of relatives' (Konig, 1974, p. 51). The distinguishing and decisive factor was the choice to share a lasting common life.

Family law has always attached a particular significance to sexual relations, whether this was to insist on physical consummation of a marriage, prohibit adulterous relationships or impute to two people the distinction of being regarded as living as 'husband and wife' (Bainham, 2002, p. 171). Traditional Catholic teaching has and continues to insist that sexual relations should only be sanctioned within marriage.

Sex within marriage has been the accepted convention, and in mainly Western or Westernized societies, 'love' has been the precondition for a couple to enter into a marriage, with the sexual relationship a primary if not the fundamental element, of a marriage.

The legal relevance of sex and sexual relations in family law

Bainham claims: 'The law's fascination with different sexualities and sexual relations apparently knows no bounds' (Bainham, 2002, p. 171). Canon law and now civil law has always insisted that in order to constitute a valid marriage there must be a proper marriage ceremony and an act of physical consummation. This is literally one act of sexual intercourse after the marriage ceremony, which must be 'ordinary and complete, and not partial and imperfect', in the words of Dr Lushington in *D-E v A-G* (1845) 1 Rob Eccl 279. The law reports illustrate in considerable detail what this is supposed to mean, and Bainham summarizes the position by saying it is 'full penetration of the vagina by the penis. Ejaculation is not required' (Bainham, 2002, p. 174). Indeed, the case of *Baxter v Baxter* [1948] AC 27, the House of Lords held that a marriage was consummated despite the husband's insistence on wearing a condom. Bainham sees great significance in *Baxter*, which he argues strengthens the case for allowing transsexuals and same-sex couples to marry because *Baxter* holds that it is only consummation *without* the need for the potential of procreation to be present [that] validate[s] a marriage. This would suggest that same-sex couples should be permitted to enter into committed relationships that are entitled to be called 'marriages'.

Historically, of course, the importance of a person's gender has been pivotal and absolutely fundamental to the very definition of marriage, or 'marriage as it is understood in Christendom' in the classic words of Lord Penzance in the nineteenth-century landmark case of *Hyde v Hyde* (1866) LR 1 PD 130 which is that 'marriage is the voluntary union of one man and one woman for life to the exclusion of all others'. This is not the place to discuss the various permutations or present-day accuracy of this well-established definition except to say that despite the enactment of the Civil Partnership Act 2004 in the UK, marriage continues to be defined as a heterosexual union although same-sex couples can now enter into 'marriage-like' domestic partnerships which are governed by similar laws to heterosexual marriage and which can be legally dissolved on the basis of very similar facts, with the exception of adultery. Further, marriages contracted outside the United Kingdom will not be recognized as 'marriages' in the United Kingdom under English law, as the case of *Wilkinson v Kitzinger* illustrates.

As far as informal domestic relationships are concerned, several legal issues have arisen in connection with means-tested social security benefits, occupation orders in relation to a family home, succession to tenancies, fatal accident claims and claims for family provision on death. The phrase 'living together as husband

and wife' and 'members of the family' have appeared in Rent Act legislation with the former phrase being interpreted by the courts as referring to a heterosexual couple so that same-sex couples cannot, in English law, be regarded as 'spouses'.

However, both American and Canadian courts have indicated that at the constitutional level, states may be required to adopt an interpretation of 'spouses' which would include same-sex partners (see *Baker Vermont* 744 A 2d 864 (1999) (Supreme Court of Vermont) and *M v H* (1999) 2 SCR 3 (a decision by the Canadian Supreme Court).

Bainham also cites the disappearance of the need for fidelity within the marital sexual obligation as another example of where the law has been in 'substantial retreat' (Bainham, 2002, p. 176). This can be seen in the law of adultery over the last few decades. Whereas the law of rape has been redefined to include anal intercourse, only vaginal penetration will constitute adultery. The advent of large-scale undefended divorce and the introduction of the 'special procedure' in 1977 in England and Wales, which turned the obtaining of divorce into an administrative procedure, meant there was no scope for any realistic judicial investigation into the truth of allegations of adultery. Hence, any investigation into adultery would be extremely unlikely to be carried out, and if it were, would be purely formalistic. Indeed, one of the reasons for the proposed change in the law of divorce in England and Wales (through the Family Law Act of 1996, which never happened) was because of the widespread acceptance that couples had colluded and falsified allegations of adultery in order to obtain a 'quickie divorce' and leave an unhappy marriage (Bainham, 2002, p. 176; Booth, 1985).

In English law, cases like *Fitzpatrick v Sterling* (see *Fitzpatrick v Sterling Housing Association* [2001] 1 FLR 571; 1 AC 27) indicate that: 'Family law has begun to attach less importance to sexual relations and is beginning to take heed of the necessity to avoid discrimination based on sexuality' (Bainham, 2002, p. 173).

Sexual relations and child support

There is another area of civil law (as opposed to criminal law) where the relationship between sexual relations and procreation is relevant. This is the area of child support, where there is legal liability for child support which can arise from just one act of unprotected sexual intercourse. Bainham sees this as perhaps the most striking example of the continued relevance of fault in modern family law. As he points out: '[T]he civil consequences that can arise from sexual relations can be extensive where they result in the conception and birth of a child' (Bainham, 2002, p. 181). Of course, it is still possible to argue that a child resulting from a casual sexual encounter should not be the responsibility of the state but a matter of individual responsibility (Krause, 1990). The argument against leaving it as a matter of individual responsibility is that the mothers concerned might have a better chance of obtaining financial support from absent/non-residential fathers if the state assumes responsibility for collecting maintenance. However, the experience of the

Child Support Agency in the United Kingdom has not been very successful in the enforcement and collection of maintenance from absent fathers.

However, there has also been a 'palpable decline in the legal significance of *parentage* and correspondingly greater emphasis on *parenting* or *parental respon-sibility* which may be exercised by those who are not genetically related to the child concerned' (Bainham, Day Sclater and Richards, 1999).

The separation of sex from marriage

Over the years, sex has extended beyond marriage and the family, since sex can be engaged in outside the marriage relationship, and it is this separation of sex from marriage which provides sociologists and historians with possibilities for further exploration and analysis. Conflicts occur when rapidly changing ideas about sex clash with the ideologies of existing institutions which move relatively slowly (Westermark, *The Future of Marriage*, 1927). This dichotomy is manifest again and again because while marital relations include sexual relations, sexual relations neither explain marriage nor exhaust its possibilities, but extend considerably beyond it (Konig, 1974, p. 51). This was confirmed in the Kinsey Report and means that sex has to be analysed in the context of sex studies as well as in the context of marriage and the family, especially in relation to procreation which plays such a significant role in the family (Konig, 1974, p. 51).

Historically, the law has sought to preserve the link between marriage, sexual relations and procreation to ensure the orderly devolution of family property (Cornish and Clark, 1989).

Extra-marital sexual relations

Attitudes towards premarital reproduction differ from country to country and sometimes vary because of social class. Christensen's study shows that in Denmark premarital sex and pregnancy is tolerated, but in Indiana (United States) marriage takes place as soon as pregnancy is determined (cited in Rheinstein, 1974, p. 53). Indeed, it is claimed that the practice of the Mormons of Utah is to get married as soon as a couple have premarital relations, without waiting for signs of pregnancy (Rheinstein, 1974, p. 53).

Premarital sex

The premarital relationship has moved into the foreground, with attitudes regarding premarital reproduction of children having changed considerably. The sexual rela-tionship has been clearly separated from the reproductive function, a factor clearly abetted by the discovery and use of effective contraceptive methods and the woman being given the power to control her own reproductive cycle and to decide when or whether to have children. Rheinstein points out: '[I]t is now known that sexuality is active for a longer time than, mainly owing to ideological prudery, was earlier thought' (Rheinstein, 1974, p. 53). He argues that this persisting sexual need is the cause of many marital crises in today's world but makes an important distinction between the pre-parental and post-parental phase. In the pre-parental phase, readily available birth control combined with the 'socio-cultural dissociation of sex and reproduction', has resulted in an increase in the number of childless marriages. With the separation of the sexual relationship from the reproductive function, a 'post-parental phase' has taken place in the relationships of more and more couples. This is characterized by a period during which the partners have grown apart after experiencing parenthood for several years, resulting in high divorce figures which have persisted for three decades. These figures have only declined recently because of the marked fall in the number of marriages, and the significant rise in the number of domestic partnerships being entered into outside marriage.

Serial mating, female-headed households and the maternal dyad

Where the biological father is absent from the family unit and the mother secures another man as her lover or husband and as father to her children, the pattern of lifelong monogamy is replaced by serial mating (a succession of sexual partners) where the child might sometimes have two 'fathers' – the mother's current lover or husband and its biological father. Serial mating also leads to female-headed households. This is where women spend periods of their lives between mates and without permanent male support for their children. This is called the maternal dyad or matrifocal unit which comprises the mother and child (Robertson Elliot, 1986, p. 18). This matrifocal unit is often cited as evidence of the non-universality of the typical biological family group.

Contemporary Western societies have been experiencing non-marital dyads with increasing frequency as marital break-ups have proliferated and this has resulted in female-headed households where the biological father, although no longer attached to the mother, is expected to continue to provide financial support for his child. Single-parent families are a regular feature of late twentieth century and early twenty-first century demographic statistics. Such families may sometimes be headed by a man but this is relatively uncommon. However, where the biological mother is absent from the family unit, father-child units have inevitably been formed.

In 1986, Robertson Elliot observed: 'Contemporary patterns of marriage, divorce and remarriage produce father-child units as well as mother-child units and remarriage families with stepmothers as well as remarriage families with stepfathers' (Robertson Elliot, 1986, p. 19). These patterns have not varied much over the past 20 years and Barlow and James could say, with supporting statistical evidence, in 2004, that 'an increasing number of couples and their children function as a family outside of the formal institution of marriage' (Barlow and James, 2004, p. 155).

Why have these changes taken place?

What is worth exploring are the reasons for these momentous changes in societies around the world, which have been traced to the impact of colonization, and the influx of ideas, cultures, languages and ideas from abroad which have made an indelible mark on various jurisdictions and in some cases, continue to do so. The broad approach of this book is to examine the family law of key common law and civil law jurisdictions within the context of their historical development and influences that have led to their 'reception' of laws which have not been indigenous to the particular region. The purpose of this enterprise is twofold: first, to see what events and influences have shaped the family law in any given jurisdiction; and second, to see how that particular region has changed since the reception of laws and the reasons for these changes.

One explanation for similarities in developments across the world has been the much-debated phenomenon of 'legal transplants' where a concept which originated in one geographical region has been received, imported, or simply copied and adopted in another geographical location, sometimes thousands of miles away, and in what appears to be a very different cultural, political and social environment.

Legal transplants in family law

> 'Ideas have wings. No legal system has been able to claim freedom from foreign inspiration.'
>
> (Hahlo and Kahn, 1973, p. 584)

As the above quotation suggests, the experience of common law, civil law and hybrid jurisdictions can be traced to similar social, cultural, political and legal changes and developments that have been replicated in and traverse various countries and continents. There is by no means consensus amongst academics over whether a 'true' transplant takes place when an idea from one jurisdiction appears in another located a considerable distance away, sometimes at the other end of the world.

Professor Alan Watson is a proponent of the view that family laws are transplantable because: (i) he dismisses objections that family laws present particular difficulties for the transplant thesis; (ii) family law is called in aid to refute any notion of a national spirit of the laws, yet this must be an illusion if identical marital property regimes exist in 'very different' societies and there are also different regimes in 'very similar' communities; (iii) massive successful borrowing is commonplace in law; and (iv) the lessons of history indicate that there is political indifference to legal policy, and political leaders are 'indifferent to the nature of the legal rules in operation' (Watson, 2000).

On the other hand, Bradley is generally critical of legal transplants and believes that Watson's claim about political indifference is exaggerated (Bradley, 2005).

He argues, using Scandinavian examples, that there is a 'consistent and systematic pattern of difference in family law that is compatible with variations in social and economic policy, and ... reflects differences in political culture and processes' (Bradley, 2005).

Bradley therefore argues that there *is* a strong political dimension which usually lies behind the emergence of an idea or policy or doctrine, and that governments might play a far more active role in shaping and reforming family law than is perhaps acknowledged by the pro-transplant supporters. As he puts it: 'Family law is political discourse' (Bradley, 2005). Bradley also highlights the importance of culture and political processes in spreading ideas from one legal system to another.

Bradley also cites Glendon as one who has expressed doubts over the feasibility of undertaking comparative family law per se, but events seem to have overtaken some of his views. In an article published in 2005, he cites Glendon's comment about whether comparative family law even exists (Glendon, 'Irish Family Law in Comparative Perspective; Can There Be Comparative Family Law?' (1997) 9 *Dublin University Law Journal* 1) but surely this has been overtaken by Glendon's excellent books and publications on comparative family law such as *The Transformation of Family Law*, published in 1989 and her masterly overview of the last three decades of family law developments in the *International Encyclopaedia of Comparative Law*, published in 2006, discussed and analysed in Part VI, pp. 360, 386, 390–91.

The debate over whether there can be or have been 'successful' legal transplants, including family laws, will doubtless continue but as I have illustrated elsewhere in some detail, the 'best interests' standard for children is perhaps the most striking example of such a transplant in a range of jurisdictions (de Cruz, 2002).

In response to the present author's research finding on the best interests standard, Bradley believes that while the 'best interests of the child' standard may have been transplanted to several jurisdictions, there are many fundamental differences in the way it is interpreted in these other areas (Bradley, 2005). As readers will readily appreciate, even when ideas or concepts have been received by a foreign jurisdiction, such concepts will inevitably be modified or adapted to the particular local conditions into which they have been introduced. This does not make them any less a legal transplant. Once the comparatist accepts this, local modifications are more easily accepted and even expected. Various other examples of the best interests standard are given in the discussion of this guideline in Part II, Chapter 4, on Asia and Africa.

Evolution of the Western family

Ancient Rome

In ancient societies, the state did not generally concern itself with matters of family life per se, although it did concern itself with the family insofar as the state was concerned with religion, and family life was determined by religious command

(Rheinstein, 1974, p. 5). Marriage appeared to be initiated by a religious ceremony but was left more or less to be determined by the customs of the time. Law did play a part in determining who was entitled to succeed to property on death or in the allocation of responsibility for what we now call tort. Law also had to determine who could marry whom. A marriage existed between a man and a woman when they were regarded according to custom and practice as having been married to each other, namely when they lived together in the manner of husband and wife and lived with all the semblance of a marital life.

The role of the law in ancient Rome was limited by the structure of Roman society and the Roman state was a 'consociation of clans rather than individual' (Rheinstein, 1972, p. 5). Law, religion and ethics appear to have existed in early Rome, where in the sphere of private law the bearer of rights was the house, represented by the pater familias or male head of the household, who was the only person recognized as an independent individual under the law. The pater familias possessed all religious rights as priest of the family ancestor cult, all economic rights as sole owner of the family property, and power of life and death over the members of the family. At his death, his name, property and authority descended to his male heirs. However, although he had considerable power within the clan, which was sanctioned by religion and convention, the pater familias could face disapproval if he abused his power. The official known as the censor could exert state control by expressing disapproval of the actions of the pater familias.

Features of the Roman system were subsequently transferred into the canon law and secular law of Europe.

The Middle Ages

In the medieval world, law was not equivalent to the norm system sanctioned by the state, because the state was not yet the exclusive political organization of the times. Other political organizations were constantly vying with each other, namely that of the emperor, the kings, the barons, the boroughs, the guilds and that of the church and its head, the Pope (Rheinstein, 1974, p. 6). Control and regulation of the marriage relation came to be taken over by the church through its unique norm system, the canon law. As Rheinstein puts it, in canon law, 'norms of basically supernatural sanction are juridified in a special sense' (Rheinstein, 1974, p. 6). The norms of the canon law were the norms of religion, hence violation of these would be a sin, resulting in punishment in the afterlife, in damnation to hell or purgatory. The church's fundamental view was that all sexual activity was sinful outside of marriage, and with 'the elevation of marriage to the dignity of a sacrament, a channel of divine grace, [it would be] strictly monogamous and indissoluble' (Rheinstein, 1974, p. 6). This indissolubility was what made it necessary for the church to create an elaborate, complex system of marriage law. The canonists thus developed their system of impediments to marriage, formalities of and preliminaries to the celebration of marriage, of nullity and of procedures in marital causes (Rheinstein, 1974, p. 6).

Secularization of family regulations

With the waning of the Middle Ages, two great movements took place: first, the secularization of the law of marriage; second, the statization of the major part of the regulation of family matters (Rheinstein, 1974, p. 7). The secularization of marriage began with the Protestant Reformation. Dominant figures such as Martin Luther, Zwingli and Calvin insisted that secular regulations conform to the Christian ideal of marriage, so that the new secular laws strictly complied with Christian teaching. A noteworthy point was that the Protestant versions of Christian teaching were stricter than Catholic teaching in the rules concerning nullity but it allowed divorce 'which was conceived of as punishment of a spouse for grave violation of marital duties, especially adultery' (Rheinstein, 1974, p. 7). As Rheinstein puts it: '[T]he door was opened for increasing secularization when Christian tradition was subjected to the critique of Enlightenment' (Rheinstein, 1974, p. 7).

The secularization of the law neither took place immediately nor did it occur in all countries at the same time. Austria saw marriage laws being included in the state's civil laws in the early nineteenth century but most Eastern European countries maintained the marriage law jurisdiction and ecclesiastical jurisdiction until the Communists took control and this happened with the Orthodox Church and other denominations. In Oriental jurisdictions, all matters pertaining to the family remained under religious law even after other parts of the law had become secularized and Westernized. Apart from in India, matters of personal status, which applied to family law matters, were left to Shariah law and other religious tribunals. In India, Hindu, Mohammedan and other religious laws were applied by the regular, secular courts (Rheinstein, 1974, p. 7). In the last half-century, a few secular governments have been steadily reforming the religious family laws on Hinduism and Islam, and Islamic countries such as Egypt have transferred jurisdiction to the secular courts. The first Islamic country where family law and family jurisdictions were completely secularized was Turkey, where it took place in 1926.

However, Christian tradition continues to be strong in the family law in Occidental countries.

The universalization of family law

When the English began to migrate to the colonies on the continent of North America, the English law they took with them was not the common law of the Royal Courts but the customary law which was still being applied in the local courts of seventeenth century England (Rheinstein, 1974, p. 12). It was only with the growth of wealth, the expansion of crafts, industry and commerce and the increasing professionalization of the men by whom legal affairs were handled that American law became increasingly identified with the common law of England. This meant it took on board its technicalities and its preoccupation with the dealings of the owners of property. Nevertheless, American law never became explicitly a law for the wealthy, since care was taken to make the courts accessible to people owning little property, especially small farmers. However, the early days of American law did not see much time spent on the needs of the poor, whose numbers coincided with new immigrants and the enslaved (Rheinstein, 1974, p. 12).

Hence, the law of marital property, succession on death, support, divorce, parental power or guardianship took special care of the needs of property owners but not of those who did not own property. This was replicated in Eastern Europe, especially Russia, where the majority of people, the peasants, were serfs until 1861. For the urban labour force of the growing industries, the old laws of the peasantry ceased to have much meaning.

On the other hand, in continental Western Europe, the monarchs were engaged in a power struggle with the nobility and therefore found it politically advantageous to pay attention to the needs of the bourgeoisie, and the monarchs' bureaucracies were more disposed to consider the needs of even the poor. Hence, welfare legislation tended to be more benevolent than the English Poor Laws of Elizabethan pedigree. In Bismarck's laws of the 1880s, social security started to be a matter which needed legislation. However, government efforts appeared to become embroiled in matters of public administration. The 'private law' of the family was concentrated on the affairs of the propertied classes. Critics of the German legislation of the turn of the century were keen to point out the new Civil Code's neglect of the poor.

Gradually, through procedural reforms, courts were made more widely accessible to those who were neither destitute nor sufficiently wealthy to pay for legal services. Family life became more protected by reforms in the law of instalment buying, garnishment of wages and housing and laws were also made which dealt with guardianship, minors' contracts, adoption, illegitimacy, divorce and welfare support. (Rheinstein, 1974, p. 13).

The individualization of marriage

Writing in 1972, Konig could say with some justification that the modern family was characterized by 'an extensive process of individualisation' (Konig, 1974, p. 380). This accounts for the nuclear family being referred to as the conjugal family because the couple is no longer the core of the group but constitutes its only permanent element (see Durkheim, 'La Famille Conjugale' (1921) 90 *Revue philosophique* 2).

Transformative forces in family law around the world

In the nineteenth century, Western nations began to grant women equal rights with men in respect of property ownership, the control of children, divorce and so on. This led to changes in the nature of the family and the rights and protections connected with it. The state began to intervene to modify parental control over their children and, at the same time, education moved from the household to the school. It could be seen that family ties and the family ambience began to loosen.

Another life-changing event that took place in the nineteenth century was the

Industrial Revolution which removed from the home economic tasks such as baking, spinning and weaving, to the factory. This had an impact on economic and social conditions in many households, as well as on the role of each spouse.

Glendon observes that in affluent modern societies, the 'principal transformative forces affecting the law of persons, formation of marriage, interspousal relations, divorce, the creation of kinship relations and the relation of parents and children' have been ideas about individual freedom, equality, and women's rights (Glendon, 2006, p. 3). Within a relatively short space of time, and well into the early twenty-first century, advances in biotechnology and genetic science will continue to have equally far-reaching effects on family relations and family law in the developed nations (Glendon, 2006, p. 3). As we approach the end of the first decade of the new millennium, her prophecies are being vindicated.

With the onset of globalization, ideas of human rights have taken hold, and these have impacted on the developing world – as can be seen in countries in Africa and the Middle East. However, the rise of traditionalist Islam should also be noted. There has also been 'an interplay between family law, identity politics and nationalism' (Glendon, 2006, p. 3).

Krause asserts that the chief trend that has transformed family life and law is 'the rapid acceleration of legal, social and economic equality for women'. He also believes that another vital trend is the 'increasing recognition of children as separate legal actors independent from their parents. Children are now seen as entitled to their fair share of rights vis-à-vis their parents and society' (Krause, 2008, pp. 1112–13). He sees the modern welfare state as the third transformative factor. He argues that the 'unintended side-effect' of [the State involvement] is that the very act of seeking to help the family where it fails its functions or falls short, has made it less necessary for the family to fulfill its traditional tasks such as socializing children and providing economic support for all its members, including the elderly.

Property aspects of marriage – general observations

As far as patterns of the husband-wife relationship are concerned, legal systems vary from traditional male predominance to full equality of the spouses (Rheinstein and Glendon, 1980, p. 5). Apart from the field of marital property, Anglo-American systems do not comprehensively treat this relationship by express statutory enactment. This means that the courts in general have had the flexibility to respond to changing social views in those areas where the life patterns of married people have legal significance (Rheinstein and Glendon, 1980, p. 5).

Katz notes that in the mid-nineteenth century, two American statutes, the Married Women's Property Acts of 1835 and 1839, finally changed the domination and control of a husband over his wife's property during marriage. The statutes allowed a married woman to acquire property in her own name, enter into contracts with others, retain her own earnings, as well as sue and be sued in her own name. However, the change which had the most significant impact on marriage was the abandonment of the unity theory of marriage, and in the last half of the twentieth century married women emerged as individuals with their own legal identity and their independent rights (Katz, 2003, pp. 62–3).

In essence, the transition from the merger of the personality of the wife with that of the husband to equality of the spouses has been achieved in the United States and in British jurisdictions.

In Oriental countries such as Japan, China or Thailand, the general position of a wife toward her husband is invariably defined by statute 'in the spirit of approximating equality' (Rheinstein and Glendon, 1980, pp. 5–6).

There are also non-Anglo-American countries, such as Scandinavia, Germany, the Netherlands, Italy, France and Austria, and former Socialist countries such as Russia, which not only pronounce but have substantially implemented the principle of legal equality (Rheinstein and Glendon, 1990, p. 6).

Apart from these countries, are countries which have modified the husband's predominance, for example, South Africa which has followed the more traditional approach, and Switzerland and Belgium whose laws are closer to the objective of achieving equality. Rheinstein and Glendon's global survey in the late 1970s indicated that, then as now, the trend of equality of the wife and husband has not been fully realized in all parts of the world, 'it is of irresistible force' and, to paraphrase them, has been gaining ground universally (Rheinstein and Glendon, 1980, p. 7). This trend has continued over the last three decades.

Community property systems

The system of marital community property originated in ancient Germanic and Celtic institutions. It allowed a wife upon the death of her husband to share in his wealth, but it avoided transfer of land from one blood line into another (see Huebner, *A History of Germanic Private Law*, Philbrick trans. 1914, pp. 629, 639). Consolidation of such ideas appears to have taken place in the later Middle Ages. By the turn of the nineteenth century, classification of matrimonial property systems according to the existence or non-existence of a community fund was widely accepted. It has clearly become increasingly untenable to sustain such a system.

This system is spread widely over many civil law countries and some parts of the United States. It consists of 'all or part of the assets of both the husband and the wife being combined in a community fund, the title to which simultaneously belongs to both spouses' (Rheinstein and Glendon, 1980, p. 36). However, the management, the profits or gains from such a fund and the power of disposition are usually the husband's, which would be limited to certain transactions by the requirement of the wife's consent or judicial authorization (Rheinstein and Glendon, 1980, p. 36). In countries such as Scandinavia, the Netherlands, Portugal, Brazil and parts of France and Germany, the community fund consisted of all the assets of both spouses, except those expressly excluded by a formal marriage contract.

The key point about these systems, which Rheinstein and Glendon highlight, is that as long as women were considered incapable of managing their own property, the husband had the power to control such a fund. This meant that its principal effect only took place when the marriage ended which, in the days when divorce was not a widespread phenomenon, would be upon the death of one of the spouses.

In the civil law countries, as the trend toward equality gained momentum, the issue became: How could the desired equality of wife and husband be combined not only with the preservation but also the expansion of the wife's share (which had always been universally one-half) in the marital property? (Rheinstein and Glendon, 1980, p. 42).

Initially, wealthy French families used the technique of the 'contrat de marriage' whereby they were able to secure to women extensive powers to deal with their own property long before such powers were incorporated into the law (Rheinsten and Glendon, 1980, p. 42). However, from 1907, a gradual process of legislative amendments began to take place, which increased equality by giving more autonomy to each spouse and eventually the need was felt for a complete revision of matrimonial property law. The next legislative amendment occurred in 1966 where the community of acquests and movables was reduced to acquests and the husband remained head of the family and manager of the community; however, his powers were reduced and the wife's participation was increased. This was followed by yet another law in 1970 (Law of 4 June 1970) which abolished the rule that the husband was the head of the family but the law retained his position as head of the community fund.

Deferred community systems

The term 'deferred community regime' is often used to describe systems which combine separation of assets while the marriage exists (or while the regime is still existing) with a system of liquidation in which the funds of the two parties, or their monetary values, are combined with the intention of distributing between the parties the sum or value so found. In the Nordic countries the fund to be divided is based on the idea of universal community, i.e. that upon marriage all the property of both spouses, present and future, is merged into one fund which upon termination is equally divided so that 'whatever the spouses own is neither his nor hers but theirs' (Rheinstein and Glendon, 1980, pp. 48–9).

In West Germany, at a time when the law relating to the right of married women to administer and enjoy their own separate property, or at least their own earnings, was in some turmoil in England and France, the German Civil Code of 1896 established a statutory matrimonial regime of a separation of ownership. This was known as the 'Mirror of Saxony' or Sachsenspiegel which consisted of a set of rules which were already highly respected in the country, especially in Northern Germany. This was the operational regime throughout the Weimer Republic and the Third Reich until 1953. Under it, the husband had the right to administer, possess and keep the income from most of his wife's real and personal property. The wife's title protected her against dispositions by the husband and a system

of publicity protected creditors. In addition, the wife had the right to administer, enjoy and dispose of a part of the property known as the 'reserved property'
(Vorbehaltsgut). This was a part of the wife's property which included her profits
and earnings acquired in the exercise of a separate occupation such as objects
exclusively designed for her personal use, property designated by the marriage
contract as reserved property and assets acquired by the wife through succession
or donation with the express condition that they become part of her reserved property (Rheinstein and Glendon, 1980, p. 48). All other property was subject to the
control of the husband and, despite protest at this regime from feminist groups,
it endured until after the Second World War. The Constitution of 1949 (art. 3)
declared full legal equality between men and women but a transitional provision
stated that laws incompatible with equality should remain in force until replaced
by new laws but no later than 31 March 1953. Consequently, no new regime of
matrimonial property was adopted before the constitutional deadline was reached
(Rheinstein and Glendon, 1980, p. 48).

The German courts subsequently held almost unanimously that since the judiciary could not make any new law of a more complex nature, the only regime
which was in accordance with the principle of equality was the regime of separation, hence West Germany adopted a separate property regime. However, the West
Germans were not satisfied with this and wished to give the married woman a
greater share of the family property than she received under the separation system
or under the old system under the Civil Code. They therefore undertook an extensive comparative study and designed a new matrimonial property regime, a deferred
matrimonial property system, which came into effect on 1 June 1958.

This system was based on the Nordic system (see above) but was altered in
important respects. Hence, instead of simply having a community property system come into effect at the termination of the marital relationship, it introduced
the Zugewinn, which meant the increase in the monetary value of the parties'
estate that has taken place during the duration of the marriage or the existence of
the regime which, by agreement of the spouses, or by judicial act, may be terminated while the marriage is still continuing. The way the system works is that the
increase, if any, of one spouse's estate is compared with the increase, if any, of
the estate of the other spouse. If the increase of one party is higher than that of
the other, he or his heir, as the case may be, has to pay to the other side one-half
of the difference (this is called Augleichsforderung, equalization claim). In calculating the difference between the final value and the initial value of each of the
two estates, the value of assets newly acquired, as well as the increase in value of
existing assets, which may be the result of conditions in the market, must also be
taken into account (Rheinstein and Glendon, 1980, p. 45).

Trends in the law of marriage in Europe

In her chapter surveying the development of Western family law over the last century and a half up to the present time, Antokolskaia talks about the new concept of

marriage, its diminishing procreative function, the change from the wife's inferior status to spouses' equality, women's emancipation, widespread female employment, and the movement from lifelong monogamy to serial monogamy, leading to the secularization and 'de-ideologisation' of marriage (Antokolskaia, 2007, pp. 242–3). However, she cautions that the 'actual level of de-ideologisation of marriage is still quite different throughout Europe' (Antokolskaia, 2007, p. 243). She identifies two opposing tendencies (or trends), namely one that avoids ideological declarations both in the definition of marriage and during the civil marriage ceremony; and the other that still exists in many European countries (she cites England and Wales), which are reluctant to remove the traditional ideological trappings from marriage.

In the case of Western European countries, she believes that the de-ideologization is in the form of emphasizing the 'contractual nature of marriage and the release of marriage from religious influence' (Antokolskaia, 2007, p. 243). In Dutch and Russian marriage law, the approach is to avoid dealing with ethical and religious aspects of marriage and to limit its scope to the more practical civil aspects. Swedish law, she points out, even allows spouses to avoid making vows for life.

Nevertheless, in the more conservative European countries, marriage retains a 'symbolic ethical and ideological meaning, a legacy from the past' (Antokolskaia, p. 244). However, for Eastern Europe, her view is that the same tendency can be explained as a reaction to communist marriage ideology.

Responding to the changes in family life – law on the books and the law in action

Rheinstein made the point in the early 1970s that the law on the books did not correspond perfectly either to the law in action or to the behaviour of the populations affected. Indeed, the legal images of the family were more in touch with the ideas and practices of the middle classes than the poor or the well-to-do (Glendon, 2006, citing Rheinstein, p. 5). Rheinstein also observed that the law in the 1970s was undergoing profound changes in three respects: (i) the social and legal status of women was being transformed, partly through modern technology, which was gradually obliterating the traditional division of labour between men and women; (ii) it was beginning to recognize the changing relations between young people and their parents; and (iii) it was paying increasing attention to the needs of previously 'neglected' groups of society: the poor, ethnic minorities and non-conformists (Rheinstein, 1974, pp.12–14). Glendon notes that the gap between family law and family behaviour widened further as the demographic upheavals that started in the mid-1960s continued (Glendon, 2006, p. 5). Lawyers then had to contend with the economic and child-related consequences of a sharp increase in marital dissolution and births outside marriage (Glendon, 2006, p. 5).

The tension between the Oriental and the Occidental way of dealing with family law

Rheinstein identifies the contrasting ways in which Oriental and Occidental societies deal with family relationships, behaviour and mores. The Oriental way is to have different laws for each of the definable groups following well-defined patterns of their own. However, the Occidental way is 'to work out legal rules which correspond to patterns of belief and behaviour which are common to all the groups and sub-groups of which the society is composed or which leave room for choice or individual formation' (Rheinstein, 1972, p. 9).

Consequently, it is essential to be aware that there are bound to be differences between the official law or state-imposed law and the actual mores being observed. Islamic, Hindu and Jewish religions have come face to face with modernity and have had to consider modifications of some of their tenets. Such tenets are the Hindu ban on the remarriage of widows, Hindu and Islamic polygamy, the Muslim husband's unlimited right to repudiate a wife, and the Jewish prohibition on marriage between a Jew and a non-Jew. As Rheinstein says: 'The relation between the family law of the books and the family law in action is even more complex in a pluralistic society, ie a society in which no single ideology is officially declared to be alone admissible' (Rheinstein, 1972, p. 9). In societies which have not experienced the full impact of industrialization, ideas of convention, religious and moral order tend to change more slowly than modes of economic life (Rheinstein, 1972, p. 8). For them family life is therefore still subject to traditional religious or customary law, yet in all other respects a system of Western origin has been adopted (Rheinstein, 1972, p. 8). Hence in countries like India, Pakistan, Bangladesh, Burma and Ceylon, family law, although modernized to a certain extent, remains 'an island of religious law – Hindu, Islamic or Buddhist – amidst a general law of Western provenance' (Rheinstein, 1972, p. 8).

Overview of divorce laws

Historical background

It might have been thought that divorce is a recent and rare phenomenon mostly limited to modern industrial societies. However, neither of these assumptions would be accurate. According to Konig, there has never been a society where there has not been either a divorce procedure or some form of functional equivalent (Konig, 1974, p. 66). As one might surmise, in some societies it was frequent and in others, rare (Stephens, 1963). In many societies, successive polygamy has been the most widespread form of marriage but this came about not only through widows and widowers remarrying but also through divorced parties remarrying.

Among the extremely patriarchal-dominated peoples of antiquity, divorce was virtually unavailable and consisted for the most part of 'repudiation', that is, of the woman by the man with the woman finding it practically impossible to obtain a divorce in her own right. It was also rare among the Chinese and Hindus. Christendom took over the theory of the indissolubility of marriage from patriarchal cultures. However, it took a long time before the forbidding of divorce and remarriage were firmly established and then there were numerous alternatives such as annulment or formal or informal separation.

Reasons or grounds for divorce

It is instructive to note the variety of reasons for the breakdown of marriage in various non-Westernized and so-called primitive communities and the reasons for a 'divorce' of some description. Konig's global survey reveals that the charge of adultery as a ground for divorce is widespread in human societies across the world (Konig, 1974, p. 59). Where the woman is regarded as the property of the man, adultery is seen as the violation of the man's property and is punished accordingly. In extremely patriarchal societies, adultery of the woman is even punished with death while the adultery of the husband is 'a standing and tolerated custom' (Konig, 1974, p. 59). In the law of the Koran, a man is allowed to have a certain number of concubines as well as four official wives. In more remote places like the Sudan, adultery is regarded as grounds for divorce, even where adultery is a common practice.

Among the Hopi Indians of Arizona, although adultery plays a role in grounds for divorce, 'the decisive factors' which can be observed as causing the breakdown of marriage are incompatibility of temperaments, laziness or stinginess (Stephens, *The Family in Cross-Cultural Perspective*, 1963, p. 231). Other more physical signs of an intention or decision to divorce may be noted. Among the Pueblo Indians in North America, if the woman simply throws the man's belongings out the door, that would be sufficient to signify a divorce. In Greenland and among the Papago in Southern Arizona, it is far more subtle and yet quite poignant. If the man simply withdraws in the evening without saying a word, the woman will return in silence to her parents' home, believing the relationship is at an end (Thurnwald, *Wesen, Wandel und Gestaltung von Familie, Verwandtschaft und Bunden*, 1932, p. 76; Underhill, *Social Organisation of the Papago Indians*, 1939). There is a long list of causes of divorce among the Muria in India (Elwin, *The Muria and their Ghotal*, 1947, p. 635):

Reasons	Number of cases
'She ran away' (with no reasons given)	23
'We quarrelled over work'	3
'She did not like me'	1
'She eloped from her parents' house before coming to me'	2
'She was a bitch'	2
'I was ill and she didn't like to stay with me'	1
'We didn't like each other'	2

Impotence	2
'I could not satisfy her'	9
'My elder wife could not stand it when I married a second'	5
'My elder wife drove out the second'	4
'She was a thief'	1
'She was of a bad character'	1

The curious fact is that there are relatively few divorces amongst the Muria, a unique, isolated tribe that lives in communal, territorial units in a forested area encircled by mountains in central India. The institution which distinguishes this tribe is the ghotul or gotul, which is a temporary co-ed dormitory for unmarried youth. It is a social club and sleeping place for the young and unmarried, between nine and 12 years of age, wherein there is complete sexual liberty until marriage. They are allowed to have sexual relations with anyone they choose but must change partners after several days. These youths tend to marry in their late teens.

The fault and no-fault divide in divorce grounds

Introduction

One of the recurrent issues in family law is the merits and demerits of fault-based and non-fault-based grounds for divorce in the more developed countries of the world. Many countries and states have been adopting no-fault grounds for divorce including several grounds beyond breakdown of the marriage. Nevertheless, many legal systems have not wished to exclude fault totally and retain it in limited situations, for example when the reason for the breakdown is considered relevant or when the concept of hardship is used (Rheinstein, 1974, p. 74).

The pure no-fault ground goes beyond the basic idea of breakdown of the marriage as it also includes divorce by mutual consent, by unilateral or by joint application, uncontested divorces and in some Eastern religious systems, unilateral repudiation of the wife by the husband (Rheinstein, 1974, p. 74).

European divorce laws

The Netherlands is typical of the no-fault divorce template in Western jurisdictions where breakdown is the solitary ground for separation and divorce. Sweden also adopts the no-fault principle as its ground for divorce, where, if the parties consent and there are no children younger than 16, an immediate divorce is possible. However, fault is still relevant when it comes to custody and property division. Ireland has introduced, via a constitutional amendment, divorce based on irretrievable breakdown, which requires the spouses to have lived apart for four years.

In Jewish law, the sole ground for divorce is the mutual agreement of both parties and the rabbinical courts only have the right to say whether the procedural requirements have been met. The husband no longer has the right to refuse to deliver the 'get' (the last piece of paperwork needed by the wife to finalize the divorce) once the courts have made an order that he should do so (Rheinstein, 1974, p. 74).

Switzerland has abolished fault as one of the grounds for divorce and introduced divorce by mutual consent.

In Germany, breakdown of a marriage may be established either based on the length of separation alone or upon the length of separation combined with a mutual agreement to divorce. A three-year separation, or a one-year separation plus a mutual agreement will constitute grounds for divorce (Rheinstein, 1974, p. 74). Rheinstein further explains that in exceptional circumstances, a German court may refuse to grant a divorce where it is in the best interests of the minor children of the couple, to preserve the marriage, or it would be an unreasonable hardship for the spouse who opposes the divorce, but both these exceptions are 'strictly construed' (Rheinstein, 1974, p. 74).

As we shall see in Part II, Chapter Two on American family law, there has been a movement in favour of the revival of fault in the context of divorce. This has sparked significant academic debate as exemplified in articles by Ellman (1997; 2000), Wardle (1999–2000) and Turnage Boyd (2005–6).

No-fault and fault grounds combined

No-fault and fault grounds have been combined in various jurisdictions in two modes. The first form is the combination of allowing no-fault divorce to be initiated by one spouse (usually the husband) but requiring fault when initiated by the other. The second form is where the system professes to have only no-fault divorce but still provide specific grounds that attribute fault to one of the spouses. Islamic divorce laws are the prime example where the husband may repudiate the wife whenever he wishes and outside any judicial control but fault is required if the wife applies for divorce. In India, Afghanistan and Saudi Arabia, Islamic laws allow repudiation as the most common form of divorce but these countries also allow divorce based on other grounds. Some Islamic countries allow the repudiation by the husband principle but require that the husband must maintain the wife during the waiting period. Most Islamic states allow divorce in cases of insanity or long absences by the husband (Rheinstein, 1974, p. 74).

The People's Republic of China purports to have no-fault divorce but has re-emphasized fault. It allows divorce by mutual consent but spouses must also agree upon custody, child support and the division of property. It recognizes the concept of adversarial divorce where spouses can agree upon divorce, but not on the ground 'that the feelings of the spouses for each other has obviously cooled down'. Under a Supreme Court ruling of 1992, this ground has been held to comprise 14 different causes of divorce, mostly characterized by fault.

Divorces based on fault per se can be found under California law. The sole ground for divorce is supposed to be no-fault, yet the breakdown of the marriage may be caused by a marital offence making the continuation of marital life intolerable. A no-fault reason such as separation will allow for a delayed divorce whereas fault leads to a quick divorce, provided the court is satisfied that some form of marital misconduct has occurred making the continuation of marital life intolerable (Vershraegen, 2004, p. 75).

A similar linking of no-fault divorce with fault in the form of marital misconduct occurs in South African law where adultery which is regarded by the petitioner as irreconcilable with the continuation of marital life is one of the factors by which irretrievable breakdown may be proven. Of course, this is also the case in England and Wales under the Matrimonial Causes Act 1973 (UK), where three of the reasons for irretrievable breakdown are fault-based conduct which must be proved, or at least a case for which must be stated in the application, without which the divorce will not be granted, despite indications that the marriage has irretrievably broken down.

Jurisdictions with explicit fault and fault grounds openly combined

Other countries have clearly set out a combination of fault and no-fault divorce. In France, there are currently three forms of divorce: divorce by mutual consent; upon a joint request or upon the request of either party; and divorce on the ground of fault. There is also the new category of divorce on the ground of 'irretrievable deterioration of married life' on the basis of de facto separation for two years.

Danish law explicitly provides for fault and no-fault grounds for divorce. The grounds are one-year separation and adultery.

Louisiana law has two separation grounds and two fault grounds. The first separation ground requires living apart after the filing of the petition for 180 days, whereas the second requires living apart for six months before the petition was filed. The couple may jointly apply for this sort of divorce and the courts have no jurisdiction to inquire about the reasons for the breakdown.

Going behind the label of 'irretrievable breakdown'

In her search for the common core of divorce laws in Europe as they developed in the last half-millennium, Antokolskaia attempts to unpick the label of 'irretrievable breakdown' and finds that the recent survey of current divorce law provided by the Commission on European Family Law reveals that that label can conceal 'virtually every type of divorce', from fault-based (such as England and Wales, Scotland, Greece and partly Poland and Bulgaria) to divorce by consent (which includes The Netherlands and Russia) (Antokolskaia, 2006, p. 325; 2007, p. 251, citing Jantera-Jareborg, 2003; Boele-Woelki, Braat and Sumner, 2003). She finds that if one goes behind the labels, there are no less than five functional types of divorce grounds: fault-based grounds; irretrievable breakdown in the narrow sense of the term; divorce on the ground of 'separation' (ie cessation of marital life as used in various jurisdictions) for a stated period of time; divorce by consent; and divorce on demand (Antokolskaia, 2006, p. 325).

The existence of fault-based grounds in any divorce law suggests there will be judicial scrutiny into any possible matrimonial offence, but for England and Wales, the implementation of the 'administrative procedure' in 1977 has meant that for the vast majority of divorce applications, it is really an administrative divorce and divorce by consent that takes place in practice, although fault-based divorce exists on paper.

Divorce based on irretrievable breakdown in the narrow sense of the term is granted when the court forms the opinion that the marriage cannot be saved, which happens in Bulgaria, the Czech Republic, The Netherlands, Poland and Hungary. But divorces will also be granted where there are no-fault grounds based on a period of separation, such as four years in Ireland, three years in Austria and two years in Belgium, even though these jurisdictions' divorce laws include the criteria of irretrievable breakdown. In jurisdictions where there is only an irretrievable breakdown criterion, there is very little possibility of a court inquiry if the case is uncontested. However, the judicial inquiry can be 'quite intrusive' in contested divorce cases in countries like Bulgaria and Poland where allocation of fault is required (Todorova, *National Report of Bulgaria*, 2003, pp. 406–8; Maczynski and Sokolowsli, *National Report for Poland*, 2003, p. 194). Antokolskaia points out that in jurisdictions where there is a requirement of irretrievable breakdown as well as statutory periods of separation, proving the breakdown is twice as difficult because even after the separation period has expired, the court still has to be convinced that the marriage has irretrievably broken down before it will grant a divorce (Antokolskaia, 2006, p. 326).

In some jurisdictions, accessibility of divorce depends solely on the length of the separation period, which varies quite significantly: six years in Austria, five years irrespective of consent in England and Wales; four years in Switzerland and Greece; three years in Italy and Portugal; two years in France and Germany; and one year in Denmark, Norway and Iceland.

Hence, having the ground of 'irretrievable breakdown' in their divorce laws appears to some jurisdictions as broad enough to justify allowing divorce by mutual consent. This happens in Austria, the Czech Republic, Denmark, Germany, The Netherlands, England and Wales, Russia and Scotland. Other countries such as Belgium, Bulgaria, France, Greece and Portugal have consent as a separate ground. In both these sets of countries, once the spouses have agreed to the divorce, courts appear to grant the divorce automatically without inquiring into the reasons for divorce but most of the states regard allowing such divorces as undermining the power of state control over divorce (Antokolskaia, 2006, p. 326).

Only Dutch and Russian law allows divorce on the basis of consent simpliciter. Other countries have a minimum period before a divorce can be granted – three years in Bulgaria, two years in Belgium, one year in the Czech Republic and Greece and England and Wales, where there is a statutory time bar.

The existence of 'irretrievable breakdown' as a ground for divorce will not prevent a court granting a divorce on the basis of the expiry of the designated minimum periods of separation, provided there is consent by both parties: two years in England and Wales, one year in Germany and in Scotland; and six months in Germany, the Czech Republic and Iceland.

In certain jurisdictions it is not permissible to grant a divorce even if the parties have agreed to divorce, unless an agreement has been reached on ancillary matters as well. This is the case with Austria, Belgium, Bulgaria, Greece, Germany, Hungary, Denmark and Portugal, so it appears that most countries are still reluctant to recognize the autonomous decisions of the spouses as a sufficient ground for divorce (see Antokolskaia, 2006, p. 326; 2007, p. 252; and Martiny, 2003, p. 536).

Divorce on demand

Divorce on demand, in the sense of each of the spouses being entitled to a divorce, by law, irrespective of the objections of the other spouse, is explicitly recognized in Sweden, Finland and Spain and indirectly in Russia (Antokolskaia, 2007, p. 252).

Fallacy of the fault/no-fault dichotomy in Europe

Antokolskaia argues that it is simplistic to suggest that Europe has been moving spontaneously towards no-fault divorce and will thus attain some sort of harmonization of their divorce laws. She maintains that with the passage of time, the reality 'is much more complicated' (Antokolskaia, 2006, p. 324). Her search for the 'common core' of the law on divorce, tracking back to the Protestant Reformation up to the present day confirms that before the Reformation the 'indissolubility of marriage' doctrine, which originated between the eleventh and twelfth centuries, formed one of the most important tenets of the canon law on marriage and divorce of the Roman Catholic Church, which was the uniform law of the whole of western Christendom. However, after the Reformation, Western Europe split into Catholic and Protestant blocs. The former continued to insist on indissolubility whereas the latter allowed full divorce and remarriage (Lacey, *Marriage in Church and State*, 1947, SPCK, p. 150). In modern times, not a single European country retains fault as the sole ground (see Martiny, 2003, p. 534), hence fault constitutes only one possible ground for divorce, albeit often the shortest route. The removal of fault as a divorce ground does not automatically mean that procuring a divorce becomes any easier (Martiny, 2003, p. 534). Thus there has not been a straightforward conversion to a no-fault law of divorce in Western jurisdictions since fault remains present in the divorce laws of European countries, if not explicitly then implicitly.

The continuing relevance of fault in contemporary Anglo-American family law

In an article published in 2003, Bainham poses the question of whether fault is dead in English family law. He examines the law relating to divorce, domestic violence, property, and children and concludes that fault continues to be relevant in a variety of contexts in English family law. Let us look at Bainham's selected areas:

Divorce

Current English divorce law (in 2009), retains fault-based grounds as well as non-fault grounds (separation) in its divorce legislation, although in everyday practice, the overwhelming majority of divorces are based on mutual consent, since divorce is predominantly an administrative procedure and has been since 1977.

Domestic violence and occupation of the matrimonial home

The basic notion in this context is that legal consequences will follow upon proof of fault, and clear evidence of physical violence (and therefore fault) will make it easier for the courts to order injunctions and non-molestation orders. However, the situation is much more problematic when it comes to the 'occupation order'. On the one hand, for victims of domestic violence, a mere non-molestation order will not be sufficient and perhaps dangerous unless an order is also made to exclude the other party from the home. On the other hand, there has been a history of over a quarter of a century during which courts have debated and disagreed over whether exclusion from a home should be a matter of 'welfare' or 'justice'. As Bainham explains, the problem has been how best to deal with a situation where the 'living conditions' of one party (usually the mother) and children have become so intolerable that there is a need to exclude the man from the family home, but there is no evidence of violence or obviously adverse conduct. It needs to be made clear that the phrase 'living conditions' does not refer to physically poor conditions but rather to an environment where the relationship has deteriorated so badly that the man needs to be removed from the house, so that the woman and her children could live in a safer environment (Bainham, 2003, p. 528).

Cases have indicated two judicial approaches in the Court of Appeal in the late 1970s and early 1980s, with one line of authority supporting the welfare approach so that even minimal physical aggression (such as shoving a person onto a sofa) sufficed for a court to order the removal of the perpetrator of that behaviour (as in *Spindlow* [1979] 1 All ER 169); and another line requiring proof of more serious adverse conduct (as in *Ellsworth* [1980] FLR 245). The issue appears to have been resolved, under the old legislation, by the House of Lords in *Richards* [1984] AC 174 where the Law Lords made it clear that both the welfare of the mother and the children *and* the conduct of the respondent were relevant considerations in the court's decision of whether to order such a removal.

Under the law to regulate domestic violence and occupation of the family home which was brought into force in 1997, a 'balance of harm' test was introduced which requires the court to ask whether, if the order is not made, the applicant or any relevant child is likely to suffer 'significant harm' attributable to the respondent's conduct (see s. 33(7) Family Law Act, Part IV). If the answer is in the affirmative, then the court must make the order unless the harm to the respondent or a child, if the order were to be made, is likely to be as great or greater when balancing one against the other. The test applies to married persons, property owners, heterosexual cohabitants and same-sex cohabitants, as amended by the Domestic Violence, Crime and Victims Act 2004, the relevant section of which came into force on 7 January 2007. Hence, as the current legislation stands, an element of fault still plays a part in determining the level of risk of significant harm which might be suffered by the applicant or child as a result of the respondent's adverse conduct.

Property and finance

Approximately half of the States in the United States give consideration to the element of fault in their determination of alimony awards and, to a somewhat lesser extent, to the allocation of property (Bainham, 2003, p. 530). The basic rationale of such laws is that consideration of fault is believed to be necessary to achieve justice in the financial consequences of divorce by allowing those aggrieved by marital misconduct to disclose details of such conduct and seek compensatory awards (Bainham, 2003, p. 530). Once England introduced separation grounds for divorce under the Divorce Reform Act 1969, the intention was to move away from having the matrimonial offence as the dominant factor. The reform of the divorce court's jurisdiction to make orders relating to property and financial matters in the early 1970s also raised the question of the extent to which the matrimonial conduct of the parties should be relevant to the exercise of the court's discretionary powers. Lord Denning gave a very clear indication of the court's approach in *Wachtel* [1973] Fam 72 when he declared that it should no longer be sufficient for adultery and other common forms of matrimonial conduct to justify a reduction in the financial award which the wife could otherwise have expected. However, he conceded that conduct which was 'obvious and gross' might be taken into account if it would be 'repugnant to anyone's sense of justice' to ignore it.

Conduct and financial provision upon divorce

Under current English law, conduct is now covered under s. 25(2)(g) of the Matrimonial Causes Act 1973 (UK) as one of the seven guidelines which the court may take into account when deciding how to exercise their discretion in any given case. The question has been what sort of conduct would be sufficient to fall under the statutory provision, and the forms of conduct which the courts have generally accepted as justifying divorce have been rather extreme and in a sense the more modern equivalent of 'obvious and gross'. Case law suggests a wide range of behaviour which Bainham has classified under five principles: (i) extraordinary conduct going beyond what might be expected in a marriage breakdown, such as firing a shotgun at the husband (*Armstrong* (1974) 4 Fam Law 156); inciting others to murder the husband under a contract killing (*Evans* [1989] 1 FLR 35); assisting the manic-depressive husband with suicide attempts not because of compassion but to get rid of him and enable the wife to cohabit with her lover (*K v K* [1988] 1 FLR 469); (ii) there must be a clear disparity in the conduct of the two parties before the court will factor in the conduct (*Leadbeater* [1985] FLR 789, where both parties were equally so disgusting in their behaviour that they cancelled each other out); (iii) exemplary conduct of one spouse may justify a larger than normal award (*Kokosinski* [1980] Fam 72); (iv) conduct which directly impinges on the family finances should be relevant (see *B v B* [1998] 2 FLR 490), for instance, dissipating the family finances and making less available for distribution; (v) financial misbehaviour will be penalized, particularly where it occurs during the course of the proceedings, in costs (*Tavoulareas* [1998] 2 FLR 418).

The House of Lords recently confirmed this approach in *Miller* [2006] UKHL 24 by declaring that conduct is only to be taken into account in exceptional cases where it satisfies the statutory criteria under the Matrimonial Causes Act 1973 – namely that it would be inequitable to disregard it, and where it can be clearly seen that one party is more to blame than the other.

Children

CHILD SUPPORT

Bainham argues that fault is not only relevant but in some cases is arguably the basis of liability for child support since liability arises from being a 'legal parent'. The legal status of being a parent, which triggers financial liability, is the result of either intentionally having a child or negligently having a child, by, for example, not taking adequate precautions with contraception (Bainham, 2003, p. 534). Perhaps as Bainham also points out, the true basis of child support is arguably welfare and it could be said that the parents are liable because the welfare of children demands that they be properly provided for financially. However, he thinks this misses the point that in the majority of cases which involve the enforcement of child support liability it is the state which is seeking to recoup from the errant father what it has already paid out in social security benefits for the child and it is really the social security system which is the prime safety net which ensures a minimum income for mothers and children and it is this which primarily protects the welfare of those children. Hence the pursuit of the father is not to secure the welfare of the child but to enforce his legal and moral responsibility to the child and the mother and he is 'conceptualised as being at fault' in not discharging this voluntarily (Bainham, 2003, p. 535).

LOSS OF CONTACT WITH A CHILD BECAUSE OF ADVERSE CONDUCT

Adverse conduct clearly has a direct impact on children if they are abused or neglected while in the care of responsible adults. This would render such persons liable to prosecution under the Children and Young Persons Act 1933 or could result in a care or supervision order under s. 31 of the Children Act 1989. Here, arguably, it is not a question of the courts merely punishing a parent for past misconduct but of looking to the future and trying to protect the child from the potentially future harmful influence of the parent. Of course, violence toward the mother may well result in loss of residence or contact with the child as illustrated in the case of *Re M (Contact: Violent Parent)* [1999] 2 FLR 321. Hence, case law illustrates that negative conduct of some gravity and a level of seriousness will often result in a father not being awarded parental responsibility or, having been awarded it, being later deprived of it.

FAULT IN ADOPTION AND CARE PROCEEDINGS

Fault is also taken into account in adoption since courts appear to have dispensed with parental consent by implicitly equating parental inadequacy with unreasonableness as shown in *Re C (A Minor) (Adoption: Parental Agreement)* [1993] 2 FLR 260.

Fault is also a pivotal consideration in care proceedings, although Bainham detects a 'marked reluctance' to call it that (Bainham, 2003, p. 537). In the House of Lords case of *Lancashire County Council v B* [2000] 2 WLR 590, the Law Lords held that where the child had been harmed by an unknown perpetrator within the care network it was not necessary for the local authority to attribute the child's significant harm to any one carer in particular. However, it was patently clear in this case that one of the carers was responsible for the child's injuries and the court took the view that the child should not be denied protection just because it was impossible to establish the actual perpetrator.

Past conduct and potential and future conduct

Bainham argues that it is important to distinguish between adverse conduct which is backward-looking and in the past and conduct which is ongoing and looks to future welfare needs (Bainham, 2003, p. 540). The principle of penalizing past behaviour appears to be continuing as far as the courts are concerned as they will often reduce the amount of property or financial awards upon divorce if the conduct is such that it would be 'inequitable to disregard' it and this also holds true of alimony awards in the United States. On the other hand, the era of the matrimonial offence appears to be long gone in the sense that the 'offences' of adultery, (mis) behaviour and desertion no longer carry the same significance as they did in the past 150 years, except that they still exist on paper and continue to provide the theoretical bases for divorce, certainly as far as adultery and 'unreasonable behaviour' is concerned, and to a far lesser extent, desertion. The era of no-fault divorce has taken hold in the sense of statutory separation periods providing legal grounds for proving the irretrievable breakdown of the marriage, with five years' separation being the threshold for granting a divorce without the need for the respondent's consent. However, matrimonial misconduct cannot be relied upon to reduce the amount of a financial award upon divorce if the 'injured party' is not substantially innocent or unimpeachable as far as conduct is concerned. If both parties are equally blameworthy, conduct will cease to be a factor to be considered in the determination of financial provision upon divorce.

As far as present and potential conduct in modern family law is concerned, 'questions of fault can become linked to questions of welfare' (Bainham, 2003, p. 541). There might no longer be an automatic refusal of a residence or contact application just because one of the parents has indulged in some form of misconduct but proof of the potential for (or history of) violence and abuse (or mental instability) on the part of the applicant parent may persuade the court to refuse an application for contact or a residence order, not because the court wishes to uphold morally upright behaviour but because there is the potentially direct threat to the welfare of the child (Bainham, 2003, p. 541). Welfare is certainly one of the court's fundamental concerns but it could be argued that the court should not be concerned solely about welfare needs but should seek to uphold individual family obligations and be open and explicit about this. Others might also argue that justice should be seen to be done so that the unimpeachable or innocent spouse should reap the benefits of his or her good behaviour and commitment to marital obligations by, for example, not committing adultery or any other matrimonial or other offence during the marriage.

Fault in American matrimonial property law

Certain American States (such as North Carolina and New York) adopted a clear policy to reject fault as a punitive ground in the distribution of property in the context of the dissolution of a marriage. Indeed, in the early twenty-first century, a majority of American jurisdictions has held that fault would only be a relevant consideration in the judicial distribution of property where it has had an economic impact on the marriage. Thus, of the 49 jurisdictions which permit the trial court to divide marital property equitably, 27 do not permit fault to be a relevant factor in their computation unless it has had an economic impact. Some writers have argued that this policy has been the consequence of the introduction of no-fault divorce, which it is argued has resulted in the substantial reduction in the amount of financial settlements received by divorced women (Parkman, 2001) and has also reduced failed marriages to a math equation by considering economic harms only and ignoring violations of physical integrity, intimacy and trust (Bennet Woodhouse and Bartlett, 1994). It should be noted that the States retain the power to consider misconduct in the allocation of marital property but the misconduct must have directly affected the amount of property available for allocation, or enlarged the needs of either spouse (Ellman, 1996). Hence, a spouse who has suffered several years of domestic violence could have this faulty conduct taken into account by proving that hospital bills were incurred or there was a loss of earnings because of serious physical abuse. However this might not be the case for adultery unless for example, the husband infected the wife with HIV which resulted in her needing money for medical expenses (Turnage Boyd, 2005–6). In short, a court would usually require evidence of extreme forms of harm and/or damage before it would consider 'faulty behaviour' on the part of either spouse. The American developments therefore have similarities with English law.

Comparative analysis of family law: pitfalls and principles

Pitfalls of comparison

In *Comparative Law in a Changing World* (de Cruz, 2007, Routledge Cavendish), I list seven major pitfalls and perils that lie in wait for any comparative enterprise:

(i)   linguistic and terminological problems;
(ii)   cultural differences between legal systems;
(iii)   the potential for arbitrariness in the selection of objects of study;
(iv)   difficulties in achieving comparability;
(v)   the desire to see a common legal pattern in legal systems – the theory of a general pattern of development;
(vi)   the tendency to impose one's own (native) legal conceptions and expectations on the systems being compared;
(vii)   dangers of exclusion and ignorance of extra-legal rules.

A detailed account of these seven points is given in the book cited above, to which the reader is referred. However, suffice to say that for present purposes they are broadly self-explanatory. Point (iv) perhaps merits a brief expansion, namely, that meaningful comparison should require that in general terms, the comparatist should be beware of drawing too many conclusions from comparing legal systems at different stages of their legal evolution, or which have markedly different cultural components. Similarly, point (vii) needs to be clarified as referring to informal customs and practices which operate outside strict law or various non-legal phenomena, such as certain economic or cultural practices which are peculiarly unique to a particular people or jurisdiction (see further, de Cruz, 2007, Ch. 7).

Methodological principles for comparative analysis

In order to make meaningful comparisons between jurisdictions of different historical backgrounds, cultures and socioeconomic profiles, a comparatist needs to observe certain principles. These include identification of the legal family to which each jurisdiction selected for comparison belongs, its legal tradition, its sources of law, mode of legal thinking, ideology and its distinctive institutions (see Zweigert and Kotz *Introduction to Comparative Law*, 1998). Two French scholars, de Singly and Commaille, suggest five rules for making meaningful comparisons of the development of family law in different European jurisdictions.

First rule: make explicit the model underlying the comparison

De Singly and Commaille (1997) argue (at p.4) that 'it is not enough to resort to the reality of observed fact' when reaching any conclusion. They contend that selecting a particular feature such as the choice of spouse as the point of comparison could be misleading as far as comparative studies are concerned. Girard (1964) has stated: 'Studies on the choice of spouse often conclude that a trend towards homogamy exists, that is, that married or cohabiting men and women have similar traits as they have similar social backgrounds and are often of the same cultural level.' Yet, de Singly and Commaille point out that 'this statement is not an acknowledgement of reality'. They argue that, in fact, there are as many homogamous marriages as there are heterogamous ones and if demographers and sociologists think that men and women choose each other because of their similarities, it is because they are comparing the observed facts to a hypothetical model of society where marriage occurs by chance, without being affected by social origins and cultural levels. The present author concurs with this conclusion but would also add that, moving away from the European stereotype, there are countries, of course, where certain marriages are arranged (such as India and Pakistan) and this applies to the more traditional Indian and Pakistani families living in Britain or in the Far East. Would-be brides have no say in their choice of partner which makes a nonsense of any model of homogamy. The results of such studies are therefore often self-fulfilling prophecies because of the limited nature of the inquiry, namely only selecting those cultures or countries where sheer familiarity with the model for comparison leads to a predictable result. The important point is that comparison should not be confined to countries within the European Union. This book observes this principle since it looks at several non-European jurisdictions.

Second rule: establish the right distance of observation

This rule derives from the leading German sociologist, George Simmel, who introduced the notion of 'variable distance' but de Singly and Commaille put it more clearly: 'One has to stand a sufficient distance away to be sure not to be oversensitive to details that might prevent a proper understanding of the overall picture' (de Singly and Commaille, 1997, p. 6).

Third rule: make theoretically significant comparisons

De Singly and Commaille agree that this rule is difficult to respect. They point out that as Jean-Claude Passeron (1991) says, the argument of 'all things being equal' cannot be followed through, since 'the language of variables' is 'deceptive because its form and strength of relations depends partly on the context' (de Singly and Commaille, 1997, p. 8). Louis Roussel (1992) observes that 'the typology of European families' is constructed according to the following criteria: fertility, marriage-rates, divorce-rates, births outside marriage and cohabitation. But this merely concentrates on the institutional dimension of family life (de Singly and Commaille, 1997, p. 8), omitting other factors such as the regulation of relationships between the sexes and the regulation of relationships between generations. The conclusions of the comparisons are 'strongly dependent on the theoretical options, which must be clarified in order to obtain more accurate findings' (de Singly and Commaille, 1997, p. 9).

Fourth rule: make statistically significant comparisons

Having reviewed the work of researchers such as Emmanuel Todd, de Singly and Commaille (1997) conclude that Todd's classification zones are based on figures that are very weak. Todd has drawn up a map of Europe which has three clarification zones: (i) where household structures are uniformly complex; (ii) zones of complexity in heterogenous countries; and (iii) other zones. Furthermore, they believe that the data limitations are not always sufficiently emphasized and the strength of the permanence of factors tends to be overestimated.

Fifth rule: do not confuse observed differences with the diversity of models

The importance of a theoretical reference model is recognized by sociologists such as Emile Durkheim, an effort must be made to pick out the 'constants' beyond infinite data variations.

Three further perspectives

In their book, *The European Family*, de Singly and Commaille analyse the European family. They ask contributors to (i) explore the relevant demography, law and policies; (ii) ask three non-Europeans to give their view of the European world as seen from their own; and (iii) to analyse the contributions of the family toward the production and reproduction of social relationships between the social classes which would include examining the modes of regulation in relation to family affairs (De Singly and Commaille, 1997, p. 17).

Other methodological viewpoints

Other commentators have suggested different ways of approaching a comparative study of family law.

The Kamba approach

Kamba puts forward a three-phased approach to comparison: (i) the descriptive phase; (ii) the identification phase; and (iii) the explanatory phase. This is perhaps the most straightforward of all the possible approaches (see Kamba, 1974).

Definition, four steps and preliminary questions: the Boele-Woelki approach

Boele-Woelki considers the usual grassroots questions of what and how the comparative enterprise should be undertaken and suggests the notion of 'framing' which she describes as 'the art of presenting an argument by strategically revealing certain information while concealing other information and hopefully presenting the package in a way that is sufficiently beautiful that no one notices (or objects to) the absence' (Boele-Woelki, 2008).

Boele-Woelki then proffers four steps and refers to a definition of the comparative process, which is derived from Kokkini-latridou who says that comparison is a scholarly process 'in which specific objects of at least two jurisdictions are set against each other in order (1) to determine their similarities and differences; (2) to explain the causes of the similarities and differences; and (3) to evaluate the solutions' (Kokkini-latridou, 1986, p. 155).

THE FOUR STEPS

The first step consists of finding similarities and differences, where two methodological rules should be applied: (i) divide the subject matter into different aspects or part problems. This is usually achieved by asking a pertinent list of questions; (ii) reintegrate the subject for comparison into its own environment by discovering the relationship of the subject with other institutions, norms and so on of the same legal system and by studying and determining the relationship between the subject and its background, whereby legal and non-legal factors might be relevant.

The second step is to explain the similarities and differences that the analysis of the comparison has revealed. A range of historical (including the reception of law), social, economic, political, geographic, and religious factors should be considered.

The third step is to evaluate the legal solutions, which Boele-Weilki sees as the essential part of the comparative research process. However, she warns that the value judgment will only have a 'relative character', meaning it will be governed by various factors. She sees these as 'the period in which [the judgment] is made, the object that was studied and the legal systems that were selected.' However, it also 'permits the comparatist to take part in the legal discourse whereas it enables others to confirm, disapprove or criticize the findings' (Boele-Woelki, 2008).

The fourth and final step is to produce the research report. Boele-Weilki again makes several caveats – no system should require preference and there is a combination of ways of presenting the findings available. Some preliminary conclusions are drawn at the end of each chapter and a final overview is presented in the closing chapter. This summarizes the main conclusions and develops some of the key issues raised, the 'big debates' of yesteryear and today, and looks ahead to the topics which we anticipate will form the major debating issues.

The chosen methodology: a combination of approaches

Ultimately, every comparatist has to make a decision as to which approach is most appropriate and this book broadly adopts the Zweigert and Kotz approach combined with certain features of the other approaches. Zweigert and Kotz take a functional approach to comparative study, which is that the only things that are comparable are those that fulfil the same function – which is to examine the history of a legal system, its mode of thought in legal matters, its sources of law, its distinctive legal institutions, and legal ideology, sometimes called its juristic style. We then make certain that the four main steps suggested by Boele-Woelki are carried out. However, in the course of our study, we also integrate Kamba's three phases; that is, we will usually describe the legal system or the rule in question in its historical, social and legal context, then identify the similarities and differences (which overlaps with Boele-Woelki's first step) before moving to the explanatory phase which is an essential component of all methodological approaches.

Further reading

Allan, G (ed) *The Sociology of the Family*, 1999, Blackwell.

Antokolskaia, M 'Convergence and Divergence of Divorce laws in Europe' (2006) 18 CFLQ 307.

Antokolskaia, M 'Comparative Family Law: Moving with the Times?' in Orucu and Nelken (eds) *Comparative Law. A Handbook*, 2007, Hart, Ch. 11.

Bainham, A 'Sexualities, Sexual Relations and the Law' in Bainham, Day Sclater, Martin Richards (eds) *Body Lore and Laws*, 2002, Hart, Ch. 27.

Bainham, A, Day Sclater, S and Richards, M *What is a Parent? A Socio-Legal Analysis*, 1999, Hart.

Barlow, A and James, G 'Regulating Marriage and Cohabitation in 21st Century Britain' (2004) 67 Mod LR 143.

Barlow, A, Duncan S, James, G and Park, A *Cohabitation, Marriage and the Law* (2005) Hart.

Boele-Woelki, K 'What Comparative Family Law Should Entail' (2008) Utrecht LR 1.

Bradley, D 'Comparative Law, Family Law and Common Law' (2003) 23 *Oxford Journal of Legal Studies* 127.

Bradley, D 'A Note on Comparative Family Law: Problems, Perspectives, Issues and Politics' (2005) 6 Oxford U Comparative L Forum 4 at http://www.ouclf.iuscomp.org.

Booth, Mrs Justice (Chair) *Report of the Matrimonial Causes Procedure Committee* 1985, HMSO.

Cornish, W and Clark, G *Law and Society in England 1759–1950*, 1989, Sweet & Maxwell.

Cretney, SM *Law, Law Reform and the Family*, 1998, Oxford UP.

Cretney, SM *Family Law in the Twentieth Century*, 2002, Oxford UP.

de Cruz, P *Comparative Law in a Changing World*, 3rd ed, 2007, Routledge-Cavendish.

De Singly, F and Commaille, 'Rules of the Comparative Method in the Family Sphere: The

Meaning of a Comparison' in Commaille and Singly (eds) *The European Family*, 1997, Kluwer Academic Publishers.

Diduck, A 'A Family by Any other Name ... or Starbucks Comes to England' (2001) 28 Int J Law and Society 290.

Diduck, A and Kaganas, F *Family Law, Gender and the State*, 2006, Oxford UP.

Eekelaar, J and Nhlapo, T (eds) *The Changing Family. International perspectives on the Family and Family Law*, 1998, Hart.

Fox Harding, L *Family, State and Social Policy*, 1996, Macmillan.

Gautier, A 'Legal Regulation of Marital Relations: An Historical and Comparative Approach' (2005) Int Jnl of Law, Policy and the Family 47.

Glendon, MA *The Transformation of Family Law*, 1989, University of Chicago Press.

Glendon, MA 'Three Decades of Legal and Social Change' in *International Encyclopedia of Comparative Law*, 2006, p. 3.

Herring, J *Family Law*, 2007, Pearson.

Kamba, W 'Comparative Law: A Theoretical Framework' (1974) 23 ICLQ 485.

Konig, R 'Sociological Introduction' in Glendon (ed) *International Encyclopedia of Comparative Law*, 1974, Mohr and Martinus-Nijhoff, Vol. IV, Ch. 1.

Krause, HD 'Comparative Family Law – Past Traditions Battle Future Trends and Vice Versa' in Reiman and Zimmerman (eds) *The Oxford Handbook of Comparative Law*, 2006, Oxford UP, pp. 1099–1129.

Martiny, D 'Divorce and Maintenance Between Former Spouses – Initial Results of the Commission on European Family Law' in Boele-Woelki (ed) *Perspectives for the Unification and Harmonisation of Family Law in Europe*, European Family Law Series No. 4, 2003, Intersentia.

Masson, Bailey-Harris, Probert (eds) *Cretney's Family Law*, 8th ed, 2008, Sweet & Maxwell.

Pinsof, WM (ed) 'Marriage in the 20th Century in Western Civilization: Trends, Research, Therapy and Perspectives' (2002) 41 *Family Process* 133 (Special Issue).

Rheinstein, M 'The Family and the Law' in *International Encyclopedia of Comparative Law*, 1974, JCB Mohr, Tubingen, Vol. IV, Ch. 1.

Shorter, E *The Making of the Modern Family*, 1976, Collins.

Standley, K *Family Law*, 2008, Palgrave Macmillan.

Verschraegen, B 'Divorce' in *International Encyclopaedia of Comparative Law*, 2004, Mohr and Martinus Nijhoff, Vol. IV, Ch. 5.

Part II

Jurisdictional survey

Chapter 1

Family law in Europe

Introduction

This chapter undertakes a comparative study of divorce, focusing on the original common law jurisdiction of England, and on France and Germany as examples of civil law jurisdictions. We trace the development of divorce law in each of these jurisdictions from a broad historical perspective, and having looked at the particular events and forces which shaped their individual development, examine their current divorce laws. We also examine the legal effects of divorce in these three jurisdictions on matrimonial property and in relation to the children of a marriage, post-divorce.

Finally, we consider whether divorce laws have converged to any extent in these jurisdictions, a topic which has been discussed in the previous chapter and to which we shall return in the final chapter.

DIVORCE LAWS IN EUROPE

England

Historical background

Before 1857, marriage in English law was indissoluble except by Act of Parliament. This process was lengthy and expensive and available to only a few people. This was because marriage at this time was governed by the canon law of the Catholic Church which did not and does not allow divorce. Ecclesiastical courts could grant a divorce a mensa et thoro but this was more in the nature of a judicial separation and, while the decree allowed the couples to separate, it did not allow them to remarry. Judicial divorce, based on fault grounds, was introduced in 1857. In his excellent survey of the law of divorce before 1857, Finlay highlights the nebulous position of marriages before that year (it was difficult to prove whether a marriage was valid), the power of the ecclesiastical courts to pronounce decrees of nullity (for example, on the basis of marriage within the prohibited degrees of consanguinity, which were sometimes called a divorce) and the mistaken belief that the abortive reform advocated in the *Reformatio Legum Ecclesiasticarum* of Archbishop Thomas Cranmer during the reign of Henry VIII, which would have introduced divorce, had been enacted but which had not (Finlay, 1978, pp. 120–1).

The Matrimonial Causes Act 1857 (the 1857 Act) conferred on the court the power to grant decrees of dissolution of marriage, nullity and so on, while retaining the fundamental principle which underpinned the basis on which a divorce had been granted under parliamentary procedure – namely, that the only ground upon which divorce could be granted was the respondent's adultery; the petitioner had to show he was free from guilt; and the court had to be satisfied that there was no connivance or collusion between the parties seeking escape from the solemn obligations of marriage. Hence, divorce was a legal remedy which was available to a legally guiltless party (petitioner) who could establish that the other party (respondent) had committed the most serious of matrimonial offences – adultery (Cretney and Masson, 2003, p. 270). It is significant that under this 1857 Act, while the husband was allowed to petition solely on the basis of the wife's adultery, the wife could not rely on her husband's adultery as the sole basis of her petition. She had to prove adultery as well as some other fault-based conduct, such as adultery plus bigamy or incest, rape, sodomy, bestiality, cruelty or desertion. This extra requirement was abolished in 1923 but adultery remained the only ground for divorce and this could be defeated by evidence of collusion between the parties.

The effect of the Second World War

From 1939 to 1945 the Second World War intervened, which inevitably led to a very difficult period for the British population, who had to bear not just the rigours and tribulations of the war but also its aftermath. As Cretney *et al.* put it, during this period: 'There were hasty weddings, enforced separations – sometimes lasting for years – and all the tensions of life in an uncertain, dangerous and deprived world. There was a divorce explosion' (Cretney *et al.*, 2008, p. 285). The figures for divorce went from 8,517 in 1939 to 14,041 in 1947 (*Royal Commission on Marriage and Divorce, Report 1951–1955* Cmnd 9678 (1956)) which is remarkable by any standards. Yet there were many people who felt they were tied to relationships which had become meaningless in which they were trapped because their legal spouse refused to petition for divorce and could not be shown to have committed a matrimonial offence as required by the law. The situation was further complicated by people in 'stable illicit unions' who wished to marry, and inter alia, legitimize their children. Pressure from an increasingly vocal population began to mount to change the law so that marriages which were mere facades could be terminated in law (Cretney *et al.*, 2008, p. 285).

However, the legal position under the 1937 Act continued up to the mid-1960s when, after the idea had taken root that the existence of broken marriages was more damaging to the institution of marriage than their legal termination, several Bills were introduced with the aim of making separation a ground for divorce (see Cretney, 2003, p. 324, 346–48), and eventually two contemporaneous reports by the Law Commission and the Church of England became the catalysts for a change in the law.

The Archbishop of Canterbury appointed a committee to investigate the formulation of a principle of breakdown of marriage, and this committee recommended that irretrievable breakdown of marriage should be the sole ground for the dissolution of marriage and that the court should carry out a detailed inquest into the facts and causes of the alleged breakdown of the marriage. The Law Commission accepted the irretrievable breakdown principle as the sole ground for divorce and stipulated the aims of the reforms which were to buttress, rather than to undermine, the stability of marriage; and where a marriage had broken down irretrievably, to enable the empty shell to be destroyed with the maximum fairness and the minimum bitterness, distress and humiliation (see *The Field of Choice*, Cmnd 3123 (1966)). However, the Law Commission did not accept that an inquest should be conducted into the couple's marital relationship.

The ground of 'irretrievable breakdown'

As a result of the Divorce Reform Act 1969, divorce law was reformed making 'irretrievable breakdown' the sole ground for divorce, which could be established by proof of one of five 'facts'. These were (i) adultery and intolerability (as one fact); (ii) the respondent behaved in such a way that the petitioner could not reasonably be expected to live with the respondent; (iii) desertion for a continuous two-year period; (iv) the parties lived apart for a continuous period of at least two years and the respondent consents to the decree; (v) the parties lived apart for a continuous period of five years immediately preceding the petition; here consent of the respondent would be irrelevant. This law eventually came into force in 1971.

Up to 1971, therefore, divorce law was based on the concept of the matrimonial offence except for insanity. Condoning and collusion were also retained as bars.

The Divorce Reform Act was eventually consolidated into the Matrimonial Causes Act 1973 which also retained the requirement that no divorce could be presented until three years of the marriage had elapsed. In 1984 this was reduced to one year by the Matrimonial and Family Proceedings Act of that year.

In 1977, a 'special procedure' was introduced which had earlier been an exceptional procedure, namely the process of administrative divorce. This procedure allows undefended divorces to be granted by the submission of completed forms and affidavits by the parties. Unless there is some reason for doubting that the marriage has irretrievably broken down, the district judge will usually grant a decree of divorce with the minimum of formality and the non-attendance of the parties. The parties need only appear in chambers if there is some dispute over the arrangements for the welfare of any minor children of the marriage. Since defended divorces have become extremely rare in England and Wales, something in the region of one in every 100 divorces, divorce is in the majority of cases a purely administrative procedure, which is in stark contrast to the pre-1977 era when parties were frequently expected to testify in court and have the public and the media be privy to the innermost facets of their marital relationship. Hence divorce went from a very private and rare occurrence before 1857 to a highly public and sometimes painful spectacle in court, until 1977 when the introduction of the special procedure to all undefended divorces removed the public element of the process; at least as far as airing a married couple's relationship in an open court was concerned.

Fault as a guiding principle – what does it mean in practice?

The English cases as reported in the English Law Reports and English media provide a rich tapestry of divorce cases and, for better or worse, they illustrate the many ways in which spouses behave with various degrees of impropriety in the course of their marital relationship. The question which exercised the earlier courts was: If the marriage had broken down, whose fault was it? Hence, one of the key themes which emerges from divorce law is the notion and principle of 'fault' which derives from canon law from which the notion of 'sin' derives, and features in the operation and application of the ground for divorce, the award of financial provision, domestic violence and allocation of property upon divorce. We shall allude to this theme from time to time in this book when casting our eye on jurisdictions across the world. The second theme which emerges from this very brief survey is that as a result of the non-enactment of the relevant part of the Family Law Act 1996, both fault-based and non-fault based facts (such as living apart) co-exist in current English divorce law and other common law jurisdictions and civil law ones like France, even in the early twenty-first century. The third theme we shall consider at the end of the book is the extent to which family law concepts can (or have been) successfully transplanted from one jurisdiction to another: if they cannot, why not? If they can, which concepts have been successfully transplanted, how and why?

Colourful case law in England

One of the side effects of the special procedure has been to remove some of the many memorable divorce cases which have been reported in the Law Reports over nearly 150 years, not least in the context of adultery as a fact proving irretrievable breakdown. As we have already seen, the law on this matter is that a petition of divorce merely alleging adultery per se is insufficient; it has to be adultery and the fact that the petitioner finds it intolerable to live with the respondent. Crucially, as established by case law, the intolerability felt by the petitioner does not have to be because of the respondent's adultery and can exist independently of the alleged adultery. This has been criticized by academics (see e.g. Freeman, 1979) and by the courts themselves. In a colourful comment in the Court of Appeal case of *Dodds v Dodds* (*Daily Mail*, 24 March 1974, unreported) Faulks, J said: '[I]f you want to get a divorce, all you have to do is fill your wife with gin, give her a complaisant obliging lodger and file your petition next day. Connivance and collusion have gone, all you have to do is to say that you find it intolerable to live with her because she wears pink knickers – or none at all! As long as you use that idiotic remark "I find it intolerable to live with her" you can get a divorce.' This is not strictly true, and Freeman points out that Faulks J himself had stated earlier in the case of *Roper v Roper* [1972] 1 WLR 1314, that a court is not bound to accept that the petitioner finds it intolerable to live with the respondent purely on the basis of the petitioner's allegation. This was supported by both Lord Denning MR and Scarman LJ in *Cleary v Cleary* [1974] 1 All ER at 501 and 503, respectively (Freeman, 1979, p. 113). The court is technically required by s. 1(3) of the Matrimonial Causes Act 1973 to inquire so far as it reasonably can into the veracity of the facts alleged by the petitioner. However, it is widely accepted that the court does not have the capability or expertise to ascertain what is really in the mind of the petitioner and the practice has long been to accept the petitioner's statements at face value. The striking feature of this adultery and intolerability 'fact' was that it conflates the notion of fault in the guise of the offence of adultery with the idea of intolerability which derives from a different philosophy and accounts for the English courts placing somewhat inconsistent interpretations on this 'fact' (Freeman, 1979, p. 113).

Roper v Roper [1972] (*also at* 3 All ER 668) was itself memorable for its facts, which were that two sets of couples lived as neighbours and eventually swapped spouses. When the arrangement was terminated and a decree was sought, the fact that adultery had been committed and that the petitioning spouse now found it intolerable to live with the other was deemed sufficient to justify a divorce, even though the feeling of intolerability was not caused by the adultery committed by the respondent. As the judge observed, the adultery had in fact been enjoyed by the parties involved. This was simply to make the point that the two limbs of this 'fact' proving divorce were independent and that the mere fact that adultery had been committed and that the petitioner was stating that the marriage was now intolerable (and therefore irretrievably broken down) were sufficient to entitle the court to grant a decree.

Case law has been most plentiful under the so-called 'unreasonable behaviour' fact and courts also helped to answer questions which were sometimes raised both by the couple who were divorcing and some members of the wider public.

The frequency of sexual relations within marriage also came under scrutiny in the 1980s. In *Mason v Mason* (1980) 11 Fam Law 143, the Court of Appeal was asked to consider whether the refusal of a wife to have sexual relations with her husband more than once a week constituted behaviour which a 'reasonable' petitioner should not be expected to endure. The couple had been married for five years when the wife, a Roman Catholic, started to refuse to have sex with the husband for fear of becoming pregnant. The husband underwent a vasectomy, but being a practising Catholic who was strictly prohibited from using artificial contraception, the wife felt constrained to have sex only about once a week on average. The husband thought he could not really test whether his operation had been successful and he left his wife to live with another woman, who was prepared to have sex more frequently with him. Ormrod LJ discharged the petition saying that it seemed to him that agreeing to have sex once a week was not 'unreasonable behaviour'.

On a more bizarre note, the 1963 case of *Lines v Lines*, reported in *The Times* (16 July 1963) bears revisiting. The husband insisted that his wife tickle him all over every night and would sulk when the tickling stopped which therefore necessitated prolonged periods of tickling. This eventually left the wife in a state of acute anxiety and uncontrollable movements in her fingers. This was deemed by the court to be 'unreasonable behaviour' enabling the wife to obtain a decree.

Another 'behavioural' cases in the 1970s was the Court of Appeal case of *O'Neill v O'Neill* [1975] 3 All ER 289 where the husband blighted his family with a long period of DIY (do-it-yourself) jobs carried out on the matrimonial home, which persistently went wrong but which were not deemed to be sufficiently serious to warrant a divorce by the lower court. However, his unfounded allegation of infidelity which questioned the paternity of the couple's children was deemed sufficiently serious to justify a decree, as this was seen by the Appeal Court as demonstrating the extent to which the marriage had broken down irretrievably.

Divorce and marriage rates in the United Kingdom

Statistical snapshots

The current divorce rate in the United Kingdom has fallen slightly as has the number of marriages celebrated annually. Where marriages used to average 350,000 a year in the 1990s, with 150,000 divorces a year, this has now fallen in England and Wales to about 244,710 marriages in 2005, and 283,730 marriages in the United Kingdom in 2005 and 155,052 divorces between 2004 and 2005 (Office of National Statistics at http://www.statistics.gov.uk). The slump reverses a previous three-year trend of an increase in the number of weddings. A change in the law from 1 February 2005 made it more difficult for non-Europeans to win the right to stay in Britain by staging a sham marriage. The Office of National Statistics issued a statement saying that it was unclear whether the change in the Home Office rules had affected the marriage figures. However, the statistics indicate that the rise in the number of marriages between 2002 and 2004 from 249,000 to 273,000 may have been the result of couples undergoing sham marriages. Indeed, according to the Office of National Statistics, the number of marriages taking place in ethnically-diverse London fell by 35 per cent between 2004 and 2005 (see http://www.news.independent.co.uk).

The remarriage rate

In 2005, remarriages (for 98,580 couples) accounted for 40 per cent of all marriages, which was a rise from the previous percentage which was approaching 33 per cent (Office of National Statistics at http://www.statistics.gov.uk). Thus, the trend in Britain is that nearly half of marriages tend to fail if they are remarriages and for third marriages it is close to 60 per cent. Nevertheless, in March 2008, it was reported that more people are getting remarried than previously although the trend for remarriages is that they have been falling and have fallen by 25 per cent in the 25 years to 2006. Between 2005 and 2006, remarriages accounted for 18 per cent of all marriages.

The fall in marriage rates

A further fall in marriage rates was reported for 2006, with the marriage rate falling by 4 per cent since 2005, to 236,980. In 2006, the number of first marriages for both people fell by more than a third since 1981, constituting just 61 per cent of all marriages in 2006. The sharpest fall in the number of marriages was in London (29 per cent) and the smallest in the North-East (3 per cent).

The number of civil marriage ceremonies in approved places such as hotels and stately homes fell in 2006 but the number of religious marriage ceremonies fell by 7 per cent and civil marriage ceremonies now outnumber religious ones. Civil ceremonies represented 66 per cent of all ceremonies in 2006, up from 65 per cent in 2005. In 1990, the figure was 47 per cent of all ceremonies.

Fall in the divorce rate

The divorce rate also fell by 7 per cent in 2006 and the divorce rate is now at its lowest level since 1984. The number of divorces granted in the United Kingdom between 2005 and 2006 fell from 155,052 to 148,141. This is the second consecutive drop in the number of United Kingdom divorces and the lowest number since 1977. It is 18 per cent lower than the highest number of divorces, which peaked in 1993 with 180,018. One in five men and women divorcing in 2006 had a previous marriage ending in divorce, a proportion which has doubled in the last 25 years. In 2007 the divorce rate in England and Wales fell to 11.9 per 1,000 married people from 12.2 per 1,000 in 2006. This means that the divorce rate is now down to the 1981 level. The number of divorces also fell to 128,534, a drop of 3 per cent on 2006 and the lowest number since 1976.

Age groups with highest divorce rates

Another statistical feature is that most divorces take place among younger people, suggesting that if a couple survive the first few years of married life, the chances of staying together increase. For the sixth consecutive year (since 2000) men and women in their late twenties had the highest divorce rate of all five age groups at 26.8 per 1,000. Looking back to 1961, the average age of marriage has increased by more than five years, to 30 for men and 28 for women.

As far as children caught up in divorce are concerned, a total of 117,193 children aged under 16 were affected by divorce in 2007, nearly two thirds of whom were under 11 years old and a fifth of the total being under five (Office of National Statistics at http://www.statistics.gov.uk).

Numbers of over-sixties getting divorced reach record high

In 2007, the fall in the divorce rate applied to men and women across most age groups. A less common demographic feature of divorce statistics was reported by the media on 30 August 2008. This was that the number of over-sixties getting divorced in 2007 reached a record high, although official figures for 2007 showed that the overall divorce rate was falling. There were 13,678 divorces among the over-sixties in 2007 compared with 12,636 in 2006 and 9,052 in 1997. This was the only age group where the divorce rate rose among both men and women.

Indeed, rates increased not just for men and women aged 60 and over, but also for women aged between 45 and 49 (Office of National Statistics, reported in [2008] Fam Law 964).

Length of marriages

The length of the average marriage, in the first few years of the twenty-first century, is around 11 to 11.5 years. Thus, in terms of duration, the average (median) duration of marriage for divorces granted in 2007 increased to 11.7 years compared with the average of 11.6 years in 2006. One in five men and women divorcing in 2007 had a previous marriage ending in divorce. This proportion has doubled in 27 years. Of those divorces granted to a sole party in 2007, 68 per cent of divorces were granted to wives and in 54 per cent of these cases the husband's unreasonable behaviour was the fact proved. For 33 per cent of the divorces granted to the husband, the fact proved was the wife's unreasonable behaviour (Divorces in England and Wales: Office for National Statistics, 2007).

Children affected by divorce

Over half (51 per cent) of couples divorcing in 2007 had at least one child aged under 16. There were 117,193 children aged under 16 who were in families whose parents divorced in 2007. Twenty per cent of these children were under five and 63 per cent were under 11.

Comparative observations – the Irish experience of marriage

In contrast with the situation in England and Wales, and as a brief excursus from the breakdown of relationships, it would appear salutary to note that marriage seems alive and well in Ireland. The Irish marriage care service published the findings from a survey, *Married Life – The First Seven Years*, based on responses from 712 couples. The survey found that more than three out of four couples were very happy with their marriage and the majority of couples agreed that their relationship of love had become stronger the longer the marriage had lasted. Among the key findings were:

(i)   the average age at marriage is rising, and among the couples surveyed the average age was 28 and the man tended to be two years older than the woman;

(ii)   56 per cent of couples knew each other for more than three years before they married; 33 per cent for one year; and 11 per cent for less than one year;

(iii) 58 per cent of couples lived with their spouse before marriage;

(iv)   joint decision making is seen as the major disadvantage of marriage;

(v)   63 per cent of couples agree strongly that their relationship has strengthened since their marriage;

(vi)   nine out of ten couples would recommend marriage to another couple.

Matrimonial property in England and Wales

Property rights during marriage – historical context

As a general rule, in view of the doctrine of unity (husband and wife became 'one' via marriage), and ironically flowing from it (since that 'one' was the husband), in almost all systems of matrimonial property law which were in effect well into the nineteenth century the general rule was that the husband had the power to control all of the couple's property irrespective of whether title was in him, in his wife or jointly in both. Consequently, he controlled anything that flowed from the use of the combined funds and he had to bear all the expenses of the family (Rheinstein and Glendon, 1980, p. 33). Even when women of full age became legally capable of managing their property, upon marriage their husbands retained their power to control these women's property. This was modified in the English common law by the contractual establishment of a married woman's separate estate in equity. Legislatures in the United States began to enact laws in the earlier part of the nineteenth century, designed to reduce or remove the disabilities of married women. However, it was not until 1870 that such a law (the Married Women's Property Act) was enacted in England, since at this time the defects of the common law became more visible than ever and the complaints of women were made known to the public and Parliament, mainly through the efforts of John Stuart Mill, whose authority was highly influential, and as Dicey put it in 1905: 'To no cause was he more ardently devoted than to the emancipation of women' (Dicey, *Law and Public Opinion in England*, 1914, p. 384).

However, it took no less than seven pieces of legislation to fully equalize the position of women with men as far as the right to own and deal with property was concerned. The Married Women's Property Act in 1870 was just the first step to effect that equalization, similar to the French Law of 1907 and the German Civil Code of 1896. It allowed married women the freedom to deal with earnings resulting from their own labour and also with certain investments. The 1882 Act which followed made the whole property, whenever and however it came to her,

her separate property (Rheinstein and Glendon, 1980, p. 41). But anomalies and unsettled points required further legislation in 1884, 1893, 1907 and 1935. It was clearly a convoluted route to achieving equality between spouses.

As a result of the 1935 legislation, the Law Reform (Married Women and Tortfeasors) Act, each spouse was given the same powers over his or her property as the other.

Current law

The separate property principle

In England and Wales, under the current law, there is no community property legislation. Instead, primarily as a result of the Married Women's Property Act of 1882, there is a system of separate property which means that the mere fact that a couple get married has no proprietary consequences, meaning any property they owned or had a right to own before the marriage still belongs to them individually, in the absence of any enforceable agreement to the contrary. Of course, during the duration of the marriage, a couple will usually jointly acquire assets, make gifts to each other and many items will be used in common by the parties. Hence, Glendon talks about the 'considerable uncertainty' surrounding the ownership rights of spouses during marriage (Glendon, 1989, p. 125). In essence, each case will be decided on its own facts, often complicated by the couple invariably failing to keep track of the exact contributions they might each have made to the acquisition or enhancement of the particular property or asset. Upon divorce, the English court has wide and far-reaching discretionary powers under the Matrimonial Causes Act 1973 to make orders with regard to the couple's assets, moveable and immoveable, including the matrimonial home.

The leading cases in this area are *Pettit* [1970] AC 777 and *Gissing* [1971] AC 886, two cases decided by the House of Lords in the 1970s which went a considerable way to establishing a baseline from which a court can decide the ownership of marital property that is not clearly identified as belonging to one or both spouses. In *Pettit*, Lord Upjohn said at 813:

> 'The rights of the parties ... must be judged on the general principles applicable in any court of law when considering questions of title to property, and though the parties are husband and wife these questions of title must be decided by the principles of law applicable to the settlement of claims between those not so related, while making full allowances in view of the relationship.'

The question of which spouse could enforce his or her right to property was resolved by the court asking what the intention of the parties was when the property was acquired. Since there is the usual problem of parties not having directed their minds to the question of ownership when a particular item was acquired, the court would simply 'impute' to the parties a constructive common intention which it considered would have been formed by 'reasonable spouses' (see Lord Diplock in *Pettit* [1970] AC 777 at 823).

The matrimonial home

As far as the matrimonial home is concerned, if both parties' names were on the deeds, there would be an equal division of the proceeds of sale of the property. However, if only one party's name was on the deed, the question would be whether the party whose name did not appear had made a contribution towards the purchase of the property which entitled her (usually the wife) to a share in the proceeds of sale of the property.

In the 1970s, there was a divergence between the House of Lords and the Court of Appeal with regard to which sorts of contributions the court would recognize in situations where only one party's name appears on the title deeds. While the Court of Appeal, usually led by Lord Denning MR, was prepared to recognize non-monetary contributions, provided they were substantial and could be linked to the acquisition of the property, the House of Lords was only prepared to recognize direct, financial contributions towards the acquisition of the property as legally entitling the non-named spouse to have a share in the proceeds of sale of the home.

In more recent times, it would appear that, for the most part, the House of Lords' approach has been followed.

Wide discretion under the Matrimonial Causes Act 1973

The English courts have a wide discretion and range of powers under the Matrimonial Causes Act 1973 which enables them to make orders for interim and final maintenance and periodical payments. These may be secured or unsecured; a lump sum order; or a property adjustment order of any interest in any asset owned by either spouse.

Distribution of matrimonial property upon divorce

The Matrimonial Causes Act 1973

The manner by which the distribution of a couple's assets is decided when they divorce is governed by statute, namely the Matrimonial Causes Act 1973. However, in typical English style, the relevant statutory provisions have to be interpreted by the courts, which have a very wide discretion under the key provision, s. 25. This statute lists seven guidelines, with no hierarchy of importance, as each case will turn on its own merits.

From the mid-1970s until 2000, the focus was on the applicant's 'reasonable needs' but this changed with the landmark case of *White v White* and cases like *Lambert v Lambert*.

Deferred community of property in English law? White and Lambert

Cretney (2003, p. 349) describes the combined effect of the decision of the House of Lords in *White v White* [2001] 1 AC 596 and the Court of Appeal in *Lambert v Lambert* [2003] 2 WLR 63 as 'dramatic' because they introduce into English law a regime of (deferred) community of property limited to acquisitions. The effect of these cases is that when a marriage is ended by divorce, and the couple have considerable financial assets, the court will, after making provision for the family's housing and other needs, seek to divide up the spouses' property so that each has an equal share. There has been some uncertainty among practitioners and academics as to whether the *White v White* approach of advocating an equal distribution in order to be fair to both parties through the 'yardstick of equality', applies only to the so-called 'big money' cases where the available assets are far in excess of an applicant's needs or whether it has a wider application to cases where the assets are not considerable or abundant, involving middle-income couples. Academic comments on these cases have been plentiful, speculating on what should or should not be regarded as the correct approach in these sorts of cases and as to what would be fair in each case.

Herring argues that seeking fairness between the parties is not only 'misguided' but 'undesirable' in this context (Herring, 2005, p. 219). He lists no less than eight interests which the state or wider community has in financial orders made on divorce which transcend the notion that such orders should be made as if they are purely a private matter between the parties. These include the state's interest in whether on divorce either party becomes dependent on welfare payments; the impact of such payments on how children and incapacitated adults are cared for by married couples; the symbolic power of financial orders; the impact of the level of spousal support on whether the child-caring spouse is employed or not, her level of happiness and self-respect and so on; the knowledge of what such orders are likely to be might even affect a party's decision whether to seek a divorce or not; the impact of such orders on how people behave following divorce; an approach based on fairness inter partes does not help to combat the poverty women face on divorce; and it is important that couples regard marriage in more mutual terms rather than as potential claimants in civil litigation, hence marriage should be viewed as a partnership of mutual obligation (see Herring, 2005).

Practitioner survey on effect of White

On the practitioner front, a small scale survey of family practitioners carried out by Emma Hitchings over a five-month period between September 2007 and February 2008, suggests that cases like *White* have not really had a significant impact on everyday cases of ancillary relief (that is, those not involving 'big money'), since every marriage/divorce is unique, hence these landmark cases, at least in the latter years of the first decade of the new millennium, appear to be of only passing relevance (Hitchings, 2008). It remains to be seen if this trend will continue.

Greater judicial recognition of the value of homemaker services in financial awards upon divorce

White v White [2001] 1 AC 596 is also notable for the statement by Lord Nicholls (p. 605): 'There should be no bias in favour of the money-earner and against the home-maker and childcarer.' He argued that to draw such a distinction would perpetuate discrimination and sent a clear message that child-rearing or home-making should not be considered less valuable but indeed equal to money-earning (Silbaugh, 1996).

The relevance of adverse conduct or fault on financial provision allocation

Current English law shows that fault or adverse conduct plays its part in the allocation of financial provision in divorce and ancillary relief proceedings, and must be considered under s. 25(2)(g) of the Matrimonial Causes Act 1973, but usually only where the conduct is extreme (personal violence towards a spouse, gross behaviour such as hiring a person to kill a spouse, child abuse within the family, treating a spouse in a particularly degrading manner, for example, imprisoning him in a caravan while the wife stays in the family home with her young lover). However if both spouses have engaged in equally disgusting behaviour, the court might disregard the conduct altogether in making the financial award post-divorce (see *Leadbeater* [1985] 1 FLR 789).

As the House of Lords made clear in *Miller* [2006] UKHL 24, conduct is only to be taken into account in exceptional cases where it satisfies the criteria under the Matrimonial Causes Act 1973; that is, where it would be 'inequitable to disregard it' and where it can be clearly seen that one party is more to blame than the other.

Several cases confirm the relevance of conduct in the allocation of financial provision upon divorce if the conduct is exceptionally appalling or is seen as intending to place the other spouse at a considerable disadvantage in physical, emotional or financial terms.

The law on children in England and Wales

For many decades the law relating to children was shaped largely by case law but the major legislation governing children is the Children Act 1989 which came into force on 14 October 1991.

General principles under the Children Act 1989

There are three general principles set out in s. 1 of the Children Act 1989 (the 1989 Act) which are designed to guide a court when it makes any decisions under the Act. The first is the welfare principle, namely when a court is determining any question with respect to the child's upbringing or administration of the child's property or the application of income from a child's property, the child's welfare shall be the court's paramount consideration. The second is the no-delay principle where in any case involving the upbringing of a child, the court must consider that any delay in determining the question is likely to prejudice the welfare of the child. The third is the no-order principle. This principle is regarded as a means of preventing cases from being brought to court unnecessarily. Hence, when a court is considering whether or not to make an order under the 1989 Act, it must not make any order unless an order would be better for the child than not making any order at all. For example, post-divorce, if parties can reach an agreement with regard to the children, there would be no need for a court order.

The best interests principle

The welfare or best interests principle made its first appearance in a statute in 1925 in the English Guardianship of Minors Act of that year. However, it had been used for many years by English judges and is traceable to at least 1857. In that year, by virtue of the implementation of the Divorce Reform Act of that year, there was a transfer of jurisdiction over divorce from the ecclesiastical to the secular courts. This created a need for guidelines for dealing with dependants of broken marriages, which had previously been restricted to the very few who could afford to pay for a divorce by a private Act of Parliament. The principle evolved through the English courts of equity (a separate court from the King's courts which developed as a means of counterbalancing the more rigid common law procedures) as a way of protecting the property of children in a legal environment where the predominant ethos was the enforcement of patriarchal authority, rather than to support child-care (see Maidment, 1984). Researchers such as Susan Maidment argue that the history of the child welfare principle should be linked to the women's movement of the nineteenth and early twentieth centuries, and she argues that the 1865 and 1925 Guardianship of Infants Acts were responsible for at least deflecting the debate about women's rights from the public to the domestic sphere by adopting a more official stance which admitted the importance of women to children. English judges have generally espoused it throughout the twentieth century, but as Freeman points out, there are family law cases even in the early 1960s where there is no mention of a child's best interests even by a judge as prescient as Lord Denning (see e.g. *Re L* [1962] 1 WLR 886). On the other hand, in 1977, Ormrod LJ in *S(BD) v S(D)* [1977] 1 All ER 656, a dispute about children, did assert categorically that the question was not about what the 'essential justice of the case requires' but 'what was in the best interests of the children' (see Freeman, 2000, pp. 441ff.)

Since 14 October 1991, the best interests principle has been enshrined in s. 1 of the Children Act 1989 (UK) which ensures that the child's welfare shall be the paramount consideration where the court is determining any question with regard to the child's upbringing. There is a checklist in s. 1(3) of the 1989 Act which includes the statement: '[A] court shall have regard in particular to (a) the ascertainable wishes and feelings of the child concerned (considered in the light of his age and understanding).' This is obviously more relevant to the older child who is capable of expressing a view.

The welfare principle has been utilized in the context of disputes over child custody (as it is still called in most jurisdictions, other than the United Kingdom which has abolished the term and uses an umbrella term such as 'parental responsibility', and 'contact' to replace what used to be called 'access' to children in the aftermath of a divorce). This is much wider than the previous notion of access.

Section 8 orders

Private law orders for a child may be made, for example on divorce, under s. 8 of the Children Act 1989. There are four types of s. 8 orders. These are: a residence order, a contact order, a prohibited steps order and a specific issue order.

A residence order may be applied for by either parent to determine with whom a child should live. Other applicants include a relative or interested person, and more than one person may share a residence order. Both separated parents could therefore have a residence order.

A contact order has replaced the old 'access' order. This order may be applied for by either party to the marriage in order to resolve a dispute over who should have contact with a child, usually after a separation or a divorce. The order would require the person with whom the child lives, or is to live, to allow the child to visit or stay with the person named in the order. This sort of order is wider than the previous type of access order as it allows the child to visit or stay with the person named in the order; or to have other forms of contact with the child such as telephone calls or letters. Grandparents, relatives and even friends can apply for such an order.

The prohibited steps order prevents a parent, while exercising his or her parental responsibility, from taking any step without the consent of the court. Hence, a court could order that a parent could not remove a child from the jurisdiction, unless the court gave its permission.

The specific issue order, as its name suggests, allows a court to give directions to determine a specific issue which may arise or have arisen in connection with the exercise of parental responsibility, such as which school the child should attend or which religion the child should be obliged to follow.

The child's welfare – the paramount consideration and other factors

Regardless of which order is applied for, the child's welfare is the court's paramount consideration and the court is obliged to consider the seven factors listed in the s. 1(3) checklist under the 1989 Act. The court may consider other factors (*Re G* [2006] UKHL 43) but this will depend on the circumstances of each case. The seven factors, apart from the ascertainable wishes and feelings of the child, include the child's physical, emotional and educational needs; the effect on the child of any change in his circumstances; the child's age, sex and background; any harm (ill-treatment or impairment of health or development) which the child has suffered or is at risk of suffering; the capability of the child's parents to meet the child's needs; and the range of powers available to the court. Courts may make shared residence orders as well as sole residence orders.

Case law has not been conclusive with regard to whether there is a maternal preference with regard to the court's allocation of parental responsibility. However, the more recent cases suggest that while babies are probably better off with their mothers, with older children there is no presumption in favour of mothers or fathers (see *Re A* [1998] 1 FLR 354). There also seems to be a strong presumption in favour of keeping a child with his or her natural parent at least to the extent that a child should not be removed from the primary care of the biological parent without compelling reasons (see *Re G* [2006] UKHL 43). Finally, siblings would normally be allowed to stay together in the same household unless there are strong reasons for not doing so (*C v C* [1988] 2 FLR 291) but the further apart in age, the weaker the presumption and there are cases where they can be separated (*B v B* [1997] 1 FLR 139).

EUROPEAN COUNTRIES

In accordance with the rest of this book, while we glance at other European jurisdictions, our focus is on France and Germany as two typical civil law countries, that is, countries which inherited the jus civile or civil law of the Romans.

Historical context

As we saw in Part I, the Introductory Overview, the present family law in Europe is to a large extent the product of the radical transformations that commenced in the 1960s and 1970s. These events have brought about several far-reaching changes to marriage, divorce, matrimonial property, the law relating to children and an equalization of the status of women and men within the marital relationship.

France

Historical background to divorce law

France is still a Catholic country, hence one might have thought that there would not be a great deal of leeway for divorce in such a jurisdiction. Nevertheless, France has had laws permitting divorce since 1792 and its 1975 Divorce Reform Law still contains a range of fault and no-fault grounds for divorce.

On 20 September 1792, at the time of the Revolution, a very liberal law on divorce was brought into force, placing the Revolution's commitment to the rights of the individual to the forefront. This law was a radical departure from what had earlier transpired, since under the ancien regime, marriage was indissoluble. The 1792 law enabled couples to divorce quickly and easily with the law acknowledging marital breakdown as well as fault. In the former, neither spouse would need to be named the guilty party to the divorce. Couples could divorce by mutual consent or one spouse could sue for divorce simply for incompatibility of temperament. A waiting period of six months was imposed before a divorce could be initiated to prevent careless use of this ground. As far as fault-based grounds were concerned, these included immorality, cruelty, insanity, condemnation for certain crimes, desertion for two years, or emigration. This was not only a very liberal law but was affordable even to the very poor and was equally available throughout France. Ideologically, it 'was not based on any double standard of sexual morality that would have put women at a disadvantage' (Plott in *Encyclopaedia of Revolution of 1848* at http://www.ohiou.edu/-chastain/dh/divorce.htm). This law was, however, clearly anti-Catholic.

When Napoleon came to power, however, divorce was made more difficult to obtain. In 1803, it was included as part of the Napoleonic Civil Code but the law was curtailed to make it much more restrictive. A sexual double standard was introduced into the law: a woman could be divorced for simple adultery but a man could not be convicted of adultery unless he brought his mistress into his home. To make it less accessible, divorce was also made more expensive and more difficult in procedural terms. This had the effect of strengthening patriarchal authority within the family and drastically reduced the number of divorces to about a tenth of their number under the 1792 law. Women continued to outnumber men as petitioners in divorce cases after 1803 which is remarkable since they were in a far weaker position than men to initiate proceedings at this time.

The Civil Code of 1804 thus upheld and reinforced the patriarchal model of a legitimate family, with its social functions being to perpetuate the species and to transmit the inheritance (patrimony). The institution of marriage was protected because the legitimate family was a centrepiece of social life.

Indeed, in 1816, when the monarchy returned to France, divorce was abolished entirely as part of the Restoration. Under Louis XVII, Roman Catholicism was reinstated as the state religion and, in accordance with its doctrine, judicial separation became the only option for couples wishing to divorce. In the aftermath of the fall of the Bourbons in the Revolution of 1831, four attempts were made to reestablish the Napoleonic law (in 1831, 1832, 1833 and 1834) via the introduction of a divorce Bill but the chamber of peers rejected any measure which would have signified a return to the Revolution and the French aristocracy was determined to reject its revolutionary past.

In 1848, another revolution took place, which brought a new attempt to reintroduce divorce in France but this proved unsuccessful as well, with some critics maintaining that 'the only moral foundation for marriage was its indissolubility' and arguing that its reinstatement would sully the purity and strength of all marriages, even those which it would not dissolve. Indissolubility was seen by many as the 'cornerstone of social order and stability' (Plott in *Encyclopaedia of Revolution of 1848* at http://www.ohiou.edu/-chastain/dh/divorce.htm).

Divorce then seemed to disappear from the public arena until the final years of the Second Empire. The 1860s saw a new mood of political liberalization and feminists like Audouard and Richer called for divorce to be reintroduced. This was given a fillip with the establishment of the Third Republic, and between 1875 and 1884 conferences were organized in towns throughout France by Naquet, a former radical socialist and now deputy from the Vaucluse, and other supporters of a new law. Women played a small part in this movement to establish a new divorce law. In 1876 and 1878, Naquet introduced a Bill, modelled on the original law of 1792, but met with either derision or little success. He abandoned the 1792 model and formulated a more conservative Bill based on the Napoleonic version which was eventually passed by the senate after the sexual double standard was deleted by removing the ground for divorce of a husband's adultery.

In the 1880s there was still widespread concern about divorce being reintroduced but eventually, with agreement of both chambers in 1884, men and women were able to divorce, re-establishing divorce in France after a period of 68 years.

Current French divorce law

Divorce is available under French law in the Civil Code, arts 229–310. The grounds for divorce are: (i) by mutual consent, upon a joint request or upon the request of either party, when accepted by the other party; (ii) on the ground of fault; (iii) irretrievable deterioration of married life, which is available after two years of de facto separation. The third ground was added in 2004, coming into force on 1 January 2005.

There is therefore a combination of fault and no-fault grounds. Under divorce by joint request, both parties may request the assistance of the same lawyer. If a party does not have sufficient income to pay for legal services, there is a right to apply for judicial aid.

The former third ground for divorce used to be by separation or by termination of the common life of the parties, and this was only available after there had been at least six years of de facto separation. This is further discussed below.

Divorce by mutual consent

There are two kinds of divorce under this head. The first is where the parties agree on the marriage breakdown and ancillary matters; the second is where the spouses are agreed about marriage breakdown but not on ancillary issues. Under the previous law, the spouses must have been married for at least six months before they could apply under this ground. Under the law of 2004 (see above and p. 60) this form of divorce is now available immediately after the parties have married.

Where the parties agree on divorce and ancillary matters, the parties must present a draft agreement to the court, with advice from an avocat. The agreement has to make provision for ancillary matters such as settlement of property, child maintenance, the matrimonial home and custody of children. The judge has to consider whether the terms are fair to both parties and make adequate provision for the children. As in other jurisdictions, the judge must discuss the possibility of reconciliation with the parties. If a reconciliation is successful, then the petition is dismissed but if unsuccessful, the judge has to wait three months to give the parties an opportunity to reflect on the implications of the divorce and, at the end of this period, the parties have to renew their application.

Guimezanes points out that the judge has no jurisdiction to pronounce on the appropriateness of the divorce but is allowed to advise the parties on its suitability. However, once the court is satisfied that the draft agreement has been entered into voluntarily and that the parties have genuinely reached an agreement, it has to confirm the agreement, subject to the requirements enunciated above, and pronounce the divorce. If the parties are no longer in agreement about ancillary matters, the court must halt proceedings and non-consensual proceedings must be started and two advocates must now be instructed if the parties had initially only instructed one (Guimezanes, 2001, p. 268).

Where the parties have agreed to a divorce but not on ancillary matters, the applicant must apply to the family judge and describe the matrimonial situation and state that the spouse 'cannot reasonably be expected to continue living with the other spouse' (Guimezanes, 2001, p. 268).

Divorce on the basis of fault

Divorce can be sought on the basis of the fault of one or both spouses. If a spouse has committed a serious criminal offence, a divorce can be granted automatically. For other cases, the judge has a discretion whether to grant the divorce depending on the particular facts. This ground covers serious and persistent violations of marital duties and obligations, rendering it intolerable for the spouses to live together (art. 242). The notion of intolerability is echoed in current English divorce legislation (see pp. 43–44). This ground is 'wide enough to cover adultery, failure to fulfil financial obligations, child neglect, desertion without reasonable cause, refusal to have sexual intercourse and cruelty' (Guimezanes, 2001, p. 270). Guimezanes explains that if both spouses have behaved unreasonably, the judge may pronounce divorce on the basis of mutual fault, even if the parties did not actually apply for divorce on this ground. This may have repercussions on the financial obligations of spouses on divorce (Guimezanes, 2001, p. 270). It should be noted that under the 2004 Act, divorce for fault will still cover repeated violations of conjugal duties that render married life unbearable and is not restricted to cases of physical violence.

Divorce after separation or termination of the common life of the parties (now abolished)

This used to be available if (i) the couple had lived apart for a continuous period of at least six years; or (ii) where the mental faculties of one of the spouses has, for at least the past six years, become so altered that life together is no longer possible, that is, so that community of life is no longer possible, and there was no longer any reasonable chance of community of life being resumed in the near future (art. 238).

Reforms in French divorce law

On 27 May 2004, the new 26 May 2004 Act on Divorce was published in the official journal and this Act came into force on 1 January 2005. This Act amends the Divorce Act 1975 to the extent that there are now three grounds for divorce with only two of the former grounds for divorce remaining, namely divorce by mutual consent and divorce for fault. The form of divorce for the 'breaking up of married life' which was open to couples after six years of de facto separation, has been abolished and replaced by the new 'divorce for irretrievable deterioration of married life' which is available after two years of de facto separation. English divorce lawyers will note immediately that English divorce legislation has had a two-year separation ground since 1973 under its Matrimonial Causes Act 1973, but this was and is subject to the consent of the respondent. In the absence of such consent, a five-year separation ground is available under English law, which can be granted irrespective of the respondent's consent.

The French ground for divorce on the basis of fault will still apply to cases of serious or repeated violation of conjugal·duties that render married life unbearable and the application of this ground will not be confined to cases of physical violence, as previously believed. Divorce by mutual consent remains but with simplified procedural requirements. In order to reduce the need for litigation, there will not be investigation of the spouses' grounds for divorcing and these need not even be expressed in the application. In addition, attempts at reconciliation are now given priority.

On 29 October 2004 a decree stipulating measures for the enforcement of the 26 May 2004 Act on Divorce was adopted. This decree enacts changes in the procedural requirements under the Code of Civil Procedure, relating to divorce and marital separation. The judge now has an important role in counselling and provides that compensatory property settlements may be temporarily enforced before the final decision is made.

Matrimonial property allocation upon divorce

Under the Napoleonic Code of 1804, France adopted a matrimonial property regime whereby there was a community of moveable property brought to the marriage, and community of property of any other kind acquired after the marriage. The parties also have the option to enter into a prenuptial agreement to decide how they would like their property to be shared in the event of a divorce. However, it is worth noting that any gift between spouses agreed upon in a prenuptial agreement will be invalid in favour of a donee spouse who is at fault in the divorce or is the applicant to a separation divorce. On divorce, the matrimonial regime must be terminated which is effected according to the regime contained in the Civil Code or that chosen by the parties in their prenuptial agreement, although any gift between spouses agreed upon in a prenuptial agreement will be ineffective in relation to a donee spouse who is at fault in the divorce or who happens to be the applicant in a separation divorce (Guimezanes, 2001, p. 272). Under art. 1540, the spouses can agree on liquidation of the matrimonial regime before the divorce has been granted, or the decree of divorce itself may deal with these issues. The matrimonial property regime in respect of the spouses terminates on the day the divorce application is presented, so that the decree of divorce has a retroactive effect. As far as third parties are concerned, the legal consequences of divorce will take effect on the day the divorce is published, which is when notice of the divorce is lodged with the municipal magistrate at the Register of Births, Marriages and Deaths (Guimezanes, 2001, p. 272).

Children

In any legal proceedings involving children, the court bears in mind three main principles: (i) The child's best interests are the prime consideration of the court when it is deciding any question relating to guardianship, custody or upbringing of a child. (ii) Strict equality between legitimate and illegitimate children must be observed, as far as possible. (iii) Emphasis must be placed on the biological and social aspects of parentage (see art. 311–11) (Guimezanes, 2001, p. 279). The mere granting of the divorce decree does not affect parental duties hence both parties remain responsible for the maintenance of any child of the family.

The best interests principle

In France, the best interests principle has been a dominant influence since the early nineteenth century. It was then called 'a general principle in law' and has been well-established in both codified law and case law, although the original version was that of the best interests of childhood rather than of the child, 'perceived as serving the general interests of society' (Rubellin-Devichi, 1992, p. 260). This was apparently the impetus for nineteenth century laws to be devised to protect children from exploitation from child labour, apprenticeship contracts, control of wet-nurses and to provide for compulsory schooling (Rubellin-Devichi, 1992, p. 261). This principle echoes the principle stated in s. 1 of the Children Act 1989 (UK) (see discussion of English law on children, pp. 54–56). From a comparativist viewpoint, the French also apply this principle when the court is deciding any question relating to guardianship, custody or the upbringing of a child. In the nineteenth century, the child came to be perceived as an individual when the law of 24 July 1889 allowed courts to deprive a father of his paternal power. Rubellin-Devichi argues that this has been 'unanimously interpreted' as a measure to protect the child and not as a form of removing a parent's power (Rubellin-Devichi, 1992, p. 260. The best interests test is also the basis of educative assistance, so if a child's health, safety or morality are in danger, a judge may be consulted. The current guiding principle for the court in cases involving children remains the child's best interests.

Parental authority, children and divorce

Unless a court orders otherwise, both parties retain and continue to exercise joint parental authority over their children even though a divorce has been granted. The court will deal with issues involving the children of the divorcing couple during the divorce proceedings but these are not final so that new orders can be made if circumstances change. Parents usually enter into an agreement concerning ancillary matters upon divorce and this agreement will invariably include sorting out the living arrangements for the children. The recognition of joint custody in 1987 has led to a reduction in the number of cases being litigated with regard to children.

The court will resolve any conflict if the parents cannot agree over custody of the children or reach an agreement which is considered to be contrary to the welfare of the children. The non-custodial parent will retain the right to participate in major decisions concerning the child, for example in relation to the child's education or health, and has a right of access. Indeed, under the new Penal Code, art. 227–5, any obstruction of the right of access to a child is a criminal offence punishable by a maximum of one year's imprisonment and a fine. The judge has the power to revoke parental authority if he or she considers that the child's welfare merits it, for instance if the parent is guilty of gross misbehaviour. As we have already seen, the judge's primary concern in cases involving children is the child's best interests. The judge may also listen to the views of a child aged 13 and above in relation to with whom the child wishes to live, but in practice the child is usually only heard when a party requests such an interview to take place (Guimezanes, 2001, p. 280). As is the case in England and Wales, and American jurisdictions, social workers and experts can be asked to report and give evidence. Parents have the right to say how their parental authority should be exercised and may also be asked for their opinion on these matters by the court. If circumstances change, the court has the right to change or vary parental authority orders, hence these are not final orders.

Duty to maintain child

There is a duty on a parent to maintain a child regardless of whether that parent has custody or parental authority but parentage has to be established. The legal obligation exists irrespective of whether the child is a marital or non-marital child. The judge will determine the amount of maintenance payable and under art. 293 of the Civil Code, the judge has the power to order periodical payments to be made to the parent with whom the child usually resides or to the parent with parental authority or to any other person who has been granted custody of the child. A maintenance order can be made during or after divorce proceedings, or when parentage is established. Criminal sanctions can be imposed for a failure to comply with a maintenance order.

The amount of maintenance ordered will depend on the financial capacity of each parent. It will usually be index-linked and may be varied depending on any changes in the financial capacity of the parents or according to the child's needs.

It is worth noting that adult children have a duty to support their parents and grandparents if they are in need of financial support (Guimezanes, 2001, p. 281).

Germany

Historical background to family law

Germany was a loose confederation of kingdoms, duchies, principalities and 39 independent city states until its unification on 23 January 1871 by Otto von Bismarck, the Prussian Chancellor. Germany was the homeland of the Protestant Reformation but even in the Holy Roman Empire of the sixteenth century, many territories adhered to Roman Catholicism or reverted to it, in accordance with the policy of the ruling house.

In the nineteenth century there were considerable differences amongst the German states, depending on whether the particular state followed the Catholic or Protestant tradition.

Prior to the legal unification of the German empire, which took place when its Civil Code came into force in January 1900, Rheinstein notes that there were three major legal approaches to divorce in the regions of Germany (Rheinstein, 1971, pp. 293–4). First, he mentions the regime of the Code Napoleon, which had been followed in the Rhineland and the Grand Duchy of Baden. The Code allowed divorce by mutual consent. Second, there was the so-called common law of Germany, which referred questions of marriage and divorce to ecclesiastical law, which would mean canon law for Catholics and Protestant ecclesiastical law for Protestants. Consequently, in places where common law applied, marriage would be indissoluble for Catholics and divorce was available to Protestants on narrow fault grounds only. This diverged from the Code Napoleon. The third approach was that of the Prussian General Code of 1794 which applied to about half of the territory of Prussia and also to a few small territories outside its boundaries.

The Prussian Code is illuminating since it allowed marriages to be dissolved by mutual consent and upon the application of one spouse, and not just for fault which was already permitted under Protestant law. The research of Heinreich Dorner, cited by Mary Ann Glendon (Glendon, 1989, p. 174) suggests that the Prussian Code bore the influence of Frederick the Great, who was an admirer of Voltaire, a staunch proponent of individual liberty which inspired the French liberal divorce law of 1792. Dorner's research unearthed a cabinet directive of 1783 which explains the rationale for the Code's principle of free divorce. The actual directive suggests that the purpose of a liberal divorce law was to enable spouses who were no longer living in harmony to divorce so that they could be free to meet other partners and produce offspring! So the main objective was to promote population growth (Glendon, 1989, p. 174). Mutual consent divorce was only to be made available when the couple was childless and unilateral divorce was to be granted when the petitioner could prove 'the existence of such a violent and deep rooted aversion, that no hope remains for reconciliation and for achievement of the purposes of marriage' (Part II, Title I, s. 1716 of the Prussian General Code) Thus, under the Prussian Code, the main purpose of marriage was expressly stated to be the procreation and upbringing of children (s. 718a of the Prussian General Code).

Once the country was unified, there was a need for a single regime of divorce and the draftsmen of the Civil Code selected a model based on the French model when divorce was reinstated in the French Civil Code of 1884. Divorce would be available only on the basis of the misconduct of one spouse and the grounds for divorce included adultery, bigamy, insanity, unnatural practices, attempt on a spouse's life, wilful desertion and a general fault ground (see the former arts 1564–87 of the German Civil Code (BGB)). Looking at these grounds, it can be seen that insanity was acknowledged as one exception to other fault-based grounds. Rheinstein's studies of divorce in Germany during the 19 years before the new code came into force and 16 years after it took effect indicate that the new law had no noticeable influence on either the incidence of divorce or the behaviour of the judges (Rheinstein, 1971, pp. 295–301).

Germany did not decide to retain the fault principle until the second half of the twentieth century. During the Third Reich, under the National Socialist regime, a new marriage law fundamentally altered the law of divorce. The grounds for divorce were altered so as to be partly fault-based and partly non-fault based. A divorce could therefore be made where the marital community of the couple had ceased to exist for three years and there was no expectation that the spouses would restore it, because of a grave irretrievable breakdown. In other words, if the couple had been separated for three years and the relationship had irretrievably broken down. After the Second World War, when the 1938 Act came under review, the Allied Control Council re-enacted it and added a hardship clause. Provisions such as divorce for 'unreasonable refusal to beget children' were deleted on the basis of being too closely associated with the National Socialist ideology. The current German state, called the Federal Republic of Germany, was founded in 1949 in the wake of Germany's defeat in the Second World War. West Germany consisted of areas occupied by British, French and American forces and East Germany was run by the then Soviet regime. The two German states existed alongside each other, following widely divergent ideologies. East Germany was much speedier in implementing reform. Unlike West Germany, women in East Germany were encouraged to work, and to obtain training so they could procure employment. State support for childcare was made available, and state benefits were also made available for single parents, predominantly women, with children. The 1938 law became the divorce law in West Germany in 1946. This provided for divorce upon proof of two types of matrimonial misconduct, namely adultery and any other 'violations of matrimonial duties' so serious that they led to disruption of the marriage and made the resumption of a common conjugal life an unreasonable expectation. Divorce was also available for two types of cases where neither spouse could be charged with fault. The first of these was divorce on the ground of the physical or mental condition of the defendant. In the second, divorce was permissible upon proof of three years' separation, with no reference to misconduct of the defendant.

The breakdown principle was much debated by the quadripartite committee on the reform of German law, established by the four allied powers to purge German law of Nationalist Socialist ideology. Their initial view was that the breakdown ground was similar to racial and eugenic aspects of the marriage law and should be deleted. However, the American member of the committee eventually persuaded his colleagues that the breakdown principle was not intrinsically sullied. He pointed out that the American state of Louisiana had a long-established non-fault separation ground based on three years' separation and Louisiana could certainly not be associated with any Socialist or Nazi policies.

Despite arguments about the use of this breakdown clause over the next few decades, it continued to play an increasingly small role in practice. In 1950 it accounted for 12.2 per cent of all divorces and in 1968 this fell to 2.2 per cent. The most popular ground was the general misconduct clause, which accounted for 93 per cent of all divorces in West Germany in 1968.

Eventually, in 1976, a new divorce law was enacted in West Germany – the Marriage and Family Law Reform Law 1976 – which replaced all the previous specific grounds with a single non-fault ground. By this statute, for the first time since 1938, a new divorce law was reinserted in the BGB.

Note that ex facie, unlike English and French statutes on divorce, this 1976 West German law does not contain any fault grounds. Fault may, however, be taken into account as part of one of the exceptions to the main law on divorce (see p. 67).

Under art. 1564 of the BGB, a valid marriage can only be dissolved by a German court upon the petition of one or both of the spouses.

The divorce rate

Germany's divorce rate has risen beyond 200,000 a year, affecting an estimated 400,000 people, and this figure does not include 170,000 school children. From the year 1991 onwards, there has been a significant increase in the number of divorces recorded and in nearly three-quarters of these, the divorce followed a one year separation period. In 2001 there were 197,498 divorces involving 153,517 children under 18.

The grounds for divorce

Irretrievable breakdown

There is only one ground for divorce under German law – the breakdown of the marriage (art. 1565(1) of the BGB). Glendon points out that this is called scheitern in the original German, which means foundering, as of a ship against the rocks, and thus figuratively, failure, and not zerrüttung (breakdown) (Glendon, 1989, p. 178). According to the definition provided in art. 1565(1) of the BGB, a marriage fails if 'the marital community of the spouses no longer exists and there can be no expectation that the spouses will restore it' (translation Martiny and Schwab, 2002, p. 1). This is the equivalent of saying there is an irretrievable breakdown of the marriage (Martiny and Schwab, 2002, p. 4), a concept which is to be found in other jurisdictions such as England and Wales and South Africa. A slightly different but more specific translation is from Dr Peter-Andreas Brand: 'A marriage is deemed to have irretrievable broken down if the spouses no longer live together and if it cannot be expected that the spouses will save their marriage' (Brand, 1997, p. 486). Whichever version one opts for, the common denominator is the irretrievable breakdown of marriage as the sole ground, although the actual physical separation is emphasized in the second translation, unlike English law which also recognizes the cessation of a common marital life, despite living under the same roof (see *Hopes v Hopes* [1948] 2 All ER 920).

However, if one looks at the relevant provision more closely, art. 1567(1) states: 'The spouses are living apart if no household community exists between them and one spouse perceptibly refuses its restoration by rejecting the marital community of life. The household community no longer exists in such cases even if the spouses live apart within the marital dwelling.' This mirrors the English approach.

Under art. 1567(2), cohabitation for a short time does not interrupt or stop the time periods specified in art. 1566.

Presumption of irretrievable breakdown

Article 1566 of the BGB clarifies the court's approach to irretrievable breakdown which is linked to periods of separation. Under art. 1566(1) of the BGB, where both spouses petition for a divorce, there is a conclusive or irrebuttable presumption that the marriage had broken down if the couple have been separated for one year. Hence, if the divorce is by mutual consent of the parties, either jointly or with the consent of the respondent, and the parties have lived apart for one year, the court must, prima facie, grant the divorce.

Under art. 1566(2) of the BGB, if only one spouse petitions for a divorce, the same irrebuttable presumption applies only if the couple has been separated for three years. Thus, because of these presumptions, the judges need not inquire as to whether the marriage has actually broken down. However, these presumptions are limited by three exceptions or hardship clauses.

The first exception is under art. 1565(2), namely, if the spouses have been separated for less than a year. In this case, the marriage may be dissolved if the continuation of the marriage would result in unreasonable hardship to the petitioner owing to causes attributable to the other spouse. Another translation of art. 1565(2) is 'unsupportable' hardship (see Glendon, 1989, p. 179). Brand suggests that examples of such hardship would be violent disputes, attempted murder drug addiction, or infectious illness. Adultery would only be a sufficiently good reason if there has been a longstanding relationship between the parties (Brand, 1997, p. 486). Divorce would only normally be permitted if the couple has been separated for a year.

The second exception is under art. 1568(1): a marriage shall not be dissolved even though it has failed if and so long as the maintenance of the marriage is a necessary exception for special reasons in the interests of minor children of the family.

The third exception is under art. 1568(2): when and as long as the divorce would result in hardship which is so severe to the party opposing the application owing to exceptional circumstances, the marriage should be continued, even after consideration of the petitioner's needs. Brand cites examples of this exception as severe illnesses, being left alone in times of particularly harsh circumstances dealt by fate, a marriage which has taken an ill-fated course and long-term joint care for a disabled child (Brand, 1997, p. 486).

To a great extent, German divorce law is, as Martiny and Schwab put it 'a combination of irretrievable breakdown and divorce by consent' (Martiny and Schwab, 2002, p. 5). However, if the couple has been separated for less than a year, the marriage can still be dissolved if it can be proven to have broken down and that maintaining its existence 'would pose an unreasonable (or unsupportable) hardship' for reasons attributable to the other spouse. This means that as long as some evidence of the other spouse's fault-based behaviour can be given, a divorce can be granted by the court if it is convinced of its authenticity. The only types of behaviour would be (possibly) acts of violence, attempted murder or drug addiction, hence fault would constitute grounds for divorce under German law in a small number of cases (Glendon, 1989, p. 180).

It needs to be borne in mind that it is only in very exceptional cases that the 'hardship clause' would apply (see the case of *BGH NJW* 1979, p. 1042 (Supreme Court, Ordinary Jurisdiction)). Of course, the hardship clause has no application if the couple has lived apart for five years (see art. 1568(2)).

As far as actual practice is concerned, in the aftermath of the reforms, the hardship clause is rarely invoked and courts rarely deny divorces on the basis of the hardship clause. The vast majority of divorces remain uncontested, as they are in England and Wales, and most petitions are brought on the basis of mutual consent of the spouses if they have lived apart for a year. On the other hand, once spouses are in full agreement that they should divorce, most opt for the breakdown clause under art. 1565, rather than the mutual consent provision under art. 1566 (Glendon, 1989, p. 181). Glendon explains that the reason for this choice appears to be to avoid the more onerous regulations required under the procedural rules for mutual-consent divorce (Glendon, 1989, p. 181). These requirements are laid down under arts 623 and 630 of the BGB which provide that spouses seeking to divorce under the mutual consent ground must produce for the court's perusal a detailed agreement on all the consequences of divorce – namely the allocation of the dwelling and household effects, spousal and child support, marital property and pension division, custody and access arrangements – and the divorce can only be granted after these matters have been settled (Glendon, 1989, pp. 181–2).

Maintenance allocation upon separation of the partners

The 2008 reforms

Before the reform of the law in this area, maintenance was calculated according to the standard of living the parties had enjoyed during the marriage. Former spouses were in a stronger position than after the reform. If they could not work or felt they did not earn enough they could ask for maintenance and their claim from the former spouse was usually perceived as stronger than a claim of the children in the former spouse's new family. However, a new Act was brought into force on 1 January 2008, called Unterhaltsrechtsanderungsgesetz, which amended certain sections of the BGB. Under this amendment a minimum amount of maintenance for children was introduced and any money earned by the breadwinner (whoever that might be) will be allocated first to the children and then be available for the spouses.

Maintenance has usually been calculated according to the standard of living enjoyed by the parties during the marriage. Indeed, this is the case if, for instance, the marriage lasted for a long time, and/or the spouse suffered economic disadvantages because of the marriage, for example, if the wife stopped work as a high-earning executive to take care of the children but cannot now get back her old job. Under the new law, maintenance can now also be calculated according to the standard of living the less well-off spouse enjoyed before the marriage. This would be the case if a former personal assistant who married her boss would have to return to work on the income of a personal assistant.

It will also be easier for a court to grant maintenance for a fixed period.

The rules have also been changed for a parent (whether married or unmarried to the other parent) who has sole care of a child. Such a parent can now ask the other parent for maintenance for the first three years of that child's life. After that period, a parent (whether married or unmarried) has to produce proof that he or she cannot work because the child needs special care. Hence, the standard for maintenance for divorced and cohabiting but unmarried spouses has been brought closer together. The courts can still make orders that favour divorced mothers and they usually do. Before these rules were brought into force, only unmarried parents could ask for maintenance for the first three years while there were no limits for divorced parents.

Matrimonial property under the BGB

Under the family law of the BGB as originally enacted, the rules of matrimonial property were based on the practice that the spouses brought to the marriage 'an interest-bearing capital sum' which was to be administered by the husband (Kotz, 1992, p. 189). Thus, the Law of the Equal Rights of Man and Woman which came into force in 1957 enacted a new statutory matrimonial property regime – the 'community of acquisitions', now inserted into the BGB in art. 1363. Under this regime, any property acquired by the spouses during the subsistence of the marriage will be divided equally between them. As long as the marriage subsists, the spouses have full control over their own property and assets and are responsible for their own debts. Thus, the division only takes place when the marriage ceases to exist, upon divorce or the death of either party. This is sometimes called deferred community of property, since it is only when the marriage terminates that the assets of both spouses will be pooled and divided equally. Until this occurs, the matrimonial property rights are the same as under English law – a separate property regime with each party retaining the rights to their separate property.

If the couple divorces, the equality principle normally applies to the extent that the spouse with the larger increase in property hands over half the difference to the other party. Basically, the partner who has earned or accrued more assets or income or property during the marriage has to hand over half the surplus to the other partner. Kotz explains that this may well be difficult to calculate or administer in practice, since spouses may disagree over the valuation of certain items or dispute who was the original owner of certain property (Kotz, 1992, p. 191).

If the marriage ends by death, then an extra quarter of the deceased's estate will be added to the statutory portion of the surviving spouse in the succession, under art. 1371 of the BGB. This rule will be applied irrespective of any increase in the property of either spouse. This is an important rule because without the operation of art. 1371, if a spouse died and there were surviving children, the normal rules of inheritance would have meant that the surviving spouse would have received a quarter of the estate under art. 1931 of the BGB. Article 1931 now ensures that the surviving spouse would receive a further quarter (Kotz, 1992, p. 191).

The objective of this regime is to ensure that the wife who has devoted her life to the family home and children and therefore not had the opportunity to earn income of her own or save any money, will have an equal share in the combined assets of the couple. In a debate which has resonance in other (mainly Western or Westernized) countries, there are counter-arguments. For instance, is this a fair system where one party who is substantially wealthy to begin with, and has accumulated even more wealth because of this initial wealth, should then have to share the proceeds of the enhanced assets with the other spouse who might not have done anything actively towards acquiring it. There is also the case of the childless couple where one party has worked extremely hard in amassing wealth while the other has done little, if anything, towards its accrual. Yet another is the perennial but significant example of placing a value on the woman whose housekeeping, bringing up the children, part-time jobs, and provision of emotional support, has made it possible for the male partner to acquire and amass wealth. If, before marriage, an engaged couple does not wish the statutory regime to apply to them, they can enter into an agreement to exclude it and keep their property strictly separate (Kotz, 1992, p. 192). The use of prenuptial contracts is gathering pace and has greater acceptability by the judiciary, even in the United Kingdom where it is not usually regarded as legally binding.

Germany therefore has a system of deferred community of property supplemented by certain statutory inheritance rights.

Children

Introduction

The BGB, as originally enacted, 'bore all the marks of the age of the conservative and patriarchal bourgeoisie' (Kotz, 1992, p. 189). Hence, decisions during the marriage were for the husband to make and it was he who exercised parental power. Illegitimate children were deliberately treated in a less advantageous way than legitimate children, as there was a fear that extra-marital affairs, which the law did not recognize, might be legalized, thus encouraging immorality and concubinage. Indeed, the non-marital child was treated as unrelated to the father and as Kotz puts it, was 'fobbed off with a claim for maintenance whose amount depended on his mother's social position' (Kotz, 1992, p. 189) and these payments ended when the child turned 16.

An important reform of the law relating to children was the Illegitimacy Act of 1969 which was enacted pursuant to the constitutional mandate in art. 6(5GG): 'Illegitimate children shall be provided by legislation with the same opportunities for their physical and spiritual development and their place in society as are enjoyed by legitimate children' (translation from Kotz, 1992, p. 192). The new provisions of the BGB recognize that the illegitimate child is related to his father in law as well as in fact. This means that the illegitimate child now has the same claim to maintenance as a legitimate child and his rights of succession are also very similar in the sense that he has an equal statutory right of succession. However, the one difference is that according to art. 1934a of the BGB, if his father leaves a surviving spouse or legitimate children, he has no claim to any part of the inheritance in kind but would have a monetary claim to the value of his portion of the inheritance (see Kotz, 1992, p. 192).

Child custody and divorce

In the early 1960s, the psychological dimensions of the best interest of the child standard were being emphasized in child psychiatric and psychological publications. Indeed, the attitude that the child's perspective should be taken into account was already being expressed when determining custody arrangements (Kalternborn and Lempp, 1998, p. 75). Kalternborn and Lempp noted that in the Germany of the 1980s, joint custody and the child's 'attachments' were seen as a 'concrete expression of the best interests standard' in accordance with art. 1671(2) of the BGB for custodial arrangements (Kalternborn and Lempp, 1998, p. 75).

The custody of young children is regulated under art. 1671 of the BGB. This provision designates the child's welfare as the paramount consideration for determining custodial arrangements after the divorce of the parents.

Parents petitioning for divorce must make a joint proposal to the court with regard to arrangements for custody, and any issues relating to custody and child support must be dealt with during the divorce proceedings. If a proposal is made, the court must accept it unless there are reasons in the child's best interests not to do so. The welfare officer will in all cases assess the children's position and report to the court. Orders for joint custody are available but are made very infrequently. The court must hear the children and will hear them on their own.

In child custody and access cases, the child's position is the main point to be emphasized. If custody is contested, the tender years doctrine is invariably used to award custody to the mother. The BGB refers to the need to consider the best interests of the child and their links to one of their parents and to other siblings. There is also frequent mention of the principles of 'continuation' and the aim of promoting 'the best possible development of the child'. These are equivalent to the maintenance of the status quo or current status of the child provisions in English law, and are a consideration in any argument for changing it in favour of the other parent (Solicitors Family Law Association).

COMPARATIVE PERSPECTIVES

Divorce laws – convergence or simply modernization?

One of the themes which we explore in the context of European jurisdictions, as with our examination of others, is whether there is any convergence in the divorce laws of these jurisdictions, primarily between European jurisdictions and England, between a civil law and a common law jurisdiction.

In Germany, the divorce grounds appear to be a combination of irretrievable breakdown and divorce by consent. However, in France there is a combination of fault and no-fault grounds, which is the broad position under English law, although there are clear differences in the actual grounds (called 'facts' under the English legislation – the Matrimonial Causes Act 1973). There is therefore considerable commonality in Germany, France and England in relation to divorce grounds, although they all operate within their own, distinctive social, legal, political and cultural contexts.

Antokolskaia distinguishes between modernization of the divorce laws of Europe, which she concedes has taken place, and convergence of such laws and believes that, at present, it appears improbable that such convergence will occur spontaneously (Antokolskaia, 2006, pp. 329–30). The issue will doubtless remain open to debate unless and until some European countries actively agree to a 'harmonization' of their laws. We return to this issue in the final chapter.

Marital property

Glendon notes: 'The marital property systems of England, France, [and] West Germany (as it then was) ... have come to resemble each other in a number of ways. In all of them, spouses are formally equal, and each spouse has substantial freedom to deal with his or her own earnings' (Glendon, 1989, p. 134). However, Glendon also emphasizes that significant differences remain. For instance, the French system imposes the most substantial restrictions on the freedom of spouses to deal with property during the marriage. Furthermore, in France, husbands and wives know from the outset that their equal co-ownership during marriage will be translated into equal property rights in the event of death or divorce. In Germany, there is separation of property during the marriage, but the spouse who has earned more during the marriage knows that upon divorce, he or she will have to give half the value of the surplus to the other spouse. It is also easier to opt out of the statutory marital property regime in France and Germany than in jurisdictions such as the United States.

On a comparative note, no proprietary consequences flow from the mere fact of marriage in England and Wales, since the doctrine of separate property applies, so each spouse retains the right to his or her own property even after the marriage has taken place. The parties are entitled to make their own maintenance and separation agreements but these are governed by contract law and can be set aside on the basis of mistake, fraud, duress or undue influence. There is also less scope for parties' private agreements to be enforced by the English courts as far as prenuptial agreements are concerned but there are now indications that this might well change and that the judiciary may be prepared to uphold such agreements in the not too distant future, provided they consider them to have been made free from duress, mistake, fraud or undue influence.

Children

The best interests of the child standard, which makes the child's welfare the paramount consideration, appears to be the common yardstick in French and German family law, in matters dealing with the custody, access, guardianship and upbringing of the child. This is, of course, the pivotal guideline in English law. Clearly, this criterion affords flexibility although it is inevitably an indeterminate guideline, subject to interpretation in every given case. However, the methods by which this general standard is applied will vary from jurisdiction to jurisdiction. It is worth noting that, in Germany, under the BGB, there is a meticulous and systematic process which takes place in the application of the best interests yardstick in cases involving children. This requires an examination of all aspects of the case akin to the checklist under the Children Act 1989 (UK), supplemented by reference to learned commentaries on the BGB provisions as well as copious illustrations of how the principle might be applied. It would not be unusual for a German court to consult more than one learned commentary on the provisions of the BGB and to call for expert evidence from social workers, child psychologists, child psychiatrists, welfare officers and other healthcare or medical staff, to assist the court in coming to a decision. Their opinions would then be given considerable weight in the court's adjudication. English courts can and sometimes do call on the above-named professionals but they rarely feature in the written judgment of the court unless their expert testimony was a crucial factor in the court's determination of the case.

American courts observe the same practice of calling for expert opinion from the kind of professionals listed above, but their written judgments will frequently cite and analyse such expert testimony which illustrates their overtly and explicitly holistic approach to such cases. This approach may well become more common in other jurisdictions in the future, but a great deal will depend on available resources, as well as the political impetus in a given jurisdiction.

Further reading

Antokolskaia, M 'Convergence and Divergence of Divorce Laws in Europe' (2006) 18 CFLQ 307.

Antokolskaia, M 'Comparative Family Law: Moving with the Times?' in Orucu and Nelken (eds) *Comparative Law. A Handbook*, 2007, Hart, Ch.11.

Bainham, A 'Men and Women Behaving Badly: Is Fault Dead in English Law?' in Dewar and Parker (eds) *Family Law: Processes, Practices, Pressures*, 2003, Hart.

Bamforth, N 'The Benefits of Same-Sex Marriage in all but Name? Same-sex Couples and the Civil Partnership Act 2004' (2007) 19 CFLQ 133.

Boele-Woelki, K 'The Legal Recognition of Same-Sex Relationships Within the European Union' (2008) 82 Tul LR 1949.

Brand, P-A 'Principles of German Divorce Law' [1997] Fam Law 486.

Cretney, SM 'Community of Property imposed by Judicial Decision' (2003) 119 LQR 349.

Cretney, SM *Family Law in the Twentieth Century – A History*, 2003, Oxford UP.

Cretney, SM and Masson, J *Principles of Family Law*, 2003, Sweet & Maxwell.

de Cruz, P 'Legal Transplants: Principle and Pragmatism in Comparative Family Law' in Harding and Orucu (eds) *Comparative Law in the 21st Century*, 2001, Kluwer, pp. 101ff.

Eekelaar, J 'Beyond the Welfare Principle' (2002) 14 CFLQ 237.

Finlay, H 'Fault, Causation and Breakdown in the Anglo-Australian Law of Divorce' (1978) 94 LQR 120.

Freeman, MDA 'Adultery and Intolerability' (1972) 35 Mod LR 98.

Freeman, MDA 'When Marriage Fails – Some Legal Responses to Marriage Breakdown' [1979] *Current Legal Problems 1978* 109.

Freeman, MDA 'Disputing Children' in Eekelaar *et al.* (eds) *Cross Currents. Family Law and Policy in the United States and England*, 2000, Oxford UP.

Gardner, S 'Family Property Today' [2008] 124 LQR 422.

Gautier, A 'Legal Regulation of Marital Relations: An Historical and Comparative Approach' (2005) 19 Int Jnl of Law, Policy and the Family 47.

Glendon, MA *The Transformation of Family Law*, 1989, University of Chicago Press.

Hamilton, C and Standley, K (eds) *Family Law in Europe*, 2001, LexisNexis.

Kalternborn, K and Lempp, R 'The Welfare of the Child in Custody Disputes after Parental Separation or Divorce' (1998) 12 Int Jo. Law, Policy and the Family 74.

Konig, R 'Sociological Introduction' in Glendon (ed) *International Encyclopedia of Comparative Law*, 1974, Mohr and Martinus-Nijhoff, Vol. IV, Ch. 1.

Maidment, S *Child Custody and Divorce*, 1984, Croom Helm.

Martiny, D and Schwab, D *Grounds for Divorce and Maintenance between Former Spouses*, 2002 at http://www2.law.uu.nl/priv/cefl/Reports/pdf/Germany02.pdf.

Masson, JM, Bailey-Harris, R and Probert, R (eds) *Cretney's Principles of Family Law*, 8th ed, 2008, Sweet & Maxwell.

Merin, Y *Equality for Same Sex Couples. The Legal Recognition of Gay Partnerships in Europe and the United States*, 2002, University of Chicago Press.

Orr, D 'In Search of the Muria Code' (2005) 77 *Geographic* 56.

Orucu and Nelken (eds) *Comparative Law. A Handbook*, 2007, pp. 241ff.

Rheinstein, M *Marriage, Stability, Divorce and the Law*, 1971, University of Chicago Press.

Rubellin-Devichi, J 'The Best Interests Principle in French Law and Practice' [1994] 8 Int Jo Law & Fam 259.

Shimmel, R and Huen, S 'The Legal Situation of Same-Sex Partnerships in Germany' in Wintermute and Andenaes (eds) *Legal Recognition of Same Sex Partners*, 2001, Hart, pp. 575ff.

Chapter 2

Family law in the United States

'The demographic changes of the past century make it difficult to speak of an average American family'

Troxel v Granville 530 US 57 (2000).

'Upon [marriage] society may be said to be built, and out of its fruits spring social relations and social obligations and duties, with which government is necessarily required to deal'

Reynolds v United States 98 US 165 (1878).

Introduction

This chapter casts a critical and exploratory eye on the American family and on family law in various United States jurisdictions. It discusses what 'the family' means in American legal and social institutions and discovers trends in divorce, property relations between spouses and cohabitants, the legal recognition of same-sex couples and in the law relating to children. The chapter compares the American experience of these topics with that of other common law regions such as the Commonwealth and England and Wales.

Preliminary observations

Family law in the United States has developed separately in each State which has its own local court and local legislature such that 'American family laws vary significantly in both substance and procedure from one state to another' (Wardle and Nolan, 1998, p. 37). Wardle and Nolan list a number of homogenizing cultural influences in the United States 'that create a tendency of similarity, if not harmony and consistency'. These include 'persuasive sister-state judicial opinions, new legislation enacted in other states that proves to be effective or popular, proposals for uniform legislation, programs of federal government support and incentives for states to take particular policy positions, federal constitutional standards, the national news and entertainment media, and special interests that operate nationally [which] have produced many multi-state and national trends in the family laws of the various states' (Wardle and Nolan, 1998, p. 37). It would appear that because of these homogenizing influences, 'students and teachers of family law in the United States often look for and find trends and general principles that are shared and prevailing rules and practices' (Wardle and Nolan, 1998, p. 37).

Historical background

The grip of the 'traditional family metanarrative', as Martha Fineman puts it, has long existed in American legal and extralegal institutions (see Fineman, 1993, p. 388). Historically, only the nuclear family has been protected and promoted by legal and cultural institutions (see Shorter, 1975; Stone, 1975; Teitelbaum, 1987). Fineman characterizes the 'veneration' of the nuclear family as 'coercive' as a result of the state's regulatory mechanisms (for example, its criminal justice system, child welfare laws, and tax codes) and as a 'privileged, if not exclusive position in regard to the sanctified ordering of intimacy' (Fineman, 1993, pp. 388–9). It has also been argued that constitutional doctrines which protect marriage, childrearing and other aspects of family life in the United States reflect and embody 'static and traditional' concepts of the family in America (see Meyer, 2002). Similarly, Richard Storrow has maintained that the constitutional law of family privacy reflects a policy of promoting nuclear families (see Storrow, 2001). To be sure, case law alone has suggested that without marriage or a biological relationship, legal recognition of a family would be unlikely (see e.g. *Moore v City of East Cleveland* 431 US 494 (1977); *Michael H v Gerald D* 491 US 110 (1989); *Village of Belle Terre v Boraas* 416 US 1 (1974)).

As Fineman reminds us: '[C]ontemporary American legal policies concerning the family are rooted in historic patriarchal structures and reflect notions of normality and morality developed centuries ago in the ecclesiastical as well as the common law courts' (Fineman, 1993, p. 389). The important point she also makes is that 'these concepts continue to influence the ways in which [American] society constructs and communicates ideological conclusions about what constitutes a "natural" family'(Fineman, 1993, p. 389).

Brief history of marriage in the United States

During colonial times, the majority of Americans followed the customs of England which meant that a religious ceremony was secondary to a civil ceremony in many of the colonies. Some colonies even gave civil magistrates the authority to perform marriage ceremonies without any religious requirements (A White Paper, 2004, p. 352). However, other colonies, such as Virginia, required the customs of the church to be followed and did not permit a civil marriage ceremony (Sears Morgan, *The Puritan Family: Religion and Domestic Relations in 17th Century New England*, 1996 ed., p. 32). A frequent and common practice was the existence of common law marriages which some States still allow today (A White Paper, 2004, p. 352). A common law marriage is defined in *Black's Law Dictionary* as: 'A marriage that takes legal effect, without licence or ceremony, when a couple lives together as husband and wife, intend to be married, and hold themselves to others as a married couple' (7th ed., 1999) and the point to note is that this sort of marriage is not recognized in English law as a marriage.

Until the Emancipation Proclamation, slaves were not permitted to marry. However slaves did marry under a religious rite in a religious ceremony, with a slave who was the leader of the church in their area officiating. These marriages were not recognized by the government of the day and slave owners retained as 'property' any children of such unions (A White Paper, 2004, p. 352).

In the seventeenth and eighteenth centuries marriage in America evolved into the monogamous one-man one-woman paradigm of today, but it was never totally accepted in American society as can be seen from Mormonism, a uniquely American religion, which allows the practice of polygamy as one of its basic tenets (A White Paper, 2004, p. 352). Utah was required to outlaw polygamy before it was allowed to enter the Union as a State but some Mormons have continued to practise polygamy in Utah and other Mormon areas of the United States (Van Wagoner, *Mormon Polygamy: A History*, 1992).

In the nineteenth century, so-called 'complex marriages' were practised by the Oneida Community in New York, under which adult members of the community were considered married to all other adult members of the community and sexual contact was regulated by the group (see Hillebrand, *The Shakers/Oneida Community (Part II)* at http://www.nyhistory.com/central/oneida.htm).

In the early part of the twentieth century the free love movement argued that monogamous marriage oppressed women and that marriage was an obsolete institution (McElroy, 'The Free Love Movement and Radical Individualism' (1996) 19 *The Libertarian Enterprise*).

There have been several changes in America's marriage laws throughout its history. Until 1930, 12 States allowed boys aged as young as 14 and girls as young as 12 to marry with parental consent (see Mintz and Kellogg, *Domestic Revolutions: A Social History of American Life*, 1998, 126, cited in A White Paper, 2004, p. 353) and as recently as 1940 married women could not make a valid contract in 12 States (Degler, *At Odds: Women and the Family in America from the Revolution to the Present*, 1980, p 333, cited in A White Paper, 2004, p. 353).

On the inter-racial front, in some States a marriage between whites and non-whites was void ab initio and as many as 40 States made such marriages a crime and 'such marriages were decried as immoral and unnatural' (A White Paper, 2004, p. 353) and this was the state of the law until 1967. In that year, the United States Supreme Court in *Loving v Virginia* 388 US 1 (1967) struck down laws prohibiting inter-racial marriage as a violation of both due process and equal protection under the Fourteenth Amendment. The court declared (at 12): 'The freedom to marry has long been recognised as one of the vital personal rights essential to the orderly pursuit of happiness.' Eleven years later, in *Zablocki v Redhail* 434 US 374 (1978), the Supreme Court affirmed that view: '[T]he right to marry is of fundamental importance for all individuals.' A majority opinion of the court held that a statute prohibiting a Wisconsin resident from marrying if the resident had an unpaid child support obligation was unconstitutional because the statute violates the Fourteenth Amendment's equal protection clause.

Divorce

Historical background

Divorce has a complex history in America. In colonial America (which refers to the period from the seventeenth century to 1776), divorce was an extremely rare phenomenon. It could be obtained only through legislative action, which was time-consuming and costly and the legislative body of the particular State would need to pass a private statute to legalize a divorce at the request of two private individuals. Several couples therefore separated without going through any legal process to dissolve their marriage; this was known as divorcing from 'bed and board' (Hall, 1989, p. 165). Legislative divorce remained the only way to secure a divorce in Virginia and Maryland as late as 1851. In 1789, Massachusetts was the first State to allow judicial divorce and it took until the end of the nineteenth century before every State except South Carolina, followed suit. It is notable that organized religion proved a formidable opponent of divorce, with the Roman Catholic Church forbidding it and Protestant denominations regarding it as an act of personal and national degeneration (Hall, 1989, p. 165). Even, when divorce was allowed by Protestants it was not without some disapproval. The mood of the times was heavily influenced by the social reformers who argued for more rigorous adherence to marital obligations and demanded limits on birth control. These reformers also regarded the increasing incidence of divorce as evidence of social decay and these views were echoed by the judges and legislators of the day (Hall, 1989, p. 165). The concept of consensual divorce was unknown to nineteenth-century America – one married party had to prove that the other party had committed a wrong sufficiently serious to warrant a rearrangement of the couple's domestic situation. Legislators no longer issued divorce decrees but continued to write statutes which described conditions under which judges could grant them (Hall, 1989, p. 365). During this era, every State legislature included adultery as a ground which justified a divorce, but also included other grounds, apart from New York which was a conservative State which stipulated adultery as the sole ground for divorce. In other States, desertion was a common ground, as well as impotence, fraud, conviction of a felony, and habitual drunkenness. Hence, adultery, desertion and cruelty were the main grounds for divorce, the precise details of which varied from State to State.

In the early 1840s, a judicial divorce became available to both husband and wife provided they stated that there were grounds for the petition. By the end of the century, cruelty was the most common ground in State statutes, but the meaning of cruelty varied from case to case. State legislatures first defined cruelty as physical harm or coercion, usually by the husband against the wife. But in 1863 in California the Supreme Court held in *Powelson v Powelson* (1863) 22 Cal. 358 that any conduct sufficient to produce ill-health or bodily pain, though operating on the mind only, should amount to legal cruelty. Judges and eventually the legislature subsequently accepted that 'mental suffering' could not only be accepted as a ground but could also be proven even if there was no deterioration in a spouse's physical health (Hall, 1989, p. 166).

A dual system of divorce developed. This meant that at one level, as far as strict law was concerned, divorce laws were as stated in the statute book. However, in reality, collusion between husbands, wives, lawyers and even judges frequently took place so that the couple would fabricate the evidence needed to obtain a divorce. Since collusion under family law (an agreement between the husband and wife to get a divorce) was prohibited under the law in all States, a number of exotic and questionable practices developed in States like New York, which only allowed a divorce on the ground of adultery right up until 1967. One such dubious practice was where the husband would register at a hotel and be only partially dressed, in his room. A woman would arrive and take off most of her clothes. A photographer would then appear and take their picture sitting on the bed together or in an incriminating or suggestive position. The woman then got dressed, pocketed her fee and left. The photographs would then be presented to the court as evidence of adultery (see Friedman, 2004, p. 63). Other similar charades were carried out in other States to establish cruelty as a ground for divorce. The wife would allege that the husband had slapped her twice or humiliated her, or otherwise made her life a misery. The husband would file no reply to these allegations and no defence. The divorce would be granted by default (Friedman, 2004, p. 63). Another way for a couple to obtain a divorce was to travel to another State which was more liberal in its divorce laws.

The economic structure began to change in the nineteenth century and millions of people began to own farms or other valuable property. Consequently, a man or woman who wanted to start a new family and leave the old one needed a divorce, or the new children would be illegitimate and the new wife regarded as a mistress with the result that the rights to the farm or the property would remain with the original or nuclear family.

In the first half of the twentieth century, there were signs that the divorce laws were not being followed and there were signs that these laws were becoming liberalized. The grounds were becoming broader and eventually divorces were being granted in some States without any grounds at all.

Katz observes that the reasons for the changes in divorce law appear to emanate from 'changes in the nature of marriage and the social and legal acceptance of formal and informal alternatives to marriage' and also changes in 'cultural norms', especially in relation to social attitudes towards divorce, population movement from one area of the country to another and 'shifts in the political climate'. These changes were also being championed by various civil rights movements, campaigning for children's rights, women's rights and father's rights. Katz also highlights the changes which occurred in the legal profession, access to legal representation, court structure and the availability of alternative methods of dispute resolution, particularly through negotiation and the wider acceptance of mediation (Katz, 2003, p. 76).

Divorce and the family in twenty-first century America

In the early years of the twenty-first century, there appears to be a growing political groundswell of opinion which is highly critical of the no-fault divorce laws in the United States. Commentators are divided on whether they favour no-fault or fault-based divorce systems but there is no shortage of reasons advanced by political and legal observers why fault-based divorce should be reintroduced as it is blamed for the high rate of divorce, the detrimental effect on children, and the dilution of family life in America (see e.g. Wardle, 2000, pp. 783ff. and sources cited therein; and Turnage Boyd, 2005, p. 609).

The modern American family

The quotation at the beginning of this chapter from Waite CJ in *Reynolds v United States* 98 US 165 (1878), a late nineteenth century decision, exemplifies the predominance of the nuclear family for over 130 years. However, as will be discerned from the opening quotation from O'Connor J in *Troxel v Granville* 530 US 57 (2000), recent changes in the law in American jurisdictions make it difficult to speak of a coherent American family law (see 'Developments in the Law: The Law of Marriage and Family' (2003) 116 Harv Law Rev 2000).

Two notable characteristics have been identified by Morrison with regard to twentieth century family life in the United States: first, Americans live significantly longer now than in the past; and second, a well-established trend of lower fertility (see Morrison, 2000, pp. 57–8). The decline in the fertility rate was a pervasive feature throughout the twentieth century, and in recent decades the average number of children born to American women has ranged from 1.8 to 2 (Bianchi and Spain (1996) *Population Bulletin* 51, No. 3). Other statistical data suggest that Americans postponed marriage in the twentieth century far more than they had in the past two centuries.

As noted in the law and family overview in the *Harvard Law Review* of 2002–3, the 'unique demographic and cultural circumstances of each state have engendered considerable variation in the [American] law governing marriage and divorce, parenthood and child support, and other aspects of family life'.

A census carried out in 2000 (see Fields and Casper, 2001) revealed the divergent forms of the modern American family, indicating that traditional family structures are less prevalent in the early twenty-first century than ever before in United States history. The so-called 'nuclear family' (a term coined by anthropologist George Murdock in 1949, to refer to a married man and woman living together in the same household) now describes less than one quarter of all United States households, constituting only 24.1 per cent of American households (see Fields and Casper, 2001, fig. 1). Notably, 26 per cent of all households are persons living alone, of which 58 per cent are women, and single parents now constitute nearly one-third of all households with children. Single mothers make up 26 per cent of families with children and single fathers make up 5 per cent of such households.

Statistical snapshots on divorce and American families – then and now

According to some researchers, divorce in the United States has been rising for more than a century and in the late 1960 it began a steep climb, with an all-time high being reached in the 1970s (Wallerstein, 2003, p. 70). As late as 1970, 40 per cent of American families conformed to the model of one wage earner, a stay-at-home wife, and two children (United States Bureau of Census, United States Department of Commerce, Current Population Reports, *Family and Living Arrangements 2003*, 2, 2004) In 2008, less than one in four families conformed to this template. Divorces quadrupled between 1960 and 1999 and single-parent families more than tripled between 1970 and 2003. One in three children are born to unwed mothers (National Centre for Health Statistics, *Preliminary Births for 2004*). In 1970, there were less than 475,000 unmarried cohabitants; in 2008 there were nearly 6 million.

The law's response to the changing American family

America in the early twenty-first century exhibits tension between individual autonomy and government regulation in all aspects of family law (see Katz, 2003).

Family law in the America of today 'reflects not only forty years of Supreme Court decisions, uniform family laws, and a trend towards federalisation, but also the changing nature of families, which are often defined by function than by form' (Elrod and Spector, 2008, p. 661). According to the Winter edition of the *Family Law Quarterly's Review of the Family Law Year 2006–7* by Elrod and Spector: '[F]ewer people are getting married; same-sex couples can enter into civil unions in numerous states; and over six million people cohabitate'. In addition, the number of children born out of wedlock has reached nearly 40 per cent; and increasing numbers of couples plan for dissolution or death by entering into premarital or postmarital contracts (Elrod and Spector, 2008, p. 661).

Reproductive technologies and the family

Elrod and Spector make the important point that assisted reproduction technology enables infertile couples to reproduce and also offers this facility to same-sex couples (Elrod and Spector, 2008, pp. 661–2).

The dearth of uniform laws or, in most States, of any law regulating assisted reproduction has tended to lead to 'widely disparate results in similar cases' (Elrod and Spector, 2008, p. 674). Thus, known sperm donors received contradictory messages from courts. For example, in *Jacob v Schulz-Jacob* 923 A 2d 473 (2007) the Pennsylvanian Supreme Court held that a man who donated sperm to enable a lesbian friend's partner to have two children and maintained a relationship with them should have been included in the couple's child support action.

In 2007, it was held in *Laura G v Peter G* 830 NYS 2d 496 (App. Div. 2007) that a husband who did not consent to his wife's artificial insemination but who held the child out as his own, was responsible for financial support. In *Khabbaz v Commissioner* 930 A 2d 1180 (2007), a New Hampshire court held that a child conceived via artificial insemination with sperm that the father had banked before his death was not 'surviving issue' under the State intestacy laws which therefore made the child ineligible for social security benefits.

Surrogacy and family law

Terminology

There are two types of surrogacy: scenario one, in which the woman carrying the baby is the genetic mother, and scenario two, in which she is not. In American legal literature, the terminology used differs from that used in British legal literature in several respects. Scenario one is described in American literature as 'traditional surrogacy' and scenario two, where the surrogate mother is implanted with the ovum and sperm from the couple who commissioned the surrogacy, is described as 'gestational surrogacy'. In British literature, scenario one would be called 'partial surrogacy' and scenario two is referred to as 'full surrogacy'. The couple wishing to pay for the surrogacy arrangement is called the commissioning couple in British literature but is called the 'intended parents' or 'contracting parents' in the United States.

Surrogacy or the practice of surrogate motherhood is now a familiar practice in many parts of the United States, although it has been officially prohibited in 11 of those States. In Dutch, the word for surrogacy is draagmoederschap which literally means 'carrymotherhood' or 'bearmotherhood' which seems particularly apt. It has been called 'technologic adoption' by Elizabeth Bartholet (1993) and has been described in market terms by Richard Posner (1987, p. 72):

> '[A] married couple ... can make an enforceable contract with another woman whereby the latter agrees to be artificially inseminated with the husband's sperm and to carry the baby to term and give it up to the couple ... [T]he father (and his wife) 'buy out' the natural mother's 'share' in their joint product.'

Despite its prominence in the 1980s with high-profile cases like *Baby M* in 1988, the impression of the prevailing picture in early twenty-first century America is that it is neither regulated nor prohibited.

Baby M and her legacy

Re Baby M

The New Jersey Supreme Court case of *Re Baby M* 537 A 2d 1227 (1988) was the first State supreme court case to test the viability of a surrogacy contract. This was a case where all parties involved appeared to want the child. The central focus was a traditional surrogacy contract (ie where the woman carrying the foetus is the genetic mother) between Mary Beth Whitehead and William Stern (the contracting or commissioning couple) which provided that Mrs Whitehead, after undergoing artificial insemination with Mr Stern's sperm, and becoming pregnant, would carry a child to term, bear it and deliver the child to Mr Stern. Mrs Whitehead also agreed to do whatever was necessary to terminate her maternal rights so that Mr Stern's infertile wife could adopt the child. Having given birth to the child, Mrs Whitehead decided she did not wish to part with her and Mr Stern therefore sought custody of the child, termination of Mrs Whitehead's parental rights and enforcement of the surrogacy contract. After different courts had heard the case, the eventual outcome was the courts' refusal to recognize the surrogacy contract on the ground that it was contrary to public policy and refused to terminate Mrs Whitehead's parental rights. But it also recognized Mr Stern as a legal parent and it pursued the line that the best interests test should govern the question of custody.

The court made the assumption that since Mr Stern had a genetic link with the child, he was a natural parent. But did this not also amount to an implicit recognition of a surrogacy contract or even the practice of surrogacy? (see Developments in the Law (2002–3) p. 2070). The court acknowledged that although unenforceable, the contract could be considered in the context of analysing the best interests of the child (see 537 A 2d 1227 at 1256 (1988)). The court's reasoning appears to be inconsistent since it will not endorse surrogacy but is prepared to look at the terms of a contract which arranges it. Ultimately, it has to find some way of ensuring the child's best interests without endorsing a commercial bargain which is contrary to the public policy of the state (see Developments in the Law (2002–3) p. 2071).

English courts have simply declined to render such contracts enforceable, and by virtue of a legislative amendment in 1990 such contracts are legally unenforceable by or against the parties entering into such arrangements (see s.1A Surrogacy Arrangements Act 1985 (UK) as amended by the Human Fertilisation and Embryology Act 1990 (UK)).

However, not all State courts have turned their face against all surrogacy contracts. In 1993, the Californian Supreme Court case of *Johnson v Calvert* 851 P 2d 776 (1993), considered a gestational surrogacy (where the woman carrying the baby is not the genetic mother) in which the intended mother, Crispina Calvert, provided the ovum, fertilized with her husband's sperm and implanted in the surrogate via IVF, and the court deemed the intended/commissioning mother to be the legal mother. This was because the gestational surrogate mother, Anna Johnson, who carried and gave birth to the child did not provide any of the child's genetic material, and the court concluded that the surrogacy agreement was not 'inconsistent' with public policy on its face, thus the case was ultimately decided on an ascertainment of the parties' intentions as manifested in the surrogacy agreement. This was because despite equally reasonable claims to parental rights under the State's governing statute, the genetic link of Crispina Calvert was stronger than that of Anna Johnson and this appeared to tilt the balance in her favour.

A year later, in *Re Moschetta* 30 Cal Rptr 2d 893 (1994), a Californian appellate court was prepared to consider the enforceability of a traditional surrogacy agreement, but declined to enforce the contract not for public policy reasons but because 'enforcement of a traditional surrogacy contract by itself is incompatible with the parentage and adoption statutes already on the books' (at 894–5).

Eight years earlier, the Supreme Court of Kentucky in *Surrogate Parenting Associates, Inc v Commonwealth ex rel. Armstrong* 704 SW 2d 209 (1986) had been prepared to analogize traditional surrogacy arrangements to conventional in vitro fertilization procedures and held that Surrogate Parenting Associates, a medical clinic that helped infertile couples arrange and execute surrogacy agreements had not breached a Kentucky law which outlawed the sale of children. In any event, this judgment did not amount to an enforcement of an actual surrogacy contract and was soon overtaken by legislation.

The next notable stage in these types of cases occurred the next year in *Re Marriage of Buzzanca* 72 Cal Rptr 2d 280 (1998) where the Californian Court of Appeal accorded parental status to the commissioning mother in a gestational surrogacy agreement even though she did not have a genetic link with the child. The statute involved was the California Family Code (s. 7613) (West 2003) which contained California's enactment of the artificial insemination provision of s. 5 of the Uniform Parentage Act. The Californian appellate court applied this statute to hold both the contracting/commissioning father and mother to be the legal parents of the child produced by the surrogacy agreement. The rationale offered was that if a husband who consents to artificial insemination is 'treated in law' as the father of the child by virtue of his consent, there is no reason why the result should be any different if a married couple consented to in vitro fertilization by unknown donors and subsequent implantation into a woman who was willing, as a surrogate, to carry the embryo to term for them (see *Re Buzzanca* 72 Cal Rptr 2d 280 at 286 (1998)). This case is particularly unusual in that the dispute focused on the dissolution of the couple's marriage and the contracting mother was the only party seeking legal recognition of parental status. This was because the contracting (or commissioning) father was seeking a judicial determination that he was not the legal father of the child and the surrogate mother also stipulated that she was not the legal mother of the child. This case illustrates the fact that the absence of a contracting mother's genetic relationship with the child does not prevent the court from declaring that she is the legal mother. *Buzzanca* reiterates *Calvert*'s premise that the surrogate mother's lack of a genetic link with the child could therefore result in conferring maternal status to commissioning or intended mothers (see Developments in the Law (2002–3) p. 2073).

On the other hand, where the surrogacy arrangement involves the surrogate sharing a genetic relationship with the child, and carrying and giving birth to the child (the traditional surrogacy arrangement), it appears highly unlikely that the courts will find the contracting or commissioning mother to be the legal parent who would be entitled to the child. In *RR v MH* 689 NE 2d (1998) the Supreme Judicial Court of Massachusetts rejected the reasoning of *Buzzanca* and refused to enforce a traditional surrogacy arrangement, refusing to accept the analogy of surrogacy to artificial insemination and distinguished the case before it from one of gestational surrogacy.

Legislative initiatives have taken place in the form of various States passing a variety of legislative initiatives aimed at regulating surrogacy (see Willoughby and Campbell, 2002, p. 104).

There is a veritable potpourri of statutes, with hardly any unifying themes. Some State legislation declares surrogacy as void and contrary to public policy, others regulate it by limiting the extent and form of compensation that can be offered, the class of women who may act as surrogates or the circumstances in which surrogacy contracts will be entertained. However, most States do not provide for legislative regulation of surrogacy.

Comparative observations on surrogate motherhood

It is not proposed to discuss in any detail the legal position on reproductive technologies or surrogacy in this book, but it is worth noting that in current English law, the legal mother is always the woman who carried and gave birth to the baby (under s. 27 of the Human Fertilisation and Embryology Act 1990 (UK)) and since surrogacy agreements are unenforceable under English law (under s.1A of the Surrogacy Arrangements Act 1985), strictu sensu, any such agreement stating the mother agrees to hand a child over could not be relied upon in court. Thus a surrogate mother would usually be allowed to change her mind and refuse to hand a child over to commissioning parents. This contrasts sharply with the United States cases of *Johnson v Calvert* and indeed, *Baby M* (for a detailed study of surrogacy laws in other countries, see de Cruz, *Comparative Healthcare Law*, 2001, Routledge). Thus, if a surrogacy arrangement is made or decided under English law, the surrogate mother retains the right to refuse to hand the child over but if the surrogacy arrangement is made in the United States, under American law, then the court may have the right to order that the baby be handed over if those were the terms of the surrogacy agreement and provided surrogacy agreements are lawful in that particular American jurisdiction. For example, in *W and W v H (Child Abduction: Surrogacy)* [2002] 1 FLR 1008 and sub nom. *(No 2)* [2002] 2 FLR 252 an English surrogate mother entered into a surrogacy arrangement in California with a married couple from California, produced twins after being implanted with an egg from an anonymous donor and, when told by the Californian court that she had no parental responsibility or rights over the children, removed the children to England. The English court ordered the summary removal of the children to California since the surrogacy agreement was valid under Californian law and the case had no real connection with England. It was also held that the children had no place of habitual residence at that time, in either England or California.

Current laws on divorce

Introduction

As we have seen, divorce has a complex history in America. Katz observes that American divorce laws and procedure have undergone far-reaching changes during the past 50 years but seem to have stabilized at the beginning of the twenty-first century (see Katz, 2003, p. 76).

As mentioned earlier in this book, divorce has replaced death as the most common endpoint of marriage (Pinsof, 2002, p. 135) hence divorce can now be seen as 'both the legal termination of the husband and wife relationship as well as the legal, social, and psychological reorganisation of that relationship and the parent-child relationship established through the marriage'. Consequently, 'while alimony and the assignment of property may continue the adult relationship, this is done on a different level from marriage' (Katz, 2003, p. 76). Nevertheless, Katz also points out that in the great majority of divorce cases, conflicts are resolved in lawyers' offices where negotiation between lawyers is carried out in an informal setting without following rules of evidence. Consequently, the cases which reach the court do so purely for 'judicial affirmation of the resulting agreement' (Katz, 2004, p. 77). As a result of this frequent occurrence, Katz makes an illuminating observation that there are in fact two systems at work in divorce practice, sometimes running in parallel and sometimes modifying or contradicting each other. One is the oral legal tradition whereby a female client is advised to adopt a course of action such as to accept a small settlement in lieu of alimony or for a male client to agree to a reasonable child visitation (access) schedule instead of seeking custody. Both courses of action may not actually be based on case law or statute but on what the lawyer believes a particular judge will do and suggests what is thought to be in that client's best interests. Hence, the lawyer may believe that the judge hearing the female client's case does not usually award alimony to a marriage which is of short duration and that a particular judge does not usually award custody to fathers. The other system is the official law, which is contained in statutes and more traditional textbooks (Katz, 2004, p. 77).

Current grounds for divorce in the United States

Introduction

As would be expected of a federal system which leaves domestic relations largely to individual States to regulate, the United States has considerable variation from

State to State in the details of divorce law (Glendon, 1987, p. 76). Where there were several grounds for divorce and a judge wanted to grant a divorce but did not have sufficiently persuasive evidence before him, he would interpret the particular ground for divorce in broad terms, so that for example, cruelty, which usually required evidence of physical force, might be extended to include emotional or mental distress without physical manifestations or acts of physical violence.

Fault

The typical grounds for divorce, while differing from State to State, have always been 'fault-based', that is, adultery, physical abuse, desertion and often cruelty. In a place like New Hampshire, simply joining the Shakers (who rejected sex) was grounds for divorce, and in Tennessee a woman who was pregnant by another man at the time of the marriage was entitled to a divorce (Friedman, 2004, p. 62). It is important to note that in States with fault-based legislation, a divorce would only be issued when one of the spouses was proven to be at fault, or had done something wrong and therefore was culpable for the action, as stated in the case of *Pennings v Pennings* 786 A 2d 622 at 625 (Me. 2001). By 1985, all 50 States had some form of no-fault divorce in place (Bradley Berry, 1998). Courts began to remove fault-based divorce arguably for two reasons: (i) because spouses perjured themselves in order to obtain a divorce even where no fault was involved because alleging fault was the only way to procure the divorce (Parkman, 2001, p. 383); and (ii) courts wanted to reduce the hostility historically associated with divorce-related litigation (Wardle, 1994, p. 741).

Lyn Wardle argued that no-fault divorce increases domestic violence between spouses, claiming that her research indicates that separated and divorced women endure the highest rate of spousal abuse because no-fault divorce causes fury and instability (see Wardle, 2003, as summarized by Turnage Boyd, 2005, p. 611).

Be that as it may, the fault-based divorce model (sometimes co-existing with no-fault grounds) still exists in 33 States: Alabama, Alaska, Arkansas, Connecticut, Georgia, Idaho, Illinois, Indiana, Kansas, Louisiana, Maine, Maryland, Massachusetts, Mississippi, Missouri, Nevada, New Hampshire, New Jersey, New Mexico, New York, North Dakota, Ohio, Oklahoma, Pennsylvania, Rhode Island, South Carolina, South Dakota, Tennessee, Texas, Utah, Vermont, Virginia and West Virginia.

This has had an impact on the assignment of children and property, and 28 States still consider marital fault when determining alimony awards: Alabama, Arizona, Connecticut, Florida, Georgia, Idaho, Kentucky, Louisiana, Maryland, Massachusetts, Michigan, Mississippi, Missouri, Nevada, New Hampshire, New Jersey, New York, North Dakota, Pennsylvania, Rhode Island, South Carolina, South Dakota, Tennessee, Texas, Utah, Virginia, West Virginia and Wyoming.

The public response to no-fault divorce

Recent surveys indicate that approximately half of all Americans are not happy with no-fault divorce and are in favour of changes which would make it more difficult to obtain a divorce. If accurate, this would be an increase in the proportion of the population against such divorces ten years ago (Parkman, 2001, p. 398). Scott and Scott also wrote, just before the turn of the new millennium, that there is 'widespread dissatisfaction with the current social and legal landscape of marriage and divorce, and a sense that marriage itself is threatened under no-fault divorce' (Scott and Scott, 1998, p. 1226).

Arguments for and against no-fault divorce

Writing around the same time, the economist Robert Rowthorn argued that no-fault divorce undermines the commitment that is key to the nature of marriage. His central argument is that marriage, like a business partnership, is an institution of trust which enables two people to have the confidence to make long-term investments in their relationship (Rowthorn, 1999, p. 661).

Wardle takes up this theme and argues: 'Survey after survey of public opinion reports that Americans believe that divorce is too easy, especially divorce of couples with children' (Wardle, 2000, p. 786). She also asserts that it is very likely that some sort of divorce reform will be adopted in many States within the next decade, and as she wrote this at the turn of the millennium, we shall see in the next few years if this prediction comes true, or whether it will take another decade before the current divorce laws are reformed.

In his response to the fault – no-fault debate, Ira Ellman has focused on and criticized four principal arguments of the proponents of fault-based divorce. These are: (i) that no fault divorce causes an increase in the divorce rate but Ellman finds no empirical evidence to support this; (ii) that fault-based divorce has a deterrent effect on marital misconduct; (iii) that no-fault divorce leads to unjust outcomes in property allocations and alimony awards; and (iv) that no-fault divorce is an aspect of wider cultural changes which reflect amoral thinking about marriage and the family. Ellman concludes that none of these arguments is well-founded (Ellman, 1997).

Residency requirements

A major procedural law was passed around the same time as the no-fault divorce laws were being enacted. This changed the trend for a one or two-year residence requirement before a person could file for divorce. Residence requirements would provide a certain amount of time to consider divorce and long residence requirements would act as a deterrent to divorce and reflect a policy of marriage being a serious undertaking which should not be dissolved easily (Katz, 2003, pp. 80–1). The statutory trend appears to be in the direction of shortening the time necessary to live in a State before one can sue for divorce, thus it has become less important to leave a State or travel to another country to obtain a divorce (Katz, 2003, p. 81).

No-fault divorce

State legislatures have steadily abrogated no-fault divorce grounds, replacing them with statutory no-fault causes such as 'irreconcilable differences, incompatibility, irretrievable breakdown of marriage, incompatibility of temperament, voluntary separation for statutorily mandated periods of time, breakdown of the marriage to the extent that the legitimate objects of marriage have been destroyed and there remains no reasonable likelihood that the marriage can be preserved, a statutorily mandated period of separation with no prospects of reconciliation and other similarly worded phrases to classify no-fault divorce'(Rigby, 2002, pp. 576–7). Spaht reports that two-thirds of divorces in the United States occur for no-fault reasons such as 'lack of connection' (Spaht, 2003, p. 13). Based on the number of divorces in 1998, in every year there were 321,420 filing for no-fault divorces when someone was at fault (Wardle, 2006, p. 617, relying on statistics cited by Parkman, 2001, p. 24).

Comparative observations on divorce

American law has had an impact on English and Commonwealth law although the impact is mainly historical (Vaver, 1978, p. 258). Vaver reminds us that when English and Commonwealth jurists and parliamentarians began to consider liberalizing divorce law they looked first to Scotland, then the United States and European law (Vaver, p. 258). When American divorce law was cited by the Gorell Commission in England, it was to demonstrate that 'contrary to the prevailing (and still persisting) view, the more liberal grounds for divorce in the United States did not have an adverse effect on public morality nor did the increased number of grounds for divorce drastically increase the incidence of divorce' (Vaver, 1978, p. 258). Indeed, Vaver argues that the 'key moment' in England's trend towards a law based on marriage breakdown came when Parliament passed the Matrimonial Causes Act 1937 which made cruelty and desertion for three years grounds for divorce. This is significant because Parliament introduced these grounds in the face of testimony to the Gorrell Commission 25 years earlier that these two grounds, if not contested, could easily be used to terminate a marriage which had broken down and that 'cruelty could be used as a convenient fiction to cover up incompatibility of temper'. The words in inverted commas are those of Professor Lawson in 1912, recorded in the Minutes of Evidence of his testimony to the Gorell Commission (see Royal Commission on Divorce and Matrimonial Causes: Minutes of Evidence, Vol. II, Cmnd 6480, para. 23,852).

Yet, while divorce laws in England and the Commonwealth were being liberalized, American divorce law went the other way and entered a conservative phase which lasted until the 1960s. Vaver remarks that it is 'strange' that in the 'liberalising phase' the exchange of ideas between Americans and the Commonwealth was minimal, despite the fact that social conditions in these jurisdictions were converging (Vaver, 1978, p. 259).

Across the Atlantic, English divorce law in 2009 is a mixture of fault and no-fault divorce grounds, which are now known as 'facts' since strictly the only ground for divorce under the governing English statute is 'irretrievable breakdown' under the Matrimonial Causes Act 1973 (UK). This single ground approach is replicated in other jurisdictions as diverse as Germany and Singapore. Fault is retained in 'unreasonable behaviour', and desertion, with the no-fault facts being separation for two years with the respondent's consent, and five years' separation, irrespective of whether the respondent consents. However, very few cases have been heard in the English family courts for many years with regard to whether irretrievable breakdown has been established in a particular case, with the main issues requiring judicial resolution focused on what was known as child custody (or the allocation of residence orders and access orders under English law) and property disputes, usually where there is 'big money' involved. Divorce in England and Wales is now very largely an administrative process for the majority of couples and has been since 1977.

Matrimonial property

Historical background

Historically, the legal status of a woman under the common law was severely restricted and this legacy carried over into early American law so that a husband's domination and control over his wife was evidenced by the fact she could not own property in her name, or enter into commercial relationships with others and could not sue her husband except in matrimonial matters (Katz, 2003, p. 62). This was changed to some extent by two mid-nineteenth century statutes, the Married Women's Property Acts of 1835 (led by Arkansas) and of 1839 (led by Mississippi). These were originally passed to allow wives to own the plantation and slaves in order to insulate the husband's original property from creditors (Chused, 1983, p. 1399–1403) but the revised Acts eventually allowed a married woman to acquire property in her own name, enter into contracts with others, retain her own earnings and sue and be sued in her own name (see Clark, *The Law of Domestic Relations in the United States*, 1987, pp. 286–305). However, despite these laws bringing a certain amount of equality to women, in reality, women still suffered from economic discrimination in the marketplace for nearly a century and a half after the 1835 (Arkansas) Act. For about four years during the Second World War, between 1941 and 1945, the economic conditions of women changed but this proved short-lived. When the veterans returned home, they resumed their places in the workforce, replacing and displacing women. Legislators appeared to be more concerned with rebuilding the American economy and providing opportunities for veterans to enter colleges and return to their jobs, than promoting equality for women. This meant displacing women who had been working in industries and had been an important part of the workforce during the war years.

Clark and Estin emphasize that the various Married Women's Property Acts (mentioned above), which were intended to place women on an equal footing with their husbands, were construed somewhat narrowly by the courts to the extent that they frequently failed to accomplish the intended reform. Indeed, they point out that it was not until the 1960s that a

> 'vigorous and effective attack upon sex discrimination began to eliminate all of married women's legal disabilities. This was accomplished by federal legislation, state legislation, the Supreme Court's broader application of the Equal Protection Clause of the Fourteenth Amendment and the adoption of the Equal Rights Amendment in about seventeen states. These amendments to state constitutions generally provide that equal rights under the law shall not be denied or abridged on the ground of sex.'
>
> (Clark and Estin, 2000, p. 8)

However, perhaps the single most important change which impacted on women's right to own property was the abandonment of the unity theory of marriage, so that in the last half of the twentieth century married women 'emerged as individuals in their own legal identity and their independent rights (Katz, 2003, p. 63).

The current law – two types of marital property regimes

There are two kinds of matrimonial property regimes co-existing in the United States – the common law system and the community property system. As Katz explains, the common law system is based on evidence of title, whereas under the community property system, which is examined more fully below, the distribution of matrimonial property is based on the principle that each spouse owns an undivided one-half interest in each community property item (see Katz, 2003, p. 87).

Nine States in America are community property States: Arizona, California, Idaho, Louisiana, Nevada, New Mexico, Texas, Washington and Wisconsin. Puerto Rico is also a community property jurisdiction and Alaska is an opt-in community property State. The situation in Alaska is that there is a separate property regime unless both parties agree that they wish it to be community property and enter into a community property agreement or a community property trust.

Puerto Rico is a self-governing commonwealth in association with the United States. It does not have any voting representation in either House of the United States Congress (Senate and House of Representatives), and Puerto Ricans cannot vote in presidential elections.

In a community property jurisdiction, most property acquired during the marriage (except for gifts or inheritances) is owned jointly by both spouses and is divided upon divorce, annulment or death. Joint ownership would thus be presumed by law in the absence of specific evidence to the contrary, with regard to any particular piece of property (http://www.familylegalgroup.com/community_property.htm).

However, the property brought into the marriage by each spouse, or which is received by gift, bequest or devise during marriage, would constitute separate property and not community property. The community property regime is believed to have originated from civil law systems (that is, from the European continent) and from Mexico, which was subject to Spanish law. Their antecedents were the Visigoths, the branch of East Germans who existed as a distinct people around the fourth century AD to 711 or 712, who sacked Rome in 410 and conquered Spain between 412 and 484.

It is important to bear in mind that the marital property systems in each of the nine States mentioned above vary greatly not only from the other 41 States but also from each other. The division of community property may be split item by item or by value (Boxx, 2005, see http://www.abanet.org).

Over the last 20 years, the number of States that have adhered (either by statute or case law) to the common law property system has declined considerably, to be replaced by the 'equitable distribution' method of allocating matrimonial property upon divorce (Katz, 2003, p. 87). In a non-community property State, the court may divide the couple's marital property using what they consider to be an 'equitable distribution'. Any separate property would be allowed to be retained by the spouse who owned it.

Thus, in jurisdictions such as California, a 50/50 division of community property is mandatory under the law (see, s. 125 California Family Code) whereas in others, for example, Texas, a divorce court may order an 'equitable distribution' of community property. This may actually result in an unequal distribution of the property, since the court would not be bound to order a 50/50 split, only what it would decide was 'equitable' in the couple's particular circumstances.

The States may be divided into the American rule States or the civil law States. In the American rule States, the income from separate property is also separate, whereas in civil law States, the income from community property is community property. In Arizona, California, Idaho, Louisiana, Nevada, New Mexico, Texas, Washington and Wisconsin, division of property occurs under community property rules. Thus, all earnings acquired during marriage and everything obtained with those earnings would constitute community property. All debts incurred during marriage, unless the creditor was specifically seeking to claim the separate property of one spouse, would be community debts. The right of a creditor to have a claim on community property in satisfaction of a debt or other obligation incurred by one or both of the spouses also varies from State to State.

Equitable distribution – the judicial approach

Katz notes that 'equitable distribution' has changed the nature of the judicial inquiry when making an assignment of property (Katz, 2003, p. 88). He points out that instead of asking the question: 'Who holds title?' several different questions are asked by the courts if they seek to effect 'equitable distribution'. These are:

What is considered marital property? What is considered separate property regardless of title? When and how was the property in dispute acquired: while the parties were single before marriage but while living together, during the marriage or after the separation? Who has contributed to the enhancement of its value or who has depreciated the property? When should it be valued (for example at the time of separation, initial court petition for divorce, at the time of the divorce trial)? and What is its value? Who should value it, the parties themselves or experts? If the property was acquired by gift or inheritance, should it be considered separate? If either of the parties enhanced the value of the gifted or inherited property during the marriage by keeping the property in good repair or rehabilitating the property, were those activities sufficient to change its nature from separate to marital?

Katz emphasizes that 'the key word to equitable distribution, is "contribution" and the ultimate question is: Who should be assigned the property?' (Katz, 2003, p. 88).

Katz further recounts that in developing a whole body of law to give courts guidance, three concepts have been devised to assist in deciding whether assets are marital or separate: tracing, commingling and transmutation. He explains these terms as follows. Tracing of assets is the determining of the source of the asset, that is, whether the asset was acquired through inheritance, gift or by the use of marital funds. Commingling occurs when separate funds are brought into the marriage but are mixed with other assets so as to be untraceable. Transmutation of an asset is a term used to describe the change in character of the property from separate to marital or vice versa, usually accompanied by use, gift or contract (Katz, 2003, p. 88).

Mixing of community and separate property

If community property is mixed with non-community property in the course of a marriage, a problem might well arise when the couple wishes to split up. If a spouse is able to distinguish which portion of the property is separate, the difficulty is resolved. However, if the two kinds of property are mixed together and are indistinguishable, the entire set of assets becomes community property.

The fundamental assumption of equitable distribution is the fact that 'marriage is an economic partnership in which there is a shared enterprise' (Katz, 2003, p. 88).

The Uniform Marital Property Act – regulation of marital property during marriage

Although today the courts have considerable discretion and extensive powers to protect and support surviving spouses in all States, only creditors have historically had occasion to question the property rights of spouses during a marriage. Nevertheless, the Uniform Marital Property Act 1983 was enacted under the sponsorship of the National Conference of Commissioners on Uniform State Laws, which regulates the marital property relations of married couples during marriage. The Act makes spouses equal co-owners of all property acquired during marriage except by gift or inheritance. This means that, as with community property regimes, for those States which choose to enact it, all property would be presumed to be co-owned (Glendon 1989, p. 130). So far, Wisconsin is the only State which has adopted the Uniform Marital Property Act.

During the marriage, the spouses retain the management and control of such property, with the exception that both spouses have a duty to act in good faith, and the consent of both spouses is required for large gifts of co-owned property (Glendon, 1989, p. 130). Glendon notes that the Uniform Marital Property Act says nothing about the division of property upon divorce or death but suggests that the statute would have 'an indirect effect' on the procedures in these situations which is to create an assumption that at least prima facie, 'the marital acquests are co-owned in equal shares' (Glendon, 1989, p. 130). Glendon perceives this Act as a statutory form of deferred community property, since the individuals have the liberty to deal with their property and incomes during the marriage, but emphasizes that an important point is that unlike community property laws generally, there is no assurance under the Uniform Marital Property Act that the couple's rights to separate and community property will be respected on divorce.

Marital property – themes and trends

A review of the past quarter of a century of the statutes and the case law dealing with equitable distribution statutes reveals that in the absence of statutory guidance, courts are more likely to divide property equally in the case of long-term marriages (15 years and longer) and less likely to presume equal division for short-term marriages (one to three years) (see Katz, 2003, p. 93). They also tend to ignore any consideration of one party being more at fault for the break-up than another in their property distribution upon divorce.

The relevance of fault in property distribution

In the early twenty-first century, a majority of American jurisdictions has held that fault is only relevant as a consideration in '[the] distribution of property where it has an economic impact on the marriage' (Turner, 2003, p. 117). Turner also points out that of the 49 jurisdictions which permit the trial court to divide marital property equitably, 27 do not permit consideration of fault that has no economic impact. According to cases like *Sparks v Sparks* 485 NW 2d 893 (1992), the divorce law of most American jurisdictions overwhelmingly favours the prohibition of traditional fault factors in the distribution of property. Alan Parkman asserts: 'The key impact of no-fault divorce has been a reduction in the compensation to a divorced spouse for their commitment to their marriage and any sacrifices that they made for its benefit' (Parkman, 2001, p. 387). Indeed, Parkman contends that after the introduction of no-fault divorce, 'the financial settlements received by divorced women declined substantially' (Parkman, 2001, p. 387). Even more scathing are Bennett and Bartless who take the view that the new no-fault paradigm reduces failed marriages to a math equation by considering economic harms only, and by ignoring violations of physical integrity, intimacy and trust (Bennett Woodhouse and Bartless, 1994).

States retain the power to consider misconduct in the allocation of marital property but as Ellman has noted, conduct is only significant if the misconduct directly affected the amount of property available for allocation, or enlarged the need of either spouse (Ellman, 1996). Turnage Boyd reflects that this means that a spouse who has suffered many years of domestic violence may well have had to incur hospital bills, or be unable to work because of serious spousal physical abuse, but that adultery might not, per se, directly affect the need for property, unless, for example, the husband infected the wife with HIV which would mean she would need money for medical expenses (Turnage Boyd, 2006, p. 621). It is recognized that men may also be the victim of spousal abuse but irrespective of which spouse is the victim, the courts' approach does seem to require an extreme form of harm and damage to have been committed for a victimized spouse to receive more than half the marital property upon divorce.

Both North Carolina (see *Hinton v Hinton* 321 SE 2d 161 (1984)) and New York have adopted a clear policy to reject fault as a punitive ground in the distribution of property. New York courts have even refused to consider abusive, violent behaviour against a spouse as a factor when distributing marital property upon dissolution of the marriage (Lee, 2002, p. 273).

The Uniform Marriage and Divorce Act 1981

Under the Uniform Marriage and Divorce Act 1981, most States consider the following factors in the distribution of property: age, health, station, occupation, amount and sources of income, vocational skills, employability, estate, liabilities, needs of each of the parties, and the opportunity of each for future acquisition of capital assets and income (s. 307, 9A ULA, Alt A (1981)).

Comparative observations on fault and financial provision upon divorce

Under s. 25(1)(g) of the Matrimonial Causes Act 1973 (UK), 'conduct' is merely one of seven factors which may be taken into account by a court in considering what financial order to make under the Act, and this factor is only taken into account by the court when it is such that it would be 'inequitable to disregard it'. In reality, the courts do not usually place much weight on the conduct of the parties unless it is extreme and unusually cruel, obvious or gross. These terms are not contained in any current English statute or case but a study of the cases bears out these adjectives. As already recounted in Part II, Chapter One, on English law, fault-based conduct would usually only be considered by a court when making a financial award if it involved extreme behaviour such as the spouse who tried to assassinate her husband (*Evans* [1989] 1 FLR 351); who made her husband sleep in a caravan rather than in a comfortable home while she slept there with a young lover (*Clark* [1999] 2 FLR 498); who attacked his wife with a razor, causing injuries that made it impossible for her to continue nursing (*Jones* [1975] 2 All ER 12); who abducted the child of the marriage causing his own imprisonment as well as causing the mother increased legal costs, loss of spousal maintenance and the loss of a child (*B v B* [2002] 1 FLR 555); who lived a life of profligacy and reckless living thereby decimating the family assets (*Martin* [1976] 3 All ER 625); and who indecently assaulted the children and lost his job as a result (*S v S* [1982] Fam Law 183).

In these cases, the courts have been known to penalize the offending party by reducing the amount they might otherwise have awarded to that party.

Appalling sexually deplorable conduct on the part of both parties (as in *Leadbeater* [1985] 1 FLR 789), if included by both parties as part of their evidence in a hearing dealing with financial provision upon divorce, has been held to 'cancel each other out' and result in the court making an award based purely on securing a fair and just award on financial terms (see Part II, Chapter One, on English law).

Children

Historical background

Over the last couple of centuries, the traditional common law rule in the United States was that in the event of custody disputes fathers retained custody of their children. However, this rule gradually fell into desuetude in the nineteenth century as patriarchy lost its predominance and the parens patriae (the father of the country) doctrine grew more popular with the public (Hall, 1989, p. 166). Under this doctrine, the courts assumed sovereign custodial power over children and other dependants in the name of the Crown. English Chancellors in the seventeenth century used the doctrine more vigorously in custody disputes involving parents accused of being grossly immoral and heretical (Grossberg, 1989, p. 236). Grossberg emphasizes that the development of parens patriae as a means of challenging paternal custody expanded 'more rapidly and fully in North America'.

Child custody disputes generally involved the right of a parent or someone acting as a parent to control a minor (Grossberg, 1985, p. 234). 'Child custody' is described by Grossberg as 'a volatile mix of parental and filial interests, rights and duties' (Grossberg, 1985, p. 234). Custody disputes usually arose after 'separation, divorce, death, or public intervention disrupted a family' (Grossberg, 1985, p. 234) just as it had in England.

Two key doctrines in child custody law

The best interests doctrine

Two important doctrines were established in child custody cases by State appellate judges in the nineteenth century. The first is the now familiar 'best interests of the child' doctrine which was first developed by Chancellor Henry De Saussure of South Carolina in the 1809 case of *Prather v Prather* 4 Des. 33 (S.C. 1809). A South Carolina mother sued for custody of her child on the grounds that the father was a known adulterer. Unusually, De Saussure did not follow the common law rule that fathers had the primary right to retain custody over their children and decided to grant custody to the mother on the grounds that this would be in the best interests of the child. After this case, custody disputes became discretionary hearings in which the judge 'balanced a newly recognised right of the mother to the child against the assessment of the needs of the child' (Hall, 1989, p. 166).

The tender years doctrine

The second major doctrine developed by the courts was the tender years doctrine which favoured granting custody to mothers especially if the children were young (that is, of tender years). In its more complete form, it 'decreed that infants, children below puberty, and youngsters afflicted with serious ailments should be placed in a mother's care unless she was proven unworthy of the responsibility' (Grossberg, 1985, p. 248). Hence, there was a judicial presumption in favour of mothers being awarded custody of their young children and in the post-Civil War era many State courts insisted that daughters of all ages were best cared for by their mothers (Hall, 1989, p. 166). In 1876, the Alabama Supreme Court declared that 'no greater calamity can befall an infant daughter, than a deprivation of a mother's care, vigilant precept and example' (*Anon 55 Ala 433* (1876)). The tender years doctrine therefore provided mothers with a presumptive advantage based on their unique status as mothers rather than on any assessment of their capability to be better carers of their children than their husbands (Hall, 1989, p. 166). The tender years presumption and maternal preference rule coexisted with the 'best interests of the child standard and were incorporated into state statutes and case law. The maternal preference could be rebutted by proof of the mother's unfitness' (Katz, 2003, p. 103, fn. 83).

Bennett Woodhouse maintains that the tender years presumption paved the way to the modern belief that custody decisions must be based on individualized assessments of the welfare of the child. She points out that courts tended to interpret the best interest standard 'through a cultural lens that focused on men and women's essential differences. Judges adopted presumptions based on gender stereotypes that reflected the division of labour in the middle-class family' (Bennett Woodhouse, 1999, p. 818). Fathers were still important in that judges were likely to find that older children and particularly boys needed the 'patronage and guidance of the economically and socially powerfully father (Bennett Woodhouse, 1999, p. 818). However, marital fault and the double standard played a leading part in rebutting gender presumptions and by the middle of the twentieth century, the old gender-based rules were being questioned and advocates for both men and women were citing the Equal Protection Clause of the Fourteenth Amendment to the Constitution.

The roots of modern American child law

Modern American child law has its roots in the turbulent 1960s when the advent of birth control pills, civil rights legislation, no-fault divorce, gender equality, and rights for children born out of wedlock competed for headlines with the Vietnam War and the war on poverty (Elrod and Dale, 2008, p. 382). Since the mid-1960s, United States Supreme Court decisions have affected nearly every area of family law, 'transforming what many had seen as ordinary family problems into debates over individual rights' (Elrod, 1999, p. 846).

During the 1970s, the Supreme Court invalidated State law schemes that distinguished between family members based on their sex, which had been an established tradition of family law (see e.g. *Reed v Reed* 404 US 71 (1971)). State courts began to strike down such provisions making it clear that gender-based custody rules would never survive constitutional scrutiny (see e.g. *Devine v Devine* 398 So 2d 686 (1981)).

Current American laws on child custody

Introduction

Each State has its own laws on child custody. California's Civil Code states that custody is granted 'according to the best interests of the child (para. 4600 California Civil Code). Other States have specific criteria listed in their statutes that are similar to the Children Act 1989 (UK) checklist and give prominence to the ascertainment of the child's wishes and feelings in determining what is best for the child. At first glance, this might not seem surprising but it needs to be borne in mind that America has moved away from its early English legal origins and the multiplicity of its influences, which includes French and Spanish receptions of law, customs and language, has led to a composite set of criteria to decide child custody cases, which is arguably a synthesis of its many influences.

The primary caretaker rule

Another rule relating to child custody law has been the primary caretaker rule, which emerged in the 1980s. The primary caretaker is defined as 'the person who before the divorce managed and monitored the day-to-day activities of the child and met the child's basic needs ... and arranging for the protection of his or her health' (Katz, 2003, pp. 104–5). The assumption would be that the primary care-taker would continue to fulfil that role after the divorce.

Clearly the emphasis would be on continuity of care and this resembles the English law approach of preserving the status quo, that is, the court would be slow to disrupt or alter the existing arrangements pertaining to the child's upbringing and welfare and would need good reasons for doing so. This would ensure stability and continuity of care for the child. Since the child would more often than not be in the care of his or her mother, the court would generally preserve the existing arrange-ment unless it was not in the best interests of the child to do so. This rule was never part of English statutory law but was implicitly developed by case law.

Academic origins and reaction to the primary caretaker rule

The popularity and growth of this presumption appears to be traceable to the work of a team of interdisciplinary team of experts, Goldstein, Freud and Solnit, whose views were first published in the early 1970s (see Goldstein, Freud and Solnit, *Beyond the Best Interests of the Child*, 1973). Their theory was that every child needs a single primary attachment figure and suffers harm when the relationship with that figure is disrupted or that figure's authority is weakened. Some scholars were prepared to adopt this approach as a means of avoiding the indeterminacy and problems of the best interests approach. It would reward the parent who has invested most in the care of the child, focus on past conduct and, where the typi-cal breadwinner/homemaker division existed in that particular family, the parents would know from the outset who would be awarded custody – the mother (Bennett Woodhouse, 1999, pp. 822–3).

Positive and negative responses to the 'rule'

Bennett Woodhouse considered the negative aspects of this rule, such as whether it was really a thinly veiled maternal preference, and whether the so-called primacy of a single caretaker concept was itself flawed, since children's relationship with the secondary caretaker might be just as important to them. A somewhat different criticism has emerged from Fineman, who argues that the primacy concept does not really favour women as it reinforces the equality myth, while undervaluing women's greater physical and emotional investments in child-rearing, and in prag-matic terms gives greater weight to the father's contribution to care-giving (see Bennett Woodhouse, 1999, p. 823 and academics such as Chambers and Fineman, cited therein).

Joint custody

Another response to the primary caretaker presumption was to argue for joint custody, a movement spearheaded by fathers' rights groups, and California even adopted a joint custody presumption when both parents agreed. The courts have the power to award either joint physical custody, where each parent was a caretaker during alternate periods of time, or joint legal custody, which gave both parents equal decision-making authority.

There was speedy acceptance of the notion of shared or joint custody although not every State adopted an outright presumption. Many States added it as an option among others, while others created a preference (Weisberg and Appleton, *Modern Family Law*, 1997, pp. 848–9). The dangers of adopting joint custody as a solution was starkly exposed in *Fisher v Fisher* 535 A 2d 1163 (1988), where two parents could not agree on their child's custody and when joint physical and legal custody was awarded the child spent several years with one and then the other. When the hearing officer decided both parents were equally fit to care for the child, he ordered joint physical and legal custody but as the parents lived in different cities, this would mean him shuttling back and forth, alternating school years between St Louis and Philadelphia. On appeal, the court overturned this order holding that such an arrangement could not possibly be in the child's best interest as the child would be less likely to establish strong friendships with other children, to participate in school activities or sports or to gain a meaningful and useful education (535 A 2d 1163 at 1166 (1988)).

Criteria for applying the best interest standard

THE UNIFORM MARRIAGE AND DIVORCE ACT 1970

Section 402 of the Uniform Marriage and Divorce Act 1970, headed 'Best Interest of Child', states:

> 'The court shall determine custody in accordance with the best interest of the child. The court shall consider all relevant factors including: (1) the wishes of the child's parent or parents as to his custody; (2) the wishes of the child as to his custodian; (3) the interaction and interrelationship of the child with his parent or parents, his siblings, and any other person who may significantly affect the child's best interest; (4) the child's adjustment to his home, school and community; and (5) the mental and physical health of all individuals involved.'

The section then declares that the court will not consider the conduct of a proposed custodian that does not affect his or her relationship with the child.

It would seem that prime importance is given to the child's age and statutes vary from simply giving consideration to the child's age, to giving increasing weight to the child as it matures, to granting overriding importance to the child who can articulate his or her wishes (Katz, 2003, p. 103, fn. 85).

Katz explains that the Uniform Marriage and Divorce Act was a model proposal for many State statutes and mandated judges to use certain statutory standards (Katz, 2003, p. 103). Some State statutes (for example in Washington) include 'elaborate schemes requiring lawyers to prepare detailed parenting plans' (Katz, 2003, pp. 103–4).

Academic criticisms of the best interests standard

American academics have criticized the best interest standard, indulging in a long-running debate over the 'indeterminacy' of 'best interests' custody adjudication (Mnookin, 1975). A leading feminist scholar, Martha Fineman, has argued that the best interest standard is based on faulty social science and the illusion of gender equality (Fineman, 1991). In addition, the level of discretion vested in judges has been highlighted by critics of the best interests standard who have cited cases which they argue have shown that 'judges often applied highly biased standards in evaluating parental fitness and were likely to base their rulings on personal prejudices that bore little or no relation to the child's welfare' (Bennett Woodhouse, 1999, p. 821). Elrod and Dale call finding the best interests of the child 'an attractive public policy and lofty objective' but 'a difficult operational standard' (Elrod and Dale, 2008, p. 392). A final criticism from family law scholars has been to question why the interest of one family member, the child, should be rated above those of other family members, potentially to the detriment of the whole family unit and Katherine Bennett has suggested replacing the standard with one that focuses on human interdependence and the parent-child relationship, evaluating it in terms of connection and responsibility (Bennett, 1988). With respect, any standard or guideline will require the exercise of evaluative discretion and, despite its flaws, the present writer believes that the best interest standard at least provides a valuable starting point and that the focus should be on the child, particularly if that child cannot speak for himself.

A response to critiques of the best interest standard has been to revert to the presumption but in gender-neutral form (Bennett Woodhouse, 1999, p. 822). As Bennett Woodhouse explains, the 'modern' presumption claims to be based not on natural law but on 'legislative or judicial generalisations identifying those situations that tend to benefit children, and those that tend to harm them' (Bennett Woodhouse, 1999, p. 822). The problem, of course, is the wide disagreement among the so-called experts about which of several competing values is of paramount importance to children. This has led to policy makers being confronted with a choice of 'diametrically opposed expert opinions' (Bennett Woodhouse, 1999, p. 822).

Key developments in child custody laws in America over the last fifty years

Elrod and Dale observe: 'The last fifty years of child custody law reflect paradigm shifts and pendulum swings in the prevailing scientific and societal view of what is in the "best interests" of a child' (Elrod and Dale, 2008, p. 381). They further note that: 'Current perspectives on custody exemplify the radical transformations of the American legal, cultural, social, and economic landscape that have inspired volatile debates and resulted in children being caught in the middle' (Elrod and Dale, 2008, p. 381). Elrod and Dale make several observations of the changes that have taken place over the last 50 years. For a start, in 1958, divorced mothers were awarded sole custody of the children in the great majority of cases whereas 50 years on, in the later years of the first decade of the twenty-first century, most children maintain contact with both parents, 'according to negotiated parenting plans' (Elrod and Dale, 2008, p. 381).

The other points made by Elrod and Dale include:

(i)   Dynamic changes have taken place in the composition of the American family as a result of the rise in the number of divorces, unwed fathers winning parental rights, and more couples, opposite sex and same-sex, choosing to live together and have children without getting married. The dissolution of these relationships and the recognition of 'parental rights' in persons not related by biology or marriage have resulted in more children being placed in the middle of adult conflicts than at any time in history.

(ii)   The universal standard when judges have to award custody in cases where two fit parents do not agree is the 'best interests of the child'. Judges have to determine whether it is in the child's best interests to be in the sole custody of the psychological parent (Goldstein *et al. Beyond the Best Interests of the Child*, 1973, pp. 37–8, 98), to have more residential time with the primary caretaker, or be placed in a shared parenting arrangement.

(iii) Two things have become apparent, as legislators, judges and parents have searched for solutions to contentious and difficult custody cases: (a) the expensive, time-consuming adversarial legal process does not work for parents engaged in hostile custody disputes; (b) as judges have found themselves ill-prepared to make future predictions about parents and their children, they have increasingly sought the advice of mental health professionals and the social sciences for help in determining the child's best interest (see e.g. Elrod, *Child Custody Practice and Procedure*, 2004, Ch. 11).

(iv)   The 1970s saw the removal of the maternal preference since sole custody (usually to mothers) was the norm until the 1970s. Changing this approach meant families became more egalitarian. The United States Supreme Court moved the States towards gender equality using the Fourteenth Amendment (see e.g. *Reed v Reed* 404 US 71 (1971) and *Orr v Orr* 440 US 269 (1979)) and recognised due process rights for unwed fathers (see e.g. *Stanley v Illinois* 405 US645 (1972) and *Lehr v Robertson* 463 US 248 (1983)). Custody law's paradigm shift to the gender-neutral best interests of the child in the 1970s meant that judges were suddenly required to make 'individualized determinations without presumptions or a clear default position' (Elrod and Dale, 2008, p. 392).

(v) Children's rights have moved from the margins of discussion to centre stage (Bennett Woodhouse, 1999, p. 815) and one of the most important rights for a child in the middle of a custody dispute is the right to be heard. Research indicates that children want to be heard on matters affecting them and that they understand the difference between providing input and making decisions. The United Nations Convention on the Rights of the Child (Art. 12) stipulates that the child's voice should be heard on all matters affecting their custody.

(vi) High-conflict cases continue to harm children and the level and intensity of parental conflict is now thought to be the most important factor in a child's post-divorce adjustment and is the single predictor of a poor outcome.

(vii) The awareness of the dramatic and long-term detrimental effects of domestic violence on children has led to all States adding the consideration of spousal abuse as a factor in custody determination. Twenty-four States have a rebuttable presumption against awarding custody to the abusive parent. When mothers raise allegations of domestic violence in custody cases, there has been a tendency for judges (and lawyers) to discount the allegations, even though research indicates that the majority of allegations are substantiated (see authorities cited by Elrod and Dale, 2008, p. 395, fnn. 75 and 76).

(viii) Fifty years ago, the law settled custody disputes by applying presumptions of what was best for children. A successful outcome was the completion of a clean break divorce and sole custody of the children awarded to their mother, whereas a successful outcome in 2008 means parents 'meeting the best psychological interests of each individual child, following a negotiated parenting plan, and developing a cooperative relationship with the other parent who possess equal parenting rights' (Elrod and Dale, 2008, p. 411). The role of the judge in child custody disputes has evolved from fault finder to settlement facilitator, with the court adopting a more rehabilitative, service-oriented model reflecting the influence of mental health professionals in custody disputes (Elrod and Dale, 2008, pp. 411–12).

In her evaluation of child custody in 1999, Barbara Bennett Woodhouse submitted that the 'future of custody law lies in perfecting the best interest standard, not in abandoning it for simpler alternatives that lack a child-centred justification' (Bennett Woodhouse, 1999, p. 815). Despite its 'operational difficulties' and indeterminacy, the universality of this standard indicates that the majority of jurisdictions regard this standard as the best starting point in any dispute involving the welfare and wellbeing of children.

Child protection and child abuse

Although child abuse and child protection is not discussed in relation to the other jurisdictions which we are examining, the history of child protection in the United States is perhaps not particularly well-known or frequently discussed in most surveys of family law in American jurisdictions. Consequently, we now take a brief look at the evolution of child protection in the United States.

Brief historical background

In his brief historical survey, Myers divides the history of child protection in America into three eras (Myers, 2008, p. 449). The first is the period from colonial times until 1875, the second from 1875 to 1962 and the third is the modern era of government-sponsored child protective services.

The first phase

Before 1875, Myers points out that many children were not protected from abuse, although criminal prosecutions were made for extreme abuse. In 1809, a New York shopkeeper was convicted of sadistically assaulting his slave and her three-year-old daughter. This case against the shopkeeper was written up and sold as a pamphlet to the public (see Southwick, H *The Trial of Amos Broad and his Wife, on Three Several Indictments for Assaulting and Beating Betty, a Slave, and her little female child, Sarah, aged three Years*, 1809). Further details of this case are given in Myers, JEB *A History of Child Protection in America*, 2004, pp. 126–7). Other cases of prosecution have been documented, for example, a year later, in another pamphlet, it was reported that a woman was prosecuted in Schenectady for murdering her newborn child but although she admitted to several people that she had killed the baby, the jury found her not guilty, in all probability because she was insane (see Schermerorn, R *Report of the Trial of Susanna*, 1810), reprinted in *Free Blacks, Slaves and Slaveowners*, 1988, pp. 211–60). In 1869, in the case of *Fletcher v People* 52 Ill. 395 (1869), an Illinois father was prosecuted for confining his blind son in the middle of winter. The Illinois Supreme Court emphatically rejected the argument of defence counsel that parents have the right to raise their children as they see fit, and declared that if a parent committed 'wanton and needless cruelty' on his child through imprisonment or inhuman beating, the law would punish him. From 1856 to 1940, Myers' research revealed that the majority of rape appeals in California involved child victims.

From about 1642, Massachusetts had a law which gave magistrates the authority to remove children from parents who did not 'train up' their children properly. Indeed, in 1866, Massachusetts passed a law which gave magistrates the power to intervene in the family when 'by reason of orphanage or of the neglect, crime, drunkenness or other vice of parents', a child was 'growing up without education or salutary control and in circumstances exposing said child to an idle and dissolute life' (see An Act Concerning the Care and Education of Neglected Children, 1866 Mass. Acts Ch. 283).

Judges had the inherent authority to stop abuse irrespective of whether a statute existed authorizing intervention (Myers, 2008, p. 450). Hence, before the growth of non-governmental child-protection societies in 1875, protection of children might have been sporadic but as we have seen, judicial intervention to protect children did occur. As Myers puts it, 'children were not protected on the scale they are today, but adults were aware of maltreatment and tried to help' (Myers, 2008, p. 451).

The second phase 1875–1962

The case of nine-year-old Mary Ellen Wilson, who was rescued from regular beatings and neglect by her guardian, took place in 1874, and sparked the start and growth of organized child protection. A religious missionary to the poor was relentless in effecting her rescue in the face of a police force which declined to investigate the situation, the absence of any child protection services or juvenile court, and child helping charities which lacked any authority to intervene. The girl was finally rescued by using a variant of the writ of habeas corpus by the lawyer of the founder of the American Society for the Prevention of Cruelty to Animals, Henry Bergh. Bergh and his lawyer then created the world's first organization devoted entirely to child protection, the New York Society for the Prevention of Cruelty to Children, of which Bergh became president, an office he held into the twentieth century. Once news of this organization spread, other States followed suit so that by 1922 there were about 300 non-governmental child protection societies in existence all over America. However, despite this number, many cities and nearly all rural areas had little or no formal child protection services. Eventually the juvenile court was created, the first being in Chicago in 1899, and by 1919 all but three States had such courts. In present times, the juvenile court is a pivotal institution in child protection cases.

One of the key deficiencies in child protection provision was that the agencies dealing with the problem were non-governmental, hence the first few decades of the twentieth century saw many calls for shifting child protection from non-governmental Societies for the Prevention of Cruelty to Children (SPCCs) to government agencies. The early twentieth century saw States creating or strengthening State departments of welfare, social services, health and labour (Myers, 2008, p. 452).

At the federal level, before 1935 there was little involvement in either child welfare policy or funding, but this changed with the creation of the Children's Bureau in 1912, the Shepherd-Towner Act which provided federal money from 1921 to 1929 for health services for mothers and babies and then the Great Depression of the 1930s, which saw President Roosevelt launch his New Deal to save the nation from economic meltdown. This led to Congress passing the Social Security Act which provided millions of dollars to States to support poor families and part of this Act contained an obscure provision which authorized the Children's Bureau to work with State public welfare agencies 'in establishing, extending, and strengthening, especially in predominantly rural areas, [child welfare services] for the protection and care of homeless, dependent, and neglected children and children in danger of becoming delinquent' (Myers, 2008, p. 453, citing the Act). This provision provided a much-needed boost for the underdeveloped social work speciality of child welfare.

In fact, the Great Depression of the 1930s spelt the end of the non-governmental SPCCs. The economic depression meant that charitable contributions dried up with the downturn in the economy and in the 1930s and 1940s many SPCCs merged with other organizations or simply shut down. Some communities saw child protection taken up by the juvenile court or the police. By 1967, nearly all States had laws which placed responsibility for child protection under government control.

The third phase 1962 to the present

As Myers notes, the 1960s 'witnessed an explosion of interest in child abuse and physicians played a key role in this awakening' (Myers, 2008, p. 454). Before the 1960s, there was little or no training provided by medical schools on child abuse and medical texts said very little, if anything, about this. Then two seminal articles appeared, the first published in 1946 by pediatric radiologist John Caffey who described six young children with bruises and fractures which he hinted were not sustained accidentally. This sparked off a steady flow of articles in which physicians highlighted the abusive origin of some childhood injuries. The high water mark of this trend was the publication in 1962 of *The Battered Child Syndrome* by pediatrician Henry Kempe and his colleagues. It was Kempe who played a major part in bringing child abuse to national attention in the 1960s and 1970s (Myers, 2008, p. 455).

Through the interest and publications of the medical profession and the media, a heightened consciousness about the existence of child abuse and the need for greater child protection emerged. News stories and journal articles caught the public imagination and this eventually led to Congress placing new emphasis on child protection through amendments to the Social Security Act in 1962.

1962 also saw the federal Children's Bureau convene two meetings which, inter alia, recommended State legislation which required doctors to report suspicions of abuse to police or child welfare agencies. These meetings were the origin of child abuse reporting laws, the first of which were enacted in 1963. By 1967, all States had reporting laws.

Another critical component of child protection is the use of foster care (Myers, 2008, p. 456) and this has also had a chequered history. In short, in the nineteenth century, foster homes were seen to be preferable to children living in orphanages or almshouses and the debate during the 1850s to the early twentieth century was between foster care versus orphanage care. Foster care became the favoured haven for child victims of abuse, and orphanages and almshouses disappeared. However, in the last quarter of the twentieth century, foster care has been criticized because over half a million children were in foster care at any point in time and too many children were marooned in such care without much hope of leaving it for more permanent families. Nevertheless, it remains the best hope for many abused and neglected children (Myers, 2008, p. 456).

Mandatory reporting of child abuse

The main elements of mandatory reporting statutes include: (i) definition of reportable conditions; (ii) persons required to report; (iii) degree of certainty reporters must reach; (iv) sanctions for failure to report; (v) immunity for good faith reports; (vi) abrogation of certain communication privileges; (vii) delineation of reporting procedures.

Concluding comment on the child protection system in the United States

The current child protection system in the United States is a vast improvement on the incomplete structure in the 1960s. Child protection systems are available across America, billions of dollars are devoted to child welfare and Myers maintains that: 'The child protection system protects children every hour of the day ... [and] As we look back across history ... the effort to protect children is not a story of failure but a story of progress and hope. [The system] is far from perfect, and much remains to be done, but ... much has been accomplished' (Myers, 2008, p. 463).

Concluding observations

General comments

Over the last 50 years, there has been a 'plethora of federal legislation, Supreme Court decisions and international treaties ... [resulting] in a federalisation of many areas of family law' (Elrod, 1999, pp. 849–51). The United States Congress has stepped into the traditionally State-controlled area of family law to address serious problems that States were either unwilling or unable to resolve; for instance, acting to deter forum shopping by enacting the Parental Kidnapping Prevention Act 1980 requiring States to give full faith and credit to custody orders made in accordance the federal law (see Elrod, 1999, pp. 846–9 for full references).

Family law has transcended local or State boundaries and has become global because of the United States' participation in international organizations such as the United Nations and The Hague Convention on Private International Law. The laws of the 50 States have also become more uniform as a result of the efforts of the National Conference of Commissioners on Uniform State Laws (for a list of the Family Law Acts it has promulgated, see Elrod and Dale, 2008, p. 383, fn. 9).

Marriage

Concluding a review of the changes in marriage that have occurred in the United States after 50 years, Estin writes:

> 'The shape of marriage has changed significantly over fifty years, but the fundamental importance of marriage has not. Marriage still matters to families and to society ... The challenge ahead is to preserve what has been constant and make room for the changes that will keep the social and legal institution of marriage alive and relevant to the lives of all our children and their children after them.'
>
> (Estin, 2008, p. 352)

Divorce

As far as the exercise of judicial discretion on divorce is concerned, an empirical study by Marsha Garrison, published in 1996, reveals what she describes as the

> 'clash of values ... that pervades issues of family and gender, the chaos that accompanies change, and ... trends that may mark the emergence of new normative and legal standards. The data provides evidence of the shift in divorce law's central paradigm, from remedial, fault-based justice to a regime focused on formal equality and dependency prevention ... [and] show us the traces of judicial personality and those thousand limitations that constrain judicial choice ... the legacy of the past, the uncertainty of the present, and tantalising hints of the future of judicial decision – making at divorce.'
>
> (Garrison, 1996, p. 527)

More than a decade on, in a review of family law in the United States in the early years of the twenty-first century, for the year 2006–7, Elrod and Spector indicated that State legislatures and courts reflected the recurrent themes of family law that dominated the day-to-day cases: 'the extent of the state's interests in marriage; the parties' freedom to contract, both before and after marriage; the state's *parens patriae* versus parental responsibilities for children; and the interface of gender and the law' (Elrod and Spector, 2008, p. 707).

Among matters we have not discussed, alimony comes to mind. In this context, it is worth noting the concept of 'rehabilitative alimony' and the fact that it is very unusual for an American court to award long-term permanent alimony to wives except in the case of a very long marriage of at least 20 years or more and only where the wife is at least 50, has been out of the commercial workplace for so long she is virtually unemployable, or is in poor health.

Property relations

Distribution of property on divorce

As far as the distribution of property upon divorce is concerned, the American system has diverged from the classic English common law approach as far as several States are concerned. A key difference has been the adoption of community property or deferred community property which is a notion usually associated with the Franco-German matrimonial systems.

Changes in the economic consequences of divorce and marital property

Oldham notes:

> '[I]n the last few decades, it became accepted in all states that a divorce court has the power to divide some or all of the spouses' property, and this routinely occurs in divorces today if the parties have property to divide. Before that time, there was no express statutory authority for equitable distribution of the parties' property.'
>
> (Oldham, 2008, p 427)

This did not mean that legal authority did not exist in any non-community property States before a few decades ago. On the contrary, between 1939 and 1948 a number of States displayed enthusiasm for a community property system so long as it provided tax advantages for married couples. These were repealed when the tax advantages were no longer available (Oldham, 2008, p. 428). In the late nineteenth and early twentieth centuries, a wealth of case law reveals that a number of States adopted statutes that gave divorce courts the power to divide property. Nevertheless, it was not until the 1970s and 1980s that a majority of non-community property States enacted equitable distribution statutes (Oldham, 2008, p. 428 and see the many cases and statutes cited in fn. 68).

Convergence of community property and common law systems

Fifty years ago, many common law States did not expressly permit property division at divorce. As of 2008, all States accept some version of a deferred community or community property system (Oldham, 2008, p. 429). Hence, the majority of States allow only certain property to be divided (frequently all acquisitions during marriage other than gifts or inheritances) and a minority permit all property to be divided. In a few community property States, marital property must be divided equally but all other States permit an equitable division of property (Oldham, 2008, p. 429).

Acceptance of premarital/prenuptial agreements

Now that premarital agreements have become acceptable, it has been possible for the rights of the economically vulnerable spouse upon divorce to be reduced through contract or even eliminated in some States. Hence, if there is no prenuptial agreement, it has become generally accepted that most property accumulated during marriage will be divided approximately equally between the spouses at divorce (Oldham, 2008, p. 446). If there are minor children, all States have established a formula for calculating the presumptive amount of child support (Oldham, 2008, pp. 446–7). In a related development, and in contrast with child support practice, in almost all States, the spousal support rules now give the United States courts considerable discretion (Oldham, 2008, p. 447). This echoes the English judicial approach where the relevant statute (Matrimonial Causes Act 1973) gives the courts a very wide discretion in deciding spousal maintenance and property division upon divorce.

Children and custody disputes

Writing in 1999, Barbara Bennett Woodhouse concluded that as far as child custody is concerned:

> '[T]he basic pattern of children residing with their mothers and visiting periodically with their fathers remains the rule, even in cases where court documents showed an order of joint physical custody … Most worrisome [sic], courts tended to award joint custody in the most highly conflicted and vigorously litigated cases … It seemed as if judges had grown tired of the fighting and saw joint custody as a compromise solution.'
>
> (Bennett Woodhouse, 1999, p. 825)

However, there are limits to its efficacy, as *Fisher v Fisher* 535 A 2d 1163 (1988) illustrates. A strong presumption favouring joint custody can, in high-conflict custody battles, risk treating the child like an item of parental property to be split 50/50 on the dissolution of the relationship (Bennett Woodhouse, 1999). Ten years on, judicial presumptions are no longer the norm and the best interests of the child has become the universal standard for courts to resolve custody disputes with most children maintaining contact with both parents in accordance with negotiated parenting plans.

As far as the American child custody scene is concerned, Elrod and Dale observed in 2008 that the trend has moved away from broad judicial discretion to a more rules-based approach. Each change that has been helpful in reducing painful family conflicts and dilemmas in some cases has been counterbalanced by frustrations and uneven results in others and not every change has necessarily signified progress. The fact is, '[n]o philosophy or process fits every child or every family' (Elrod and Dale, 2008, p. 418) but even though forming the perfect child custody law has been elusive, 'the stakes are too high to stop trying' (Elrod and Dale, 2008, p. 418).

Consequently, in Barbara Bennett Woodhouse's opinion, Americans should take seriously their fiduciary duty to the next generation and engage in the difficult work of putting flesh on the bones of best interest, in search of a child custody law that is both just and workable' (Bennett Woodhouse, 1999, p. 832).

Further reading

American Bar Association for Family Law 'A White Paper: An Analysis of the Law Regarding Same-Sex Marriage, Civil Unions, and Domestic Partnerships' (2004) 38 FLQ 339.

Bartholet, E *Family Bonds: Adoption and the Politics of Parenting*, 1993, Houghton Mifflin.

Bennett Woodhouse, B and Bartless, K 'Sex, Lies and Dissipation: The Discourse of Fault in a No-Fault Era' (1994) 82 Geo LJ 2525.

Bennett Woodhouse, B 'Child Custody in the Age of Children's Rights: The Search for a Just and Workable Standard' (1999) 33 FLQ 815.

Bradley Berry, D *The Divorce Sourcebook*, 1998, McGraw Hill.

Bumpass, L and Lu H-H 'Trends in Cohabitation and Implications for Children's Family Contexts in the United States', 2000, *Population Studies*, Vol. 54, pp. 29ff.

Chused, R 'Married Women's Property Law 1800–1850' (1983) 71 Geo LJ 1359.

Clark, HH and Estin, AL *Domestic Relations – Cases and Problems*, 2000, West Group Publishing.

Cott, N *Public Vows: A History of Marriage and the Nation*, 2000, Harvard UP.

Ellman, IM 'The Misguided Movement to Reform Divorce and Why Reformers Should Look Instead to the American Law Reform Institute' (1997) 11 Int Jnl of Law, Policy and the Family 216.

Ellman, IM 'Divorce' in Katz, Eekelaar and MacLean (eds) *Cross Currents*, 2000, Oxford UP, pp. 444ff.

Elrod, LD and Dale, MD 'Paradigm Shifts and Pendulum Swings in Child Custody: The Interests of Children in the Balance' (2008) 42 Fam LQ 381.

Elrod, LD and Spector, RG 'A Review of the Year in Family Law 2006–07: Judges Try to Find Answers to Complex Questions' (2008) 41 Fam LQ 661.

Estin, AL 'Golden Anniversary Reflections: Changes in Marriage After Fifty Years' (2008) 42 FLQ 333.

Fields, J and Casper, L *America's Families and Living Arrangements: Population Characteristics*, 2001, US Census Bureau, US Department of Commerce.

Friedman, LM *Law in America*, 2002, Modern Library.

Friedman, LM 'Looking Backward: American Law in the Twentieth Century' in Freeman, MDA (ed) *Current Legal Problems*, 2002, p. 649.

Fineman, M *The Illusion of Equality: The Rhetoric and Reality of Divorce Reform*, 1991, University of Chicago Press.

Fineman, M 'Our Sacred Institutions: The Ideal of the Family in American Law and Society' (1993) Utah LR 387.

Garrison, M 'How do Judges Decide Divorce Cases? An Empirical Analysis of Discretionary Decision Making' (1996) 74 North Carolina LR 401.

Garrison, M 'The Decline of Formal Marriage: Inevitable or Reversible?' (2007) 41 FLQ 491.

Glendon, MA *Abortion and Divorce in Western Law*, 1987, Harvard UP.

Glendon, MA *The Transformation of Family Law*, 1989, Univ of Chicago Press.

Grossberg, M *Governing the Hearth*, 1985, Chapel Hill.

Hall, K *The Magic Mirror – Law in American History*, 1989, Oxford UP.

Jacob, H *Silent Revolution. The Transformation of Divorce Law in the United States*, 1988, University of Chicago Press.

Katz, Eekelaar and McLean (eds) *Cross Currents*, 2000, Oxford UP.

Katz, S *Family Law in America*, 2003, Oxford UP.

Katz, SN 'Five Decades of Family Law' (2008) 42 FLQ 295.

Krause, H D 'Marriage for the New Millennium: Heterosexual, Same Sex – Or Not At All?' (2000) 34 FLQ 271.

Meyer, D 'Self-Definition in the Constitution of Faith and Family' (2002) 86 Minn LR 791.

Mnookin, RH 'Child-Custody Adjudication: Judicial Functions in the Face of Indeterminacy' (1975) 39 *Law and Contemporary Problems* 226.

Morrison, DR 'A Century of the American Family' in Katz, Eekelaar and Maclean (eds) *Cross Currents*, 2000, Oxford UP, pp. 57ff.

Myers, JEB 'A Short History of Child Protection in America' (2008) 42 FLQ 449.

Ohs, A 'The Power of Pregnancy: Examining Constitutional Rights in a Gestational Surrogacy Contract' (2002) 29 Hastings Const LQ 339.

Parkman, AM 'Reforming Divorce Reform' (2001) 41 Santa Clara L Rev 379.

Pinsof, WM 'The Death of "Till Death Us Do Part": The Transformation of Pair-Bonding in the 20th Century' (2002) 41 *Family Process* 135 (*Marriage in the Twentieth Century in Western Civilisation*, Special Issue).

Phillips, R *Untying the Knot*, 1991, Cambridge UP.

Posner, R 'The Regulation of the Market in Adoptions' (1987) 67 Bu L Rev 59.

Rigby, K 'Report and Recommendation of the Louisiana State Law Institute to the House Civil Law and Procedure Committee of the Louisiana Legislature Relative to the Reinstatement of Fault as a Prerequisite to a Divorce' (2002) 62 La L Rev 561.

Rowthorn, R 'Marriage and Trust: Some Lessons from Economics' (1999) 23 Cambridge Jo. Economics 661.

Shorter, E *The Making of the Modern Family*, 1975, Basic Books.

Spaht, KS 'Revolution and Counter-Revolution: The Future of Marriage in the Law' (2003) 49 Loyola LR 1.

Stanworth, M (ed) *Reproductive Technologies: Gender, Motherhood and Medicine*, 1987, Polity Press.

Stone, L 'The Rise of the Nuclear Family in Early Modern England: The Patriarchal Stage' in Rosenberg (ed) *The Family in History*, 1975, University of Pennsylvania Press.

Storrow, R 'The Policy of Family Privacy: Uncovering the Bias in Favour of Nuclear Families in American Constitutional Law and Policy Reform' (2001) 66 Mo LR 527.

Sugarman, SD 'What is a "Family"? Conflicting Messages from Our Public Programs' (2008) 42 *Family Law Quarterly* 231.

Teitelbaum, L 'The Legal History of the Family' (1987) 85 Mich L R 1052.

Turnage Boyd, K 'The Tale of Two Systems: How integrated Divorce Laws can Remedy the Unintended Effects of Pure No-fault Divorce' (2006) 12 Cardozo Jo Law and Gender 609.

Wardle, LD 'Domestic Violence and the No-Fault Divorce Culture' (1994) Utah LR 741.

Wardle, L and Nolan, L 'United States of America' in Pintens (ed.) *International Encyclopaedia of Laws*, Vol. 4, Family and Succession Law, No. 11 (latest update, 1998).

Wardle, LD 'Divorce Reform at the Turn of the Millennium: Certainties and Possibilities' (2000) 33 Fam LQ 783.

Wardle, LD 'Marriage and Domestic Violence in the United States: New Perspectives about Legal Strategies to Combat Domestic Violence' (2003) 15 St Thomas L Rev 791.

Willoughby, K and Campbell, A 'Having my Baby: Surrogacy in Colorado' (2002) 31 Colo Law 103.

Chapter 3

Family law in Australia and New Zealand

Introduction

This chapter looks at family law developments in Australia and New Zealand. These are both common law jurisdictions, for the reasons given in the text that follows.

AUSTRALIA

Historical background

Australian family law is based primarily on the English common law system not least because of its history and its British roots, and is traditionally classified as a common law jurisdiction. This means that the laws of settlements peopled by settlers from the United Kingdom were predominantly grounded in case law (mainly English law) rather than in comprehensive codes or statutes. From Australia's federation in 1901 until the mid-twentieth century, marriage and divorce laws were inherited from England and 'reflected English law as it developed over that period' (Harrison, 2002, p. 2). Between 1857 and 1864 all colonies except New South Wales adopted the English Matrimonial Causes Act 1857. But, as Harrison points out, the laws of the colonies, and, after federation, the States, developed somewhat differently in the decades that followed, particularly in formulating different grounds for divorce. The Commonwealth Constitution of 1901 enabled the Commonwealth to legislate in respect of 'marriage; divorce and matrimonial causes; and in relation thereto, parental rights and the custody and guardianship of infants'. But it was not until the Matrimonial Causes Act 1959 that 'the first comprehensive exercise by the Commonwealth of those powers' was undertaken, which was followed in 1961 by the Marriage Act (Harrison, 2002, p. 3).

This Act unified the law of divorce and associated issues across Australia. Before looking at this Act in further detail, we reflect on the nature of the Australian family and family structures in Australian history from the time of the Australian federation in 1901.

The family and family structures in Australian history

Historian Patricia Grimshaw regards the Australian family as having been 'born modern' and relatively unencumbered by kinship and community (Grimshaw, 1979, p. 412) and, since the 1970s, a growing body of research suggests that even in the short course of Australian history since federation took place in 1901 there have been substantial changes and variations in family structures (see Gilding, 2001, p. 6).

As in other Western-influenced and Western-oriented jurisdictions, Michael Gilding observes that there is now far more uncertainty about what the 'family' means than ever before. He notes the shift from the household economy of the late nineteenth century, to the child-centred nuclear family of the mid-twentieth century, to the more recent proliferation of households (see Gilding, 1991).

In a survey of Australian families from 1901 to 2001, Michael Gilding looks at Australian families at the time of federation when they were 'relatively enmeshed in wider relationships and solidarities' and highlights three aspects to these wider relationships. First, the wealthiest households produced many goods and services in the home which are now purchased throughout the market. Second, households across the class spectrum consistently accommodated extended kin as required. Women and children were especially vulnerable in the absence of a welfare state, as were the unemployed and disabled. Third, working-class households were commonly crowded and economically precarious and crowding 'promoted life on the streets' (Gilding, 2001, p. 6).

On 1 January 1901, the Constitution of Australia came into force and this is when the six separate British self-governing colonies of New South Wales, Queensland, South Australia, Tasmania, Victoria and Western Australia came together as a federation. The movement for federation had begun in the late 1880s, when nationalism began to manifest itself among Australians, many of whom were by then native born. The final successful effort to establish a Federal Council was achieved in 1883 at an intercolonial conference called to debate the strategies needed to counter the activities of the German and French in New Guinea and New Caledonia. This eventually led to the formation of the Federal Council of Australasia which was formed to represent the affairs of the colonies in their relations with the South Pacific Islands.

Following debate and discussion in the wake of federation in 1901, a cautious introduction of welfare support was implemented for the elderly and the disabled, as well as a 'living wage' based on the amount required for a man 'to lead a human life, to marry, and to bring up a family' (Ryan and Conlon, 1975, p. 50).

Low birth rate crisis

Gilding observes that the most controversial aspect of family life a century ago was the declining birth rate. The birth rate started falling in the 1880s, fell sharply in the

1890s and by the 1900s there was a 'growing moral panic about the declining birth rate' (Gilding, 2001, p. 8). This led to the setting up of the Royal Commission on the Decline of the Birth Rate and on the Mortality of Infants in New South Wales of 1903. The Royal Commission consisted of senior public servants, politicians, doctors and businessmen but there was not a single woman on the Commission. The findings in the Final Report, predictably, were that the reason given for people for restricting procreation is that they could not conveniently afford to rear more than a certain number of children but that this was not the 'real reason'. Expert witnesses referred to the 'unwillingness to physical discomfort, the strain and worry associated with childbearing and childrearing; and a love of luxury and of social pleasures, which is increasing' which amounted to 'selfishness' (Royal Commission, 1904). This clearly referred to women's selfishness (Gilding, 2001, p. 8). The Commissioners warned of the 'dire consequences' to health of contraception for women – derangement of the nervous system; frequent distress of mind and body; impairment and sometimes ruin of the general health; and inflammatory diseases which disabled the reproductive organs (Royal Commission, 1904).

Moralistic criticisms were also launched against birth control, most notably by the clergy, in terms reminiscent of more recent times, about birth control lowering the whole view of what marriage is about and turning marriage into a mere sexual compact (Archbishop of Sydney in Royal Commission, 1904). The Royal Commission called the use of birth control an attack on the value of the family as the basis of social life and said that it jeopardized Anglo-Saxon sovereignty and Australian imperial prospects in the nearby region (Gilding, 2001, p. 8). Gilding's study on the Australian family has unearthed several points about the debate in the early twentieth century over birth control. First, he notes that the debate over birth control illustrated that 'there is a long history of moral panics around the family'; second, this debate appeared to centre on what was 'natural' – with the implication that having an unlimited number of children was natural, birth control of any sort 'unnatural' and nature would somehow punish unnatural practices; third, the public debate about the future of the family was overwhelmingly conducted by men, a situation some commentators called 'public patriarchy', which is a situation hard to imagine occurring today. Gilding further notes that 'there may be a long history of moral panics but the character of these moral panics has changed' (Gilding, 2001, p. 8).

Reasons for changes in the Australian family

By the postwar decades of the 1950s and 1960s, the Australian family had undergone considerable changes, not least in their structure but with the nuclear family reaching its apogee and being more widespread than ever. Gilding's study (see Gilding, 2001) offers several reasons for this. First, households with domestic servants had all but disappeared, young women did not enjoy domestic service and were leaving it in huge numbers to take up jobs in the expanded manufacturing, retail and service sectors. The disappearance of these women from domestic service meant the upper and middle classes were forced to reorganize themselves and women of all classes became 'housewives' (Gilding, 2001, p. 8). Second, the growth of the welfare state led to the family been less required to accommodate extended kin in times of difficulty, as government pensions permitted the elderly and disabled to maintain independent households. Third, the 'long boom' of the 1950s and 1960s promoted marriage and family formation with more marriages taking place than previously and people getting married younger than ever before. This meant that there were fewer unmarried women (and to a lesser extent men) who stayed at home to look after their parents, and fewer unmarried men (and to a lesser extent women) who entered into lodgings with another family. However, the notion of 'the family' became a pivotal and common reference point in government reports and the social sciences and this was a reference point which was 'heavily normative' (Gilding, 2001, p. 9). Hence the converse side of the 'family' was the broken family so that by definition, the broken family was not really a family but merely 'a fragment of the family', caused by 'family breakdown' (Gilding, 2001, p. 9).

The non-traditional 'traditional' family

An illuminating insight by Gilding is that although conservative politicians at the turn of the new century often refer to the traditional family of the post-war decade, in reality the post-war families in Australia at this time were not 'traditional' in the sense of the archetypal nuclear family of the male as breadwinner and woman as housewife (see Gilding, 2001, p. 9). This traditional family was not the stereotypical family of pre-industrial societies, and it was also far more homogeneous across social classes (Gilding, 2001, p. 9).

The changing family – partnership, democracy and the waning of patriarchal authority

By 1948, fuelled by the increase in the number of marriages being entered into by more young couples than ever before, a 'baby boom' took place. This allayed the moral panic surrounding birth control, which eventually came to be regarded not as a threat to the family but as a form of family planning and, by 1948, a eugenics organization responsible for birth control called the Racial Hygiene Association renamed itself the Family Planning Association. However, anxieties still beset the post-war decades and these were reflected in the publication in 1957 of the first Australian study of the sociology of the family – *Marriage and the Family in Australia*, edited by the anthropologist Professor A.P. Elkin (Elkin, 1957). This study focused particularly on the changing character of marriage and the rising divorce rate, which in the last years of the Second World War had risen to unprecedented levels. Borrie, one of the contributors to the Elkin book, observed that divorce and juvenile delinquency had replaced the birth rate as maladjustments threatening the family, but was encouraged by the fact that the divorce rate had fallen since the end of the war.

The roles of husband and wife

A social scientist contributor to Elkin's book, Fallding, reported his research revealed that the majority of couples in his small-scale sample were in patriarchal marriages which accepted the division between breadwinner and housewife as natural and justified the authority of men. But this view of marriage was challenged by couples who framed their marriage in terms of partnership which emphasized equality, at least in principle. However, these marriages appeared to be more unstable than the patriarchal ones to the extent that they involved partnership and equality (Fallding, cited in Elkin, 1957).

Elkin himself observed in his book that by the late 1950s the primary functions of the family had changed, with the main function now being 'the provision of an emotionally satisfying centre' for the development and health of the individual, a function which required a more democratic partnership form of marriage, one that was more demanding than the former [patriarchal] authoritarian form. Elkin recommended that marriage be viewed as a vocation which required 'special training' (Elkin, cited by Gilding, 2001, p. 9).

Gilding also observes that the 'most striking' aspect of the new approach was its emphasis upon the family as a social institution. The family was no longer regarded as an entity to be left to the vagaries of nature and was, as Reiger observed 'a set of rational and manipulable social practices' (Reiger, cited by Gilding, 2001, p. 9). Furthermore, there has been a significant change towards the notion of patriarchal authority in the family, which could no longer be taken for granted and a noticeable trend towards partnership and democracy in families.

New millennium Australian families

Diversity in family structures began to characterize the nature of families across the Western world in the 1970s and Australia is no exception. Gilding suggest five main reasons for this: (i) the breakdown of the old division of labour between breadwinner and housewife; more women began to delay marriage and having children and were more willing and able to leave marriages; (ii) governments in the 1970s introduced additional parents' benefits for women (in 1973) and for men (in 1979), which was the last major extension of the welfare state; these state benefits meant single mothers were more able to keep their children and women were more able to leave violent and unhappy marriages; (iii) the prolonged education of children with more children completing secondary school and going on to university; prolonged education meant children joined the workforce at a later age, the cost of having children rose, the fertility rate progressively declined and it became more acceptable to have one child or none at all; (iv) the sexual liberation movements challenging the traditional family with feminism promoting equality and democracy in marriage; and (v) the ethic of 'individualisation' – the pursuit of autonomy and self-fulfilment becoming more widespread; this fuelled the exploration of new relationships, lifestyles and sexualities and marriage and children came to be regarded as 'personal choices, not destiny – or necessity' (Gilding, 2001, p. 9, citing McDonald, 1988, pp. 40–7 and Beck, 2000, pp. 164–74).

Diversity in families – then and now

Australian family structures have now gone full circle, going from diversity in families to nuclear families and now a return to diverse families (Gilding, 2001, p. 9). However, as Gilding also points out, household diversity at the time of federation 'involved relationships and solidarities beyond the nuclear family – including extended kin, neighbours, servants and lodgers' (Gilding, 2001, p. 9) whereas a 100 years later, diversity is 'associated with single-parent families, stepfamilies, and childless couples'. In 1901, never getting married meant living with parents or extended families, or working as a servant, or living in lodgings. In the early twenty-first century, it often means living as an unmarried couple or living in a serial relationship or living in a same-sex relationship (Gilding, 2001, p. 9).

Changing nature of family law in Australia

Harrison observes:

> 'The changing nature of family law broadly reflects the patterns of social change experienced over the last century, particularly since the end of the Second World War. Increased secularisation, increased choice (particularly for women) and recognition of family violence and its consequences are illustrated respectively in the removal of various legal barriers to divorce, in the propensity for women to initiate divorce proceedings, and in the growing emphasis on family violence in case law and legislation.'
>
> (Harrison, 2002, p. 2)

Nicholson and Harrison also mention the abandonment of ecclesiastical remedies and the strong influence of constitutional law, political decisions and case law on the development of family law. They also emphasize that 'what amounts to "family law" for particular purposes is dependent on the century-old Constitution, rather than on any popular understanding or acceptance of the term' (Nicholson and Harrison, 2000 at http://www.austlii.edu.au/au/journals/MULR/2000/30/html).

Australia was fortunate enough to enjoy years of economic stability during the 1950s and 1960s, accompanied, as we have seen, by very high marriage and fertility rates and low rates of marriage breakdown (McDonald, 1984), but during the 1960s a number of changes, such as the availability of reliable and accessible birth control, began to give women more choice.

Consequently, by the late 1960s and early 1970s, McDonald observes that there emerged a more 'assertive, anti-authoritarian and individualistic approach' to social issues in Australia, just as it did elsewhere (McDonald, 1984). This was also a time when there was an 'increased emphasis on human rights, and the questioning of a number of beliefs previously held as sacrosanct' such as the permanence of marriage.

An increasing number of complaints was in evidence with regard to the 'intrusiveness, embarrassment and cost associated with divorce proceedings' (Harrison, 2002, p. 3). Eventually, there was an increase in the levels of retention and workforce participation rates among women, accompanied by the advent of equal pay and anti-discrimination legislation, spearheaded successfully by the women's movement. The traditional division of labour in and outside the home began to be seriously challenged (Harrison, 2002, p. 4).

The court structure

Federal and State jurisdictions

Unlike the United Kingdom, Australia has a Federal government and State government structure and a written Constitution. Laws covering areas such as divorce, orders for children, property division and spousal maintenance are primarily dealt with under the Family Law Act 1975 but there are numerous other laws affecting couples in marriages and in marriage-like relationships, as well as legislation in each Australian State which permits property settlements between de facto couples and this includes same-sex couples in jurisdictions such as Queensland and Tasmania. In essence, there is a bifurcation of legislative responsibility between the States and Territories and the Commonwealth of Australia.

Two key distinguishing features of Australian family law have been, first, its introduction of no-fault divorce under its Family Law Act 1975 and, second, its establishment, in January 1976, of a specialist Family Court of Australia, which promoted a holistic approach to dispute resolution and a family court complete with in-court conciliation and counselling. This is a separate federal specialist court with an 'integrated court-attached counselling service [and] an emphasis on litigation as a … last resort' (Harrison, 2002, p. 1). This dual role in counselling and mediation distinguishes it from courts in many overseas jurisdictions. The 1975 Act also contained a direction that judges should be appointed 'on the basis of their suitability (by reason of training, experience and personality) to deal with family law matters' (Harrison, 2002, p. 1).

The Family Court of Australia is a superior court of record which exercises original jurisdiction in all States and Territories except Western Australia, and exercises appellate jurisdiction throughout Australia (see Family Law Council's Statistical Snapshot of Family Law, 2003–5).

The Family Court of Australia has jurisdiction to hear matters relating to divorce and matrimonial causes (mostly applications for parenting orders relating to both nuptial and ex-nuptial children), the distribution of property following marriage breakdown, and welfare (see *Secretary, Department of Health and Community Services v JWB and SMB* (1992) FLC 9–293; *Minister for Immigration and Multicultural and Indigenous Affairs v B* (2004) 206 ALR 130). The court also hears matters arising under the Marriage Act 1961 (Cth), the Child Support (Assessment) Act 1989 (Cth) and the Child Support (Registration and Collection) Act 1988 (Cth). However, the Family Court cannot determine certain disputes which would usually be associated with family law, such as child protection, juvenile justice and adoption. It also has no power to hear financial disputes between de facto or same-sex couples. Many States and Territories have separate laws dealing with the rights of de facto and same-sex couples involved in financial disputes when their relationship breaks down (Nicholson and Harrison, 2000).

Matters not within the Constitutional power of the Commonwealth, as a result of the bifurcation of responsibilities between the Commonwealth and States and Territories, are the responsibility of the States and Territories under legislation which is neither consistent nor uniform. These States and Territories have separate laws dealing with child welfare, adoption and juvenile justice but, somewhat confusingly, the Commonwealth Parliament retains power under s. 122 of the Constitution to exercise full legislative powers as far as the Territories are concerned (see Nicholson and Harrison, 2000).

The jurisdiction of the Family Court is exercised by judges, judicial registrars, senior registrars and deputy registrars with all but the judges exercising delegated jurisdiction (Harrison, 2002, p. 7).

Family Court of Western Australia

This is a State court created in accordance with the Family Law Act (see s. 41 Family Law Act 1975). It exercises the same jurisdiction over children and property disputes between de facto couples.

Federal Magistrates Court

The Federal Magistrates Court has jurisdiction over the dissolution of marriages; applications for spousal maintenance; all parenting orders, including disputed applications about where children will live (complete residence jurisdiction was given on 27 December 2000); enforcement of orders; location and recovery orders; and matters concerning questions of parentage. It possesses unlimited jurisdiction in property matters but unlike the Family Court of Australia does not have jurisdiction to hear matters regarding adoptions or applications concerning the nullity or validity of a marriage. Notably, it does not exercise any family law jurisdiction in Western Australia (see s. 40A Family Law Act).

Despite restrictions on their jurisdictional powers, Harrison remarks that 'by virtue of geography and cost, state and territory Magistrates' Courts are frequently the most appropriate venue for minor family law disputes, and particularly for domestic violence orders' (Harrison, 2002, p. 9). However, State Magistrates' Courts are not equipped to provide conciliation services in matters involving children or property. There is also a wide variation in the nature and quality of their premises and facilities across the country, so much so that 'security concerns, inadequate privacy and the uncomfortable combination of civil and criminal proceedings are also issues of concern' (Harrison, 2002, p. 9).

Divorce

Historical development

Divorce was uncommon in Australia until the 1970s – which followed the divorce pattern in England. The small number of people affected by this meant that divorce reform was not a priority but this changed in the years leading up to the passing of the Australian Family Law Act 1975.

For instance, in 1961, the Matrimonial Causes Act came into effect and unified the law of divorce and associated issues across Australia. This Act provided a list of 14, mainly fault-based grounds which, prima facie, would enable divorce to be granted. However, considerable discretion was given to the presiding judge in the granting of divorce, irrespective of the proof of the ground in question. Ancillary relief was only possible where divorce proceedings were being sought concurrently or had been completed (Harrison, 2002, p. 5).

Current demographic perspectives

In the past few years, the demographic trend has been that two out of every five marriages in Australia will end in divorce. The early indications in the early twenty-first century are that the divorce rate is undergoing a long-term upward trend with divorces representing about 13 per thousand married men and women (Australian Bureau of Statistics). In 1988, 41,000 divorces were granted in Australia but in 2002, 54,000 were granted. Yet, in 2002, there was a 2.4 per cent decrease in the number of divorces granted and there has actually been a decline in the annual number of divorces across Australia with each successive year, apart from Western Australia where the number of divorces granted increased between 2002 and 2003 and again between 2004 and 2006, only falling in 2003 and 2004. Indeed, across Australia, between 2005 and 2006, the number of divorces decreased by 2 per cent, from 52,399 to 51,375. Taking a longer-term view, divorces in 2006 represented a decrease of 2.1 per cent on the number granted in 1996 but it was a 30.3 per cent increase on the number granted in 1986 (39,417). In 2006, the highest number of divorces granted of all the Australian States and Territories was in New South Wales (14,482), followed by Queensland (12,175) and Victoria (12,110) (Australian Bureau of Statistics at http://www.abs.gov.au).

Fault-based divorce

Under the Australian Matrimonial Causes Act 1959, there were no less than 14 grounds available for a divorce or dissolution of marriage to be granted, including adultery, desertion, cruelty, habitual drunkenness, imprisonment and insanity.

However, to succeed using one of these grounds, a spouse had to prove marital fault. Obtaining proof of any of these grounds required hiring a solicitor and/or private detective to collect evidence to support the petition. This involved considerable expense which meant those less wealthy could not afford to take their case to court. The solitary no-fault ground was separation for more than five years. The court had a discretion under s. 37(1), (2) and (3) of the 1959 Act to refuse a divorce on the ground of separation if granting the divorce would 'in the particular circumstances of the case, be harsh and oppressive to the respondent, or contrary to the public interest'; if the petitioner had not made 'provision for the benefit of the respondent, whether by way of settlement of property or otherwise' (for example spousal maintenance); or if the petitioner had committed adultery. This last proviso appears to penalize the petitioner for conduct even though the couple might have lived apart for five years and did not have any specific requirements relating to when the adultery must have occurred or whether it might have been condoned.

On the other hand, as Donaldson points out, the system was 'designed to permit genuinely injured spouses to end their marriages but ... was also intended to protect the institution of marriage by not permitting bored or disillusioned spouses to divorce at will' (Donaldson, 2004). There was, she further notes, no possibility under the 1959 statute to allow couples to consent to a divorce.

Under s. 40 of the 1959 Act, collusion (that is, behaviour intended to pervert the course of justice) was a bar to a divorce. Nevertheless, couples were known to conspire to end their marriages by divorce by fabricating their evidence to establish one of the grounds (see Donaldson, 2004). Under s. 39, two bars to a divorce being granted were condonation (forgiving the offending conduct) and connivance (inferred permission to engage in the offending conduct). In addition, under s. 43, a spouse needed court permission to bring proceedings for divorce if the parties had been married for less than three years.

The mood and attitude towards the 1959 Act eventually changed so that 'both the public and the legal profession' came to the conclusion that the 1959 Act was in need of 'drastic reform and that the principle of matrimonial fault on which it was based, should be replaced by one which reflected current standards'. The existing procedures were seen as 'too cumbersome and caused unnecessary expense' (see comments of Attorney-General in Cabinet Submission No.777, November 1973). Reform was therefore inevitable.

'No-fault divorce' under the Family Law Act 1975

The implementation of the Family Law Act 1975 on 5 January 1976, which repealed the 1959 Act, meant the sole ground of divorce became that the marriage has 'broken down irretrievably' (s. 48(1)). This ground is satisfied if a spouse can satisfy the court that 'the parties separated and thereafter lived separately and apart for a continuous period of not less than 12 months before the filing of the divorce application' (s. 48(2)). The Family Law Act is 'best known as the statute that abolished fault as a factor relevant to the granting of a divorce' (Harrison, 2002,

p. 1). It is important to note that under s. 48(3) a decree 'shall' not be made if the court is satisfied that there is a reasonable likelihood of cohabitation being resumed. However, as Dickey points out, the Family Law Act 1975, 'unlike its predecessor, is not primarily about divorce' and he highlights its three main features, in addition to the setting up of the court, as '(i) setting out the principal rights, duties, powers and liabilities between spouses and between parents and children; (ii) providing for the enforcement of those rights; and (iii) providing the requirements for dissolution of marriage' (Dickey, 1990, pp. 45–6).

In 1975, 94 per cent of the total of 24,257 divorce petitions granted were based on just four grounds, namely, desertion, adultery, separation and cruelty (see Finlay *et al.*, 1997, p. 25).

As happened in the United Kingdom when the Special Procedure was implemented in 1977, obtaining a divorce in Australia is now an administrative exercise for most couples. They simply have to fill in an application form and pay a filing fee. There is no necessity to go to court if the couple does not have a child under 18 years old or the parties make a joint application. If the couple do have a child under 18, the court cannot grant a divorce unless it is satisfied that 'proper arrangements in all the circumstances' have been made for the care, welfare and development of the child (s. 55A Family Law Act).

A common practice is that divorcing couples will usually agree that they separated on a particular date (Donaldson, 2004). It is therefore normally unnecessary for an applicant to prove that separation occurred on a specific date. The applicant merely makes a sworn statement or affirms that the date is correct. However, if the respondent disagrees with any details provided by the applicant, or cites a different date of separation, both parties must then present evidence, in the form of signed statements (affidavits) from witnesses. However, fault need not be proved by either party. If parties have been married for less than two years, they must usually attend counselling before filing a divorce application (s. 44(1B) Family Law Act).

Donaldson also emphasizes that 'separated' spouses can continue 'to reside in the same residence' or render 'some household service' to each other, despite the marriage being at an end (see s. 49(2) Family Law Act) (Donaldson, 2004). Apparently, a married couple may live 'separately and apart' as a result of imprisonment or work but the court may not consider the couple to be 'separated' for the purposes of obtaining a divorce.

Unlike the 1959 Act, the 1975 Act prohibits the publication of details of family law cases which would identify parties, associates or witnesses (s. 121) although there are some exceptions. This provision is intended to protect the privacy of the parties.

The Family Law Act 1975 also separates principal relief from ancillary relief which means that a divorce can be granted independently of the institution of proceedings for the disposition of proceedings relating to children and property (Harrison, 2002, p. 1).

Property relations

Matrimonial property

Under s. 4(1) of the Family Law Act 1975, property is defined in these terms: '"Property" in relation to the parties to a marriage or either of them, means property to which those parties are, or that party, is, as the case may be, entitled, in possession or reversion.' The issue of what may be regarded as matrimonial property is dealt with by s. 79 which allows the court the power to alter property interests for married parties.

As under English law, Australia has a separate property regime and marriage per se has no effect on spousal property rights. However, upon separation, the Family Court has a broad discretion to alter the property rights of the parties, provided the outcome is just and equitable, taking into account various direct and indirect and monetary and non-monetary contributions which each spouse has made to the marriage. It can also take into account a number of adjustment factors listed under s. 75(2) of the Family Law Act. These include whether each party has the care and control of a child under 18 and the income, property and financial resources of each party and their physical and mental capacity for appropriate gainful employment (Harrison, 2002, pp. 13–14). These requirements are similar to those listed in the English Matrimonial Causes Act 1973 but are not identical.

If the case does not involve spousal maintenance, the court is required to make such orders as will finally determine the financial relationships between the parties to the marriage and avoid further proceedings between them, which is the equivalent of the clean break principle familiar to English legislation.

The main issues the court has faced relate to its discretionary powers in determining financial disputes between the spouses because it is said this allows insufficient weight to be given to the value of non-financial contributions, usually made by a wife, especially in 'big money' cases; it is an uneven approach to the consideration of s. 75(2) adjustment factors (Young, 1997, Graycar, 2000); and superannuation is omitted from the property pool (Nicholson and Harrison, 2000). Superannuation is a compulsory retirement savings scheme paid from earned income. The omission of superannuation has now been addressed by the Family Law Legislation (Superannuation) Act, passed in 2002, so that superannuation is now defined by the Act as property and the court has been given the power to make orders in respect of the interest and to bind trustees of the funds to any order the court makes (Harrison, 2002, p. 14).

Alteration of property interests

As mentioned above, courts have the power under s.79 of the Family Law Act 1975 to alter the nature of the property interests of the 'parties to a marriage'. The law relating to de facto couples and same-sex couples is discussed below.

Section 79 provides:

'In proceedings with respect to the property of the parties to a marriage or either of them, the court may make such order as it considers appropriate altering the interests of the parties in the property, including an order for a settlement of property in settlement in substitution for any interest in the property and including an order requiring either or both of the parties to make, for the benefit of either or both of the parties or a child of the marriage, such settlement or transfer of property as the court determines.'

During the subsistence of the marriage, parties may bring property proceedings at any time but if they apply for divorce (or annulment) proceedings, property or maintenance applications must be brought within a year of the decree nisi becoming absolute, or within a year of the decree of nullity being made, unless the court grants leave in cases of hardship or circumstances of need (s. 44(3) and (4) Family Law Act). If parties consent to proceedings being instituted outside the time limit, the court's permission to do so need not be sought. On the other hand, if the court is satisfied that the consent was obtained by fraud, duress or unconscionable conduct, it may dismiss the proceedings, as allowing proceedings to continue in these circumstances would be a miscarriage of justice (s. 44 (3AA)).

The court is only supposed to make an order under s. 79(2) if it is satisfied that, in all the circumstances, it is just and equitable to make an order. Section 79(4) lists seven factors, all of which the court is to consider when deciding whether a property order should be made in relation to parties to a marriage. These include: (a) the financial contribution made directly or indirectly by a party to the marriage or a child of the marriage to the acquisition, conservation or improvement of any of the property of the parties to the marriage ... (b) the contribution, other than a financial contribution made directly or indirectly; (c) the contribution made by a party to the marriage to the welfare of the family constituted by the parties to the marriage and any children of the marriage, including any contribution made in the capacity of homemaker or parent; (d) the effect of any proposed order upon the earning capacity of either party to the marriage; (e) matters referred to in s. 75(2) where relevant (see above); (f) any other order made under the Act affecting a party to the marriage or a child of the marriage; (g) any child support under the Child Support (Assessment) Act 1989 that a party to the marriage has provided, is to provide or is liable to provide ... for a child of the marriage.

The three-step approach

Despite the broad discretion provided by Pt VIII of the Family Law Act, Harrison notes that a line of Full Court decisions has formulated and developed a three-step process for determining these matters which has given more predictability to the process of financial allocation of assets, namely: (1) identify and value the property in dispute; (2) consider the contributions of the parties; (3) consider whether any adjustments are necessary in the light of the s. 75(2) factors (see *Ferraro v Ferraro* (1993) FLC 92–335; *McLay v McLay* (1996) FLC 92–667).

Thus, under s. 79(4) the factors under (a), (b) and (c) have been regarded by the courts as the 'contribution' factors which they usually consider first, and then the rest, under (d) to (g), would be considered, especially (e) which are the s. 75(2) factors (see above). Family Court judges have referred to this approach as the *Pastrikos* approach, after the leading case of that name. In *Pastrikos* (1980) FLC 90-897, the Full Family Court declared that under s. 79, the court has to embark on a dual exercise, the first part being to determine the nature and value of the property of the parties in issue, noting that usually the whole of the property of the parties would be relevant. It then stated that the next step would be for the court to proceed to make some assessment of the extent of each party's contribution to those assets. Its final observation was that a party's contribution need not be tied down to a specific asset but may be assessed as a general contribution to the property of the parties. The second part of the process involves considering the financial resources, means and needs of the parties and the other guidelines listed in s. 75(2).

Some cases like *Davut and Raif* (1994) FLC 92–503 even suggested that this approach was the preferred approach and that if a judge deviated from it, this would have to be justified, not as an error but because a proper consideration of s. 79(4) warranted such an approach.

The four-step approach

However, more recently, in *Hickey* (2003) FLC 93-143, the court outlined what appears to be a four-step approach to determining property orders. Nicholson CJ, Ellis and O'Ryan JJ observed that the preferred approach involved: first, [making] findings as to the identity and value of the property, liabilities, and financial resources of the parties at the time of the hearing; second, the court should identify and assess the contributions of the parties within the meaning of s. 79(4)(a),(b) and (c); third, the court should assess all the relevant factors including the matters referred to in s. 75(2) [the *Pastrikos* approach]; fourth, the court should consider the effect of these findings and determine and resolve what order is just and equitable in all the circumstances of the case. This now appears to represent the most recent approach taken by the courts in deciding whether to make an order altering married parties' property interests.

Spousal maintenance

The Act also sets out the circumstances under which one spouse has an obligation to support the other and, as in similar jurisdictions, spousal maintenance may be sought. If the court agrees to make an order, spousal maintenance is usually payable as a lump sum or periodic sum, which may or may not have a cut off period, but it should be noted that spousal maintenance applications are very rarely sought (Behrens and Smyth, 1999). There have only been a few reported cases where spousal maintenance has been awarded (see *Best v Best* (1993) FLC

92–418; *Mitchell v Mitchell* (1995) FLC 92–601; *Clauson v Clauson* (1995) FLC 92–595).

Children

Introduction

As with any other Westernized or Western-influenced jurisdiction, the Australian family law framework covers parenting arrangements and seeks to ensure the best interests of the child (which is now the norm in the majority of jurisdictions across the world) particularly if children are at risk or their parents or carers are separating. Laws governing child protection are mainly dealt with on a State and Territory basis, under State and Territory legislation. Parenting arrangements are covered by the Family Law Act 1975.

Australia also has a child support scheme, which is administered by the Federal government under which parents can either reach private agreements or can be required to make payments to the person with primary responsibility for the child. The Child Support (Assessment) Act 1989 was implemented in 1989 under which child support is administered by the Child Support Agency Australia.

Australia has also signed up to international obligations and is a signatory to The Hague Convention on the Civil Aspects of International Child Abduction, which is covered under the Family Law Act 1975.

Legislation relating to parents and children in parenting disputes

Amendments to legislation on children

In 1996, a number of amendments were made to the provisions relating to children's matters, strongly influenced by the English Children Act 1989 and, to a lesser extent, by the United Nations Convention on the Rights of the Child. Under the Australian Family Law Act, s. 60B(2), certain key principles are enunciated which apply, except when it is or would be against the child's best interests:

(a) children have the right to know and be cared for by both their parents, regardless of whether their parents are married, separated, have never married or have never lived together; and

(b) children have a right of contact, on a regular basis, with both their parents and with other people significant to their care, welfare and development; and

(c) parents share duties and responsibilities concerning the care, welfare and development of their children; and

(d) parents should agree about the future parenting of their children.

Parental responsibility for children remains unaffected by the parents' separation or the children's living arrangements.

Research findings on the effect of the 1996 reforms

Research findings by Rhoades, Graycar and Harrison on the efficacy of the 1996 reforms of the Family Law Act 1975 in their first three years were not encouraging on a variety of fronts. They reported:

(i) encouraging shared parenting after separation is not a realistic option for Family Court clients who are in dispute over their children. Families with workable shared parenting arrangements tended to arrive at them without resort to the law and were not even aware that the law had changed to encourage such arrangements. For those clients in the system who found co-operation between the parents impossible, often because of family violence, the shift in emphasis to shared parenting has increased the opportunities for dispute and affected children's welfare and often, their safety;

(ii) the inclusion in the Family Law Act of a child's "right of regular contact with both parents" has created a climate where judges and lawyers are more likely than before to agree or seek contact, sometimes in circumstances where there are serious concerns about the safety of children and their carers. Orders suspending contact have rarely been made at interim hearings since 1996, despite the high rate of allegations of violence and child abuse in these matters. However, at final hearings, where all the evidence is heard, the number of "no contact" orders has not changed, suggesting that children are spending periods of time in situations subsequently determined to be unsafe for them;

(iii) there is tension between the "right of contact" provisions, the need for all decisions about children to be made by reference to their best interests, and new provisions that require judges to ensure that parenting orders do not expose children or their carers to an "unacceptable risk of violence" or conflict with existing family violence orders;

(iv) there has been an increase in the number of applications for parenting orders and also for enforcement of those orders, particularly by some non-residence fathers who see the "right to contact" as belonging to them rather than to their children;

(v) changes in terminology have not been widely accepted and have made little or no difference to the behaviour of parents or their lawyers' (Rhoades, Graycar and Harrison, 2000 cited by Harrison, 2002, pp. 17–18).

Despite these negative findings, the Australian government has pressed ahead with reforms such as introducing a presumption of equal shared parental responsibility culminating in further reforms being made to the Family Law Act 1975 in 2006 by the Shared Parenting Responsibility Act.

Amendments to the Family Law Act 1975 by the Family Law Amendment (Shared Parental Responsibility) Act 2006

The most recent significant changes to have occurred in the family law system have been implemented by the Family Law Amendment (Shared Parental Responsibility) Act 2006 (the 2006 Act) which amended the Family Law Act 1975 and was passed on 22 May 2006, most of which came into force in July 2006. This latest amendment to the Family Law Act 1975 demonstrates the Australian government's determination to ensure the rights of children to grow up in a safe environment with the love and support of both their parents, and particularly to protect children from family violence (Family Law Council, *Statistical Snapshot of Family Law 2003–5*, Family Law Council Report). It was, like the Family Law Act, influenced by the United Nations Convention on the Rights of the Child, which Australia ratified on 17 December 1990, and is also largely based on the Children Act 1989 (UK), although there are clear differences.

The 2006 amendments apply to any matter involving children that were in court on or after 1 July 2006. A key object of this law is to ensure that the best interests of children are met by ensuring that 'children have the benefit of both of their parents having a meaningful involvement in their lives, to the maximum extent consistent with the best interests of the child' (at http://www.comlaw.gov.au/Legislation/Act1.nsf/0/1D1968BB157D8090CA257178000B0A56OpenDocument).

Thus the primary aim of this Act is to ensure that the courts always have the 'best interests of the child' as the paramount consideration.

The main changes, as outlined in the Family Law Amendment (Shared Parental Responsibility) Act 2006 (as listed in Family Law Council, *Statistical Snapshot of Family Law 2003–5*, Family Law Council Report) are to:

    (i)   introduce a new presumption of equal shared parental responsibility;

    (ii)   require the court to consider whether a child spending equal time with both parents is reasonably practical and in the best interests of the child. If it is not appropriate, the court must consider what constitutes substantial and significant time;

    (iii)   make the right of the child to know their parents and be protected from harm the primary factors when deciding the best interests of the child;

    (iv)   require parents to attend family dispute resolution sessions and make a genuine effort to resolve their dispute before taking a parenting matter to court. This requirement does not apply where family violence or abuse is in issue;

    (v)   strengthen the existing enforcement regime by giving the courts a wider range of powers to deal with people who breach parenting orders;

    (vi)   require the court to take into account parents who fail to fulfil their major responsibilities;

    (vii)   amend the existing definition of family violence to make clear that a fear or apprehension of violence must be 'reasonable';

   (viii) provide for a less adversarial approach in all child-related proceedings;

    (ix)   increase the emphasis on parenting plans to encourage parents, where possible, to reach suitable agreements outside the court system; and

    (x)   improve recognition of the interests of the child in spending time with grandparents and other relatives.

A best interests checklist

Section 60CA of the Family Law Act 1975 provides that in deciding whether to make a particular parenting order in relation to a child, a court must regard the best interests of the child as the paramount consideration. Section 60CC contains a list of matters the court must consider when making a parenting order. The primary considerations are: (a) the benefits to the child of having a meaningful relationship with both of the child's parents; (b) the need to protect the child from physical or psychological harm from being subjected to, or exposed to, abuse, neglect or family violence.

Under s. 60B(2)(a) 'children have the right to know and be cared for by both their parents, regardless of whether their parents are married, separated, have never married or have never lived together' and under s. 60B(2)(b) 'children have a right to spend time on a regular basis with, and communicate on a regular basis with, both their parents and other people significant to their care, welfare and development (such as grandparents and other relatives)'.

Children also have the right to enjoy Aboriginal or Torres Strait Islander culture, including the right to maintain a connection with that culture and to have the support, opportunity and encouragement necessary to explore the full extent of that culture, consistent with that child's age and developmental level and views and to develop a positive appreciation of that culture (see s. 60CC(6))

The 2006 amendments also abolished terms such as 'custody' and 'access' as the United Kingdom did in October 1991 when the Children Act 1989 (UK) was brought into force. 'Residence' has replaced 'custody' and simply relates to a 'person/persons with whom a child is to live'. Thus, the residence order does not vest a person with sole decision-making power for day-to-day matters and does not remove any aspect of the non-residential parent's responsibility for the child. 'Contact' replaces 'access' and refers to 'the time a child is to spend with another person or persons'. A 'specific issues' order is required if it is sought to give one parent (or a third person) sole day-to-day or long-term parental responsibility for a child.

Comparative observations on the best interests test

The United States

As Part II, Chapter Two on the law in the United States explained, s. 402 of the Uniform Marriage and Divorce Act contains a checklist dealing with the best interests of the child. This contains five guidelines and declares that the conduct of a proposed custodian will not be considered by a court unless that conduct affects the proposed custodian's relationship with the child. There has been a burgeoning of checklists, both judicial and statutory, listing factors to consider in determining the child's best interests, with some States including 11 or more factors (see Elrod, *Child Custody Practice and Procedure*, 2004–9, Ch. 11).

England

The Children Act 1989 UK introduced a welfare checklist (on 14 October 1991 when the Act came into force) under s. 1(3), which lists various statutory guidelines intended to assist a court in determining any question in relation to the upbringing of a child, They leave scope for judicial discretion and interpretation and must be read together with two other key statutory guidelines, namely that delay is likely to prejudice the welfare of the child (s. 1(2)) and that the court should not make any order unless doing so would be better for the child than making no order at all (s. 1(5)).

Relevance of domestic violence

Judges must ensure that orders for residence and contact do not expose any person to an 'unacceptable risk' of family violence, 'to the extent that it is possible to do so consistently with the child's best interests being the paramount consideration'. The court must also ensure that any order it makes in this context is consistent with a family violence order and in order not to expose any person to a risk of family violence, may order any safeguards which it considers necessary for the safety of those affected by the order (see s. 60CG Family Law Act 1975).

Reasonable apprehension of violence

As far as the degree of apprehension of violence is concerned, the 2006 amendments now make it necessary for a person to 'reasonably' fear for or be apprehensive about his or her personal wellbeing or safety in order to satisfy the requirement of being a victim of 'family violence'. However, the Act does not contain any definition of what 'reasonably' means in this context, although an explanatory note in the statute states: 'A person reasonably fears for, or reasonably is apprehensive about, his or her personal well-being or safety in particular circumstances if a reasonable person in those circumstances would fear for or be apprehensive about, his or her well-being or personal safety.' In practical terms, therefore, it will ultimately be left to the court's discretion as to what might or might not be a 'reasonable' fear, in individual cases.

As far as case law is concerned, the Full Court has found that evidence of violence may justify a refusal of contact to a father where it is likely to impact adversely on the mother's capacity to care for the children (see e.g. *In Marriage of JG and BG* (1994) 18 Fam LR 255; *In Marriage of Patsalou* (1995) 18 Fam LR 426; *In Marriage of Jaeger* (1994) 122 Fam LR 209).

Problems faced by women who allege domestic violence

Graycar and Morgan highlight the problems that women face should they raise the issue of domestic violence when they apply for a residence order upon the breakdown of the marital relationship. The problem is that such women become vulnerable to negative evaluation by the courts and counsellors of their parenting abilities. Specifically, these women have encountered three problems: first, they tend to be subjected to assessments by judges and counsellors that are based on a 'misleading stereotype' of 'battered women' and the nature of domestic violence; second, even when a woman's evidence of abuse is accepted, the court may fail to acknowledge the effects of that abuse on the mother's care giving; third, a woman may find herself being blamed for the violence she has lived with because judges may sometimes regard the relationship between the woman and the man as one of 'high conflict' or 'co-dependence' rather than abuse and that the woman was in some way responsible for being in a violent relationship in the first place (see Graycar and Morgan, 2002, p. 271).

Child Support Scheme

The Commonwealth government introduced Stage One and Stage Two of a child support scheme which brought considerable changes to Australia. There is a child support scheme which is administered by the government, whereby parents can reach private agreements; or the Child Support Agency has the power to order payments to be made to the person who has primary care of the child. Child support has been administered by the Child Support Agency Australia since 1989, under the Child Support (Assessment) Act 1989. The Child Support Agency was originally set up within the Taxation Office and moved to the Department of Family and Community Services on 30 June 2001.

Comparative perspectives on child support schemes

Child support in the United Kingdom

As is well documented, England experienced a torrid time when it came to implementing and enforcing a child support system in relation to the non-residential parent and it has proved the bete noir of politicians, political parties and governments. The principle has been accepted by the main political parties but the question of whether a child has a legal right to support has not been as self-evident or as clear cut as might have been supposed, and indeed led to a polarization of opinion between academics (see e.g. Wikely, *Child Support*, 2006, and Bromley, 1992, p. 651) and even within the judiciary (see the House of Lords' majority opinion in *Kehoe* [2005] 2 FLR 1249 and the dissenting opinion of Baroness Hale). The Child Support Act 1991 and the Child Support Agency it created has operated since the early 1990s in the United Kingdom but it has been beset by a range of problems, in terms of enforcement and delays as well as poor monitoring and inadequately trained staff. This led to widespread criticism and the agency was abolished in July 2008 to be replaced by a Child Maintenance and Enforcement Commission.

Conclusions on Australian family law

Divorce Australian style

The present Australian system of divorce is simpler than the fault system which previously existed, is less expensive with less delay and is less embarrassing than the 1959 regime, although there is still some cost involved and a social stigma surrounding divorce. Donaldson argues that although marriage is 'a hallmark of society requiring protection' it is not necessarily undermined by a no-fault divorce system. Returning to a fault-based system would not necessarily achieve happy marriages or social stability, whereas the current system 'may alleviate some angst and expense from the end of some marriages' (Donaldson, 2004).

Challenges faced by the Australian Family Court

Nicholson and Harrison (2000) submit that the Australian Family Court faces a number of challenges in the twenty-first century. These include: jurisdictional issues, such as the limited jurisdiction of the Family Court; constitutional challenges, such as High Court challenges to the validity of provisions of the Family Law Act; the family court structure; providing an effective and fair child support scheme; maintenance and alteration of property interests; dealing with parenting disputes and the rise in applications for parenting orders while trying to minimize disputes between parents; child protection issues and how best to protect children who are the subject of abuse concerns in the light of Australia's fragmented family law system which, inter alia, has involved an overlap between jurisdictions so that there should not be an application waiting to be heard in a children's court while a parenting order is being sought in the Family Court; and dealing with self-represented litigants.

Nicholson and Harrison make the telling point that while Family Court orders apply across Australia, State Children's Court orders only apply within the boundaries of the State in which they are made.

NEW ZEALAND

Historical background

New Zealand may be classified as a common law jurisdiction as a result of its historical antecedents. The whole body of existing English law, both legislative and common law, as well as English constitutional conventions, was received into New Zealand on 14 January 1840. Hence, for a considerable period, the Parliament at Westminster (in England) legislated for New Zealand. However from 1865 New Zealand received limited legislative powers of its own. In 1931, the United Kingdom Parliament passed the Statute of Westminster to facilitate the acquisition of independence for the Dominions (former colonies) by removing the restrictions on their legislative powers. It was only in 1947, however, that New Zealand passed the Statute of Westminster Adoption Act, the effect of which was to accept full responsibility for its own future.

New Zealand is a constitutional monarchy, the monarch being Queen Elizabeth II, although she is represented for most purposes in New Zealand by a Governor General. Unlike Australia, it operates as a unitary, not federal entity and is also unicameral, having only one House of Representatives, with no Upper House. It does not have a written Constitution in the sense of one single, authoritative and established legislative instrument which enunciates the powers of the various branches of government. However, it does possess a number of constitutional documents which collectively list some of the rights of citizens, and other civil rights are protected by common law. New Zealand has a representative government.

New Zealand courts

Since 2003, final appeals from lower New Zealand courts are no longer sent to the Privy Council which sits in London. The Supreme Court, established by the Supreme Court Act 2003 (NZ), is now New Zealand's highest appellate court. Below this court sits the Court of Appeal, and below that is the High Court of New Zealand, which has seats in main centres throughout the country. The court of first instance, with centres in most towns and cities, is the District Court.

Despite these momentous changes, New Zealand continued to look to the United Kingdom Parliament at Westminster for sources of its own legislation and to the superior (higher) English courts for precedents in its own courts. Thus, House of Lords and English Court of Appeal decisions remain highly persuasive and English decisions are still cited frequently in New Zealand courts. In the last 20 years, however, New Zealand has started to look at other jurisdictions for legislative models, especially in the commercial arena. The present trend is now to look at North America rather than the United Kingdom for sources of legislation.

New Zealand courts are prepared to consider authorities from a number of other common law jurisdictions, especially Australia, Canada, the United Kingdom and the United States. New Zealand lawyers are familiar with researching the law across several jurisdictions and are more receptive than are British lawyers to considering the relevance of laws in other jurisdictions.

Divorce

The first legislation on divorce, the Divorce and Matrimonial Causes Act, was passed in 1867, and it was simply an adaptation of an English Act of 1857. The grounds were adultery by the wife; and adultery by the husband provided this had been committed together with certain aggravating circumstances. In other words, an act of adultery simpliciter by the husband was not sufficient to constitute grounds for divorce under this Act. No wider grounds were permitted by the English authorities and it was only in 1898 that adultery by either husband or wife became a legal ground for divorce and new grounds were then introduced, including desertion for five years (which was reduced to three in 1919) and non-compliance with a decree of restitution of conjugal rights. This led to abuse of the procedure by those seeking a quick divorce and since 1953 non-compliance has been reduced to three years which has led to this ground becoming practically a dead letter.

However, under the 1867 Act, a decree of judicial separation was obtainable by either the husband or wife (similar to a divorce a mensa et thoro) on the grounds of adultery, cruelty and desertion without cause for two years.

In 1907, additional grounds were introduced and an important amendment was made in 1920 when a divorce could be obtained, at the court's discretion, by either party, after three years' separation under a court order or an agreement. The impact of this amendment was somewhat diminished in 1921 when the court was required to refuse a decree if the respondent proved that the separation was due to the petitioner's wrongful conduct. This same restriction was utilized in 1953 when a provision was passed which allowed divorce after seven years of living apart without likelihood of reconciliation. This gave rise to criticism and the living apart ground was removed by the Matrimonial Proceedings Act 1963, which came into force on 1 January 1965.

The 1963 Act made further changes, so from 1 January 1965 the grounds available are: adultery; artificial insemination of the respondent wife without the husband's consent; desertion for three years; habitual drunkenness for three years with failure to support, or neglect of domestic duties (as the case may be), or cruelty; conviction for murder or certain attempted murders; insanity and confinement for this reason for certain periods without likelihood of recovery; non-compliance for three years with a decree of restitution of conjugal rights; separation by court order or agreement for three years; living apart for seven years without likelihood of reconciliation; conviction of certain offences; rape, sodomy, or bestiality (wife's petition).

The most common ground has been three years' separation, followed by adultery and then desertion. Apparently, the trend over several years has been that the majority of divorces have been initiated by wives' petitions but almost twice as many divorces are granted to husbands for the wife's adultery than vice versa (see McLintock, 1966, and http://www.TeAra.govt.nz/1966/D/DivorceAnd Separation/en).

Matrimonial property

Historical background

New Zealand and England used to share a strong preponderance of judicial discretion in their attempt to achieve justice between the parties. This discretionary element was replaced by the Matrimonial Property Act 1976 which introduced an equal division of matrimonial property, subject to exceptions, including a right of the parties to contract out of the Act. Separate property, namely gifts, bequests and property owned before marriage, was not divided equally. This was a deferred community or deferred participation system. Nevertheless, cases like *CIR v Van Doorme* [1983] NZLR 495 and *Roberts v Roberts* [1994] NZLR 200, suggested that rights to 'community' or 'matrimonial' property need not always be deferred until the end of the marriage but could crystallise during the course of a happy marriage.

Upon the death of one of the parties, some jurisdictions award the survivor a prescribed share of the property although common law countries have tended to opt for freedom of testation. The Family Protection Act 1955 (NZ) permits a wide range of judicial discretion to determine the amount that can be awarded to a claimant who challenges the terms of a will. The rules of common law and equity have been developed in New Zealand for claimants who have been in de facto relationships, or de facto partners (unmarried cohabitants) as they are called. As in other common law jurisdictions, the law of trusts, in particular the constructive trust, has been adapted and redefined to 'allow for the dictates of modern society' (Atkin, 2003, p. 174). Again (as in England and Wales), this has meant that the results have been difficult to predict, and some claimants have emerged from disputes with little or nothing (Atkin, 2003, p. 174).

The reforms in 2002

Major changes to the laws relating to the property of married and de facto couples came into force on 1 February 2002 through new rules which amended the Property (Relationships) Act 1976. From that date, the property of de facto couples (including same-sex couples) who decide to terminate their relationship has been divided according to the same equal-sharing rules as those which regulate the property of married couples. This applies for the purposes of inheritance (whether a party dies testate or intestate), division of property at the end of a relationship, and for the payment of maintenance. The key legislation is the Matrimonial Property Act 1976, renamed the Property (Relationships) Act 1976 by the Property (Relationships) Amendment Act 2001. A change in terminology was adopted, and 'matrimonial property' has become 'relationship property'. The courts have also been given new discretionary powers to award compensation for 'economic disparity' where there is likely to be a significant discrepancy in the income potential and living standards of the two separating parties (Atkin, 2003, p. 175). It is important to note that this legislation allows parties to contract out of the Act (Pt 6) and it has subsequently been extended to de facto couples but only applies if both parties agree (Atkin, 2003, p. 176).

The Property (Relationships) Act 2001, with one important proviso, applies the same rules on property division to married and unmarried couples. The proviso is the 'threshold to be crossed' (Atkin, 2003, p. 177) before the court has jurisdiction to intervene. If the parties are married, or there has been a void marriage, this is sufficient for a court to intervene. If the marriage is one of short duration, which usually means the parties have lived together for less than three years, if certain conditions are satisfied (such as one party owning the house before the parties began living together), then the property may be divided on the basis of contribution, rather than equally. The court has the power (under s. 2E) to consider a marriage lasting longer than three years as one of short duration, but this has rarely been exercised. Hence, courts have jurisdiction to intervene for all marriages, regardless of their duration, but the length of the marriage modifies the rules. Nevertheless, regardless of the duration of the marriage, provisions relating to occupation orders and those aimed at preventing the improper disposal of property are all available.

Widowed parties

The law under the Property (Relationships) Act 1976 has been extended to cover widowed parties. Hence, under s. 82 of the Law Reform (Testamentary Promises) Act 1949, the deceased's property is presumed to be relationship property, available for division, unless there is evidence to the contrary. Since the deceased cannot offer any direct evidence, the survivor has, in the first instance, to remove any problems relating to classifying property so that the onus is on the estate to prove otherwise. If it happens that the survivor is not adequately provided for under the terms of the deceased's will or in relation to jointly owned property, s. 88 of the abovementioned Act enables the survivor to have an unqualified (unconditional) right to apply for an order under the Property (Relationships) Act. However, the deceased's personal representative is required to obtain permission from the court to apply, which will be granted only if refusal would cause 'serious injustice'. As discussed above, this phrase is not easy to define or to interpret with any degree of consistency but it is pivotal to determining the balance between competing parties (Atkin, 2007, p. 226).

According to the Court of Appeal case of *Public Trust v Whyman* [2005] 2 NZLR 696, the previous judicial approach of Heath J (in *Kinniburgh v Williams* [2004] NZFLR 467) of interpreting 'serious injustice' as injustice that had to be intolerable and the kind that the court could not in conscience countenance, was possibly to be confined to the facts of that case. Accordingly, it declared that the test of 'serious injustice' could be interpreted directly, without a need to put any gloss on the words and that Heath J went too far in suggesting that the injustice needed to be 'intolerable'. It argued that if that had been intended by Parliament it would have suggested that leave be granted if necessary to avoid 'intolerable injustice'. The Court of Appeal refused to define the term but the upshot of its decision is that it has become easier for personal representatives to lodge a successful claim so that beneficiaries and family members will have a much better chance of success than they would have had under the approach of Heath J. Indeed, in the *Whyman* case, the deceased's de facto partner was pitted against his minor children who were living with his divorced wife. His property was in joint names with the de facto partner which meant that in the absence of property proceedings, the property passed to her as the surviving partner. To complicate matters, he had cancelled a life insurance policy intended to benefit the children, apparently over a dispute about access to the children, and the estate was therefore described as largely 'devoid of assets'. The High Court held that this was not a situation of 'intolerable injustice' but this decision was reversed on appeal.

Trusts and companies

There has been considerable use of family trusts in New Zealand, for family, business and professional reasons. Farms have usually been placed in the name of a trust and it has also been a way of running a professional practice but even for non-farmers, trusts have long been established as a useful way of providing security, particularly for children. Trusts no longer offer a way of avoiding payment of estate duties since these were abolished in the 1990s. However, they are useful for serving as protection against creditors and avoidance of the relationship property division rules. Property owned by a trust or company is not regarded as owned by a party in a relationship breakdown and would not prima facie be regarded as available for division under the Property (Relationship) Act 1986. This can work to the serious disadvantage of the party who does not have property held under a trust or by a company.

Under the 2001 reforms, s. 44A-F of the 1976 Act enables the courts to make compensatory adjustments where relationship property has been placed under the control of a trust or company. However, subject to one exception, the courts cannot make orders relating to the trust. The exception concerns situations where there is insufficient property (relationship or separate) to pay compensation, in which case the court may make an order in relation to the income from the trust but not from its capital. This does not apply to companies. Atkin reports that the 2001 reforms have led to considerable litigation, the result of which, so far, is that the courts will construe the 2001 innovations liberally and that the measure of their success has been spasmodic (Atkin, 2007, pp. 233–6).

Maori and property

The Treaty of Waitangi 1840 between the settlers and the indigenous Maori is based on an agreement allowing the Queen of England to establish a form of governance in New Zealand, while simultaneously ensuring that the Maori tribes could retain control over their transitional lands and fisheries. Atkin observes that in modern times the Treaty has come to be seen as a 'partnership' between two peoples and is often referred to as the 'constitutional foundation of the nation'. Indeed, he calls it 'a vital reference point in the development of policy and law reform' (Atkin, 2003, p. 181).

As far as Maori are concerned, the most important relationship is with the family or whanau along with the tribe (iwi) and sub-tribe (hapu). Hence relationships between spouses and parents are secondary (see Hall and Meiga, 2002). Neither the 1976 Act nor the 2001 reforms pay much regard to traditional Maori concepts.

The traditional Maori attitude to property is communal rather than individualist, thus traditional Maori land is exempt from the property division rules of the 1976 Act. However, as far as all other property is concerned, a couple, one or both of whom are Maori, will on separation divide their property according to the same rules as everyone else.

One exception to this was covered by the 2001 reforms. This applies to family chattels, which are to be divided equally irrespective of their origin. Family chattels apply to a wide range of items, including furniture, cars and pets and, as we shall see, possibly works of art. The 2001 reforms amended the definition of family chattels to exclude 'heirlooms' and 'taonga', but while the first of these words may be familiar to most readers, 'taonga' would not be. According to Atkin, this translates into English as 'treasures' and may relate to precious Maori artefacts or like heirlooms, items that have been passed down over time. However, the word has a wider meaning than this and is even used of children (Atkin, 2007, p. 236).

The meaning of the word 'taonga' was explored in *Perry v West* [2004] NZFLR 515 where neither party was Maori. The wife had in her possession a painting by one of New Zealand's greatest artists, Colin McCahon. The husband had bought the painting shortly before the parties' marriage, using money received as a student prize. When they separated, the parties had drawn lots for two McCahon paintings, the husband retaining the other one. He now claimed that the paintings were not family chattels but 'taonga'. Laurenson J rejected the husband's argument but his decision was bad on the facts, not the law. As a matter of law, the judge accepted that 'taonga' was not limited to Maori items but could be extended to property of New Zealanders of other ethnicities. Atkin regards this as surprising because the use of a Maori word by the legislature suggested that this would bear a specialized Maori meaning of special significance to the Maori population (see Atkin, 2007, p. 236).

Laurenson J also thought that an item could be 'taonga' through having special significance, attaching for a range of reasons, such as it being 'sacred and inviolate' at one end and being 'deserving of respect' at the other. It could be of special significance to the individual concerned or because its significance was ascribed by others, for example if someone had made a gift of the item. The distinction was important because it was suggested that the husband intended to sell the painting if it came back to him. In the second category, the learned judge believed that the nature of the gift might be quite 'inimical' to the recipient's receipt and possession of the object for it even to be sold for a monetary return. In the first case, if the individual had acquired the object without reference to others, simply because it was of special significance to him or her, then decided to sell it, that would not necessarily indicate that the object had not, to that point, been regarded as an object of taonga to the owner.

On the facts of the case, Laurenson J thought that the painting may have been taonga when originally bought but subsequent dealings indicated that it had lost any such quality. Drawing lots for the paintings and confirming this in a subsequent agreement counted against the paintings being taonga to the husband. It was therefore held to be a family chattel and would fall within the pool of property to be divided.

Atkin argues that while this line of reasoning makes sense from the parties' subjective point of view, a McCahon painting, like a Rembrandt, should have special significance as ascribed by others and should have been regarded as a taonga or treasure (Atkin, 2007, p. 237).

Economic disparity

Although deferred community is the dominant principle regulating property rules in New Zealand, so that the common property rule is enforced only upon the parties' separation, the 2001 Act created new discretionary reforms to be used where there is economic disparity. Section 15 allows a general power which enables the court to adjust the shares in relationship property to compensate the disadvantaged party. Section 15A applies where the advantaged party's actions during cohabitation have enhanced the value of that party's own separate property. As Atkin observes, the economic disparity compensation 'intentionally leads to unequal division in an equal division regime' (Atkin, 2007, p. 238).

In his study of the policy as evidenced by case law, Atkin finds that while the policy may be justified, its implementation is problematic. There are still doubts about the awkward insertion of economic disparity powers into a deferred community regime and there are underlying problems.

First, the Court of Appeal has identified a

'conceptual problem whether the provisions are properly to be regarded as being directed to economic equalisation in the larger sense of that term, on the breakdown of the relationship; or whether they are to be regarded as being directed to the loss of opportunity (by way of earning capacity) that one party has had to embrace [because] of the division of functions in the relationship.

There are then the consequential problems of the appropriate ways of calculating awards' (*Nation v Nation* [2005] NZLR 103 at [162]).

The thrust of the court's first argument appears to be that while there may appear to be a formal equal division of property, this may not translate into actual equality in reality. Hence the court might award formal unequal division to achieve equality in reality. The court's second argument focuses on the loss suffered by the lower income earner rather than on the gain made by the higher income earner. This is supposed to deal with providing compensation for the person who has given up a career in order to support the other party, or to care for the children, or for some reasons associated with domestic life. Even here, there are difficulties as several questions can be posed since, as with the first argument, considerable speculation is involved. Atkin poses several questions which might arise: How do we know whether the party would have continued with the career? With what success? And with what return? Should we not take benefits gained by the relationship as well as the losses incurred? (Atkin, 2007, p. 239).

Second, there is considerable scope for argument over the practical implementation of the law. Atkin reports that his analysis of judgments in the New Zealand Family Law Reports over the years 2002–6 reveals that seven claims have been successful, nine have been unsuccessful and one returned to the Family Court for more evidence (Atkin, 2007, p. 241). This suggests something like a 50/50 chance of success and his perusal of several unreported cases reveals similar findings. He points out that 'anecdotally, many property disputes are now settled with an economic disparity component contained in them' (Atkin, 2007, p. 241).

Third, many of the unsuccessful claims fail to clear the jurisdictional hurdles.

Conclusions on matrimonial property in New Zealand

While the original 1976 reforms introduced a form of deferred community into New Zealand law, the 2001 reforms introduced the principle of equality and sought to achieve greater equality of division of assets upon separation. However, it also brought a highly discretionary element into the scheme by allowing the court to award compensation for economic disparity. Overall, the reforms have been a mixed bag and it will probably take another few years before definitive judicial rulings indicate the relative success or failure of the reforms to matrimonial property division upon separation of the parties. The inclusion of de facto relationships has led to the predictable squabbles over whether a de facto relationship existed, and so far the trend seems favour including rather than excluding such relationships. The inclusion of widowed parties has not sparked a plethora of cases and the main area of dispute will centre on the circumstances in which the personal representative might be allowed to apply. On the other hand, there has been a solid stream of cases involving trusts.

Children

The best interests or paramountcy principle in New Zealand family law

The paramountcy principle in New Zealand statutory law appears in s. 23(1) of the Guardianship Act 1968 which reads:

'In any proceedings where any matter relating to the custody or guardianship of or access to a child, or the administration of any property belonging to or held in trust for a child, or the application of the income thereof, is in question, the Court shall regards the welfare of the child as the first and paramount consideration.'

It adds that the court shall have regard to the conduct of any parent only to the extent that such conduct is relevant to the welfare of the child.

Subsection (1A) provides that regardless of the age of the child, in cases involving the allocation of custody of the child, there shall be *no presumption* (emphasis added) that the placing of a child in the custody of a particular person will best serve the welfare of the child, purely because of that person's gender. This provision was introduced in 1980 to dispel any gender-based assumptions which might have suggested whose parental care would best serve the welfare of the child.

Comparing this to English law, it will be noted that the New Zealand Parliament has enshrined in statute that there is no presumption of a maternal preference in custody disputes. This has never been placed on a statutory footing in English law, although case law suggests that this is now the legal position. In *Re A (Children: 1959 UN Declaration)* [1998] 1 FLR 354, the English Court of Appeal made it clear that although there is still a presumption that babies are better off with their mothers (see *Re W (A Minor) (Residence Order)* [1992] 2 FLR 332), as far as the other (older) children are concerned, there is no principle or presumption in favour of mothers or fathers (see *Re S (A Minor) (Custody)* [1991] 2 FLR 388).

Scientific evidence, as far as it can be relied upon, appears to support the maternal preference principle in relation to babies as far as the benefits of breastfeeding are concerned. Psychological evidence seems to suggest that there is no convincing evidence that girls are better off with mothers and boys with fathers (see Downey and Powell, 1993) but there is some evidence to suggest that children prefer to be brought up the parent of the same sex after divorce (Kalternborn and Lempp, 1998).

Wishes of the child to be ascertained

Section 23(2) requires the court to ascertain the wishes of the child where it is possible to do so, which shows a clear intention on the part of the New Zealand legislature to prioritize the child-focused nature of proceedings by declaring: 'In any proceedings under subsection (1) of this section the Court shall ascertain the wishes of the child. If the child is able to express them, and shall ... take account of them to such extent as the Court thinks fit, having regard to the age and maturity of the child.'] → *New Zealand has a more child-focused legal position*

This replicates one of the requirements under the English Children Act 1989, s. 1(3) (a), and also statutorily implements what may be termed the well-known 'Gillick competence' requirement under English law which is that the child's view would only be asked or considered if that child possesses 'sufficient age and understanding' as the English statute puts it, for the court to do so.

New Zealand, it is the "Gillick" it is not

It designed to be "far-reaching" – Gillick is not

However, this provision goes much further in its range of application than the English statute by the use of phrases like 'any proceeding' and 'any matter' followed by the phrase 'relating to' which indicates that the New Zealand legislature has manifested a clear intention to make the paramountcy principle applicable in an all-encompassing manner. Indeed, the New Zealand courts have said that any person or court who exercises any power conferred by the Act should at all times treat the interests of the child or young person as the first and paramount consideration. This is supported by several cases for example *Re J (An Infant)* [1996] 2 NZLR 134; *T v AG* (1999) 18 FRNZ 48; [1999] NZLR 886 and *P v D* (1996) 14 PRNZ 470 (see *The 'Child Paramountcy Principle' in the Family Law Act*, 2004, Family Law Council, Australia).

Case law

Paramountcy and the New Zealand Bill of Rights – Re J

In *Re J* [1996] 2 NZLR 134 there was an apparent conflict between the New Zealand Bill of Rights Act 1990 and the paramountcy principle in s. 23. The Court of Appeal recognized the paramountcy of s. 23. The case involved parents who asserted that a right to withhold a blood transfusion on religious grounds and freedom of religion and conscience were rights entrenched in the Bill of Rights. The parents submitted that their rights under the Bill of Rights precluded the court from overriding their withholding of consent to the transfusion. Gault J rejected the argument and specifically refuted two presumptions that were said to underlie it: (i) that intrusion by the court to protect the child's rights was indistinguishable from intrusion by the court to uphold any other right; and (ii) that the parent's rights were superior to the child's rights. Gault J held that the rights created under the Bill of Rights must be defined so as to exclude doing anything likely to place the child's life, health or welfare at risk.

Paramountcy and natural justice – T v AG

In *T v AG* [1999] NZLR 886 a father accused of sexual abuse applied to allow a psychologist retained by him to view police videotapes of interviews with the children. Counsel for the child had recommended access not to be granted. The court held that the paramountcy principle displaced the principles of natural justice.

Paramountcy and cultural considerations – P v D

In *P v D* (1996) 14 FRNZ 470 the High Court held that the psychological health of the child will take precedence over more abstract cultural concerns. Although the court accepted that cultural factors form part of the matrix of decision-making, they do not take priority over welfare considerations. Consequently, the safety, health and wellbeing of the child must carry greater weight than deeply held cultural values or broadly accepted cultural practices.

⤷ is this the same with Gillick?

Paramountcy more important than procedural considerations

Section 23 impacts on more than just the substantive rights relating to custody decisions. It affects aspects of procedure under the Guardianship Act 1968. This may be discerned from a line of decisions which espouse the policy that lengthy or repeated litigation may be detrimental to the interests of children with the result that potential litigants are turned away or proceedings are struck out. Four cases may be noted.

The first is *T v M* (1988) 5 NZFLR 252 where litigation was 'stopped in its tracks' and Judge Inglis QC emphasized (at 253) that: 'The direction that the welfare of the child is to be treated as the first and paramount consideration must necessarily apply at all stages of the proceedings.'

The second is *Lynskey v Walsh (No. 2)* (1999) Auckland, FP975/95 which suggests that a judge should, as a prerequisite to making custody decisions, in accordance with s. 23(2), ascertain the wishes of the child.

A third case is the High Court case of *D v H* [2000] 2 NZLR 242 where Robertson J sounded a cautionary note in declaring that the touchstone for exercising the power is that there is evidence of actual abuse of process and the court is satisfied that there has been a course of persistent vexatious proceedings instituted.

A fourth case is *M v R* [1991] NZLR 382 which highlighted the procedural significance of s. 23 in relation to the disclosure of family reports. The court held that where disclosure of such reports is sought, the paramount considerations which should be given to the child override any right of a parent to access such a report.

CONCLUDING COMPARATIVE PERSPECTIVES

Australia

The pattern of development in Australian family law was broadly in keeping with other Westernized or Western-influenced countries around the world, but there were some notable differences.

Fault continues to play a part, albeit greatly reduced, in both Australian and English family law relating to divorce and financial proceedings, and the reasons for the diminishing of fault in the non-permanence of marriage will vary, although the waning of the influence of the Christian church can be noted to be fairly prominent.

Obtaining a divorce in Australia is now an administrative procedure, which has been the case in England since 1977. Similarly, Australia has a separate property regime as far as matrimonial property is concerned, and the statutory guidelines are similar to that of English law, but not identical. Indeed, there appears to be a more detailed and meticulous approach under Australian law to determining financial provision for the parties upon divorce and making property orders for the parties (for example the three-step and four-step approach). A recurrent theme in financial proceedings has been the argument that insufficient weight has been given to the value of non-financial contributions, usually made by the wife, especially in big money cases. This certainly echoes developments in English case law.

As with other jurisdictions, the best interests of the child standard is used by Australian courts and legislation, although the best interests checklist is not as detailed or as extensive as the English statutory model. On the other hand, a very detailed list of factors has been introduced by the Family Law Amendment (Shared Parental Responsibility) Act 2006 which seeks to ensure that the best interests of children are met by ensuring that they have the benefit of both their parents having a meaningful relationship in their lives 'to the maximum extent consistent with the best interests of the child'. One of the key requirements is to introduce a new presumption of shared parental responsibility, and the court has to consider how this is to be achieved, through providing for a less adversarial approach to child-related proceedings and, echoing the United States' approach, increasing the emphasis on parenting plans, to encourage parents to reach suitable arrangements outside the court system.

The bifurcation of courts, and geographical differences in the quality and availability of facilities and premises, and the attendant problems and inequalities that these bring, add to the concerns that continue to exist for Australian family courts.

New Zealand

The Family Law reforms in New Zealand constitute 'an attempt to ensure that family law, broadly defined, more closely reflects and responds to the reality of domestic living arrangements in a modern society' (Atkin, 2003, p. 184). Inevitably, these reforms were the subject of debate and controversy when they passed through the New Zealand Parliament, but in the end, the objective of complying with and introducing stronger support for human rights appears to have won the day.

As far as the law relating to children is concerned, it would appear that the paramountcy or best interests of the child principle is actually given a higher priority than the New Zealand Bill of Rights or principles of natural justice, cultural or procedural considerations, at least as far as the New Zealand courts are concerned. This echoes a similar approach adopted by the English courts which tend to focus more on giving effect to the best interests of the child in any given case than on enforcing or giving effect to the rights given to adults under the European Human Rights Convention, which they tend to acknowledge towards the end of judgments almost as a mere formality but not to the extent of giving them optimum attention and consideration (see Part V on the impact of human rights law on family law).

Further reading

Altobelli, T 'The Family Home in Australian Law' Australian Institute of Family Studies Conference, 2000, at http://www.aifs.gov.au.

Atkin, B 'The Rights of Married and Unmarried Couples in New Zealand – Radical New Laws on Property and Succession' (2003) 15 CFLQ 173.

Atkin, B 'Reflections on New Zealand's Property Reforms Five Years on' [2007] Int Survey Fam Law 217.

Behrens, J and Smyth, B 'Spousal Support in Australia: A Study of Incidence and Attitudes' (1999) Working Paper No. 16, Australian Institute of Family Studies, p. 7.

Dickey, A *Family Law*, 2nd ed, 1990, Law Book Company.

Donaldson, M 'A Question of Fault: A Short History of Australian Divorce Law since 1959', 2004, Parliamentary Library Research Note No. 38.

Family Law Council's Statistical Snapshot of Family Law 2003–5.

Felhberg, B 'Spousal Maintenance in Australia' (2004) 18 Int Jnl Law, Policy and the Family 1.

Finlay, HA, Bailey-Harris, RJ and Otlowski, MFA *Family Law in Australia* 5th ed, 1997, Butterworths.

Gilding, M *The Making and Breaking of the Australian Family*, 1991, Allen & Unwin.

Gilding, M 'Changing Families in Australia 1901–2001' (2001) 60 *Family Matters* 6.

Graycar, R and Morgan, J *The Hidden Gender of Law*, 2002, The Federation Press.

Harrison, M 'Australia's Family Law Act: The First Twenty-Five Years' (2002) Int Jnl of Law, Policy and the Family 1.

McDonald, P 'Can the Family Survive?' (1984) Discussion Paper 11, Institute of Family Studies, p. 7.

McLintock, AH (ed) 'Divorce and Separation' in *An Encyclopaedia of New Zealand*, 1966 at http://www.TeAra.govt.nz/1966/D/DivorceAndSeparation/en.

Nicholson, A and Harrison, M 'Family Law and the Family Court of Australia: Experiences of the First 25 Tears' [2000] *Melbourne University Law Review* 30 at http://www.austlii. edu.au/au/journals.MULR/2000/30/html.

Sheehan, G and Hughes, J 'The Division of Matrimonial Property in Australia' (2000) 55 *Family Matters* 28.

Willmott, L, Mathews, BP and Shoebridge, G 'Defacto Relationships Property Adjustment Law – A National Direction? 2003, Lexis Nexis.

Chapter 4

Family law in Africa and Asia

Introduction

This chapter looks at the development of marriage, divorce, marital property and the law relating to children in selected hybrid or mixed legal systems in Africa and Asia. The rationale for examining these countries within the same chapter is that they have a common denominator – they are all non-Western post-colonial regions. Hence, apart from having a mixture of legal systems and foreign (Western) influences, countries like India, Hong Kong and Singapore may all be labelled as common law jurisdictions, as they rely on case law as their main (received/inherited) source of law, supplemented by statutes. Another common feature of these countries is they all have a tradition of recognising and applying customary or indigenous laws from time to time, alongside more formal written laws.

The common characteristics and themes for each of these regions will subsequently be discussed in greater detail as our exploration proceeds, but in keeping with the approach in the rest of this book, we commence our survey with a brief historical introduction to the sources of law in the selected regions. From a comparative lawyer's point of view, a foray into these jurisdictions immediately raises questions about the feasibility of a comparison with say, a common law or civil law jurisdiction. Are not Asian and African jurisdictions so patently different in their cultural, sociological, linguistic and political infrastructure from Western-oriented systems that differences rather than similarities would be the norm, which would render any comparison nugatory? Therein lies the endless fascination of the comparative enterprise as we explore the rich history of Asian and African countries and examine the influence of their colonial past and seek to discover their unique cultural and social laws and lore, expecting differences but also encountering more commonalities with Western-based systems than might be realized at first blush.

Having examined the reception of customary law and statutory or written laws in Africa and Asia, we will return to the question of legal transplants, and consider whether legal concepts which originate from overseas jurisdictions, and which have been adopted, adapted, and made part of the existing tapestry of local laws, can legitimately be called successful legal transplants and applied to local situations and cases over a period of time. The issue of whether these foreign concepts have improved or worsened the indigenous society remains a separate issue for debate.

AFRICA

Introduction

We begin with the African continent, a geographical region of tremendous diversity, multi-faceted historical background and a region which experienced a reception of laws originating from foreign countries. Menski argues that 'African law' is 'merely a kind of ethnic label and the collective term "African laws" comprises ... many different types of legal systems' (Menski, 2006, p. 380). It has been questioned whether such an entity as 'African law' exists.

In response, a leading African judge and author, M'Baye, is very clear in stating that Africa has a system of law per se, which 'affects every aspect of life' (M'Baye, 1970, p. 139) and in a sense it therefore permeates everything that occurs in everyday life. Thus as Gonidec points out: 'Instead of saying that there is no law in the so-called primitive societies, one might just as well say that everything is law' (Gonidec, 1960, p. 8). Hence the notion of law in African societies is more widely conceived than in European societies but undoubtedly exists, with 'different functions, techniques, and characteristics' (M'Baye, 1970, p. 139). Cotran, whose research on marriage in Africa is discussed later on in this chapter, also concurs with Gonidec that his research of the Equatorial African tribes in Kenya reveals that the African systems of law form a unit (Cotran, 1963, p. 213).

Writing in the 1960s, Allott said 'African law is not ... a single system, even one with variant schools, but rather a family of systems which share no traceable common parent'. Nevertheless, he observed that 'more fundamentally, African laws reveal sufficient similarity in procedure, principles, institutions, and techniques for a common account to be given of them' (Allott, 1968, p. 131).

Allott was also of the opinion that African law no longer means the indigenous customary laws deriving from antiquity but includes the modern statutory laws as well, and thus 'African law is the totality of African legal systems' (Allott, 1965, p. 219).

African law is thus multi-faceted, comprising the old customary base, constantly evolving, influenced by Christianity and Islam, and geographically limited by its concepts (M'Baye, 1970, p. 140). It is also 'the system of law which the new independent African States are trying to enlist into the services of de-colonisation, unity and development ... a system of law in a state of flux' (M'Baye, 1970, p. 140).

African law is not 'the law of the African continent'

M'Baye is careful to distinguish between African law and the 'law of the African continent'. It is not possible to include in the same family of legal systems all the countries of the African continent stretching from Algiers to Capetown. He explains that the Maghreb States, and Egypt and Libya, are orientated towards the Middle Eastern world by the race and religion of their inhabitants and belong to the Muslim family of legal systems (M'Baye, 1970, p. 140). On the other hand, the South African Republic must also be excluded from the geographical area of African law, because of its political system and it has adopted a legal system of Western inspiration (M'Baye, 1970, p. 140). This is why South Africa is dealt with separately in this chapter. On the other hand, Madagascar, despite its Asiatic origins, has undergone, in M'Baye's words, a 'political, economic, social and cultural evolution similar in all respects to Black Africa' and as Ramangasoavina observes, 'their legal institutions reveal a juxtaposition of Asiatic and African features, making it logical to include it in the territorial domain of African law' (M'Baye, 1970, p. 140; Ramangasoavina, 1962, p. 330). Hence the term 'African law' for present purposes refers to the domain which covers the peoples of Black Africa, Ethiopia, the Sudan, Somaliland and Madagascar.

The oral tradition

The oral African legal tradition as far as its customary laws are concerned should also be noted in contrast to its relatively recent written laws, contained in statutes. Indeed, 'African civilisation is essentially oral' (M'Baye, 1970, p. 149). What this strongly suggests, in the present writer's opinion, is that there will inevitably be differences between tribes and regions simply because of geographical and demographic differences and the distance between villages, tribes and communities, resulting in different interpretations of certain customs and practices and variations in the way these customs have been practised or observed. On the other hand, the existence of long-standing family ties or collaborations between tribal communities will, in a sense, narrow the distance between geographically separated societies. African customary law is handed down from generation to generation by means of the memories of the ancients who are the clerks of the court in the African legal organization (M'Baye, 1970, p. 150). The accuracy of the information is therefore uncertain – making the rules sometimes difficult to ascertain precisely, and they will inevitably be distorted according to the subjectivity of their reporters (M'Baye, 1970, p. 150). Nevertheless, oral evidence remains extremely important in African law. It is also important to note that the great Sudan empires knew about writing and used it (Diop, 1960, p. 87).

Historical background

Reception of foreign law

Allott divides African legal history into three periods: pre-colonial, colonial and post-colonial (Allott, 1975). Menski argues that unlike the assumption made by most authors that colonial legal systems simply intervened in traditional African legal arrangements and destroyed them, 'it is much closer to reality that much of traditional African law became invisible unofficial law as a result of colonisation' (Menski, 2006, p. 382). However, Africa did experience non-African influences even in the pre-colonial period, predominantly from the spread of Christianity and Islam. Ethiopia was Christianized in the fourth century but the main conversion took place during the nineteenth century.

African customary law developed in response to the demands of traditional societies when they set themselves up 'everywhere from the desert to the dense forest' (M'Baye, 1970, p. 140). The anarchies, chieftaincies and states were set up on both sides of the equator, moulding the law 'according to the needs of the respective civilisations they supported: forest civilisation, paleonegroid civilisation, Sudanese civilisation'. In their turn, 'they experienced the influence of the modern world' (M'Baye, 1970, p. 140).

In the 1980s, it was estimated that about 30 per cent of Africans south of the Sahara were Christian (see David and Brierley, 1985, p. 553). These numbers have grown with the increased popularity of Christianity since then. In the eleventh century, the countries of Western Africa were partly converted to Islam and in the fourteenth and fifteenth centuries, Islam had spread to Somaliland and reached the Indian Ocean. By the 1970s and 1980s, about 35 per cent of the inhabitants of Black Africa and 45 per cent of Western Africa were Muslim (David and Brierley, 1985, p. 553).

Differences between English and other forms of colonization

In the nineteenth century, all Africa came under European rule. However, there was a difference between the English and the other countries in their method of colonialism. The English adopted a policy of indirect rule which meant that they mainly allowed the native population to continue self-rule, but under British control. On the other hand, the French, Spanish and Portuguese, adopted a policy of assimilation, a centralized form of administration, basically accepting an African as French, Spanish or Portuguese, provided they were prepared to give up their African culture and adopted the culture of whichever European power was in control of the region. This continued until the end of the colonial period. The effect of these policies, as described by David and Brierley, was: '[T]he states that emerged from the former British Empire now consider themselves to be Common law countries, and those issuing from the French Empire or Belgian Congo, as well as Rwanda and Burandi and the former Spanish and Portuguese possessions, now belong to the Romanist legal system' (David and Brierley, 1985, p. 556).

As David and Brierley further explain, a two-fold development had taken place to bring about these changes. First, there was a reception of a modern legal system which was needed to regulate the many issues arising from 'the transition to a new civilisation ... for which native customs were unable to provide practically useful solutions'; second, there was a 'transformation of customary law in those areas where it had already constituted a complete system of rules and concepts, either because the colonial power in question had not considered it sufficiently civilised or because the law itself may have been forced to adapt to the changes taking place' (David and Brierley, 1985, p. 556).

The main period of decolonization began after the Second World War, as pressure from various independent movements, political parties and trade unions, as well as from the United States, led to almost all of Africa being decolonized by 1980.

The meaning of 'family' in the African context

Before examining notions of the family and family law in Africa, it is important to be aware that the word 'family' in Africa describes something quite different from the English nuclear family, even though the latter concept has itself undergone a transformation in the last 30 years or so and could well be branded an anachronism in many parts of twenty-first century Britain. As Murdoch explains, the African unit usually refers to a '*polygamous family* – consisting of two or more nuclear families affiliated by plural marriages – ie having one married parent in common' or an '*extended family*, consisting of two or more nuclear families affiliated through an extension of the parent-child relationship rather than of the husband-wife relationship – ie by joining the nuclear family or a married adult to that of his parents' (Murdoch, 1960, p. 37). As a result of these phenomena, Nhlapo points out that this has 'profound implications' on the way children are brought up, because the African child brought up in these conditions will have any number of people to call father, mother, brother or sister. Although blood relatives would obviously be included, the list may extend to neighbours and other members of the village (Nhlapo, 1998, p. 12).

Typically, however, the 'family' in Africa refers to the extended family rather than the nuclear family. Even in the most unsophisticated systems of tribal law, there still exists 'an elaborate network of principles, rules and regulations concerning such matters as courtship, the marriage ceremony, childbirth, the relationship of husband and wife, the relationship of parent and child, the domestic dispute settlement and succession'. Indeed, the notion of family 'impinges upon almost every area of community life, including property ownership and even civic status' (Nhlapo, 1998, p. 9).

Family law in the African context

Nhlapo declares that 'the importance of family law in traditional African systems cannot be sufficiently emphasised'. Thus, matters such as 'marriageable age, consent and equality within marriage are closely tied up with the very structure of traditional society' (Nhlapo, 1989, p. 9). He then reminds the reader that geographically the vast majority of African peoples, as much as 90 per cent in some African countries, live in rural areas and regard themselves as subjects of customary law (Nhlapo, 1989, p. 20). Thus the family unit is central to traditional thinking that customary family law is the 'best developed branch of customary law for most African communities' (Nhlapo, 1989, p. 9).

Nhlapo also highlights another highly significant feature of African family law, namely that family matters are closely tied to issues of women's rights. He contends that the topic of women's rights is not popular in Africa (see Nhlapo, 1989, p. 10). He does not, however, say whether men or women regard it as unpopular but highlights the point that the idea of sex equality is of comparatively recent origin even in advanced societies and also presents a rationale for the nature of African marriage and warns against evaluating the traditional African marriage out of its cultural context (Nhlapo, 1989, pp. 10–13). Before considering his contextual arguments, let us look at the nature of traditional African marriage and the ways in which it has changed over the last few decades.

Marriage

Marriage under African customary law

We have already seen that Africa is a diverse continent and each region has its own particular customs and customary law. In one sense, it is misleading to generalize and to speak of 'African customary law' in the light of its diversity. However, as will be seen in this section, there are sufficient common characteristics of African marriage, for example, to justify the use of the general term 'African family law'. Let us first consider whether the term 'marriage' is appropriate to our discussion.

The classic definition of marriage in the nineteenth-century English case of *Hyde v Hyde* (1866) LR 1 P&D 130 is the 'voluntary union of one man and one woman to the exclusion of all others'. Almost every single word of this definition is inapplicable to marriages contracted under traditional African customary law (Allott, 1960, p. 213). Cotran notes that there are at least four differentiating features in marriages contracted in African societies. First, in many African societies marriage was not a voluntary union, especially for the brides; second, the union was not for life because it might easily be dissolved without any court involvement or intervention; third, the marriage was 'not so much a union between a man and a woman, as an alliance between two family groups'; and fourth, customary marriages were potentially polygamous (Cotran, 1968, p. 15). Cotran goes so far as to say that it is 'impossible to put forward a definition which would cover marriage as recognised and known under a multitude of African customary laws'. This is because they differ in aspects such as their 'political and social structure, kinship groupings, descent systems, and economic way of life'. Indeed, Professor Phillips, another expert on African customary law, maintains, in the context of African customary law, that 'not only is there a vast diversity in matters of detail between the customs of different tribes and localities' but that it is not even possible, except to a very limited extent, to trace any broad uniformity of basic principles underpinning such law (see Phillips, 1971, p. 5). Nevertheless, Phillips concedes that, subject to a recognition of endemic diversity in customary law, the main distinguishing feature of African customary marriage from European marriage is the toleration and even approval of polygamy.

General characteristics of traditional African marriage

Despite this diversity, Cotran lists seven distinctive features of traditional African marriage, six of which derive from Professor Phillips' *Survey of African Marriage and Family Life*, 1953, pp. xii–xiii. The first is its polygamous nature, with no restriction on the number of wives. This is permitted by all customary laws in Africa and these laws not only allow such marriages but encourage a man to have 'as many wives as he pleased'. It was known that rich men or chiefs had 'fifty or even a hundred wives simultaneously' (Cotran, 1968, p. 17). The second is the role played by the spouses' families at almost every stage of the matrimonial relationship, called the 'collective' aspect of the marriage transactions or the alliance between two family groups. In these situations it was the spouses' families and not the spouses who negotiated and concluded the agreement. The consent of the spouses' families would be the legal prerequisite to the marriage. Thus the dissolution of the marriage, if initiated by the wife, would be practically impossible unless the family cooperated in carrying it out. The third feature is the 'complex formalities and ceremonial' that surround such marriages. These vary from one societal group to another, from a series of rituals to ceremonies which lasted many months. As Cotran explains, this created problems from a legal point of view since it would be difficult to determine which of these ceremonies fulfilled legal requirements and which were purely social; and at precisely what stage the marriage came into existence (see Cotran, 1968, p. 17).

The fourth characteristic of traditional African marriage was its provision for the payment of goods or services by the bridegroom or his family to the wife's family at a point before, at the time of or after the marriage. This is known as 'brideprice,' a controversial practice which has provoked predictable criticism. These include branding the practice as 'wife purchase' as in the mere purchase of cattle, strongly rebuffed by writers such as Radcliffe-Brown (1950, p. 37) who argue that the idea that an African buys a wife in the way an English farmer buys cattle is the result of 'ignorance … or blind prejudice'. Another theory is that brideprice is a form of compensation to the woman's family for the loss of one of its members and provides security for the maintenance of the marriage by the respective families. Yet another rationale is that it is symbolic, to seal the marriage contract, or it is child price or a compensation for the transfer of a woman's reproductive capacity and her issue to the husband's family. In Cotran's opinion, in which he concurs with Radcliffe-Brown, 'with very few exceptions, the payment of brideprice was traditionally not a mere compensation, but the means or one of the means by which a marriage became legally valid' (see Cotran, 1968, pp. 18–19). It is perhaps useful to note that brideprice is not a uniquely African institution but was also a feature of the social systems of European societies in earlier times (see Phillips, 1971, p. 5).

The fifth general feature of African marriage is 'its emphasis on the procreation of children as the prime end of marriage' (Cotran, 1968, p. 19). It can be observed that this is a traditional function of Christian and in particular Catholic marriage, so we can see an obvious link with a classic, traditional function of Western marriages. However, Cotran explains that African societies go to great lengths to express their desire for procreation, illustrated in practices such as polygamy; delaying the final marriage ceremony until the woman conceives; performing elaborate magical rites and sacrifices which are meant to stave off the barrenness of a wife or impotence of a husband; the levirate union (widow-inheritance); sororate unions and woman-to-woman marriages where the biological father is a third party (such as the Onitsha local custom, see p. 173; and the fact that most matrimonial disputes focus on custody or 'ownership' of the children (Cotran, 1968, p. 19).

The sixth characteristic of African marriage has been the inferior social and legal status of the wife as compared with the husband in the marriage relationship. This is evident in polygamous practices, the payment of brideprice, the fact that a woman's consent was always relatively unimportant to the marriage, and the levirate union. Hence, for most customary laws, the tradition has been that a wife's authority and rights over her children, her rights of ownership and disposal of property, her right to sue and be sued in her own name have all been severely limited. As we shall see, several of these features changed in modern African society.

The seventh and final feature of customary marriage relates to divorce. There has been a perception that divorces could be obtained on demand and according to the husband's will. However, Cotran's meticulous research into the marriage laws of East Africa has revealed that this is not the case. Divorce was virtually unknown and only occurred in exceptional cases, for instance where there were no children from the marriage. Moreover, since marriage has been the union of whole families, the suggestion that marriages were easily dissolved at the will of the husband 'could scarcely be further from the truth' (Cotran, 1968, p. 19).

Be that as it may, Cotran concedes that two factors distinguish divorces in customary law from English or European law. First, the provision in customary law for conciliatory machinery and arbitration, and the availability of inter-familial divorce by agreement between the families without the need for judicial pronouncement; and second, in most customary laws, although grounds for divorce are required, they are not as clear cut or as rigid as under English law. Indeed, unlike English law, under most customary laws, several factors may be taken into account including the existence of children, the ability of the wife's family to return the brideprice and a consideration of whether remedies other than divorce are available (Cotran, 1968, p. 20).

Changes in the nature of African marriage

Cotran classified the changes in the nature of African marriage into two categories: the first, as a result of indirect causes and the second as a result of government legislation. It is important to be aware that in the late 1960s, when the survey was conducted by Cotran, the extent of changes varied greatly from one part of Africa to another, and sometimes even within different districts of the same African country (Cotran, 1968, pp. 20–31). This situation has not changed radically, and some of the differences and variations would depend, and still do, on the amount of contact a particular community has had with the outside world and the extent to which the influences of religion, education and Western influences have impacted on a particular region.

Indirect causes of changes in African marriage – religion and cultural contact

Cotran identifies five key changes.

Diminution of the influence of the family

First, Cotran cites the 'dying influence of the family or kinship group in the marriage relationship and the movement towards individualism' (Cotran, 1968, p. 21). He explains how this was reflected in three key aspects of African marriage. The first was in relation to consent; the second was the change in the nature and practice of brideprice; and the third was the curtailment or omission of the extended ceremonies. As far as consent was concerned, the situation in the mid 1960s had changed to the extent that, generally speaking, the choice of partner would be left to the spouses. The practice of infant-betrothal has been on the decline and even where it did occur was subject to the consent of the spouse upon reaching majority. In addition the fact that young men could afford to pay for their own brideprice meant their families no longer had the power to veto the choice of a bride by refusing to pay the brideprice. The practice that eventually developed in the 1960s, which has continued into the early twenty-first century, is that men frequently married without the consent of their family.

However, on the issue of consent, Nhlapo recounts the notorious 'red ochre' custom in Swaziland which attempts to trick a girl into marrying a certain man. Under its customary law, a marriage comes into being in Swaziland if a bride has gone through a ceremony where her face has been smeared with red ochre by female members of the groom's family, a ceremony usually performed at dawn on the wedding day or near the cattle byre. The full consent of all concerned will normally have been obtained but there is a custom whereby a prospective groom lures a girl to his home, on some pretext, and persuades her to spend the night there. He then arranges for the elderly women in the homestead to wake the girl at dawn, take her to the cattle byre and smear her face with red ochre. A beast is then slaughtered and an envoy is sent to the girl's home with a special cut of meat, to be delivered with the announcement that the girl is now the man's wife. In most cases, the girl would have been a known lover who would have visited the prospective groom several times. But Nhlapo informs us that in a 'significant' number of cases, women were tricked into staying overnight and fell victim to the early morning raid when they had no intention of marrying the man at all (Nhlapo, 1989, p. 16). Consent from the girl would therefore not have been obtained in this case and apparently this dubious ceremony still takes place even in contemporary times.

Change in brideprice

The second aspect was the change in the nature of brideprice from a payment of goods or services to one of cash, which in one stroke removed its traditional significance as a means of cementing the bond between the spouses' families. This also rendered obsolete the detailed rules relating to the method of payment, replacement and return of the brideprice on death or divorce, particularly with regard to cases where the bulk of the brideprice was formerly payable in cattle.

Change in the marriage ceremonies and formalities

Various practices such as the 'capture of the bride', the ceremonial defloration of the bride, feasting, presentations and similar ceremonies have become obsolete or changed substantially, in urban communities particularly.

Change in the status of women

African women have been fighting for legal emancipation for a considerable time and continue to do so. Women's organizations have grown considerably and some of the legal restrictions applicable to women in the matrimonial relationship have been removed. Various aspects of the marriage relationship have changed significantly, namely: (i) a woman's consent is now almost always obtained before a marriage is entered into; (ii) the custom of the levirate or widow-inheritance is breaking down and where practised the consent of the widow is obtained; (iii) women can now sue and be sued in African or local courts and a wife may now obtain a divorce without the consent of her family.

Changes emanating from the increased accessibility of divorce

The rate of divorce has increased considerably since divorce has been made more accessible. In addition, families have played a far less important role in conciliation and arbitration. Neither of these consequences has been desirable for African society, and indeed, any society. The African or local courts have imitated the superior courts in establishing more rigid grounds for divorce rather than using the traditional approach of considering all the circumstances of the case (Cotran, 1968, pp. 21–2).

Legislative changes – the statutory form of marriage

The British colonial policy with regard to customary marriages was to pass territorial and local legislation which would seek to carry out a 'civilizing mission' by expressly recognizing customary marriages and making provision for persons who were previously subject to customary law to marry under an enactment providing for a monogamous or English-type marriage. The idea was that through education and missionary influence, the monogamous influence would prevail (Cotran, 1968, p. 23). Thus, most colonies and protectorates had a territorial Marriage Ordinance on the statute books which regulated marriage in accordance with the general principles of English law (Cotran, 1968, p. 24). Territories such as Kenya and Uganda also had a simplified procedure to convert a customary marriage into a monogamous one. But these Marriage Ordinances went further than merely making available an alternative form of marriage. They also stipulated that if Africans chose to accept this statutory option, they would also be accepting all other aspects of the English law relating to marriage; namely, the rules of English law on age, prohibited degrees, consents and form. Additionally, during the continuance of the Ordinance marriage the law of bigamy applied to a customary marriage under penalty of five years' imprisonment. Even more radical was the provision in territories like Malawi and Nigeria that if a person who was previously subject to customary law contracted a statutory marriage and subsequently died intestate, the English law of succession would be applied to his property.

As Cotran points out, these Ordinances sometimes went even further. First, even though customary law was expressly recognized, the legislature and the judges of the superior courts made every attempt to emphasize that statutory marriages were superior to customary marriages. Second, under legislation which enacted general territorial law, a marriage under customary law would not be recognized under a particular enactment. Thus, for example, the Penal Code of Uganda provided that for the purpose of the Code, which represented the criminal law of the territory, a wife who was married under customary law was not recognized as a wife in law, so that rules governing conspiracies and compulsion, for instance, did not apply to these women.

In keeping with the culture and practice of the time, such Ordinances were more notable for their non-enforcement than for their observance. The move to encourage monogamy instead of polygamy failed, since Africans who married under such enactments continued to take subsequent wives under customary law and the penal provisions regulating this form of bigamy were never enforced (Cotran, 1968, p. 25). Nevertheless, Cotran argues that one revealing attitudinal shift may be observed as a result of the introduction of these Marriage Ordinances: they inculcated the notion of the superiority of the Ordinance marriage and the inferiority of the customary marriage, and Africans among the educated classes, while not willing to abhor the customary marriage, began to regard the Ordinance or statutory marriage 'as a sign of prestige and respectability' (Cotran, 1968, p. 25).

Local legislation was also introduced to regulate the application of customary marriage, with measures such as seeking to enforce the registration of customary marriages and divorces and attempting to control the payment of brideprice. Unfortunately, none of these legislative measures proved very successful and indeed, apart from these enactments, there was a lack of government initiative in dealing with the major problems arising from the application of the customary laws of marriage. Neither was there any government-led systematic study or recording of the customary marriage laws, which thus remained mostly unwritten and treated by the courts as a matter of fact rather than of law (Cotran, 1968, p. 26).

Customary law in the period of independence

Once independence was attained by many of the ex-colonial territories in the 1950s and early 1960s, the newly independent African governments adopted policies which constituted direct interference in these matters (Cotran, 1968, p. 26). This was done in three ways.

First, projects were initiated by countries such as Tanzania, Kenya, Malawi, Zambia, Bechuanaland, Swiziland, Basutoland, Sierra Leone and Eastern Nigeria to record and restate the different customary marriage laws in the country.

Second, the different customary marriage laws were unified. Eventually, a schedule was attached to the Local Customary Law Declaration Order 1963, which dealt with brideprice, marriage, divorce and the status of children. Examples of the kinds of laws adopted by all the patrilineal tribes of Tanzania are: (i) a girl is free to marry without parental consent after she reaches 21 (previously it was only clear that she was unable to marry until she reached that age); (ii) payment of brideprice was not essential to the validity of a marriage; (iii) no customary divorce would be valid unless it is registered and a divorce certificate obtained. However, irrespective of how worthy and progressive such reforms have been to Tanzania, the information gleaned from Cotran is that many Tanzanians have never heard of these unifications, or if they have they think they apply only to districts other than theirs (Cotran, 1968, p. 28).

The third method of reforming the marriage laws was to introduce a new law of marriage which attempts to integrate or unify the different systems of marriage within a country, whether they were statutory, customary or religious (Cotran, 1968, p. 28).

Cotran cites the example of Ghana which attempted to introduce a Marriage, Divorce and Inheritance Bill which proposed that a man might register only one marriage, and would bestow public recognition only on the wife whose name appears on the Register. However, there was no legal provision which prevented the man from marrying subsequent wives under customary law. Only one registered wife would be entitled to inheritance under the new law. The concept of arbitration and attempted reconciliation in divorce matters was preserved and a husband or wife could petition any High Court for a divorce. On receipt of a petition, the judge was to appoint and chair a divorce committee to arbitrate in the matter and attempt a reconciliation. The objective was to discourage divorce, approach marriage in a constructive way, to accentuate reconciliation and the sanctity of marriage.

However, this Bill never became law because of opposition from many quarters when it was introduced in 1962 and again in 1963. Cotran believes the moral of Ghana's failed Bill is clear: no matter how important and desirable African governments feel it is to unify and reform their marriage laws, they cannot achieve their aims if they are not supported by public opinion. Cotran suggests that the concept of family arbitration should be revived and made the basis of divorce in a new integrated law, where a monogamous and polygamous marriage is given equal recognition. In his opinion, this would be the 'only way of producing a law which would be in line with the requirements and conditions of the people of Africa' (Cotran, 1968, p. 33).

Women's rights and African traditional marriage in their cultural context

Nhlapo offers several insights into the unique position of women in traditional African society and also makes some comparative observations regarding the Westernized woman or the woman in Western-influenced societies. To begin with, he emphasizes the consequences that flow from African customary marriage law, covering the points we have discussed in the above section detailing the characteristics of African marriage. But he then declares that 'in most African countries reaction to any type of "women's movement" tends to be hysterical, thus effectively obscuring the issues and preventing the laying down of the proper foundations for enlightened reform' (Nhlapo, 1989, p. 10). This sort of reaction, he argues, fails to recognize that there may be a great difference between the needs of the African woman and those of the Western feminist and contends that 'the difference is attributable to social and cultural factors', which serve to highlight the pivotal position of the family in African thinking. Nhlapo then offers his interpretation of Western feminist theory, by first stating that such a theory sees economic and psychological discrimination as the two factors responsible for the disadvantageous position of women. However, he then says: 'Hostility to both marriage and the family seems to be a recurring theme in feminist theory' (Nhlapo, 1989, p. 11). He considers most of this hostility to be directed at childcare, housework, romantic love and the inequality of the partners, in that order. This is where he sees the problem lies as far as comparisons are concerned, since his view is that 'most African cultures see the family unit as the basic building block of society' and African philosophy aims to preserve and strengthen this family unit. He cites Anne Oakley's comment that 'bearing children is a biological capacity whose implications women are unable to avoid' (Oakley, 1981, p. 32) which he interprets as meaning that if an alternative were available, Oakley believes that Western women would not necessarily choose the option of giving birth to children. Nhlapo argues that in contrast, no traditional-minded African woman would willingly be childless, and that abortion and contraception, where practised, are solely to prevent premarital pregnancy. Moreover, children in traditional African society still fulfil the classic roles of providing prestige for the parents; a source of labour; a means of strengthening the family by alliances forged through marriage; to provide insurance for old age; and to help to transmit property.

Nhlapo then makes his key argument that whereas the Western woman has the choice of whether to marry or not and whether to beget or not, 'this is largely denied her African counterpart' (Nhlapo, 1989, p. 12). Furthermore, no adult African woman is willingly unmarried. Through customs such as polygamy it is possible for most women, including widows, to find husbands. Further, in a society where technology and the economy is underdeveloped, running the home is a full-time occupation, so that the average African woman does not have the opportunity to take part in public life or leisure pursuits, unlike her Western counterpart.

Perhaps this is a somewhat sweeping statement as far as women in the West are concerned but Nhlapo is obviously dealing in generalities.

Nhlapo then warms to his theme by addressing the issue of the division of labour in African society. By this he is referring to the 'strict demarcation' between 'men's work' and 'women's work' and submits that 'by and large, the spouses go about their separate social lives in circles of their own sex' (Nhlapo, 1989, p. 12). Of course, this sort of behaviour is not peculiar to African women as Arab, Turkish and some Greek communities also have this practice of separate lives.

Nhlapo also notes that this sort of social arrangement gives African women greater freedom than their counterparts in the industrialized world, which they cherish. Another difference identified by Nhlapo is that African society does not have the literary and media promotion of romantic love as a prerequisite for marriage. As he puts it: 'In Africa, respect, the need for security, obedience to parents may all play a part in persuading a woman to marry a particular man' (Nhlapo, 1989, p. 12).

For these and other economic reasons – such as a serious lack of resources – Africa is not about to search for alternatives to the African family model, especially if the intention is for the state 'to take responsibility for child care and to allow women (married or single) greater personal fulfilment' (Nhlapo, 1989, pp. 12–13).

South Africa

Type of legal system

As indicated earlier, South Africa merits separate and special consideration from the rest of the African continent and indeed what is usually classified as African law. South Africa's legal system is traditionally classified by comparative lawyers as a mixed or hybrid legal system. This is because it has inherited a considerable imprint from Roman-Dutch civil law as well as English common law. The mix also includes African customary law which is recognized as a source of law under s. 21(3) of the Constitution of the Republic of South Africa 1996. Writers such as du Plessis argue that it is more appropriate to consider South Africa as being a pluralist system 'in which the civil law/common law mixture and customary law are separate components' (du Plessis, 2006, p. 667).

Status of marriage

Three statutory laws

There are currently three statutory laws which provide for the status of marriage in South Africa. These are the Marriage Act 1961, the Recognition of Customary Marriages Act 1998 (the 1998 Act) and the Civil Union Act 2006 (the 2006 Act). The first two statutes provide for the civil registration of marriages solemnized according to the traditions of indigenous tribes and the third allows the 'voluntary union of two persons, which is solemnised and registered by either a marriage or civil union'. The 2006 Act effectively allows same-sex marriage. Couples who marry under the 2006 Act have a choice as to whether their union is called a civil partnership or a marriage partnership. If the latter is chosen, couples will enjoy the same privileges as those married under the Marriage Act 1961. If there is proof that a couple married under the terms of any of these three statutes, that marriage will be legally valid and no individual or organization may treat such couples as unmarried.

The Recognition of Customary Marriages Act 1998

The Recognition of Customary Marriages Act 1998, which came into force on 1 November 2000, confers full recognition on African customary marriages and regulates their celebration, registration, proprietary consequences and dissolution. It also permits polygamy within customary marriage and has retrospective effect, since it gives full recognition to all customary marriages celebrated prior to its enactment.

Hence, under this Act, all African customary unions are recognized as legal unions, polygamy is retained and there is an attempt to protect wives in customary marriages. All existing (that is, at the time of commencement of the Act) customary unions which are valid at customary law are accorded legal recognition for all purposes, under the Act. For customary marriages intended to take place after the Act, a range of requirements for validity is enunciated, requiring, for instance, that both prospective spouses must be over 18 and must freely consent to be married to each other under customary law (see s. 2(2) and s. 3). There is also provision for registration but a failure to register does not invalidate the marriage (s. 4).

Section 6 of the 1998 Act states that a wife in a customary marriage has full status and capacity, including the capacity to acquire assets and to dispose of them, to enter into contracts and to litigate, in addition to any rights and powers that she may have under customary law. This, the section makes clear, is on the basis of equality with her husband and subject to the matrimonial system governing the marriage. Although spouses who married at customary law may also marry one another at civil law, provided neither is a party to a customary marriage with another person, those who have married at civil law are not competent to enter into any other marriage (s. 10(1) and (4)) and the language implies that such a subsequent marriage would be void.

The Act has provoked a 'flood of academic writing' (Sinclair, 2002, p. 420) and the issues it raises (as listed by Sinclair) are: (i) Does this statutory attempt to bring customary marriages in line with civil marriages create a contest between the constitutional right to culture against the right to equality? (ii) Which aspects of customary law infringe other rights in the Constitution? (Sinclair, 2002, p. 420).

Promotion of Equality and Unfair Discrimination Act 2000

The Unfair Discrimination Act 2000 establishes special equality courts with powers to make a range of orders providing relief to victims of unfair discrimination. The Act is potentially provocative because it explicitly provides that no person may unfairly discriminate against any person on the ground of gender, and this includes gender-based violence, female genital mutilation, any practice which impairs the dignity of women and any policy which limits access of women to land rights, finances or other resources (s. 8). Patriarchy, which is central to African customary law, may fall foul of the Act, hence lobolo, the paying of a brideprice, which is seen by some as patriarchal and amounting to a sale of women, might arguably be covered by the Act. The list of practices prohibited by the Act, at least in one writer's opinion, 'appears to wipe out the entire system of customary succession', as it is based on patriarchy (see Pieterse, 2000, p. 633). Pieterse also believes that any decision to ban lobolo should not be taken lightly. Bohler suggests that the equality courts will provide a less formal way of dealing with discrimination cases and will actually help to develop customary law (Bohler, 2000) but the Act may be interpreted as seeking to ensure compliance with the Constitution and with South Africa's obligations under international law (Sinclair, 2002, p. 420). This Act also requires the abolition of the 'system preventing women from inheriting family property' (male primogeniture in the law of intestate succession) which could also prove controversial. It remains to be seen how the courts will interpret the mandates of the Act (Knoetze, 2003). Pieterse believes that the eradication of African customary law risks leaving a chasm between the lived customs of the people and the official version of their laws and the precipitous winds of change may well bring stormy weather (Pieterse, 2000).

Matrimonial property

Section 7(2) to (4) of the Recognition of Customary Marriages Act 1998 also makes it clear that a customary marriage entered into after the commencement of the Act, in which the husband is not already a partner in another customary union, is a marriage in universal community of property unless this is excluded by an antenuptial contract. Antenuptial contracts are valid and enforceable in South Africa.

The husband in a customary marriage who wishes to enter into another customary marriage must apply to the court for approval of a written contract regulating the future matrimonial property system governing his marriages. This is the result of the operation of s. 7(6) to (9) of the 1998 Act.

A person who is a marriage officer appointed under the terms of the Marriage Act and who has an objection of conscience, religion or belief to marrying same-sex couples may object in writing to the government, after which she or he will be granted an exemption from performing such marriages. However, a marriage officer whose appointment includes performing marriages under the terms of the Civil Union Act may not be exempted from performing same-sex marriages. Persons who have an objection to performing such ceremonies may resign from their office as marriage officers, or a particular organization as a whole may inform the government that their members no longer wish to be recognized as marriage officers on the basis of their objection to same-sex unions.

Same-sex marriage in South Africa

The equality clause contained in s. 9 of South Africa's Constitution prohibits unfair discrimination on a non-exhaustive list of grounds, including prohibitions against discrimination on the grounds of sexual orientation and of marital status. The landmark case on same-sex unions and the meaning of family life, decided by the Constitutional Court, was *National Coalition for Gay and Lesbian Equality v Minister of Home Affairs* (2000) (2) SA 1 (CC). This case dealt with a failure to exempt gay and lesbian couples from onerous conditions specified in South African immigration laws, in contrast to benefits extended to spouses of a particular category of persons. The Constitutional Court held that the failure to extend benefits to spouses of partners in same-sex unions contravened the Constitution because it constituted 'overlapping or intersecting discrimination on the grounds of sexual orientation and marital status'. The court further affirmed that s. 10 of the Constitution recognized and guaranteed that everyone has the right to have their dignity respected and protected. Ackerman J held that the message contained in the offending legislation was that gays and lesbians lacked the inherent humanity to have their family and family lives in same-sex relationships respected and protected. This legislation, opined the learned judge, perpetuated and reinforced existing prejudices and stereotypes. As far as the prerequisites of a 'family' or 'family life' were concerned, the essential element singled out by the court was whether the relationship constituted a permanent life partnership, based on the physical, moral and spiritual community of life which comprises the consortium omnis vitae. Sloth-Nielsen and Heerden query how far beyond the traditional idea of the nuclear family this concept would be interpreted (see Sloth-Nielson and Heerden, 2003, p. 131).

In any event, subsequent case law has continued this trend. Hence, in *Satchwell v President of the Republic of South Africa* (2001) (12) BCLR 1284, the Transvaal High Court declared unconstitutional certain provisions of the Judges Remuneration and Conditions of Employment Act 88 of 1989 and conferred spousal benefits such as pension rights, travelling and subsistence allowances upon the same-sex life partners of judges. The orders made by Kgomo J were mainly confirmed by the Constitutional Court (see *Satchwell v President of the Republic of South Africa*

(2002) (9) BCLR 986 (CC)). However, an important qualification to the High Court orders was added by Madala J when he declared that s. 9 of the Constitution does not require benefits provided to spouses to be extended to all same-sex spouses if no reciprocal duties of support have been undertaken.

In 2005, the Constitutional Court of South Africa decided that the exclusion of same-sex couples from the common law definition of marriage and the statutory marriage formula was unconstitutional as it violated the rights of such couples to equality.

Same-sex marriage was made legal in South Africa on 30 November 2006 with the enactment of the Civil Unions Act which was passed by the South African Parliament earlier in November. South Africa is the first country in Africa to legalize same-sex marriage. It is worth noting that same-sex couples now have the right to adopt children (see *Du Toit* (2001) (12) BCLR 1225 (T) discussed at p. 168 under Children).

Divorce

Grounds

Under the South African Divorce Act 1979 (the 1979 Act), a marriage may be dissolved by a court by a decree of divorce on two possible grounds. The first is irretrievable breakdown; the second is mental illness or the continuous unconsciousness of a party to the marriage. A court may grant a decree on the ground of irretrievable breakdown of a marriage if it is satisfied that the marriage relationship between the parties has reached such a state of disintegration that there is no reasonable prospect of the restoration of a normal marriage relationship between them. A court may accept as proof of irretrievable breakdown of a marriage: (a) that the parties have not lived together as husband and wife for a continuous period of at least one year immediately prior to the date of the institution of the divorce action; (b) that the defendant committed adultery and that the plaintiff finds it irreconcilable with a continued marriage relationship; or (c) that the defendant has in terms of a sentence of a court been declared an habitual criminal and is undergoing imprisonment as a result of such sentence.

The 1979 Act also stipulates that if it appears to the court that there is a reasonable possibility that the parties may become reconciled through marriage counselling, treatment or reflection, the court may postpone the proceedings in order that the parties may attempt reconciliation. If a divorce action is not defended and is postponed to allow the parties an opportunity to be reconciled, the court may direct that the action be tried de novo, that is, as a new trial, on the date of resumption thereof, by any judge of the court.

A court may refuse to grant a decree of divorce if it appears at the proceedings that, despite the granting of a decree, one of the spouses will not be free to remarry unless another marriage is dissolved in accordance with the prescripts of that party's religion or the religion of either of them; or unless a barrier to the remarriage of the spouse concerned is removed.

As far as safeguarding the interests of children are concerned, a court will not grant a divorce unless it is satisfied that the provisions made with regard to the welfare of any minor or dependent child of the marriage are satisfactory or are the best that can be made in the circumstances (s. 6(1)). A court may order an investigation which it may deem necessary to be carried out and may order any person to appear before it and may order the parties or any one of them to pay the costs of the investigation and appearance.

Courts dealing with family law

The court system dealing with family law is fragmented. In practice, a two-tier system operates. The wealthiest litigants use the High Courts, which are staffed by judges, and the poorer litigants use the family courts, which are staffed by magistrates (van der Merwe and du Plessis, 2004, p. 137). However, on paper there are several courts available to those seeking redress or support in relation to their family situation. The High Courts deal with divorce and custody and have exclusive jurisdiction for Hague Convention matters. At regional court level, the Divisional Courts have jurisdiction to grant divorces and ancillary relief. However, these courts do not have jurisdiction to deal with maintenance, custody or access if issues relating to these matters are not connected to a divorce action. Uniquely, South Africa has Special Maintenance Courts, which are the most extensively used courts of all the courts dealing with family law issues. These courts deal specifically with claims of child and spousal maintenance. There are also Special Children's Courts which deal exclusively with matters of child welfare. The 'overcrowding, inefficiency and bureaucracy [of these courts] is well documented' (van der Merwe and du Plessis, 2004, p. 137). The Constitutional Court, the ultimate court of appeal in South Africa, has declared that the administrative problems within the maintenance system constitute a denial of human rights of women and children. Clearly, more resources are urgently required to improve the facilities and quality of South African legal remedies in this field (van der Merwe and du Plessis, 2004, p. 137). This is made even more pressing in the light of research by the University of Cape Town which suggests that the divorce rate is as high as 50 per cent in certain sectors of the population (van der Merwe and du Plessis, 2004, p. 138).

Children

The best interests principle

Article IV of the African Charter on the Rights and Welfare of the Child provides: '[I]n all actions concerning the child undertaken by any person or authority the best interests of the child shall be the primary consideration.' Although the Executive Committee of the United Nations High Commission for Refugees has stated that 'all actions taken on behalf of the child as well as by the principle of family unity', there is no definitive guidance or criteria for deciding what is in a particular child's best interests.

The welfare principle in cases involving children has been incorporated in the Bill of Rights of the 1996 South African Constitution, and it remains a key principle in common law. Historically, South Africa's common law derives from its heritage of Roman-Dutch law whereby the custody of children was a matter left to the discretion of judges (see Voet, 1965, originally published 1698; The *Commentary on the Pandects*, Gene trans., 25.3.20). The discretion was usually based on what judges regarded as being in the best interests of the child. Nineteenth-century case law also appears to support this in, for example, *Simey v Simey* (1881) 1 SC 171 at 176.

The principle is also a key element of the Convention on the Rights of the Child which was ratified by South Africa on 16 June 1995. It is also part of the African Charter on the Rights and Welfare of the Child, ratified on 7 January 2000, which provides: '[i]n all actions concerning the child undertaken by any person or authority the best interests of the child shall be the primary consideration.'

Under the South African Constitution, s. 28(2) stipulates that 'a child's best interests are of paramount importance in every matter concerning the child'. Section 28(1) also enunciates a fairly extensive list of specific children's rights which include rights to parental care, family care or alternative care, rights to be protected against abuse and ill-treatment, rights to shelter, healthcare, nutrition and rights to legal representation in designated circumstances. However, a child has no right to vote or stand for political office but older children can apply for the right to freedom of religion and conscience (see Bonthuys, 2006, p. 40). Bonthuys further emphasizes that the Constitution does not contain any explicit family rights or parental rights 'nor does it specifically protect the family as a social institution' (Bonthuys, 2006, p. 24). By this is meant that the family per se is not specifically mentioned as warranting special constitutional protection. However a body of case law from the Constitutional Court indicates that the family has indirect protection through the rights to dignity of its members (see e.g. *Re Certification of the Republic of South Africa* (1996) (4) SA 744 (CC) paras 98–102 and *Booysen v Minister of Home Affairs* [2001] 7 BCLR 654 (CC)).

Bonthuys has argued that the inclusion of the best interests principle and a detailed list of children's rights in the South African Constitution has led to two sets of tensions. The first arises between the case-by-case application of the best interests principle and the general, principled application of human rights and constitutional norms. Bonthuys notes that the application of the principle in case law (see *V v V* (1998) (4) SA 169 (C) 187ff.) highlights the fact that the best interests of a particular child would depend on the surrounding circumstances and that each case should be decided on its own merits. The second set of tensions arises from the need to balance the rights and interests of children with the rights and interests of other family members and the needs of society in general (see Bonthuys, 2006, pp. 24–5).

Application of the best interests principle by the courts

Bonthuys' survey of the relevant case law suggests three conclusions. First, some courts ignore completely the best interests principle (see e.g. *Mthembu v Letsela* (1997) (2) SA 936 (T); (1998) (2) SA 675 (T) and *Van Zijl v Hoogenhout* [2004] 4 All SA 427 (SCA)); second, other courts assume that the common law as it stands accurately reflects the best interests of the child (e.g. *Van Rooyen* (1999) (4) SA 435 (C) and *Jackson* (2002) (2) SA 303 (SCA)); and third, a group of courts uses the best interests principle to revise or drastically change the rules of South African common law.

The most remarkable example of such a case is *Laerskool Middelburg v Departementshoof Mpumalanga Departement van Inderwys* (2003) (4) SA 160 (T) where the governing body of an Afrikaans school mounted a challenge to the decision by the Department of Education to change the school into a dual medium school to accommodate (mainly black) pupils. Despite the fact that the administrative action was clearly illegal as the statutory procedures had been ignored, the court held that the constitutional best interests principle meant that the rights of those pupils who had already been admitted to the school should outweigh the interests of the school, the application of administrative law and single language schools in general. Further, her analysis of cases like *du Toit v Minister of Welfare and Population Development* (2003) (2) SA 198 (CC) suggests that despite the rhetoric of the courts, the best interests principle is not being used as an independent or fundamental constitutional right, at least not in the same manner as other rights in the South African Bill of Rights (see Bonthuys, 2006, pp. 26–8). In *du Toit*, the Constitutional Court struck down provisions in the Child Care Act 1983 which prohibited the joint adoption of children by same-sex couples. The court took the view that the situation that was created by only one partner to the same-sex union having a legal relationship with the adopted children was not in the best interests of those children whose rights the care-givers sought to enforce and protect (Sloth-Nielsen and Heerden, 2003, p. 133).

Bonthuys notes that South African courts have increasingly begun to utilize the terminology of children's rights even in cases where the straightforward application of the common law rules and standards would have sufficed, for example in cases such as *B v S*, where the Supreme Court of Appeal articulated the common law right of access thus: '[I]t is the child's right to have access, or to be spared access, that determines whether contact with the non-custodian parent will be granted' (see *B v S* (1995) (3) SA 571 at 582a, followed in *T v M* (1997) (1) SA 54 at 57 and see Bonthuys, 2006, p. 33).

Natural father's right to access extra-marital children – legislation

Decisions such as *B v S* (1995) (3) SA 571 led to the promulgation of the Natural Fathers of Children Born out of Wedlock Act 1997, which confirmed the common law position that *the natural father may, on application to the High Court, be granted access to, or custody or guardianship of, his extra-marital child if he can satisfy the court that this is in the best interests of the child* (s. 2) (emphasis added). In considering the father's application, the court, under s. 2(5), must take into account 'where appropriate', a non-exhaustive list of factors including the degree of commitment that the applicant father has shown toward the child. A point of comparison may be made with the English law position where, as well as considering factors such as the degree of attachment between the applicant and the child and the reasons for the father's application, the courts will also seek to ascertain a non-resident unmarried father's degree of commitment in the context of whether to grant him parental responsibility (see *Re H* [1991] 3 All ER 185).

Right to consent to adoption of non-marital child

Another piece of legislation worth noting is the Adoption Matters Amendment Act 56 of 1998 which amended s. 18(4)(d) of the Child Care Act so as to provide for the granting of consent by both parents to the adoption of a child born out of wedlock, provided that the natural father has acknowledged himself in writing to be the child's father and has made his identity and whereabouts known.

Parental rights and parental responsibilities

In the same way as it transpired in English child law in the mid to late 1980s, judicial language has also shifted from parental rights to parental responsibilities, even though these 'responsibilities' remained the same as the parental rights (see *Heysteck* (2002) (2) SA 754 (T) at 757B-G; *Tyler* [2004] 4 All SA 115 at para 24 (see below); *Krugel v Krugel* (2003) (6) SA 220 (T) at 223D). However, case law indicates that judges still regard parental rights as very relevant to the ascertainment of the child's best interests and parental rights have been articulated as part of the best interests of children (Bonthuys, 2006, p. 33). An example of this is the *Tyler* case where a man and his second wife removed a baby from the care of the man's teenage daughter and argued in court that they would be better able to care for the child. This was despite the fact that there was no evidence that the teenage mother was inadequate or unable to provide for the child. However, it was clear that the daughter could not provide the level of care which her father and stepmother could afford. The common law rule was that the mother had rights of custody unless this could be shown to be detrimental to the child. The court reformulated the rule as: '[T]he biological bond between a child and his or her natural parent is one of the most important factors still to be considered when the issue of what is in the best interests of the child is under consideration' (see *Tyler* [2004] 4 All SA 115 at 128b-c (NC)). The court's decision was to award custody to the biological mother.

Another noteworthy feature of the South African courts' approach is to regard the best interests of children as interwoven with the rights and interests of other family members, especially parents. In *V v V* (1998) (4) SA 169, the High Court held that 'access is ... not a unilateral exercise of a right by a child, but part of a continuing relationship between parent and child'(at 189D-E) and thus the idea of the best interests of the child is seen as part of an interlocking set of relationships with the child (see *Hugo* (1997) (4) SA 1 (CC) at para. 110 and *Bannatyne* (2003) (2) SA 363 at para 29)

Bonthuys argues that her survey reveals two key points. First, the cases do not contain any analysis of the other constitutional rights of children or any attempt to balance the best interests or the rights of children against the constitutional rights of other family members such as parents. Second, even where the courts do use the principle to justify changes to the common law, there is no authoritative analysis of what is in the best interests of children and why. Bonthuys argues that, in essence, the courts appear to be using the best interests principle as a blanket principle to justify their decisions; it is easier to use the broad notion of best interests rather than attempt to define concepts such as parental care or abuse; it also means they do not have to deal with constitutional rights; where the focus is on parents, it enables the courts to say that even if they have not considered the children's rights, they have considered their needs. The best interests principle also provides the courts with 'a relatively easy way of deciding cases where it is difficult to choose between competing parental rights or societal interests' (Bonthuys, 2006, p. 31).

Problems in the application of the best interests principle

Nevertheless, Burman argues that the concepts inherent in the best interests standard are foreign to a large section of the South African population and she regards it as 'an import from an alien world' (Burman, 2003, p. 29). Thus, although South Africa has officially adopted the best interests standard as the desirable standard for legal decisions regarding children, there are major problems with its operation. First, this standard conflicts with religious law and customary law that is widely observed in the country; and second, the prevailing social conditions in South Africa, especially HIV and AIDS, are adversely affecting the operation of the standard and the problems are likely to increase. Even worse, the legal acceptance of the standard has given those in power the false impression that children's interests are being protected in every situation.

Morocco

At the opening of its Parliament, Morocco's King Mohammed VI announced a landmark reform granting women new rights in marriage and divorce. He emphasized that the aim is to draw up a modern family law which is consistent with the spirit of their tolerant religion. Among the objectives identified was to give 'true authority to women to exercise it in accordance with their choice and interest on the basis of the interpretations of the Koranic verse which prevents forcing women into marriage without their consent'.

Nigeria

Introduction

Nigerian family law merits attention in this brief conspectus of aspects of family law in the African continent for its somewhat conflicting approach to child custody (see below) and because of the somewhat bizarre custom which allows a marriage between a dead man and a living spouse and a 'woman to woman' marriage. It should be noted that the Nigerian system may be classified as a common law jurisdiction, with cases as its main source of law supplemented by statutes. However, as is the case with several post-colonial countries, the courts recognize and apply local customs mutatis mutandis.

Marriage between the dead and the living – 'weird and unnatural' customary law?

In *Okonkwo v Okagbue* (1994) 9 NWLR 301, the Nigerian court was asked to adjudicate on an Onitsha local custom. This permits a marriage between a dead man and the living, and the plaintiff asked that the court declare this custom to be repugnant to natural justice, equity and good conscience. Nnanyeiugo Okonkwo died in 1931 survived by five sons, the plaintiff being one of them. He was also survived by two sisters, the first and second defendants. Both women were married but had no children and had since separated from their respective spouses and returned to their father's house. In 1961, 30 years after Okonkwo died, the first and second defendants (the surviving sisters) 'married' the third defendant (another woman) on behalf of their deceased brother, Okonkwo. The third defendant bore six children who answered to the name Okonkwo. However, the plaintiff (one of the surviving sons) and his brothers refused to accept the children as their deceased father's children.

The extended family was unable to resolve this dispute, and the plaintiff instituted a case in the High Court asking the court for (i) a declaration that by Onitsha native law and custom the first and second defendants could not by themselves marry the third defendant in the place of their dead brother, Nnanyelugo Okonkwo, and the alleged marriage was null and void; (ii) a declaration that the third defendant was not the wife of the late Mr Okonkwo; (iii) a court order stating that all the six children of the third defendant were not the children of the late Mr Okonkwo; (iv) a declaration that the said children of the third defendant therefore could not inherit the personal or real property of the late Mr Okonkwo.

The High Court held that the marriage of the third defendant to the deceased man was valid under Onitsha native law and custom and that the six children of the third defendant were therefore perfectly legitimate and belonged to the Okonkwo family. The court dismissed the plaintiff's action. On appeal, the Court of Appeal upheld the trial court's judgment. The plaintiff appealed to the Supreme Court.

The Supreme Court unanimously allowed the appeal and held that the purported marriage between the third defendant and the deceased was null and void. The court declared that 'marriage is a union between a man and a woman who are both living'. Since one of the essentials of marriage under customary law is the element of procreation, it is necessary that the parties to the marriage must be together physically. The court further held that the Onitsha custom which allows a woman to be 'married' to a deceased man as in the present case, was repugnant to natural justice, equity and good conscience. A dead man could not give his consent and could not consummate the marriage with any woman purported to have been married to him.

All three Supreme Court judges unanimously condemned the Onitsha custom, both with regard to a purported 'marriage' between someone already deceased and because it was in reality a union between women, as repugnant to natural justice, equity and good conscience. Uwais JSC declared that the first and second defendants' purported marriage of the third defendant purportedly on behalf of the deceased 30 years after his death, was a 'fiction and a fallacy for it was impossible for the dead to be married to the living'. In his opinion, what happened was a purported 'marriage' between a woman and two women, which he found repugnant to natural justice, equity and good conscience. Ogundare JSC held that a marriage can only be contracted between two living persons, and a dead man was incapable of fathering children. Consequently, the 'marriage' between the third defendant and the deceased was void and the six children of the third defendant were not to be regarded as the children of the deceased Mr Okonkwo. He added that it would amount to encouraging promiscuity to hold otherwise; consequently, any custom which permits the practice was not consonant with public policy and good conscience. Mohammed JSC was equally scathing and described the marriage between the dead and the living as 'weird and unnatural' and condemned the custom which permitted a 'woman to woman marriage' as repugnant to natural justice, equity and good conscience.

The law report makes no mention of the identity of the biological father of the six offspring who were produced in this case. On this point, the present author notes that there is no suggestion or evidence received by the court that any magical or supernatural forces, from the living or dead, might have been responsible.

Despite this ruling, it needs to be noted that this custom is still being widely practised not only amongst the Onitsha population but in many parts of Ibo land and Isham. As Uzodike informs us: 'No court decision has yet succeeded in stopping the practice' (see Uzodike, 2000, p. 344).

Children in Nigerian law

Under s. 71(1) of the Nigerian Matrimonial Causes Act 1970, 'in proceedings with respect to the custody, guardianship, welfare, advancement or education of children of a marriage the court shall regard the interests of those children as the paramount consideration and subject thereto, the court may make such order in respect of those matters as it thinks proper'. In custody disputes, therefore, it has been made clear that 'the question is no longer who has the better right or claim to the children or whose claim is superior by virtue of the common law or customary law rights ...' (see (1997) 3 NWLR 472). Case law indicates that the most important consideration is the interest and welfare of the children (see Uzodike, 2000, p. 340). It is important to note that under customary law in Nigeria the husband has exclusive rights to the custody of the children but this is not the prevailing cultural attitude, although the patriarchal customary law position is doubtless difficult to eradicate from the judges' minds. Indeed, in *Oyelowo v Oyelowo* (1987) 2 NWLR 239, Nsofor JCA's view was that while the children's interest is the paramount consideration, it is not in the children's interest to be kept away from their father's family where they 'rightly' belong. The net result of such an approach if followed by the majority of the judiciary is that custody would always be granted to the father on the basis that it is the father's family with whom the children belong.

Same–sex unions

South Africa

Same-sex marriage was made legal in South Africa on 30 November 2006 with the enactment of the Civil Unions Act. This passed through the South African Parliament earlier in November. South Africa is the first country in Africa to legalize same-sex marriage, through its Civil Unions Act, which creates a separate kind of marriage by allowing opposite sex and same-sex couples to choose whether to register a civil union or marriage.

Concluding comments on African family law in the early twenty-first century

General observations

In the late twentieth century and the early years of the twenty-first century, Africa remains a complex continent, almost defying classification and rationalization because of its multi-faceted cultural mix, diverse regions and heritage. As far as African society is concerned, it also retains its apparent bias of customary law and practice in favour of males. Under the Black Administration Act and some former homeland laws, chiefs' courts have not been allowed to hear cases of nullity, divorce or separation arising out of a civil marriage. Rural women continue to be unhappy about the administration of land by traditional leaders, claiming that women are traditionally disadvantaged by the customary law of land holding and its administration by traditional leaders.

Indeed, the inferiority of the African woman's status has been a historical fact and ingrained in African society as a result of a dominant patriarchal society.

It is problematic to define family or household in South Africa because of the 'fluidity, mobility and dispersion of caring relationships' which exist in this jurisdiction. However, it appears that it has experienced a 'remarkable liberalisation of family law through the application of constitutional principles', and 'heterosexual domestic partnerships will be given some recognition and protection' (Sloth-Nielsen and van Heerden, 2003, p. 140). Even more remarkably, in less than a decade, its courts have allowed joint adoption by same-sex couples and statutory recognition may shortly be given. There are even proposals by a special Parliamentary Select Committee to recommend that a same-sex couple may act as a commissioning couple for a surrogacy parenthood arrangement and have access to other alternative reproductive techniques.

As a result of statutory reform and the influence of modernity, there now exists a multitude of legally recognizable family forms, such as 'common law marriages, customary unions, same-sex life partnerships, domestic partnerships (heterosexual and homosexual) and religious marriages' (Sloth-Nielsen and van Heerden, 2003, p. 140).

Matrimonial property in African legal systems

One source of anachronism and potential confusion lies in the area of matrimonial property. The Matrimonial Property Act 88 of 1984 was not adopted in several of the homeland territories. Homelands consist of several independent regions which exist within the old Republic of South Africa, each with its own set of laws governing homeland citizens. Under the law enacted by the Transkei Marriage Act, the husband's marital power still exists. The 1984 Act was made applicable in the homeland territories with effect from 1 April 1997 and is not retrospective with regard to marriages contracted before this date. Hence there is a multiplicity of matrimonial property regimes, each one applicable according to the date of the marriage and the place where it was contracted.

South African courts have not been enthusiastic about applying the Bill of Rights in the context of customary law and marriages governed by religious laws. Sloth-Nielsen and van Heerden argue: 'The stated paramountcy of the Bill of Rights has not prevented a tangible tension in judicial pronouncements between constitutional values such as equality and dignity, on the one hand, and the need to respect diverse traditions and cultures, on the other' (Sloth-Nielsen and van Heerden, 2003, p. 141). According to these commentators, this creates the possibility of exacerbating vulnerability rather than ameliorating it. The deserted Muslim wife and the illegitimate daughter under customary law are cited by them as cases in point.

Children in South Africa

Best interests test adopted

As far as South African children are concerned, the guideline of the best interests of the child has been officially adopted as the guiding criterion, in keeping with most of the rest of the world, in conformity with the South Africa Constitution, s. 28(2), which states: 'A child's best interests are of paramount importance in every matter concerning the child.' As recently as 2006, Bonthuys, among others, suggested that Robert Mnookin's criticisms of this principle, despite being made in 1975, still hold true in the early twenty-first century, namely that '[d]eciding what is best for a child poses a question no less ultimate than the purposes and values of life itself' (Mnookin, 1975, p. 260). Matters are not helped by the fact that 'social and psychological parenthood may be more common in an extended family or a family where a divorce has occurred' (van der Merwe and du Plessis, 2004, p. 139). These writers were referring to South Africans but their comment applies equally to many parts of Africa.

Difficulties in applying the best interests test

Bonthuys has observed that 'the best interests standard originates in and has long formed part of South African common law' (Bonthuys, 2006, p. 24). She points out various difficulties in its implementation and application but Burman goes even further by arguing that her reviews of South African law show that 'given South Africa's heterogeneity, there is virtually no agreement on what values should dictate the choice between alternatives for the child even in normal situations'. She continues, tellingly, that '[t]hese are not normal times' (Burman, 2003, p. 37) because there are no alternatives available as far as decision making for children is concerned. Chief among the factors which remove these choices is the size of the AIDS epidemic in South Africa, not helped by the fact that other parts of Asia and Africa are facing similar crises. Other limiting factors are the social conditions in South Africa – the economic situation of women, drink, drugs, violence, and the size of the prison population (Burman, 2003, p. 38). Those segments of the population who do not accept the best interests standard regard it as a 'foreign import' which 'distorts the operation of their legal systems and perverts the way society provides for its members' (Burman, 2003, p. 38) Since the Convention on the Rights of the Child was not adopted by South Africa with any interpretative declaration, it cannot limit its operation to selected sections of the community. The most damaging aspect of the adoption of this standard is that it deludes the people in power into believing that the interests of children are being taken care of, whereas the reality is different (Burman, 2003, p. 38). In a word, this is a case where a legal transplant has taken place but in the opinion of some South African legal experts is not appropriate to the particular circumstances and problems of South Africa.

Other writers on South Africa observe that there is evidence that responsibility for children is 'increasingly being separated from social and biological parenthood, largely due to the HIV/AIDS crisis' (van der Merwe and du Plessis, 2004, p. 139).

Concluding comments on the South African family

van der Merwe and du Plessis describe the South African family as

> 'extremely heterogeneous, without uniformity of lifestyle, morality, child-rearing practices or religion … Many families maintain relationships across long distances. Furthermore, many domestic arrangements are in a continual state of flux, with some members migrating to urban areas to sustain the household and children being cared for by relatives or grandparents in rural areas or following their mothers to urban areas.'
>
> (van der Merwe and du Plessis, 2004, p. 166)

ASIAN COUNTRIES

In the course of their history, several Asian countries came under colonial rule or colonial influence in some form or other, and this impacted on their laws with regard to family law. For the purposes of the present chapter, we shall only examine countries which are of comparativist interest in the sense that their laws have either undergone significant reform or they have 'borrowed' or 'received' laws from other countries. Examples will be taken from common law jurisdictions such as Singapore, Hong Kong and India. In each case, a brief historical excursus is undertaken to place the development of that jurisdiction's family law in historical context. It needs to be emphasized that the present writer does not purport to provide an exhaustive or comprehensive account of the family law of the region, which has been achieved in some measure by writers such as Hooker, but merely to outline the basic legal heritage of selected jurisdictions in the region before moving on to highlight recent reforms or developments which resonate with trends or themes in other countries.

Hong Kong

Introduction

Hong Kong is usually classified as a common law jurisdiction as it was a British colony for several decades and inherited English law over the colonial period. However, as with its other branches of law, the family law of the former British colony of Hong Kong was reformed post-1997, that is, after the transfer of sovereignty in that year from Britain to the People's Republic of China (PRC) and the extension to Hong Kong of a series of international human rights treaties. The plurality of Hong Kong's legal heritage needs to be borne in mind since from the British colonial period until 1971 two systems of family law operated in juxtaposition to each other. This was the Chinese system of family law and the received

English common law system. The main purpose of the 1971 reforms was to achieve 'a gradual integration of the Chinese system' and the English common law system 'with the latter occupying a more dominant position in this process' (Rwezaura and Ho, 2002, p. 181). The process of trying to combine the two systems is still evident in the early years of the twenty-first century; primarily in the courts, where judges continue to grapple with intricate questions involving the applicability of Chinese customary law as it was practised in the former colony and mainland China during the last century.

The concubinage issue

The 'union of concubinage' was abolished on 7 October 1971 along with customary marriages, by the Marriage Reform Ordinance. However, neither the status or rights of concubines lawfully taken before that date are affected, nor are the status or rights of their children, whether born before or after that date (s. 5(2)(b) Marriage Reform Ordinance). The intention was to close the 'Chinese chapter' of the marriage system in Hong Kong.

However, as Liu puts it: '[T]he actual demise of customary marriages, [and] unions of concubinage … is yet to come about.' At the moment, the courts are dealing with various aspects of customary marriage and, because of increased life expectancy, claims from the children of unions of concubinage are likely to continue for decades into the twenty-first century.

Inheriting the estate – the widow or the concubine?

Some of the most difficult and enduring problems have centred on immigration law and policy involving family members on both sides of the border. There is also the problem of the mainland mistresses of Hong Kong married men and their children. Thus, a recent issue, which also occurred in jurisdictions like Singapore, is: Who shall inherit the estate – the widow or the concubine? (see Rwezaura and Ho, 2002, p. 184).

The case of *Ng Kuk Mui v Yu Bik Fong Rebecca* (1997) HCAP 2/97 is an example of a pattern of cases in which Chinese men migrated from mainland China to Hong Kong, separating from their families in China and founding new family units in Hong Kong. Madam Ng Kuk Mui applied for a grant of letters of administration after the death of her husband when these had previously been granted to Yu Bik Fong on her application as the surviving child of the union between the deceased, Yu Kau Sun, and her mother, Madam Mok. The first issue was whether the plaintiff was the lawful kit fat (principal) wife of the deceased which would entitle her to the letters of administration. The court accepted that she was. The second issue was whether she was lawfully married to the deceased. The court held that the relationship between the defendant's mother, Madam Mok and the deceased, was not a lawful marriage under Chinese customary law. This was because it was proved that the deceased had already been married in China in 1945 before coming to

Hong Kong in 1956 when he began to cohabit with Madam Mok. The deceased's first marriage to the plaintiff had not been dissolved. The court could not decide, because of lack of evidence, whether Madam Mok could be regarded as a concubine of the deceased because of her cohabitation with him. Her status was therefore regarded as a mistress but this proved irrelevant because of an amendment in the law implemented in 1993, entitling illegitimate children to inherit from the intestate estate of their father (see Intestate's Estate Ordinance, Cap. 73).

Concubine de jure and concubine de facto

Chan Chiu Lam v Yau Yee Ping [1998] 2 HKC 569 was another case which came before the courts to determine whether the surviving children had a right to inherit the estate of their late father's concubine. Under the relevant legislation, a child of the union of concubinage is deemed to be the child of a valid marriage. The relevant issue was whether the plaintiffs were the children of a valid marriage to which the deceased's last husband and another female were parties. The trial court held that they were but this was reversed by the Court of Appeal which found that the union of concubinage between the last husband of the intestate and another female, which produced the plaintiffs, was not a valid marriage. Therefore the plaintiffs were not entitled to inherit the estate of their late father's concubine.

The Court of Appeal drew an important distinction between a de facto and de jure concubine. A concubine de facto, although in accordance with Chinese customary law, was not recognized by the 1931 Civil Code of the Republic of China. As Rogers JA expressed it, a concubine de facto was no more than a mistress. Hence it did not make any difference that the law gave a mistress certain rights including the right to maintenance. Since the plaintiffs were the issue of a union not legally recognized by the law of the parties' domicile – that is, the Republic of China at the time – Hong Kong courts, applying the common law principles of private international law, were bound to hold that the plaintiffs did not qualify to inherit the estate of Madam Chu Li, the intestate. The Court of Appeal also noted that the rules of private international law applied in Hong Kong recognized the efficacy of legislation which removed the capacity to contract a polygamous marriage previously enjoyed under the personal law of the parties. The same rule would have applied if there had been a foreign law, which was the Chinese Civil Code, abolishing the institution of concubinage.

Once again, this was a dispute between the children of Chinese parents who had migrated to Hong Kong as adults having been previously married in mainland China. Their entitlement to inheritance rights had to be decided by the application of legal principles of Chinese state law. The Court of Appeal held that although the Chinese Civil Code 1931 was silent on the subject of concubines, the omission was a deliberate policy decision to abolish such unions (Su Yigong, 'The Application of Chinese Law and Custom in Hong Kong' (1999) 29 HKLJ 267). Rwezaura and Ho highlight the fact that this decision is also notable for 'drawing a clear distinction between the law governing capacity to marry (that is, the law of domicile) and the law relating to formal validity of the marriage (that is, the law of the place of celebration)' (Rwezaura and Ho, 2002, p. 186). A final point of clarification came from Ribeiro JA who declared that once a person's law of domicile is established, the common law rules of conflict of laws must be applied, rather than Hong Kong law simply because the person was of Chinese ethnicity and resident in Hong King, despite his or her foreign domicile.

The mainland mistresses

The opening up of mainland China for trade, especially the creation of special economic zones, created opportunities for Hong Kong people to travel regularly to China on business. As a result of these business ventures, some Hong Kong men established relationships with mainland women in what has been called 'second homes' and their partners have become known as bao ernai or mistresses. This has led to women soliciting social welfare services for assistance. The situation has been debated by legislators and academics and various laws have been proposed but it has not been resolved. It is now over a decade since the debate began and neither the law to prohibit nor the law to legalize these unions has been enacted. It has been reported that the numbers of children born in these unions has risen markedly and an academic has commented that several villages in Southern China have become known as 'lover's nests' where most of the women are mistresses to Hong Kong men (see Khun Eng Kuah-Pearce 'The Cultural Politics of Mainland Chinese Migration to Hong Kong' (2001), paper presented at Conference on Immigration Law & Policies, University of Hong Kong, 24 February, at pp. 16–17). As Rwezaura and Ho observe, 'whether the mainland mistress is indeed a concubine or merely a by-product of the burgeoning market economy of China is ... of little significance to those families directly affected' (Rwezaura and Ho, 2002, p. 190). This problem continues to pose a challenge to Hong Kong's government, its social welfare system, and its immigration department. In addition, the change in the law has meant that the children of the unions are lawful children of their Hong Kong fathers, hence it is now irrelevant whether their mothers are wives or concubines (Rwezaura and Ho, 2002, p. 190). In places such as Shenzhen and Huizou, 'concubine villages' exist where hundreds, if not thousands, of young mainland women live in spacious apartments in high-rise complexes, paid for by their lovers.

Many of these women have children, so the kinds of disputes discussed above will no doubt continue for many years to come.

Divorce

Establishing irretrievable breakdown

As with many common law jurisdictions, the ground of irretrievable breakdown of the marriage has to be established under the Matrimonial Causes Ordinance before a divorce can be obtained. This is because Hong Kong has generally followed developments in English law, adopting in 1972 what English law had introduced with its Divorce Reform Act 1969. Evidence of such breakdown could be demonstrated by proof of: (i) the respondent committing adultery and the petitioner finding it intolerable to live with the respondent; (ii) the respondent behaving in such a way that the petitioner cannot reasonably be expected to live with the respondent; (iii) separation; that is, living apart for two years being the minimum period (if both parties consent to the divorce) or living apart for five years (without the need to prove consent by the respondent to the divorce); (iv) desertion for not less than two years. The time bar was two years; that is, the marriage had to have lasted for a minimum of three years before an application could be made.

Liberalizing divorce

In May 1995, Hong Kong enacted four major changes to its divorce law through the Matrimonial Causes (Amendment) Ordinance 1995. The changes comprised: (i) a new procedure for divorce by joint application to the court, based on either of two grounds, namely that the parties have lived apart for one year or that they have given one year's joint notice of intention to divorce without living apart; (ii) the minimum period of living apart prior to divorce has been reduced from two years to one year (with consent) and from five years to two years (without consent); (iii) the minimum period of desertion is reduced from two years to one year; and (iv) the time bar for divorce applications is reduced from three years to one year.

Division of matrimonial property and assets upon divorce

The law in Hong Kong under the Matrimonial Proceedings and Property Ordinance does not specify a percentage when allocating marital property and assets post-divorce. In fact, the matrimonial proceedings law in Hong Kong replicates the Matrimonial Causes Act 1973 (UK) in the version that existed before it was amended by the Matrimonial and Family Proceedings Act 1984, except that it does not make any reference to a minimal loss principle and reference to conduct is in general terms only. Thus it has the same seven guidelines which provide the framework within which the discretion of the court may be exercised. However, the task of the court is not helped by the fact that the Ordinance does not provide a specific target which the court should seek to achieve, since there is no reference to the minimal loss principle (that is, to place the parties in the financial position in which they would have been if the marriage had not broken down and each had properly discharged his or her financial obligations and responsibilities towards the other).

In *C v C* [1990] 2 HKLR 183, the Hong Kong Court of Appeal declared that the omission of a target provision in the Matrimonial Proceedings and Property Ordinance had been deliberate. However, the intention of the Hong Kong legislature has always been to follow English examples so the 'target' provision would always be in the background of Hong Kong law. But its deliberate omission meant that there was 'a lower duty on the court and lowers the significance of this element. [The omission] may then diminish a wife's claim and operate marginally in favour of the husband' ([1990] 2 HKLR 183 at 188).

If both parties have contributed in their own way and have similar needs, the capital may be divided equally but if the court perceives the wife as needing a house to accommodate herself and any minor children and the husband has sufficient income to accommodate himself, it may award the bulk of the capital assets of the spouses to the wife. A short marriage with a husband who is extremely wealthy will usually mean that the court may allow that husband to keep the majority of his assets. A clean break may also be awarded, despite the absence of a specific clean break provision, if the parties are wealthy (according to *C v C* [1990] 2 HKLR 183), or if there are no children of the marriage and the parties are able to earn a living (see *Lai Lai-hing v Lai Kwai-ping* [1995] 1 HKC 654 and *Fei Tai-chung v Gloria Fei* (1995) Court of Appeal Action No 170 of 1994) or for example, if there is considerable bitterness and hostility between the parties but the amount of the lump sum will depend on the particular circumstances of the case. A clean break can also be awarded if there are children as in *Murphy v Murphy* (1992) Court of Appeal, Civil Appeal Action of 1992 and *Hui I-mei v Cheng Yau-shing* (1996) Court of Appeal, Civil Appeal Action No 157 of 1996.

In the light of the *White* case (*White v White* [2000] 2 FLR 981), decided in 2000, English courts now strive, in so-called 'big money' cases (where available assets far outstrip the parties' reasonable needs) to make a 50/50 award wherever possible, adopting the yardstick of equality. It remains to be seen whether Hong Kong courts will follow suit in similar cases as they usually either award a clean break once and for all payment, or lifelong maintenance, or a deferred clean break.

Children and child custody

The first and paramount consideration – the welfare principle

Under s. 3(1) of the Guardianship Ordinance (HK) in any proceedings relating to the custody or upbringing of a minor the court shall regard the welfare of the minor as the first and paramount consideration and shall give due consideration to the wishes of the child, 'having regard to the age and understanding of the minor and to the circumstances of the case' and 'any material information including any report of the Director of Social Welfare available to the Court at the hearing'. The meaning of 'first and paramount' is interpreted in line with leading English authorities such as *J v C* [1969] 1 All ER 788. It has been noted by Athena Liu that Hong Kong courts have, for many years, followed guidelines (a) to (f) under s. 1(3) of the Children Act 1989 (UK), but there is no checklist of factors under the Guardianship Ordinance which the court must consider. Consequently, the weight attached to these factors will vary from case to case and have to be understood 'in the light of the unique local circumstances and culture' (Liu, 1999, p. 251).

Conclusions on Hong Kong family law

The geographical and cultural proximity of Hong Kong to mainland China has resulted in a constant flow of people between the two jurisdictions and inter-marriages and de facto unions have resulted. The social cost of the continued practice of concubines will take its toll in the years ahead and will pose an ongoing challenge to the courts and the political leaders in Hong Kong.

Hong Kong's divorce laws have continued to follow the English reforms, up to a point, and social and economic consequences have followed suit, as in England. On the positive front, there has been a movement away from the adversarial style towards a more administrative and bureaucratic model with minimal judicial participation and a recognition that couples should have the freedom to end their marriage (Rwezaura, 1998, pp. 201–2). Of course this means that the focus then shifts to post-divorce issues like financial support and the protection and care of minor children. On the negative side, the divorce law lacks adequate facilities for a cost-effective and humane resolution of post-divorce issues (Rwezaura, 1998, p. 202). Rwezaura points out that Hong Kong lacks an effective system of mediation that can be brought into play when the couple submits its joint notice of intention to divorce, despite the fact that there are statutory provisions for mediation.

As with Anglo-American law, conflict over money and child custody now takes centre stage rather than the attempt to prove that grounds for divorce exist.

With regard to financial provision upon divorce, the Hong Long legislation replicates the former version of the Matrimonial Causes Act 1973 (UK) (before the 1984 amendment), hence has no target provision such as the minimal loss principle. However, the courts appear more than capable of applying those guide-lines, aided by reference to English authorities, and is by no means inhibited or restricted by them.

In relation to child custody and child welfare, the Hong Kong courts have followed broadly the checklist of factors enumerated in s. 1(3) of the Children Act 1989 (UK), even though their legislation does not contain a checklist of any description and their basic guideline is that the child's welfare is the first and paramount consideration for the court in all matters relating to the minor child's custody or upbringing.

Unsurprisingly, therefore, Hong Kong family law has a great many similarities with English law albeit somewhat frozen in a past incarnation of its divorce legis-lation. But it is also unique in its interpretation of customary law and the vexed question of inheritance and concubinage. The proximity of Hong Kong to mainland China continues to shape the development of Hong Kong family law. As we have seen, even after 1997 the 'plural heritage of the law and the continuing influence and dominance of English common law and its interaction with Chinese culture and Chinese customary law' (Rwezaura and Ho, 2002, p. 206) is still evident in a variety of circumstances redolent of its colourful past. So, in comparative terms, there is both an element of convergence and divergence.

India

Introduction

India is another country of diversity with a plethora of religions. Its Constitution was enacted on 26 November 1949 and resolved to constitute India as a Union of States and a Sovereign, Socialist, Secular, Democratic Republic. One billion Indians live in 28 States and seven Union Territories within India, and the population comprises multicultural societies 'professing and practising different religions and speaking different local languages' (Malhotra and Malhotra, 2007, p. 102).

Systems of law in India

As Malhotra and Malhotra remind us, the oldest part of the Indian legal system is the one consisting of personal laws governing the Hindus and the Muslims. Hindu personal law has undergone changes by a continuous process of codification but Muslim personal law has remained relatively untouched by legislation (see Malhotra and Malhotra, 2007, p. 103). However, India is predominantly a common law jurisdiction, the result of British imperial rule over many years.

Marriage

The Hindu Marriage Act 1955 is a statute intended to amend and codify the law relating to marriage among Hindus. Ceremonial marriage is essential under this Act but it does not make the registration of marriages compulsory. This is mainly because Hindu marriages and most marriages in India have always been performed in public with wide publicity. Section 8(5) of the Hindu Marriage Act 1955 provides that failure to register a Hindu marriage shall in no way affect its validity. Even where compulsory registration of marriage is laid down under the rules, non-registration does not affect the validity of the marriage and failure to comply attracts only a nominal fine.

The Special Marriage Act 1954 was enacted by the Indian Parliament to provide a special form of marriage in certain cases, for the registration of such and certain other marriages and for divorces under this Act. Solemnization of marriage by registration under this Act may be resorted to by Hindus, non-Hindus and foreigners marrying in India who opt out of the ceremonial marriage under their respective personal laws. Unlike the 1955 Act, registration is compulsory under this statute. Non-Hindus can obtain a divorce under this Act and indeed, it governs people of all religions and communities in India, regardless of their personal faith (Malhotra and Malhotra, 2007, p. 104).

Family Courts

The Family Courts Act 1984 provides for the establishment of Family Courts with a view to promoting conciliation in disputes and to secure a speedy settlement of such disputes relating to marriage and family matters (Malhotra and Malhotra, 2007, p. 105). In addition, some parallel community and religious courts continue to exist, despite the organized, well regulated and established hierarchy of judicial courts in India. These unrecognized and unauthorized courts are not part of the judicial system and the judicial courts have expressed regret over their existence.

No absolute right to marry

Mr X v Hospital Z (1999) All India Reporter SC 495 is a landmark decision on the right of a patient suffering from a contagious venereal disease to marry. In the case, a doctor had claimed compensation from the Apollo Hospital in Chennai. The hospital discovered he was HIV-positive and this was disclosed to the would-be bride's family which responded by calling off the marriage. The doctor submitted that the hospital had violated medical ethics by disclosing his medical condition to the bride's family which then resulted in his social ostracism (see Malhotra and Malhotra, 2001, p. 115). The Supreme Court of India held that so long as the person is not cured of the disease or impotency, his right to marry cannot be enforced through a court of law. The court held that if a man's marriage has been cancelled owing to his being an AIDS patient, his right to marry will remain a suspended right. He would not be entitled to claim compensation from the hospital which had disclosed his medical condition to the would-be bride's family. There is clearly no absolute right to marry.

Divorce

There is a three-tier divorce structure in India which applies to most of its communities. This comprises fault grounds, the breakdown theory and the mutual consent principle. These provide the codified and statutory grounds for divorce in India (see Malhotra and Malhotra, 2007, p. 110). Some case law suggests that the ground of irretrievable breakdown rarely succeeds. This was the effect of two High Court decisions, *Yudhister Singh v Sarita* (2004) Hindu Law Reporter (1) 228 and *Kakali Dass v Dr Asish Kumar* (2004) Hindu Law Reporter (1) 448 and one Supreme Court decision *Sham Sunder v Sushma* (2004) (8) SC 166.

On the other hand, other Supreme Court of India decisions suggest that the Apex Court has recommended that 'irretrievable breakdown of marriage' should be added as a ground of divorce on the statute book. In *Naveen Kohli v Neelu Kohli* (2006) Judgments Today (3) SC 491, the Supreme Court of India recommended to the Union of India that it should seriously consider adding irretrievable breakdown of marriage as a ground for divorce to the Hindu Marriage Act. Indeed, the Apex Court applied the irretrievable breakdown principle in *Durga Prasanna v Arunhati*

(2005) (7) SC 596 following the precedents of the last five years (Malhotra and Malhotra, 2007, p. 110).

As far as customary divorce is concerned, spouses may invoke a valid custom which permits divorce. To be valid and binding the custom must be of immemorial existence, reasonable, certain and continuous; it should also be in existence that the right existed since living memory. The custom must also be ancient and invariable, established by clear and unambiguous evidence and must usually be proved by direct evidence.

In the past few years, particularly in the city areas, more marriages appear to be ending in divorce. In 1997, only 216 cases of divorce were filed in a typical district court but in 2005 the number was between 900 and 1,000. Statistics indicate that the number of divorces doubled between 2001 and 2004. This may be attributed to the fact that divorces have been made easier with the amendment of the Hindu Marriage Act, particularly the amendment in 2003. This allowed a petitioner to seek a divorce from the place where he or she last lived, unlike the previous rule which required that a divorce application had to be sought either from the place where the couple last lived or the place where the wedding ceremony took place.

Children

The best interests test

The received colonial laws from British rule in India partly coincided with and partly differed from the indigenous laws of the region. In order to introduce uniformity, the best interests test was adopted and this undermined the cultural and religious pluralism of the region. The concept of best interests of the child derives from India's colonial heritage. The Guardianship and Wards Act 1890 requires a court to determine custody according to the welfare of the minor child. Section 17 of the 1890 Act lists guidelines for determining whether an order is in the best interests of the child. The court must have regard to the age, sex and religion of the child and the character and nearness of kin to the child. As Goonesekere points out, these guidelines have encouraged courts to 'give weight to factors such as kinship relationship of wider family members, and the "morals" of a parent, particularly of the mother' (Goonesekere, 1994, p. 127). This provision has apparently influenced law and policy in the post-independence period and established child-centred standards, despite reflecting the English law of the time, by declaring that the father had superior parental rights, which would prevail unless he was unfit to be a guardian. Indian courts have continued to give preferential status to the father, although there are sufficient precedents to support awarding custody to the mother where this has been in the child's interests (Goonesekere, 1994, p. 127). This law still applies to Bangladesh and Pakistan.

In more recent times, this uniformity of approach is danger of being weakened by a heightened sense of religious and ethnic awareness. Paternal authority continues to dominate and the exploitation of female children, child marriage and infanticide continues to occur. Indeed, infanticide and child abandonment are regularly reported in the Indian press, and child marriage is one area where notions of the child's welfare have not been invoked to either declare such marriages void or to modify personal laws. Nevertheless, all countries in the South Asian region have ratified the United Nations Convention on the Rights of the Child, signifying their commitment to upholding this standard in their home jurisdictions.

Custody disputes

In the case of a dispute between a father and mother over the custody of a child, the court seeks to strike a 'just and proper' balance between the requirements of the welfare of the minor children and the rights of their parents. In *Om Prakash Bharuka v Shakuntala Modi* (1993) All India Reporter 38, there was a custody dispute between the mother and father of three minor children, and custody had been granted to the mother. The wishes of the children had been ascertained. They refused to go and stay with their father. The court held: '[M]erely because the father loves his children and is not shown to be otherwise undesirable cannot necessarily mean that the welfare of the children would be better promoted by granting custody to him.' Indeed, the wife might be 'equally affectionate towards her children and equally free from blemish, and ... because of her profession and financial resources, may be in a position to guarantee better health, education and maintenance for them'. In short, 'while giving [sic] custody of the children, the welfare of the children should be regarded as a paramount consideration'.

Conclusions on divorce law in India

On the issue of a possible reform of the existing law on divorce in India, Indian commentators Malhotra and Malhotra argue that where the marriage has irretrievably broken down, this ground needs to be incorporated in the statute book as an additional ground for divorce, but only in cases where both parties to the marriage jointly petition the court. They see two possible benefits from this: first, if parties have irreconcilable differences and wish to part amicably, an option will be available to them to part legally and logically without resorting to a protracted and time-consuming legal battle on trumped up grounds; second, the number of cases of recourse to ex parte divorce in foreign jurisdictions by non-resident Indians against spouses on Indian soil may diminish once a definite option of irretrievable breakdown is available to spouses resident in India (Malhotra and Malhotra, 2007, p. 111).

Sri Lanka

Sri Lanka is a particularly instructive jurisdiction to examine, as it is a mixed jurisdiction; having been a British colony and therefore receiving English common law yet also having experienced the reception of Roman-Dutch law. This law, while accepting the husband's marital power over his wife and children, also accepted the overriding responsibility of the courts to act as parens patriae in order to safeguard the interests of children. As Goonesekere explains, this meant that the courts, acting as the 'upper Guardian of minors' could deprive the father of any or all of the incidences of parental power and, as was the case in France, this was seen as being in the best interests of the children (Goonesekere, 1994, p. 120). Dutch jurists have claimed that the courts are the guardians of minors so that they could deprive a parent of all or any of the components of parental power if necessary. Goonesekere argues: 'A comparison of the received and indigenous legal heritage in South Asia shows that indigenous systems reflected some child-centred concerns that were not found in the early English Common law and Roman-Dutch law.'

Modern-day Sri Lanka still experiences 'sweeping paternal authority, exploitation of girl children [sic], child marriage and infanticide' (Goonesekere, 1994, p. 124). However, the child's best interests are identified with 'the personal rights of the father or mother and the concept has been developed by the judiciary without any legislative intervention' (Goonesekere, 1994, p. 131).

Singapore

Historical background to family law in Singapore

Singapore was founded as a British settlement in 1819 and is classified as a common law jurisdiction. Being at the confluence of South-East Asian trade routes, at the base of what was then the Malayan Peninsula, it was populated not just by Chinese settlers but also by Malays, Indians and a smattering of other ethnic groups, including Jews. Singapore joined Penang, and a few years later was joined by Malacca, and the three eventually became known as the Colony of the Straits Settlements. As a result of this grouping, it was considered appropriate to treat the law of Singapore as a part of the law of the Straits Settlements. The lawmakers of these Settlements were dealing with a multi-religious and multicultural mix of inhabitants including Chinese and Muslims (predominantly Malays, Arabs, and Indians) as well as Hindus, Christians, Parsis and Jews. However, by virtue of the Second Charter of Justice of 1826, the business of the courts built up and it became clear that the judges felt obliged to apply the law of England while still dealing fairly with native custom (see Freedman, 1968, p. 50). The famous case of *Spottiswoode* (see *Choa Choon Neoh v Spottiswoode* (1869) 1 Ky 216) is illustrative. Here, Sir Benson Maxwell said:

'In this Colony [Singapore], so much of the law of England as was in existence when it was imported here and is of general (and not merely local) policy, and adapted to the conditions and wants of the inhabitants, is the law of the land; and further, that law is subject, in its application to the various alien races established here, to such modifications as are necessary to prevent them operating unjustly and oppressively on them.'

Somewhat ironically, 'alien races' applied to all the non-English, but one section of the population, the Malays, did claim to be part of the indigenous population.

Indeed, as Freedman explains, 'when British rule came to be extended from the Straits Settlements to the Malay States in the last quarter of the nineteenth century, the special position of the Malays came to be reflected in the Colony' (Freedman, 1968, p. 51). This was why 'Islamic family law became established almost in its entirety in the Straits Settlements and this is the only separate family law left in Singapore' (Freedman, 1968, p. 51). Since no statutes were enacted to clarify the extent to which the accommodation of non-English laws was to be applied, it was left to the judges to decide, and they made up the law on an ad hoc basis as they went along. In essence, they held that the Chinese were polygamous, that widows and daughters were entitled by English rules to shares of an intestate's estate, that adopted sons were not entitled to such a share, and that property could not be tied up indefinitely in order to provide for ancestor worship (Freedman, 1968, p. 51).

Freedman maintains that despite the acceptance that the Chinese were polygamous, the brand of polygamy that was sanctioned was not the type that the Chinese of the time actually practised. This was because they 'turned concubines or secondary wives into spouses of virtually equal status with major wives' (Freedman, 1968, p. 51). This came about largely through judgments made in relation to the disposal of the estates of people who died intestate. Thus, through a series of judgments, English law was applied such that the widow of a man who died without making a will, was granted half or a third share of his property, depending on whether the deceased had left issue. Applying traditional Chinese law would have meant that a widow had no claims to an outright share since family property vested in males.

Even more significantly, since secondary wives were given equal status by the English judges presiding in the Straits courts, the widow's half or third share was divided equally among all widows, including secondary wives. Sir Benson Maxwell appears to have been the first to preside over and posit certain principles in a series of decisions beginning in 1867 in a case (only subsequently reported in the 1893 Law Reports) called *Re Lao Leong An* (1893) 1 SSLR 1. Here he said: 'The first wife is usually chosen by the husband's parents of a family of equal station, and is espoused with as much ceremony and splendour as the parties can afford: while the inferior [sic] wives are generally of his own choice made without regard to family connection.' He then adds: 'But that they are wives not concubines seems to me clear from the fact that certain forms of espousal are always performed and that, besides, their children inherit in default of the issue of the principal wife, and that throughout the Penal Code of China they are treated to all intents and purposes as well as the first.' This continued until the *Six Widows' Case* of 1908 (see *Choo Eng Neo v Neo Chan-Neo* (1908) 12 SSLR 120) which marked the culmination of a series of cases in which the interpretation of 'polygamous' with regard to the Chinese meant equality of treatment for both principal and secondary wives, at least as far as inheritance of an intestate's estate was concerned.

The tricky question which had to be resolved by the Straits courts at this time was: How do you distinguish a concubine (that is, a secondary wife) from a mere mistress (or 'keep' as she was called in the Straits language of the time)? As far as the Chinese were concerned, the main reason for needing to make this distinction was to decide on the legitimacy of the plentiful children who resulted from these informal unions. The Chinese tradition was to consider children legitimate if they were recognized as such by their father. Such recognition did not reflect on the status of their mothers as the man's companions. However, in order to find that a child was a legitimate heir, and therefore entitled to a share in the property upon the father's death, the Straits courts had to find that the child's mother was a wife. The judges initially demanded that there had to be evidence of some sort of marriage ceremony, and in the 1930s there had to be some evidence of cohabitation and repute in order to prove the existence of a secondary marriage. However since the Second World War, the courts began to accept that a secondary marriage could be established where there was merely evidence of an intention to form such a union (Freedman, 1968, p. 52).

The Women's Charter and the influence of foreign law

The original statute passed in Singapore, the Women's Charter 1961, replicated England's Matrimonial Causes Act 1937. Singapore then introduced separation as a ground for divorce in 1967, which followed the similar legislative step taken in Australia and New Zealand. The ground adopted in Singapore was that the parties had to have lived separately for not less than seven years and were unlikely to be reconciled. This was a no-fault ground and broke with the usual tradition of matrimonial fault as the basis of the divorce laws.

The impact of the Women's Charter in Singapore

It is probably true to say that the Women's Charter, a statute which was introduced for the first time in 1960, played a significant role in the development and reform of family law in Singapore. Nevertheless, one major change had already been made to Singapore family law – the Muslims Ordinance 1957, which had already made provision for a Shariah court and which prohibited the registration of divorces other than those by mutual consent except by order of this court. In 1960, this 1957 Ordinance was amended again to restrict Muslim polygamy. It is also important to realize that up to the late 1950s, family law was largely irrelevant to Singapore Chinese who by then formed the majority of the population. As Freedman puts it 'they married, divorced, adopted and disposed of their property according to the rules *they* recognised' (emphasis added) (Freedman, 1968, p. 56). He adds that when large properties were left by an intestate, 'some dissatisfied widow or child could invoke the law of the courts to secure a share; but most of the time family disputes were settled outside the framework of the legal system, narrowly defined, and by principles the courts might well have refused to accept' (Freedman, 1968, p. 56). Thus, it was only when the Singapore Chinese began to perceive law as an instrument of social change and when it was placed in their hands as an instrument of political change that 'a new chapter opened in the history of family law' in Singapore (Freedman, 1968, p. 56).

It is important to note that until the enactment of the Women's Charter, customary laws existed alongside Muslim or Islamic law as adapted to local conditions and as interpreted by the local Shariah courts, and of course, English common law as received under the 1826 Charter of Justice. The Singapore courts developed local principles of marriage from religions such as Islam, Hinduism and Judaism, and also from local custom, which was mainly Chinese custom (see Leong Wai Kum, *The Family Law Library of Singapore* (CD-ROM), Singapore, Butterworths, 1991, pp. 69–86; for the body of principles developed, see pp. 112–26 and 87–104). As the colony developed, the local legislature began to enact versions of the prevailing marriage statute in England (Leong, 1991, pp. 138–48).

The modern law of marriage in Singapore thus began in 1961 with the enactment of the Women's Charter as the main marriage and family legislation for all non-Muslims, irrespective of their ethnicity or religious affiliation (Leong, 2000, p. 257).

Hence, once the Women's Charter was enacted, two systems of family law co-existed, one for Muslims and the other for non-Muslims which was governed by the Charter.

Historical background to divorce in Singapore

Judicial divorce was introduced in Singapore in 1910 by the Straits Settlements Divorce Ordinance which replicated the Matrimonial Causes Act 1857 (UK). This permitted a spouse to be freed from the bonds of matrimony only upon proof of the commission of a grave matrimonial offence by the respondent. This meant that, as under the English law of the time, the law differentiated between husbands and wives in its application. For example, while adultery per se was sufficient for a husband to obtain a divorce, a wife required aggravated forms of adultery by the husband before she could obtain a divorce from her husband. So there had to be adultery with cruelty, or bigamy with adultery, or incestuous adultery or adultery coupled with desertion before she could obtain a divorce under this law in both Singapore and in England. In 1941, two further grounds were made available; namely, desertion without cause for a period of three years immediately preceding the presentation of the petition, and cruelty. So Singapore adopted the classic fault-based approach towards divorce, usually but not always adopting the equivalent English statute as its template.

Growing dissatisfaction with the existing law, and law reform taking place in other countries, led to Singapore liberalizing its divorce laws in 1980. This was done by replacing the fault-based approach and making irretrievable breakdown the sole ground for divorce.

Current divorce law in Singapore

The sole ground for divorce for non-Muslim marriages

Under the current Women's Charter, divorce for non-Muslims is permissible under Singapore law on the sole ground that a court is satisfied that a marriage has irretrievably broken down. If the parties are Muslims or have been married under Muslim law, they are not permitted to apply for a divorce from the Family Courts, but must apply to the religious Shariah court.

A minimum period is usually required before a divorce petition may be filed. Consequently, under s. 94(1), divorce petitions are not usually allowed to be filed unless three years have passed since the date of the marriage and the filing of the petition. However, the court will allow a writ for divorce to be filed before three years have passed if the case is one of exceptional hardship suffered by the plaintiff or there is exceptional depravity on the part of the respondent under s. 94(2). Section 94(3) provides that in determining whether to grant leave to present a petition before the expiration of three years, the court shall have regard to the interests of any children of the marriage and to the question of whether there is a possibility of reconciliation between the parties. The Singapore courts would usually follow English judicial precedents in their interpretation of exceptional hardship and exceptional depravity. These cases, such as *Fay v Fay* [1982] AC 835, suggest that the facts would have to be extraordinary and unusual, and there must be evidence of ill-health, or of nervous sensitivity or tension resulting in severe emotional mental stress or breakdown. There should also be evidence of the particular circumstances which have been alleged constitute the exceptional character of the hardship suffered. The court can also take into account past and present hardship and the 'hardship arising from having to wait until the specified period has elapsed' (as indicated by Ormrod LJ in *C v C* [1980] Fam 23 at 28).

This provision no longer exists in the equivalent English legislation, as the English Law Commission believed that such a provision caused bitterness and humiliation and recommended its abolition. Their solution was to recommend a one-year bar which was taken up by the British Parliament and remains the current law in England.

Five facts evidencing irretrievable breakdown under Singapore divorce law

Section 95 of the Women's Charter sets out five facts, the establishment of which may entitle the court to infer that the marriage has irretrievably broken down. These are:

- that the respondent has committed adultery, and the petitioner finds it intolerable to live with the respondent;

- that the respondent has behaved in such a way that the petitioner cannot reasonably be expected to live with the respondent;
- that the respondent has deserted the petitioner for a continuous period of at least two years immediately preceding the filing of the writ;
- that the parties to the marriage have lived apart for a continuous period of at least three years immediately preceding the filing of the writ and the respondent consents to a judgment being granted;
- that the parties to the marriage have lived apart for a continuous period of at least four years immediately preceding the filing of the writ.

If none of the facts can be established, then, strictly speaking, the court cannot grant a divorce even if the marriage is clearly at an end (*Richards* [1972] 3 All ER 695 and *Stringfellow* [1976] 2 All ER 539). However, the establishment of just one of the facts means the court must grant a decree, unless it would not be just and reasonable to do so (s. 95(2) Women's Charter). Indeed, as Leong Wai Kum has pointed out, 'in the vast majority of divorce suits brought in Singapore, the courts act solely upon allegations and evidence that one side presents to it' (Leong, 1990, p. 217) and, in reality, Singapore practically has 'divorce by mutual consent of the parties' (Leong, 1990, p. 217). Consequently, cases which do reach the courts focus on the allocation of matrimonial property upon divorce and on post-divorce custody and access arrangements for the children, very much as currently occurs in England and Wales.

The fault element in Singapore divorce law

In accordance with the fault-based approach to divorce under the Women's Charter the petitioning spouse must also be free from moral blame in order to be granted a divorce. Hence, a petition based on adultery would be dismissed if the respondent had been an accessory to, or connived at, or condoned the adultery (s. 86(2)(b)) or was guilty of wilful neglect or misconduct conducing the adultery (s. 86(2)(iv)). The petition would also be dismissed if the petitioner had committed any matrimonial offence himself or herself such as adultery, cruelty towards the other spouse, desertion or separation without reasonable excuse (s. 86(2)).

In 1941, the ground of incurable insanity was introduced and in 1967 living apart for seven years was also introduced as a ground but they had little impact, in view of the stringent requirements which had to be proved (Chan, 2008, p. 93).

Application of divorce law in Singapore: 1984–2003

Chan's survey of the way in which Singaporean and English couples utilized their divorce law over a 20-year period between 1984 and 2003 is an illuminating exercise in comparative law. Here are some of the findings from her analysis:

    (i)   Singapore's crude divorce rate is low compared with other more developed countries in Europe, Oceania as well as within Asia, but it has, in common with many countries around the world, seen a spectacular rise in the number of marriages ending in divorce.

(ii)   For Muslim divorces, there was an increase of 210 per cent between 1980 and 2000.

(iii)   Three periods in which non-Muslim divorces increased coincided with administrative changes which appeared to facilitate the procurement of divorces. The first period spans 1990 to 1991, reforms included extended court hours and the introduction of pre-trial conferences in civil cases reduced waiting times for the disposal of new divorce cases; the second spans 1995 to 1998 which coincides with the setting up of the specialized Family Court in Singapore on 1 March 1995 (waiting time was also cut for the Family Court); the third period of increase in 2002 (of 14.8 per cent) coincides with the changes in the income criteria for those eligible for legal aid in 2001.

(iv)   A study of statistics over this 20-year period suggests that reliance on desertion and adultery has decreased over the years. Living apart is the most common ground, reaching a high in 1991 but this has undergone a downward trend since 1995. However, the ground of unreasonable behaviour has increased over the years, surpassing living apart in 2003. The percentage of divorces granted on allegations of fault exceeded those relying on the non-fault based fact of living apart for the first time in 1999. These statistics are in line with the experience in England where a majority (71 per cent) of petitions in 1985 relied on allegations of fault and the allegation of unreasonable behaviour was also the most common (40 per cent). The rapid decline in adultery and desertion in divorce petitions also occurred in England in the late 1980s.

(v)   Husbands preferred to rely on the non-fault based fact of living apart in their petitions (64.6 per cent between 1990 and 2003) with unreasonable behaviour being only 24.1 per cent. Wives were more inclined to cite unreasonable behaviour than husbands. On the other hand, adultery was as likely to be cited by husbands as by wives in their petitions between 1990 and 2003. In England, the tendency has been for adultery to be more frequently relied upon by husbands than by wives in the period between 1976 and 1986.

(vi)   There is a correlation between divorce and early marriages; those who marry at a young age are over-represented in the divorce statistics (see e.g. Monahan (1953); Gibson (1974); Leete (1979); Bumpas, Martin and Sweet (1991); and for Singapore, see Tan (1977) and *Subordinate Courts of Singapore* (2003) Research Bulletin No. 31) This is a common phenomenon in most jurisdictions but in Singapore this trend was overtaken, between 1984 to 2003, by a shift towards divorce by older couples.

(vii)   Research studies indicate that divorce is most likely to occur when a couple is in their mid-life with teenage children, with this being the lowest point of marital satisfaction and in Singapore divorce is most likely to occur for husbands aged between 30 to 44 and for wives aged between 25 and 39. For both husbands and wives, the shift towards divorce by older couples has, in keeping with worldwide trends (Bair, 2007) increased in recent years compared with previous decades (Chan, 2008, p. 108). Bair suggests that this is a worldwide phenomenon which occurs because people are living longer, with healthier lifestyles and have more disposable income (Bair, 2007). This is obviously only applicable to countries whose populations exhibit these traits.

(viii) The duration of marriages in Singapore also confirms the shift towards divorce taking place among older couples. Chan offers three possible explanations for this: first, the existence of the three-year time bar in Singapore before a divorce can be presented would dampen divorce rates; second, government policy requires couples who jointly purchase public housing to occupy it for at least five years before selling it (it would be surrendered to the government for a loss if the five year period is not fulfilled); third, Singaporeans, living in an Asian society, may have greater tolerance for the difficulties in their marriages than their Western counterparts (Chan, 2008, p. 109).

Matrimonial property

The basis of the law relating to the division of marital property in Singapore is the English common law but this has been overtaken from time to time by legislation, primarily the Women's Charter. Thus, in 1981, the Women's Charter gave Singapore courts the power to adjust property rights upon dissolution of a marriage. This power, contained in s. 100, which became s. 106 in the revised edition of the statute, was derived from a Kenyan report submitted in 1968 which was the source of identical Malaysian legislation. In 1993, Leong Wai Kum reported that 12 years after its enactment, the norm appeared to range from 35 per cent to 45 per cent of the matrimonial assets being awarded to the spouse who was full-time homemaker and child carer, but in 2000 she observed that the homemaker and child carer who was also in employment could get 50 per cent of the matrimonial assets (Leong, 1993, 2000).

In 1996, the provision was revised further to state '[t]he court shall have power ... to order the division between the parties of any matrimonial asset ... in such proportions as the court thinks just and equitable'. The provision (now s. 112) lists seven guidelines, which are not exhaustive, for the court to consider when it decides to exercise its powers under this section, namely: (a) the extent of the contributions made by each party in money, property or work towards acquiring, improving or maintaining the matrimonial assets; (b) any debt owing or obligation incurred or undertaken by either party for their joint benefit or for the benefit of any child of the marriage; (c) the needs of the children (if any) of the marriage;

(d) the extent of the contributions made by each party to the welfare of the family, including looking after the home or caring for the family or any aged or infirm relative or dependant of either party; (e) any agreement between the parties with respect to the ownership and division of the matrimonial assets in contemplation of divorce; (f) any period of rent-free occupation or other benefit enjoyed by one party in the matrimonial home to the exclusion of the other party; (g) the giving of assistance or support by one party to the other party (whether or not of a material kind), including the giving of assistance or support which aids the other party in the carrying on of his or her occupation or business; (h) the matters referred to in s. 114 so far as they are relevant.

The Singapore equivalent of s. 25 of the Matrimonial Causes Act 1973 – comparative perspectives

Section 114, the Singapore equivalent of s. 25 of the English Matrimonial Causes Act 1973, lists factors the court should take into account when it is determining the amount of maintenance to be paid, including: the income, earning capacity, property and other financial resources which each of the parties to the marriage has or is likely to have in the foreseeable future; financial needs, obligations and responsibilities which each of the parties has or is likely to have in the foreseeable future; the standard of living enjoyed by the family before the breakdown of the marriage; the age of each party to the marriage and the duration of the marriage; any physical or mental disability of either of the parties to the marriage; the value to either of the parties to the marriage of any benefit (for example, a pension) which, by reason of the dissolution or annulment of the marriage that party will lose the chance of acquiring. Section 114 then contains the form of words of an earlier version of s. 25 of the Matrimonial Causes Act 1973 which, having regard to the parties' conduct, sought to place them in the position they would have been if the marriage had not broken down and the parties had discharged their financial obligations and responsibilities towards each other. This was known as the minimal loss principle and was repealed by the British Parliament, with conduct placed as one of the factors which the court should consider if it was conduct which it would be 'inequitable' for the court to disregard. English courts no longer seek to place the parties in the position they would have been in had the relationship not broken down but at least on paper, and ex facie, Singapore courts would be expected to do so.

Giving weight to non-financial contributions

Singapore courts have always given credit for homemaking and childcare in the context of the division of matrimonial assets upon divorce, as the cases of *Shirley Khoo v Kenneth Mok Kong Chua* [1989] 2 MLJ 264 and especially *Ng Hwee Keng v Chia Soon Hin William* [1995] 2 SLR 231 and *Chan Yong Keay v Yeo Mei Ling* [1994] 2 SLR 541 illustrate. There have been the odd exceptions but, by and large, the courts have interpreted fairness in division of marital assets as representing marriage to be an 'equal partnership of efforts' (Leong, 2002, p. 190). In *Yah Cheng Huat v Ong Bee Lan* (1995, Div Pet. 1147/1995, unreported), a case where the marriage lasted 21 years, and a spouse who was homemaker and carer also worked and contributed financially to the family, the court was content to divide the proceeds of the parties' former matrimonial home equally. Prakash J declared that when the marriage was good, the parties worked together and accumulated their assets jointly without drawing any distinction between them. Once it had broken down, without any way of determining who earned what share of the assets, 'the fair division of the home would be to divide it equally between the parties' (see Leong, 2002, p. 391).

Conduct in maintenance awards

When considering conduct as relevant in awarding maintenance and the division of matrimonial assets, the courts have generally ignored allegations of impropriety, as in cases like *Tan Bee Giok v Loh Kum Yong* [1997] 1 SLR 155 and *Yip Mei Ling Agnes v Tan Thiam Chye* [2003] SGDC 99.

Children

General introduction

As with other jurisdictions, the best interests principle ('courts will endeavour to reach a decision in the best interests of the child') has become the guiding principle for state courts in many parts of Asia and Africa.

Paramount consideration to be welfare of the child

Where the court is determining who should have custody of the child, s. 125 of the Singaporean Women's Charter states: '[T]he paramount consideration shall be the welfare of the child, and subject to this, the court shall have regard (a) to the wishes of the parent of the child; and (b) to the wishes of the child, where she is of an age to express an independent opinion.'

Clearly, para. (b) is the statutory enshrinement of the *Gillick* principle (see *Gillick v West Norfolk and Wisbech Area Health Authority* [1985] 3 All ER 402 (HL)) by the Singapore Parliament whereby, in its equivalent statutory form in the Children Act 1989 (UK), a child who possesses 'sufficient age and understanding', something the court would have to determine in individual cases, has several rights to make up his own mind whether to agree to certain procedures. These include the right to refuse medical or psychiatric assessment under s. 43(8), and the *Gillick* principle has been extended to matters such as the child's right to choose their own solicitor. However, the English courts have stopped short of allowing a child the right to die, particularly in cases where the child is suffering from a psychotic and psychological illness; and in situations where the child has refused life-saving treatment or their parents have objected to life-saving blood transfusions. In these cases, the child has no right to refuse life-saving medical treatment despite the *Gillick* principle. It remains to be seen whether the Singapore courts would follow suit and restrict the application of the *Gillick* principle, as well.

=> parent/child relationship in Singapore more equal/ circle => may allow right to die.

The Maintenance of Parents statute

A fairly novel Singapore statute involving parents and children is the Maintenance of Parents Act 1995 (Cap. 167B), revised in 1996. In keeping with Confucian ideology, this statute is: 'An Act to make provision for the maintenance of parents by their children and for matters connected therewith.' This statute is intended to give persons domiciled in Singapore, aged 60 or above, the right to obtain maintenance from their children. Section 3 allows any person who is unable to maintain himself adequately to apply to court for maintenance from any or all of his or her children. 'Child' is defined in s. 2 to include an illegitimate, adopted or stepchild. Under s. 3(4) a parent is unable to maintain himself or herself if their total or expected income and other financial resources are inadequate to provide them with basic amenities and basic physical needs including but not limited to shelter, food and clothing.

Even in cases where a person is below the minimum stipulated age of 60, this Act shall apply to that person if the Tribunal is satisfied that he or she is suffering from infirmity of mind or body which prevents them from maintaining themselves, or makes it difficult to do so, or that there is some other special reason. This clearly allows the Tribunal some discretion in deciding whether to order that one or more of that person's children pay them a monthly allowance or any other periodical payment or a lump sum for their maintenance.

An applicant does not have to seek maintenance from all of his or her children.

In the light of Singapore's British colonial heritage and antecedents and Westernized lifestyle and the strong influence of English law and culture, this is prima facie a revolutionary statute in Singapore's family law. However, it must be remembered that Singapore is a unique mixture of Western and Eastern culture and ideology. Hence, although it developed initially as a British outpost in the Far East, the bulk of its population are Chinese who form about 85 per cent of the population and who practise a variety of religions, including Buddhism. The main religions, co-existing in an atmosphere of religious tolerance, are Buddhism, Judaism and Christianity. Singapore has a relatively young population, enjoying a high standard of living, with its Confucian roots never having been fully homogenized into a pseudo-Western culture or ideology. Filial piety has therefore remained an extremely strong characteristic which, even early on in its history, had built up a strong network of extended families. When one bears in mind the smallness of the island, and the geographical proximity of families even for those who marry and move out of the original family home, the closeness of family ties is much more

[handwritten margin notes:]
= children are part of not family of western family structure
impact of children
= child maintenance of parents

understandable. Weekend outings often include parents, grandparents, aunts and uncles, so that despite individual religious practices and beliefs, restaurants, food centres and shopping centres are generally child-friendly and much more geared to families than in Britain, Europe or the United States. The extended family is very much alive in Singaporean society, though not as widespread as in past decades.

Given these factors, an Act which requires children to maintain their parents would not be regarded as radical as it might first appear. Claims would not be made unless the parent was unable to maintain themselves through age or infirmity and the offspring were clearly able to provide financial support which was superior to that of the parent.

Concluding comparative perspectives

Recurrent themes

Several recurrent themes emerge from our study of these Asian and African jurisdictions. They range from the notion of the arranged marriage; the extended families who played an active part and, in some cases still play an active role in the formation and dissolution of the marriage; the brideprice; the status of the secondary wife or wives and the concubine in cases of intestate succession; and the quest by women for equality with men and increased recognition of their inherent worth as women, a movement which has been taking place for several years. Both regions have, in some measure, received foreign law through colonization and most countries have regained independence resulting in an inevitable impact on their customary and statutory laws.

African law and African marriage practices

We have seen how African law is sui generis, and that the African conception of law is essentially different from European law. We have also examined African law separately from South African law, because of its particularly unusual mixed legal heritage. We have observed how individualism has grown apace for young potential bridegrooms in many of the regions of Africa, so that they are far more independent than ever before. Their ability to pay the necessary brideprice out of their own earnings has given them independence from their kinfolk and they have gained the power to make a cash payment in lieu of any obligation to live with the wife's family for a trial period or to perform services to gain the bride. However, even in modern times, Nhlapo confirms that marriage still involves entire families (or clans) of the intending spouses (Nhlapo, 1989, p. 16). Indeed, in cases where child-betrothal still occurs, the arrangement is entered into because of the need to merge or strengthen the ties between two families rather than because of the interests of the married couple (Nhlapo, 1989, p. 16). Hence, the couple marries into not only immediate families but a network of traditionally large extended families, with the network extending much further than in typical European familial networks.

The marital power of the African husband over his wife remains considerable, even in the twenty-first century, especially in regions where only customary law still applies, under which a husband's marital powers over his wife cannot be excluded by prenuptial contract. The husband retains the ultimate right to decide matters pertaining to the person and property of his wife. He has the final say on her clothes, associates, whether she may seek employment, and even whether she may consult a doctor. It also includes the right to administer corporal punishment, and this would certainly breach the non-discrimination and personal dignity provisions of the African Charter when it comes into force (Nhlapo, 1989, p. 16).

Singapore law, divorce and fault

As Leong notes, there is 'substantial similarity' between the marriage laws of England and Singapore, which is unsurprising since Singapore received English law in 1826 via the Second Charter of Justice. However, this reception only extended to the common law of marriage in England becoming part of the basic law of Singapore, as the Marriage Act of 1823 was not received because of its provisions which were incompatible with local (English) parish structures (Leong, 2000, p. 257). On the question of trends in divorce, as far as countries like Singapore are concerned, the trend in divorce petitions 'shows a continued reliance on allegations of fault on the part of the respondent' (Chan, 2008, p. 115), which is also the trend observed in England, Canada, and Australia. Chan surmises that the reasons for this trend could be because of a genuine belief that divorce is unacceptable unless the other party to the marriage is to blame for the marital breakdown, a misconception that an advantage might be gained in ancillary proceedings if one is innocent, or because the parties did not wish to delay their divorce by living apart for the requisite period of time (Chan, 2008, p. 115).

Legal transplants

On the issue of legal transplants, there is little doubt that the influence of the British in parts of Africa and Asia has led to a reception of foreign law but only to the extent that a Western-based form of marriage and the Western-derived rules which govern that form of marriage co-exist in parts of Africa and in parts of Asia such as Hong Kong, India and Singapore. As far as the law relating to children is concerned, the best interests test has made its appearance in one form or another but does not carry much significance where the cultural and social structure of a particular community retains its strong patriarchal bias and where any disputes involving children are not taken to Western law-based tribunals for resolution.

Further reading

Allott, A *Essays in African Law*, 1960, Butterworths.

Allott, A 'The Future of African Law' in Kuper and Kuper (eds) *African Law: Adaptation and Development*, 1965, University of California Press.

Allott, A 'African Law' in Derrett (ed) *An Introduction to Legal Systems*, 1968, Sweet & Maxwell.

Anderson, JND (ed) *Family Law in Asia and Africa*, 1968, Allen & Unwin.

Armstrong, A, Beyani, C, Himonga, C, Kabeberi-Macharia, J, Molokomme, A, Ncube, W, Nhlapo, T, Rwesaura, Stewart, J 'Uncovering Reality: Excavating Women's Rights in African Family Law' (1993) 7 Int Jnl of Law, Policy and Family Law 314.

Bartholomew, GW 'English Law in Partibus Orientalium' in Harding (ed) *The Common Law in Singapore and Malaysia*, 1985, Butterworths, pp. 3ff.

Bohler, N 'Equality Courts: Introducing the Possibility of Listening to Different Voices in South Africa' (2000) 63 THRHR 288.

Bonthuys, E 'The Best Interests of Children in the South African Constitution' (2006) 20 Int Jnl of Law, Policy and Family Law 23.

Chan, Wing-Cheong 'Trends in Non-Muslim Divorces in Singapore' (2008) 22 Int Jnl of Law, Policy and Family Law 91.

Chanock, M 'Neither Customary nor Legal: African Customary Law in an Era of Family Law Reform' (1989) 3 Int Jnl of Law, Policy and Family Law 72.

Cotran, E 'The Changing Nature of African Marriage' in Anderson (ed) *Family Law in Asia and Africa*, 1968, Sweet & Maxwell.

de Cruz, P 'Maintenance, Marital Property and Legislative Innovation' in Bainham (ed) *The International Survey of Family Law*, 1996, pp. 401ff.

de Cruz, P 'Legal Transplants: Principles and Pragmatism in Comparative Family Law' in Harding and Orucu (eds) *Comparative Law in the 21st Century*, 2001, Kluwer, pp. 101ff.

Freedman, M 'Chinese Family Law of Singapore: The Rout of Custom' in Anderson (ed) *Family Law in Asia and Africa*, 1968, Allen & Unwin.

Fishbayn, L 'Litigating the Right to Culture: Family Law in the New South Africa' (1999) 13 Int Jnl of Law, Policy and Family Law 147.

Goldblatt, B 'Case Note: Same-Sex Marriage in South Africa – The Constitutional Court's Judgment' (2006) 14 *Feminist Legal Studies* 261.

Goonesekere, S 'The Best Interests of the Child: A South Asian Perspective' (1994) 8 Int Jnl of Law, Policy and Family Law 117.

Herbst, M and du Plessis, W 'Customary Law v Common Law Marriages: A Hybrid Approach in South Africa' (2008) 12 EJCL at http://www.ejcl.org/121/art121-28.pdf.

Hinz, MO 'Family Law in Namibia: The Challenge of Customary and Constitutional Law' in Eekelaar and Nhlapo (eds) *The Changing Family. Family Forms and Family Law*, Hart, 1998, p. 139.

Knoetze, E 'Emancipation of the African Woman: Fact or Fallacy?' in Dewar and Parker (eds) *Family Law: Processes, Pressures and Practices'*, 2003, Hart, pp. 491ff.

Leong Wai Kum 'Common Law and Chinese Marriage Custom in Singapore' in Harding (ed) *The Common Law in Singapore and Malaysia*, 1985, Butterworths pp. 177ff.

Leong Wai Kum 'Formation of Marriage in England and Singapore by Contract: Void Marriage and Non-marriage' (2000) 14 Int Jnl of Law, Policy and the Family 256.

Leong Wai Kum 'Singapore – Supporting Marriage Through Description as an Equal

Partnership of Efforts' in Bainham (ed) *The International Survey of Family Law*, 2002, pp. 379ff.

Liu, Athena AC *Family Law for the Hong Kong SAR*, 1999, Hong Kong University Press.

Malhotra, A and Malhotra, R 'Some Perspectives on Indian Family Law' in Bainham (ed) *The International Survey of Family Law*, 2001, pp. 115ff.

Malhotra, A and Malhotra, R 'Hindu Law and Uniform Civil Code – The Indian Experience' Part I in Bainham (ed) *The International Survey of Family Law*, 2007, pp. 101ff.

Menski, W 'African Laws: The Search for Law', in *Comparative Law in a Global Context. The Legal Systems of Asia and Africa*, 2006, Cambridge UP, Ch. 6.

Mnookin, RH 'Child Custody Adjudication: Judicial Function in the Face of Indeterminacy' (1975) 39 *Law and Contemporary Problems* 225.

Morolong, S 'Overview of Recent Developments in the Law of Marriage in Botswana' in Bainham (ed) *The International Survey of Family Law*, 2002, pp. 67ff.

Murdoch, GP 'The Universality of the Nuclear Family' in Bell and Vogel (eds) *A Modern Introduction to the Family*, 1960, Routledge, p. 37.

Nhlapo, RT 'International Protection of Human Rights and the Family: African Variations on a Common Theme' (1989) 13 Int Jnl of Law, Policy and the Family 1.

Nyamu-Musembi, C 'Sitting on Her Husband's Back with Her Hands in his Pockets': Commentary on Judicial Decision-Making in Marital Property Cases in Kenya' in Bainham (ed) *The International Survey of Family Law*, 2002, pp. 229ff.

Ong, DSL 'The Singapore Family Court: Family Law in Practice' (1999) 13 Int Jnl of Law, Policy and the Family 328.

Pieterse, M 'The Promotion of Equality and Prevention of Discrimination Act 4 of 2000: Final Nail in the Customary Law Coffin' (2000) 117 SALJ 627.

Phillips, A (ed) *Survey of African Marriage and Family Life*, 1953, Oxford UP.

Phillips, A *Marriage Laws in Africa*, 1971, Oxford UP.

Radcliffe-Brown (ed) *An Introduction to African Systems of Kinship and Marriage* 1950, Oxford UP.

Rwezaura, B 'Law, Culture and Children's Rights in Eastern and Southern Africa' in Ncube (ed) *Law, Culture, Tradition and Children's Rights in Eastern and Southern Africa*, 1998, Dartmouth.

Rwezaura, B and Ho, R 'Hong Kong Family Law: Moving Forward with its plural heritage' in Bainham (ed) *The International Survey of Family Law*, 2002, pp. 181ff.

Sinclair, J 'South Africa – Ebb and Flow: The Retreat of the Legislature and the Development of a Constitutional Jurisprudence to Reshape Family Law' in Bainham (ed) *The International Survey of Family Law*, 2002, pp. 393ff.

Sloth-Nielson, J and van Heerden, B 'The Constitutional Family: Developments in South African Family Law Jurisprudence under the 1996 Constitution' (2003) 17 Int Jnl of Law, Policy and the Family 121.

Teshome, T 'Reflections on the Revised Family Code of 2000' in Bainham (ed) *The International Survey of Family Law*, 2002, pp. 153ff.

van der Merwe, CG and du Plessis, JE (eds) *Introduction to the Law of South Africa*, 2004, Kluwer Law International.

Zoke, ENU 'Developments in Nigerian Family Law: 1991–1997' in Bainham (ed) *The International Survey of Family Law*, 2000, pp. 325ff.

Chapter 5

Family law in the Russian Federation

Introduction

Before we look at the progress of family law in the Russian Federation from the mid-1990s to the early 2000s, it is instructive to bear in mind a few salient background features about the Russian Federation as it exists in the early twenty-first century. Since the collapse of the old Soviet Union in 1990–1, and the consequent disintegration of the old Soviet Socialist Republics into a Commonwealth of Independent States, Russia has evolved into a country of contradictions. On the one hand, it retains its general sources of law which lie in several codes that provide detailed enactments on a range of topics most closely associated with civil law countries. These codes cover civil law and procedure, criminal law and criminal procedure, family law and a host of other areas of law. There was also an old Russian Constitution that was superseded in 1993 by a new Constitution which, at least in its explicit terms, seeks to turn Russia into a democratic socialist state. On the other hand, although 74 years of state control have not been easy to shrug off, Russia has gone from a country racked by rampant inflation to one that is currently enjoying economic success and whose oil reserves have played a significant part in achieving considerable wealth and economic stability. Alongside these developments, Russia has also become far more capitalist in its outlook, at least in a strata of its society which has begun to trade and bargain on an international scale and to make optimum use of scarce resources.

As leading Russian commentators (Antokolskaia, 2000, 2001; Khazova, 2001) report, the result of the major political changes in Russia has been a comprehensive revision of the whole of the private law field, and adoption of a new Constitution. In 1995, part of this revision process included the adoption of a new Russian Family Code, adopted by the Russian Parliament in December 1995 and which came into force on 1 March 1996.

Historical background

The family in Soviet and Russian society

The family was seen by the communists as a 'bourgeois manifestation and an economic and legal entity based on the inequality of the spouses and the dependence of the wife and children on the husband' (Butler, 2003, p. 419). The intention was thus to transform the family into an association based on the free will of its members. In the early post-revolutionary years, the way in which such a transformation was to be achieved was a subject of lively debate but by the mid 1930s, the family was once again viewed as a 'legal and economic entity, a core unit of present and future society' (Butler, 2003, p. 419) and this remained the view until the end of the Soviet era. The communists were anxious to establish the principle of equality between the spouses as soon as possible, and this is clearly manifested in the Family Code of 1918.

As Khazova points out, however laudable this was in theory, and enduring as the idea has been over three or four generations, the main reason for the drive for equality of the sexes was to enable women to participate in the labour market, to provide much-needed human resources to a country in economic meltdown. 'According to the new social order, everybody, irrespective of their sex, was supposed to work, and the right of a woman to claim maintenance from her husband only because of her status as a wife was abolished as a "bourgeois survival of the past".' 'Alimony was declared to be "not a charity"' (Khazova, 2002, p. 352). Quoting Gemkin, she emphasizes that 'the State could not allow one spouse to be a parasite at the expense of the other' (Gemkin, 1949, p. 440) since this would be incompatible with the proletarian philosophy. Hence, Khazova claims that Russia is the first country in the world to declare 'full equality between a man and a woman, to give women equal political and civil rights and to equalize them with their husbands in family relations' (Khazova, 2002, p. 354). But this equalization, which dates from the 1917 Revolution, meant that neither women nor society were prepared economically or psychologically for such equality, since 90 per cent of Russian families fitted the patriarchal model.

We shall return to this principle of sex equality when we discuss the 1995 Russian Family Code.

Civil marriage and divorce did not exist in pre-revolutionary Russia as the population was subject to the canon law or ecclesiastical rules of the religion to which they belonged. However, the Bolsheviks were keen to 'break the authority of the Church' and wanted to secularize marriage and divorce (Butler, 2003, p. 419). Civil marriage was therefore introduced in 1917 and since then legal validity was accorded only to civil solemnized marriages.

The 1918 Russian Family Code

In 1918, a year after the Revolution, the first Russian Family Code 1918 was adopted. These laws 'transferred the acts of civil status from the jurisdiction of the Church to that of the State, denied legal force to religious marriages and established that the only form of legal marriage was civil (secular) marriage' (Khazova, 1998, p. 73). They also simplified the conditions of marriage and abolished most of the obstacles to it. In 1918 irreversible breakdown was the only ground which entitled spouses to divorce but procedure was also simplified so that mutual consent between the spouses entitled them to divorce in the state agencies for the registration of civil status, known as the Department of Registration for Civil Acts. This effectively introduced divorce on demand. If one party did not consent to the divorce, the other could apply to the court for a divorce. Another significant legislative change was to remove the subordinate status of women so that they would be considered by law to be equal to men. However, the Code did not alter the matrimonial regime of separation of property. This was justified at the time, as motivated by the intention to protect women's rights, declare women independent and no longer subordinate to or dependent on their husbands. However, it was not fair to housewives who did not own property and had no personal earnings. The 1918 Code also abolished marriage contracts, which remained forbidden until the Russian Federation Civil Code was enacted in 1995.

Antokolskaia notes that by 1926, long-term cohabitation outside marriage had acquired 'virtually the same legal status as formal marriage' (Antokolskaia, 2000, p. 26). Johnson explains that the recognition of cohabitational unions outside marriage had a practical value (Johnson, 1969, p. 172). In the troubled era of the war, the Revolution and the Civil War, many men had disappeared and many unconventional unions were formed, so that in recognizing these unions as legal unions, the women became entitled to maintenance whenever she needed it and was unable to work, so both she and her children would have inheritance rights if the man died.

Further codifications

This system of recognition was preserved in the 1926 Code of Law governing Marriage, The Family and Guardianship, promulgated in that year. Divorce procedure was simplified again so that a party's mere unilateral intent was sufficient to terminate a marriage (Antokolskaia, 2000, p. 27). By the mid 1930s, the family appeared to regain its status as a permanent primary social, legal and economic entity which was worth preserving and this recognition continued until the end of the Soviet era (Butler, 2003, p. 419). However, Antokolskaia points out that by 1944 the legal recognition of forms of informal marriage was no longer practised. The main change introduced by the 1944 Edict, which came into force on 8 July 1944, was that only registered marriages were to be recognized as bestowing the status of husband and wife with their attendant matrimonial rights and duties (Johnson, 1969, p. 172). De Facto unions, or factual unions which had commenced before the law came into force, could be registered retrospectively. Divorce policy became more formalized and bureaucratic so that only a court could grant a divorce under the Edict and the courts were obliged to seek to reconcile the parties before granting a divorce. If reconciliation was not possible, the case would proceed to a new judicial hearing. No grounds for divorce were specified by the Edict, but the policy was to make divorce more difficult again. Hence, spouses had to present sufficient evidence of the irreversible breakdown of their marriage. In line with the state policy to preserve the stability of the family, the courts also had the power to dismiss a petition even if the parties both wished to have a divorce. Fees payable to the state for a divorce were increased considerably and by construing the evidence couples presented very narrowly, the courts effectively 'forced parties to separate and form a new sustained unregistered partnership, and possibly have children therefrom' (Butler, 2003, p. 422). This Code allowed de facto unions which had commenced before the law came into force to be registered with retrospective effect, but aside from rights acquired prior to July 1944 cohabitation outside marriage was not recognized. Judicial practice in relation to divorce was subsequently relaxed in the 1950s and in 1965 the Family Code was amended to vest decisions to grant divorces, maintenance and custody in the people's courts.

This law was replaced by the new Code entitled Basic Principles of Marriage and Family Law which came into force on 1 October 1968 and then the new Family Code of 1969 made divorce much more accessible. Irreversible breakdown was retained as the general ground for divorce but spouses were not required to present evidence of such breakdown and irreversible breakdown was presumed. The court, as under the 1918 Code, retained the power of dismissing a petition even if this was against the wishes of the parties (Antokolskaia, 2001, p. 28).

Unmarried cohabiting unions were again not recognized by the subsequent Code on Marriage and Family 1969. Johnson explains this was again for practical reasons. Once social conditions had stabilized, the liberal attitude towards these unions became a source of confusion and it became difficult to say when a de facto 'marriage' existed, which led to the eventual abandonment of such recognition (Johnson, 1969, p. 172). This position was preserved by the 1993 Russian Constitution with art. 38 declaring that 'motherhood and childhood shall be under the defence of the State' (see Butler, 2003, pp. 419–20).

The Code on Marriage and the Family 1969 of the Russian Federation was replaced on 1 March 1996 by the Family Code of the Russian Federation of 8 December 1995 which was amended 15 November 1997, 27 June 1998 and 2 January 2000.

As we can see, family law appears to be one of the most revised areas of legislation in Russia.

Marriage

The legal requirements for marriage (noted by Butler, 2003, p. 425) are:

    (i)   mutual agreement of the intending spouses;

    (ii)   spouses must be aged 18, which in exceptional circumstances may be reduced to 16 or 14;

    (iii) neither spouse must be already legally married;

    (iv) the spouses are not relatives in direct line of ascendance or descendance, full or half-brothers or sisters, or adoptive and adopted persons;

    (v)   neither spouse must lack dispositive legal capacity as a consequence of mental disturbance as determined by a court.

Divorce: disappearances, postcards and the influence of in-laws

An examination of the Soviet laws relating to some of the procedures and grounds for divorce provides a revealing insight into Soviet society and Soviet families and divorce and nullity procedure (see Johnson, 1969). For example, a marriage was mistakenly recorded as having taken place where the official mistook a witness or a friend to be one of the parties wishing to be married; and the register also showed that the intended bridegroom was married to the bridesmaid in the course of the ceremony rather than to the intended wife. This was later regarded as a 'non-existent marriage' in view of the absence of consent and rather than institute proceedings for a decree of nullity, administrative proceedings were instituted to have the entry on the register cancelled.

Another illuminating instance is the case of the spouse who disappeared without trace. If a spouse disappears and is not heard of again for a considerable period, a procedure exists whereby the law could pronounce that the missing spouse was missing, presumed dead. Such a pronouncement, in the form of a decree, would have the legal effect of activating measures for securing that person's property and allowing payments to be made out of it for the benefit of those whom he had a duty to support (Johnson, 1969, p. 182). However, such a decree did not dissolve a marriage but would give the resident spouse a ground for divorce. After such a divorce was obtained, then either spouse would be free to remarry. Once a person was declared missing, further proceedings could be taken to have them presumed dead; or independent proceedings could be taken for a presumption of death to be declared. It is worth noting that once a presumption of death had been made, this was sufficient to dissolve the marriage even thought that person was later found to be still alive. Hence, a man who reappeared after he was presumed dead could not contest the validity of the second marriage his ex-wife might have contracted. In these circumstances, if the wife had contracted the second marriage only in the belief that her first husband was dead, and she now wishes to resume conjugal relations with her first husband, this was sufficient ground for bringing divorce proceedings against the second husband to enable her to remarry her first husband. The courts have decided that in these distressing circumstances, it was up to the woman to decide which husband she wished to live with (Johnson, 1969, p. 182). However, in terms of legal validity, if the woman preferred to live with her first husband, the first marriage was no longer valid, which meant that she had to divorce her second husband and enter into a marriage ceremony with her first husband if she wished to be legally married (Johnson, 1969, p. 182).

'Postcard divorces' were also permissible until the Code of 1918. In order to obtain a divorce, a party simply had to go the Civil Status Registry and announce that he wished to terminate the marriage, giving the necessary details of the union. For a nominal fee, the other spouse was then sent a postcard by the Registry informing her that the marriage had been dissolved and that she had a right to apply to a People's Court (a local/regional court) for the settlement of any dispute over the children and maintenance (Johnson, 1969, p. 178). Postcard divorces were abolished in June 1936, after which both parties were required to attend at the Registry and the fees were raised considerably. This brought about a sharp reduction in the divorce rate but the principle remained that it was possible to obtain a divorce if you could afford to purchase one.

Finally, it appears that in-laws and relatives were responsible for the break-up of some marriages. For instance, in the late 1960s, while 96 per cent of divorces were granted, the 4 per cent which were refused included cases where the court came to the conclusion that the trouble between the spouses arose mainly because of interference by their relatives. In these circumstances, the court considered whether the source of trouble between the spouses was really attributable to disputes between wife and mother-in-law or husband and mother-in-law. If this were found to be the case, the court would refuse a divorce in order to enable the couple every opportunity to save the marriage by administering an admonition to the relatives in question to allow the couple to live their lives without interference from them.

The 1995 Russian Family Code

In an attempt to bring Russian family law in line with the situation in the early 1990s, a time of immense political, social and economic changes, the Russian Family Code 1995 was adopted. There was the new Russian Federation Constitution 1993, the new Civil Code 1994, and the United Nations Convention on the Rights of the Child and the 'new' Russia was seeking to promote the ideas of freedom and values associated with perestroika (Khazova, 2002, p. 347). However it was never intended to be truly revolutionary and was formulated with conservatism in mind, and a return to more traditional norms was the underlying rationale.

In general terms, the Russian Family Code 1995, with its eight parts and 170 sections (articles) is, as Khazova puts it, an 'attempt to enlarge citizens' rights in family relations and to increase the number of dispositive rules' with the legislator seeking to 'extend the limit of permissive options in the field of family law, reducing the number of imperative rules'. It concerns 'different aspects of family relations; property relations between the spouses while the marriage lasts and after its dissolution, divorce procedure' (Khazova, 1998, p. 76).

However, the intention was to preserve those positive family law provisions which were accumulated during the Soviet era, which included progressive features (such as equality of spouses, equality of all children, whether marital or non-marital, and no-fault divorce) which were all introduced between 1917 and 1918. Indeed, as Butler wrote in 1998, there were 'surprisingly few changes' to the Family Code in the post-Soviet era (Butler, 1998, p. xxii).

The Code reiterates the constitutional provision that the family is under State protection and 'enlarges the formula to include fatherhood' (Butler, 2003, p. 423). The Code no longer makes ideological references to the 'communist' family and the new Code seeks to minimize state intervention in the private lives of spouses as much as possible. It aims to 'strengthen the family, structure family relations on feelings of mutual love and respect' (Butler, 2003 p. 423).

The principles guiding family policy include the 'voluntariness of the marriage union of man and woman, the equality of the rights of spouses ... the settlement of intra-family questions by mutual consent, [and] the priority of family nurturing of children' (Butler, 2003, p. 423). Butler argues that although the latest Code has omitted ideological components, 'in substance' there is unlikely to be any changes in the equality of spouses since this simply reinforces the previous position whereby each Russian citizen has the right to choose his or her own surname, occupation, profession, and place of residence and the mutual requirement of mutual consent to resolve intra-familial issues maintains the existing position (Butler, 2003, p. 423).

It might look as if this Code is wholly supportive of maintaining the marriage relationship but further reading gives a different impression. Indeed, under art. 22 of the 1995 Family Code, the court should 'dissolve the marriage without disclosing the reasons for divorce'. As Antokolskaia emphasizes, this article also makes it clear that 'a judge can no longer suspend divorce, refuse to grant it, or even examine the motivation for divorce' and the courts now only have the jurisdiction to hear cases in two limited instances: if there are minor children involved; and where there is no mutual consent to a divorce (Antokolskaia, 2000, p. 28).

Thus, in the first case, even where both spouses agree to divorce, a court hearing is still required if minor children are involved. As with the law in England and Wales, the court has to approve any arrangements involving minor children.

The second case is where one of the spouses wishes the marriage to continue. Under art. 22, 'marriage has to be dissolved if it is proven that further family life of the spouses is not possible', hence if one spouse is objecting to the divorce the court will require proof of the irreversible breakdown of marriage. The procedure, however, does not require spouses to reveal why they either support or oppose the divorce and if the spouses refuse to discuss their private life in court, the court's only option under art. 22(2) is to postpone the divorce for up to three months in order to give the couple the opportunity to be reconciled. When this period has expired, the court is obliged to dissolve the marriage if one spouse is still requesting a divorce. Antokolskaia regards the liberalization of the divorce law as an indication that the state has decided that it wishes to reduce intervention in the private lives of spouses as much as possible and that it should be left to the spouses to decide for themselves if there were reasons which they regarded as sufficient for them to be divorced (Antokolskaia, 2000, p. 28).

Antokolskaia also highlights the five main areas covered by the Family Code 1995: (i) marriage and divorce law; (ii) marital property; (iii) paternity determination; (iv) parental rights; and (v) minors' rights. Topics under (iii), (iv) and (v) are discussed at pp. 215, 217 and 218, respectively.

Marriage and divorce law

The 1995 Family Code did not make any changes to the area of marriage and divorce law. Hence, cohabitants do not acquire any spousal rights on separation, in terms of property division, alimony or inheritance. Indeed, according to art. 244(3) of the Civil Code, cohabitants 'cannot unilaterally elect to hold their property as community property' (Antokolskaia, 2000, p. 27). Further, marriage for persons of the same sex is not available and this rule prevents informal same-sex unions from being accorded marital status and leading commentators like Antokolskaia believe this is not expected to change in the foreseeable future. The age at which a couple can marry has been changed so that they must be at or above the age of majority. Although this is officially 18, authorized state bodies can reduce the age to 16 in special circumstances. Marriageable age was the subject of considerable debate in the Russian Parliament and eventually the wording of the relevant provision allowed regional legislation to specify special circumstances which would justify lowering the age to 16. There is no lower limit and, somewhat surprisingly, less than a year after the Code's enactment, the central regions of the Russian Federation, including Moscow, passed laws permitting marriage to take place from the age of 14 if the bride was pregnant or she had already given birth to a child. This was unexpected because the southern and Asian regions might have been expected to have passed such laws.

Another case where the 'special circumstances' rule was utilized was in the context of the formal requirements for a legal marriage to take place. Under the new Code, there is, for the first time, no need for any waiting period to take place before a marriage ceremony can take place. Hence, under art. 11(1) Pt 3, the ceremony can take place on the day an application is presented at a state agency for the registration of civil status. However, this is only permissible as an exceptional case in special circumstances, three of which are designated by the Code: (1) pregnancy of the bride; (2) birth of a child; and (3) threat to the life of one of the parties. The third exception has clearly been enacted in response to the events in Southern Russia, to the war in Chechnja in particular. But it also covers situations where there is a danger to a person's life, such as an imminent departure on a dangerous expedition or undergoing a risky surgical operation (Khazova, 1998, p. 83).

Questions have also arisen in connection with same-sex couples and their demands to legalize their relationships. In this context, Russian family law has always proceeded on the premise of a heterosexual relationship being the basis of a legal marriage and this has always been an implied condition of a marriage

(Khazova, 1998, p. 83). The new Family Code affirmed this position by stipulating as a general principle (art. 1(3)) but also as a condition to marriage in art. 12(2): 'To conclude a marriage it is necessary to obtain mutual voluntary consent of a man and a woman to be married ...' This appears to echo public opinion polls conducted by the Levada Centre in 2005, which indicated that the majority of Russians oppose same-sex marriage although they would support a ban on sexual orientation discrimination (at http://www.GayRussia.ru).

Marital property

In pre-revolutionary times, under Imperial Russian Law, a regime of separate property existed, thus a husband and wife owned their own property separately. Indeed, a married woman was allowed to enter into any civil transaction and freely dispose of her own assets (Antokolskaia, 2000, p. 29) and a husband had no right to administer or deal with his wife's property (Johnson, 1969, p. 176). However, it is important to remember that the Imperial law did not apply to the peasants and neither did the Soviet Family Codes and the law relating to collective farm households was the applicable law for these citizens. Moreover, in practical terms, separation of property gave the husband a privileged position since he would go out to work and earn wages whereas the wife usually stayed at home, did the housework and looked after the children, hence in the event of the breakdown of the marriage, the wife could not have the benefit of what her husband had earned. Hence it was thought that sex equality would be better achieved by the introduction of community of property, a limited form of which was brought in by the Family Code 1926. Under this Code, all property acquired during marriage was considered community property. The community property regime has remained until present times.

Under art. 256(2) of the Civil Code and arts 33 and 34 of the Family Code, property acquired by the spouses during marriage are regarded as a common asset. This property is jointly owned and non-community property is premarital property, property acquired during marriage as a gift, through inheritance or some other cost-free transaction as well as items of individual use except jewellery and other similar luxury items. The judge is also empowered under art. 38(4) of the Family Code to award the status of separate property to assets that were acquired after separation of the spouses but this would only apply to the period before all the divorce formalities were fulfilled (Antokolskaia, 2000, p. 30).

Community assets can be divided by the court when a couple divorce or during the marriage. The 1995 Family Code created history by allowing spouses to create a contractual regime of marital property by entering into a marriage contract. This can be entered into at any time before or after a marriage is solemnized. It also requires notarization and authentication in writing in order to be valid, and if it was entered into before the marriage was celebrated it will come into force at the time the marriage is registered. However, despite this momentous innovation, the Family Code provision creating this marriage contract is not without limitations. For instance, it does not provide possible contractual regime models, so inexperienced spouses and notaries have no template for a marriage contract. The marriage contract must also comply with the general requirements of legal capacity and not be entered into under undue influence for civil transactions under the Civil Code. A marriage contract cannot include provisions which govern minor children and cannot restrict the right of a spouse who is disabled or needy to make a claim for maintenance (Antokolskaia, 2000, p. 31).

Law which applies in the case of overlap or where no family legislation exists

The Russian Family Code does not claim to be exhaustive in two respects: certain family relations are governed by other federal legislation and the subjects of the Federation have the right to adopt their own Family Codes and other family laws which are not inconsistent with the Russian Family Code (Butler, 2003, p. 424). Indeed, some Republics within the Federation have enacted their own Family Codes. This is the result of family law now being under the joint jurisdiction of the Russian Federation and the subjects (that is, the Republics) of the Federation. To deal with this, the Russian Family Code rules that civil legislation shall normally apply 'where it is not contrary to the essence of family relations, to the property and personal non-property relations named in the Family Code between members of a family which are not regulated by family legislation' (Butler, 2003, p. 424).

However, if neither family nor civil legislation provides the relevant legislation, and there is no agreement of the parties:

> '[T]he norms of family and/or civil law regulating similar relations apply to such relations unless this is contrary to the essence of family relations etc as stated above. If no such norms exist, rights and duties of family members will be determined by proceeding from general principles of family or civil law and principles of humaneness, reasonableness and justice' (Butler, 2003, p. 424).

Operation of the Russian Family Code 1995–2000

In her review of the Family Code 1995 after it had been in operation five years, Olga Khazova offers several illuminating insights. For instance, she believes the fact it was drafted in some haste and was intended to be conservative in approach accounts for some of its main deficiencies. On the substantive front, she discusses the deficiencies of the Code in relation to (a) child maintenance; (b) surrogate motherhood; (c) maintenance agreements; and (d) sex equality (Khazova, 2002). We shall now discuss these areas, noting the law and its alleged deficiencies.

Child maintenance and child welfare

According to art. 24(1) of the Family Code, when dissolving a marriage the spouses may submit to the court an agreement dealing with whom the child will reside and the payment and amount of the children's maintenance. The critical wording here is 'may submit' but they are neither obliged to do it in principle, nor to do it in written form. Khazova informs us that in practice this rule does not achieve its aim, which is to ensure the children's interests receive proper protection under the law, despite the fact that the new rule is supposed to have remedied the previous law which only required the court to be informed informally if the spouses had come to an agreement on the custody and upbringing of the children (Khazova, 2002, p. 349).

Article 24(2) of the Family Code states that if there is no agreement between the spouses with regard to the questions specified in art. 24(1), or if the agreement violates the interests of children, then the court is obliged to determine with which of the parents minor children will reside after divorce and what amount of alimony shall be received for their children.

The problem is that in practice if there is no written agreement or obvious dispute, the judge will be prepared to accept what he or she is told in court, that there is consent between the parties, and there will be no investigation as to whether there is any consent, or whether any such agreement exists or whether the child will get any such maintenance. Hence, this part of the Code has apparently been far from effective.

Surrogate motherhood

The Family Code is the first piece of legislation to contain provisions on surrogate motherhood. Article 51(4) provides: '[A] married couple, who have agreed to implantation of an embryo in another woman in order for the gestation of a child, can be registered as the child's parents only if this woman (surrogate mother) gives her consent to such a registration.' Hence, as Khazova explains, this means that under Russian law, the surrogate has the right to keep the child (Khazova, 2002, p. 350).

As Antokolskaia also points out, the Family Code 1995 gives priority to the interests of the surrogate mother who is given a chance to change her mind (under art. 51(4) of the Family Code). Thus after the birth of a child, the surrogate mother may either (i) confirm her consent before the implantation of the embryo and hand the child over to the commissioning couple with whom she contracted; or (ii) withhold her consent and register herself as the mother (art. 51(4) Family Code). Once the surrogate mother confirms her consent, it becomes irrevocable and once the couple is registered as the child's parents, the registration cannot be challenged in the future (Antokolskaia, 2000, p. 35).

There is no requirement under the Code for the surrogate to be a single woman so she may be a married woman. However, the Code is silent on the surrogate's husband or partner and does not address the 'husband-related' consequences of her becoming a surrogate mother. Khazova takes the view that this constitutes a gap in the legislation, since no provision in the Code or in any other Russian legislation requires the surrogate's husband to be asked if he wants to have the baby or not, and thus, strictly speaking, no one in the fertility clinic would be obliged to obtain his consent to the use of assisted reproduction techniques in relation to his wife. This means if the surrogate does decide to keep the baby, her husband will automatically be regarded as the child's father which brings all the legal consequences of paternity (Khazova, 2002, p. 350).

The provision also talks about a 'married couple' in this context. Yet, under the Fundamentals of Russian Federation (RF) Legislation on Citizens' Health 1993, art. 35 provides for the right of every woman to benefit from assisted reproduction. Consequently, art. 51 as it stands not only restricts the right of those who are not married to have access to a surrogate motherhood program but also restricts the right of de facto couples (that is, unmarried couples) to be registered as the legal parents of their child if a child is born as a result of the surrogacy arrangement.

Birth registration for parents of children born through artificial insemination

Butler points out that if married persons have given their consent in writing to artificial insemination or the implantation of an embryo, then in the event of the birth of a child to them as a result of these methods they will be entered as parents in the book of birth registration (Butler, 2003, p. 432).

Comparative observations on surrogate motherhood

It should be noted that in English law, the surrogate mother is also allowed to change her mind about handing over the baby who has been produced by a surrogacy agreement. The legal basis for this is straightforward – surrogacy arrangements are unenforceable in English law, and the woman who carried the baby in the womb, irrespective of whether the pregnancy was created via IVF or sexual intercourse with the commissioning husband, remains the legal mother under the Human Fertilization and Embryology Act 1990, until an adoption order is made. This is not the legal approach taken in many American jurisdictions, which will differ depending on the State in which the surrogacy has taken place. In California, for example, where there has been a full surrogacy (that is, where the commissioning couple has provided both sperm and ovum) and the surrogate mother has no genetic input, the Appeal Court in *Johnson v Calvert* 286 Cal Rptr 369 (1991) held that the (full) surrogacy agreement is enforceable and should be treated as any other contract, to give effect to the intention of the parties. The mother would have been treated as the legal mother of the child in English law.

Maintenance agreements

According to Butler, spouses have a duty to support each other from the moment their marriage is registered (see Butler, 2003, p. 430). This appears to be borne out by art. 89(1) of the 1995 Code which states that 'the spouses are obliged to maintain each other'. However, Khazova argues that there is no legal obligation for spouses to maintain each other in Russian law, unless there are special justifying circumstances, such as old age, pregnancy, incapacity to work or a disabled child in the family. This is because in the first instance, the intention was to give spouses the freedom to make their own agreements and to solve their financial problems themselves. However, what happens in practice is that in the overwhelming majority of cases, if the spouses do not attain the pension age or are not disabled, if they have no disabled child in the family to look after, or if the wife is not pregnant, and if the woman is young enough and can work (even if they have five children of the marriage), they cannot receive a maintenance order from the court (Khazova, 2002, p. 351).

A married woman who has decided to stay at home and devote herself to her family will not acquire the right to claim alimony from her husband during the marriage or after it has been dissolved simply by virtue of her status as a wife (Khazova, 2002, p. 351). Neither the husband nor wife will be entitled to any payments, either compensatory, rehabilitative or even for a short period, which would assist in helping to make the adjustment to the new financial situation.

Article 99 of the Code states that 'an agreement concerning the payment of alimony (amount, conditions, and procedure for payment of alimony) is made between the person obliged to pay alimony and the recipient thereof …'. Khazova interprets this as meaning that this section only concerns those who are obliged to provide maintenance by law and does not cover those who maintain their spouse or other family member voluntarily, while not being legally obliged to do so. Indeed, she emphasizes that the list of family members in Russian law who are under this duty is short, and 'strange though it may seem, does not include the spouses themselves in the majority of cases' (Khazova, 2002, p. 351).

Sex equality

As we mentioned at the beginning of our very brief historical survey of Russian family law, the abolition of discrimination against women or economic dependency on men was part and parcel of the post-revolutionary plan to introduce equality between the sexes, thus popularizing the idea that for women to become truly free from economic dependency on their husband, both in theory and in practice women had to go out and join the workforce. This ideology survived the decades of Soviet rule, but in the light of the revolutionary changes which took place in the early 1990s, women have experienced high unemployment and considerable hardship. This was brought about by the collapse of social services, and the resulting high cost of services in the private sector, which resulted in a slump in women's income.

In addition, Khazova observes that there appears to be a considerable number of women who are shunning the labour market and who wish simply to stay at home, look after the children and fulfil the traditional role of the housewife. She believes that she is witnessing a 'restoration of the housewife role in Russia', a new trend in the early twenty-first century, which has acquired the label of 'patriarchal renaissance'. She interprets this phenomenon as a natural reaction to many years of double-employment and women being forced to be separated from the family (Khazova, 2002, p. 353).

Khazova suggests that the best way to deal with this new social reality is to restore the institution of spousal maintenance, so that a married woman who stays at home and is dependent on her husband will not be left without any financial support in the event of divorce or conflict in the family which results in withdrawal of financial support by her husband (Khazova, 2002, p. 353). This helps the economically weaker partner in the event of divorce or separation to cope with the situation (for example to find a job or acquire new skills).

To have to rely on an agreement or contract between the spouses does seem wholly inadequate and Khazova argues that 'there must be a clear mechanism stipulated by the law' to protect the housewife or spouse whose income is much lower than the other's (Khazova, 2002, p. 353). Her view is that maintenance should be a 'right, expected and earned' (Diduck and Orton, 1994, p. 681).

Butler remarks that assuming there is no maintenance agreement between the spouses, and support is refused, the category of spouses who have the right to demand alimony in a judicial proceeding from the other spouse who possesses the means to pay includes: a needy spouse lacking labour capacity; a wife while pregnant and within three years from the day of birth of a common child; and a needy spouse who has cared for a disabled child until the child reaches 18 or for a common disabled child' (Butler, 2003, p. 431). He also points out that the duty to support a spouse may be removed or altered by court decision. A court may make such a ruling if a spouse loses the capacity to work through abuse of alcohol or drugs; as the result of the commission of an intentional crime; or if the marriage was of a short duration. This unworthy conduct must be proved by the other spouse on the basis of judicial decisions or other evidence, and it may have occurred before or after the marriage (Butler, 2003, p. 431).

Children

Paternity

As in many countries around the world, illegitimate children in Russia suffered discrimination, not least in the nineteenth century. This discrimination never completely disappeared although the stigmatizing slowly diminished. The first Russian Family Code 1918 granted children born out of wedlock equal rights with legitimate children. If a putative father refused to acknowledge paternity, the Code gave the court the power to establish paternity by court decision (Antokolskaia, 2000,

p. 33). Then came a rather one-sided legislative provision in the Family Code 1926 which declared that a mother who lodged a paternity suit did not have to prove her case because the burden of proof shifted to the father. To strengthen the case further, an instruction letter from the Civil Department of the Supreme Court of the Russian Socialist Federal Soviet Republic of 11 June 1929 stated: '[E]very child must have a father in order to be able to claim alimony from him.' Yet in 1944, the pendulum swung the other way, with the Act of 8 July 1944 declaring that paternity could not be voluntarily established nor could the courts establish paternity by decision (Uzak Prezidiuma Verhovnogo Soveta SSSR, Ved. SSSP, 1944, No. 37, 1944) It took until the Code of 1969 before both institutions were restored, and this Code attempted to strike a balance between the interests of children born out of wedlock and those of putative fathers (see art. 45(3)).

The most recent change occurred in the mid 1990s. Under art. 48(4) of the 1995 Family Code, if a child is born within a lawful marriage the mother's husband is presumed to be its father. This presumption can be challenged by the husband, the mother or the child's natural father. As in English law, it is a delicate balancing of competing interests and it is often undesirable to allow a paternity test to be carried out on the basis of a claim by an alleged biological father who is not currently married to the child's mother, as it disrupts a family's stability and might not be in the best interests of a child. Antokolskaia argues strongly that accepting a paternity claim creates an irreconcilable conflict between a mother and her lawful husband, who are caring for the child and enjoying a family life with the child and the interests of the child's biological father. She believes that 'such claims should be satisfied only in exceptional cases' when for example the judge feels that establishing a relationship with the biological father would serve the interest of the child because he happens to be a better influence on the child than the mother's lawful husband (Antokolskaia, 2000, p. 33).

If a child is born of unmarried parents, and they do not make joint application to register the birth, the origin of the child from a specific person (fatherhood) may be established in a judicial proceeding which relies on the statement of one of the parents, trustee (or guardian) of the child or upon the statement of the child when he or she attains majority (Butler, 2003, p. 432). The court will take into account any evidence which it considers to be reliable, confirming the origin of the child from a specific person (Butler, 2003, p. 432).

In cases where the putative father denies paternity, the mother, the guardian and the adult child may file a claim before the court. If the putative father wishes to have his paternity established and the mother refuses to acknowledge it, the father may petition to have his paternity established in court.

An adult child may bring an action to establish paternity against the putative father or, if the mother prevented the registration, also against her. If the putative father is deceased, then a special proceeding may be held to establish a legal fact, that is, paternity. In trying to establish paternity, the court will take into account the cohabitation and keeping of a common household by the child's mother and the defendant before the birth of the child, or the joint upbringing or support of the child, or any reliable evidence which confirms the acknowledgment of paternity by the defendant. This may include witness testimony concerning statements by the defendant or blood tests (Butler, 2003, p. 432) or even genetic expertise.

If it is not possible to determine paternity in the proceedings, or the mother refuses to name the father, the child's name will be entered in the birth register under the mother's surname and whatever forenames she may choose. This will prevent the embarrassing blank spaces that appeared in such cases under the pre-1968 legislation which thereby disclosed the illegitimacy of the child. The mother will not qualify for paternity support but will be entitled to state benefits for unmarried mothers.

Children born out of wedlock will now have equal rights and duties with regard to parents and relatives as children born to a married couple (Butler, 2003, p. 432).

Antokolskaia notes that under the Family Code the couple who have a child using in-vitro fertilization are presumed to be the child's parents and cannot contest parenthood in the future by relying on the fact that the birth was the result of assisted reproduction techniques. The Code does not allow the establishment of paternity or the maternity of the donors, or even the disclosure of their names (see Antokolskaia, 2000, p. 34). Antokolskaia sees this approach as old-fashioned and undesirable because sometimes discretion might be needed to allow the disclosure of the biological origins of the child for identification and treatment of inherited diseases; or the child may have a strong desire to know its biological parents. She suggests that the better solution would be for the Code to allow the court to order disclosure of a child's biological origins if the child presents a claim and a compelling argument for disclosure (Antokolskaia, 2000, p. 34).

Some comparative observations on paternity

On a comparative note, English law as it currently stands would tend to order a paternity test unless it is not in the best interests of the child (see e.g. *Re H* [1996] 2 FLR 65; *Re T (Paternity: Ordering Blood Tests)* [2001] 2 FLR 1190; *Re H and A (Children) (Paternity: Blood Tests)* [2002] 1 FLR 1145). English law also recognizes the two opposing views that apply to this difficult issue: that the child has a right to know its origins; and the competing right of the child to have the stability of his or her family protected.

Parental rights under the Russian Family Code

In the era prior to the Russian Revolution, Russian law granted parental authority not only with respect to minor children but also over adult children (see Svod Zakonov Grazhdanskikh, arts 161–8). After the Russian Revolution, the development of parental rights was 'rather contradictory' (Antokolskaia, 2000, p. 35). Hence, both parents acquired equal rights with respect to their children but parental functions were considered mainly societal duties. Under the Family Code, parents

[handwritten: → Russia take it on a right-by-right basis. ↗ Gillick competence a less convincing factor.]

have the right to decide on their children's upbringing and education (art. 65(1)). Parental discretion must be based on mutual consent and must consider the wishes of the children (Antokolskaia, 2000, p. 35). Presumably, this refers to older children. Antokolskaia highlights art. 65 of the Code which limits parental discretion by stating that parents should not cause any harm to the physical, psychological or moral development of their children. If this article is violated, the state will limit the parents' discretion and utilize special public bodies to exercise control over the wellbeing of the child, usually through the Guardianship and Curatorship Department.

Under art. 61(1) of the Code, both parents are given equal parental authority irrespective of whether they are married, whether or not they are living together with the child and whether paternity was acknowledged voluntarily or by court decision, which is in accord with art. 18 of the Convention on the Rights of the Child 1989. Antokolskaia considers this rule to be 'troublesome' because it grants full parental authority to some parents who have no desire to establish relations with their child (Antokolskaia, 2000, p. 36). She argues that this rule can be disruptive and can empower a reluctant parent to refuse consent where it is needed, even for relatively trivial matters such as taking the child abroad for holidays. Only a court would be able to terminate such a disruptive parent's rights.

The other problematic scenario is where one of the parents is not living with the child but wishes to play a part in the child's upbringing and education. Although the mother and father have equal rights, if they are separated the courts tend to place children with their mother, which means that non-residential fathers cannot exercise access rights without the cooperation of the mother, and this has generated 'considerable social tension' (Antokolskaia, 2000, p. 36). This situation is also a common problem in Western countries, including England and America. In Russia, separated fathers who feel they have been marginalized and wish to have greater scope to exercise their parental rights have formed an organization that campaigns for equal rights for fathers, called A Group for Equal Treatment of Divorced Fathers. Under the Family Code, the court has been given the power, in art. 66(3), to transfer child custody from the mother to the father in those cases where the mother grossly disobeys the court and refuses to let the father exercise his rights.

Rights of minors

Chapter 11 of the Family Code contains special rules relating to the rights of minors, which is something of a novelty in Russian law (Antokolskaia, 2000, p. 36). According to one of the experts who worked on the 1995 Code, the United Nations Convention on the Rights of the Child 1990 was the inspiration for the new rules, which moved away from the old attitude of children being merely passive subjects of parental care (Anotokoloskaia, 2000, p. 37). *[handwritten: → As late as 1995 the change came in Russia]*

As a legal successor to the former Soviet Union, Russia became a party to the International Convention on the Rights of the Child which was ratified on 16

August 1990 (Vedomosti Verkhovnogo Soveta SSSR, 1990, No. 26b, Item 497). After the Convention was ratified, Russia tried to bring its domestic legislation in line with international obligations in the field of children's rights. Apart from signing the Optional Protocol to the International Convention on the Rights of the Child on the Involvement of Children in Armed Conflict it also passed the Federal Law on Basic Guarantees of the Rights of the Child in the Russian Federation in July 1998, which repeats all the provisions of Convention on the Rights of the Child. Various pieces of Russian legislation do not follow the definition of children provided by the Convention.

Under art.1 of the Convention on the Rights of the Child everyone under the age of 18 is recognized as a child. However, most specialized health care programs in Russia do not include children older than 14, or older than 16 if a child is disabled. Parental consent is required for medical procedures to be carried out on children under 16 and tax legislation treats minors under 16, and between 16 and 18 years of age, differently.

Age range changes for different things → some degree of legal difference is present

Child's right to express his or her opinion

The Russian Family Code follows the Convention on the Rights of the Child by allowing a child the right to express his or her opinion, and in accordance with the Convention, does not prescribe a minimum age when this right may be expressed. Consequently, in theory at least, all Russian children have the right to express their opinion in relation to any family decision that touches the child's interests as soon as the child is able to formulate an opinion. This right also exists in any administrative or court procedure and the age of the child is only relevant when it comes to the evaluation of the child's opinion (Antokolskaia, 2000, p. 37).

However, the age of ten is given special significance in terms of at what age the child's opinion must be considered. Under art. 12 of the Convention, a child's opinion will be considered in the light of its ability to formulate an opinion.

Similarly, under art. 57 of the Family Code, if a child is ten years old, that child's opinion must be considered. Consequently, although a child who is under ten years old must be given the opportunity to be heard, parents and officials are not obliged to follow the child's opinion. On the other hand, if a child who is ten years old expresses an opinion on a family decision and this opinion is not followed, those who disregarded this opinion must provide an adequate explanation for their motivation. The classic example is if a child has expressed its wish to stay with its father after a divorce but the judge considers it is better for that child to stay with its mother, the judge will have to clarify why overruling the child's wishes is in the child's best interest.

There are certain decisions which cannot be made against the child's wishes, if that child is aged ten or above. A child aged ten years or older must consent to a proposed change in its first or family name and, if adoption is to be established, if adoptive parents are to be registered as natural parents, or if the child is to be placed with foster parents (see arts 59(4), 132, 134(4), 154(3) Family Code). Hence, for

Therefore more child-focused than Gillick factors. All 10+ year olds, not just some i.e.

these situations where the child's 'most serious' interests are involved, affect its identity, or cause a complete change in its living conditions, its explicit consent would be required (Antokolskaia, 2000, p. 37).

A child also has the right to maintain contact with his or her parents and other family members, particularly in divorce cases. Importantly, a child can also refuse such contact which, in a situation of parents in dispute on this issue, will force the court to look at access or visitation rights from the point of view of the child, rather than that of the parents.

Under art. 56(3) of the Code, children are also given the right to protect themselves against their parents or others in cases of abuse. Children of any age may seek protection in the Department of Guardianship and Curatorship at their own initiative. Once a child is aged 14, he or she is entitled to lodge a direct action to the court and to initiate a procedure of terminating or limiting the parental rights of abusive parents (Antokolskaia, 2000, p. 38).

Comparative observations

Under the Children Act 1989 (UK), a child who is '*Gillick* competent' (see *Gillick v West Norfolk and Wisbech Area Health Authority* [1985] 3 All ER 402 (HL) – that is, possesses 'sufficient age and understanding' – has the right to apply in their own right to a court to discharge a care order, challenge an emergency protection order, refuse to submit to a medical assessment or examination, and has the right to choose their own legal representation, provided the child possesses the necessary maturity to weigh the longer term against the short term consequences and to participate as a party without representation by a guardian ad litem (under *Re S* [1993] 3 All ER 36, a Court of Appeal case involving an 11-year-old boy). The mature child also has the right to apply to the court for a s. 8 order (a residence order, contact order, specific issue order and prohibited steps order) provided the court is satisfied the child has sufficient understanding to make the proposed application. These rights are not tied to a minimum age for the child and it is up to the court in every instance to decide whether the particular child possesses the requisite maturity to make these decisions which involve serious consequences, and some of which will involve a radical change in the child's living arrangements, or an interference in the child's physical integrity. Under English law, a court has the power to override a child's wishes if it believes the child's decision is not in his or her best interests (*Re W (A Minor: Medical Treatment)* [1992] 4 All ER 627). For example, for children suffering from anorexia nervosa, or those suffering from psychotic mental problems – situations which have arisen frequently in connection with a child's life being at risk. Children who are perceived as suffering from a mental disorder who choose to die by, for example, refusing life-saving treatment or food, will not be allowed to do so by the English courts, even if that requires forcefeeding the child (see e.g. *Re C (Detention: Medical Treatment)* [1997] 1 FLR 180). In all cases where the child's welfare and upbringing is directly concerned, the child's welfare is the paramount consideration.

Impact of the upheavals of 1990 on children in R

The economic and social crisis of the 1990s had an inevitab
and children's rights in Russia. Until 2003, payment of so
encountered constant delays and, although money was ι
parents with minor children, it did not significantly affect their ευ
because of the insignificant amounts being received and inflation (La_v
of Congress at http://www.loc.gov/law/help/child/rights/russia.php). The typ.
cal problems associated with the implementation of Russian legislation and the
functioning of government institutions are unfortunately exemplified in the area
of children's rights protection. These problems are:

> '[A] lack of separation of powers between the federal and regional levels of
> authorities; contradictions within the legislation; no defined division between
> federal and state budgets in relation to the payment of state subsidies to
> children; maintenance of social support institutions; and absence of working
> mechanisms that would provide for rehabilitation and integration of children
> with disabilities.'
>
> (Law Library of Congress at http://www.loc.gov/
> law/hekp/child/rights/russia.php)

Russian Federal Law on Basic Guarantees of the Rights of a Child

In addition to the Family Code 1995, the rights of a child are regulated by the
Federal Law on Basic Guarantees of the Rights of a Child in the Russian Federation
of 24 July 1998, as amended 20 July 2000, and international treaties of the Russian
Federation.

Conclusions

In the 'new' Russia of the early twenty-first century, Russian legislation 'continues
to adhere to the earliest decrees on family law' (Butler, 2003, p. 431) which means
that the blood relationship, the birth of children, remains the sole basis for the rights
and duties for parents and children. As art. 38 of the 1993 Russian Constitution
states, 'motherhood and childhood and the family shall be under the protection of
the State', which indicates the central importance the family has in Russian law,
both as 'a legal and economic entity ... and a core unit of present and future society' (Butler, 2003, p. 419). The 1995 Family Law Code reflects the history and
the contradictory and complex nature of modern-day Russian society. Specialist
academics have commented on its application and efficacy. Butler's account of
Russian law presents a comprehensive, authoritative and systematic account of all
important aspects of Russian law, almost entirely a 'black letter' account in the

e that he presents 'the law' as it stands but he also cross-references previous ws, and charts their development, albeit briefly. He has also presented the historical background to the law or area he happens to be discussing, so it is not true to say there is no socioeconomic or sociopolitical analysis. The work of Khazova and Antokolskaia is didactic and analytical and both present accounts of Russian family law which offer different insights and are certainly illuminating. Khazova's more recent writing reflects concerns and problems which have resulted in the Family Code not achieving its aims and the resulting hardship which both children and women have suffered. It appears that speedy legal reforms and discerning judicial interpretations of the law are needed to ameliorate the problems that Russian women and children have been facing. Russia is again undergoing a change of focus and continues to have an uneasy relationship with its ex-constituents and the West. Russia's unique political history and culture may always tend to overshadow its social policy, but since the Revolution it has sought to achieve commendable social objectives to which some Western jurisdictions continue to aspire.

Further reading

Antokolskaia, M 'The New Aspects of Russian Family Law' (2000) 13 Cal Western Int LJ 23.

Antokolskaia, M 'The Process of Modernisation of Family Law in Eastern and Western Europe' (2000) 4 *Electronic Journal of Comparative Law*.

Antokolskaia, M 'Russian Law from a Comparative Law Perspective' (2001) 8 Maastricht Jo Comp L 339.

Butler, W *Soviet Law*, 1993, Butterworths.

Butler, W 'The Russian Family Code' in *Russian Family Law*, 1998, Simmonds & Hill Pub Ltd.

Butler, W *Russian Law* 2003, Oxford UP, Ch. 10.

Diduck, A, Orton, H 'Equality and Support for Spouses' (1994) 57 Mod LR, p. 681.

Gemkin, DM, Novitski, IB, Rabinovitch, NB *History of Soviet Civil Law (Istoria sovetskogo grazhdaskogo prava)*, 1949, VIYUN, Moscow.

Johnson, E *An Introduction to the Soviet Legal System*, 1969, Methuen, Ch. 8.

Khazova, O 'The New Codification of Russian Family Law' in Eekelaar and Nhlapo (eds), 1998, Hart, Ch. 4.

Khazova, O 'Five Years of the Russian Family Code: The First Results' in Bainham (ed) *The International Survey of Family Law*, 2002, Jordan, pp. 347ff.

Khazova, O 'Allocation of Parental Rights and Responsibilities after Separation and Divorce under Russian Law' (2006) 39 Fam LQ 373.

Chapter 6

Family law in Japan
The Japanese family – between tradition and modernity

Historical background

The Japanese legal system is based on the civil law system and also bears the marks of influences from American law (Oda, 1992, preface). However, as Professor Oda points out, comparativists are yet to agree on the position of Japanese law within the world's legal system. He emphasizes that contrary to the views of leading comparativists, it is inaccurate and meaningless to put Japanese and Chinese law in the same category on any basis except geographical. Unlike China, Japan did not turn to socialism in 1949 and its legal system cannot be regarded as part of the socialist legal family. Indeed, despite introducing some legal institutions from China, the Chinese influence on Japanese law is minimal. Indubitably, Japanese law has been influenced by various foreign legal systems, mainly Romano-Germanic and latterly American, which was the consequence of the outcome of the Second World War. Foreign law was received into Japan in three stages. The first stage was in the seventh to eighth century when Japan imported the Chinese political and legal system. Nevertheless, the legacy of China is minimal in contemporary Japanese law. The second stage took place between the overthrow of the Tokugawa Shogunate in the mid nineteenth century and the early years of the twentieth century when the country completed its industrialization (Oda, 1992, p. 7). The third stage began after the Second World War and continued during the period of the Allied occupation when some laws were amended or even replaced by laws based on American law. However, Oda observed that there was a strong civil law influence even in the late twentieth century (Oda, 1992, p. 8) although Japanese lawyers still have a perception that they are working within a predominantly Westernized system of law. Japan might therefore arguably be characterized as a hybrid jurisdiction.

Evolution of family law

Japanese family law is contained in Part IV of the Japanese Civil Code which was originally enacted in 1896 and again in 1898. However, it was in 1868 that Japan began its modernization after 200 years of self-imposed isolation from the outside world (Isono, 1988, p. 183). The country had been divided into several semi-autonomous feudal fiefs which owed allegiance to the Shogun. It had to be united to form a state ruled by a strong central government. This innovation was brought about not by a revolution of the rising bourgeosie but by a change of polity led by the lower stratum of the samurai class who had been less than satisfied with what they regarded as the stagnant society under the Shogunate of the Tokugawa family. They gave a touch of legitimacy to their revolt by inviting the Emperor, who had been kept in obscurity, to be the sovereign of the new regime with the title of Meiji. Hence the innovation was also a restoration of the supreme authority of the Emperor which had been ignored by the Shogun for more than 250 years (Isono, 1988, p. 183). Various methods of imitating Western culture then took place for about ten years or so, which included the imbibing of some democratic ideas, but eventually the leaders of the modernization decided that they wished to 'keep the Japanese soul and adopt Western technology'. An ideology was formulated to transform a people whose identity had been shaped by membership of relatively small and closed communities which curtailed their individualism by portraying the Japanese state as a large family with the Emperor as the head of the family, 'with his subjects as His children who were enjoined to obey him with filial piety' (Isono, 1988, p. 184).

The extended family (iye) with common ancestors was deeply rooted in the traditional Japanese value system and their version of it was not the Western concept of an extended family. In fact, iye was based on the vertical line, not on the tie of husband and wife. Hence, the status of the head of the family as the representative of the long line of ancestors was transmitted to the eldest son, while the younger son was allowed to set up a branch iye which was subordinate to the main iye, or was occasionally adopted by another iye with no male child. The daughter was given in marriage to another iye and not really to the husband. Hence, there could be a succession of men but the iye was supposed to last forever. There was a strict hierarchical structure under the supreme authority of the head of the family, with filial piety being the basis of all moral teaching. Under this system, every family member was subject to the control of the head of the family and women were always subordinate to men. There would be a sole legal heir to the head of the family. Only the father had legal control over the children.

The Imperial Family was presented as the main iye, the founder of which was the grandson of the Sun Goddess and all Japanese iye were the branch iye, which could trace the origins of their ancestors who were members of the divine line at some time in the past. This fiction managed to secure unconditional loyalty to the government who ruled in the name of the Emperor.

A modern system of compulsory education was implemented which inculcated the idea of ruler as father figure and the fiction of common ancestry of a nation. The divine origin of the Emperor was also a deeply ingrained notion in the Japanese psyche. The political leaders under Emperor Meiji realized that Japan needed to modernize rapidly or be reduced by Western powers to a colonial or semi-colonial state, as was the case with nearly all the other countries of Asia. The Tokugawa Shogunate had been forced to accept a series of unequal treaties and one of the most urgent tasks for the Meiji leaders was to compile a modern code of law.

Creation of family law through legal reform

Matsushima submits that Japanese family law can be said to be created and developed through three major legal reforms (Matsushima, 1998, p. 85). The first was the establishment of the Japanese Civil Code in 1898, around the same time as the promulgation of the Meiji Constitution. This was the birth of modern law, based on the paternalistic iye system. The second was the family law reforms instituted in 1947 following the Second World War and the creation of Japan's present democratic constitution, which resulted in the abolition of the iye system and the introduction of the principle of equality between men and women. The third was carried out in the period from 1990 to the present day, during which the progress in legal reform has reflected 'changing family circumstances, such as a falling birthrate, an increase in the aged population, greater numbers of working women and a decline in common values in Japanese society' (Matsushima, 1998, p. 85).

The Civil Code of 1898

Under the Civil Code, Meiji family law was characterized by a focus on the iye system and its origins lay in the koseki system which was a form of family register (see p. 232). Among the other characteristics of the iye, discussed above, the responsibility of the head of the family to support family members extended to supporting workers when they were ill, lost their jobs or retired in the cities and to reducing the welfare burden for companies and the state. This contributed to the rapid rise of capitalism in Japan. However, although this stabilized society, it also hampered social solidarity and retarded the development of the social security system (Matsushima, 1998, p. 89).

Other disadvantages of the iye system were that citizens were forced into blind obedience to the Meiji government, women were not given the right to vote and girls were unable to receive higher education. Married women were not given any legal capacity.

The Revised Civil Code of 1947

The growth of the nuclear family occurred in the period after the First World War and by 1920 more than half the population were members of a nuclear family, such that there was a gap between iye and the family member household. After its defeat in the Second World War in 1945 Japan was forced to undertake democratic reforms by the Allied forces. This led to a new Constitution which expressly provided for the principles of equality under the law (art. 14 Constitution), the dignity of individuals and the equality of the sexes in the family (art. 24 Constitution). All laws in breach of the Constitution were rescinded at this time. This also spelt the end of the iye system, which had been built on a principle of inequality (Matsushima, 1998, p. 90).

Matsushima lists the various revisions that were made:

(i) provisions relating to the head of the family were removed;

(ii) marriage is now based on the free agreement between two individuals;

(iii) provisions which required the consent of the parents and head of the family were nullified;

(iv) the wife's legal incapacity was abolished so that she now had equal rights with her husband to hold assets and manage them;

(v) the husband and wife are to support each other mutually and to share the expenses of married life;

(vi) divorce, where the wife was previously subjected to unfair treatment, was made free and equal for both husband and wife;

(vii) the couple can now choose the family name of either the husband or wife;

(viii) the surviving wife now always becomes the legal successor;

(ix) parental rights may be exercised jointly by the father and mother;

(x) adoption was for the welfare of the child rather than mainly to continue the family line;

(xi) the approval of the Family Court would be required when a minor child is adopted;

(xii) the system of a sole legal heir was abolished and a system of equal inheritance now exists whereby all children receive an equal amount, irrespective of whether they are male or female. All legitimate children now have equal rights and share an equal obligation; for example, the duty to support elderly parents must be shared equally by all the children. An illegitimate child is entitled to inherit only half the amount to which a legitimate child is entitled.

Reforms from the 1990s onwards

Up to the 1970s, the basic family unit of industrial society was one where the husband was responsible for being part of the workforce and his wife cared for him and his children. The concept of the legally married family was seen as the ideal family unit in most people's minds. However, during the 1970s families changed in several ways. For example, the population started to age at a rate unprecedented anywhere else in the world. According to the United Nations, a country which has over 7 per cent of its population aged over 65 is an 'ageing society'. It took only 25 years for Japan to have more than 14 per cent of the population aged over 65 years of age. This outstripped France which took 150 years, Sweden which took 85 years and England which took 45 years to reach the same percentage of 'elderly' people. Families declined in size as a result of an increase in the divorce rate, which created single parent (mother or father) families, and the number of single-parent (unmarried) households has been increasing; as it is in countries such as England and Wales. In Japan, the number of single mother households was 1.5 million in 1975 but increased to 2.3 million in 1979. The number of single father households, a phenomenon not very common in Western societies, rose in Japan from 0.2 million in 1975 to 0.4 million in 1990. Since 1975 there has been a great increase in the number of women joining the workforce. By 1991, the number of women whose occupation was that of housewife fell below 30 per cent of the adult female population. By 1997, some 40 per cent of women were participating in the workforce in one form or another, and this has brought about a change in the conventional perception of husbands and wives having a fixed division of roles. Indeed, as with Western societies, family circumstances have become diverse and the nuclear family has ceased to be the only model for family law. Significantly, even the perception of what a family is has diversified. Some opinion polls in the late 1990s suggested that more than 70 per cent of the younger generation did not support the idea of fixed roles for men and women and sought individual freedom and dignity even inside the family (Matsushima, 1998, p. 92).

Human Rights International Conventions

The shape of family law was also changed by various human rights movements. The Universal Declaration of Human Rights 1948 and the International Covenant on Civil and Political Rights 1966 provided the impetus for these movements. Women's rights received a boost from events such as the International Women's Year, held every year since 1975, and the International Plans of Action that follow these years. Several measures were implemented as a result. Japan signed the United Nations Convention on the Elimination of All Forms of Discrimination Against Women and revised the Nationality Law abolishing the law whereby only children with a Japanese father were eligible for Japanese nationality. A system was introduced so that both men and women could pass their citizenship to their children.

Marriage

The 'Ie' was the household or basic unit in Japanese society, and it typically consisted of grandparents, their son and his wife and their grandchildren.

Marriage in Japan usually takes the form of a civil marriage and is legalized by virtue of filing the appropriate notification. A wedding ceremony performed by a religious or fraternal organization is not an essential element for a legal marriage. A man has to be at least 18 years old, a woman at least 16 before they may legally marry. However, a minor could marry by obtaining the consent of his or her parents. Under the Civil Code of Japan, bigamy is prohibited (art. 732). A woman would not be permitted to remarry within six months of the day of dissolution or cancellation of the previous marriage, except where she becomes pregnant and gives birth to the child before the day. Lineal relatives by blood, collateral relatives within the third degree of kinship by blood (that is, between one and one's sibling, uncle, aunt, nephew or niece by blood) may not marry, except between an adopted child and his or her collateral relatives by blood through adoption.

Divorce

Four types of divorce

Four types of divorce are permissible in Japan. The first is divorce by agreement (kyogi rikon), based on mutual agreement; the second is divorce by mediation in a family court (chotei rikon), in cases where divorce by mutual agreement cannot be resolved; third, divorce by decision of the family court (shinpan rikon), which is divorce finalized by a family court where divorce by mediation cannot be established; and fourth, divorce by judgment of a district court (saiban rikon).

In cases where divorce cannot be resolved by the family court, a couple may apply to the district court for a decision. Here, the application for arbitration is a prerequisite. Once the case has been decided, the court will issue a certified copy of the divorce and a certificate of settlement, which is attached to the divorce registration.

It would seem that the last two methods are rarely used, as the traditional approach has been that dissolution of a marriage should be a private matter and that recourse to the law is not an appropriate option. It also seems that Japanese law is the only example of a real divorce by mutual consent since the divorce is treated in the same way as the entry into marriage. Both are regarded as contracts and there is no state intervention apart from the formal requirement of registration. The parties only need to state who is the custodian of any children of the marriage and all other consequences of divorce would seem to be irrelevant (see *International Encyclopaedia of Comparative Law*, Vol. 5, p. 80)

Custody

Joint custody of children is terminated once a divorce has been finalized. Where a divorce has taken place by agreement, the husband and wife must determine which parent will have custody of each child. For other types of divorce, custody is determined by the mediator or judge, and there is usually a strong maternal preference on the part of the judiciary; that is, a preference for custody of the children to be awarded to the mother, particularly with regard to children born after the divorce.

Family Courts

The Japanese Family Court was established on 1 January 1949, as a specialist court for family affairs and juvenile delinquency cases. These family courts have jurisdiction in the first instance over all intra-familial disputes, including divorce and child custody. A mediation system is employed by the family courts and it is obligatory to go through the conciliation procedure in the Family Court. There has been discontent with the Family Court but it has survived nearly 60 years. It has a panel of commissioners who are in charge of both the legal and emotional sides of the conflict. Although one of three commissioners should be a judge, in practice, this only happens at the last session to ensure there is no breach of the law. Commissioners are supposed to be selected from qualified attorneys and people who are specially equipped with the knowledge and expertise to handle family problems. They are also supposed to be persons of high moral standard and insight, and their age range has tended to be from 40 to 70. However, there is no adequate screening process to check their suitability. Most of the male commissioners are attorneys and most of the women commissioners are housewives who are college-educated (Isono, 1988, p. 201). No special training in social work or counselling is required apart from a short series of lectures on the basics of law and counselling. Commissioners are remunerated. The Family Court continues to be based on the paternalistic view that family problems should not be aired or settled in the formal courts of law. On the other hand, paternalism does not have the same resonance as it does in Western societies, and a benevolent and protective attitude on the part of a more experienced or eminent personage is welcomed. Japanese commentators draw an analogy with the company and the benevolence of the boss, and the fact that an employee sees himself personally responsible for the 'after-care' service to customers, such as servicing and maintenance of a product out of office hours or on weekends, to develop the customer's brand loyalty to a product or a company. However, when this is transferred to the family, an excessive devotion to work 'often results' in neglect of family life (Isono, 1988, p. 202). Isono believes one of the greatest challenges to Japan will be whether it can retain the typically Japanese social and economic system in spite of its rapidly expanding international contacts and continue to live in harmony with the other members of the family of nations in the present world (Isono, 1988, p. 202).

Guardianship for adults

Changes in welfare legislation

In 2000 there were major changes in welfare legislation. First, the Law on Public Care Insurance for the Elderly came into force on 1 April 2000. Second, the Law on Guardianship for Dependent Adults was promulgated on 8 December 1999 and came into force on 1 April 2000. Japan has a reputation for a long life expectancy and as every industrialized country is facing an ageing society, Japan is no exception. Hence, the welfare of the elderly is becoming an increasingly important issue (Niijima, 2001, p. 237). The elderly have greater economic independence and are better off than their predecessors because of improvements in the social security system and company pension schemes. The ongoing concern is how to manage and protect the assets of the elderly when many suffer senile dementia or Alzheimer's.

Problems with the old law

Niijima describes a number of problems which existed under the old system which the new Guardianship Law seeks to address. First, there were only two types of classification available, either incompetent or quasi-incompetent, and it was only possible to be declared incompetent if all mental function ceased (the actual wording being 'chronically mentally disturbed' (former art. 7 Civil Code). A quasi-incompetent was one who was mentally unstable but not totally disturbed, or a spendthrift (under the former art. 11, Civil Code). The degree of loss of function clearly varied from person to person yet once someone was declared incompetent they would lose the power to deal with their assets. This was seen as inadequate in protecting the rights and interests of persons who had been declared incompetent, since they would lose the power to manage their assets regardless of the degree of mental function they retained. Those deemed quasi-incompetents were placed under curatorship, and consent was required to perform certain legal acts. However, if the quasi-incompetent performed an act without the curator's consent, the curator had no right to rescind such an act. It was also perceived that the curator was not acting as an agent of the quasi-incompetent person and the protection was inadequate.

Second, the spouse of the incompetent would normally be the first person to be appointed as the guardian. In many cases, they would be old and unable to provide adequate care and management of the assets of the incompetent.

Third, there was only provision for one guardian to be appointed. This person had the responsibility for providing for both the care and management of the assets. It was again perceived as too difficult for a guardian (even if not an elderly spouse) to undertake both these responsibilities. A more flexible system was therefore needed.

Third, Niijima points out that the terms 'incompetent' and 'quasi-incompetent' (in Japanese 'kinchisan' or 'jun-kin-chisan') are regarded as discriminatory language in modern Japanese society. Moreover, people adjudicated as incompetent or quasi-incompetent are recorded as such in the Family Register (koseki). Koseki is a registration system under which every family is registered with the government.

Statistics

Statistically speaking, in 1998 there were about 1 million elderly people suffering from senile dementia and about 2 million people suffering from mental disability, however only 1,700 determinations of incompetence and 251 determinations of quasi-incompetence were made (Judicial Statistics, 1998).

The new guardianship law

Three types of protection have been introduced by this law.

Guardianship

On the face of it, guardianship simply corresponds to the old nomenclature, being also applicable to people who have lost their mental capacities. However, there are several significant innovations. As Niijima explains, the Family Court has the power to make an order to commence guardianship for a person who is habitually incapacitated owing to mental disorder. Under the amended art. 7, an application can be made by the person wishing to be declared incompetent, the spouse, any relative up to the fourth degree of relationship, the guardian for a minor, the supervisor of the guardian for a minor, the curator, the supervisor of a curator, the assistant, the supervisor of the assistant or a public prosecutor. A medical test is required before a medical order will be made. Another innovation is that more than one guardian can be appointed in cases where the court considers it necessary. Different guardians can be appointed for different functions; for example, one for management of assets, another for physical care. Importantly, the spouse is no longer the automatic guardian and the Family Court now has a discretion to appoint an appropriate guardian (Niijima, 2001, p. 239).

The court is required to take all the circumstances into consideration, such as the mental and physical condition of the person, the lifestyle and assets of the person, the personal history, occupation and any interest between the person and the guardian. Unusually, a corporation may be appointed as a guardian, which is likely to be one which specializes in welfare business. However, if a corporation is appointed, the court must consider the suitability of the corporation. Under art. 9, the emphasis is on respecting the wishes of the person needing a guardian, hence despite the powers of rescission and power of attorney, the person under guardianship should be allowed to independently carry out actions limited to those required for day-to-day living. Even more unusually, a new legal term 'guarded person' has been coined to replace the word 'incompetent' (Niijima, 2001, p. 240).

Curatorship (hosa)

Curatorship (hosa) is applicable to people who are classified as 'feeble-minded'. The Family Court has the power to appoint a curator for a person whose capacity to make a reasonable judgment has been gravely limited due to a mental disorder. The order may be made on the application of the persons named in the previous section. The curator is given the right to consent to important legal acts listed in the Civil Code, which, under the new art. 12, para.1, include borrowing money or becoming a guarantor, transactions concerning real property and movables of significance, receiving or investing funds, and initiating litigation. A new art. 12, para. 4, enacts that any such act done without the consent of the curator is voidable and may be rescinded. Unlike the old system, the curator may now have a power of attorney for specified legal acts if the court has given this power on application. If the power of attorney is applied for by someone other than the person him or herself, then the consent of that person is required before such a power of attorney will be granted.

General aid (hojo)

The court may make an order to commence general aid (hojo) for a person whose capacity to make a reasonable judgment is insufficient due to mental disorder. This covers people who are not feeble-minded but who for example might have slight senile dementia, the intellectually or mentally disabled, autistic people and others who require care. It is believed that this new type of protection would cover most mentally disabled people who were not covered by the old system because their degree of disability was not severe enough to warrant protection. Applicants will be the same sorts of people as listed in (i) Guardianship above.

Guardianship by agreement

New form of protection of the elderly

A new form of protection of the elderly has been created by the Law on Guardianship by Agreement 1999. This is called 'guardianship by agreement' whereby a person chooses his or her guardian and a contract is concluded between the person and the agent before the person's capacity for judgment has deteriorated. A notary public should be present to conclude a written contract to ensure its authenticity (art. 3). Under the new system, the guardian appointed by the person is supervised by the supervisor of the guardian who monitors the guardian's conduct. The court has the power to appoint the supervisor of the guardian on the application of the person, their spouse, any relative up to the fourth degree of relationship or the guardian. The supervisor has a duty to report regularly to the Family Court how the guardian is conducting affairs and the court has the power to order the supervisor to review the conduct of the guardian and to make a report to the court if necessary. The guardian may also be removed by the court if they have preformed any unjust act or gross misconduct (Niijima, 2001, p. 241).

Registration changes

Under the Japanese registration system, birth, marriage, divorce, adoption and death, as well as declarations of incompetence by the court, are recorded in the Family Register (koseki), as is the relationship between each person. The koseki carries considerable legal and social significance, which is why the Japanese would prefer to keep the koseki as socially respectable as possible, and could account for the low divorce rate in Japan (Niijima, 2001, p. 242). A record of being deemed 'incompetent' would deter people from using the system of guardianship for adults, as the persons recorded as such in the register would be the object of social prejudice. Nevertheless, there is a need to have a system which discloses a person's capacity to act for the protection of the other party in a legal transaction such as a contract. An act performed by a ward would be voidable under the new art. 9 of the Civil Code. Consequently, under the new law, records of the three new types of statutory guardianship and guardianship by agreement are to be registered with the Register Office and not in the Family Register.

This means that if requested, the Register Office can issue a certificate to prove a person is under guardianship and name the guardian.

Comparative observations on special care of the elderly

Another Asian law which requires special care of the elderly is the law in Singapore which requires children to care for their parents when they are no longer able to do so (see Part 2, Chapter 4 on Asia and Africa). And, as we have seen, German law also requires adult children to provide for their parents and grandparents if they are in financial need.

Children

Under the present law, a child born to a legally married couple is regarded as legitimate and a child born to an unmarried couple is regarded as illegitimate. As mentioned earlier, an illegitimate child is entitled to inherit only half the amount to which a legitimate child is entitled. This is the result of the proviso to art. 900(4) of the Japanese Civil Code. Reforms have been suggested despite the fact that a Supreme Court judgment of 5 July 1995 held that the provision was not unconstitutional. The court held that the principle of respecting legal marriage was reasonable legislation, and the decision regarding which inheritance system to adopt was a question for the legislature. However, the judgment was delivered with ten judges in favour and five against. Four judges suggested that this provision in the Civil Code should be reformed.

The rate of illegitimate births in Japan is extremely low compared with the West, being only 1.2 per cent in 1995. The reason is thought to be the strong social discrimination and prejudice against illegitimate children and single mothers in Japan (Matsushima, 1998, p. 97). Matsushima remarks that if a woman becomes pregnant before marriage, in most cases either the father marries the woman 'and they become a model married family' or, if that is not possible, the woman has an abortion.

Conclusions

The Japanese adult guardianship provisions are novel in the East and no equivalent system exists in other Eastern jurisdictions, but there are the enduring power of attorney and lasting power of attorney systems used in countries such as England and Wales. These laws, which seek to protect and promote the wellbeing of the elderly, might serve as a possible template for other Eastern jurisdictions which do not have an insurance or care policy specifically aimed at looking after the elderly, as the issues raised by an increasing population of elderly citizens need to be addressed by more and more countries. These laws demonstrate the importance placed by Japan on the welfare of the elderly and their respect for the dignity and self-determination of the elderly. It remains to be seen how effective the provisions will be in the years to come.

Matsushima draws several conclusions from his survey of the evolution of Japanese family law (see Matsushima, 1998, pp. 85–101). First, he points out that 'Japanese law is characterised by the way its reforms were inspired by foreign systems'. He explains that the two fundamental changes in the evolution of Japanese family law were both influenced by pressures from the West. The first change occurred in 1899, with the promulgation of Japan's first modern constitution which was brought about by the end of the warrior society and by the opening of the country to foreign trade for the first time after a policy of isolation lasting 250 years.

The second set of changes comprised fundamental changes to the legal system, which were brought about in 1945 by the defeat of Japan in the Second World War when political and military pressure from Allied forces of Western Europe and America forced Japan to abandon its feudal past and discriminatory family law and replace it with a more egalitarian law. This went hand in hand with the enactment of an American-style Constitution, also the result of the policies of the Allied forces occupying Japan.

The second conclusion drawn by Matsushima is that Japanese family law, compared with the family law of Western countries, was very much influenced by political ideology. Whereas family law in the West developed via a series of amendments to address human rights issues and to bring about equality between men and women, Japanese family law was used by the government of the day to regulate human relations in a uniform manner. The iye was used to maintain the totalitarian nature of the country and personify its legal policy. The gap between law and reality widened as 'capitalism marched relentlessly onward after the end of the First World War' (Matsushima, 1998, p. 98) and democracy movements became more active and began to have more impact.

The third conclusion drawn by Matsushima is that the present family law system in Japan is both progressive and flexible. Indeed, he points out that the comprehensive reform carried out after the Second World War was premised on the dignity of the individual and the equality of the sexes to the extent that the law was significantly more advanced than the reality of the family life it regulated (Matsushima, 1998, p. 99). Clearly, deep seated changes have taken place in Japanese society but Matsushima sees the flexibility of the law as another reason for its longevity since, for example, the present family law 'entrusts the settlement of family relations, including family disputes, to the parties concerned in reaching their own agreement' and 'this recognises the autonomy of private life' (Matsushima, 1998, p. 99). Matsushima gives a range of examples to illustrate this, namely: the basis of marriage is grounded in the mutual consent of both parties; the surname is to be decided after discussion by the couple in the marriage; parental authority over children is to be exercised jointly by father and mother; husband and wife are expected to cooperate with each other and provide mutual assistance; the couple is supposed to share marital expenses; and divorce by consent is possible. It is only when the couple cannot come to a mutually acceptable agreement that the case is transferred to the Family Court. The system has also stood for non-interference by the state but this has meant that inequalities of power between men and women continue to exist, with women being in a weaker position than men. Although the improvement in the economic status of women as well as an increase in the educational opportunities for women and the advancement of women in the workplace has led to the enactment of the Equal Employment Opportunity Act, inequalities continue to exist in practice. This is the background to separate surnames for husband and wife, the discrimination between marital and non-marital children and the fact that the courts have been asked to play a more positive part in divorce settlements.

The fourth conclusion Matushima draws is that the function of the family is under re-examination. It has to be said that this particular facet of the Japanese family is by no means unique and has been replicated in several societies across the world. However, Matsushima's view in 1998 was that Japanese society was shifting towards a 'borderless and multi-cultural society' (Matsushima, 1998, p. 100).

Further reading

Higuchi, N 'Parenthood under Japanese Law' in Bainham *et al.* (eds) *Frontiers of Family Law*, 1995, Wiley.

Isono, F 'The Evolution of Modern Family Law in Japan' (1988) 2 Int Jnl of Law, Policy and the Family 183.

Matsukawa, T 'The Japanese Family between Tradition and Modernity' in Commaille and de Singly (eds) *The European Family*, 1997, Kluwer Academic, pp. 139ff.

Matsushima, Y 'The Development of Japanese Family Law from 1898 to 1997 and its Relationship to Social and Political Change' in Eekelaar and Nhlapo (eds) *The Changing Family*, 1998, Hart, Ch. 5.

Niijima, K 'Japan: Guardianship for Adults' in Bainham (ed) *The International Survey of Family Law*, 2001, p. 237.

Noda, Y 'Japan: Its Past and Present' in Tanaka (ed) *The Japanese Legal System: Introductory Cases and Materials*, 1977, Univ of Tokyo Press.

Oda, H *Japanese Law*, 1992, Butterworths.

Part III

Cohabitation, informal unions and civil partnerships in comparative perspective

Introduction

This chapter discusses the development of the law relating to unmarried heterosexual and homosexual cohabitation or informal domestic partnerships in common law and civil jurisdictions within and outside the United Kingdom. Both same-sex and opposite-sex cohabitation in the common law jurisdictions of the United States, Australia and New Zealand are examined. In keeping with the rest of the book, while we review the legal position in a range of jurisdictions, we have selected France and Germany as examples of civil law countries that have introduced legislation that affects such informal unions, comparing them with the English common law position. We also consider Sweden as an example of a jurisdiction which has its roots in the continental or civil law tradition and whose main source of law is codified law or statutes. Sweden first introduced a Cohabitee Act in 1987 and again in 2003.

An initial point to note is that both common law and civil law countries have encountered similar problems. Even now, approaching the end of the first decade of the twenty-first century, there is no universally accepted statutory or social definition of heterosexual non-marital cohabitation, only different descriptions for different purposes. This is perhaps inevitable given the changeable and diverse nature of this social phenomenon.

Terminology

For purposes of this and related discussions, the term 'cohabitation' refers to unmarried heterosexual cohabitation, in circumstances resembling a 'marriage-like' relationship. In jurisdictions such as Australia, the term 'de facto relationships' has traditionally been used to denote unmarried heterosexual couples who live together. However, the term 'domestic partnership', introduced into Australian legislation in 1999, includes a de facto relationship, and the definition of 'de facto relationship' has also been widened to include same-sex couples.

The problems with the legal regulation of cohabitation

Cohabitation has always posed problems as far as legal regulation is concerned. To begin with, there is the problem of definition – how should one define cohabitants? How long should their relationship or association have lasted in order to merit legal recognition of some description, for example in the area of property rights? In brief, the law has been clear about the regulation of marriage but not about the status of cohabitation. The lack of a universal definition about what sort of cohabitation should be legally recognized has meant that English courts initially did not recognize cohabitational relationships outside marriage. This was in keeping with the contemporary social mores and existing law of the time, and courts needed to be more inventive when they wished to grant some sort of legal redress to a situation which they thought merited such legal imagination. This need arose in relation to property and financial provision rights and remedies and, as Barlow *et al.* describe it, 'overall, cohabitation law is acknowledged to be complex, confusing and often illogical' (Barlow *et al.*, 2005, p. 6). The law has tended to look for 'marriage-like' relationships, to see if a man and woman have been living 'as husband and wife', often for a minimum prescribed period of time, and whether there has been sexual intimacy before deciding that the couple in question may have property rights or social security benefits. Thus, whether a couple would be treated as cohabitating would depend on 'the statutory or judicial definition of cohabitation adopted in the context in which [an applicant] is seeking to rely on such a status' (Barlow *et al.*, 2005, p. 7). In more recent legislation, such as the Adoption and Children Act 2002, a couple is defined under s. 144(b) as 'two people (whether of different sexes or the same sex) living as partners in an enduring family relationship'. After considerable debate, unmarried couples have now been allowed to adopt under the Adoption and Children Act, which would have been considered unthinkable just a few years ago.

COMMON LAW JURISDICTIONS – OPPOSITE SEX COUPLES

Cohabitation in Britain

When an unmarried cohabitational relationship of an opposite sex couple breaks down in England and Wales, the courts do not have the power to invoke the Matrimonial Causes Act 1973, since the couple are not married to each other, and can exercise relatively limited powers to resolve any disputes the couple may have over property and children.

In April 2007, the latest census revealed that 2 million couples were living together and that the prediction was that the number of cohabiting households would grow from one to six to one in four by 2031 (*The Times*, 26 April 2007).

In their empirical study of British public attitudes towards cohabitation and marriage in Britain, Barlow *et al.* identify what they see as the reason behind some of the ambivalence or uncertainty of the law towards informal marriage-like unions, namely that 'formal marriage has always been the epicentre of family law' particularly after Lord Hardwicke's 1753 Act removed legal recognition from informal 'common-law marriage' (see Barlow *et al.*, 2005, p. 6). As they point out, the 1970s and 1980s saw a 'more inclusive or neutral approach to regulating marriage-like cohabitants'. Indeed, Lord Denning presided over and decided several cases where he invoked principles from the Court of Equity in order to award cohabitants a share in the proceeds of sale from the homes in which their names were not on the deeds but to which they had made non-financial contributions (see *Eves* [1975] 3 All ER 768). The 1990s saw a 'return to family values' under the Conservative government and this movement of 'strengthening families' was reinforced by the succeeding Labour government.

Barlow *et al.* argue that in Britain, as a result of a 'lopsided development' in the law relating to cohabitants, 'the law accepts that married families should be regulated in a special and privileged way but is unclear about the status of cohabitation' (Barlow *et al.*, 2005, p. 6) This has resulted in either treating cohabitants as married, or ignoring the relationship completely, or treating them as individuals or treating them as a couple but in a way which is inferior to their married equivalents (Barlow *et al.*, 2005, p. 6).

Three main areas of contention

There are three main contexts in which the inconsistency of the law regarding cohabitation has been noted: first, during the relationship; second, upon breakdown of the relationship and third, on the death of a cohabitant (Barlow *et al.*, 2005, pp. 8–13).

During the relationship

There are several situations where anomalies exist which are exposed during the relationship. The Family Law Act 1996 provides married couples and civil partners with the right to occupy the matrimonial home but this right is not given to cohabitants of either a rented or owner-occupied home. Indeed, an occupation order granting occupation rights to a 'non-entitled' cohabitant who is not an owner or tenant of the family home can be made for a maximum of 12 months, but this is usually an order which will be sought as a result of domestic violence (see s. 36).

A key distinction between a cohabitant father and a married father is that only the married father has automatic parental responsibility under the Children Act 1989 for his child on birth. An unmarried father therefore cannot take formal decisions relating to his children, such as giving consent to medical procedures or adoption. However, the unmarried father's right to be consulted on such matters can be acquired by entering into a parental responsibility agreement (in a prescribed form) with the mother which must be signed and witnessed. A British Social Attitudes (BSA) national survey suggested that only 5 per cent of cohabitant fathers in England and Wales had done so, which means that the majority have duties and obligations but no positive legal status in respect of their child (Barlow *et al.*, 2005, p. 8).

On relationship breakdown

There is no equivalent divorce procedure under statute for cohabitants whose relationship has broken down, irrespective of the contribution made to the relationship by the non-property owning cohabitant, whether there are children from the relationship or whether it has lasted a considerable number of years. There is thus no duty to pay maintenance to a former cohabitant, or to redistribute property between the partners according to family law principles when cohabiting partners separate. Instead, strict property rules normally operate. *Burns v Burns* [1984] Ch 317 is the classic example of the woman who cohabited with her partner for 19 years, and raised their children but never married him, who, when they separated, ended up with no beneficial interest in their family home because her name did not appear on the deeds to the house and she could not establish a constructive trust which would have given her a share in the property. Indeed, had her name appeared on it, she would have been entitled to a half-share in the property. Had she been married, and they split up, the division of assets would have been made, where assets exceed needs, on the basis of a 'yardstick of equality', provided there was no 'stellar contribution' by one party to the marriage.

On the death of a cohabitant

If a cohabitant dies intestate, that is, without making a will, the surviving cohabitant will have no automatic right to inherit a share of the estate, whereas the surviving spouse or civil partner will. As far as tenancy succession is concerned, certain rented family homes, such as those protected by the Rent Act and assured tenancies, will automatically be transferred to a cohabitant on the death of the tenant partner irrespective of how long the couple have cohabited, which basically treats the couple as if they were married. However, the cohabitant of a secure tenant will only qualify if they have lived with the deceased tenant for at least 12 months prior to the death under s. 87 of the Housing Act 1985. Thus, under s. 46 of the Administration of Estates Act 1925, it is only a spouse who will automatically inherit all or some of their spouse's estate where their husband or wife dies without making a will. Nevertheless, both a spouse and cohabitant of at least two years' standing have the right to make a claim for financial provision under a deceased partner's estate if there has been no or inadequate provision made for them by will, under s. 1(1)(a) and (bA) of the Inheritance Act 1975. The difference is that a cohabitant is limited to such financial provision 'as it would be reasonable in all the circumstances for the applicant to receive for his [sic] maintenance'. A spouse is not limited to merely a maintenance claim and would expect to receive a more generous award equivalent to a sum awarded upon divorce.

The spouse or civil partner of one killed in an accident may claim damages under the Fatal Accidents Act 1975. A cohabitant can also make such a claim if he or she had been living with the deceased for at least two years immediately before the death. Unlike a spouse, cohabitants cannot receive statutory bereavement damages.

Case law on cohabitants – from *Hammond v Mitchell* to *Stack v Dowden*

Introduction

English cases on cohabitation have a colourful history. The stories have ranged from Playboy bunny mistresses to unmarried women who contributed manual labour to enhance property intended as a joint home but, despite being initially given a share, were then refused more equal shares in the proceeds of sale of such property. Promises were apparently made between the cohabiting lovers during the course of their relationship but the court needed more than mere assertions of promises to award shares in the property once the couple separated. Dominant doctrinal themes appear to have been the notion of the constructive trust, proprietary estoppel, common intention and contribution. The concept of 'detrimental reliance' also appears to underpin these other principles. There was a set of cases decided in the 1970s, 1980s and 1990s of women who had physically worked to enhance joint property which was not in their names, and other cases such as *Hammond v Mitchell* [1992] 2 All ER 109 where the female cohabitant was denied a share of the proceeds of certain property in the absence of the common intention of the parties that she should do so. Arguably, the most unsatisfactory case involving cohabiting couples where the woman was not given any share in the property is *Burns v Burns* [1984] Ch 317, involving a couple who cohabited for 19 years, who had children from the union but never married, where the woman's name was not on the title deed. The woman (who took her partner's name), raised the children, worked part-time and paid some of the household bills, but could not establish a common intention (express or inferred) sufficient to establish a constructive trust under which she and her partner shared ownership of their family home. The Court of Appeal held that she had no beneficial interest in the property since the home had been purchased in the partner's name and there was no other legal remedy available to her. The woman's subsequent appeal was dismissed by the House of Lords in 1988. This decision has been partly counterbalanced by the cases of *Midland Bank v Cooke* [1995] 2 FLR 915 and *Oxley v Hiscock* [2004] EWCA Civ 546.

The physical contribution cases – *Eves* and *Cooke*

In two cases involving unmarried cohabitants, the women carried out considerable manual labour on the property and were given untruthful reasons why their names were not included on the title deed. In *Eves* [1975] 3 All ER 768, the woman carried out manual work on the property which included using a sledgehammer to break up concrete, demolishing and rebuilding a shed, and renovating the house. The cohabiting couple had two children from their relationship and the man gained her confidence by saying that he intended to put the house they had moved into in their joint names but that it was not possible until she was 21. This was untrue and the Court of Appeal took the view that the man's statement amounted to recognition by him that she was entitled to a share in the house. Hence, although she did not make any financial contribution, she contributed in many other ways to the property in question and looked after the children. The Court of Appeal was prepared to award one-quarter of the proceeds of sale of the property to the woman and three-quarters to the man. In *Cooke v Head* [1972] 2 All ER 38, the man bought the plot of land and arranged and paid the mortgage and the woman undertook considerable manual labour, including working a cement mixer and demolition. The woman's name did not appear on the deed but the court was prepared to award one-third interest for the value of her labour.

The car salesman, the bunny girl and the Spanish hacienda

In *Hammond v Mitchell* [1992] 2 All ER 109, the couple, who never married, first met by chance in Epping Forest. He was a married man of 40, a second-hand car trader, separated from his wife, and she was a 21-year-old single Essex girl, employed at a high salary by the Playboy club as a croupier. Their conversations led to further meetings and they started living together in 1977. There was a mutual love of the good life (a term used in evidence to the court), namely a succession of luxury cars, comfortable holidays abroad, dining out in restaurants, gaming in casinos and racing and raising greyhounds. They also shared a love of dealing for dealing's sake in the market place and a delight in bargain hunting. In 1979, the man bought a bungalow for them both and their child. At the time of the purchase, he told the woman that the bungalow must be put in his name as he was having tax problems connected with his ongoing divorce but assured her: 'Don't worry about the future because when we are married it will be yours anyway and I'll always look after you and the boy.' In subsequent years, the woman participated in the man's business activities, including two speculative ventures involving considerable financial risk. She generally helped the man with his English and Spanish businesses, and brought up their two children but made no contribution to the purchase price.

The court held that the woman was entitled to a half share in the English house but no share in the house in Spain. It would appear that the court was prepared to accept that a brief conversation held many years before the parties split up had taken place as alleged by the woman and she was therefore entitled to a share since she had apparently acted, to her detriment, in reliance on the statement made by the male cohabitant. There are clearly difficulties in proving an oral agreement and as Waite J put it in *Hammond* [1992] 2 All ER 109 at 121:

'The tenderest exchanges of a common law courtship may assume an unforeseen significance many years later when they are brought under equity's microscope and subjected to an analysis under which many thousands of pounds of value may be liable to turn on this fine question as to whether the relevant words were spoken in earnest or in dalliance and with or without representational intent.'

*Male cohabitants also denied share in property if common intention
not proved*

On the other hand, the courts have been consistent by denying a share of property to a male cohabitant whose name did not appear on the deeds and who did not make any direct financial contribution to the purchase of the property. In *Thomas v Fuller-Brown* [1988] 1 FLR 237, the man, a builder by trade, moved in with a woman who owned the property and he carried out various acts of DIY around the house and even added a new storey to the property, enhancing its value. However, the court seemed to think that the DIY jobs were the sort of things a man would do around the house and the building work was not done because the man believed he had an interest in the property. The difficulty was that the man seemed to spend most of his time at home and the woman had apparently encouraged him to make himself useful and did not make any promises to him that he would have a share in the property as a result of any work in did on it. The man was not entitled to a share in the property.

Stack v Dowden – a twenty-first century cohabitation case

This case was reported in April 2007 as 'Unmarried couples come closer to winning legal divorce rights' which is, of course, an inaccurate use of legal terminology since unmarried couples do not enter into legal matrimony and therefore do not need a divorce when they separate. However, irrespective of the media's inaccuracy in terminology, this case was decided by the House of Lords, the highest domestic appellate tribunal in England and Wales, and its pronouncements have to be taken seriously.

Stack v Dowden [2007] 1 FLR 1858 involved a heterosexual unmarried couple who lived together for 20 years, and had four children from the union. Throughout the relationship the woman, an electrical engineer, earned more than her male cohabitant, a freelance builder. The couple moved into a house in 1983, bought in the woman's name for £30,000 that she paid from her savings and a mortgage in her name. In 1993, they bought another property which was registered in both their names for £190,000, using £66,000 from the sale of their previous home, a £65,000 mortgage and £59,000 in savings. However, in October 2001, the relationship broke down and the male partner moved out although the woman remained in the property. He was then granted a court order giving him half the proceeds of the house, worth £770,000. The woman appealed. The Appeal Court found that both parties intended to have an interest in the property but there is no evidence of any agreement or discussion between them as to the quantum of those shares. The court went on to infer a common intention from the parties' conduct. The fact that the woman had contributed a much larger share of the purchase price was of critical significance. The Court of Appeal awarded her 65 per cent of the proceeds of sale and the man 35 per cent.

The man's appeal to the House of Lords was dismissed. The Law Lords agreed that the parties' beneficial shares in the property should reflect their financial contribution towards it. In the absence of any express agreement, the courts need to find evidence of a common intention between the parties as to how the property would be owned.

Two points should be noted. First, the House of Lords made it clear that in a domestic context, in the case of a property registered in joint names, where there was no express declaration of the trusts of their respective beneficial interests, 'equity follows the law' which means that the presumption is that the couple own the property in equal shares. This is a firm presumption and rebutting it would not be easy. Hence the claimant seeking to establish that the equitable interests are held other than equally has a heavy burden to discharge. The presumption of equality will only be discharged in very unusual cases. Secondly, however, this case was itself held – unanimously by all five Law Lords – to fall into the very unusual category. Hence the Law Lords, despite their pronouncement of a general principle, were prepared to declare that the parties were entitled to unequal shares because it had been established that the woman made the greater financial contribution. The Law Lords made it clear that it was only in rare circumstances that a survey of the parties' conduct may give a clearer indication of what proportion of the shares were intended and demonstrate an inferred common intention that those shares should be unequal. The conduct need not be limited to direct financial contribution. Nevertheless, it is clear that, in this case at least, the principle that direct financial contribution (according to well-established resulting trust principles from earlier cases) made the difference to the ultimate allocation of the proceeds of sale for the parties despite the initial presumption of equality which followed from property registered in both parties' names.

Both names on a deed can lead to half-share under constructive trust

FOWLER V BARRON

In *Fowler v Barron* [2008] EWCA Civ 377 (Court of Appeal) ex-fireman Mr Barron lived together with Miss Fowler for 23 years, from 1983 to 2005. They purchased a property in joint names in 1988 to provide a home for themselves and their son, born in 1987. They did not take legal advice as to the consequences of the joint purchase and they did not discuss or enter into any agreement as to how the property should be held. The man paid the deposit, mortgage payments and the household bills and was therefore under the impression that he could claim the house as his. The lower court found that there was a resulting trust which could be valued by the respective contributions of the parties and since the woman had not made any such contributions the claim for a beneficial interest must fail. However, on appeal, the Court of Appeal disagreed and held that the judge had erred in that he applied the test for a resulting trust rather than for a constructive trust as is required under *Stack v Dowden* [2007] 1 FLR 1858. Accordingly, as the tenancy was in joint names, the onus was on the respondent to rebut the presumption of shared beneficial ownership, which he failed to do. Consequently, the court held that the woman had a 50 per cent share in the property regardless of her lack of quantifiable contribution. As Baroness Hale said in *Stack* at [69], on which the Court of Appeal relied: 'In law, "context is everything" [and] when a couple are joint owners of the home and jointly liable for the mortgage, the inferences to be drawn from who pays for what may be very different from the inference to be drawn when only one is owner of the home.'

Siblings living together not entitled to tax exemption for married couple and civil partners

BURDEN V UNITED KINGDOM

Burden v United Kingdom [2008] STC 252 was decided by the Grand Chamber of the European Court of Human Rights. Two unmarried sisters born in 1918 and 1925 had cohabited for 31 years in a property owned in their joint names. The sisters claimed that the survivor would have to pay 40 per cent inheritance tax on the property and she should have the right to a tax exemption on the death of the other sister on the ground that she should qualify on the same basis as a spouse or a civil partner and that the sisters had been prevented from entering into a civil partnership because they were sisters and therefore closely related to each other.

Two articles of the European Convention on Human Rights were asserted. Under art. 1, there is an entitlement to the peaceful enjoyment of possessions: 'No one shall be deprived of his possessions except in the public interest and subject to the conditions provided for by law and the general principles of international law.' Article 14 is a prohibition against discrimination.

Their claim was rejected by the chamber and the Grand Chamber, both ruling there was no violation of art. 14 taken with art. 1.

The European Court found that the relationship between siblings is qualitatively different from that between spouses or civil partners. One of the defining characteristics of the connection between siblings is consanguinity, whereas one of the defining characteristics of marriage or civil partnerships is that it is forbidden to close family members. A marriage and civil partnership confer a special status on those who enter into them. The determinative feature is the existence of a public undertaking carrying with it a body of rights and obligations of a contractual nature. Hence, the absence of such a legally binding agreement between the applicant and her sister rendered their relationship of cohabitation fundamentally different from that of a married or civil partnership couple. They could not be compared to a married couple or civil partners, even if the sisters had chosen to live together all their adult lives and this tax relief did not discriminate against the siblings.

Possible reforms?

In 2007, the Law Commission published a report which stated they had considered various means of reforming the law on cohabitation, and had suggested that cohabitants should have the right to apply for a share of a partner's money, property or pension. The Commission made several recommendations in its 2007 Report (*Cohabitation: The Financial Consequences of Relationship Breakdown No. 179, LC 2007* at http://www.lawcom.gov.uk/docs/lc307.pdf).

Definitional recommendations

The Law Commission suggests that persons should be cohabitants for the purposes of being eligible to apply for financial relief on separation where:

    (i)   they are living as a couple in a joint household; and
   (ii) they are neither married to each other nor civil partners.

Signposts

They also offered six signposts or guidelines:

   (1) existence of a joint household;
   (2) stability of the relationship;
   (3) financial arrangements;
   (4) responsibility for children;
   (5) sexual relationship;
   (6) public recognition of the relationship.

Application

The Commission recommended that the new statutory regime should only apply if the parties have not agreed to an opt out scheme, which must be in writing, signed by both parties and making clear the parties' intention not to apply the statute. They also declared that it would be inappropriate to apply the Matrimonial Causes Act scheme to unmarried cohabitants. They also recommended that their proposed scheme would apply only if the couple satisfied eligibility requirements; that is, they had a child from the relationship, lived together for a specified number of years (recommended not less than two but not more than five years); and the applicant had made qualifying contributions to the relationship giving rise to enduring consequences. The cohabitant would have the right to apply under the scheme if, as a result of qualifying contributions that the applicant has made, he or she suffered a significant economic disadvantage or the other gained a significant advantage from the relationship. The court would have the power to set aside an opt-out agreement if its enforcement would cause manifest unfairness.

Meaning of 'qualifying contribution'

The Commission described 'qualifying contribution' as 'any contribution arising from the cohabiting relationship which is made to the parties' shared lives or to the welfare of members of their families. Contributions are not limited to financial contributions, in particular to the care of the parties' children following separation'. Examples given included:

(i)   care for children of both parties, both during and after the relationship;

(ii)   care for other members of their families, including children who are not children of both parties and elderly relatives (whether or not they are members of the parties' joint household);

(iii)   financial support of the family;

(iv)   activities (whether financial or non-financial) which enhance the value of, or enable the respondent to acquire or retain, capital assets, including savings and investments;

(v)   unpaid work in the respondent's business;

(vi)   funding professional and other training; and

(vii)   giving up secure accommodation in order to commence cohabitation

(LC 2007, paras 4.34, 4.44).

Retained benefit

Retained benefit may take the form of capital, income, or earning capacity that has been acquired, retained or enhanced (LC 2007 para. 4.35).

Comparative perspectives – the Scottish legal position

In Scotland, which is a civil law jurisdiction, unmarried couples appear to be in a better position than their English counterparts. Since 2006, either party can make an application to the courts for a lump sum payment to compensate for any financial disadvantage suffered as a result of the relationship or to cover the costs of looking after a child.

We now turn to the development of heterosexual cohabitation in the United States, which is a predominantly common law jurisdiction.

The United States – domestic partnerships outside marriage

Nancy Cott argues: 'The married as well as the unmarried bear the ideological, ethical and practical impress of the marital institution, which is difficult and impossible to escape' (Cott, 2000, p. 3). Cott argues that in the nineteenth century marriage was all-pervasive, influencing the state's definition and debates over citizenship, political rights of former slaves, Native Americans, Asian immigrants and women. Indeed, she contends that: 'The whole system of attribution and meaning that we call gender relies or to a great extent derives from the structuring provided by marriage.' In the 1990s, in six States (Florida, North Carolina, North Dakota, Mississippi, Virginia and West Virginia) cohabitation was illegal (Ihara and Warner, *The Living Together Kit: A Legal Guide for Unmarried Couples*, 1997). However, after the United States Supreme Court decision in *Lawrence v Texas* 123 S Ct 1472 (2003) the validity of such laws is in some doubt.

To be sure, the United States has experienced a surge in cohabitational couples living outside marriage in domestic and quasi-marriage relationships and the number of such couples has geometrically increased during the past four decades. Cohabitational relationships outside marriage for opposite sex and same-sex couples has proved a strong competitor to marriage. With the fading away of 'living in sin' as it used to be called, the stigma associated with such relationships has virtually disappeared, at least in urban centres. As Friedman puts it in relation to such partnerships: 'What was once an object of gossip and scandal hardly raises an eyebrow in the early twenty-first century' (Friedman, 2004, p. 67).

Possible reasons for the rise in cohabitation in American jurisdictions

Champlin has suggested various reasons for the rise in cohabitation. These include: the 'greening' of America with its antipathy towards institutions of any type; the legalization of abortion; the common acceptance and practice of contraceptives; a common toleration, even approval, of cohabitation; the growing mobility in American culture; the delay of marriage due to graduate studies and the training for professions; and the accelerating rate of divorces (Champlin, 2003).

Cohabitation statistics

In the majority of American States there is no legal definition of cohabitation and demographers have developed various methods of identifying cohabitation in order to measure its prevalence. The most helpful definition appears to be that of the Census Bureau which describes an 'unmarried partner' as '[a] person aged 15 years and over, who is not related to the householder, who shares living quarters and who has a close personal relationship with the householder'. There was a huge surge in the number of unmarried couples living together in the 1960s and 1970s. In 1960 there were 439,000, by 1984 the number had increased to 1,988,000 and in 1998 the Census Bureau total was 4,200,000. By the early 1990s, cohabitation outside marriage was well-established in American family life (Kennedy and Bumpass, 2007). It has grown from being a somewhat rare relationship into a normal part of adult formation, rapidly spreading to families with children so that by 1995, nearly two-fifths of all children could expect to experience 'maternal cohabitation' during childhood. Indeed, by 1995, 45 per cent of women aged 19–44 had lived with an unmarried partner (Bumpass and Lu, 2000). Cohabitation has usually been a short-lived state with just over half of all cohabiting couples married within ten years (Bumpass and Lu, 2000). Chandra's research indicates that the numbers increased to encompass half of all women aged 15–44 in 2002 (Chandra *et al.*, 2005).

In 2005, the Census Bureau reported 4.85 million cohabiting couples, which was up more than 1,000 per cent from 1960 when there were 439,000 such couples. A survey published in 2000 found that more than half of newlyweds have lived together, at least for a short period, before getting married. The cohabiting population includes all ages, but the average cohabiting age group is between 25 and 34. However, this statistic has no special significance, since the average marriage population is in this range.

Legal status of couples who cohabit outside marriage

States such as California have laws that recognize cohabiting couples as 'domestic partners', where such couples are defined as people who 'have chosen to share one another's lives in an intimate and committed relationship of mutual caring' including having a common residence, and are the same sex or persons of opposite sex if one or both of the persons are over the age of 62. A Domestic Partners Registry was created (http://www.ss.ca.gov/dpregistry) which grants domestic partners limited legal recognition and some rights similar to those of married couples.

Fifty years ago it was illegal in every State for adult lovers to live together without being married. However, in the early twenty-first century, there are five States (Mississippi, Virginia, Florida, North Dakota and Michigan) where cohabitation by opposite-sex couples is still a crime but anti-cohabitation laws are seldom enforced (and struck down by judges, as occurred in North Carolina by Judge Alford). The widely held view is that, since *Lawrence v Texas* 539 US 123 (2003), laws making cohabitation illegal are unconstitutional.

Case law on heterosexual cohabitation

Without the rights framework that exists within the marriage relationship, predictable issues have arisen in relation to property rights, custody disputes over children and parental rights, and some disputes have reached the courts.

A series of 'palimony' cases, so-called by the media because of drawing an analogy between a pal's rights and the rights of a divorcing spouse, have been decided culminating in 1976 with the well-known case of *Marvin v Marvin* 134 Cal Reptr 815 (1976), involving the Hollywood actor Lee Marvin. 'Palimony' is a misnomer since a spouse has a right to share in marital property based on his or her status as a spouse whereas a pal has no automatic legal right to property or support based on his or her status as a non-marital partner (see Laskin at http://www.palimony.com/7/html).

Hence a non-marital plaintiff has to establish a basis for a claim such as an express or implied contract (see the cases mentioned below, *Marvin* 134 Cal Reptr 815 (1976), and especially *Marvin* 122 Cal App 3d 871 (1981)).

Cases pre-Marvin

In *Trutalli v Meraviglia* 215 Cal 698 (1932), a California court established that non-marital partners may lawfully enter into a contract concerning the ownership of property acquired during the relationship, and ruled that an agreement between cohabitants that all money be paid to the man to be invested for their joint benefit is enforceable, so long as it is not based upon the illegal and immoral agreement of the plaintiff and defendant to live and cohabit together as man and wife, outside marriage. This sort of principle then continued with *Padilla v Padilla* 38 Cal App 2d 319 (1940) and *Hill v Estate of Westbrook* 95 Cal App 599 (1950), with the memorable line in the latter (at p. 603): 'The law does not award compensation for living with a man as a concubine and bearing him children.' In *Updeck v Samuel* 123 Cal App 2d 264 (1954), another California court held that an oral contract between a man and a woman based on consideration that they are living together as husband and wife, where both parties are legally married to other spouses, is void ab initio because it is founded on an immoral consideration and calls for them to live in a state of adultery.

Several cases then followed a similar line, until *Beckman v Mayhew* 49 Cal App 3d 529 (1975), which held that a cohabitant was entitled to an equitable lien on the man's real estate, where she had co-signed a promissory note with him, the proceeds of which were mainly used to purchase materials used in improving the property. It also held that the Family Law Act did not apply to cohabitants.

This case was followed in *Marvin v Marvin* 134 Cal Reptr 815 (1976).

Marvin v Marvin

The most high-profile palimony case that reached the courts was *Marvin v Marvin* 134 Cal Reptr 815 (1976), heard by a Californian court, involving the late movie star, Lee Marvin and a female cohabitant, Michelle. The couple had in fact entered into an oral agreement which it was claimed had been to the effect that: '[W]hile the parties lived together they would combine their efforts and earnings and would share equally any and all property accumulated as a result of their efforts whether individual or combined.' Michelle further claimed that they had agreed to hold themselves out to the general public as husband and wife, and that she would 'further render her services as companion, housekeeper and cook'. She argued that she had given up a lucrative career as an entertainer and singer to devote herself full time to Lee Marvin; that she had lived with the defendant for six years and had fulfilled the obligations under the agreement. When they split up, the woman sought a declaration of constructive trust to claim one-half of the property acquired during the course of the relationship. Under the law as it stood before the case, it looked as though the woman did not have much chance of success and indeed, the California Supreme Court confirmed that Michele could not enforce an agreement that rested upon 'illicit meretricious consideration' which Friedman calls a 'smarmy term for a long-term sexual affair' (Friedman, 2004, p. 68). Neither could they enforce a contract to pay for the performance of sexual services which would be an agreement for prostitution and unlawful for that reason. But in the present case, the court ruled that the parties could lawfully agree to pool their earnings and to hold all property acquired during the relationship in accord with the law governing community property. In the present case, the terms of the contract as alleged did not rest upon any unlawful consideration. It was therefore held that the complaint furnished a suitable basis upon which the trial court could render declaratory relief.

The court also added that in the absence of an express agreement, it could look to a variety of other remedies to protect the parties' legitimate expectations. It reviewed a range of possible remedies from using conduct to infer an implied contract, a constructive trust, resulting trust and even a quantum meruit (as much as he deserved) to reflect the reasonable value of household services rendered. But its central and telling point was that: 'The mores of society have ... changed radically in regard to cohabitation that ... [the court] could not impose a standard based on alleged moral considerations that have apparently been so widely abandoned by so many.' The trial judge awarded the plaintiff $104,000 but the case went on appeal and the California Appeal Court declared that an unmarried cohabitative relationship has no community property claim but merely a contract claim. Since there was no evidence of an enforceable contract between Marvin and his cohabitee, the court deleted the award and sent the case back for trial in the lower court. At that second trial, Michelle's case was dismissed.

Post-Marvin developments

The *Marvin* case is still regarded as a landmark seminal case. Some States followed it, some curtailed its possible effect. Simply by allowing the case to be heard (in 1976), the California Supreme Court sparked similar cases in 15 other States. By the time the case reached its final stage in 1979, there were 1,000 palimony suits pending in California alone. Since *Marvin*, the California courts have been very careful to distinguish Marvin actions from domestic relations actions, holding that an award of spousal support may not be based on the parties' cohabitation before marriage (see *Re Marriage of Bukaty* 180 Cal App 3d 143 (1986)); and that a *Marvin* case may not be processed in the superior court under the special family law rules (see *Schafer v Superior Court* 180 Cal App 3d 305 (1986)); and that jurisdiction standards applicable to domestic relations cases do not apply to *Marvin* actions (see *Kroopf v Guffey* 183 Cal App 3d 1351 at 1357–8 (1986)).

Some ambiguity still appears to persist regarding what *Marvin* stands for, as arguably illustrated by the California Appeal Court in *Taylor v Fields* 178 Cal App 3d 653 (1986). The plaintiff, Taylor, had a relationship with a married man, Leo, for 42 years. When Leo died, Taylor sued his widow, alleging breach of an agreement by Leo to take care of Taylor financially. The Court of Appeal declared that the relationship alleged by Taylor was nothing more than that of a legally married man and his mistress. Hence the alleged contract rested on meretricious consideration and was unenforceable. However, the court then held that the fact that the parties did not live together was the main reason for denying Taylor recovery. The court then noted (at 661) that in *Marvin*, and the cases cited therein, the courts upheld agreements where parties had lived together and which were not based on meretricious consideration. It then reviewed cases where cohabitants had claimed loss of consortium or wrongful death, including a case where the right to sue for loss of consortium had extended to cohabitants who engaged in 'stable and significant' relationships. It then concluded that cohabitation between the parties was a prerequisite to recovery in a Marvin action and that 'Taylor's contract with Leo is unenforceable because there is no showing of stable and significant cohabitation' (at 666). The fact that Taylor asserted that she and Leo occasionally spent weekends together and registered as husband and wife was 'inadequate to bring their relationship within Marvin principles' (at 663).

Laskin criticizes this statement as a 'profound misunderstanding of Marvin' because the Marvin principle is to treat non-marital cohabitants 'as we do any other unmarried persons' principally by enforcing their contracts. So in effect the court in *Taylor v Fields* illogically held that 'one must be a cohabitant to be treated like a non-cohabitant' (that is like 'any other unmarried persons'). As Laskin points out, if this were followed to its logical conclusion, no contract would be enforceable unless the contracting parties live together (Laskin at http://www.palimony.com/7.html). This criticism appears to have been justified when we note subsequent cases such as *Milian v De Leon* 181 Cal App 3d 1185 (1986) and *Bergen v Wood* 14 Cal App 4th 854 (1993) which did not pursue the approach of *Taylor v Fields*. Indeed, in *Milian*, the court stated: 'Cohabitation is not a prerequisite to the finding of an implied agreement between unmarried persons concerning their property' (at 1193).

The Friedman case

Two contrasting cases may be noted. The first is *Friedman v Friedman* 29 Cal App 4th 876 (1993), in which the California Appeal Court held that there was no evidence of an implied contract for support despite a 21 year relationship, two children, marriage plans and post-relationship payments of $190,000. An immediate comparative observation may be made with the infamous 1984 English case of *Burns v Burns* [1984] Ch 317 where the couple cohabited for 19 years in all, without ever getting married, despite the woman taking the man's name, looking after their children and performing duties which a legally married spouse would normally fulfil. The English Court of Appeal held that as all the property and the home were in the man's name, the female cohabitant would not be entitled to any share of the property or assets.

Byrne v Laura

The second case, *Byrne v Laura* 52 Cal App 4th 1054 (1997), involved probate proceedings in which the decedent's unmarried cohabitant sought to enforce an oral agreement that the decedent would support her for the rest of her life and that some day she would have all his assets. The California Court of Appeal reversed a summary judgment for the defendant and held that (i) an oral promise of support is enforceable; (ii) a contract of support was not too uncertain to enforce; and (iii) a contract that all assets would someday be the plaintiff's was enforceable, although the agreement would be subject to the Statute of Frauds, and either the Civil Code, Probate Code or a trust for real property. It should be emphasized that the court appeared to find that there was evidence which showed the decedent expected to provide for the plaintiff's support and that expectation should be fulfilled. The court also found that equitable estoppel to assert the Statute of Frauds is a question of fact and the trier of fact could find that the plaintiff had seriously changed her position by moving in with the decedent, performing the duties of a spouse and retiring from her job. An illuminating observation from the court is that even if the plaintiff performed the services out of love that does not defeat an argument for equitable estoppel. It is not necessary that her services be 'unequivocally referable' to the contract so long as she 'seriously' changed her position and would suffer 'unconscionable' injury, which in this case must refer to detriment.

COMPARATIVE PERSPECTIVES ON HETEROSEXUAL COHABITATION

The clear comparative point that should be noted in relation to *Marvin* is that it reflects the legal approach in English law as far as remedies for unmarried cohabitants are concerned. American courts are also prepared to consider using implied, constructive and resulting trusts to provide some sort of remedy in the absence of evidence of an enforceable contract between unmarried cohabitants. However, they are also prepared to consider a quantum meruit claim which the English courts have not usually included in their range of possible remedies for unmarried cohabiting couples. In classic common law style, the law has been and continues to be shaped by the judiciary without definitive or specific statutes on cohabitation governing the resolution of any disputes.

Further comparative perspectives

Common law v civil law approaches

It has been clear from the outset of this book that it is important not just to make comparisons but to make meaningful comparisons, to recognize similarities and differences but to always place them in context. We can look at common law jurisdictions, so named because they have a common law heritage, and therefore adopt a common law approach of having case law as their main source of law, inevitably supplemented by statute law as in the United States, but always requiring judicial interpretation of statutes. We look at civil law jurisdictions conscious of their different approaches, being primarily Code-based, Code-orientated and Code-dominated. Courts in civil law countries rely heavily on the illustrations in their many Codes to interpret the law and their style of judgment is different from the typical common law jurisdiction judgment. But at root, people appear to face the same problems as far as relationships are concerned – in order to show their commitment to one another they would like some sort of ritual or indication to manifest this commitment, but if they are opposed to marriage what do they do? How can they validate their union? How has the law in other jurisdictions responded to the needs of such couples, if they feel the need, for example, to protect the children of such unions?

Making incorrect comparative links and assumptions?

Auchmuty raises several points in relation to using comparative data in a meaningful way. For instance, she argues that the globalisation of the same-sex marriage movement has meant that arguments from one jurisdiction are being applied to another jurisdiction with little consideration for the different social and legal context (Auchmuty, 2008, p. 488). She believes this dubious application of ostensibly comparing the situation in ostensibly similar jurisdictions is compounded by the fact that the 'general public' has a 'muddled grasp' of the law and 'their assumption that marriage makes a much greater legal difference in the UK than it actually does' (Auchmuty, 2008, p. 488). She points out that one does not have to be married in the United Kingdom for one's relationship to be recognised by banks, insurance companies and the tax office or in relation to one's pension scheme or gym. Moreover, civil partners have the same recognition as spouses and in most cases, in practice, so do unmarried cohabitants (opposite-sex or same-sex) including in hospital. However, some of the benefits which marriage does confer in the United States, such as transferable health benefits, do not apply and are irrelevant in the United Kingdom. Her most telling conclusion is that comparative data may be – and has been – usefully employed in legal argument, but she believes its use is limited when other countries' laws, conceptualizations of marriage and social practices 'are so very different from the British' (Auchmuty, 2008, p. 489).

One response to this is that the comparative law enterprise is not only about finding similarities in data between the objects of comparison in different legal systems but also to identify differences (see Part I for a detailed discussion of methodology) and so long as the comparatist is aware of the limitations of the comparative data, and is sufficiently aware of the social, cultural and political elements which form the backdrop to this data, the danger of drawing the wrong conclusions from the comparison can be anticipated and averted.

Australia

Introduction

Passing legislation to deal with a social phenomenon such as cohabitation is not the usual approach taken by common law jurisdictions like England and the United States, but it has been the Antipodean response, as we shall see. While there is no uniformity in Australian legislation, there appears to be a trend towards widening the scope of coverage of the various pieces of legislation in its constituent States and Territories. The common law jurisdiction of Australia has a regime under the Property (Relationships) Act 1984 (NSW) which is specifically aimed at heterosexual cohabitants. This statute has been in operation for about a quarter of a century with New South Wales being the first to introduce such a regime in 1984, and Victoria following suit in 1987, but with a more limited scheme than the New South Wales model. The New South Wales Act was amended to include same-sex relationships in 1999 when the name of the Act was changed from the De Facto Relationships Act 1984 to the Property (Relationships) Act 1984.

Basic approach of legislation dealing with de facto relationships

This Act's basic approach has been to prescribe a minimum number of years before such couples might qualify for legal recognition and to shorten the qualifying period if there are children from the relationship.

De facto relationships statutes

New South Wales was the first Australian legislature to introduce a statute, the De Facto Relationships Act 1984, to deal with the proliferation of unmarried heterosexual relationships that were in existence in the early 1980s, calling such relationships de facto relationships. Victoria passed similar legislation in 1987 by amending its Property Law Act 1958, although with a more restrictive scheme. The Northern Territory passed its De Facto Relationships Act 1991. The Australian Capital Territory passed the Domestic Relationships Act 1994 which was noticeably different from other States' property regimes at the time, in that it covered same-sex relationships, as well. South Australia passed the De Facto Relationship Act 1996.

In 1999, New South Wales amended its legislation to include same-sex relationships. This was followed by Queensland passing amendments to its Property Law Act 1974 in 1999 to include same-sex relationships in its first de facto property scheme. This approach was followed in the Tasmanian Relationships Act 2003 and Victoria amended its Property Law Act 1958 to refer to 'domestic partner irrespective of gender'. The Northern Territory De Facto Relationships Act mentions a 'marriage-like' relationship but South Australia's De Facto Relationships Act is restricted in operation to a 'man and woman'.

New South Wales renamed its De Facto Relationships Act the Property (Relationships) Act 1984, which came into force on 28 June 1999, and its definition of 'de facto spouse' includes a cohabiting same-sex couple.

Definition of 'domestic relationship' under the New South Wales Act

Section 5(1) of the Property (Relationships) Act 1984 introduces the concept of a 'domestic relationship' which it defines as (a) a de facto relationship; or (b) a close personal relationship (other than a marriage or a de facto relationship) between two adult persons, whether or not related by family, who are living together, one or each of whom provides the other with domestic support and personal care. Section 5(2) makes it clear that a close personal relationship will not be taken to exist between two persons where one of them provides the other with domestic support and personal care for fee or reward or on behalf of another person or organization.

Section 5A of the Act clarifies what 'related by family' means by stating that persons are related by family if (a) one is the parent, or another ancestor of the other, or (b) one is the child, or another descendant, of the other, or (c) they have a parent in common. Previously, s. 3 of the Act applied only to those couples 'living together or having lived together as a husband and wife on a bona fide domestic basis although not married to each other'.

Under s. 4(1) of the amended Property (Relationships) Act 1984 a de facto relationship is a relationship between two adult persons:

(a) who live together as a couple; and
(b) who are not married to one another or related by family.

In s. 4(2), determining whether two persons are in a de facto relationship, all the circumstances of the relationship are to be taken into account, including such of the following matters as may be relevant in a particular case:

(a) the duration of the relationship;
(b) the nature and extent of common residence;
(c) whether or not a sexual relationship exists;
(d) the degree of financial dependence or interdependence, and any arrangements for financial support, between the parties;
(e) the ownership, use and acquisition of property;
(f) the degree of mutual commitment to a shared life;
(g) the care and support of children;
(h) the performance of household duties;
(i) the reputation and public aspects of the relationship.

Section 14 provides for a party to a domestic relationship to apply to a court for an order for the adjustment of interests with respect to the property of the parties, or either of them, or for the granting of maintenance, or both. Section 14(2) provides that these applications can be made in addition to remedies or relief under any other law. Section 20(1) provides that a court may adjust the interests of the parties to a domestic relationship in property as seems just and equitable.

To come within the scheme, s. 17 stipulates that the applicant must satisfy the court that the parties have lived together in a domestic relationship for no less than two years. Alternatively, s. 17(2) provides that a court may make an order where it is satisfied (a) that there is a child of the parties to the application; or (b) that the applicant has made substantial contributions to the acquisition, conservation or improvement of any of the property of the parties; or to the capacity of the homemaker or parent, or to the welfare of the other party, or to a child of the parties or child accepted by the parties into the household, whether or not the child is a child of one of them (see s. 20), for which the applicant would not be adequately compensated; and the applicant has care and control of a child of the respondent and serious injustice would result if the court fails to make an order.

New Zealand

New Zealand is another common law jurisdiction and again, somewhat unusually for such a jurisdiction, has passed legislation dealing with (heterosexual) cohabitation (called 'de facto relationships' in their law), as well as same-sex relationships.

The human rights dimension in New Zealand law

Within the last 30 years, New Zealand has undergone certain changes which have enabled it to develop a 'human-rights culture' (Atkin, 2003, p. 176). First, the Human Rights Commission Act 1977 introduced anti-discrimination laws, focusing on gender and race discrimination but also including marital status and religion. Second, the Human Rights Act 1993 extended the anti-discrimination grounds to include sexual orientation, which is defined as 'a heterosexual, homosexual, lesbian, or bisexual orientation' (s. 21(1)(m) Human Rights Act 1993). 'Marital status' was defined as being single, married, married but separated, divorced, widowed, or living in a relationship in the nature of a marriage under s. 21(1)(b) of the Human Rights Act 1993 (Atkin, 2003, p. 176). The phrase 'in the nature of a marriage' clearly covers de facto relationships since the growth of such relationships has led to a demand that they be recognized within domestic law.

The New Zealand Parliament decided in 2001 that a more sweeping reform of the law was required. Although the path to reform was far from smooth, new laws were finally brought into force in February 2002.

The property reforms in 2002

Major changes to the laws relating to the property of married and de facto couples came into force on 1 February 2002 through new rules which amended the Property (Relationships) Act 1976. From that date, the property of de facto couples (including same-sex couples) who decide to terminate their relationship has been divided according to the same equal-sharing rules as those which regulate the property of married couples. This will apply for the purposes of inheritance (whether a party dies testate or intestate), division of property at the end of a relationship, and for the payment of maintenance. The key legislation is the Matrimonial Property Act 1976, renamed the Property (Relationships) Act 1976 by the Property (Relationships) Amendment Act 2001. In effect, the new Property Relationships Act 2001 gives the Court jurisdiction only if the parties are married, or there has been a 'void marriage'. However, if the couple is heterosexual and living together and unmarried, the general law applied unless their relationship ended after 1st February 2001. There are also exceptions to the 3-year rule which is discussed under the next section (see p. 259). A change in terminology was adopted, and 'matrimonial property' has become 'relationship property'. The courts have also been given new discretionary powers to award compensation for 'economic disparity' where there is likely to be a significant discrepancy in the income potential and living standards of the two separating parties (Atkin, 2003, p. 175). Atkin calls this a 'leap in the dark' for New Zealand law because there was some ambivalence about whether this would genuinely advantage women who had put their careers on hold during the bringing up of their children or would advantage many men. It appears that so far there has not been a surge of litigation as a consequence of this legislation. It is important to note that this legislation allows parties to contract out of the Act (Pt 6) and it has subsequently extended to de facto couples but only applies if both parties agree (Atkin, 2003, p. 176).

Thus, the Property (Relationships) Act 2001, with one important proviso, applies the same rules on property division to married and unmarried couples. The proviso is the 'threshold to be crossed' (Atkin, 2003, p. 177) before the court has jurisdiction to intervene. If the parties are married, or there has been a 'void marriage' this is sufficient for a court to intervene. If the marriage is of short duration, which usually means the parties have lived together for less than three years, or if certain conditions are satisfied (such as one party owning the house before the parties began living together), then the property may be divided on the basis of contribution, rather than equally.

The situation on jurisdiction with regard to de facto relationships involving unmarried opposite-sex couples is quite different.

De facto relationships: unmarried heterosexual couples

The 2006 New Zealand census did not necessarily provide clear-cut findings. Atkin points out that in part this was because a large number of people, 207,075, did not answer the marital status question on the census questionnaire. The category of 'partnered' was ticked by 48,174 people and 'other partnerships', mostly de facto (that is, unmarried opposite-sex couples) relationships, accounted for 379,956 people (see Atkin, 2007, p. 221). The 2001 census findings are that there were 300,846 couples living in de facto relationships, compared with 247,847 in 1996 and 87,960 in 1981 when statistics were first collected. In 2001, 10,134 people were in same-sex relationships, compared with just 6,520 in 1996. Male partnerships involved 4,464 men and female partnerships involved 5,670 women.

The status of heterosexual couples who cohabit in 'marriage-like' relationships but remained unmarried has also undergone legislative changes in New Zealand.

Certain key factors were also noted by Atkin (see Atkin, 2007, p. 222):

(i)   The new rules apply only to de facto relationships which ended after 1 February 2002, which is when the 2001 amendments came into force. It is therefore important in transitional cases to know whether a relationship ended before or after the cut-off date. If it ended before 1 February 2002, it would have to be decided under the old law.

(ii)   Most de facto relationships must last three years before the Family Court has jurisdiction to hear applications, subject to certain exceptions (see below). Hence the beginning and ending of the relationship will be crucial in determining whether there has been sufficient passage of time and the particular relationship qualifies.

(iii) The automatic right to apply under the Act expires three years after the ending of a relationship. Later applications are dependent on the court granting an extension of time.

The exceptions to the three-year rule in (ii) (above) are set out in s. 14A of the Property (Relationships) Act 1976. These include: first, if there is a child from the relationship; or second, the applicant must have made a 'substantial' contribution to the relationship. In both these circumstances, despite the relationship not lasting three years, the court may have jurisdiction. This legislation is based on Australian legislation (s. 17 Property Relationships Act 1984 (NSW), where the relevant period is two, not three years). As far as 'substantial' is concerned, the case law has not, so far, been decisive. Thus, one case has said the party must have contributed more than 50 per cent to the relationship to rank as 'substantial' (*M v H*, Tauranga Family Court, FP 070/210/03, 19 May 2004), whereas another has said that the contribution need not have been too far beyond the norm (see *LS v ZJ* [2005] NZFLR 932 at [66]).

Jurisdiction will probably ultimately depend on whether the court is satisfied that failure to make an order would result in 'serious injustice', but this is a term which the courts have been reluctant to define in any definitive way (see the comments of Ronald Young J in *Schimdt v Jawad* [2006] NZFLR 410). Chisholm J mentioned a 'relatively high threshold' but in the event was prepared to hold that the test had been met in order for the parties not to have to revisit the same issue in civil proceedings (see *S v W* [2006] NZFLR 699 at [133]–[137]). Hence the matter remains one for each court to determine according to the individual facts of a case.

Defining de facto relationships

Defining a de facto relationship has proved problematic, as it has been in other jurisdictions, since those in such relationships will inevitably rely on the factual nature of their association in order to establish their right to have court intervention in their favour. If the relationship has been characterized by periods of cohabitation and non-cohabitation, there will clearly be scope for dispute. The pivotal question will be whether the parties (whether same-sex or opposite sex) lived together as a couple within the period required under the legislation, and s. 2D of the Property (Relationships) Act 1976 provides a list of non-exclusive factors which seek to assist in determining this issue; namely, duration, nature and extent of common residence, sexual relations, finances, property, the 'degree of mutual commitment to a shared life', children, household duties, reputation and public aspects of the relationship. Section 2D(3) makes it clear that no single factor is an essential condition in order to prove the existence of a de facto relationship. Atkin argues that therefore two people may be found to be in a de facto relationship even though they do not reside in the same place, nor do they need to be financially interdependent, which is a requirement if they are to qualify for social security support (see *Ruka v Department of Social Welfare* [1997] NZLR 154, cited by Atkin, 2007, p. 223).

Love in the Pacific

Although there was no initial surge of applications on this issue, there is now a steady stream of cases, which are usually determined on their individual facts. An instructive case is *Scragg v Scott* [2006] NZFLR 1076, a decision from a two-judge High Court. The facts were that the parties started seeing each other in the 1990s, after the woman's marriage had broken down. Their relationship blossomed into a full sexual relationship. The man had business on the island of Guam in the Pacific Ocean and the woman lived with him whenever she was in Guam, and he lived with her whenever he was in New Zealand. The man was extremely generous to the woman with gifts and she was largely dependent on him. The man then started another relationship in Guam without the knowledge of the first woman, in 2000, which was before the new law came into effect. The first court held that there was a de facto relationship which lasted until July 2002, which meant that the new law applied. This decision was upheld on appeal. Gendall J and Ellen France J commented (at [31] and [37]) on the task of ascertaining whether a de facto relationship existed saying, inter alia:

'The complexity and diversity of human nature and behaviour is such that many types of association may properly fall within the category of de facto relationship as envisaged by Parliament. For there to be a relationship there must be an emotional association between two persons … [t]he test must inevitably be evaluative, with the Judge having to weigh up as best he or she can all of the factors – not just those contained in s. 2D, but also any others there may be – and applying a common sense objective judgment to the particular case … Generalizations are to be avoided because every case is fact specific.'

Atkin highlights the fact that the learned judges emphasized that the inquiry is essentially a factual one which will differ from case to case (Atkin, 2007, p. 223). This variability of decisions is, of course, more typical of family law cases than those in other branches of the law. Two unusual cases illustrate this point further.

The pimp and the prostitute

In *Dravitzki v Methven*, the court had to decide whether a pimp and a prostitute were in a de facto relationship for the purposes of the legislation. It was decided that it was a 'parasitic business relationship' up until the time when the woman ceased being a prostitute at which point it became a de facto relationship (see *Dravitzki v Methven* (2006) FAM 2004-043-000714, 18 January 2006).

The odd couple

In the second case, *PZ v JC* [2006] NZFLR 97, a 41-year-old student boarded with a 78-year-old who in due course died. Although there had apparently been intimacies, it was held that the relationship lacked the necessary commitment to be a de facto relationship.

Level of commitment the critical factor

The level of commitment appears to be the critical factor but the judges in *Scragg v Scott* [2006] NZFLR 1076 were not prepared to lay down a definitive rule, and while they conceded that sexual fidelity may be a factor, they were equally clear that it all depends on the particular circumstances of a given case and 'mere unfaithfulness cannot, of itself, and without more, end a de facto relationship which has already formed and which continues though having necessary characteristics' (see *Scragg v Scott* [2006] NZFLR 1076 at [44] and [59]). However, Atkin observes that a situation like *Scragg* could be complicated and perhaps this necessitated Mr Scragg's argument that there was not one de facto relationship, but several, each lasting short periods of time. The legal effect of such an argument is that a short duration relationship is likely to fall outside the Act but the judges were not prepared to accept this argument. Hence common residence is only one factor and not an essential requirement. Consequently, the fact that the parties have physically separated does not necessarily bring the relationship to an end. This means that under this legislation, the question of whether a de facto relationship has ended will depends on the same process which ascertains whether a couple is living apart, which has always been a difficult computation.

Atkin supports the courts' approach on the basis that the courts should not too readily accept that a relationship had ceased when the parties had reunited to form a new relationship as this would defeat the purpose of the Act which is to provide a rational basis for the division of property (Atkin, 2007, p. 224).

Before the 2001 reforms took effect, same-sex couples in New Zealand were not covered by legislation but could invoke common law and equity to divide their property in the same way as opposite-sex couples but the 2001 reforms now apply equally to gay and lesbian de facto relationships.

The 2005 reforms on civil unions

In April 2005, civil unions (for same-sex couples) were established as a legally recognized form of relationship so that civil union couples who break up are now treated in the same way as married couples under the Property (Relationships) Act.

Canada

In Canada, another common law jurisdiction, under the Modernization of Benefits and Obligations Act, SC 2000, the law has over a number of years recognized parity between the obligations and benefits of spouses and cohabitants. Nevertheless, the Canadian Supreme Court held in *Attorney-General of Nova Scotia v Walsh* (2002) 4 SCR 325 that it was not unconstitutionally discriminatory for Provincial legislatures to discriminate against unmarried couples in terms of marital property laws.

LEGAL RECOGNITION OF SAME SEX RELATIONSHIPS

Introduction

The legal recognition of relationships between same-sex couples has attracted considerable attention on a global scale for more than ten years. Indeed, the decision whether to permit same-sex couples to formalize their relationship has been one of the most controversial issues within Europe, the United Kingdom and the United States. These same-sex unions have been called registered partnerships, civil partnerships, life partnerships and civil unions. The term 'registered partnership' is used in the Scandinavian countries, the Netherlands, Czech Republic and Switzerland. Denmark was the first country in the world to offer registered partnerships to same-sex couples commencing on 7 June 1989. Since then, several countries have followed suit, with France introducing their unique civil pact of solidarity (pacs) in November 1999, Germany a registered partnership (called a life partnership) in August 2001, and Finland in the same year; and the United Kingdom introduced the Civil Partnerships Act to formalize unions between same-sex partners in October 2005.

Common law jurisdictions

As the law currently stands in Britain, same-sex couples cannot enter into a legal 'marriage' but they may enter into a civil partnership, which will have almost identical legal consequences.

Same-sex unions/civil partnerships in England and Wales

Nature of a civil partnership in England and Wales

A civil partnership is a relationship between two people of the same sex, formed when they register as civil partners of each other, which ends on death, dissolution or annulment. Civil partnership became legal in England and Wales with the passing of the Civil Partnership Act 2004, which came into force on 5 December 2005.

The Civil Partnership Act 2004

Formation and registration

A civil partnership will be formed as soon as both individuals have signed the civil partnership document in the presence of a registrar and two witnesses. No religious service is allowed to take place during the registration, and in any event, the registration cannot take place in premises that are either designed for, or are in use mainly for, religious services.

Eligibility

Each party to the civil partnership must be of the same sex and be at least 16 years of age. Any party below 18 years of age will usually need parental consent, except in Scotland where such consent is not required. The parties to the proposed partnership must not be within the prohibited degrees of relationship. A party who is already in a marriage or civil partnership is ineligible to register.

Legal consequences of civil partnership

The position of civil partners in relation to financial arrangements replicates that of married partners.

The ground for dissolution of a civil partnership

As is the requirement with a marriage, no application for dissolution may be made in England and Wales until a year has passed since the formation of the civil partnership, except in Scotland. Similarly, the sole ground for dissolution is irretrievable breakdown. Section 44 of the Civil Partnership Act 2004 declares that the court may not make an order of dissolution unless the applicant satisfies certain 'facts' which prove the breakdown of the relationship. These facts are identical to those for divorce under the Matrimonial Causes Act 1973 except for adultery. Hence, there is respondent's behaviour, two years' separation with respondent's consent, two years' desertion or five years' separation. The court is bound to make a dissolution order if the applicant satisfies the court of any of these facts, unless it is not convinced that the partnership has broken down irretrievably. The s. 5 defence is also available, so the order would not be made if it would cause the respondent to suffer grave financial or other hardship if the dissolution order were made and it must be wrong in all the circumstances to order the dissolution. In divorce proceedings, this defence very rarely succeeds and it will probably be the same with civil partnerships. Bamforth has suggested that adultery should be included as a 'fact' proving irretrievable breakdown but be rephrased as a concept directly analogous to adultery since the law is seeking to deal with the consequences of sexual infidelity (see Bamforth, 2007, p. 133). Nevertheless, adultery may be cited as an example of unreasonable behaviour.

Unlike a marriage, a civil partnership may not be ended for non-consummation or venereal disease. There is clearly the difficulty of defining non-consummation in the case of a same-sex relationship in the same terms as an opposite-sex relationship.

Same-sex civil partnerships not regarded as same-sex marriages under English law

The stated object of the Civil Partnership Act 2004 (UK) was to put same-sex couples on an equal footing before the law as married couples. However, whether this was achieved was the subject of considerable discussion in *Wilkinson v Kitzinger* [2007] 1 FLR 295. This was a case brought by an English professor, Susan Wilkinson, who married her English partner, Celia Kitzinger, in 2004 at a time when they were both living in Canada. At that time, same-sex marriage was possible in a number of Canadian States, including British Columbia where they were living. When they returned to live in England, they wished to have their marriage recognized in English law. Ms Wilkinson applied for a declaration of validity under the Family Law Act 1986. The High Court (Sir Mark Potter P) held that although Ms Wilkinson had capacity under Canadian law and thus was able to contract a marriage recognized as being valid in that jurisdiction, she did not have capacity according to United Kingdom law because the law in this jurisdiction does not permit same-sex marriages. Ms Wilkinson had argued that same-sex marriages appeared to have an inferior status under the 2004 Act and English law, to which the President of the Family Division replied:

> 'Abiding single sex relationships are in no way inferior, nor does English law suggest that they are by according them recognition under the name of civil partnership … Parliament has not called partnerships between persons of the same sex marriage, not because they are considered inferior to the institution of marriage but because, as a matter of objective fact and common understanding, as well as under the present definition of marriage in English law, and by recognition in European jurisprudence, they are indeed different' (at [121]).

The court further held that the distinction between civil partnerships and marriage which could be seen as discriminating between same-sex couples was not in breach of the Human Rights Act as it fell within the margin of appreciation.

Are civil partnerships losing their gloss?

According to fairly recent statistics, civil partnerships may already be losing their appeal. After the Civil Partnership Act 2004 came into force in December 2005, registrations in the first few months outstripped predictions but numbers have actually fallen. There were 55 per cent fewer in 2007 than in 2006 (see 'Civil partnerships' in National Statistics Online, 2008 at http://www.statistics.gov.uk/nugget.asp).

The United States – civil partnerships and same-sex unions

Marriage between persons of the same sex, a politically divisive issue, is recognized in two States in the United States, Massachusetts and Connecticut. However, the federal government does not recognize same-sex marriage since the federal Defence of Marriage Act expressly prohibits federal recognition of such marriages. However, the Act does not prevent individual States from defining marriage as they see fit. The social movement to obtain rights and responsibilities in the United States began in the 1970s, reaching its height in the 1990s. Massachusetts has recognized same-sex marriage since 18 November 2003 and Connecticut since 10 October 2008.

Maine, Hawaii, the District of Columbia, Oregon, Washington, and Maryland allow same-sex couples to enter into legal unions which offer varying aspects of the rights and responsibilities of marriage under their individual State jurisdictions.

From 1 January 2009, Vermont, New Jersey and New Hampshire introduced legal unions for same-sex couples which are defined as offering all the rights and responsibilities of marriage under State law.

It is worth noting that from 1 January 2009, 30 States have, through constitutional amendments, explicitly banned the recognition of same-sex marriage, restricting 'civil marriage' to mean a legal union which can take place only between a man and a woman. More than 40 States explicitly allow marriage to take place legally only between two persons of the opposite sex.

Australia and New Zealand

Australia

The De Facto Relationships Act 1984 was amended to include same-sex relationships in 1999 when the name of the Act was changed to the Property (Relationships) Act 1984.

New Zealand

As mentioned above, the Human Rights Act 1993, applicable to New Zealand, extended the anti-discrimination grounds to include sexual orientation, defined as 'a heterosexual, homosexual, lesbian, or bisexual orientation' (s. 21(1)(m)).

Before the 2001 reforms took effect, same-sex couples in New Zealand were not covered by legislation but could invoke common law and equity to divide their property in the same way as opposite-sex couples but the 2001 reforms, brought in by the amending Property (Relationships) Act 2001, has now amended the law so that under the Property (Relationships) Act 1976, the main piece of legislation, the rules for married couples now apply equally to gay and lesbian de facto relationships. Hence the property of same-sex couples who decide to terminate their relationship will be divided according to the same equal-sharing rules as those which regulate the property of married couples. These changes took effect in February 2002.

Civil unions of same-sex couples of short duration are also covered by the Property (Relationships) Act 1976 subject to the s. 14A exceptions: a relationship lasting less than three years might be considered by the court if there is a child from the relationship (not impossible even for same-sex couples via assisted reproduction techniques); if the applicant made a substantial contribution to the relationship ('substantial' not defined, and subject to the court's interpretation); and the court is satisfied that failure to make an order would result in 'serious injustice', which is not defined, and therefore each case depends on its individual facts and is subject to the court's interpretation and discretion.

The 2005 civil unions reforms in New Zealand

In April 2005, civil unions for same-sex couples were established as a legally recognized form of relationship so that civil union couples who break up are now treated in the same way as married couples under the Property (Relationships) Act 1976.

CIVIL LAW JURISDICTIONS – DOMESTIC PARTNERSHIPS OUTSIDE MARRIAGE BETWEEN OPPOSITE SEX AND SAME SEX COUPLES

France

Marriage, the family and cohabitation trends

Marriage is no longer as popular in France as it used to be. Whereas in the 1970s there were nearly 400,000 marriages per year, with a peak being reached in 2000 of 305,000, in 2006 the number fell to 274,400, a decrease of 30 per cent. The current rate of marriage is the lowest since 1995. It is also a choice which is being exercised increasingly later in life. Hence, in 2004, the average age of marriage was 29.5 for women and 38.6 for men (see Godard, 2007, p. 310). These figures place France ahead of most European countries with only Sweden, Finland, Norway and Denmark having comparable rates. Cohabitation is the preferred choice of many couples and a National Assembly report states that cohabitations are more frequent and last much longer than they used to be (National Assembly Report, 26 January 2006). An even more notable point is that in the early twenty-first century, nine out of ten marriages start with cohabitation whereas in the early 1970s the figure was one in six. The report also states that cohabitation is becoming a common form of communal life, involving not only a marginal part of the population but is particularly widespread among men and women who have already experienced a 'rupture of union' (Godard, 2007, p. 311). As far as children are concerned, in 2005, 48.4 per cent of children were born outside wedlock whereas the figure was only 7 per cent in 1970.

Unmarried couples were not given any legal recognition in the Civil Code 1894 but it became increasingly difficult to ignore the rise in unmarried cohabitation amongst the French population. Indeed, as Godard notes, case law gradually took account of the existence of opposite-sex partnerships during the 1970s and 1980s and acknowledged some of their rights in areas such as social security and housing but did not resolve questions relating to property or taxes (Godard, 2007, p. 311). Any rights granted heterosexual couples were not extended to same-sex couples.

Case law

In 1989, the Cour de Cassation refused to extend to cohabiting same-sex couples the travel concessions that were granted to family or unmarried partners of the opposite sex of their employers (see Soc.11 July 1989 D. 1990.582, JCP 1990. II21553).

The same claim was made in England in 1998, in *Grant v South West Trains Ltd* [1998] All ER 193, against South West Trains Ltd, and the Court of Justice of the European Communities decided:

> 'The refusal by an employer to allow travel concessions to the person of the same sex with whom a worker has a stable relationship, where such concessions are allowed to a worker's spouse or to the person of the opposite sex with whom a worker has a stable relationship outside marriage, does not constitute discrimination prohibited by art. 119 of the EC Treaty or Council Directive 75/117/EEC of 10 February 1975 on the approximation of the laws of the Member States relating to the application of the principle of equal pay for men and women.'
>
> (cited by Godard, 2007, p. 311)

In 1997, the Cour de Cassation refused the transfer of a lease to a homosexual partner because: 'cohabitation can only result from a stable and continuous relationship having the appearance of a marriage, therefore between a man and a woman' (see Civ 3e, 17 December1997, D.1998.111).

Godard points out that this situation became critical for same-sex couples during the AIDS epidemic as AIDS sufferers were not entitled to benefit from their partners' social welfare cover or transfer leases. Indeed, families of sick or deceased partners could reject them and they could have their hospital visiting rights restricted, with many also being excluded from funeral services (Godard, 2007, p. 312).

The French registered partnership

Background to pacs (civil pact of solidarity)

No discussion of domestic relationships and partnerships in France would be complete without a discussion of the unique pacs or registered partnerships which have been made available for both same-sex and opposite-sex couples who wish to live together but do not wish to opt for the institution of marriage.

A proposal for a registered partnership for same-sex couples was first introduced in May 1990 followed in 1992 by a new proposal, but none of these proposals was discussed in the French Parliament.

The introduction of pacs was preceded by a heated debate, with conservative opponents of the reform tabling more than 1,000 amendments, with one of them speaking for more than five hours, displaying a Christian Bible in the Assembly. As Godard describes it: 'Homophobia was clearly demonstrated in the streets, in the media and in the Parliamentary speeches'(Godard, 2007, p. 312). The Senators believed that the introduction of a definition of cohabitation wide enough to include same-sex partnerships would avoid creating the status of a civil pact of solidarity specifically for same-sex couples.

Pacs defined

However, in 1999, the French Parliament adopted the pacte civil de solidarite (pacs) or 'civil pact of solidarity' which is a form of registered partnership or civil union between two adults who may be same-sex or opposite sex for organizing their lives together and who may register to regulate their relationship (see Act No. 99–944 of 15 November 1999, amending the French Civil Code).

The Act of 15 November 1999 contains a definition of cohabitation in art. 5615–8, which reads: '[C]ohabitation is a de facto stable and continuous relationship characterised by a communal life, between two persons of different sexes or of the same sex living together as a couple.' This signifies the recognition of non-married couples, making marriage just one of the options available and no longer the norm.

Pacs brings rights and responsibilities but these are fewer than marriage. This is a contract between two individuals which is stamped and registered by the clerk of the court.

In the words of Borrillo and Fassin, pacs 'is now part of the culture. As evidenced by acceptance in the French language: the acronym *Pacs* is no longer capitalized and both the noun – *les pacses* – and the verb – *se pacser* – have entered everyday parlance' (Borrillo and Fassin, 2004, p. 19). In 1999, there were 6,139 pacs registered (seven dissolutions), in 2002 there were 22,108 (620 dissolutions) and in 2005 there were 59,248 (8,464 dissolutions).

Main provisions of pacs

The provisions of pacs are not part of the section on marriage in the Civil Code. However, under art. 515–12, the prohibitions for pacs are similar to those applicable to marriage so that a pacs is not allowed 'between ascendants and descendants in direct line, between relatives by marriage in direct line and between collaterals until the third degree inclusive'. It is worth noting, as Godard does, that unlike marriage, no relaxation of this rule is allowed; this prohibition can be removed to allow a marriage, for serious reasons, between uncle and niece, aunt and nephew, under art.164 (Godard, 2007, p. 313). Partners may not be bound by another pacs or by marriage, just as art.147 prohibits bigamy in marriage.

Marriages are advertised and conducted in town halls, in the presence of at least two witnesses, followed by a religious ceremony if the spouses so wish, but pacs are merely recorded by the clerk of the court of first instance (tribunal d'instance).

Apparently, the venue for the registration was a response to the strong dissension against the recognition of same-sex marriage, particularly manifested in 1997 by a petition against same-sex marriage, signed by 15,000 mayors, which persuaded the government to keep away from town halls (Godard, 2007, p. 320, fn. 15).

Dissolution of pacs

Dissolution of a registered pacs may be effected without judicial intervention by means of an administrative procedure which is based on the mutual agreement of the pacses or by a unilateral declaration of one of them. Termination of a pacs may be effected with two months' notice. Indeed, there is no requirement to even inform the tribunal d'instance when there is a marriage or death of a person bound by pacs. Hence, automatic dissolutions are not recorded. Godard's research suggests that dissolution is usually consensual, with more than 80 per cent of dissolutions occurring at the request of the two partners and only 5 per cent effected by the unilateral request of one of the partners. Eleven per cent result from the marriage of one of the partners (Godard, 2007, p. 320, fn. 21).

No obligation of fidelity is created between the pacses and no maintenance obligations continue after the dissolution.

Another revealing principle is that in the event of conflict between the partners after the dissolution, the case will be dealt with by a judge of the tribunal de grande instance who normally deals with contracts, not the judge who normally deals with family law matters such as divorce (juge aux affaires familiales). This was the ruling of the Appeal Court of Douai in 2003, because art. 587–7 does not specify which judge has the jurisdiction to deal with such cases (Cour d'Appel de Douai, 27 Fevrier 2003, AJ Famille 2003 p. 313; RTD Civ. 2003 p. 684 obs. J. Hauser).

In March 2007, the Cour de Cassation held that a same-sex marriage which had been concluded in France in 2004 was not valid under French law and that a marriage can only take place between a man and a woman (Cour de Cassation [cass. ass. plen] Mar. 13, 2007, Bull. civ. 1, No. 76). The court declared that this principle does not violate any provision of the European Convention on Human Rights and in fact was affirming the decision of the local court and the intermediate appellate court.

Statistics on pacs

Not only has pacs become increasingly popular but the number of pacs registered has increased each year, except in 2001. Apart from that year, pacs has increased every year since 1999. In 2000, 40,100 pacs were signed, though the rate of increase in that year was slightly lower than the increase between 2002 and 2003. In 2005, 60,500 pacs were signed, which was a 50 per cent increase on 2004 and in the first quarter of 2006 about 57,500 pacs were signed (see Hughes, Davis and Jacklin, 2008, pp. 221–2). As Hughes, Davis and Jacklin observe, these figures do not distinguish between opposite sex and same-sex couples but 'taken in conjunction with the decline in the rate of marriage, they surely point to the *Pacs* having a considerable degree of popularity with heterosexual couples, for since the creation of the status in 1999, some 263,600 *Pacs* have been signed' (Hughes, Davis and Jacklin, 2008, p. 222).

Comparing the divorce figures with pacs' figures, in 2004, the total divorce rate was 45 per 100 marriages whereas in 2006, some 33,600 pacs had been dissolved since 1999, which is 12.8 per cent of the pacs signed (Hughes, Davis and Jacklin, 2008, p. 222).

Conclusions on pacs

The ambiguity of pacs is that, although it was conceived as a contract, it is considered by many as a marriage for same-sex couples who are not allowed to 'marry' in any other way, and this may be the reason why the French legislature is giving more rights to pacses (Godard, 2007, p. 314). Godard argues that the next step should be taken so that a new category of civil unions should be created for same-sex couples which would distinguish homosexual unions from marriage but give them the same rights and protections as a married couple. These rights would be autonomous and not derived from pacs or marriage (Godard, 2007, p. 319). However, as Probert puts it: 'Pacs has the potential to appeal to a wide cross-section of those couples that have chosen not to marry and to provide a more attractive means by which they may regulate their joint lives' (Probert, 2001, p. 267).

Introducing this new mechanism of a pacs as an alternative to marriage was controversial but it has since become popular, although mainly with heterosexual couples (Godard, 2007, p. 314). Same-sex couples are gradually being granted more rights and opposite-sex couples are beginning to take advantage of these changes so that pacs might be seen as resembling marriage in more ways than before. A Pacs couple is recognized as a unit for most tax, insurance and social security purposes in France. However, pacs and marriage simply represent different levels of commitment and perhaps for some, reflect different phases of their relationship. Godard concedes that if pacses were given exactly the same rights as married couples, it would be necessary to impose on them the same obligations, so that ultimately, it might be better to maintain the current situation and 'keep a flexible status such as Pacs alongside marriage ... [which] would provide a legal status for the relationship but would, at the same time, allow freedom for rupture' (Godard, 2007, p. 319). Godard also remarks that perhaps the United Kingdom's solution is the 'optimum solution' as it passed the Civil Partnership Act 2004 since, in her view, the request for a same-sex marriage option by the homosexual lobby is more a request for equality of respect rather than a demand for equivalence of status (Godard, 2007, p. 320). With respect, if cases like *Wilkinson v Kitzinger* [2007] 1 FLR 295 are anything to go by, same-sex couples would like to be able to enter into a fully-fledged marriage because they believe that anything less is seen as an inferior way of sealing a loving relationship (see p. 266 and p. 281 for a discussion of *Wilkinson v Kitzinger*).

Germany same-sex unions – registered/life partnerships

In Germany there was a notable failure in attempts to achieve improved treatment or comprehensive legal recognition for same-sex partnerships through litigation. This led to a shift in focus to achieving these aims through legislative reform (Schimmel and Heun, 2001, p. 588).

The culmination of this campaign for legislative reform is that Germany now allows registered partnerships for same-sex couples, who must be aged over 18 and not blood relatives, as of 1 August 2001, under the Life Partnership Act (Eingetragene Lebenspartnerschaft). This Act creates a new concept in German family law, a 'life partnership' open only to same-sex couples and requiring registration (Shimmel and Huen, 2001, p. 589). It permits a same-sex couple to enjoy several rights which are enjoyed by married, opposite-sex couples. Since its enactment, the Life Partnership Act has been upheld by the Federal Constitutional Court of Germany, which held that the law is in conformity with the Basic Law (Grundgesetz) and that these partnerships are entitled to equal rights with those accorded to married couples. Under the Act, the partners are obliged to care for and support one another and to live together. They also have a duty to support one another. In effect, the partners are acknowledged as relatives who have not only mutual maintenance but also alimony obligations towards each other.

Spousal rights have also been granted in the field of tenancy. Hence, if one partner dies, the surviving partner is allowed to stay in the dwelling and take over the lease.

Under the Life Partnership Act registration is carried out by making a declaration before a state agency; although the law does not specifically mention which, and merely recommends using the same agency as for heterosexual couples, which would be the registry office. It allows state governments to choose which authority may carry out the registration and permits them to pass an additional law to specify details and requirements of the registration process (Merin, 2002, p. 146).

The Life Partnership Act

Arrangement of the partners' assets

The Act allows two ways for the life partners to arrange their assets. The first is to found an Ausgleichsgemeinschaft, wherein 'assets in the possession of the life partners at the beginning of the life partnership or acquired during the existence of the life partnership, do not become community property'. If the partnership is ended, any assets in excess of those acquired by the individual partners are divided equitably. This post-dissolution rule is very similar to the principle which governs heterosexual married couples. The second option is the Lebenspartnerschaftsvertrag (life partnership agreement) which requires certification by a notary in the presence of both life partners in order to be valid. If either the partnership agreement or the agreement to found an Ausgleichsgemeinschaft is invalid or unenforceable, the partners' assets, under s. 6(III), are deemed to be separate.

Inheritance rules

The life partners are also entitled to inherit from one another. If the deceased partner's immediate family is alive and entitled to inherit, the surviving partner receives one-fourth of the total inheritance. If the deceased's second degree relatives (grandparents, cousins etc) are alive and entitled to inherit the surviving partner receives one-half of the total inheritance. In both cases, the surviving partner inherits the household goods (Hausrat) and any objects which form part of the partnership household, unless they are fixtures of a parcel of land. There is also an entitlement to any gifts given to the partners jointly to commemorate the partnership, prior to the division of the estate.

Note that under s. 10(I), if the surviving partner is inheriting alongside the decedent's immediate family, the partner only gets the household goods and wedding gifts prior to the division of the estate if they are necessary for the surviving partner in order to run the household in a reasonable manner. Under s. 10(II) the surviving partner inherits the entire estate if there are no first or second degree relatives or grandparents. However, the surviving partner is not entitled to inherit from the deceased partner if both partners had agreed to dissolve the life partnership or one partner had petitioned to dissolve the partnership and the other did not contest the petition. The same rule applies if one partner had petitioned to dissolve the partnership because its continuation would constitute an 'undue hardship' which is the effect of s. 10(III) of the Act.

The life partners may also make out a joint will and a will made out by one partner to benefit the other is permissible within the same limitations as with a heterosexual marriage. If one life partner writes the other partner out of his or her will, the surviving partner may obtain an obligatory share (Pflichtteil) of the estate in the amount of one half of the estate to which the survivor would otherwise have been entitled which is either one-fourth or one-eighth of the estate.

Other rights

There is also the right of health insurance and hospital visitation, and one partner now has the right to make decisions for the other in the event of the other's disability. In addition, as in the case of a married couple, they have the right to change their names to the same surname, and have the right of shared custody over each other's children and are eligible for social benefits for children. Hence, if one partner is unemployed, this partner will receive higher unemployment payments if there are children in the registered partnership. Relatives of one partner are considered in-laws of the other partner. The partners are not required to testify against each other in criminal proceedings (Merin, 2002, pp. 146–7). Immigration and naturalization rights are also provided, so a residence and work permit may be obtained for a foreign partner as with married couples (Merin, 2002, p. 147).

Dissolution of the partnership

It is also worth noting that this form of partnership can only be dissolved through a court proceeding where the court will also determine property allocation and division, and this will be according to similar rules as those applicable to divorce. Dissolution of the partnership may take place, provided 12 months have passed since both partners declared their intent to dissolve the partnership, 36 months have passed since one partner served the petition to dissolve the partnership or if it would cause undue hardship for one of the partners to continue the partnership by reason of some characteristic of the other partner. If one partner is unable to secure his or her own financial wellbeing, the other may be required to pay maintenance after the dissolution of the partnership. The amount of the maintenance will be calculated on the basis of the conditions existing during the partnership, as well as circumstances that prevent the partner seeking maintenance from obtaining employment that would reasonably secure his or her own financial wellbeing.

Further amendments

Further amendments were passed by the Bundestag (the lower house of the German Parliament) on 12 October 2004, using the Life Partnership Law (Revision) Act (Gesetz zur Überarbeitung des Lebenspartnerschaftrechts). These allowed step-child adoptions, simplified the alimony and divorce rules but excluded allowing the same tax benefits to same-sex partners as in a marriage.

By October 2004, 5,000 couples had registered their life partnerships.

Sweden

In the 1980s, Sweden was a pioneer country in creating a statute which regulated the property rights of heterosexual and same-sex cohabitants or 'cohabitees' (as it referred to them) as defined under the statute. This was the Cohabitees (Joint Homes) Act 1987. This Act applied for 16 years but it has now been replaced by the Cohabitees Act 2003.

The Cohabitees Act 2003

The Cohabitees Act 2003 is virtually identical to the Cohabitees (Joint Homes) Act 1987 but its innovative feature is a new definition of cohabitees which is generally applicable and clearer than the previous definition. The definition enunciated under the 2003 Act is that cohabitees refers to 'two people who live together on a permanent basis as a couple and who have a joint household'. The Governmental Explanatory Guide (the Guide) on the statute makes it plain that it is of no importance whether the cohabitees are of opposite or of the same sex. It requires three criteria to be fulfilled for a person to qualify as a cohabitee, namely: (i) the cohabitee must live with his or her partner on a permanent basis; (ii) the cohabitee and his or her partner must live together as a couple; (iii) the cohabitee must share a household with his or her partner. Thus, the first requirement makes it clear that the relationship must not be of short duration, the second that the parties have to be living together in a relationship which normally includes sexual relations and the third suggests sharing household chores and expenses. Two siblings living together would not meet these criteria.

The 2003 Act does not apply to relationships where either of the cohabitees is married or a registered partner. The Guide explains that cohabitees may conclude a written agreement to keep their financial affairs separate and such that the rules on division of property contained in the 2003 Act shall not apply to their relationship. They may also agree to be selective about which property is covered by the 2003 Act and exclude certain property from the division of property. This agreement must be signed by the cohabitees or the prospective cohabitees but need not be registered or attested. The 2003 Act only applies to the joint home and joint property. Under the Act, 'home' refers to permanent dwellings such as houses and apartments and any equipment which is normally part of the home such as furniture and goods. However, since the Act only applies to the home and furniture it does not include other property such as bank assets, shares, cars and boats. Summer houses are also not covered by the Act. These excluded items fall outside the division of property and the cohabitee who owns such property will retain ownership after the couple has separated.

Rules applicable during the cohabitational relationship

During the relationship, each cohabitee owns and manages their own property and is responsible for their own debts. As with married couples or registered partnerships, there are limitations on a cohabitee's rights to dispose of their property. Thus, there is no right to give away, sell, mortgage/pledge or let the joint home unless the other cohabitee consents. The same rule applies to giving away, selling or pawning joint household goods. The Guide does not explain what a 'joint household' item actually is but presumably it means an item that is intended to be used by both parties, irrespective of who paid for it.

A useful innovation which is allowed under this 2003 Act is that if the cohabitees live in property of which one of them is the registered owner or for which he or she holds the site leasehold, they may enter in the (Land) Register that the property is their joint home by applying to the registration authority which is the district court. A note to this effect entered in the register can be a guarantee that the cohabitee who owns the property does not sell or mortgage it without the other cohabitee's consent.

Termination of a cohabitee relationship

According to the Guide, a cohabitee relationship ends 'when the cohabitees or one of them enters into matrimony or registered partnership, if they separate or if one of them dies'. It also ends if one of the cohabitees applies to the district court to appoint an executor 'to divide the property or for the right to remain in a joint home included in the division of property'. The relationship also ends if one of the cohabitees institutes an action 'to take over a joint home not included in the division of property'.

Request for division of property

The Guide explains that when a cohabitee relationship ends, a division of property shall be made at the request of either of the cohabitees. If there is no request for a division of the property upon termination, then each cohabitee retains his or her own property. If the cohabitee relationship is terminated by the death of a cohabitee, only the surviving cohabitee may request a division of property. The heirs to the deceased cohabitee do not have the right to make such a request.

Division of property

Under the statute, a division of property includes the cohabitees' joint dwelling and household goods if the property 'was acquired for joint use'. It does not matter who paid for the property. Hence, unlike under English law, no resulting trust principles would apply whereby the party who paid for property would be entitled to have its proportional value awarded to them. However, the rules on division of property would not apply if one of the parties has moved into the other party's house, even if the couple shared amortization and other costs. It should be noted, nevertheless, that if such a dwelling has been sold and the money used for a joint new home, the new dwelling will be included in the division of property (see the Guide).

Before the division of property takes place, a deduction shall be made to cover debts. Anything that remains shall in principle be divided equally between the cohabitees. Under the statute, the cohabitee 'most in need of the dwelling or household goods' (this phrase is not explained in the statute) is entitled to receive the property if this is 'reasonable'. The term 'reasonable' is not explained under the statute either. If it turns out that the other cohabitee does not receive other property from the joint home to the same value, the cohabitee taking over the dwelling or household goods shall pay the corresponding sum of money.

Two exceptions to the 50/50 division would be made if: (a) the division into halves is not considered 'reasonable', with special weight given to the duration of the relationship (in special cases, each party may simply be allowed to retain their own property); and (b) there is the 'base amount' rule which only applies in the event of the death of one cohabitee and means that out of the property to be divided the surviving cohabitee always (provided there is sufficient property) receives as much as corresponds to two price base amounts.

Rules relating to taking over the other cohabitee's dwelling

Under the 2003 Act, a tenant-owner (condominium) right or tenancy that was not acquired for joint use but which nevertheless has been used jointly would not be included in the division of property. However, the cohabitee who most needs the dwelling may take it over from the other cohabitee. The tenor of the Guide suggests that a cohabitee with children who are her sole or primary responsibility would take priority, since the Guide makes it clear that one cohabitee being allowed to take over from the other is an extraordinary step if the cohabitees have no children. Even if this did take place, the party taking over the dwelling 'shall fully compensate the other for the value of the dwelling' (see the Guide). Cohabitees have no right to agree to remove the right to take over the dwelling. The issue of taking over the dwelling may also require resolution if the rules on division of property under the 2003 Act have been removed under an agreement made by the parties.

The cohabitee wishing to take over a tenancy or tenant-owner right must submit such a claim no later than one year after the termination of the cohabitee relationship. However, if the cohabitee wanting to take over leaves the dwelling, the claim must be submitted no later than three months thereafter. The period of one year's grace does not apply if the cohabitee who possesses the dwelling dies and the surviving cohabitee remains in it.

There is no right of inheritance given to the surviving cohabitee in the event of death but cohabitees are entitled to make a will to this effect.

There is also no obligation to maintain one another, not even after a very long relationship.

Children

For a child whose parents are not married, paternity must be specially established. This also applies to parents who are unmarried cohabitees. As in the majority of Western-influenced jurisdictions, when a child is born the mother is automatically granted custody of it. The parents may obtain joint custody by applying to the tax authority or the social services committee with regard to confirmation of paternity and registering the fact that they have joint custody.

Cohabitees are not allowed to jointly adopt a child.

Norway

Norway, another civil law jurisdiction, also introduced a Joint Household Act in 2002 under which cohabitants qualify if they have lived together for a minimum of two years or if they have or are expecting a child together. This Act is not restricted to sexual relationships and does not provide for sharing the value of jointly used assets as in Sweden but only regulates the right to take over the home or household goods on the death or at the termination of the relationship.

European perspectives – harmonization of family law

In April 2007, European Union justice ministers announced that they had agreed a new European Union regulation on jurisdiction and applicable law in matrimonial proceedings called Rome III. The present position is that every member state applies its own rules as to which law is applicable to a divorce where the spouses are of different nationality or where the couple live abroad. Hence, a German-Dutch couple who lived in Germany is allowed to be divorced in Germany under German law. However, if the Dutch spouse petitioned for divorce in the Netherlands, Dutch law could be applied which could lead to a different outcome. The European Commission says that the new regulation would avoid this uncertainty by providing uniform rules for determining the law applicable to divorces with an international dimension. Subject to some limitations, it would give spouses the right to choose both the court with jurisdiction in a member state as well as the applicable law. Hence, a French court may be chosen by a couple to be the forum for a divorce in relation to which Spanish law is applied. From a British perspective, the United Kingdom government has the right to opt out of proposals relating to European civil and family justice and has exercised that right with regard to Rome III. However, the United Kingdom government has also said that it intends to remain involved in the negotiations, as it retains the right to opt-in once the regulation has been drafted.

European Union ministers also announced that they have agreed to take measures to improve existing arrangements for the cross-border recovery of maintenance orders made within the European Union. Ministers have agreed on the guiding principles that are to shape future negotiations for finalizing the terms of a regulation making court maintenance decisions by any member states enforceable in all other member states without having to take intermediate measures. Council President and Federal Minister of Justice Brigitte Zypries announced that a central authority will be set up to support European Union citizens entitled to maintenance to recover any arrears (Family Law Bulletin, May 2007).

International overview

Civil partnerships, domestic partnerships and registered partnerships (with varying benefits and rights) are available in: Andorra, Argentina, Brazil, Croatia, Czech Republic, Denmark, Finland, France, Germany, Iceland, Israel, Luxembourg, Mexico, New Zealand, Norway, Portugal, Slovenia, Sweden, Switzerland, United Kingdom, the Australian States of Tasmania and Western Australia and, in the United States, California, Connecticut, Hawaii, Maine, New Jersey and Vermont and the District of Columbia (Washington DC).

Global perspectives on same-sex partnerships

Since 2008, same-sex marriages have been recognized nationwide in the Netherlands, Belgium, Spain, Canada and South Africa. The Netherlands is the first Western country to legalize gay and lesbian marriages. In addition, both opposite-sex and same-sex couples have the option to enter into a registered partnership instead of a marriage. As of 1 January 2009, Norway also recognizes such relationships. Same-sex marriages conducted abroad are recognized in Israel, France, Aruba, Netherlands, Antilles and the States of New Mexico, New York and Rhode Island. In contrast, no country of the United Kingdom recognizes same-sex marriage but all its countries allow the formation of civil partnerships to same-sex couples and that have all the consequences of marriage. As we saw in *Wilkinson v Kitzinger* [2007] 1 FLR 295 in English Law, a lesbian couple who sued for the recognition of their marriage which had been contracted in Vancouver, British Columbia, Canada, in 2003 lost their case in the English High Court. The English court held that the couple's marriage could be recognized as a civil partnership in England and Wales but not as a marriage.

Convergence or non-convergence?

Terminological and comparative distinctions

Apart from ambiguity and a lack of consensus in formulating or agreeing a definition for opposite-sex unmarried couples who cohabit, Bradley points out that even the designation of a law as a 'registered partnership' is misleading if it is taken to imply uniformity (Bradley, 2001, p. 23). He explains that Scandinavian registered partnership laws are restricted to same-sex relationships and heterosexual relationships are treated differently in that jurisdiction (for details see Bradley, 1996, pp. 95–105, 151–60, 213–22). On the other hand, laws in France and the Netherlands cover a range of relationships but these 'vary substantially in content' (Bradley, 2001, p. 23). Bradley also notes that the pacs differs significantly from the Dutch partnership model and while the commitment to equality in the Netherlands led to complete assimilation of marriage and extra-marital cohabitation, the French law on pacs is merely a 'shadow of marriage' (Bradley, 2001, p. 37). Hence, there may well be superficial convergence but no substantive convergence since each jurisdiction has its own unique features and characteristics.

Reforming the law on cohabitation?

Barlow and James list several reasons why a case can be made that cohabitation is in need of reform, such as the separation of sex and childbearing (as well as other functions and effects of traditional marriage) from the institution of marriage, some empirical evidence that there is private commitment to a relationship by couples despite this commitment not being made in public through the exchange of marriage vows at a ceremony, the decline of marriage and the rise of cohabitation outside marriage (Barlow and James, 2004, p. 153). There is also the rise in births registered to mothers who are unmarried.

Clearly, some jurisdictions have been more willing and speedier than others in reforming the law relating to cohabitation for same-sex and opposite-sex couples. Barlow and James argue that in twenty-first century Britain, although the social acceptance of heterosexual cohabitation as a parenting and partnering structure on a par with marriage has been achieved almost universally over the last two decades, piecemeal reform of the law has left it in a state of 'confusion, uncertainty and complexity' (Barlow and James, 2004, p. 143). They assert that the way forward is for the law to be reformed to protect the function rather than the form of relationships.

In addition, they argue that cohabitation, at least for heterosexuals, has taken on the functions of marriage and conversely, marriage has become more companionate, and more akin to unmarried cohabitation, since it has broken out of its patriarchal mould and become more a partnership of equals 'whose often still different and gender oriented roles are on divorce more equally valued' which was acknowledged by the House of Lords in *White* [2000] 2 FLR 981 and by the Court of Appeal in *Lambert* [2003] 1 FLR 139 (Barlow and James, 2004, p. 153). Since marriage for so many couples is no longer necessarily a lifelong commitment, it may be time 'to regulate what families actually *do* rather than what form they take' (Barlow and James, 2004, p. 153).

Hence, if a relationship is performing the functions of marriage, it should be treated like marriage at least in the sense that the rights of married couples and long term cohabitants should be equalized. As Baroness Hale has put it: '[I]t is the relationship rather than the status that should matter' (Hale, 2004, p. 421).

Barlow and James propose providing better legal information and setting up a Civil Partnership Register, which is now common in Europe, although it may take several forms. They also acknowledge the need to safeguard the autonomy and preserve the freedom of choice of cohabitants who do not want to be treated as married, by recommending that a couple have the right to opt out of the proposed regime.

Opting out could be achieved either by making cohabitation contracts lawful, as proposed in Scotland, or through the combination of a French pacs-style Civil Partnership Register which could provide cohabitants with a 'true alternative legal status to marriage' (Barlow *et al.*, 2005, p. 117).

Further reading

Auchmuty, R 'What's So Special about Marriage? The Impact of Wilkinson v Kitzinger' (2008) 20 CFLQ 475.

Barlow, A, Duncan, S, James, G and Park, A *Cohabitation, Marriage and the Law* 2005, Hart.

Barlow, A and James, G 'Regulating Marriage and Cohabitation in 21st Century Britain' (2004) 67 *Modern Law Review* 143.

Bradley, D *Family Law and Political Culture*, 1996, Sweet & Maxwell.

Bradley, D 'Regulation of Unmarried Cohabitation in West-European Jurisdictions – Determinants of Legal Policy' (2001) 15 Int Jnl of Law, Policy and the Family 22.

Bjornberg, U 'Cohabitation and Marriage in Sweden' (2001) 15 Int Jnl of Law, Policy and the Family 350.

Clarke, L and Edmunds, R 'H v M: Equity and the Essex Cohabitant' [1992] Fam Law 523.

Collier, R 'A Hard Time to be a Father?: Reassessing the Relationship between Law, Policy, and Family (Practices)' (2001) 28 Jo Law and Society 520.

Cretney, SM *Same Sex Relationships*, 2006, Oxford UP.

Curry-Sumner, I *All's Well that Ends Registered?* 2005, Intersentia.

Deech, R 'The Case Against Legal Recognition of Cohabitation' (1980) 29 ICLQ 480.

Gardner, S 'Rethinking Family Property' (1993) 109 LQR 263.

Gibson, C 'Changing Family Patterns in England' in Katz, Eekelaar and Maclean (eds) *Cross Currents: Family Law and Policy in the US and England*, 2000, Oxford UP.

Hale, B 'Unmarried Couples in Family Law' [2004] Fam Law 419.

Kiernan, K 'The Rise of Cohabitation and Childbearing outside Marriage in Western Europe' (2001) Int Jnl of Law, Policy and the Family 1.

Martin, C and Thery, I 'The PACS and Marriage and Cohabitation in France' (2001) 15 Int Jnl of Law, Policy and the Family 135.

Merin, Y *Equality for Same-Sex Couples*, 2002, University of Chicago Press.

Olah, LS 'Policy Changes and Family Stability' (2001)15 Int Jnl of Law, Policy and the Family 118.

Ostner, I 'Cohabitation in Germany – Rules, Reality and Public Discourses' (2001) 15 Int Jnl of Law, Policy and the Family 88.

Pawlowski, M 'Joint Ownership and Beneficial Entitlement: Stack v Dowden' [2007] Fam Law 606.

Richards, C 'The Legal Recognition of Same-Sex Couples – The French Perspective' (2002) 51 ICLQ 305.

Sheldon, S 'Unmarried Fathers and Parental Responsibility: A Case for Reform?' (2001) 9 *Feminist Legal Studies* 93.

Swedish Government Publications *Cohabitees and their Joint Homes. A Brief Presentation of the Cohabitees Act.*

Wintemute, R and Andenaes, M (eds) *Legal Recognition of Same-Sex Partnerships*, 2001, Hart.

Wright, W 'The Tide in Favour of Equality: Same-Sex marriage in Canada and England and Wales' (2006) Int Jnl of Law, Policy and the Family 249.

Ytterberg, H 'A Swedish Story of Love and Legislation' in Wintermute and Andenaes (eds) *Legal Recognition of Same-Sex Partnerships*, 2001, Hart.

Part IV

Domestic violence – a comparative survey

Introduction

Some form of violence in the home, or 'domestic violence', probably existed in households around the world long before statistics began to be collected, and the Western world, in particular, has experienced a discernible change in the perception of what is unacceptable behaviour between spouses – and latterly, partners – in domestic relationships. One of the difficulties in dealing with this phenomenon stems from the fact that it always occurs behind closed doors and was invariably regarded as a 'domestic' incident and therefore a 'private' issue in which state authorities had no business intervening and was consequently not the province of the police, being not a matter involving 'the public' at large. The public/private divide and non-visibility of domestic violence continues to be a problem and masks the extent of the problem. It is not always possible to gauge the true extent of such violence in homes, especially since it also appears to be seriously underreported, as suggested in the 2003 British Government White Paper (see *Safety and Justice: The Government's Proposals on Domestic Violence*, 2003, Home Office). Another part of the problem was that women were traditionally seen as inferior to men and subject to them, indeed even as chattels and the property of men to deal with as they pleased. This was compounded by the economic dependence of women on men, which meant that even if women suffered from and wished to leave an abusive relationship they were constrained by economic necessity not to do so. As Edwards puts it: 'The legal construction of the marriage contracts has furthered [the wife's] vulnerability' (Edwards, 1996, p. 191). The notion of a man and woman being 'one flesh' once they married also conspired to reinforce the non-interventionist attitude of the state, which meant that for the police to intervene would be seen as a last resort.

This attitude and perception underwent considerable change in the late 1970s, the 1980s and 1990s and legislation subsequently passed in certain countries has reflected a more enlightened and progressive view of the problem. As Lorna Smith notes, interest in the subject has been shown by a variety of disciplines: psychology, sociology, law, medicine, social work and criminology (Smith, 1989, p. 1). To a certain extent, this shows the complexity of the subject and the multi-faceted nature of the problem, where each discipline can throw its own shaft of light to illuminate the domestic violence prism.

Scope of chapter

This chapter offers a brief global glimpse into this serious and disturbing phenomenon, while looking a little more closely at Germany, France, Russia, South Africa, Australia and Japan, representing a mixture of civil, common law and hybrid jurisdictions. Some issues apply to all jurisdictions and to all families, while others are arguably confined to certain countries because of their particular cultural and social heritage.

Definitional issues

The definition of domestic violence has posed its own terminological difficulties although a generalist approach would be to regard the term as covering any sort of violence within the family. This has led to several definitions being used by different jurisdictions over the last century. Rawstorne simply defines it as 'violence within the family' (Rawstorne, 2002, p. 25), an all-embracing definition which would include both violence between adults and also that perpetrated by adults towards children. Of course, as Summers and Hoffman point out, 'family violence encompasses not only violence between female and male partners or same sex partners but also child abuse and elder abuse. Domestic violence, more specifically, refers to the abuse by one person of another in an intimate relationship' (Summers and Hoffman, 2002, p.xii). These relationships can involve marriage partners, partners living together, dating relationships (Berry, 1998), and even former spouses, former partners, and former boyfriends or girlfriends (Chalk and King, 1998). The abuse itself 'may take the form of physical violence, emotional abuse, sexual abuse, and even stalking' (Summers and Hoffman, 2002, p.xii). The law in England and Wales has responded to stalking with the Protection from Harassment Act 1997 (UK) (see p. 292). In 2003, the British Home Office defined domestic violence as: 'Any violence between current and former partners in an intimate relationship, wherever and whenever the violence occurs. The violence may include physical, sexual, emotional and financial abuse' (*Safety and Justice: The Government's Proposals on Domestic Violence*, 2003, Home Office).

The ongoing dilemma

The ongoing dilemma which bedevils domestic violence is: How should the law best deal with this problem? In other words, is the civil law or criminal law best able to deal with domestic violence as far as the victim and perpetrator is concerned? Both branches of the law bring difficulties and it has proved very difficult to strike a balance between civil and criminal solutions.

Domestic violence in England and Wales

The situation in England and Wales

As far as the British scene is concerned, Rawstorne has observed that 'domestic violence has been marginalized and trivialized, ignored or diverted to civil or lower, less important courts'(Rawstorne, 2002, p. 25). This is borne out by the chequered development of domestic violence legislation and the sometimes quirky case law. The case law has ranged from relatively minor acts of violence being deemed sufficiently serious to warrant court intervention in cases such as *Spindlow* [1979] 1 All ER 169, to cases where far more serious and persistent acts of violence do not appear to have deterred the female victims from repeatedly resuming contact with the alleged perpetrators of the violence. The interpretation of terms such as 'molestation', for which no legislative definition exists, has also exercised the courts over the years, where, apart from harassing, pestering or annoying a domestic partner, the courts also interpreted the sending of semi-nude photographs of an ex-partner to the press without that partner's permission as amounting to molestation (see *Johnson v Walton* [1990] 1 FLR 350). The 'undertakings' that perpetrators were required to give to the courts were persistently breached and women appeared to have endured prolonged periods of physical abuse (see e.g. *Hussain* [1986] 2 FLR 271). The one flesh doctrine or doctrine of unity, whereby marriage rendered a husband and wife 'one person in law', that person being the husband, was also largely responsible for the impossibility of committing marital rape by the husband and it was as recently as 1991 when the House of Lords finally ruled that it was possible for a man to commit rape on his wife (see *R v R* [1991] 4 All ER 481).

Historical perspectives

Summers and Hoffman claim that domestic violence has been a common occurrence throughout recorded history. 'In many societies, women were traditionally considered the property of the man; his duty was to discipline her and the children (and slaves) with thorough beatings. The only concerns about this related to the thickness of the stick that the law allowed for the beatings' (Summers and Hoffman, 2002, p. xiii). Hecker notes that in early English law, a husband's rights over his wife extended to complete control of her property and over her daily affairs which, apart from the right to correct and chastise, also gave the husband the right to 'give his wife a severe beating with whips and clubs' (Hecker, 1910). Hecker also contends that it was a right practised by most men irrespective of their social class. Hence it was both socially and legally acceptable for husbands to use physical force against their wives and only force used to excess brought any social or legal disapproval or condemnation. However, assuming she was able to do so, the wife had no right to beat her husband. The basis of this right was the doctrine of unity of the spouses.

Pleck observes that the development of domestic violence as a social problem has a very uneven history (Pleck, 1987). Martin has described the historical roots of wife beating as ancient and deep, going back to the first monogamous pairing relationships which she argues brought about the subjugation of one sex by another (Martin, 1978). The subjugation of women to their husbands was sanctioned by the church and wives were counselled that increased devotion and submissiveness were the means of avoiding 'disciplinary' chastisement (Smith, 1989, p. 3). One of the earliest reported English cases was that of Margaret Neffeld of York. This woman brought witnesses before an ecclesiastical court to testify that she had been attacked by her husband who had wielded a dagger, wounded her and broken her bones (Baur and Ritt, 1983; Freeman, 1979). Despite the evidence presented, the court held that the then equivalent of a modern-day judicial separation had not been made out and the woman was compelled to continue to live with her husband.

The Dobashes conducted an examination of the sociohistorical roots of domestic violence and maintain that for centuries husbands have used violence, both systematically and severely, to dominate, punish and control their wives, simply as a husband's prerogative (Dobash and Dobash, 1981). Indeed, the Dobashes discovered community attempts to control such behaviour dating from the fifteenth century when public shaming and ridicule were used by local people to change the behaviour of offending members of their community. Dobash and Dobash note that such measures were rarely exercised if powerful members of the community were involved. In addition, the community only appeared to express opprobrium for cases of savage and severe treatment, and lesser forms of violence appear to have been acceptable and condoned (Dobash and Dobash, 1981).

Research on domestic violence began in the 1960s and achieved more prominence and a higher profile in the 1970s, This led to significant legislation being passed to deal with the problem.

Domestic violence and related legislation in the 1970s and 1980s

The 1970s saw three pieces of important legislation: the Domestic Violence and Matrimonial Proceedings Act 1976, the Domestic Proceedings and Magistrates' Courts Act 1978 and the Housing (Homeless Persons) Act 1977. The 1976 Act was available in the County Court and the High Court and the 1978 Act in the magistrates' court. Both Acts were intended to provide legal remedies, but were different in their scope and application and the way in which they were interpreted and implemented was at best complex and at worst, confusing. They were certainly not sufficiently integrated to form a coherent set of remedies. The upshot of these two Acts was that domestic violence victims continued to be inadequately protected. The 1978 Act introduced new powers for magistrates to issue orders to protect women from physical violence but the Act was only available for married persons; the 1976 Act (which applied only to complaints brought in the High Court and County courts) was available to married and unmarried couples, covered non-physical violence and also included a power of arrest to be attached to ex parte orders, which the 1978 Act did not. Part of the difficulty in the implementation of these Acts is that they were essentially civil remedies with some criminal sanctions tagged on. In a sense, this was not surprising because of the ubiquitous debate over whether civil or criminal remedies are most effective to curb or prevent domestic violence and because, for instance, a husband could not be convicted of raping his wife until 1991 when the case of *R v R* [1991] 4 All ER 481 was decided, and it took a decision by the House of Lords to make this momentous change in the law.

The 1977 Act included specific provisions to help persons who had become homeless as a result of domestic violence. In the 1980s, the Matrimonial Homes Act was passed which included further options for protecting married persons from domestic violence, such as ouster and exclusion orders.

The current law in England and Wales

Domestic violence in England and Wales is currently dealt with under both the civil law and criminal law. The main civil legislation is contained in Pt IV of the Family Law Act 1996, as amended by the Domestic Violence, Crime and Victims Act 2004. The Housing Act 1996 and the Children Act 1989 also provide forms of protection for victims of domestic violence. The criminal law may be invoked under three main statutes, namely the Offences Against the Person Act 1861, the Sexual Offences Act 2003 and the Protection from Harassment Act 1997.

The Family Law Act 1996

The Family Law Act 1996 makes non-molestation orders and occupation orders available to a long list of 'associated persons'. There is still no statutory definition of molestation, so it remains a matter for judicial interpretation. Under s. 62(3) those who may apply for non-molestation orders include married and ex-spouses; cohabitants or former cohabitants; civil partners; persons who live or have lived in the same household (other than merely because they were the other's employee, tenant, lodger or boarder); a list of eligible relatives; those who have agreed to marry one another; those with whom they have or have had an intimate relationship that is or was of significant duration; in relation to any child; and if they are parties to the same proceedings.

A 'relevant child'

A 'relevant child' is defined under s. 62(2) of the 1996 Act. This refers to: any child who is living with or might reasonably be expected to live with either party to the proceedings; any child in relation to whom an order under the Adoption Act 1976, Adoption and Children Act 2002 or the Children Act 1989 is in question in the proceedings; and any other child whose interests the court considers relevant.

In deciding whether to grant an order the court will consider all the circumstances including the need to secure the health, safety and wellbeing of the applicant, and of any relevant child.

Criteria for occupation orders

In deciding whether to grant occupation orders, the court will consider all the circumstances: the housing needs and resources of the parties and of any relevant child; the financial resources of the parties; the likely effect of any order on the health, safety or wellbeing of the parties and of any relevant child; and the conduct of the parties in relation to each other.

Balance of harm/significant harm test

A central statutory guideline is the balance of harm/significant harm test. Under s. 33(7), if it appears to the court that the applicant or relevant child is likely to suffer significant harm attributable to the conduct of the respondent if an order is not made, the court shall or may make the order unless (a) the respondent or any relevant child is likely to suffer significant harm if the order is made; and (b) the harm likely to be suffered by the respondent or child in that event is as great as, or greater than, the harm attributable to the conduct of the respondent that is likely to be suffered by the applicant or the child if the order is not made.

This suggests that the court will have to weigh the consequences of making the order against those of not making the order. If the harm caused by making the order is as great or greater than that which is likely to result from the respondent's conduct, then the court will not make the order.

The 1996 Act's definition of significant harm is the same as that which exists under the Children Act 1989; that is, it refers to ill-treatment or the impairment of health; and in relation to a child, refers to ill-treatment or impairment of health or development; 'health' includes physical or mental health.

In enforcing non-molestation and occupation orders, the court must attach a power of arrest to its order if it appears to the court that the respondent has used or threatened violence against the applicant or the child, unless it is satisfied that the applicant or child will be adequately protected without such a power of arrest.

Housing Act 1996

A local authority is empowered under the Housing Act 1996 to apply for an order to exclude a tenant who is being violent towards another tenant.

The Children Act 1989

The Children Act 1989 gives the courts powers of arrest to remove a suspected child abuser from the home under s. 8. The court will be permitted to make such an order for the perpetrator to be excluded as part of an application for an emergency protection order or an interim care order for the child. The court has to receive a statement from the local authority that there is reasonable cause to believe that the child is likely to suffer significant harm if the suspected abuser is not removed from the home.

The Protection from Harassment Act 1997

The Protection from Harassment Act 1997 creates two criminal offences: criminal harassment and putting people in fear of violence (or the aggravated indictable offence of harassment). Criminal harassment means the pursuit of a course of conduct that amounts to harassment and which the accused knew or ought to have known amounts to harassment of the victim.

The offence of putting people in fear of violence refers to the pursuit of a course of conduct which causes the victim to fear (on at least two occasions) that violence will be used against him or her and which the accused knows or ought to know would cause the victim to so fear. The penalty is a fine or up to five years' imprisonment and the court can make restraining orders to prevent further harassment. An actual or apprehended breach of the prohibition against harassment of another under s. 1 may also be the subject of a claim for damages.

Although this Act was initially prompted by stalking (the obsessive harassment of one person by another) it has gone beyond stalking and requires a course of conduct which must have taken place on at least two occasions (as required under s. 7(3) of the 1997 Act). As the Court of Appeal clarified in *R v Hills* [2001] 1 FLR 580, a course of conduct requires proof of a cogent link between the two or more incidents constituting harassment. In the *Hills* case, the two cases of assault were six months or so apart and the evidence had not established the link between the two assaults.

Civil remedies are also provided for restraining violent persons who do not come within the list of 'associated persons' under the Family Law Act 1996, and it is possible to apply for damages for harassment offences under this Act. There is no provision to make occupation orders and claims are limited to non-molestation orders.

Effect of the Domestic Violence, Crime and Victims Act 2004

A key reform of the Domestic Violence, Crime and Victims Act 2004 is that assault has been made an offence punishable by up to five years' imprisonment (see Pt 2, s. 10). However, this Act repealed part of s. 41 of the Family Law Act 1996 which required courts to have regard to the non-married status of cohabitants or former cohabitants. It also amended s. 36 of the 1996 Act to oblige courts to have regard to the level of commitment between cohabitants or former cohabitants when considering whether to make a s. 36 occupation order. In addition, it amended the definition of cohabitants in the 1996 Act to include same-sex couples; and amended the previous definition in the 1996 Act of 'associated persons' to include non-cohabiting couples who have or have had an intimate personal relationship with each other of a significant duration, so it can also cover couples who never lived with each other but have had a close personal relationship. This is clearly a very wide definition attempting to cover practically all possibilities.

The Domestic Violence, Crime and Victims Act 2004 introduced new statutory provisions for undertakings. While these have not been criminalized, with any breach only constituting a contempt of court, the court may now issue a warrant of arrest in the event of an alleged breach. The courts have always been reluctant to accept undertakings where there has been actual or threatened violence and this position is further emphasized with the amendments of the 2004 Act, which now limits the use of undertakings even more. The court is now restricted from accepting an undertaking where it appears to the court that the respondent has either used or threatened to use violence against the applicant or relevant child. Hence the best way to protect the applicant or relevant child would be to apply for a non-molestation order, the breach of which is punishable by criminal sanctions. If the respondent denies violence or threats of violence, and gives an undertaking not to harm the applicant, there would probably a fact-finding hearing.

The effect of another amendment by the Domestic Violence, Crime and Victims Act 2004 is that it is the police and eventually the Crown Prosecution Service who decide whether to pursue the matter or not. An alleged offender may be arrested because of an initial complaint but the Crown Prosecution Service may decide not to proceed with the case because of lack of evidence or a shortage of resources. Although the victim may consider pursuing the matter in the civil courts, the Legal Services Commission has given no commitment to provide legal aid for proceedings which may be pursued through the criminal courts.

Effect of using a non-molestation order rather than an occupation order

As a result of the Domestic Violence, Crime and Victims Act 2004, Soni points out that it now makes a difference whether an applicant who has split up from her violent partner and has moved away taking her children with her uses a non-molestation order or an occupation order. If a non-molestation order under s. 42 of the 1996 Act is used, and this is breached, then this is a criminal offence and will have to be pursued in the criminal courts, whereas if the applicant applies for an occupation order under s. 33(g) of the 1996 Act and this is breached, this will not constitute a criminal offence and will be dealt with by the civil courts (Soni, 2007).

In effect, as Soni emphasizes, the applicant who does not want the matter to be criminalized no longer has the option to obtain a remedy in the civil family proceedings courts. She is forced to pursue the matter in the criminal courts where the focus is on punishing the offender rather than protecting the applicant. This means that the matter will usually be heard in open court within the criminal system, unless a special measure application is made, and this may well deter women from reporting the matter in the first place. On the other hand, the family court is a closed court with privacy and anonymity being preserved and this 'is absolutely vital for an applicant from an ethnic minority' who may be concerned about bringing 'shame' or 'dishonour' to her family (Soni, 2007).

Soni also notes that the new subsections (3) and (4) of s. 42 of the 1996 Act (inserted by the Domestic Violence, Crime and Victims Act 2004) make it such that an individual who has been punished for contempt in family proceedings may not be convicted of an offence in the criminal courts and vice versa. This avoids a form of double jeopardy.

Current statistical perspectives

According to British government statistics ranging over the past few years, domestic violence accounts for about 16 per cent of all violent crime in Britain at a cost of more than £23 billion a year (see Home Office, *Crime in England and Wales 2004–2005*, 2005, cited in Kury & Smartt, 2006, p. 382). Another research study which surveyed one London borough claims that 'domestic violence affects one in four women, and one in six men in their lifetime' (Stanko *et al. Counting the Costs: Estimating the Impact of Domestic Violence in the London Borough of Hackney,* 1998, Crime Concern).

The situation in Britain in 2008

Even in 2008, it has been reported that the new domestic law has failed to protect women at risk adequately. On 14 April 2008 *The Times* reported that thousands of women continue to be at risk of assault because new laws to curb domestic violence have backfired, deterring victims from seeking help. Since legislation was introduced in July 2007 to criminalize domestic abuse, it was claimed by judges that 'at least 5,000 women' failed to report violent partners. As we have seen above, under the amendments introduced by the Domestic Violence, Crime and Victims Act 2004, the relevant section of which came into force on 1 July 2007, a breach of a non-molestation order became a criminal offence and therefore under the jurisdiction of the criminal courts. Battered wives, and sometimes husbands, remain reluctant to seek a court order because this might give their partners a criminal record and potentially, a prison sentence of up to five years. A *Times* report of 14 April 2008, quoting Judge John Platt, stated that non-molestation orders had fallen by between 25 per cent and 30 per cent since the implementation of the above amendment. The judge in question has been a circuit judge with over 20 years of dealing with domestic violence cases. However, the Crown Prosecution Service has denied this and in fact claimed that the numbers of cases and the conviction rate has been higher than in previous years. These statistics are from before the time the Domestic Violence, Crime and Victims Act reform was introduced.

On the practical front, a number of Specialist Domestic Violence Courts have been brought into operation in Britain, and it can only be hoped that this will be an improvement on the previous legal and other responses to this ongoing problem in society.

Australia

Introduction

Australia ranks as a common law country, by virtue of its history and its continuing links with the 'mother country', and is therefore an appropriate jurisdiction to be considered after our overview of the law in England and Wales.

There are apparently 'more experts, consultants, practitioners, activists, bureaucrats and academics working on domestic violence in Australia than ever before' (Pickering, 2002, p. 1). Pickering also remarks '[i]t seems that we have never known so much about domestic violence and never before have we done so much about it', but, and this is surely the position in every jurisdiction in which we examine this phenomenon, '[domestic violence] remains impervious to expert "knowing"' and 'the extent of such violence in Australian society is impossible to measure' (Pickering, 2002, p. 1). It is a matter of record that feminists have been contributing in new ways to understanding, investigating and preventing domestic violence throughout the 1970s, 1980s and 1990s.

Research into domestic violence in Australia

The Commonwealth government's task force, the Partnerships Against Domestic Violence, has carried out a comprehensive study of domestic violence in Australia. It surveyed more than 280 people from different cultural and linguistic backgrounds, with participants being Indigenous Australians and a mix of ethnic groups including Vietnamese, Cantonese, Tagalog, Turkish and Arabic. A report published in 2000, *Awareness of Domestic and Family Violence in the Diverse Australian Community*, stated that across the groups, people had a 'sound level' of domestic violence, which was seen as including physical, psychological and emotional abuse. In Indigenous communities, domestic violence is readily linked to sexual abuse. According to the Australian Bureau of Statistics, in Australia, females were more likely than males to have been assaulted by someone known to them (see Recorded Crime in Australia, 1997) and females represent 79 per cent of sexual assault victims, with almost half the victims being under 20 years of age. The offender is most commonly a non-family member known to the victim. A nationwide survey conducted in 1996 found that 7.1 per cent of women interviewed had experienced violence in the past 12 months (most of it at home) and 23 per cent of women who had ever been married or in a de facto relationship had experienced domestic violence (*Women's Safety Australia*, Australian Bureau of Statistics, 1996). Behrendt has observed that the majority of assaults in which alcohol is often a factor are not reported (Behrendt, 2000).

Domestic violence and Aboriginal women

Aboriginal women are significantly over-represented in official victimization statistics (Pickering and Alder, 2000, p. 222) and the number of Indigenous women killed by their partners was greater than the number of men who died while in custody (*Equality Before the Law: Justice for Women*, Australian Law Reform Commission, 1994). In some Queensland communities, one in three Aboriginal women die from injuries inflicted through domestic violence, and 16 per cent of all homicide victims are Aboriginal women (Behrendt, 2000). Pickering argues that, to date, the Australian justice system has not shown any consistent interest in intervening to prevent and respond to violence in Aboriginal women's intimate relationships. Police statistics continue to show that Aboriginal women are much more likely to be victims of reported violent crime than non-Aboriginal women.

Contributing factors identified by Pickering are financial pressure and economic difficulties, drug and alcohol abuse. Barriers to women reporting such abuse include the shame and fear felt by these women as well as a lack of financial support and suitable services to cope with the consequences of disclosure (Pickering, 2002, p. 4).

The problem with trying to reform domestic violence laws in Australia

Stubbs asserts that the major problem with trying to reform the law as a response to domestic violence is that 'the women most able to utilise that protection remain those who are most informed and financially able, residing in urban settings and belonging to dominant cultural groups'. On the other hand, 'women from culturally diverse backgrounds, indigenous women, and women living in rural and remote settings are the least protected' (Stubbs, *Women, Male Violence and the Law*, Institute of Criminology Monograph Series, Sydney, 1994). So far, law reform has not proved to be effective for women victims of domestic violence.

Current laws dealing with domestic violence

Pickering notes that research on police responses to domestic violence complaints suggests that historically women have had great problems in getting police protection in Australia (Pickering, 2002, p. 5). However, while this may still be a problem in many cases, all Australian jurisdictions introduced legislation throughout the 1990s to provide more protection to the victims of domestic violence. This protection was in the form of orders, variously known as restraining orders, apprehended violence orders, intervention or protection orders. The main innovation was domestic violence protection orders and these take precedence over Family Court injunctions. In New South Wales they are known as apprehended violence orders, and are available for a range of violent offences, including domestic violence. The detail of the legislation varies from State to State but they all provide for a court order, to be made on the balance of probabilities, to protect the victim from further violence. The breach of such orders (which are essentially civil remedies, but sometimes regarded as quasi-criminal orders), has been made a criminal offence and the police may arrest without a warrant a person who has contravened a protection order. It is important to realize that these orders are aimed at restraining the future behaviour of the perpetrator, not past actions. Past actions and assaults should be dealt with by the usual criminal law remedies. The advantage of such orders is that they may be utilized if a target is likely to be subject to violence on the balance of probabilities, which is the civil standard and a lower standard than that required by the criminal law and therefore ostensibly easier to establish.

Seddon points out that such orders have been considered cheaper and more efficient than other forms of injunctions and have been regarded as more effective in the way that they can deal with particular forms of violence (Seddon, *Domestic Violence in Australia: The Legal Response*, 1993, Federation Press). For example, they can deal with conduct not normally dealt with by criminal law, such as telephoning and then following someone in a car. In fact, a whole range of behaviour has been criminalized for which these orders provide protection.

Nevertheless, research findings on the effectiveness of these orders have found that women report mixed experiences. Although they have generally enabled women to cope more effectively with violence in their lives, they have not been of much use where there are respondents of multiple domestic violence protection orders. Stewart has argued for more 'situational and rehabilitative responses', so that an offender continues to be prevented from future violence rather than the law continuing to focus solely on victims escaping from such relationships, particularly for serial offenders (Stewart, 2000, pp. 77–90).

Germany

Introduction

We now consider a civil law country's response to domestic violence by looking at Germany. Despite German law acknowledging equal standing and rights of married women and men through the First Right to Marriage Reform Act of 14 June 1976 (Ehereformgesetz), which came into force in 1977, measures to deal with domestic violence took a much longer time to be implemented, the German Parliament reacting somewhat tardily to changing social norms and public attitudes towards this phenomenon.

German Penal Code and other laws

The German Penal Code prescribes severe penalties for crimes of violence against human beings and this includes crimes of marital and domestic violence. Nevertheless, domestic violence is still not treated as a crime prosecuted by private indictment, thus the police and prosecution are obliged to institute criminal proceedings whenever they are informed that an incident of violence has occurred. In addition, a statute was implemented on 1 January 2002 which illustrates further legislative measures to combat violence towards women. This is the Act to Improve Civil Court Protection in the Event of Violent Acts and Unwelcome Advances and to Facilitate Allocation of the Marital Home in the Event of Separation. The short title of the Act is the Protection from Violence Act 2000, which acts as a 'protection for victims of violence, persecution, and other unreasonable acts (such as stalking) and for the facilitation of legislation relating to the allocation of the domestic and marital home during divorce proceedings' (see Kury *et al.*, 2006). This Act provides for the eviction of one (married) partner from the marital home in cases of domestic violence, via an exclusion order, a ban on harassment and a restraining order. Smartt has pointed out that this Act only protects those who are legally married and only where the domestic violence offence occurs in the marital home. Hence, cohabitants who fight in the pub, for instance, would not be protected (Smartt, 2001, p. 230).

The courts are also permitted, under the Act, to prescribe other protective measures that prohibit the offender from entering the marital home, or visiting certain places where the victim stays, such as the workplace, contacting the victim by telephone, and others. The statute also contains a provision on allocation of the dwelling if the victim lived in the same dwelling with the offender for a long time. To reinforce these provisions and ensure the victim easy access to those protective measures, the relevant provisions of procedural and enforcement statutes have also been amended (http://www.legislationonline.org).

Punishing marital violence

Under the German Penal Code, offences of rape and sexual coercion are governed by ss 177–9, according to which they are punishable if a person using force or threat of physical violence coerces a person to have sexual intercourse or engage in other sexual acts. In 1977, an amendment was brought in to widen this definition to include marital rape, so that rape could constitute an offence within marriage. As recent as this seems, it is significant to note that an English court, namely the House of Lords, only recognized marital rape in 1991(see *R v R (Rape: Marital Exemption)* [1991] 4 All ER 181). Section 179 of the German Penal Code also provides for punishment of 'physical' or 'psychological' sexual abuse inflicted on a person who is incapable of resisting the offence. Under German law, rape is punishable by not less than two years' imprisonment and up to a life sentence. This penalty is raised to not less than ten years if the rape resulted in death, even if the perpetrator did not cause the death intentionally.

Other related criminal laws

Yet another statute, the Act of 1998 to Protect Witnesses in Questioning in Criminal Proceedings and to Improve Victim Protection, provides for the use of video in criminal proceedings to protect the victim from the stressful procedure of direct testimony and from having contact with the offender. The Act on Settlements between Offenders and Victims in Criminal Law and s. 1(55a) of the Code of Criminal Procedure allows criminal proceedings to be discontinued if a settlement is reached between offender and the victim.

The police perspective on domestic violence

All 16 German district police forces have their own domestic violence regulations but these forces differ in their willingness to implement the regulations (Kury *et al.*, 2006, p. 397). In 1987, Bergdoll and Namgalies-Treichler reported a change in attitudes amongst some German police forces from the late 1980s onwards (Berdoll and Namgalies-Treichler, 1987, p. 62). The main aim of the police then was usually to provide mediation and advice and to calm things down but not, presumably, to take any other sort of action. In 2005, Steffen pointed out that 'abused wives and women cannot presently rely on the help and support of the police, neither can they rely on the help and support from other formal authorities – something they ought to be able to hope for and rely on since domestic call-outs are rather unpopular with the police and yet such emergency call-outs are increasing in frequency' (Steffen, 2005, pp. 17–36, p. 158). Indeed, Stumper *et al.* noted in 1990 that as recently as 1975 calling out the police to attend what was called a 'domestic problem' would only have exacerbated the situation, especially when it came to laying charges against the perpetrator, since police interference in such matters was regarded as a purely secondary measure even in the most violent of domestic assaults (Stumper *et al.*, 1990, p. 704.

'Platzverweiz' – another method of combating domestic violence

In 2005, another legislative measure was introduced to combat domestic violence, which forms part of the Protection from Violence Act 2000. This is a court or police order (Platzverweiz) which places an injunction, exclusion, displacement or banning order on the perpetrator but only for a short duration. The word derives from the world of sport's red card and sin bin, to which a person who commits a foul is sent for a short time. This is a civil order but once breached has criminal law consequences. It initially last for ten days but the victim may ask the courts for an extension or variation (Kury and Obergfell-Fuchs, 2005). This order can include: taking away the house keys, doorstep curfews or reporting regularly to the local police station. Police statistics from the Land-Baden-Wurtenburg for 2005 show that this measure has been used for several victims of domestic violence and is proving to be reasonably popular. Of the 8,966 domestic–related distress calls received, 2,968 Platzverweis measures were ordered.

France

Criminal Law

Domestic violence is also recognized as a crime in France, another civil law country. Violence committed by a husband or partner is defined in the French Criminal Code as an 'aggravating circumstance' to the physical crime. This aggravating circumstance will be applicable to instances of murder, manslaughter and rape with the maximum penalty being 30 years to life imprisonment.

The maximum punishment for violence by a husband or partner resulting in the victim's inability to work for more than eight days is five years' imprisonment and a fine of around 76,000 Euros. If the woman is unable to work for up to eight days, the maximum punishment is three years' imprisonment and a fine of around 46,000 Euros.

Marital rape is recognized as a crime and carries a maximum punishment of 15 years in prison. In a national survey on violence against women, only 1 per cent of women reported rape by their husband or partner.

Violence against women in immigrant communities

It has been suggested that domestic violence is particularly likely to occur to immigrant women in France. It would appear that the national domestic hotline in France is the only source of statistics on violence within the immigrant population. According to Mihalich's research in 2000, more than 20 per cent of the women who called this number in 1999 were foreign-born, with 8.3 per cent from the Maghreb and 3.9 per cent from Black Africa (see Mihalich, 2001). The proportion of callers from North Africa is disproportionate to their forming only 1.2 per cent of the French population. Mihalich argues that certain socioeconomic conditions militate to make immigrant women particularly vulnerable to domestic violence. First, many immigrants in France come from Islamic countries, particularly Algeria, Morocco and Tunisia. These countries have gender inequalities institutionalized though Muslim tradition and personal status laws. As Mihalich states: 'The belief that women provoke violence and deserve to be beaten is transmitted across generations, as women come to believe they are at fault' (Mihalich, 2001). Second, immigrant women in France are often extremely isolated, with the majority lacking competence in the French language; 57 per cent of Algerian women (as opposed to 16 per cent of Algerian men) and 65 per cent of Moroccan and Tunisian women (as opposed to 40 per cent of their male counterparts) do not speak French.

Other measures

The French Parliament has raised the age at which women can get married, from 15 to 18, as part of a package of measures to combat domestic violence (BBC News: http://news.bbc.co.uk/go/pr/fr/-/1/hi/world/europe/4838090.stm) and there are plans to introduce more severe penalties for marital rape and assault which will be extended to married partners, cohabiting couples and even to ex-partners.

JAPAN

Introduction

Watanabe reminds us: 'The idea of a male-dominated society still holds in today's Japanese society ... [and] is deeply rooted'(Watanabe, 2002, pp. 83, 90). This is both an ethic and a vestige of their feudal society but the idea has weathered over time.

Historical background

Under the feudal ethos, a husband would be allowed to hit his wife as a means of discipline, and a wife would be supposed to obey her husband since she belonged to him. This rule also meant that no one would be allowed to say anything about the husband's behaviour, no matter how violent or unreasonable it may be. Hence, marital or domestic violence would be regarded as 'mere quarrel' between husband and wife, rather than a crime (Watanabe, 2002, p. 83). Unless the violence caused death, women were expected to endure it and it was not considered a social problem.

However, the male dominated society has begun to decline in its pervasiveness and 50 years on from the Second World War equality of the sexes has been accepted in Japanese society, and domestic violence has gradually been recognized as a social problem (Watanabe, 2002, p. 84). United Nations' activities relating to violence against women has led to public organizations intervening in domestic disputes even though there used to be a rule against such involvement for public agencies. Thus, 'in a society in which men dominate women in social, economic, and physical terms, acts of violence against women who are in vulnerable positions are now being regarded as crimes rather than personal problems' (Watanabe, 2002, p. 84).

The contemporary situation

Domestic violence is now considered a serious problem because contemporary Japanese are far more conscious of human rights than were past generations. However, the government does not yet have women's refuges specifically for victims of domestic violence, and only around two dozen private shelters are available nationwide (Watanabe, 2002, p. 92). Other problems highlighted by Watanabe included the inadequate availability of opportunities for consultation, a lack of change in men's attitudes generally, private support organizations being operated by volunteers and a lack of financial support. Some of these problems were addressed by a law which came into force in 2001.

Prevention of Spousal Violence and Protection of Victims Law

In 2001, the Prevention of Spousal Violence and Protection of Victims Law was passed. It contains restraining orders and protection orders similar to those that exist in the United States. This law was adopted in April 2001 and came into force in October 2001. Under this law, it is prohibited for a person to inflict physical harm or bodily injury upon another person, even between spouses. Violence between spouses is called 'spousal violence'and may take various forms. The 'spouse' may include male or female and includes unmarried partners and former spouses in cases where violence is inflicted both before and after a separation. 'Violence' includes not only physical but (after an amendment in 2004) also psychological and sexual violence, however protection orders apply only to physical violence.

Protection orders

Where there is a grave threat that a victim could suffer serious harm to life or body from renewed spousal violence, a protection order may be issued to the abused by a district court, initiated by a written petition to the court. There are three types of protection order: (i) an order to prohibit an approach; (ii) an order to vacate; and (iii) a stay-away order related to children,

Under an order to prohibit an approach, the court may prohibit a perpetrator from approaching a victim and his or her children, or loitering in the vicinity of the victim's residence, other than the place where the abuser and victim have been living together, workplace, schools or any other places frequented by the victim and the victim's children.

Under an order to vacate, the court may order the perpetrator to vacate, for a two-month period, the residence shared as the main home with the victim and not to loiter in the vicinity of the victim's residence. Despite the two-month limit, the victim can keep renewing the request for such an order so that it can be extended.

Under a stay-away order, the court may forbid the abuser from approaching non-adult children who are living with the victim, or from loitering in the vicinity of their residence, school or other place, until the order has expired.

Violation of a protection order by the abuser is punishable by imprisonment with hard labour of up to one year, or a fine of not more than 1 million yen.

Victims can contact the Spousal Violence Counselling and Support Centre, known as the SV Centre, for details of the requisite procedure. The SV Centre is a specialized agency supporting victims of spousal violence.

Under the 2001 law, local government is supposed to provide financial assistance to organizations which assist victims of domestic violence and it provides for the national government to establish new facilities to assist victims.

As Oshita explains: 'The significance of the new Law at the time was that it recognised domestic violence as a crime and made it state responsibility to address it' (Oshita, 2006). Apart from providing protection regulations and legal sanctions, which were found effective as short-term protection for women from abusive husbands, the law was important not only for the women victims of domestic violence seeking protection but also for 'Japanese society because it established that violence is not tolerable even at home between a couple' (Oshita, 2006).

Women's groups formed a network and a lobby in response to the weaknesses in the law, which at the time included: not covering violence by a divorced partner or a boyfriend, protective measures were short term without providing long-term support for women to enable them to restore their lives, and the absence of specific provision for migrant women. A group called Solidarity with Migrant Workers (SMJ) combined with the Japanese National Network on Revising the Law was formed in 2003, comprising women victims of domestic violence, their support groups and shelter staff, aiming to raise awareness among the members of the Japanese Parliament and ministries on the plight of victims of domestic violence and to lobby for the first amendment of the law in 2004. As a result of persistent lobbying an amendment was made in 2004 which included the need to respect the human rights of domestic violence victims regardless of their nationality. Immigration laws were partly relaxed to prioritize protection of victims over the visa status.

However, further gaps were identified by the network after the first amendment came into effect in December 2004. These included: the need for protection to be extended to include threats by phone, fax or email; divorced partners and boyfriends should be covered by the law; the police being slow to respond to cases and unwilling to arrest perpetrators of domestic violence; the need for local government to improve their bureaucratic procedures and provide all information and services available at one stop centres; children's training programs on domestic violence should be developed and conducted to prevent domestic violence in the long term; the need to revisit the 2004 amendment to respect the human rights of victims regardless of their nationality as it had proved insufficient to persuade the police to protect victims without a valid visa (Oshita, 2006).

These deficiencies were to be addressed in the second amendment, intended to take place in 2007.

Current statistics

The annual rate of murder cases in which a husband kills his wife through the use of violence has been 100 to 120, and about 40 per cent of these murdered women had been abused by their husbands ('Marital Violence no. 1', *The Asahi*, November 11, 1998, p. 23). Approximately 30 per cent of female victims of murder have been killed by a husband or male cohabitant.

Concluding comment

To eradicate this problem, it will be necessary to improve 'judicial, administrative, medical, and welfare networks' (Watanabe, 2002, p. 92). The move for gender equality, which has been gathering momentum in Japan, and the laws to protect victims of domestic violence, which have also begun to address the counselling and other supportive measures essential to make these laws work, although by no means completely effective in their operation, present strong evidence that this complex and hardworking nation has begun to make strides in tackling domestic violence in its society.

South Africa

Historical and cultural background to the domestic violence problem

In 1999, the racial mix in South Africa was made up of Africans/Blacks (33,239,879), Whites (4,538,727), Coloureds (mixed race) (3,792,631), Indians/Asians (1,092,254) and others (390,815). All these racial groups, according to van der Hoven, have certain traditions, norms and attitudes which perpetuate violence towards women. Indeed, van der Hoven argues that the 'domination of and violence toward women are ingrained in the tradition of family relationships in South Africa' (van der Hoven, 2002, p. 130). Hence, within the black communities in South Africa, certain traditions have been identified by van der Hoven as contributing to domestic violence, particularly wife abuse, namely: indoctrination by initiation schools; the lobola (dowry) system; the patriarchal family system and women's economic dependency on men. In each of these cases, either the indoctrination of adolescents into manhood, which encourages both domination over and violence towards women; or the payment by the bridegroom's family of a brideprice or dowry to compensate the bride's family for the loss of the bride, which had the effect of making the husband feel the wife was his possession to use and abuse as he pleased; or the practice of polygamy, which meant men could procure several wives but women were supposed to remain faithful to only one husband, who frequently abandoned their families and left the women to fend for themselves, has resulted in a culture where violence towards women has been both tolerated and accepted.

Van der Hoven explains that as women became more enlightened and better educated in more recent times, they started to move into the labour market and their male partners have seen this as a challenge to male authority. Consequently, having grown up in families which have accepted the element of violence towards women, and sometimes fuelled by alcohol, men have been violent towards these women, wishing to reassert their dominance and to put the women in their place (van der Hoven, 2002, p. 131).

Whether or not one accepts the validity of all these assertions, there is little doubt that South African women who face problems in their home environments will have had such problems compounded by their particular cultural, economic and geographical situation.

The incidence of domestic violence in South Africa

A very bleak and depressing picture is painted of the incidence of domestic violence in South Africa, indicating it poses a very serious social problem, despite the implementation of a comprehensive law in 1999. In 1994, Margaret Lessing was moved to write that there has never been more wife battering, more child abuse, more physical violence, more family murders or more ill-treatment of the elderly than was being reported at that time (Lessing, 1994).

Statistics on domestic violence and the pre-1998 Act situation

Before the implementation in 1999 of the Domestic Violence Act 1998, battered women had to initiate charges against the perpetrator for acts such as assault, assault with intent to cause grievous bodily harm, kidnapping, rape, indecent assault or attempted murder. No category of crime existed under any legislation for 'domestic violence' or 'wife abuse' (van der Hoven, 2002, p. 127 and sources cited therein). Indeed, as in every other jurisdiction, it is difficult to make an accurate estimate of the full extent of the problem since it would, by definition, usually occur while hidden from public view. The Government Gazette, which contains statistics of reported incidents, estimates that one in six South African women is battered by a male partner (Government Gazette, 1997, p. 73). Other statistics suggest that almost half (48 per cent) of sexual offences and assaults occur inside private dwellings, one in every four South African women is assaulted by a boyfriend or husband every week (NICRO Women's Support Centre, 1998, p. 1) and violence against the female partner is cited in more than a third of divorce cases in South Africa (Beijing Conference Report 1995, p. 44). This occurs across all socioeconomic and racial groups (van der Hoven, 2002, p. 127).

Wide definitions of 'domestic violence 'and 'domestic relationship' under the Domestic Violence Act 1998

Under s. 1(viii) of the South African Domestic Violence Act 1998 (No. 116 of 1998), domestic violence is comprehensively defined to include not just physical abuse but also sexual abuse, emotional, verbal and psychological abuse, economic abuse, intimidation, harassment, stalking, and damage to property. The definition also includes 'entry into the complainant's residence without consent, where the parties do not share the same residence; or any other controlling or abusive behaviour toward a complainant, where such conduct harms, or may cause imminent harm to, the safety, health or well-being of the complainant'.

Section 1(vii) of the 1998 Act has a very broad definition of 'domestic relationship' which it defines as a relationship between a complainant and respondent in any of the following ways: that the parties were or are married to each other, including marriage by any law, custom or religion; that they (whether of the same sex or opposite sex) live or lived together in a relationship in the nature of a marriage, although they never married each other or were ever able to marry each other; that they are parents of a child or are persons who have or had parental responsibility for that child (whether or not at the same time); that they are family members related by consanguinity, affinity, or adoption; that they are or were engaged, dating, or in a customary relationship, including an actual or perceived romantic, intimate or sexual relationship of any duration; or they share or recently shared the same residence.

Under the 1998 Act, a duty is placed on the South African Police Service to inform a victim of his or her rights at the scene of an incident of domestic violence. A police officer has the right to arrest a person, without warrant, at the scene of an incident of domestic violence who he or she reasonable suspects of having committed an offence containing an element of violence against a complainant.

The 1998 Act also allows a protection order to be granted subject to confirmation, depending on whether the alleged perpetrator appears in court on the return day. The Act also allows the seizure of firearms and other dangerous weapons at the scene of the alleged domestic violence.

In granting a protection order, a court may also issue a suspended warrant for the arrest of the respondent. This means that such a warrant would remain in force unless the protection order is set aside. Consequently, if the respondent breaches the protection order, he or she will be arrested by the police. The complainant or respondent has the right to apply for the protection order to be amended or set aside.

The 1998 Act also provides that proceedings must be held in camera. The penalty for domestic violence suggests it is a serious crime, since a perpetrator can be sentenced to five years' imprisonment.

Thus, this Act was enacted to provide a simple, speedy and cost-effective procedure to protect its victims.

In 2001, two years after the implementation of the 1998 Act, van der Hoven could still declare: 'In South Africa, violence against women and children is widespread and on the increase' (van der Hoven, 2002, p. 125). Indeed, the incidence of crimes of violence in South Africa has been recorded as extremely high, with the country having the highest murder and rape statistics in the world (SAPS Crime Information Analysis Centre, 1999) and this trend being reflected in domestic violence (van der Hoven, 2002, pp. 126–7).

Current measures to deal with domestic violence

A number of facilities now exist which provide a service for victims of domestic violence. There is a Rape Crisis Shelter for Battered Women in Cape Town, opened in 1986, six shelters for abused women in Johannesburg, Port Elizabeth, Cape Town, Kimberley and two in Durban. An advice desk has been operating in Durban since June 1989. This provides a wide range of services such as a hotline to deal with crisis calls on a 24-hour basis; shelter services; support and counselling services for abused women, men and children; support groups for women, men and children who have witnessed domestic violence.

A significant deficiency of the 1998 Act is that it did not provide for compulsory state-sponsored rehabilitation and counselling programs for perpetrators of domestic violence. Fedler has pointed out that 'experience worldwide indicates that these programmes cannot be relied upon to stop the violent behaviour of the abuser' (Fedler, South African Law Commission, 1997, p. 113). Abusers can use counselling as a form of manipulation instead of change, and joint counselling can perpetuate the power of one party over the other (van der Hoven, 2002, p. 136).

Unlike the previous government, the South African government which came into power in 1994 committed itself to eradicating the problem of domestic violence, which given its endemic nature, was a formidable objective. It pledged to comply with the Beijing Platform, which is an agenda for action in women's empowerment, and entrenched the rights to gender equality and freedom from violence in the Constitution of 1996 and started work on a Charter of Rights for victims of crime.

Comments on the South African situation

Despite the Domestic Violence Act 1998, several problems continue to exist in relation to the protection of victims from domestic violence, including the passivity of battered women, flaws with the current counselling system, and the lack of state support for mandatory rehabilitation and counselling programs for perpetrators of domestic violence.

Russia

Introduction

The perception of domestic violence in the Russian Federation has changed since the time of the Communist regime (pre-1989). As Voigt and Thornton explain, domestic violence was believed to be a rare occurrence, stemming mainly from an individual's abnormal personality in combination with alcohol abuse (Voigt and Thornton, 2002, p. 98). Voigt and Thornton assert that 'it was not until the 1980s that "family crime" became a topic worthy of data gathering and it was during the period of *glasnost* (openness) and *perestroika* (restructuring) under Mikhail Gorbachev that domestic violence began to emerge in public discourse', although it still mainly regarded as a secondary problem and one associated with alcohol abuse (Voigt and Thornton, 2002, p. 98). In fact, Voigt and Thornton suggest that it was largely due to the efforts of major women's organizations in large cities such as Moscow and St Petersburg, as well as criminological investigators, that awareness of the prevalence of domestic violence was maintained.

The post-1989 developments

After the former Soviet Union collapsed and began to fragment in 1989, domestic violence became part of the national agenda in Russia. The deteriorating socioeconomic conditions and the erosion of public support appear to have had a detrimental effect on the institution of the family in Russia, and in response the Russian Federation declared 1994 the Year of the Family. Voigt and Thornton report that this focused attention on all aspects of the family, and 1994 will be remembered as the year in which a mini-survey conducted in that year revealed that a one-child family had become typical; the birth rate, marriage rate and number of children per family were all in decline. In contrast, the survey suggested that the number of divorces, single-parent families and unwed mothers was increasing.

The growing divorce rate (two thirds of marriages ending in divorce) has contributed to more economic hardship and emotional stress, leading to more domestic violence. In the aftermath of divorce, many couples have had no alternative but to live in very cramped conditions and to continue to share living quarters because of the severe housing shortage (Russian Association of Crisis Centres for Women, 1997). Indeed, Voigt and Thornton emphasize that there have sometimes been three-generation households living in these cramped housing conditions, and most single-parent families and pensioners on the poverty line are women (Voigt and Thornton, 2002, p. 100). A sociologist, Tanya Zabelina, when interviewed by the *Moscow Tribune*, expressed the view that domestic assault and battery and other forms of violence against women have always existed but they are now more brutal as a result of the increasing stresses in the living environment, exacerbated by growing unemployment and alcoholism (Clarke, 1995).

The frequency of spousal homicide

Another extremely worrying phenomenon was spousal homicide, with more than half the victims being women. In 1994 it was reported that approximately 15,000 women were murdered by their husbands annually (Human Rights Watch Report, 1997). These sorts of statistics galvanized the Russian Federation into enacting a new family policy by decree of the president of the Federation in 1996. This addressed the plight of Russian children, the overall quality of family life in Russia, and led to a Code which emphasized assisting families in their difficulties – resulting in 'a national effort to enhance and expand the system of social support for families, especially women and children, resulting in a significant growth of facilities and shelters' (see Centre for Europe's Children: Russian Federation, p. 7, cited by Voigt & Thornton, 2002, p.99).

The position of Russian women is somewhat paradoxical at the moment. The Soviet Constitution declared women and men legally and politically equal but women have had a heavy burden placed on them since; despite having the 'freedom' to take on full-time jobs, they are still responsible for practically all household and cleaning duties (Fastenko and Timofeeva, 2004, p. 113). A study conducted in 2000 by Arai, Perlitsh and Erdyneev suggested that there are idealistically high expectations of women as good mothers, wives, housekeepers and dedicated professionals. Yet, Fastenko and Timofeeva maintain that widespread sexual harassment and age discrimination in the workplace still exist, which make it very difficult for many women to find and maintain employment, despite their high educational attainments and work experience (Fastenko and Timofeeva, 2004, p. 113).

The legal response

The 1994 Code of Civil Law of the Russian Federation, the 1996 Code of Criminal Law in the Russian Federation and the 1997 Code of Criminal Procedure of the Russian Federation all address protection against violence in the family.

Concluding comments on the Russian situation

Voigt and Thornton have observed that 'Russia represents a classic illustration of anomie, a condition of normlessness or social chaos owing to rapid social changes with accompanying disruption of the social structure' (Voigt and Thornton, 2002, p. 103). This upheaval has been inimical to harmonious family life, particularly in view of the traumatic economic, social and political changes Russia underwent following the disintegration of the Federation and separation from the former Soviet Republics, with which it is still coming to terms. Under these circumstances, it is remarkable and commendable that domestic violence has reached the national agenda and that positive legal and social measures have been made to tackle the problem.

The United States

Historical background

There were some early laws against spousal abuse in the United States which date from the mid nineteenth century. From around 1875, American society started to be less tolerant of a husband's use of force against his wife (Epstein, 1999) and in 1850 the first law against wife beating was passed in Tennessee. The flaw in this and other early statutes was that there was an underlying theory that in the absence of serious injury or life-threatening violence, the state should avoid intervention in the domestic realm (Rapoza, 2004, p. 454).

The next milestone in public concern over family violence was Kempe, Silverman, Steele, Droegmuller and Silver's (1962) description of the 'battered child syndrome' – injuries such as burns, broken bones, and fractures attributable to parents' maltreatment of the child. As Brienes and Gordon note, by 1957, the huge attention generated by this publication resulted in mandatory child abuse reporting laws in all 50 States (Brienes and Gordon, 1983). During the 1960s and 1970s the feminist movement led to the establishment of many battered women's organizations (Fagan, 1995). In the 1970s the American justice system began to regard the problem seriously and to treat domestic violence as a crime. Indeed, one of the first battered women's shelters was opened in 1974 in St Paul, Minnesota based on the premise that wife abuse was a social problem rather than a purely private and personal one.

Yet it was only in the 1980s, when high profile media coverage of battered women and the results of the Minneapolis Domestic Violence Experiment, 'drastically changed' public opinion and legal approaches to domestic violence cases (Rapoza, 2004, p. 454). This experiment showed that 'domestic violence recidivism was substantially less for men who were arrested as compared with men who were dealt with using other tactics' (Sherman and Berk, 1984). Not all studies mirrored this finding (see for example Tolman and Edleson, 1995) but the 'arresting of batterers and the criminalization of domestic violence was evidence of American society taking more seriously the rights and needs of battered women' (Rapoza, 2004, p. 454).

In their study of domestic violence in the United States, Summers and Hoffman survey the legal response, the police response and make several observations on protection orders, highlight the use of panic buttons and mention the work of the model court programs.

The legal response to domestic violence in the United States

In 1984, the federal government passed the Family Violence Prevention and Services Act, which 'provides federal funds to help local communities and states, co-ordinate research and provide training with regard to stopping domestic violence' (Summers and Hoffman, 2002, p. 181). The Victims of Crime Act was also passed, which 'provides funds to state agencies for compensating victims of crime and provides assistance to victims of domestic violence' (Summers and Hoffman, 2002, p. 181).

In 1994, the Crime Act was passed which makes a gender-motivated crime a violation of women's civil rights and gives the woman the legal right to sue the perpetrator. These statutes look beyond providing merely local State protection by making it a federal crime for abusers to cross State lines to commit domestic violence, by making protection orders enforceable across State lines and by providing criminal penalties for interstate stalking. This means that a woman can move to another State and still have the protection of the law against an abusive ex-partner or intimate.

These statutes also make funding available for States and local communities to establish shelters, counselling programs and various prevention programs, such as crisis hotlines, and education and training for police and justice system workers who deal with victims of domestic violence (Summers and Hoffman, p. 182)

The police response

As in many other jurisdictions, American police officers were reluctant to intervene in domestic disputes until the climate of awareness changed and domestic violence began to be taken more seriously. However, with the change in attitude which recognized domestic violence as unacceptable in society, about half the States in the country enacted mandatory arrest laws, which allow police officers to make an arrest at the scene of domestic violence if there is 'probable cause'. This means there must be evidence that a person has been injured or abused (Summers and Hoffman, 2002, p. 182).

Protection orders/restraining orders

Summers and Hoffman point out that in the United States protection orders or restraining orders are court orders which prohibit any further abuse, contact, or the harassment of a victim, and exist in most local and State jurisdictions. There are also ex parte protection orders that may be issued in an emergency for which the victim can apply without the abuser needing to be present in court for the application hearing. If issued, they can be in effect from 30 to 60 days and can result in imprisonment if the order is violated. Many areas allow police reports on domestic violence to be sent directly to the prosecutor's office which then issues a protection order and proceeds with criminal prosecution without the need for the victim to be involved (Summers and Hoffman, 2002, p. 182). A permanent order or injunction may last up to three years and can include provisions for evicting the abuser from the home, financial support, and child custody (Summers and Hoffman, 2002, p. 182). Summers and Hoffman make the important point that these protection orders are intended to protect the victim from further harm and do not involve criminal prosecution or punishment of the offenders. Some States have even more far-reaching protection orders which can divide up a couple's property or require the perpetrator to pay restitution for damages as well as spousal and child support (Summers and Hoffman, 2002, p. 183).

Panic buttons

Panic buttons are a particularly novel and useful warning device to prevent domestic violence that is regarded as imminent (see Summers and Hoffman, 2004, p. 183). They are used in many cities of the United States and are small electronic devices which, when pressed, send a high priority message to the police. They are for individuals at high risk of domestic violence from, for example, an intimate who is violating a protection order or who has just been released from jail. Summers and Hoffman note that in Cambridge, Massachusetts, police respond in two or three minutes (Summers and Hoffman, 2002, p. 183).

Model court programs

There are 18 model court programs across the United States which are said to represent the most successful court programs in the intervention and reduction of domestic violence (see *Family Violence: State-of-the-Art Court Programmes,* National Council, 1992). The programs emphasize 'the co-ordination of the efforts of law enforcement, prosecution, and the courts with social services, medical services and various treatment programmes' (Summers and Hoffman, 2002, p. 183). Summers and Hoffman report that many of these comprehensive programs are operated by 'private, non-profit organisations and provide direct services to victims such as shelter, counselling, therapy, legal assistance, court advocacy, and referrals to other agencies for matters such as housing' (Summers and Hoffman, 2002, p. 183).

Husband abuse

Although there is ample evidence that it exists (see Cook, 1997; Hines and Malley-Morrison, 2001; Steinmetz, 1977) intimate partner violence against males in the United States has been largely ignored. From surveys conducted in the United States, Americans seem to show greater approval for violence perpetrated by a wife toward a husband than by a husband toward a wife (Strauss, Kaufmann-Kantor and Moore, 1997). Approval of a husband slapping a wife decreased from 20 per cent in 1968 to 10 per cent in 1994, yet approval of a wife slapping a husband appeared to remain constant at 22 per cent.

Concluding observations – looking to the past and to the future

In her review of domestic violence reform in a special issue of the Family Law Quarterly which reviews 50 years of family law in the United States, Elizabeth Schneider maintains that no aspect of [American] family law has had more dramatic change than the law of domestic violence (Scheneider, 2008, p. 353). Fifty years ago it was simply invisible, being neither recognized as a subject of study nor as a legal problem (Schneider, 2008, p. 354). Fifty years on, it is recognized as a serious harm, a 'harm within intimate relationships that has an impact on every aspect of the law, including criminal law, torts, reproductive rights, civil rights, employment law, international human rights, and especially family law' (Schneider, 2008, p. 254). Schneider's review includes the following observations. (i) There now exists a greater understanding of what domestic violence is and who experiences it. Instead of including only the original idea of physical abuse there is now the 'core concept' of the 'exercise of power and control', so that domestic violence includes a wide range of behaviours including physical abuse, verbal abuse, threats, stalking, sexual abuse, coercion and economic control. (ii) Lawyers, judges and other professionals still tend to see a physical focus, minimize other aspects of abuse, and fail to see the other elements of power and control as abusive and connected with physical abuse. (iii) Domestic violence is 'overwhelmingly' a problem for women, but some continue to argue it affects men and women equally. (iv) Deep and pervasive attitudes affect every aspect of domestic violence and make the question "Why don't they leave?" the central question. This reflects a failure to understand the nature of the problem. Women's efforts to free themselves from the problem 'often precipitates and exacerbates abuse and puts women and children at risk'. The pervasiveness of women-blaming continues. (v) Domestic violence affects same-sex relationships as well. (vi) Intractable problems surround the protection of abused women and the prevention of violence. (vii) Despite considerable changes in the imposition of criminal sanctions, criminalization has proven to be very problematic, being too crude a remedy and because it requires too much from women who wish to end the violence but not the relationship. Such women do not want to subject their partner or family to criminal sanctions. Special problems have been identified for non-white women and immigrant women in obtaining police protection. Family privacy has also been cited as a reason which has historically prevented intervention. (viii) Prevention of violence is very difficult not least because this sort of violence occurs within a 'gendered context'. There is a need for education and outreach to assist women to recognize signs of abuse and 'not to confuse them with ... romance and the desire for intimacy' (Schneider, 2008, pp. 356–9).

Italy

The patriarchal model has been writ large in Italy, where there is a view that religion has maintained domestic violence as an isolated and personal and private matter and not a widespread social problem. Historically, the Catholic Church and the state have regarded domestic violence as personal and private. The advice to battered women would traditionally be to return to their abusing partners, and it is all-important to preserve 'the family', so that domestic violence has been overlooked or even considered normal.

Concluding observations

In England and Wales there have been notable signs of progress in dealing with domestic violence in terms of a more coordinated law. A much more comprehensive set of laws covers conduct such as stalking and other forms of harassment and also a wider range of perpetrators (including 'associated persons' such as ex-spouses, former cohabitants, relatives, same-sex and opposite-sex partners) than before. The Home Office definition even includes persons who may carry out 'financial abuse', which is not specifically covered in any of the definitions we have looked at in other jurisdictions.

As far as a more global overview is concerned, each country we have looked at varies in its perception of the contributing factors to domestic violence. In England and Wales, some of the risk factors include: gender inequality, poverty, social exclusion, having a criminal background, and having experienced abuse as a child (Summers and Hoffman, 2002, p. xiii). Families have been classified as patriarchal and women have a subordinate status, which has been the seedbed for those families' problems.

Russia (and Germany), unsurprisingly, identify major political change as a contributing factor (Summers and Hoffman, 2002, p. xiii), with Russia experiencing social chaos and disruption and facing a critical phase in its history where its basic institutions (such as the family, economy, government, education and religion) have been and continue to be in a state of flux and transition. Economic and structural stress have also been identified by South Africa as contributing factors, which appear to compound the indigenous male-dominated culture which has, whether wittingly or not, encouraged violence towards women.

Our study of France and Australia highlights the special problems faced by the immigrant female population as far as domestic violence is concerned, where ethnic minorities appear to be high-risk targets of such violence. In Australia, most citizens appear to see domestic violence as rooted in the aggressive nature of men yet the Indigenous or native population see it as learned behaviour.

In the United States a variety of responses have been made to deal with the problem of domestic violence. Apart from protection orders and restraining orders, a range of measures have been and are being implemented to protect victims and to deal with offenders. The use of a panic button seems particularly appropriate in cases of imminent danger. In retrospect, there can never be adequate compensation for the families of those victims who have lost their lives through homicide or taken their own lives but as the 'dynamics of this violence' and its contributing causes are being better understood, treatment and prevention programs are showing signs of making progress in measuring the prevalence of the violence and evaluating the interventions (Summer and Hoffman, 2002, p. 183).

Schneider's survey of the American scene over the last 50 years echoes most of the findings and observations of other commentators like Summer and Hoffman, while emphasizing the intractable nature of the problem and mirroring the current difficulties faced in seeking to protect women in other jurisdictions, including Britain, by using criminal sanctions as the central solution.

The suffering of thousands of women (and to a lesser extent, men) and children from this complex and incipient problem is being seriously addressed in the United States and for the many who have suffered from domestic abuse for many years without receiving adequate protection or relief for many years, there appears to be light at the end of the tunnel.

Overall, this overview has revealed that endemic and entrenched problems remain, namely: the difficulty in persuading victims (predominantly female) to make complaints, testify in court or to leave violent and abusive relationships. Another disturbing finding is the passivity of certain female victims, especially those from ethnic minorities or who are immigrants in certain countries and therefore more vulnerable to such abuse and open to exploitation.

All jurisdictions continue to try to bridge the public/private divide that has bedevilled this social problem, seeking to provide more effective protection through criminal sanctions – which in some cases deter victims from using the tougher laws because of the wish to avoid giving their partners a criminal record and a prison sentence. The state, through the police and the counselling agencies, must continue to provide support where it is needed until this appalling scourge of our times is eliminated.

Further reading

Behrendt, L 'Aboriginal Women and Crime' in Rafter (ed) *Encyclopedia of Women and Crime*, 2000, Phoenix Press.

Berdoll and Namgalies-Treichler '*Frauenhaus im ländlichen Raum*', 198 *Schriftenreihe des Bundesministeriums fur Jugend, frauen, Familie und Gesundheit*, 1987.

Dobash, RE and Dobash, R *Violence Against Wives*, 1982, Open Books.

Dobash, RE and Dobash, R *Women, Violence and Social Change*, 1992, Routledge.

Edwards, S *Sex and Gender in the Legal Process*, 1996, Blackstone.

Fastenko, A and Timofeeva, I 'Russia' in Malley-Morrison (ed*) International Perspectives on Family Violence and Abuse*, 2004, Lawrence Erlbaum Associates.

Hague, G and Malos, E *Tackling Domestic Violence*, 1996, Rowntree Foundation.

Home Office *Safety and Justice: The Government's Proposals on Domestic Violence*, 2003.

Kury, H and Smartt, U 'Domestic Violence: Recent Developments in German and English Legislation and Law Enforcement' (2006) 14 *European Journal of Crime, Criminal Law and Criminal Justice* 382.

Lewis, R, Dobash, R, Dobash R and Cavanagh, K 'Law's Progressive Potential: The Value of Engagement with the Law of Domestic Violence' (2001) 10 Social and Leg Studies 105.

Lessing, M 'Women and Violence' in Lessing, M (ed) *South African Women Today*, 1994, Longman.

Mihalic, L 'No Exit: The Plight of Battered Maghrebi Immigrant Women in France', 2001, SOS Femmes Accueil at http://www.sosfemmes.com.

O'Hanlon, L 'Violence Against Women in France' *Report to the Committee on the Elimination of Discrimination Against Women*, Benniger-Budel (ed), 2003, OMCT (The World Organisation Against Torture).

Oshita, F 'Japanese Women's Groups Lobbying for Changes in the Law for Legal Protection of Migrant Women – Victims of Domestic Violence' (2006) 19 *Asia Pacific Forum on Women, Law and Development: Forum News.*

Martin, D 'Battered Women: Society's Problem' in Chapman and Gates (ed) *The Victimization of Women*, 1978, Sage.

Mooney, B *Gender, Violence and the Social Order*, 2000, Macmillan.

Pahl, J *Private Violence and Public Policy*, 1985, Routledge.

Pickering, S and Alder, C 'Challenging Reforms for Feminists and the Criminal Justice System' in Chappelle and Wilson (eds) *Crime and the Criminal Justice System in Australia: 2000 and Beyond*, 2000, Butterworths.

Pickering, S 'Australia' in Summers and Hoffman (eds) *Domestic Violence – A Global View*, 2002, Greenwood Press.

Pleck, E *Domestic Violence.The Making of Social Policy Against Family Violence from Colonial Times to the Present*, 1987, Oxford UP.

Rawstorne, S 'England and Wales' in Summers and Hoffman (eds) *Domestic Violence – A Global View*, 2002, Greenwood Press, Ch. 3.

Schneider, EM 'Domestic Violence Law Reform in the Twenty-First Century: Looking Back and Looking Forward' (2008) 42 FLQ 353.

Smith, LJ *Domestic Violence*, 1989, Home Office Research Study.

Soni, B 'Domestic Violence and Family Law: A New Era' [July 2007] *Family Law Week* at http://www.familylawweek.co.uk.

Steffen, W 'Gesetze Bestimmen die Taktik: Von der Reaktion auf Familienstreitigkeiten zur Umsetzung des Gewaltschutzgesetzes. Veränderungen im Polizeilichen Umgang mit Häuslicher Gewalt – Zugleich ein Beispiel für die Praxisrelevanz Kriminologischer Forschung' in Kury and Obergfell-Fuchs (Hrsg). *Gewalt in der Familie Für und wider den Platzverweis*, 2005, Frieburg, pp. 17–36, 58.

Stumper, A, Gemmer, K, Hamacher, H-W, Salewski, W 'Verhinderung und Bekampfung von Gewalt aus der Sicht der Polizeipraxis, Gutachten der Unterkomission V' in Schwind and Baumann (eds) *Ursache, Prävention und Kontrolle von Gewalt, Analysen und Vorschläge der Unabhängigen Regierungskommission zur Verhinderung und Bekämpfung von Gewalt (Gewaltkommission)* 1990, Berlin, II.

Summers, RW and Hoffman, AM (eds) *Domestic Violence – A Global View*, 2002, Greenwood Press.

van der Hoven, AE 'South Africa', in Summers and Hoffman (eds) *Domestic Violence – A Global View*, 2002, Greenwood Press, Ch. 10.

Voigt, L and Thronton, WE 'Russia' in Summer and Hoffman (eds) *Domestic Violence – A Global View*, 2002, Greenwood Press, Ch. 8.

Walklate, S 'What is to be Done about Violence Against Women?' (2008) 48 Brit J Criminol 39.

Watanabe, N 'Japan' in Summers and Hoffman (eds) *Domestic Violence – A Global View*, 2002, Greenwood Press, Ch. 7.

Wilson, E *What is to be Done About Violence in the Home?* 1983, Penguin.

Website sources

Domestic Violence Laws of the World at http://annualreview.law.harvard.edu/population/domesticviolence

Women's aid website at http://www.womensaid.org.uk/what_is_dv.htm

Part V

The impact of human rights law on family law

Introduction

This chapter looks at the impact of human rights law such as the European Convention on Human Rights on the development of family law in various jurisdictions. The main focus will be on Britain but some comparisons will be made with other European countries. Unlike other chapters which have explored the historical background to the development of family law in a particular jurisdiction, this chapter attempts to show how one piece of international legislation has affected the practice of family law in the United Kingdom and other European countries.

Since its implementation in October 2000 in Britain, the Human Rights Act 1998 has been invoked in family law cases ranging from corporal punishment to recognition of a sex-change and in relation to an alleged violation of the right to respect for privacy and family life. This chapter examines the implications and impact of the Human Rights Act on the aforementioned areas by looking at relevant case law in England and Wales and selected European jurisdictions.

When the Human Rights Act was implemented in Britain in October 2000 the legal community appeared to respond with ambivalence. As far as the law relating to children is concerned, academic writers have argued that the principles of the Human Rights Act and the welfare principle may well be conflicting rather than complementary (Herring, 1999) and that, to date, relatively sparse amounts of case law acknowledge that children are sometimes not accorded rights under the European Convention on Human Rights, since the judicial focus remains firmly in favour of parental/adults' rights. Similarly, there is scant recognition (except by academics) that the family courts in England are not necessarily meeting the demands of the Human Rights Act in this context (Fortin, 2006). We shall return to these viewpoints later on in this chapter.

It is also worth noting that the Human Rights Act is not the only human rights law relevant to the courts and policy makers in the United Kingdom. There is also the United Nations Convention on the Rights of the Child and the Convention on the Elimination of all Forms of Discrimination Against Women. In Northern Ireland, the Belfast Agreement of 1998 and the Northern Ireland Act 1998 emphasize human rights and equality as part of the peace building process and impose further rights obligations on the institution of the devolved administration.

However, this chapter continues the highly selective approach taken in the rest of the book so that we concentrate on the Human Rights Act and its impact on English law, although there will be references to other jurisdictions.

The 'rights' debate – a few preliminaries

This book is not a vehicle for jurisprudential or philosophical ruminations on the language and discourse of rights, although rights are mentioned and discussed. As Halpin puts it, the debate about rights confronts 'a bewildering disarray of issues and opinions' (Halpin, 1997, p. 105) which, if taken up in any detail, could deflect us from our main objective, which is to examine how family law has been affected and influenced by human rights law. There are, of course, several levels of rights and categories of claim. Honderich describes a right as a justified claim to the protection of a person's important interests (Honderich, 1977, p. 777). He argues that they may be justified by rules, morals, law or other norms. However, rights only become legal rights if they will be enforced by the state or its organs and institutions. Archbold points out that human rights are often seen as both legal and natural rights and their enshrinement in international instruments such as the Preamble to the Universal Declaration of Human Rights sometimes suggests that they have an intrinsic quality derived from the dignity of a human being (Archbold, 2000, p. 189). Archbold also reminds us that positivists might say that rights are derived from the fact that they are set out in national and international documents which have legal effect (Archbold, 2000, p. 189).

THE HUMAN RIGHTS ACT 1998

History and implementation

History

In 1950 the Convention for the Protection of Human Rights and Fundamental Freedoms, commonly known as the European Convention on Human Rights, established the 'first international complaints procedure which enabled an individual to have access to international courts against the state' (Swindells et al., 1999, p. 3). As Swindells eloquently puts it, this Convention 'grew out of the ashes of the twentieth century's second horrifying World War and the barbarities of the Holocaust' (Swindells, 2000, p. 55). The Human Rights Act incorporates the Convention into English domestic law by providing a statutory scheme whereby English law is enacted, interpreted and amended so that it is compatible with the Convention. The main effect of this incorporation is that Convention rights can be invoked against the state in the English domestic courts without having to plead a case in Strasbourg, as was previously required. In addition, a single, full-time European Court of Human Rights replaced the two international bodies which were previously responsible for applying the Convention, namely, European Commission of Human Rights (the Commission) and the European Court of Human Rights (the European Court). As Lord Lester describes it, the Human Rights Act is a 'fundamental constitutional measure of great contemporary significance' (Lord Lester, 1998, p. 665).

Implementation

Under the Human Rights Act, so far as it is possible to do so, English domestic legislation must be read and given effect so as to be compatible with the Convention rights. The courts are supposed to act in a way which is compatible with the Convention rights and must take into account Convention case law. The key requirement is therefore compatibility. This is to be found in s. 2 of the Human Rights Act which provides that when deciding any question which has arisen in connection with a Convention right, it must 'take into account' the judgments, decisions and opinions of the European Court of Human Rights. However, case law leading up to the implementation of the Human Rights Act in English law has suggested it requires a 'broad purposive approach' (*Golder v United Kingdom* (A/18) (1975) 1 EHRR 524). Its provisions should be interpreted so as to make its safeguards practical and effective (*Loizidou v Turkey* (1995) 20 EHRR 99, para.72). As Swindells *et al.* explain, the Convention has been given a 'dynamic or evolutive interpretation' (Swindells, 1999, p. 5) and is a 'living instrument' which must be interpreted in the light of present-day conditions (*Tyrer v United Kingdom* (A/26) (1978) 2 EHRR 175).

Rules of domestic family property law which breach the Convention

Archbold identifies several rules of domestic family law which breach the Convention. The first is the rule relating to the equal rights of spouses within marriage. The Government White Paper *Rights Brought Home* Cmnd 3782 (1997) recognized that this domestic rule breaches art. 5 of Protocol 7 of the Convention. The United Kingdom could not therefore ratify that particular article. The White Paper declares the government's intention to amend the law to accord with the Protocol and to ratify it. Three technical rules of family property law breach the Protocol.

The first is the somewhat antiquated common law duty of the husband to maintain his wife. This rule has been rendered obsolete and nugatory because of the subsequent statutory enactment of reciprocal statutory duties to maintain each other as laid down in s. 1 of the Domestic Proceedings and Magistrates' Court Act 1978, and s. 27 of the Matrimonial Causes Act 1973, but it has not been formally or statutorily repealed as such, hence continues to exist under English law.

The second rule is the law relating to ownership of housekeeping money, which differs according to whether the money was provided by the husband or wife. Under the Married Women's Property Act 1964, any savings made from an allowance given by the husband to the wife and any proceeds from them will belong jointly to both spouses. This rule does not apply in Northern Ireland where the common law rules that ownership of the savings and proceeds belong to the husband alone (see *Blackwell v Blackwell* [1943] 2 All ER 579). In the United Kingdom and Northern Ireland, if the wife gives an allowance to the husband, a rebuttable presumption of a resulting trust will be created so that the savings or their proceeds will be inferred to belong only to the wife.

The third rule is the presumption of advancement which infers that a gift by a man to his wife or child is intended as a gift (see *Silver v Silver* [1958] 1 WLR 259). On the other hand, for historical reasons, transfers by a woman to her husband are not presumed to be a gift, and the presumption of resulting trust, whereby a rebuttable presumption arises so that where one person, *A*, provides all or part of the money to purchase something in the name of another, *A* will be entitled to a share in the property proportional to the amount of the contribution (see the leading cases of *Gissing v Gissing* [1971] AC 886 and *Pettit v Pettit* [1970] AC 777).

Interpreting the Human Rights Convention

Two principles are applied by the European Court of Human Rights in interpreting the Convention: the doctrine of the margin of appreciation and the principle of proportionality.

The margin of appreciation

This doctrine means that when making a decision which involves a Convention right, a state has a measure of discretion, which is subject to the ultimate supervision of the Convention organs. The courts do not apply this in a rigid manner, hence the scope of the margin of appreciation will vary from case to case and from article to article. The basis of this doctrine is that states and national courts are in a better position than international judges to strike an appropriate balance in the furtherance of legitimate public purposes in their own jurisdiction.

The principle of proportionality

In essence, proportionality requires a reasonable relationship between the means employed and the aim sought to be realized (see *Ashingdane v United Kingdom* (A/93) (1985) 7 EHRR 528, para. 57). It was expressed in *Soering v United Kingdom* as: 'Inherent in the whole Convention is a search for a fair balance between the demands of the general interest of the community and the requirements of the protection of the individual's fundamental human rights' (see (A/161) (1989) 11 EHRR 439, para. 59).

The test of proportionality, the right to marry and immigration

An example of the application of the test of proportionality is the case of *Baiai v Secretary of State for the Home Department* [2007] 2 FLR 627 (Court of Appeal) and [2008] Fam Law 994 (House of Lords). Here the appeal courts had to consider whether a rule (s. 19(3)(b) Asylum and Immigration Act 2004) which requires persons subject to immigration control to obtain the Home Secretary's written permission to marry in the United Kingdom, unless they intended to enter into an Anglican marriage, was compliant with art. 12 of the Convention. The Court of Appeal held that the policy was a breach of the European Convention on Human Rights since it breached art. 12, (the right to marry) and was discriminatory under art. 14 since it discriminated against persons who wished to enter into a non-

Anglican marriage. It was further held that although art. 12 did not guarantee an absolute right to marry, it was recognized as an important and fundamental right which was not lightly to be interfered with. Significantly, it also held that although immigration control was a legitimate ground for interfering with art. 12, it did not mean that the state had the liberty to choose whatever means of controlling immigration it considered prudent or necessary, irrespective of the effect on art. 12. The scheme was considered to have failed the test of proportionality.

On appeal by The Secretary to the House of Lords, the appeal was dismissed.

The House of Lords held that the right to marry was a strong right. It had no second paragraphs permitting interferences or limitations necessary in a democratic society or for specified purposes. It was subject only to national laws governing its exercise. The Strasbourg case law adopted a restrictive approach to national laws. Such laws may lay down rules of procedure and substance based on generally recognized considerations of public interest, such as capacity, consent, prohibited degrees and bigamy. However, national laws governing the right to marry cannot injure or impair the substance of the right and cannot deprive a person of full legal capacity of that right nor substantially interfere with its exercise.

The Law Lords conceded that a national authority could properly impose reasonable conditions on the right of a third country national to marry in order to ascertain whether a proposed marriage was one purely of convenience and, if it was, to prevent it. Article 12 protected the right to enter into a genuine marriage, and did not grant a right to secure an advantage by going through a form of marriage for purely ulterior reasons. The scheme under s. 19 of the Asylum and Immigration Act 2004 (requiring written approval from the Secretary of State) could be justified only to the extent that it operated to prevent marriages of convenience which, because they were not genuine, did not attract the protection of art. 12. If s. 19 restricted the right to marry to a greater extent than that, it was disproportionate.

It agreed that s. 19 was discriminatory in distinguishing between Anglican and other marriages. Apart from that, s. 19, when read alone, was not legally objectionable. It was open to a member state, consistently with art. 12, to seek to prevent marriages of convenience. On the other hand, there was nothing in the text of s. 19 which authorized or required the withholding of permission to marry in the case of a marriage which was not a marriage of convenience. The text gave no indication of the grounds on which permission to marry could be refused. The current operation of s. 19(3)(b) (the section in question) was disproportionate. The section should be read as referring to a person who has the written permission of the Secretary of State to marry in the United Kingdom, such permission not to be withheld in the case of a qualified applicant seeking to enter into a marriage which is not one of convenience. The application for, and grant of, such permission should not be subject to conditions which unreasonably inhibit the exercise of the applicant's right under art. 12 of the European Convention.

Clearly, the statutory provision in this case was flawed and could not be upheld as it had not been confined in its operation to marriages of convenience; that is, marriages contracted with the sole aim of circumventing entry and residence rules, and could not therefore be interpreted as compatible with art. 12 of the European Convention. The judgments of the Law Lords emphasized the fundamental nature of the right to marry and the restricted scope allowed to national laws to curtail this right (see *Bailey-Harris* [2008] Fam Law 995 and *Douglas* [2007] Fam Law 806).

Principles justifying interference with Convention rights

Convention case law has determined that there are four underlying principles which justify an interference with a Convention right. The interference must: (i) be in accordance with the law; (ii) serve a legitimate aim; (iii) be necessary in a democratic society; and (iv) not be discriminatory (Swindells *et al.*, 1999, p. 7)

The family provisions of the European Convention on Human Rights

How does the European Convention on Human Rights perceive the family? Articles 8 and 6 are of primary importance in the field of family law with art. 8 dealing directly with family law. Articles 12 and 14 are also relevant and we return briefly to art. 12.

Article 12 –the right to marry

Article 12 deals with the right to marry and found a family but case law has declared that this does not include the right to dissolve a marriage; that is, there is no right to divorce under this article (*Johnston v Ireland* (A/112) (1986) 9 EHRR 203). In addition, it does not include same-sex couples but it might be argued that it may be available to allow same-sex couples to adopt. This provision appears to suggest that a conjunctive interpretation should be placed on it; that is, there is a right to marry and found a family as part of the consequence of marrying, rather than a right to marry and a separate right to found a family.

Article 6 – the right to a fair trial

Article 6 provides for everyone to have the right to a fair trial within a reasonable time by a fair and impartial tribunal in the determination of 'civil rights or obligations' in connection with any criminal charge brought against an individual. Case law such as *Airey v Ireland* (A/32) (1979) 2 EHRR 305 suggests that this right must be 'real and effective, not theoretical and illusory'.

This article applies to private law family cases (*Airey v Ireland* (A/32) (1979) 2 EHRR 305), as well as to public law decisions such as placing children in care (*Olsson v Sweden (No. 1)* (1988) 11 EHRR 259). Decision making has to be transparent, parents must be involved and there has to be disclosure to parents of all relevant documents. This was made clear in cases such as *Re G* [2003] 2 FLR 42 and *Re M* [2001] 2 FLR 1300, where Holman J declared that the case had brought home to him the 'heavy responsibility and wide discretion the Human Rights Act has placed upon courts to consider, after the event, the lawfulness of a decision-making process' and opined that it was possible to make a freestanding application under s. 6 and s. 7 of the Human Rights Act 1998, and the court had the power to grant relief if it was appropriate under art. 8.

Article 6 is also relevant to cases involving parental contact with children, fostering and adoption, where state action is directly determinative of the rights; child abduction; domestic violence cases, secure accommodation applications and ancillary relief applications (see cases cited by Swindell *et al.*, 1999, p. 24)

It was made clear in *Re L (Care: Assessment: Fair Trial)* [2002] 2 FLR 730 that art. 6 extends to all stages of the proceedings; that is, judicial and administrative. The parent's right to a fair trial is absolute and, unlike art. 8, cannot be qualified by reference to or balanced against any rights under art. 8.

The main focus of our discussion, however, is on art. 8, which we now examine in detail.

Article 8 – a key family law provision

Article 8(1) states:

> 'Everyone has the right to respect for his private and family life, his home and his correspondence.'

This article talks about the right to 'respect' for private and family life, home and correspondence, so that any interference with this right would, if proven, constitute a violation of art. 8. It implies a positive and negative obligation and applies to the family unit and its individual members, including parents and children. The key objective of this article appears to be to protect the individual against arbitrary interference by public authorities but there is no definition of 'family life' in the Convention.

Article 8(2) states:

> 'There shall be no interference by a public authority with the exercise of this right except such as is in accordance with the law and is necessary in a democratic society in the interests of national security, public safety or the economic well-being of the country, for the prevention of disorder or crime, for the protection of health or morals, or for the protection of the rights and freedoms of others.'

This article sets out the conditions under which the state may interfere with the enjoyment of the right such that the onus is on the state to demonstrate that interference was justified. The interference has to be: (a) in accordance with the law;

(b) necessary in a democratic society; (i) in the interests of national security, public safety or the economic well-being of the country; (ii) for the prevention of disorder or crime; (iii) for the protection of health or morals; and (iv) for the protection of rights or freedom of others.

As Swindells *et al.* note, the Convention cases heard by the European Court have adopted the practice of considering each of the following stages in turn: the scope of the right, the nature of the interference which is alleged to restrict the enjoyment of the right, the lawfulness of the interference, the legitimate aims of the interference and the necessity for the interference in a democratic society, namely 'whether there are relevant and sufficient reasons for the interference, which are proportionate to the restrictions on the enjoyment of the right when taking into account the margin of appreciation' (Swindells *et al.*, 1999, p. 38).

The Human Rights Act, family life and the concept of the family

As de Mello *et al.* explain, in order to mount an argument that there has been a breach of the right to respect for family life, the first stage will be to establish the existence of family life. Once this has been established, then the second stage can be explored; namely to see whether there has been interference with the right to family life (de Mello *et al.*, 2000, p. 233). The reason for this is because the Convention does not seek to guarantee the right to acquire family life, only the maintenance of it once it is in existence, as indicated in *Application No. 12513 v United Kingdom* (1989) 11 EHRR 46. Hence the reality of a subsisting relationship is the pivotal point, not the mere fact of blood relations. The European Court's ongoing interpretation of art. 8 and 'family life' can be gleaned from its case law, which we now examine.

No definition of family life in the European Convention

There is no definition of family life in the Convention. The concept has been described by the European Court as 'autonomous and freestanding' and it has been interpreted widely. For example, the right to family life of both de jure and de facto families is protected (see *Keegan v Ireland* (A/290) (1994) 18 EHRR 342 and *Marckx v Belgium* (A/31) (1979) 2 EHRR 330, para. 11). The European Court's interpretation will depend on the individual facts of each case and its particular circumstances. For instance, the European Court will look at de facto family ties such as applicants living together, in the absence of any legal recognition of family life (*Johnston v Ireland* (A/112) (1986) 9 EHRR 203, para. 19). The European Court has accepted that the range of relationships recognized as familial is increasing and that 'family life' is not confined to relationships based on marriage (*Keegan v Ireland* (A/290) (1994) 18 EHRR 342). Indeed, the European Court of Human Rights has said that the Convention is a 'living instrument' which requires interpretation in the light of social changes (*Selmouni v France* (2000) 29 EHRR 403), hence the courts must adapt to changing social conditions when interpreting family law. This was reiterated by Mr Justice Munby, writing extra-judicially on the interpretation of art. 8 on the family and family life, when he said that there were very profound changes in family life in recent decades which have been driven by four major developments: (i) enormous changes in social and religious life; (ii) the lack of interest in or even a conscious rejection of marriage as an institution – statistics demonstrate 'a striking decline in marriage'; (iii) a sea-change in society's attitude towards same-sex unions; and (iv) enormous advances in medical and in particular, reproductive, science so that reproduction is no longer confined to 'natural' methods and many children are born a result of 'high tech' IVF methods, 'almost inconceivable a few years ago' (Munby, 2005, p. 503).

Question of fact whether 'family life' exists

As with domestic courts, it will be a question of fact whether family life exists, depending on the real existence of personal ties as indicated in *K v United Kingdom* (No. 11468/85, Commission decision of 15 October 1986, Decisions and Reports (DR), p. 199 at 207).

Family life can exist between non-biological parents and children

In *Marckx v Belgium* (A/31) (1979) 2 EHRR 330, para. 61 the European Court ruled that signatory states had a positive obligation to amend their civil codes so that they would be in line with the protection of family life in art. 8 and the non-discriminatory rule in art. 14. Indeed, the European Court interpreted these two articles as giving any child born outside marriage the right to have filiation established with its mother and to enjoy from birth a normal family life.

Similarly, in *X, Y and Z v United Kingdom* [1997] 3 FCR 341 it was again held that family life can be found to exist between non-biological parents and children. It also held that the length of the relationship would also be taken into account and, for couples, whether they have demonstrated their commitment to each other by having a baby together.

As explained in *Kroon v The Netherlands* (A/297-C) (1994) 19 EHRR 263, para. 32, once a family tie is shown to exist with a child, the state must act to develop that tie and legal safeguards must be established to integrate that child into his or her family at the moment of birth or as soon as practicable after the birth.

Mere biological relationship insufficient to attract art. 8 protection

In *Lebbink v The Netherlands (Application No. 45582/99)* [2004] 2 FLR 463 the European Court held that mere biological kinship without other legal or factual elements which indicate the existence of a close personal relationship would not be sufficient to attract the protection of art. 8.

Family life is not restricted to relationships based on marriage or blood, or legally recognised relationships

Abdulaziz, Cabales and Balkandali (A/94) (1985) 7 EHRR 471, is a landmark case where the European Court rejected the United Kingdom government's submission that art. 8 of the European Convention did not apply to an immigration case. It declared that there is no obligation on the state to admit alien spouses of the applicant to join them. However, it held that measures taken in the field of immigration may affect the right to respect for family life under art. 8 in circumstances where the exclusion of a person from a state might prevent him from joining his lawfully resident spouse.

Cohabitation is not a sine qua non of family life between parents and children

The European Court has found the existence of 'family life' even where the couple do not live together, as was held in cases such as *Kroon v The Netherlands* (A/297-C) (1995) 19 EHRR 263. Here, the applicant and her partner of several years had a child together. She had been married earlier but that relationship had broken down very quickly and she had no contact with her husband for seven years. Under Dutch law, the husband was presumed to be the father of the child. All attempts to alter that failed, as the presumption of paternity could only be rebutted by the husband if he denied paternity. The father of the child did not wish to cohabit with the mother or wish to marry her. The mother complained that she was unable to get the father's paternity recognized and that the law was discriminatory, since only the husband could deny paternity in breach of Arts 8 and 14.

The European Court held that there was a violation of art. 8, declaring that 'family life' is not confined to marriage-based relationships and may encompass other de facto 'family ties' where parties are living together outside marriage.

Similarly, in *Singh v Entry Clearance Officer, New Delhi* [2005] 1 FLR 308, the European Court held that the potential for the development of family life was not confined to relationships based on marriage or blood or to formal relationships recognized in law. That potential was relevant in determining whether family life already existed.

Factors which might establish the existence of 'family life'

In the case of a natural father and his child born outside marriage, the European Court has declared that in ascertaining the existence of family life, relevant factors may include cohabitation, the nature of the relationship between the parents and his interest in the child (*Keegan v Ireland* (A/290) (1994) 18 EHRR 342, paras 17–18).

However, in *Berrehab v The Netherlands* (A/138) (1988) 11 EHRR 322, the European Court held that in general, cohabitation is not a sine qua non of family life between parents and children and that 'family life' is not extinguished just because the parents and children no longer lived together.

Family life can include relationships between near relatives

Marckx v Belgium (A/31) (1979) 2 EHRR 330 also indicated that family life can include relationships between near relatives such as between grandparents and grandchildren, and respect for this means that those ties must be allowed to develop normally. This was confirmed in *Price v United Kingdom* (1998) No. 12402/86, Decisions and Reports (DR) 55, p. 224 at 234), where such relationships were seen as within the scope of family life especially if they played a considerable part in that family's life. In *Boyle v United Kingdom* (1995) 19 EHRR 179 it was held that it could include a relationship between nephew and uncle. *Gaskin v United Kingdom* (1990) 12 EHRR 36 also suggested that it can include a relationship between foster-parent and foster-child.

The bond between natural parents and children is a strong indicator of family life

A child born of a marital union is ipso jure part of that relationship. Hence, from the moment of the child's birth, and by the very fact of it, there exists between the child and its parents a bond amounting to family life which subsequent events cannot break, apart from exceptional circumstances. This was the finding in *Ahmut v The Netherlands* (1997) 24 EHRR 62, where there was a refusal by the Netherlands authorities to grant a residence permit to a Moroccan minor which would have allowed him to live with his father. The European Court had to consider whether the bond between the applicants amounted to 'family life'. The European Court held that the bond between the applicants was established. Indeed, it emphasized that the bond between natural parents and children is a strong indicator of the existence of family life and that a bond which signifies family life cannot be broken by subsequent events, except in exceptional circumstances.

Removal of child from parent by the state must not destroy the natural bond between parent and child

In the case of *K and T v Finland* [2001] 2 FLR 707, the European Court held that the removal of a child from the parents must not be done in such a way as to destroy the natural bond. The state had to consider the long-term prospects, declared that there should not be a presumption in favour of permanent separation and that it was particularly important for very young children to maintain the family tie.

Hence, in *Johansen v Norway* (1996) 23 EHRR 33, the European Court made it clear that family life does not end when a child is taken into care or if the child's parents divorce (see *Berrehab v The Netherlands* (A/138) (1988) 11 EHRR 322).

Power of court to restrain publicity in children cases recast as art. 8 rights

The power of a court to restrain publicity in cases relating to children has been recast as part of the rights under art. 8 (see *Re S* [2005] 1 AC 593). With the enactment of the Human Rights Act 1998, there is now no necessity to consider any earlier case law which explored the court's inherent jurisdiction to restrain publicity. The court's power to restrain publicity to protect a child's private and family life now derives from rights under the European Convention on Human Rights, which provides a more direct approach. Of course, the earlier cases may provide an indication of how to strike a balance between privacy and freedom of expression (Department of Constitutional Affairs, *Review of the Implementation of the Human Rights Act* at http://www.justice.gov.uk/docs/full_review.pdf).

Transsexuals, the right to marry and the definition of a 'marriage' in law

English law has traditionally adhered to a sexual definition of a 'man' and 'woman' as far as defining a legal marriage is concerned, perhaps most famously (or infamously) in the case of *Corbett v Corbett* [1971] P 83, otherwise known as the April Ashley case, decided in 1970. The respondent April Ashley, a post-operative male-to-female transsexual, was born a male, but underwent female sex assignment surgery before her marriage to Corbett. When the marriage failed, the petitioner, Corbett, sought a decree that the marriage was void in view of the fact that both parties were persons of the male sex, which contravened s. 11(1)(b) of the Matrimonial Causes Act 1973. Ormrod J ruled that sex for that purpose is to be determined by the application of chromosomal, gonadal and genital tests where these are congruent and without regard to any surgical intervention. Another ground for declaring the marriage void was because a transsexual was incapable of consummating the marriage in the context of ordinary and complete sexual intercourse.

Corbett has been criticized by the medical profession and academics from other disciplines but remained the law in Britain until 2004, despite its reasoning and conclusions not being followed in courts in other jurisdictions, as well as being subjected to criticism by the European Court of Human Rights. But until 2002, judicial criticisms did not affect the United Kingdom's position on the immutability of gender ('once a man, always a man'), in the sense that it constituted a breach of the right to marry and found a family under art. 12 of the European Convention on Human Rights.

However, in 2002, two cases (*Goodwin* [2002] 2 FLR 487 and *I v United Kingdom* [2002] 2 FLR 518) were decided by the European Court of Human Rights that finally persuaded the British government to institute legislation to address their position on gender, which culminated in the Gender Recognition Act 2004.

Gender issues, discrimination and human rights

We now examine some seminal cases from the United Kingdom relating to gender issues, discrimination and human rights – *Ghaidan, Goodwin, I v United Kingdom and Bellinger*.

Ghaidan v Godin-Mendoza

In *Ghaidan v Godin-Mendoza* [2004] 2 FLR 600, the defendant had lived in a long-standing homosexual relationship with the deceased who was a protected tenant of a flat owned by the claimant. After the tenant's death, the claimant appealed to the county court claiming possession of the flat. The judge held that the defendant did not succeed to the tenancy because para. 2 of the Rent Act 1977 (as amended) applied only to heterosexual couples. The tenant appealed to the Court of Appeal on the ground that the difference in treatment as to succession rights granted to the survivor of heterosexual relationships and the survivor of homosexual relationships by para. 2 of the Rent Act infringed art. 14, read in conjunction with art. 8 of the European Convention. Furthermore, the court had a duty under s. 3 of the Human Rights Act 1998 to give effect to legislation in a way that was compliant with European Convention rights. The appeal was allowed and the claimant appealed to the House of Lords.

It is worth noting that under Sch. 1, para. 2(2) of the Rent Act, a person who was living with the original tenant 'as his or her wife or husband' is treated as the spouse of the original tenant. In the earlier case of *Fitzpatrick v Sterling* [2000] 1 FLR 271 (discussed in Part II, Chapter One on English law), the House of Lords decided that this provision did not apply to persons living in a same-sex relationship. The question in *Ghaidan v Godin-Mendoza* was whether this reading of para. 2 can survive the coming into force of the Human Rights Act. In *Fitzpatrick*'s case, the original tenant had died in 1994.

In *Ghaidan v Godin-Mendoza*, the House of Lords dismissed the appeal by the claimant (Lord Millett dissenting). It held that, since art. 14 guaranteed that the rights set out in the European Convention should be secured without discrimination, and art. 8 guaranteed the right to respect for a person's home, it was common ground that art. 14 was engaged in the present case. Here, a majority of their Lordships held that the grounds for according different treatment to the survivors of heterosexual and homosexual relationships could not withstand scrutiny. Consequently, it followed that the relevant paragraph of the Rent Act, when construed without reference to s. 3 of the Human Rights Act, violated the tenant's European Convention rights under art. 14, taken together with art. 8.

In addition, s. 3 of the Human Rights Act required that 'so far as it is possible to do so, primary legislation and subordinate legislation must be read and given effect in a way which is compatible with the Convention'. It remained to be seen whether it was possible under s. 3(1) to read para. 2 of the Rent Act in a way which was compatible with the European Convention. The policy object of the Housing Act

1988 in extending security of tenure to the survivors of couples living together but not married could offer no justification for excluding homosexual partners. On that basis, it was possible under s. 3 to read para. 2 of the Rent Act in a way which was compatible with the European Convention, as though the survivor of a homosexual relationship was the surviving spouse of the original tenant.

Goodwin v United Kingdom

In *Goodwin v United Kingdom* [2002] 2 FLR 487, the applicant had undergone reassignment surgery and lived in society as a woman, but remained for legal purposes as a male. She was unable to obtain a birth certificate that showed her status as a female. This impacted on her life in the area of employment, social security, pensions and marriage and she had suffered numerous discriminatory and humiliating experiences. The applicant claimed in the European Court that the refusal to give legal recognition to her gender reassignment violated her right to respect for her private life under art. 8 of the European Convention on Human Rights, her right to marry under art. 12 and the cause of several discriminatory experiences and prejudices under art. 14.

The British government submitted that a fair balance had been struck between the rights of the individual and the general interest of the community, that, to the extent that there were situations where a transsexual might face limited disclosure of their change of sex, these situations were unavoidable and necessary. Evidence established an emerging consensus within contracting states in the Council of Europe on providing legal recognition following gender reassignment and a continuing international trend towards such legal recognition.

The European Court held that there had been violations of Arts 8 and 12 and no separate issue had arisen under art. 14. The United Kingdom government, having failed to respond to earlier warnings by the European Court that the relevant legal measures should be kept under review, had failed to respect the applicant's right to private life in breach of art. 8. There had also been a breach of art. 12 because it was 'artificial' to claim that post-operative transsexuals had not been deprived of the right to marry because they were able to marry a person of their former opposite sex. The applicant lived as a woman and would only wish to marry a man but had no way of doing so. The applicant was entitled to claim that the very essence of her right to marry had been infringed. There was no justification for barring the transsexual from enjoying the right to marry under any circumstances.

I v United Kingdom

I v United Kingdom [2002] 2 FLR 518 was decided by the European Court together with *Goodwin*, since it also involved a post-operative transsexual who lived in society as a woman but remained for legal purposes as a male. She was unable to obtain a birth certificate that showed her status as female and had been required on a number of occasions to show her original birth certificate. The applicant also claimed that there had been a breach of Arts 8, 12 and 14 on the same basis as in *Goodwin* and the British government responded in the same way as in that case.

The European Court held that there had been violations of Arts 8 and 12, and delivered the same reasons as stated in *Goodwin* (see above).

Bellinger v Bellinger

Subsequently, the issue was again reviewed in domestic law, by the House of Lords, in *Bellinger v Bellinger* [2002] 1 FLR 1043 where the appellant was a male-to-female transsexual who had undergone treatment culminating in 1981 in gender reassignment surgery. She and a man went through a ceremony of marriage in May 1981. In 2001, she sought a declaration that the marriage was valid from its inception. That application was refused by the trial judge and by a majority of the Court of Appeal, in accordance with the decision in *Corbett v Corbett* [1971] P 83. The applicant sought, in the alternative, a declaration that s. 11(c) of the Matrimonial Causes Act 1973 was incompatible with Arts 8 and 12 of the European Convention.

The House of Lords held that the recognition of gender reassignment for the purposes of marriage was part of a wider problem which should be considered as a whole and was altogether ill-suited for determination by courts and court procedures. These matters were pre-eminently a matter for Parliament, more especially when the government had already announced its intention to introduce primary legislation on that difficult and sensitive subject. Indeed, as Lord Nicholls pointed out (at 1052):

> 'Recognition of Mrs Bellinger as a female for the purposes of s. 11(c) of the Matrimonial Causes Act 1973 (the 1973 Act) would necessitate giving the expressions "male" and "female" in the Act a novel, extended meaning: that a person may be born with one sex but later become, or become regarded as, a person of the opposite sex. This would involve a major change in the law, having far-reaching ramifications. It raises issues whose solutions call for extensive inquiry and the widest possible public consultations and discussion.'

Accordingly, the court would not make a declaration that the marriage celebrated by the appellant in 1981 was valid, and the appeal on that point was dismissed.

However, the Law Lords were prepared to rule that s. 11(c) of the 1973 Act, which did not recognize gender reassignment for the purposes of marriage, was clearly incompatible with Arts 8 and 12. The European Court of Human Rights so found in July 2002 in *Goodwin* and the government had so accepted. It was desirable in a case of such complexity that the House of Lords as the court of final appeal should formally record that the present state of statute law was incompatible with the European Convention. The declaration of incompatibility would be made as sought.

Some critical observations on Ghaidan, Goodwin and Bellinger

Diduck argues that cases like *Ghaidan*, *Goodwin* and *Bellinger* illustrate the law's ambivalence in this area and represent 'an incorporation ... of the politics of family practices into a law in which old family certainties and meanings are sustained' (Diduck, 2003, p. 204). It is certainly true that there is an enduring tendency of the English Law Lords to be reluctant to move away from well-established norms and to recognize, interpret and apply the culture of human rights within the framework of the Human Rights Act, and therefore the European Convention, to families and family policies. Diduck makes the point that although *Mendoza*, *Goodwin*, *I* and *Bellinger* may result in 'justice' for an increased population, 'they have not resulted in a new vocabulary or new categories for intimate lives as much as they have simply expanded the meaning of family' (citing Smart and Silva, 1999, p. 10 and Diduck, 2001). Indeed, she declares that these cases are an example of change 'being both embraced and spurned by law, of continuity both maintained and disrupted' (Diduck, 2003, p. 200). In her view, *Bellinger* [2002] 1 FLR 1043, for example, illustrates the 'intransigence of law, of the normative family, and of normative familial identities'. Thus, despite having acknowledged that English marriage law was incompatible with human rights principles, the Law Lords were still not prepared to grant the requested declaration that the 1981 marriage between Mr and Mrs Bellinger was valid. It rejected the idea that sex/gender was a matter of individual choice and experience; these cases illustrate 'law's reluctance to embrace fully the potential to re-imagine what family or marriage means' (Diduck, 2003, pp. 203–4).

The present writer agrees that English judges appear to have a problem with incorporating the culture of rights into a long-established ideology and religious-based philosophy. (In *Bellinger*, Lord Nicholls even cited the Church of England Book of Common Prayer of 1662, which states that the first cause for which marriage was ordained was the procreation of children.) A tradition that has lasted for several centuries is not easily discarded or abandoned. Advances in medical technology have made it possible for persons 'trapped in the wrong body' as transsexuals have said they are, to escape this entrapment and live as they would want to, in the gender that they wish. In modern times, cases like *Bellinger* need the concept of marriage to be broadened, but to expect highly conservative judges from a generation that never countenanced (or approved) same-sex marriage to be willing to adopt a more radical definition of a legally valid marriage is surely expecting too much, too soon. In any event, the law generally speaks for the majority of the population, and for the majority it is still important to adhere to traditional norms of familial relationships. The problem arises if the law unwittingly assists the exploitation of transsexuals who cannot then be legally raped because of the non-recognition of their change of sex. This travesty of justice would have been allowed to continue and the Gender Recognition Act 2004 now addresses this, since the practical effect of a gender recognition certificate is to provide a transsexual person with legal recognition in the acquired gender.

The Gender Recognition Act 2004

The Gender Recognition Act 2004 (UK) provides under s. 1, that a person of at least 18 years of age can apply to a Gender Recognition Panel for a gender recognition certificate on the basis of living in the acquired gender or having changed gender according to the law of another country. The effect of s. 9 is that the certificate signifies that the person's gender becomes, for all purposes, the acquired gender. That person can then acquire a new birth certificate which reflects the acquired gender and is able to enter into a valid marriage or valid civil partnership in his or her new gender.

Same-sex marriage not recognised in the United Kingdom despite Arts 8, 12 and 14

Another instance of the European Convention rights being invoked arose in the case of a same-sex couple wishing their overseas marriage to be recognized as a marriage under English law. In *Wilkinson v Kitzinger (No. 2)* [2007] 1 FLR 295, W, the petitioner, and K (the respondent) were a lesbian couple who lived in England but had married in Canada. They wished to have their Canadian marriage legally recognized as a valid marriage in the United Kingdom. They applied to the Family Division for a declaration as to marital status under s. 55 of the Family Law Act 1986. They submitted that ss 212–18 of the Civil Partnership Act 2004 (which treats overseas marriage as a civil partnership) and s. 11(c) of the Matrimonial Causes Act 1973 (requiring parties to a marriage to be male and female) violated Arts 8, 12 and 14. Alternatively, they argued that the common law definition of marriage should be developed to include same-sex marriage; and they sought a declaration that the relevant statutory provisions were incompatible with Arts 8, 12 and 14 of the European Convention on Human Rights.

Sir Mark Potter, President of the Family Division, dismissed the application. He made several points. First, he rejected the argument that *Goodwin* meant that art. 12 should now be interpreted as a 'living instrument' stressing that there were clear limitations on the 'living instrument' doctrine and it could not be applied to bring within the scope of the Convention issues plainly outside its contemplation.

Second, this was not an area where there was European-wide consensus on the subject. Only the Netherlands, Belgium and Spain have passed laws providing for same-sex marriage. Having noted the authorities which bar English courts from interpreting Convention rights more generously than the Strasbourg court, he found no violation of art. 12, which he declared should be interpreted in the traditional sense of applying to a marriage between a man and a woman.

Third, on the possible violation of art. 8, he ruled that the European Court does not regard same-sex relationships as 'family life' and the right to family life did not extend to childless same-sex couples. The difference in treatment of same-sex couples was reasonable, legitimate and proportionate and falls within the margin of appreciation accorded to Convention states.

Fourth, he cited the enactment of the Civil Partnership Act as the United Kingdom's move to recognize the rights of individuals to make a same-sex commitment to one another. This was a policy choice creating a legal status for same-sex couples but which also demonstrated support for traditional marriage.

In rejecting the reasoning of Canadian cases which found that denial of same-sex marriage violated the general anti-discrimination provision of the Canadian Charter of Rights and Freedoms, the learned judge declined because those cases were decided in a context in which same-sex partners had no means of accessing the rights and duties of civil marriage, as they now can under English law via a civil partnership.

Further case law illustrating interpretation of the Human Rights Convention

Article 8, family life and immigration cases

Scope of art. 8 extended in immigration cases

In *Slivenko v Latvia* [GC] No. 48321/99, ECHR 2003-X, the European Court extended autonomous human rights protection under art. 8 to the applicants' 'network of personal, social and economic relations'. The applicants were a former Soviet army officer and his family who had lived in Latvia most of their lives and who contested their deportation from Latvia after their claims for residence rights under the 1994 Russo-Latvian Treaty on troop withdrawal were rejected. The European Court accepted that the applicants' removal did constitute an interference with their rights under art. 8, since they had been removed from the country where they had developed, 'uninterruptedly since birth, the network of personal, social and economic relations that make up the private life of every human being' (para. 96).

Thym observes that the case law of the European Court of Human Rights in respect for private and family life 'demonstrates its new readiness to extend the protective reach of art. 8 in the field of immigration' (Thym, 2008, p. 111). Thus, the European Court no longer confines the application of that article to situations of cross-border migration in expulsion and family reunion cases but has extended it to the legal conditions for leave to remain. This is illustrated in cases like *Sisojeva v Latvia*, 2007, 15 January (s. III.B) and *Rodrigues Da Silva and Hoogkamer v The Netherlands*, 2006, 31 January (s. III.C), where the European Court concluded that the contracting parties had violated their obligations under art. 8 by refusing to regularize the applicants' illegal stay.

Thym believes that 'this extension of the Convention to the legal status of immigrants under the heading of private life independent of the existence and preservation of family bonds raises important questions about the general interaction of the Convention with national and European immigration laws' (Thym, 2008, pp. 111–2). Thym argues that this means that in future, the court will have to 'strike a careful balance between the requirements of effective human rights protection and the preservation of the contracting parties' margin of appreciation and the corresponding respect for the normative structure of national immigration law' (Thym, 2008, p. 112). Thus, certain immigrant families have been given long-term resident status via the extension of the ambit of art. 8 of the European Convention of Human Rights. This has tended to be for second-generation immigrants, who had often been born in the Western European reception states or joined their migrant parents at a young age, which some academic observers believe to be part of the Strasbourg Court's 'hidden agenda' (see Cholewinski, 1994, pp. 287ff). An illustrative case with regard to the concept of family interference is *Slivenko v Latvia* [GC] No. 48321/99, ECHR 2003-X, which has been discussed at p. 338 in another context.

Separation of core family from non-dependent parents does not constitute interference with 'family life' under art. 8 in immigration cases

In immigration cases, the courts will not be willing to find family life exists between parents and adult children unless they can demonstrate additional elements of dependence (*Slivenko v Latvia* [GC] No. 48321/99, ECHR 2003-X). In the *Slivenko* case, the core family in the eyes of the European Court was the spouses and minor children, but not the elderly parents of the applicants, described by the court as 'adults who did not belong to the core family' and who were not shown as being dependent members of the applicants' family. Thus, in the context of immigration in Europe, the European Court appears to have 're-conceptualised the notion of family life' (Thym, 2008, p. 87) in certain situations, and case law within the last few years has 'widened the reach of human rights to the legal conditions for leave to remain, effectively granting applicants a human right to regularise their illegal stay' (Thym, 2008, p. 96).

Article 8, care proceedings, parental rights and local authority decisions

Article 8 guarantees substantive rights to parents involved in care proceedings but also grants procedural guarantees. *Re L (Care Assessment: Fair Trial)* [2002] 2 FLR 730 confirmed that art. 8 imposes positive obligations of disclosure on the local authority and guarantees fairness in the decision-making process at all stages of the proceedings. Case law has also established that while art. 8 contains no explicit procedural requirements, the decision-making process leading to measures of interference must be fair and such as to afford due respect to the interests safe-guarded by art. 8 (per Munby J in *Re G (Care: Challenge to Local Authority's Decision)* [2003] 2 FLR 42).

Article 8, custody, contact and residence disputes

The European Court of Human Rights has enunciated several principles in the subject of children being separated from one of their parents in the context of contact and residence disputes. The Strasbourg jurisprudence contains four main principles. The first is the principle enunciated in *Kosmopolou v Greece* [2004] 1 FCR 427 at [47]: '[T]he mutual enjoyment by parent and child of each other's company constitutes a fundamental element of family life, even if the relationship between the parents has broken down, and domestic measures hindering such enjoyment amount to an interference with the right protected by Article 8 of the Convention.'

The second principle deals with the possible detrimental effects of the passage of time and has been stated in several cases but particularly in *Hoppe v Germany* [2003] 1 FLR 384 at [54] that: '[I]n cases concerning a person's relationship with his or her child, there is a duty to exercise exceptional diligence in view of the risk that the passage of time may result in a de facto determination of the matter.' Indeed, as the court in *Glaser v United Kingdom* [2001] 1 FLR 153 at [93] said: 'It is ... essential that custody and contact cases can be dealt with speedily.' This was reiterated in *Sylvester v Austria* [2003] 2 FLR 210 at [69]: '[T]he court reiterates that effective respect for family life requires that future relations between parent and child not be determined by the mere effluxion of time.'

The third principle is that in private law cases, as well as in public law cases, art. 8 includes what was described in *Hokkanen v Finland* (1994) 19 EHRR 139, para. 55 as 'a right for the parent to have measures taken with a view to his or her being reunited with the child and an obligation for the national authorities to take such action'. There have been repeated declarations by the European Court that national authorities have an obligation to take measures to facilitate contact by a non-custodial parent with their child and this means they must do their utmost to facilitate cooperation between the parents (see *Glaser, Kosmopolou* and *Hokkanen* as well as *Ignaccolo-Zenide v Romania* (2000) 31 EHRR 212 and *Nuutinen v Finland* (2000) 34 EHRR 358).

The fourth principle is the general one stated in *Hornsby v Greece* (1997) 24 EHRR 250 at para. 40 and *Saffi v Italy* (1999) 30 EHRR 756 at paras 63, 66, which is that the right of the court would be illusory if a contracting state's domestic legal system allowed a final, binding judicial decision to remain inoperative to the detri-ment of one party. The European Court thought it 'inconceivable' that art. 6(1) should describe in detail procedural guarantees afforded to litigants for proceed-ings that are fair, public and expeditious, without protecting the implementation of judicial decisions. Execution of a judgment must be regarded as an integral part of the trial for the purposes of art. 6 and it cannot be unduly delayed.

As Munby J explained in *F v M* [2004] EWHC 727, other cases have clarified that these positive obligations 'extend in principle to the taking of coercive measures not merely against the recalcitrant parent but even against the children', for example where the parent living with the child acts unlawfully (see *Ignaccolo-Zenide v Romania* (2000) 31 EHRR 212, para. 106). In *Hansen v Turkey* [2004] 1 FLR 142 at [106] the European Court declared: 'Although measures against children obliging them to re-unite with one or other parent are not desirable in this sensitive area, such action must not be ruled out in the event of non-compliance or unlawful behaviour by the parent with whom the children live.' However, the *Ignoccolo* case at para. 94 also recognized that 'any obligation to apply coercion can only be limited since the interests, rights and freedoms of all concerned must be taken into account, and more particularly the best interests of the child and [his or her] rights under Article 8 of the Convention'. This principle has been consistently recognized in Strasbourg jurisprudence.

In *Sylvester v Austria* (2003) 37 EHRR 417 at paras 59–60, the test set out by the European Court was:

> '[W]hat is decisive is whether the national authorities have taken all the necessary steps to facilitate execution as can reasonably be demanded in the special circumstances of each case. In examining whether non-enforcement of a court order amounted to a lack of respect for the applicant's family life the court must strike a fair balance between the interests of all persons concerned and the general interest in ensuring respect for the rule of law.'

It then emphasized that the swiftness of the implementation determined whether the measures taken had been adequate and the national authorities cannot shelter behind an applicant's lack of action (see *Ignoccolo* (2000) 31 EHRR 212, para. 111). Indeed, Munby J emphasizes in *F v M* [2004] EWHC 727, para. 34 that, as defined by the court in *Sylvester v Austria*, the obligation on the court to enforce its own court orders is more onerous than had previously been suggested in *Glaser v United Kingdom* [2001] 1 FLR 153.

Munby J makes the telling point that English courts can no longer complacently assume that 'our conventional domestic approach to such cases meets the standard required by Article 6 and 8' (*F v M* [2004] EWHC 727, para. 35).

Prohibition of discrimination in relation to the substantive rights in the Convention

Article 14 of the Convention states that the enjoyment of the rights and freedoms set forth in the Convention shall be secured without discrimination on any ground such as sex, race, colour, language, religion, political or other opinion, national or social origin, association with a national minority, property, birth or other status. This is a non-exhaustive list and it is a unique provision since it has no independent existence, complements other provisions and has effect only in relation to 'the enjoyment and freedoms' safeguarded by those freedoms (Swindells *et al.*, 1999, p. 61). According to cases like *Rasmussen v Denmark* (A/87) (1985) 7 EHRR 377, para. 21), it only applies if the facts fall within the ambit of one or more of the substantive articles.

Children, 'best Interests' and the Human Rights Act 1998

The Human Rights Act and the best interests/welfare principle

It is widely known amongst family lawyers that the 'best interests' test so central to decision making in relation to children is in practice an indeterminate standard, and, as Kennedy points out, it encourages a less than rigorous approach to decision making. In his opinion:

> 'It allows lawyers and courts to persuade themselves and others that there is a principled approach to law. Meanwhile, they engage in what to others is a form of "*ad hocery*". The best interests approach of family law allows the courts to atomise the law, to claim that each case depends on its own facts. The court can then respond intuitively to each case while seeking to legitimize its own conclusion by asserting that it is derived from the general principle contained in the best interests formula.'

> (Kennedy, 1992, p. 395)

Fortin expressed the hope in 1999, pre-implementation of the Human Rights Act 1998, that the incorporation of the Act into the United Kingdom domestic courts would inject a 'far greater rigour' into judicial decision making than hitherto (Fortin, 1999, p. 237). She also suggested that the best way forward would be to apply the welfare principle as a qualification to the individual rights set out in art. 8 of the European Convention (Fortin, 1999, p. 250). Eekelaar responded to this suggestion by identifying two limitations of such an approach: first, this might place the interests of the child too low; second, the welfare principle may operate in the same way as the orthodox approach, and only lip service may be paid to other relevant interests with the interests of others being protected 'under the guise of the child's welfare' (Eekelaar, 2002, p. 242). Eekelaar has also argued that there is an 'uneasy tension between retaining the orthodox English position' regarding the welfare or best interests principle and a modified application that takes into account the structure of the European Convention rights (Eekelaar, 2002, p. 237).

Herring has argued that as far as reconciling the application of the welfare principle with the principles of the European Convention on Human Rights under the Human Rights Act is concerned, neither an approach based purely on rights nor on welfare would be satisfactory, as the courts applying the Convention have found (Herring, 1999, p. 235). Instead, he proposes a 'relationship-based' approach which 'reconceptualises' the welfare approach, so that the courts would be required to ascertain what would be the best set of relationships for parent and child, based on mutual cooperation and a respect for each other's rights (Herring, 1999, p. 235).

In an article published in 2006, Fortin argues that the English family courts are not meeting the demands of the Human Rights Act. She submits that a reinterpretation of the paramountcy principle or best interests principle under the Children Act 1989 should be accompanied by a radically different judicial approach to evidence relating to children's best interests (Fortin, 2006, p. 299). As Bainham has pointed out, in many areas of law involving children, little attempt has been made to articulate children's rights as rights (Bainham, 2002). Part of the problem lies in the wording of art. 8 of the Convention, which encourages parents to view any grievances they may have with the state over their child's upbringing from an adult standpoint (Fortin, 1999, p. 357). Fortin argues that this causes adults and the courts to lose sight of the fact that the focus of the dispute is the children and it is they who may have rights and interests of their own 'which need proper assessment and deliberation' (Fortin, 2006, p. 300).

Fortin's central criticism in her 2006 article, regarding the application of the Human Rights Act by courts in cases involving the ascertainment of a child's best interests, is that only when children themselves are the applicants do the courts find it essential to consider the children's position as fully fledged rights holders. This means that where younger children are involved, arguments relating to the children's interests are only part of a discussion which focuses on how infringement of adults' rights might best be justified (Fortin, 2006, p. 326). It needs to be said that what the courts are doing is actually giving due weight to the requirements of art. 8(1) of the Convention, which necessitates independent consideration of the rights of the child's parents. This, in essence, highlights the potential incompatibility between art. 8(1) and the welfare principle under English law.

In an article published in 2005, Choudhry and Fenwick also note that resistance to the Human Rights Act is strongly marked in cases in relation to disputes involving children and argue that the failure of the courts to take account of European Convention arguments could only be justified if there was no conflict between the demands of the welfare principle and those which the Convention guarantees but that 'in fact, the approach of the European Court of Human Rights differs considerably from that of the UK courts since it seeks to balance the rights of different family members' (Choudhry and Fenwick, 2005, p. 453). Whereas the paramountcy principle under English law automatically requires the child's welfare to be given priority over the rights of other family members. They therefore suggest that given these competing approaches and demands, it is time to adopt a new model of judicial reasoning in the context of disputes over children – the 'parallel analysis' or 'ultimate balancing act' (Choudhry and Fenwick, 2005).

This approach would require a consideration of the rights of all parties involved in disputes over children, in accordance with the requirements of art. 8(2) of the Convention, in parallel with each other and these interests would then need to be balanced against each other to see which should prevail, in accordance with the test of proportionality. As Jane Fortin puts it, the English courts apparently see no need to consider 'whether the infringement of the parent's rights is proportionate to the child's immediate needs' (Fortin, 2003, p. 59). Hence Choudhry and Fenwick's approach would require the courts to weigh the proportionality of such an infringement.

Restraining factors on the use of the Human Rights Act 1998

Harris-Short argues that the restraining factors of opposition to rights-based reasoning in family law cases and the notion that Parliament rather than the courts should be responsible for making any changes to complex sociolegal issues have had an effect on three key areas of English family law: first, the legal regulation of intimate adult relationships; second, the public law on children; and third, private disputes over children.

Appraisal of the Human Rights Act in private law family cases

For the first two years after the implementation of the Human Rights Act in 2000, only a relatively small number of significant private law family cases reached the courts in which the art. 8 rights of the parties had been engaged. Private law cases deal with actions brought by 'private individuals' such as parents, carers and children themselves, against each other, in relation to legal questions concerning children, most commonly relating to contact and residence. A survey of such cases conducted by Bonner, Fenwick and Harris-Short, published in 2003, indicates that two key cases, *Payne v Payne* in the Court of Appeal (see [2001] 1 FLR 1052) and *Re B (Adoption: Sole Natural Parent)* [2002] 1 FLR 196 in the House of Lords sent a clear message to the lower courts: that the Human Rights Act does not require any change to the traditional welfare-centred approach of domestic family law (Bonner *et al.*, 2003, p. 584). This might well have been seen as a welcome defence of the welfare principle. Nevertheless, Bonner *et al.* point out that Lord Justice Thorpe was being highly selective in *Payne v Payne* when he purported to rely on *Johansen v Norway* (1996) 23 EHRR 33 in declaring that 'particular weight should be attached to the best interests of the child ... which may override those of the parent' as he actually omitted the full quotation from *Johansen* [2001] 1 FLR 1052 at [29] which read: 'In carrying out the balancing exercise, the Court will attach particular importance to the best interests of the child, which, *depending on their nature and seriousness*, may override those of the parent.' The full quotation including the omitted phrase (italicized above), actually accepts the possibility of the welfare principle *not* being given paramount importance, as it is understood in English law. This approach has been confirmed in subsequent decisions of the European Court (see for example *Buchberger v Austria, Application No. 32899/96* and *Sahin v Germany* [2002] 1 FLR 119).

Butler-Sloss LJ also takes the same view in *Payne* (see [2001] 1 FLR at [82]) that *Johansen* is authority for the principle that the child's welfare is the 'overriding' consideration.

However, as this survey only reflects the judicial approach in the first two years after the Human Rights Act's implementation, Bonner *et al.* emphasized at the outset that this could only be a stocktaking rather than anything more definitive (Bonner *et al.*, 2003, p. 549). Even at this stage, the authors declared that the reasoning on which the defence of the welfare principle has been based has been 'extremely disappointing', that 'judicial reasoning under the Human Rights Act is most conspicuous by its absence' and that the specific duties placed on the court by ss 3, 4 and 6 of the Act have been largely glossed over or ignored and the demands of the Convention or its case law have not been subjected to sufficiently rigorous scrutiny. They also note that there is a strong body of opinion that 'rights-based discourse' has no place in the context of private family disputes (Bonner *et al.*, 2003, p. 584).

In the same vein, in an article published in 2005, Sonia Harris-Short points out that two key factors were always likely to have a restraining influence on the use of the Human Rights Act in British family law cases: first, a strong resistance to rights-based reasoning in the family law context; and second, the fact that 'legal regulation of family life often gives rise to sensitive questions of public policy, traditionally regarded as the responsibility of Parliament rather than the courts' (Harris-Short, 2005, p. 329). Her review of post-implementation Human Rights Act cases suggests that there is a 'marked failure' in many of the private law family cases to engage with the European Convention arguments 'in any sustained or convincing manner' (Harris-Short, 2005, p. 353). The courts have shown a reluctance to confront the issue of the potential incompatibility between the welfare principle and art. 8 of the Convention. This is because art. 8(1) requires independent consideration of the rights of the child's parents whereas the paramountcy principle means that in matters relating to the upbringing of a child, the child's welfare must be the court's *only* consideration (Harris-Short, 2005, p. 353). This is required under the Children Act 1989 and under English case law of the highest authority (see *J v C* [1970] AC 668 at 697 per Lord Guest, at 710–11 per Lord MacDermott and at 727 per Lord Donovan). Consequently, the rights of others, including the child's parents, should not to be accorded serious weight, unless they have a direct bearing on the child's best interests (Harris-Short, 2005, p. 353).

Harris-Short further observes that the standard approach, which the courts have been utilizing in cases where the upbringing of a child is directly in issue, is to give detailed and careful consideration to the welfare test and the child's best interests and then, at the end of the judgment, to turn somewhat dismissively to art. 8 and conclude that it has no material effect on the decision which has been based on considerations of welfare (Harris-Short, 2005, p. 354).

Hence, it is only in cases involving matters of procedure or evidence where the courts have more readily accepted the language of rights, possibly because these cases do not impact on the ideology of the family but are more concerned with the smooth administration of justice, or the right to a fair trial (Harris-Short, 2005, p. 359).

Case law review

The unmarried mother – Belgium

Marckx v Belgium

In *Marckx v Belgium* (A/31) (1979) 2 EHRR 330, an unmarried Belgian mother and her infant daughter claimed that the state had breached their rights under Arts 8 and 14 because, unlike a married mother, she had no automatic legal bond with her daughter, but had to execute a formal deed of recognition. Despite having such a deed, her daughter was still disadvantaged in terms of inheritance rights or intestacy from her mother's family line. The court reaffirmed that the right to respect for family life applied to both 'illegitimate' and 'legitimate' families equally. Further, it may go so far as to impose positive obligations on states rather than just preventing interferences.

The unmarried father

McMichael v United Kingdom

McMichael v United Kingdom (A/308) (1995) 20 EHRR 205, a Scottish case, dealt with the unmarried father's legal position. Under the law, unmarried fathers are not automatically accorded parental responsibility. However, unmarried mothers and married fathers acquire parental responsibility automatically. The case concerned the disclosure of documents in proceedings to free the applicant's child for adoption. The unmarried father complained that his rights had been violated by reason of his initial lack of rights in respect of either custody or standing in the care proceedings preceding the adoption proceedings. The European Court held that there had been no violation of art. 14 or art. 8 in this regard and that the difference in treatment of married and unmarried fathers was not discriminatory, as the purpose behind it was to provide a mechanism for identifying meritorious fathers who might be accorded parental rights, thereby protecting the child and the mother. Thus, the legislation had a legitimate aim and the principle of proportionality had been respected in terms of the means employed in achieving that aim.

This case has been criticized by Branchflower (1999) on the grounds that the court did not carry out a full analysis of the justification for the clear differential treatment of the unmarried father, and seems to say that Convention rights are only available to those who deserve them, which conflicts with *Marckx* which held that there should be no discrimination between married and unmarried mothers on the ground of 'unmeritoriousness' and the case did not test whether the child's rights had been breached under the Convention.

Keegan v Ireland

In *Keegan v Ireland* [1994] 3 FCR 165, an unmarried father had lived with the child's mother before the birth and planned to marry her. But the relationship ended before the birth and the father subsequently paid one visit to see the child in the hospital.

The court emphasized that 'family life' exists between parents and biological children from the moment of birth; thus exclusion of parents from the life of the child can only be justified in exceptional circumstances.

Hence, considerable weight is attached to the blood tie.

Article 12 does not confer a right to marry

Johnston v Ireland

In *Johnston v Ireland* (A/112) (1986) 9 EHRR 203, a Quaker complained that since Irish law did not allow him to obtain a divorce, he was therefore compelled to cohabit with a person outside marriage and that this was a breach of art. 12 which deals with the right to marry. However, the court held that art. 12 does not encompass a right to a divorce even when it may be a necessary prerequisite to a further marriage. Encountering difficulty or a delay in obtaining a divorce will not constitute grounds for a violation of the right to marry under art. 12.

The right to family life under art. 8 – The Netherlands

Berrehab v The Netherlands

Berrehab v The Netherlands (A/138) (1988) 11 EHRR 322 involved a complaint relating to whether the expulsion of an alien leading to the separation from his child and inhibiting contact between them amounted to a violation of the right to family life under art. 8. The European Court stated that in determining whether an interference was 'necessary in a democratic society', the court makes allowance for the margin of appreciation that is left to the contracting states. In this connection, it accepts that the Convention does not in principle prohibit the contracting states from regulating the entry and length of stay of aliens. The established case law of the European Court interpreted 'necessity' to mean that the interferences correspond to a pressing social need and this had to be proportionate to the legitimate aim pursued. Family life is not extinguished if the parents and children no longer live together.

The right to use art. 8 for alleged breach of access rights – Finland

Hokkanen v Finland

In *Hokkanen v Finland* (1994) 19 EHRR 139, where the father had not been able to exercise his access rights to his daughter due to the non-compliance of the grandparents, the European Court held that the national authorities must do their utmost to facilitate the cooperation of all concerned. The child's grandparents had deliberately obstructed the father's contact with the child over a three-year period, despite the father's repeated applications to the court.

This case reiterated that art. 8 includes 'a right for the parent to have measures taken with a view to his or her being reunited with the child and an obligation for the national authorities to take such action' (para. 55). However, the European Court made it clear that the obligation to facilitate reunion is not absolute, since the reunion of a parent with a child who had not lived for some time with other persons may not be able to take place immediately and may require preparatory measures being taken to this effect. The nature and extent of such preparation will depend on the circumstances of each case, but the understanding and cooperation of all concerned will always be an important ingredient.

The European Court took pains to point out that the child could not be coerced into being reunited with the natural parent because 'the interests as well as the rights and freedoms of all concerned must be taken into account, and more particularly the best interests of the child and his or her rights under Article 8 … Where contacts with the parent might appear to threaten those interests or interfere with those rights, it is for the national authorities to strike a fair balance between them' (para. 58). It further emphasized that if the child had become sufficiently mature for her views to be taken into account, contact should not be granted against her own wishes (para. 61).

Public law cases

In public law cases, where the state has an interest in intervening in the family in the best interests of the child, the Human Rights Act tends to be involved only in procedural issues and situations relating to parental involvement in decision making where state authorities make a decision on placing a child into care. There have been difficult cases involving the need for the state authority to remove a child at birth from a mother who poses a risk to her child because of her treatment of her other children and the equally controversial question of whether the mother and her partner should be given notice of the intention to remove that child in order to protect it from future harm.

Removal of children from their parents by the state
– United Kingdom

Under English law, children may only be taken away from their parents by the state if the conditions set out in s. 31 of the Children Act 1989 are satisfied, that is, if the local authority can establish that the children have suffered or are likely to suffer significant harm as a result of parental default.

Strasbourg jurisprudence has also appeared to give the child's welfare priority over parental rights. For example, it said in *Yousef v The Netherlands* [2004] 1 FLR 210 at [73]: 'In judicial decisions where the rights under Article 8 of parents and those of a child are at stake, the child's rights must be the paramount consideration. If any balancing of interests is necessary, the interests of the child must prevail.'

This seems to follow the paramountcy principle in English law. However the English court cannot make a care order simply because the requirements of the Children Act have been fulfilled, but has to consider art. 8 of the European Convention on Human Rights. This was made clear in *Re B* [2003] 2 FLR 813.

Re B (Care: Interference with Family Life)

In *Re B (Care: Interference with Family Life)* [2003] 2 FLR 813 at [34] the English Court of Appeal held (per Thorpe LJ) that where an application is for a care order empowering the local authority to remove a child from the family, the judge in the family court may not make such an order without considering the European Convention on Human Rights, art. 8 rights relating to the adult members of the family and of the children of the family and 'must not sanction such an interference with family life unless he is satisfied that it is both necessary and proportionate and that no other less radical form or order would achieve the essential end of promoting the welfare of the children'.

This is why the European Human Rights Court in Strasbourg has repeatedly stated, as in *Haase v Germany* [2004] 2 FLR 39 at [93]: 'The taking into care of a child should normally be a temporary measure to be discontinued as soon as circumstances permit and any measures of implementation of temporary care should be consistent with the ultimate aim of reuniting the natural parent and child.'

Taking a newborn baby into care – Germany

Hasse v Germany

In *Hasse v Germany* [2004] 2 FLR 39 the European Court held that the taking of a newborn baby into care is an extremely harsh measure. There must be extraordinarily compelling reasons before a baby can be physically removed from its mother. The European Court declared that 'it is incumbent on the competent national authorities to examine whether some less intrusive interference into family life at such a critical point in the lives of the parents and the child is not possible' (at [101]).

Comparative observation on removal of baby at birth

In 1987, in the English pre-Children Act case of *Re D* [1987] 1 All ER 20, a baby born to a drug addict mother was removed at birth from the care of its mother as it was born suffering from drug withdrawal symptoms (see de Cruz, 1987). Under s. 31(2) of the current Children Act 1989, such a removal would still be permitted provided the local authorities reasonably believed that the baby was in danger of future significant harm. However, even if the local authority was aware of a pregnant drug addict who was taking an excess of unsuitable drugs, English law would not permit making the foetus a ward of court under its wardship or inherent jurisdiction, as the foetus does not have legal personality in English law (*Re F (in utero)* [1988] Fam 122).

Removing the child without involving the parents – United Kingdom

Bury Metropolitan Borough Council v D

A more recent case involving taking a newborn baby into care is *Bury Metropolitan Borough Council v D* [2009] EWHC 446, decided on the 4 March 2009, where the English High Court had to deal with an application by a local authority to remove a baby from the care of its mother as soon as it was born, without involving the mother or her partner in that decision, because the mother had shown herself to be violent to a previous child and it was argued that there would be a risk to the child if she knew that the child would be removed at birth. Munby J identified the issue as: '[W]hether, despite the requirements of Article 8 of the European Convention, it is lawful for the local authority not to involve the mother and her partner fully in the birth planning for her future child as would normally be required.'

The court noted that the European Court of Human Rights has recognized that there are exceptional occasions when it would be inappropriate for there to be such parental involvement, and there have been a number of cases where the court has recognized not merely that the removal of children under an emergency protection order or its equivalent is in principle entirely compatible with the Convention, but moreover, that there may be such cases where a without notice application may be justified, as in for example *Venema v The Netherlands* [2003] 1 FLR 552 and *Haase v Germany* [2004] 2 FLR 39 (see above).

The European Court's approach was spelt out very clearly in *Venema v The Netherlands* [2003] 1 FLR 552 at [93] where it said:

'The court always accepts that when action has to be taken to protect a child in an emergency, it may not always be possible, because of the urgency of the situation, to associate in the decision-making process those having custody of the child. Nor, as the Government point out, may it even be desirable, even if possible, to do so if those having custody of the child are seen as the source of an immediate threat to the child, since giving them prior warning would be liable to deprive the measure of its effectiveness. The court must however be satisfied that the national authorities were entitled to consider that there existed circumstances justifying the abrupt removal of the child from the care of its parents without any prior contact or consultation. In particular, it is for the respondent State to establish that a careful assessment of the impact of the proposed care measure on the parents and the child, as well as the possible alternatives to the removal of the child from its family, was carried out prior to the implementation of a care measure.'

The European Court repeated the same point in *Haase v Germany* [2004] 2 FLR 39 in almost exactly the same words.

In the *Bury* case, having carefully considered the law and accepted the evidence which indicated that the mother was given to impulsively violent and dangerous acts, Munby J decided to grant the declaration that the local authority's proposed course of action was lawful.

National authorities must try to reunite a family swiftly – Norway

If a child has been separated from one or both of her parents, the European Court has held, in for example *Johansen v Norway* (1996) 23 EHRR 33, that there is an obligation on the national authorities of the state concerned to reunite the family as soon as possible if, post-separation, such a reunion is seen to be in the best interests of the child.

Johansen v Norway

In *Johansen v Norway* (1996) 23 EHRR 33, the European Court of Human Rights held that there is an obligation on the national authorities to work towards the reunification of the family as speedily as possible while simultaneously protecting the best interests of the child in cases where the child has been separated from one of his or her parents and placed in foster care. The European Court also recognized that the competent national authorities enjoyed a 'wide margin of appreciation' in assessing the necessity of taking a child into care when 'necessary in a democratic society' within the terms of art. 8(2) and the level of appropriateness for intervention would vary from country to country depending on family traditions and state intervention into family affairs. It also stressed that it could not substitute its decisions on such matters for those of the domestic authority and consideration of the child's best interests was of crucial importance. *A fair balance was to be struck between the interests of the child in remaining in public care and those of the parents in being reunited with her* (emphasis added). The European Court declared that in carrying out this balancing exercise, it will attach 'particular importance to the best interests of the child, which, depending on their nature and seriousness, may *override* those of the parent' (emphasis added).

Damages and the Human Rights Act

The issue of the award of damages for a breach of a provision of the European Convention on Human Rights has cropped up in a few cases, for example in the 2007 case of *Re P* (the following account of this case is taken from English and Cross, 2007 at http://www.familylawweek.co.uk/site.aspx?I=ed1789).

Re P

In the case of *Re P* [2007] EWCA Civ. 2, the Court of Appeal dealt with a case of a care plan designed to effect a rehabilitation between a mother and her child. It considered whether the first instance judge had been correct in considering that a declaration of breach of art. 8 was 'just satisfaction' where a mother had been insufficiently involved in the decision by the local authority to abandon a care plan for her rehabilitation with her child. The mother's appeal was based on a number of Strasbourg cases which she claimed entitled her to damages in addition to the declaration. She lost her appeal, but their Lordships appeared troubled by the question of these loss of opportunity cases and the issue of whether they should be dismissed without a damages or compensatory award.

In *Re P*, the appellant had been in local authority care since the age of six. In January 2004, aged 16, she gave birth to M. The appellant was separated from M in March 2004 as a result of concerns for M's wellbeing. In December 2004, the respondent local authority sought to reunite mother and child. A care plan was negotiated, and a care order by consent was drawn up. The plan allowed the mother six months to demonstrate capacity to parent M. At the same time, plans to arrange for M's adoption were to be taken. The care plan envisaged M's removal in emergency circumstances or in the event of a general failure to progress. The appellant was to be kept fully informed and clearly warned and to be allowed to mount a legal challenge. Following the consent order, the appellant's care of M deteriorated and she became violent and threatening. In January 2005, the local authority decided to remove M as a matter of emergency and to abandon the care plan. The appellant's solicitor was contacted prior to the separation of mother from child, but the appellant was not herself informed. M was removed on the 6 January and later released for adoption.

The appellant sought a declaration of a breach of her rights under art. 8 and damages under s. 8 of the Human Rights Act 1998 and art. 41 of the Convention arising from her insufficient involvement in the decision-making process.

The first instance judge held that there had been a significant breach in M's procedural rights in the decision to abandon the care plan without her consultation. However, M's removal had been lawful as a matter of emergency and it was not in M's best interests to attempt further rehabilitation. The judge found that a declaration was 'just satisfaction', as the concept of damages did not sit easily with the welfare jurisdiction of family law. The term 'just satisfaction' suggests that a declaration is appropriate and sufficient legal redress.

Court of Appeal decision

The mother appealed to the Court of Appeal against the refusal to award damages. Despite the breach being purely procedural, there were several precedents which supported the award of damages in such circumstances, and the appellant relied on *W v United Kingdom* (1987) 10 EHRR 29 and *Venema v The Netherlands* [2003] 1 FLR 552.

W v United Kingdom and *Venema* are cases which stand for the principle that where a serious decision – such as the removal of a child from its mother – is being taken, it is incumbent on the local authority to involve the parent to a degree sufficient to provide him or her with the requisite protection of their interests. *Venema* involved a child being removed because it was suspected that the mother was suffering from Munchausen's Syndrome by Proxy. Here, the Strasbourg Court observed that there was 'wholesale failure' to consult the parents or to give them a proper opportunity to dispel concerns by challenging the reliability, relevance or sufficiency of the information upon which the authorities were acting. For breach of these violations, damages of 15,000 euros were awarded to the applicants jointly as compensation for the distress and anxiety resulting from feelings of frustration and injustice.

However, in his leading judgment in *Re P*, Thorpe LJ declared that in those cases, damages had been awarded for the loss of opportunity and the distress caused by the lack of judicial remedy or injustice. In *Re P*, the appellant had not suffered a loss of opportunity as the lower court judge had found that it 'distinctly probable' that, even if she had been invited to the meeting, the same conclusion – to remove M – would have been reached. In addition, her outrage had preceded or flowed from the removal of M but there was no evidence that the exclusion from the decision had caused any independent or additional injury. While the local authority had been wrong to proceed to adoption without consulting the mother, she did not have capacity to consent at the time and her solicitor had been closely involved. She had been given the opportunity to issue legal proceedings but had failed to do so in time. Consequently, while the jurisprudence of the European Court of Human Rights indicated that damages were sometimes to be awarded where art. 8 rights had been infringed by shortcomings in procedures, 'the breach ranked low on the spectrum of severity, and in this case did not justify monetary compensation' (see English and Cross, 1997, at http://www.familylawweek.co.uk).

Indeed, in contrast with the cases relied upon by the appellant, legal means of redress had been available to the applicant in this case, even if not employed. As the court stressed: 'Factually, the cases were also very different in terms of the severity of the breach.' In *W v UK*, the most extreme of the cases cited, the authorities restricted and then terminated the applicant's access to the child without any discussion or warning. The applicant had no means of legal redress, and the child was put up for adoption. Hence, as English and Cross reiterate, in comparison with previous authorities the breach in *Re P* was indeed on the lower end of the 'scale of severity'. Hence the bases upon which awards of damages were justified by the Strasbourg Court were not present in the appellant's case. It was also clear that the outcome would not have been different even if the appellant had been consulted, which is why the appeal was unsuccessful (English and Cross, 1997).

The views of Wilson LJ in *Re P* have also been highlighted by English and Cross. Wilson LJ declared: '[T]he firm negative phraseology of s. 8(3) of the HRA ... namely "No award of damages is to be made unless ..." is a feature of our domestic law not reflected in the Convention itself, which might therefore place the decisions of the European Court of Human Rights at one remove from us.' However, the learned Lord Justice rejected this impression. English and Cross argue that it is not self-evident that the difference between s. 8(3) of the Human Rights Act and art. 41 of the Convention is one of style rather than of substance. In fact, they point out that *Re P* follows a line of authorities 'that seek to emphasise that a declaration of a breach of human rights should be considered "just satisfaction" and that no more should be required by way of legal redress' (English and Cross, 1997).

Further, cases such as *Anufrijeva v Southwark London Borough Council* [2004] 1 AC 604; *R (Mambakasa) v Secretary of State for the Home Office* [2004] QB 1124; *R(N) v Secretary for the Home Office* [2004] QB 1124 have held: 'Where an infringement of an individual's human rights have occurred, the concern will usually be to bring the infringement to an end and any question of compensation will be of secondary, if any, importance.' This principle was reiterated by Lord Bingham in *R (Greenfield) v Secretary of State for the Home Department* [2005] UKHL 14, where he emphasized that the focus of the Convention is on the protection of human rights and not the award of compensation.

Concluding observations

This chapter has excavated different terrain from the other chapters in this book by examining the impact of a major international treaty, the European Convention on Human Rights, on the domestic law of several European and British jurisdictions, as illustrated and indicated by their case law. Nevertheless, it has maintained a comparative perspective because it has compared the way an issue arising in a domestic context has been decided by an international tribunal, applying a set of international norms, and has also looked at the way some domestic courts have dealt with the same issue.

Bonner's study of art. 8, two years after the implementation of the Human Rights Act in Britain, suggests that the family law cases reveal 'a willingness to (mis) read ECHR rights, as explained in ECHR jurisprudence, to preserve traditional approaches' (Bonner, 2003).

In an article in the *Human Rights Quarterly* in 2008, Greer argues that the European Convention on Human Rights (the Convention) is in danger of experiencing a severe overload of applications. He maintains that although the Convention is widely regarded as the most successful experiment in the transnational, judicial protection of human rights in the world, it 'faces a potentially fatal case overload crisis' (Greer, 2008, p. 680). For most of its first 30 years it was virtually ignored and only 800 or so individual complaints a year were received by the Strasbourg institutions, whereas towards the end of the first decade of the twenty-first century, the annual average has reached 40,000. In March 2009 Lord Hoffman, one of the most senior law lords, launched an extraordinary attack on the European Court of Human Rights. In a lecture to the Judicial Studies Board, he accused the European Court of trivializing and discrediting human rights. He said he had no difficulty with the text of the European Convention or its adoption as part of United Kingdom law in the Human Rights Act 1998, or being used as a standard against which a country's compliance with human rights can be measured, but the problem was with the European Court which, he said, had not been able to resist the temptation to 'aggrandise its jurisdiction and to impose uniform law on member states', that a judicial body was not entitled to introduce new concepts, and that the European Court did not enjoy the constitutional legitimacy in the United Kingdom which the Supreme Court enjoyed in the United States. He said that as of 1 November 2008, there was a backlog of 100,000 applications pending, of which 60 per cent were from five countries – Russia, Turkey, Romania, Ukraine and Italy. Without a summary mechanism to deal with hopeless cases, he predicted that the European Court would drown in its own workload (see Lord Hoffman, *The Universality of Human Rights,* Judicial Studies Board Annual Lecture, March 2009).

But perhaps the last word, at least for now, should go to Munby J, who, in a public lecture in 2005, said:

> 'We need to analyse more carefully ... how we balance the interests of children and parents when their Article 8 rights come into conflict ... The Human Rights Act 1998 has given the judges new tools with which to meet the emerging needs of an ever-changing society. But many of the most pressing reforms require legislation. Will Parliament be able to meet the challenge? I should like to hope so, but I am not sanguine.'
>
> (Munby, 2005, pp. 508–9)

Further reading

Archbold, Claire 'Family Law-Making and Human Rights in the United Kingdom' in Maclean (ed) *Making Law for Families,* 2000, Hart.

Bainham, A 'Can We Protect Children and Protect Their Rights?' [2002] Fam Law 279.

Bonner, D, Fenwick, H and Harris-Short, S 'Judicial Approaches to the Human Rights Act' (2003) 52 ICLQ 549.

Branchflower, G 'Parental Responsibility and Human Rights' [1999] Fam Law 34.

Choudhry, S and Fenwick, H 'Taking the Rights of Parents and Children Seriously: Confronting the Welfare Principle under the Human Rights Act' (2005) 25 Oxford J Legal Studies 453.

de Cruz, SP 'Protecting the Unborn Child – Re D' (1987) 17 Fam Law 207.

de Mello, L (ed) *Human Rights Act 1998. A Practical Guide*, 2000, Jordans.

Diduck, A 'A Family by any other Name ... or Starbucks comes to England' (2001) 28 Jo Law and Society 290.

Diduck, A *Law's Families*, 2003, LexisNexis, Ch. 8.

Fenwick, H 'Clashing Rights, the Welfare of the Child and the Human Rights Act' (2004) 67 Mod LR 889.

Fenwick, H, Phillipson, G and Masterman, R *Judicial Reasoning under the Human Rights Act*, 2007, Cambridge UP.

Fortin, J 'Rights Brought Home for Children' (1999) 62 Mod LR 350.

Fortin, J 'The HRA's impact on Litigation involving Children and their Families' (1999) 11 CFLQ 237.

Fortin, J *Children's Rights and the Developing Law*, 2003, Lexis-Nexis Butterworths.

Fortin, J 'Accommodating Children's Rights in a Post Human Rights Era' (2006) 69 Mod LR 299.

Fottrell, D 'Human Rights Act and Family Law' at http://www.hrla.org.uk.

Greer, S 'What's Wrong with the European Convention on Human Rights?' (2008) 30 *Human Rights Quarterly* 680.

Harris-Short, S 'Family Law and the Human Rights Act: Judicial Restraint or Revolution?' (2005) 17 CFLQ 329.

Herring, J 'The Human Rights Act and the Welfare Principle in Family Law – Conflicting or Complementary?' [1999a] CFLQ 223.

Kennedy, I *Treat Me Right*, 1992, Oxford UP.

Lester, Lord 'Opinion: The Art of the Possible – Interpreting Statutes under the Human Rights Act' [1998] EHRLR 665.

Munby, Justice 'Families Old and New – the Family and Article 8' (2005) 17 CFLQ 487.

Smart, C 'The "New" Parenthood: Fathers and Mothers after Divorce' in Silva and Smart (eds) *The New Family?* 1999, Sage.

Storey, H 'The Right to Family Life, and Immigration Case Law at Strasbourg' (1990) 39 ICLQ 328.

Swindells, H, Neaves, A Kushner, M and Silbeck, R *Family Law and the Human Rights Act 1998*, 1999 Jordan.

International websites

European Court of Human Rights –Strasbourg at http://www.echr.coe.int
United Nation Convention on the Rights of the Child at htpp://www.unicef.org/crc/

Part VI

Common themes, key debates and comparative overview

'All things change and nothing stays the same
This was Anaxogoras' well-known claim'

Frank Murphy A Summer's Walk, 2006

The changes to family law and society in the jurisdictions we have been looking at, wrought by phenomena such as industrial revolutions, world wars and ever-developing technology, appear to be almost inevitable as we approach the end of the first decade of the twenty-first century. Hence, the claim of the pre-Socratic philosopher Anaxogoras holds as true today as it did in ancient times, for moment-ous change has indeed occurred in family law, sex and society in common law and civil law countries across the world, as well as in hybrid jurisdictions such as South Africa and Russia. Diversity in the typical family, changes in the composition of the marital dyad, the decline in the number of heterosexual marriages, the advent of divorce replacing death as the most common endpoint of marriage, the spectacular rise in cohabitation outside marriage, the legal recognition of the status of children born outside marriage, the phenomenal number of single-parent families and the legal recognition of same-sex relationships as civil unions in a growing number of jurisdictions are all endemic to society in the early twenty-first century in Western and Western-influenced jurisdictions.

This chapter reviews and reflects on the common themes and trends we have encountered in our survey of the development of the family, marriage, unmarried cohabitation, divorce, matrimonial property, financial provision upon divorce, child custody and domestic violence. We begin, however, by considering the great debates in family law as highlighted by Krause.

The 'great debates' in family law – past, present and future?

Krause's 'great debates' in family law

In his contribution to the *Oxford Handbook of Comparative Law*, Krause reviews what he regards as the past and present 'great debates' in family law and looks ahead to those of the future. We shall consider his views and then look more closely at some of the major areas, such as marriage, divorce, marital property and children.

The past

Divorce

Krause begins by saying that in the last 50 years, 'reform efforts in country after country have departed from conditioning divorce on the commission by one mar-riage partner of a marital offence – such as adultery or cruelty – and have moved to an almost total disregard of marital fault' (Krause, 2008, p. 1113). As far as the West is concerned, he observes that divorce has moved from being simply unavailable, to difficult (on fault grounds only), to easy to obtain (as a result of being uncontested and on consensual fault grounds) and now even past no-fault grounds (Krause, 2008, p. 1113). As a result of the state requiring little more than one party's unilateral decision to divorce the other as far as many courts are concerned, 'the relevant focus of the divorce process has shifted almost entirely from status (whether divorce may be obtained) to the economic consequences, because divorce is freely available but not for free, and to allocating child custody and support. Indeed, he believes: 'Divorce, through its legal and social consequences, now all but defines the legal meaning of marriage and with that, Western family law' (Krause, 2008, p. 1113).

Krause identifies two great family law reforms in the last 50 years. The first is in relation to the allocation of the economic consequences of failed marriages. Here, as far as the spouses inter se are concerned, there has been a shift from alimony or periodical support for a dependent ex-spouse to division between the ex-partners of marital property. However, as he also notes, even in wealthy countries, there is the problem of inadequate assets being produced by the typical marriage to divide upon divorce and in the longer term, spousal support is rarely sufficient to provide for a new spouse, family or lifestyle (Krause, 2008, p. 1113). It may be added that in England and Wales, the current trend, at least for 'big money' divorces, where the couple's assets far outstrip its reasonable needs, the House of Lords has advocated adopting a principle of equality and fairness between spouses in the court's awards of financial provision (for a fuller discussion of this see Part II, Chapter One on English law).

The second reform is the allocation and enforcement of child support responsibility after divorce, as well as for the vastly increased numbers and proportion of children born outside marriage (Krause, 2008, p. 1114). Hence, 'the absent parent is fully legally liable and increasingly held accountable for marital and non-marital children. Non-marital children are equal' (Krause, 2008, p. 1114). Predictably, the problem of inadequate resources rears its head. It may be noted that Europe is generally more generous than the United States and Britain in its child allowances and tax benefits. In Britain there have been several problems of enforcement and administration in relation to child support over many years, with the government-backed Child Support Agency recently being abolished and replaced by a Child Support Commission, and government policy now firmly in favour of encouraging private arrangements between mother and absent parent.

Current and future debates

Krause then discusses seven areas he says form the bases of current and future debates in family law: (i) downgrading marriage and upgrading cohabitation alternatives; (ii) decoupling strictly legal civil marriage from the traditional legal-cultural-religious-historical significance of marriage; (iii) redefining the state's secular interests in civil marriage; (iv) same-sex relationships; (v) the future of marriage and whether legal marriage is still relevant; (vi) assisted reproduction, artificial insemination, IVF, embryo transplantation and surrogate motherhood; (vii) abortion and contraception. We shall consider these areas in the light of other relevant academic commentary on them.

Marriage – downgrade and replace with cohabitation alternatives?

Krause pinpoints the relaxed attitude towards marriage, family formation and sexual companionship becoming legally and socially accepted in the West as the reason for 'high-flying divorce statistics' and falling marriage rates (Krause, 2008, p. 1114). In the United States, the number of cohabiting couples is currently over 4 million, and in France, more than 40 per cent of births are to unmarried mothers. With the trend towards cohabitation clearly up and rising, cohabitation appears to offer several attractions, such as avoiding potentially costly legal procedures to terminate the relationship and avoiding the likely considerable financial consequences of divorce; the opportunity to make private arrangements which can be less restrictive and more flexible in making antenuptial contracts; avoiding traditional male dominance in marriage; and avoiding the costs incurred in remarriage (Krause, 2008, p. 1115). Several questions are posed by Krause: (i) How should the law define the legal position of unmarried partner vis-à-vis partner and that of unmarried couples vis-à-vis society? (ii) Short of marriage, what level of marital-like rights and obligations should be imposed on, or granted to unmarried partners? (iii) Short of documented marriage, how may it be proven efficiently – in terms of cost and predictability of consequences – that a legally significant, though not married, relationship exists or existed? (iv) Must or should another country or a sister state that itself does not recognize a cohabitation status (or indeed, same-sex marriage or partnership) recognize a legal status created in another state or country? (Krause, 2008, p. 1115).

'Decoupling' civil marriage from religious tradition

Krause argues that the only way to make progress in any sensible adaptation of marriage and family to current conditions is for civil marriage to be distinguished from 'the continuing romance with religious images of marriage as a status of supra- and super-natural virtue' (Krause, 2008, p. 1116). He therefore suggests a decoupling of the strictly legal meaning of marriage from the traditional legal-cultural-religious-historical significance of marriage (Krause, 2008, p. 1116). Doubtless the debate over the religious v secular significance of marriage will continue into the next decade and beyond.

The state's secular interests in civil marriage

Krause believes that a pragmatic, secular concept of marriage should guide the legislator once it is accepted that the state has a legitimate interest in adapting secular marriage to the modern world. Here he believes the question should be 'What does this or that union do for society, and what rights should society provide in return?'

He suggests that the focus should be on the 'appropriate mix of private ordering' (allowing the partners to express their own voluntary, autonomous decisions) and 'public ordering (based on social objectives that justify imposing limits on or providing incentives for the partners' choices)' (Krause, 2008, p. 1116).

The legal treatment of same-sex relationships

Krause observes that throughout the West, an 'emotional debate' has been taking place over the legal treatment of same-sex partners. Hence, marriage or partnership rights have been debated or enacted in Australia, Brazil, Canada, Costa Rica, Israel, New Zealand, South Africa, parts of the United States and much of Europe (Krause, 2008, p. 1116 and see Andenas and Wintemute (eds), *Legal Recognition of Same-Sex Partnerships: A Study of National, European and International Law*, 2001). For further details of the countries which have legalized same-sex relationships see Part III on informal unions and cohabitation.

It may be noted that in the United States, Massachusetts is the sole State which recognizes actual *marriage* for same-sex couples, and by court decision this is now a State constitutional mandate (see *Goodrich v Department of Public Health* 798 NE 2d 941 (Mass. 2003)). In contrast, over 30 States now provide by legislation or constitutional amendments that only heterosexual marriage is to be recognized as legal marriage. Indeed, until 2003, when the United States Supreme Court ruled that such a law was invalid, nearly a dozen States still criminalized homosexual conduct (see *Lawrence v Texas* 539 US 558 at 573 (2003)). So the topic remains a live issue and a continuing bone of contention in the United States.

Other common law jurisdictions such as Britain have passed legislation which recognizes civil partnerships of same-sex couples. New Zealand has only recognized legal effects in terms of property rights accruing from cohabiting relationships and has stopped short of legalizing same-sex marriage. On the civil law system front, Germany has provided a close equivalent of marriage through domestic/life partnership legislation and France recognizes a contractually based legal status of cohabitation for both same-sex and opposite sex couples, called pacs (see Part III).

Marriage – will it be relevant in the future?

In an earlier article, Krause argues that marriage has been 'shaken by the widespread abandonment of fundamental traditional social understandings and the failure of visible alternatives for ongoing social functions and needs' (Krause, 2000, pp. 271–2). Indeed, feminists such as Martha Fineman and Nancy Polikoff advocate the abolition of marriage altogether (Polikoff, 2003; Fineman, 2000). Nearly eight years later, he argued that much of the current controversy over whether traditional marriage (with all its legal effects) should be extended to same-sex couples may be 'misdirected' and suggests that the rational test for providing legal preference to intimate partners is whether there is a measurable gain for society or a compelling social need for protective intervention (Krause, 2008, p. 1120).

English academics have also raised the issue of whether legal marriage will continue to be relevant (see for example Probert and Barlow, 2000; Dewar, 2000) and it has been debated extensively in the pages of the *Family Law Quarterly* by American academics such as Martha Garrison, Elizabeth Scott, Milton Regan and Krause himself.

In a more recent publication, Krause asserts that sensible law would result in relation to both same-sex and opposite-sex couples if the social purposes of marriage and other intimate relationships were more 'consciously, openly, and rationally defined and legal consequences tailored accordingly' (Krause, 2008, p. 1121).

Assisted reproduction, artificial insemination, in vitro fertilisation, embryo transplantation, surrogate motherhood

In the areas of assisted reproduction, contraception and abortion, the common theme has been that Western family law, with its more traditional moralities, has struggled to keep up with the new ethical challenges posed by medical advances, capabilities and the new technology (Krause, 2008, p. 1121). Assisted reproduction techniques have brought benefits to couples otherwise unable to beget children, and this has required the law to define the respective rights and interests of the various parties involved. Artificial insemination, in vitro-fertilization (IVF) and embryo transplantation challenge traditional definitions and understandings of what it means to be a parent. Krause lists four possible claimants to family status in these cases; namely: (i) the married mother's husband when the mother conceives a child by artificial insemination with semen donated by another man; (ii) the woman who carried a child through pregnancy and childbirth where the pregnancy resulted either from (a) her artificial insemination with the intending father's semen or (b) the transplantation of a fertilized ovum (embryo) stemming from another woman, such as the wife of the intending couple; (iii) the donor of the semen; and (iv) the donor of the ovum or embryo. Krause adds that with human cloning becoming likely in the future, perhaps scientists should also be included in this list (Krause, 2008, p. 1122)!

In Western Europe, legal approaches to these possibilities have not been uniform. In European law, there has been a greater willingness to regulate access to reproductive technologies than in United States law, which has been somewhat inconsistent and varies greatly. In Europe and the United States it is widely accepted that a child born to a married woman through artificial insemination is legally the husband's legitimate child; most jurisdictions have followed the approach of the Uniform Parentage Act 1973, which provides that a husband who consents to the artificial insemination of his wife under the supervision of a licensed physician 'is treated in law as if he were the natural father' (s. 5(a) Uniform Parentage Act 1973). In Europe, most jurisdictions prohibit the husband who has consented to the use of Artificial Insemination by Donor (AID) from challenging paternity (see Blair and Weiner, 2003, p. 1014).

Less common is the fact that some United States and European jurisdictions have applied the same rule to unmarried partners. In 2002, the Uniform Parentage Act was revised to expand its coverage to unmarried couples but, as of 2005, only three States had adopted this change (Krause, 2008, p. 1122). As Krause observes: 'One may generalise that the trend has been toward assigning parentage based on parties' intent' (Krause, 2008, p. 1122).

From a comparative perspective, it may be noted that as far as surrogacy arrangements are concerned, certain States in the United States recognize some surrogacy agreements as legally enforceable contracts and, if it appears that the parties entered into such an agreement voluntarily, the surrogate mother would not normally be permitted to change her mind about handing over the child, as this would not be giving effect to the parties' contractual intentions. On the other hand, since English law regards surrogacy arrangements as unenforceable (under s. 1A Surrogacy Arrangements Act 1985), this allows the surrogate mother to change her mind and keep the child once it has been born, despite the surrogacy arrangement, provided the court considers this to be in the child's best interests.

Contraception and abortion

A detailed consideration of abortion and contraception, is beyond the scope of this book. However, there is little doubt that these two topics have and will continue to be among the list of divisive issues in family law. In the United States, contraception is in fact merging with abortion in the debate over 'Plan B', 'the morning after pill', also known as RU-486 (Krause, 2008, p. 1123). Abortion plays a particularly disputed role in the United States, 'where *judicial interpretation* of a federal constitution entirely silent on the subject, generally allows for ... wider access to abortion than does European law (Krause, 2008, citing Blair and Weiner, 2003, pp. 1062–88, 1123). The United States approach is to set the limit for abortion (thus the viability of the foetus) at about two trimesters (six months). Krause points out that 'in starkest contrast', Germany's constitutional court has held that life begins at conception but has also allowed substantial exceptions to be made to that principle through legislation (see Krause, 2008, p. 1123 and see BverfGE 39 (1975), 1 (1–68) (Germany) for further details).

Professor Mary Ann Glendon published a comparative study of abortion in the 1980s wherein she makes the observation that although the United States has 'less

regulation of abortion in the interest of the foetus than any other Western nation …
[it] provides less public support for maternity and child raising. And, to a greater
extent than in any other country, [United States] courts have shut down the legislative process of bargaining, education, and persuasion on the abortion issue'
(Glendon, *Abortion and Divorce in Western Law*, 1987, p. 2).

Krause adds that the United States courts have, on constitutional grounds, also
shut down the marital process of bargaining on the issue. In 1976, the United States
Supreme Court held that State law would not require the husband's consent to his
wife's decision to have an abortion in *Planned Parenthood of Central Missouri
v Danforth* 428 US 52 at 71 (1976) and in 1992, it ruled that the State could not
rule that the husband at least be notified if his wife wished to have an abortion
in *Planned Parenthood of Southeastern Pennsylvania v Casey* 505 US 833 at
896(1992). Krause makes the further point that the 'vehemence and emotionality'
of the abortion debate in the United States becomes more understandable when
one learns that State statutes seeking to prohibit the practice of so-called 'partial
birth abortions' have so far failed to persuade the United States Supreme Court of
their constitutionality. Hence, in *Carhart v Stenberg* 530 US 914 (2000), the United
States Supreme Court held unconstitutional a Nebraska statute that prohibited
'partial birth abortions', with the court holding that the statute placed an 'undue
burden' on a woman's right to elect abortion because its language covered not only
the 'dilation and extraction' method of abortion but also the 'dilation and evacu-
ation' method of abortion, which is the most common form of abortion used in
the second trimester of pregnancy. Krause poses the question whether notification
to the husband after an abortion takes place should be seen as an equally serious
burden. He argues that among husbands so disposed, post-abortion notifications
may pose an even greater risk of violence (Krause, 2008, p. 1124).

In comparative terms, Europe has effectively reached the same delicate balance
as the United States. Ruling on a case that emanated from England, *Paton v United
Kingdom* (1981) 3 EHRR 408, the European Commission on Human Rights held
that a husband has no legal grounds under the European Convention on Human
Rights to demand that his wife consult him before electing to have an abortion. Any
right that the potential father might have had under art. 8's protection of family
life was outweighed by the potential mother's superior interests in her private life
and bodily integrity, described by the Commission as 'the right of the pregnant
woman … the person primarily concerned in the pregnancy and its continuation
or termination'.

Comparative overview

Let us now list some common themes that have emerged from our comparative
survey of common law, civil law and hybrid jurisdictions. These include:

(i)   the transformation of marriage in the last three decades;
(ii) the spectacular rise in the incidence of cohabitation;

(iii)   the increasing legal recognition of same-sex unions/relationships;
(iv)   the transformation of the family in Western society;
(v)   the fault/no-fault debate in divorce law;
(vi)   the equalisation of women's rights to matrimonial property;
(vii)   the adoption of the best interests of the child guideline in most jurisdictions.

All of these themes have been examined and discussed in varying measure throughout this book but it is now proposed to revisit some of them and to develop some of the ideas that have been mooted in earlier chapters, placing them in comparative perspective.

Marriage

Marriage and society – global transformations in the twentieth century

Pinsof observes that during the twentieth century, human life was transformed in a number of significant ways. These changes occurred primarily in the West but also took place in certain industrially developed parts of Asia, South America, and Africa (Pinsof, 2002, p. 135). Most notable was the fundamental transformation concerning the termination of a marriage, whereby prior to the twentieth century the common endpoint of marriage was death, but during the twentieth century the most common endpoint of marriage became divorce (Pinsof, 2002, p. 135).

Yet Cretney points out that at the beginning of the twentieth century, in England for example, the legal remedy for marital breakdown was not divorce but legal separation orders (Cretney, 2000, p. 2). Hence, at least in Britain, the public perception that divorce was the inevitable remedy for marital breakdown only started to take hold towards the latter half of the twentieth century. As we have seen in Part Three, the Second World War may well have been the most influential catalyst for the movement towards the liberalization of divorce although the unusual levels of prosperity in the 1960s will have engendered a more enterprising and laissez-faire attitude to marriage and relationships in general.

Pinsof pinpoints the possible reasons and conditions which led to the more widespread acceptance of divorce in particularly Western and Westernized jurisdictions by declaring that the shift from death to divorce as the most common termination point of marriage was perhaps 'associated and driven by three major factors: the increased lifespan in Western civilisation, the shift in the biopsychosocial roles of women; and legal and social value changes' (Pinsof, 2002, p. 139).

Until the Second World War, the marital paradigm prevailed which meant the nuclear family, which was a heterosexual monogamous couple married for the first time, with the husband the sole breadwinner and the wife-mother performing the homemaker role – cooking, cleaning, washing and looking after the children as the norm. The prevailing economic situation in many jurisdictions meant that the man was the sole wage-earner, and the widespread lack of opportunities for women to secure even part-time employment meant that within the family, the 'standard authority structure' and roles of parties within marriage was that the husband-father should have the ultimate say in decision making and should be responsible for providing the material needs of the family. On the other hand, the wife-mother was expected to fulfil her role as the carer of the household and children, with procreation being the purpose of marriage (Glendon, 2006, p. 5).

According to Pinsof, marriage has been a form of pair-bonding (a term from ethology – see Eibl-Eibesfeldt, *Human Ethology*, 1989) predicated upon the existence of a heterosexual relationship between the partners, which defines the couple as potentially procreative. This appears to have been the pattern for Europe, North America, Australia, and New Zealand – European-American civilization (Pinsof, 2002, p. 136). Glendon also observes that the prevailing assumptions were that family solidarity and the community of life between spouses were emphasized over the individual personalities and interests of family members (Glendon, 2006, p. 4). Divorce was only permitted for very serious reasons such as extreme cruelty, adultery, desertion or in some jurisdictions, insanity.

In the mid 1960s, family behaviour changed in the developed countries, at a pace that took even professional demographers by surprise, not because the phenomena were new but because their 'scale was unprecedented' (Glendon, 2006, p. 4). These changes went hand in hand with broader social changes, some of which we discuss below in the context of British society. On a more global basis, as far as Westernized civilizations were concerned, these changes included a rise in geographical mobility, the increased labour force participation of married women and mothers of young children, increased control over procreation, and greater longevity. By the end of the 1980s, the major demographic indicators appeared to have stabilized in the developed countries but remained at their new high or low levels, registering only modest rises or declines (Bahr, 2002, pp. 5–6; and see further Fukuyama, *The Great Disruption*, 1999, for a discussion of the social, economic and political implications of these changes). As Glendon notes, as well as these changes, came 'less quantifiable but no less momentous shifts in the meanings that men and women attribute to sex and procreation, marriage, gender, parenthood, kinship relations and to life itself' (Glendon, 2006, p. 4). Even more remarkable was that these changes have taken place in less than 20 years (Roussel, *Demographie – Deux Decennies de Mutations dans les Pays Industrialises* in Meulders-Klein and Eekelaar (eds), *Family, State and Individual Security*, 1988, pp. 37–41). In the developing countries where globalization was disrupting well-entrenched customs and patterns of family organization, 'family law was often at the centre of religious, ethnic and political strife' (Glendon, 2006, p. 4).

Marriage and the family in the twenty-first century

Towards the end of the twentieth century and in the first few years of the twenty-first century, in North America, Europe, Japan and Australia, birth rates and marriage rates have fallen precipitously, while divorce rates, the number of children born outside marriage, and the incidence of non-marital cohabitation have risen to high levels. Women have also joined the paid workforce en masse which has had an impact on parental roles and property relations between partners.

A new concept of 'family'?

At the heart of these momentous changes has been 'a basic redefinition of family from a unit defined exclusively by blood and procreation, to a unit increasingly defined by intentionality – what the participants intend' (Pinsof, 2002, p. 152).

The family – then and now

There is abundant evidence that across the world, in common law and civil law countries, the last three decades, commencing from the mid 1960s, have seen turbulent change in families and family law. The nature of marriage, the incidence of cohabitation outside marriage, the rates of divorce, the relationship between husband and wife, and the relationship between parent and child have all undergone significant changes. Two other significant developments have occurred in the law's attitude towards gender, homosexuality and adultery and their impact on the granting of a divorce; and the legal and social recognition of same-sex unions. There have also been new techniques of artificial insemination.

Yet another widespread tendency, according to Glendon, is the policy to decrease state regulation of marriage formation and dissolution, more so in the Anglo-American jurisdictions than in the civil law systems (Glendon, 2006, p. 7). In the Romano-Germanic legal systems, the trend has been to have closer judicial supervision of parties' agreements in relation to support, property division and custody upon divorce (Glendon, 2006, p. 7).

The decline of marriage and the rise of cohabitation

In 2007, it was accurate for Marsha Garrison to observe that marriage is in decline all over the industrialized world (Garrison, 2007, p. 491). Krause has also made the comment that as the twentieth century drew to a close 'no social institution was under greater pressure than marriage and the family' (Krause, 2000, p. 271). However, American academics such as Estin and Morrison still argue that marriage as an institution retains its fundamental importance and should be part of social policy in any society (see Estin, 2008, p. 352; Morrison, 2000, p. 79).

In England and Wales, there is statistical evidence to suggest that marriage rates have declined between 1979 and 1995 and despite a rise in 2000 (of 1.7 per cent) there has been a fall in the numbers of marriages in the early twenty-first century. Indeed, at least statistically speaking, there appears to be a long-term downward trend. Alongside this trend has been a spectacular increase in cohabitation outside marriage since the mid 1990s, and available statistics say that 25 per cent of all non-married adults aged between 16 and 59 currently cohabit outside marriage (*Social Trends* 33, 2003, The Stationery Office).

The number of marriages contracted in 2005 (244,710) was the lowest since 1896, when the British population was half the current size. This rate was down by 10 per cent since 2004. The 2006 figures showed that there were 4 per cent fewer marriages than in 2005, being 236,980 in total, and this represents the lowest number of people getting married since 1862, the year when records began. There were also fewer divorces on record, which is hardly surprising since fewer people were getting married in the first place.

On the cohabitational front, in the ten years from 1996 to 2006, the number of cohabiting couples increased by 65 per cent or 900,000. They are currently the 'fastest-growing family type in the UK' (Curtis, 2007; *The Guardian*, 5 October 2007, p. 13). The trend in the early years of the twenty-first century was that 29 per cent of all women under 50 were cohabiting, which was in stark contrast to 11 per cent in 1979, and this number is expected to double by 2021 (Shaw and Haskey, 1999).

Law and the family – is there a new pair-bonding paradigm?

In the early twenty-first century, a new pair-bonding paradigm has begun to emerge which integrates the implications of the death-to-divorce transition but sees law struggling to keep pace with it (Pinsof, 2002, p. 151). This includes new structures formed by cohabitation outside marriage and non-marital co-parenting. Attempts have been made to determine and enforce the rights and mutual obligations of non-marital partners, the legal obligations and rights of unmarried fathers to their children, the access rights of the parents and siblings of divorced or never-married parents to their grandchildren and nephews or nieces and the rights of same-sex couples to marry (Morrissey, 2002).

Nevertheless, the legal community has responded to the new pair-bonding phenomena with ambivalence, with many legal experts calling for sweeping changes in the law.

Glendon observes that family law has become a 'testing ground for various ways of re-imagining family relations and, at times, an arena for struggles among competing ideas about individual liberty, human sexuality, marriage and family life, and responsibility for the care of the very young and the frail elderly' (Glendon, 2006, p. 4).

The courts and legislatures in many countries, especially in America and Britain, have responded to these changes by emphasizing and applying values such as equality and individual liberty. Hence, under the influence of the equality principle, most distinctions between marital and non-marital children have been abolished, as well as most (but not all) legal differences between the rights and responsibilities between husbands and wives and mothers and fathers. Indeed, Glendon asserts that the principle of non-discrimination has been invoked to assimilate the legal treatment of informal cohabitants or same-sex relationships to marriage (Glendon, 2006, p. 4).

Nevertheless, the present writer notes that not all vestiges of the legal heritage have been removed, as for instance, campaigners for fathers' rights will testify in the context of contact with their children post-separation.

At the beginning of the twenty-first century, courts and legislatures have been grappling with the problem of how to determine 'when differential legal treatment should be banned as discriminatory, and when it should be regarded as an appropriate response to important differences' (Glendon, 2006, p. 4).

JURISDICTIONAL REVIEW

England and Wales

Family law in Britain over the last 125 years

In an article published in 2005, which reviews some of the key characteristics in British families and family law over the last 125 years, Mr Justice Munby mentions three great pillars on which traditional family law (in Britain) was founded. The first was the basis of the family being a marriage that was Christian (or if not Christian, then its secular or other religious equivalent) and at least in theory, a lifelong union (Munby, 2005, p. 487). This meant the typical family was reflected in the *Hyde v Hyde* template 'as understood in Christendom ... defined as the voluntary union for life of one man and one woman, to the exclusion of all others' (see *Hyde v Hyde* (1866) LR 1 P&D 130 at 133). The second was the unequal relationship between husband and wife, as typified in various cases like *Durham v Durham* (1885) 10 PD 80 at 81, in which Sir James Hannen P talked about the man offering his 'protection' as part of the nature of marriage in return for the 'submission' of the woman. Even as late as the middle of the nineteenth century, the husband had the right to his wife's consortium whereas she had the duty to give him her society and her services (Munby, 2005, p. 488). The third pillar was the unregulated control of the father over the relationship of parent and child. Hence, while the father had virtually absolute power over the child as its legal guardian, the mother, unlike that of an errant father, was in a far from secure position and any moral failing on her part was enough to warrant her permanent separation from her child. Hence, an adulterous wife would be denied not only custody of but also access to her children, which was regarded as having a 'salutary effect in the interests of public morality' (*Seddon v Seddon* (1862) 2 Sw &Tr 640 at 642 per Sir Cresswell Cresswell). This was a particularly notorious illustration of the judicial attitude in the nineteenth century, as the husband in this case had also been guilty of misconduct conducing to his wife's adultery, described as a 'most unfavourable character' by the learned judge who, in the same breath, also said that the wife should suffer the consequences of her conduct.

Changes in English family law in the late twentieth and early twenty-first century

Over the last 125 years, there have been profound changes in British society and in English family law. Munby describes the history of family law in the past 125 years as being the history of first, the emancipation of the married woman; second, the partial emancipation of the child; and third, a revolution in sexual mores.

Munby identifies four major developments as the reasons for these changes. The first is the enormous changes in the social and religious life of Britain, and he says we now live in a 'secular and pluralistic society', which is also a multicultural community of many faiths (Munby, 2005, p. 503). The second, he argues, is an increasing lack of interest in and sometimes even a conscious rejection of marriage as an institution; at the same time, divorce is virtually permitted on demand. Third, there has been a sea-change in society's attitudes towards same-sex unions, so that within the learned judge's professional lifetime, there has been a change in attitude towards such unions from treating them as perversions which should be stamped out by the criminal law to an acknowledgment that these unions are entitled not only to respect but also to equal protection under the law (*Ghaidan v Godin-Mendoza* [2004] 2 AC 557). Fourth, there have been enormous advances in medical, and especially reproductive, science so that reproduction is no longer restricted to 'natural' methods, resulting in many children being born today as a result of 'high tech' IVF methods which could not have been imagined before.

Barlow and James argue that '[m]arriage has simply lost its power to hold people together' (Barlow and James, 2004, p. 178) and offer reasons for this loss of power. They assert: 'The social structures which gave it this power have been greatly weakened by lack of religion, women's financial independence, state support for lone parents, separation of sex from marriage and of child-bearing from marriage, ease of divorce [and] ease of cohabitation' (Barlow and James, 2004, p. 178).

Problems with attempts to reform cohabitation

As we have seen from our preceding survey of the law relating to cohabitation, there have always been difficulties surrounding any state attempts to reform cohabitation. Douglas, Pearce and Woodward argue that their study of the progress of cohabitants' disputes, and the views of clients and practitioners involved, shows that the 'current law produces significant injustice' affecting both men and women (Douglas *et al.*, 2009, p. 46). However, attempts to reform cohabitation run into at least two difficulties; one primarily ideological, the other judicial but both politically contentious. The first approach, in their view, might have been to conceive the issue in terms of whether cohabitants should be 'entitled' to claim property or support from each other. This would focus the debate on whether cohabitation is sufficiently similar to marriage to justify greater recognition or protection and end discrimination against those who do not marry, and 'whether in so doing, the law will diminish the significance and privileged position occupied by marital status'.

The second approach would be to encourage a broader recognition of 'contributions' which show that a claimant has 'earned' a share of property, but this appears to present an obstacle to reform because the courts have shown a reluctance to make more explicit forays into an area which has clear policy implications.

They suggest a third way of dealing with the problem of unfairness, which is to re-conceive the issue as one of unjust enrichment which would enable the legal process to 'focus on doing justice between the individual partners' (Douglas *et al.*, 2009, p 47).

The need to address problems with the existing law

Writing extra-judicially, Justice Munby sees the 'most pressing problem' in family law as being to address the inadequacies of the existing law when dealing with anything other than the traditional family founded on a marriage, since [English] family law has now trifurcated. There is one family law for those of different sexes who have married; another for those of the same sex who choose to enter into a civil partnership; and a third, or perhaps virtually no family law at all, for those couples who, for whatever reasons, choose neither to marry nor to enter into a civil partnership, which he argues causes hardship to many; both adults and children (Munby, 2005, pp. 508–9).

Europe

The past

Goody writes: 'The past of the European family influences its present, both its continuities and discontinuities ... there is no end to the family; some kind of sexual coupling and child care is essential for the vast majority of humankind' (Goody, 1999, p. 1). The early roots of the European family lie in the classical Mediterranean civilizations of Greece and Rome as well as in the Germanic and Celtic tribal societies that dominated much of the north and west of the continent when those civilizations flourished to the south. Both strands have been held responsible for significant aspects of the family in later Europe, especially Rome for family law (Goody, 1999, p. 2).

The influence of the Catholic Church

The influence of Christianity was far-reaching and enduring. It affected countries such as India and parts of Africa which adopted the Christian faith through the influence of foreign and local missionaries, and where divorce was deemed impossible. Goody reminds us that Europe 'began to differ substantially from Asia and from the surrounding Mediterranean when it adopted Christianity with its very specific selection of new norms' (Goody, 1999, p. 10). These were not merely diacritical features which were not solely intended to differentiate Christians from

Jews and pagans but were specifically designed to establish and maintain the church as a major organization in society (Goody, 1999, p. 10).

Common features of family law in European countries – an historical snapshot

Goody lists common features of the typical historical pattern of family life which his research revealed. These are the general points relating to kinship, family and marriage. First, he claims there is virtually no society in the history of humanity where the nuclear family was not important, in the vast majority of cases as a co-residential group. Second, even in regions where the family is not jurally monogamous, it often has been monogamous in practice, with the basic unit of production and reproduction being always relatively small. Third, even where unilineal descent groups exist, there has always been the element of consanguinal (bilateral) ties between both parents, including the one through whom descent is not reckoned. Hence, Goody explains, even in patrilineal societies, the mother's brother has always been an important figure. Fourth, in no society have the ties between mother and child (and, in the vast majority, between father and child) been unimportant, sentimentally or jurally, even though in some cases those ties have been somewhat minimalized (Goody, 1999, pp. 2–3). In classical times, Greece and Rome both gave some emphasis to unilineal descent groups (patrilineal groups and clans) but these 'largely disappeared under the impact of the German invaders with their bilateral kindreds and under pressure from the Christian Church which weakened all wider kinship groups by effectively limiting their extent and initiating an alternative system of ritual relations, of godparenthood' (Goody, 1999, p. 3). All this eventually diminished in importance, until the effective range of kin relations in Europe became barely more than the descendants of a grandparental couple; that is, immediate uncles and aunts (siblings of parents) and their children (first cousins) (Goody, 1999, p. 3).

The links with more modern familial relationship networks are clearly discernible.

Key changes in the nature of the family in Western society

In his 2005 lecture, Justice Munby, writing extra-judicially, notes that the nature of the family 'has further been transformed in particular by three technological as well as sociological developments: first, the general use of contraception, secondly, the legalisation of abortion and, most recently, advances in reproductive science' (Munby, 2005, p. 483).

Munby believes that contemporary Britain is a largely secular society and is increasingly diverse in religious affiliation (Munby, 2005, p. 493). Krause believes that in contemporary times, and in many countries, 'a secular, pragmatic view of the family is spreading' (Krause, 2008, p. 1113). He argues that the looser interpretations of marriage and the family and the 'decreasing everyday relevance of religion' have brought about new, more reason-based solutions (Krause, 2008, p. 1113). Clearly this would not apply to those countries, such as Brazil, Argentina and parts of Asia and Africa, which continue to have religion as a dominant guiding influence in their everyday activities.

The present – the continuing relevance of fault

Despite the considerably diminished influence in Britain first of the Catholic Church and then of the Anglican Church, there is no doubt that the concept of fault, originating from the notion of sin, continues to manifest itself in family law, albeit to a negligible extent in divorce, usually only playing a subsidiary role in the English courts' allocation of financial provision upon divorce and in isolated aspects of criminal law. This is comprehensively analysed by Bainham who charts the past and present influence of fault in the context of divorce, domestic violence and occupation of the family home, in property and financial matters, in disputes and cases involving children (see Bainham, 2003 and Part I for a discussion of Bainham's analysis).

Fault continues to be relevant to French law, and indeed, the element of fault and accountability in divorce cases has re-emerged in the United States as a reason for apparent dissatisfaction with the current divorce laws and the body of opinion that wishes to curb or even reverse the no-fault divorce laws in many American jurisdictions. This has provoked strong responses from academics in both the no-fault and fault camps to argue the case for each stance (see Part II, Chapter Two on family law in the United States for a discussion of the arguments for and against no-fault divorce).

Africa and Asia

In Asian and African jurisdictions, common themes include the arranged marriage (which used to be the practice of Western aristocracy until recently), and in African societies, the role of the extended families who played (and in some cases, still play) an active part in the formation and dissolution of marriage, the brideprice (again a practice carried out in the West by the wealthy classes), and the vexed status of the secondary wife and the concubine, particularly in cases of intestate succession. There is also the ongoing quest by women for equality with men and for greater recognition of their worth as women. The African male retains considerable marital power over his wife, especially in cases where customary law prevails. Substantial similarity exists between the family laws of other common law jurisdictions such as Singapore, Hong Kong, India and English law, mutatis mutandis. Variations can be found where former colonies such as Singapore have introduced unusual statutes, for example the Maintenance of Parents Act 1995, which gives parents above 60 who are unable to maintain themselves financially the right to claim maintenance from their children.

Same-sex marriage was recognized in South Africa in November 2006. This echoes the legal changes that have taken place in Belgium, Canada, the Netherlands and Spain.

Other jurisdictions

Socialist and post-socialist countries

The more recent reforms in family law in the Russian Federation were discussed in some detail in Part III, Chapter Five. However, it is worth noting that while Russia and the socialist countries of Eastern Europe were worth separate and special consideration in the 1960s, they have since begun their historic transition towards market economies and more democratic forms of government, which might suggest they will reflect more typical Western patterns in their family lives. Nevertheless, it is claimed that Russia is the first country in the world to declare 'full equality between a man and a woman, to give women equal political and civil rights and to equalize them with their husbands in family relations' (Khazova, 2002, p. 354). But this equalization, which occurred immediately in 1917 through the Revolution, meant that neither women nor society were prepared either economically or psychologically for such equality, with 90 per cent of Russian families corresponding to the patriarchal mould. Ironically, state economic and social policy over the last few decades has made it almost impossible for women to stay at home to be housewives and the current reality is that married women who do stay at home and who are totally dependent on their husbands may be left without any financial support in the event of divorce or conflict in the family (Khazova, 2002, p. 353). This is because there is no mandatory legal obligation (as opposed to a moral one) between the spouses to maintain each other in Russian law, unless there are special justifying circumstances. Hence a restoration of the housewife role is being sought in the Russia of today, and a 'patriarchal renaissance' is apparently required to protect the women who need financial support for themselves and their families.

DIVORCE

The fault/no-fault dichotomy in divorce law – convergence or divergence?

As we have seen from the common law and civil law jurisdictions we have examined, the grounds for divorce have not simply swung from fault-based to non-fault-based, despite the apparent liberalization and so-called modernization of divorce. Jurisdictions like France and the United Kingdom continue to have both fault and no-fault grounds in their divorce laws. In addition, jurisdictions that purport to have purely no-fault divorce in fact still retain fault grounds for certain purposes allied to the post-separation and/or divorce process. Indeed, Antokolskaia's review of the divorce laws of the countries of Western Europe, which we alluded to at the beginning of this book (see Part I), suggests to her that the question of whether family law within Europe has been and is converging, remains controversial. She points out, agreeing with Willekens (see Willekens, 1997, p. 60), that the mere choice of a period of investigation can be 'decisive' for the outcome of one's research, and that 'the different appreciation of the convergence/divergence tendency often has to do with the examination of too short time-spans' (Antokolskaia, 2006, p. 308). This would mean that it would be quite easy to fall into the trap of 'selectiveness' by focusing only on those periods which tend to affirm one's starting point (Antokolskaia, 2006, p. 308).

Antokolskaia argues that the issue of whether there was a convergence tendency in the period of the early Reformation is a 'question of perception', since two contrasting events took place. On the one hand, the main event in Western Europe was the transformation from the uniformity of Roman Catholic canon law to the Protestant-Catholic dichotomy in the first place, and the mutual diversity among the Protestant laws in the second place. On the other hand, the Reformation was an extra-national phenomenon, so the states influenced by the same denomination or Reformation ideology had similar divorce laws. Nevertheless, she observes that a clear divergence of family laws occurred as a result of the Reformation because, if nothing else, in the Protestant countries, divorce, for the first time after centuries of dominance by Catholic doctrine, was permissible again (Antokolskaia, 2006, p. 311).

She concedes that 'the history of divorce law during the last half-millennium clearly shows a general development of divorce law in Europe in the same direction: from more restrictive to more permissive' (Antokolskaia, 2006, p. 327). Indeed, she notes that the 'choices, the ideological background and the political colour of the principal participants in the divorce debates are the same everywhere' (Antokolskaia, 2006, p. 327). However, she also observes that there has been a significant divergence in the 'profundity and pace of modernisation of family laws from one European country to another' but argues that it is important to separate the question of whether there has been a tendency towards modernisation of divorce laws in Europe from the issue of whether there has been a convergence of divorce laws (Antokolskaia, 2006, p. 327).

History has shown that there has been an undeniable tendency towards modernization but Antokolskaia found no clear indication that the level of similarity of divorce laws in Europe will greatly increase in the near future and thus it is not very probable that harmonization of family law will take place through 'spontaneous convergence' (Antokolskaia, 2006, pp. 329–30).

There has also not been any clear-cut swing from fault to no-fault divorce grounds in the various jurisdictions and a combination of these grounds still exist, despite expectations that fault as a ground for divorce would disappear altogether. Although there has been a movement away from adultery as the dominant, and initially only, ground for divorce in most jurisdictions, fault-based behaviour continues to be a factor in many divorce laws around the world, if not explicitly then certainly as an available ground for obtaining a divorce. This is borne out by various surveys of several jurisdictions, especially that of Konig and Glendon (see Part I). As a matter of statistical interest, 68.6 per cent of divorces in England and Wales are granted on the basis of fault grounds (Lowe, 2003, p. 103). As Antokolskaia puts it, 'in spite of all the optimistic expectations that were derived from the no-fault reforms, no substantial common core has so far emerged' (Antokolskaia, 2007, p. 253).

England and Wales

Fault and no-fault grounds co-exist in the current divorce laws of England and Wales, as a consequence of the non-enactment of the Family Law Act 1996 which would have abolished fault-based grounds altogether. Three of the statutory 'facts' which are available to establish irretrievable breakdown involve fault-based conduct under the current Matrimonial Causes Act 1973 (UK). Divorce has become an administrative procedure since 1977, and very few cases reach the courts, except where there is a dispute over property and children. The vast majority of divorces take place by mutual consent of the parties and a recent survey reveals that fault-based grounds constitute around 68 per cent of the petitions which are granted a divorce (Lowe, 2003, p. 103). Most parties tend to opt for the shortest route to a divorce and this has been a fairly consistent trend over the years.

The United States

The movement for the return to fault-based divorce

Our study has revealed that there appears to be a movement among certain sections of the population for a return to fault-based divorce. However, there is no consensus in the United States as to whether divorce laws should return to the 'fault era' with more accountability and attention being paid to conduct and behaviour within a marriage.

In California, although the sole ground for divorce is supposedly breakdown and therefore based on no-fault, the breakdown of the marriage can still be stated as having been caused by a marital offence making the continuation of marital life intolerable. This indicates that the old fault principle is still there under the guise of breakdown (Verschraegen, 2004, p. 75). The crucial feature under this law is that a no-fault reason such as separation allows for a delayed divorce, but if a fault reason is pleaded, this leads to a quick divorce, provided the judge is satisfied that marital misconduct has occurred making marital life intolerable. A similar link of fault in the form of marital misconduct and no-fault can be found in jurisdictions such as South Africa and, indeed, in England and Wales.

Until the 1960s, all American jurisdictions (theoretically) required proof of fault by the respondent before the petitioner could obtain a divorce (see Foster, 'Divorce Reform and the Uniform Act' (1973) 18 *South Dakota Law Review* 572). States then began to accept unilateral no-fault divorce and currently practically all

States accept no-fault divorce (see Weitzman, *The Divorce Revolution*, 1985, and Parkman, *No-Fault Divorce: What Went Wrong?*1992).

Oldham notes that during the past 50 years, American society has changed in many ways, inter alia, with an increased divorce rate and the length of time marriages have lasted when couples reach the point of divorce also (on average) having increased, 'thereby making it more precarious to be an economically vulnerable partner in a romantic relationship' (Oldham, 2008, p. 446).

Europe

In France, divorce grounded on fault is the most prevalent, because this will allow an immediate divorce. Apparently parties regard grounds based on mutual consent as too cumbersome, yet divorce by mutual consent will entitle parties to a divorce without the need to prove that the parties agree on the consequences of the divorce. The parties simply need to agree certain facts leading to the breakdown of the marriage (Verschraegen, 2004, p. 75).

Asia and Africa

Former British colonies, for example India and Singapore, have divorce laws which resemble English divorce laws. They have embraced the notion of irretrievable breakdown as one of the fundamental grounds which would justify a divorce, but they have also retained fault grounds. Indeed, in Singapore, as in England, Canada and Australia, the trend in divorce petitions (as recently as in 2007) is that there is a continued reliance on allegations of fault on the part of the respondent. India has a three-tier divorce structure, comprising fault grounds, the breakdown theory and the mutual consent principle.

In South Africa, one of the factors by which irretrievable breakdown may be proved is where adultery is pleaded by the petitioner as irreconcilable with the continuation of marital life.

Other jurisdictions

Divorce in Russia has borne the imprint of a civil law mentalité, the effects of its Revolution and, more recently, the post-Revolution experience of dialectical materialism, communism and socialism, followed by the abandonment of its particular brand of socialism at the end of the 1980s. In the twenty-first century, Russia has retained its legacy of a civil law type of jurisdiction by promulgating and reforming its laws in the form of comprehensive Codes which are authoritative, comprehensive and declaratory, and which reflect some of its earlier ideological principles. Russia has experienced customary law, a monarchy, postcard divorces and has latterly adopted a more Westernized divorce law (see Part II, Chapter Five on Russian law).

MATRIMONIAL PROPERTY

General observations

Those systems of matrimonial property law which were universally in effect far into the nineteenth century 'were characterised by ... the general rule that the husband had the power to control all of the couple's property irrespective of whether title was in him, in his wife, or jointly in both' (Rheinstein and Glendon, 1980, p. 33). The husband had control of all the fruits of the combined funds and bore all the expenses of the family. Even following the marriage of single women of full age who had become legally capable of managing their property, their husbands retained the power to control the property of his wife. Changes eventually came about with the Industrial Revolution but the process of transformation was slow and gradual and 'nowhere did it acquire impetus until the very structure and spirit of society were transformed by industrialization and urbanization or by revolution' (Rheinstein and Glendon, 1980, p. 40). The notion of fault continues to play a part in both English and American jurisdictions but in their own way, and in mainly exceptional cases. It is only considered a relevant consideration by courts where the 'faulty conduct' is extreme and/or causes some form of serious harm, loss or injury.

England and Wales

Equal distribution of matrimonial property upon divorce?

The manner in which the distribution of a couple's assets is decided when they divorce is governed by statute, namely the Matrimonial Causes Act 1973. However, in typical English style, the relevant statutory provisions must be interpreted by the courts, which have a very wide discretion under the key provision, s. 25. This statute lists seven guidelines, with no hierarchy of importance, as each case will turn on its own merits.

From the mid 1970s until 2000, the focus was on the applicant's 'reasonable needs' but this changed with the landmark case of *White v White* [2001] 1 AC at 605 and cases such as *Lambert v Lambert* [2003] 2 WLR 63.

The effect of White and Lambert – deferred community of property?

Cretney describes the combined effect of the decision of the House of Lords in *White v White* [2001] 1 AC 596 and the Court of Appeal in *Lambert v Lambert* [2003] 2 WLR 63 as 'dramatic' because they introduced into English law a regime of (deferred) community of property limited to acquisitions. As we saw in Part II, Chapter Five on Russian Law, the effect of these cases is that when a marriage is ended by divorce, and the couple have considerable financial assets, the court will, after making provision for the family's housing and other needs, seek to divide up the spouses' property so that each has an equal share. There has been some uncertainty among practitioners and academics as to whether the *White v White* approach of advocating an equal distribution in order to be fair to both parties through the 'yardstick of equality', applies only to the so-called 'big money' cases where the available assets are far in excess of an applicant's needs or whether it has a wider application to cases where the assets are not considerable or abundant, involving middle-income couples. Academic comments on these cases have been plentiful, speculating on what should or should not be regarded as the correct approach in these sorts of cases and as to what would be fair in each case.

Herring argues that seeking fairness as between the parties is not only 'misguided' but 'undesirable' in this context (Herring, 2005, p. 219). He lists no less than eight interests which the state or wider community has in financial orders made on divorce which transcend the notion that such orders should be made as if they are purely a private matter between the parties. These include the state's interest in whether on divorce either party becomes dependent on welfare payments; the impact of such payments on how children and incapacitated adults are cared for by married couples; the symbolic power of financial orders; the impact of the level of spousal support on whether the child-caring spouse is employed or not, their level of happiness and self-respect and so on; the knowledge of what such orders are likely to be might even affect a party's decision on whether to seek a divorce or not; the impact of such orders on how people behave following divorce; an approach based on fairness inter partes does not help to combat the poverty women face on divorce; and it is important that couples regard marriage in more mutual terms rather than as potential claimants in civil litigation hence marriage should be viewed as a partnership of mutual obligation (see Herring, 2005).

On the practical front, a small scale survey of family practitioners carried out by Emma Hitchings over a five-month period between September 2007 and February 2008, suggests that cases like *White* have not really had a significant impact on everyday cases of ancillary relief (that is those not involving 'big money'), since every marriage/divorce is unique, hence these landmark cases, at least in the latter years of the first decade of the new millennium, appear to be of only passing relevance (Hitchings, 2008).

Greater judicial recognition of the value of homemaker services in financial awards upon divorce

White v White [2001] 1 AC 596 is also notable for the statement by Lord Nicholls at 564: 'There should be no bias in favour of the money-earner and against the home-maker and childcarer.' He argued that to draw such a distinction would perpetuate discrimination and sent out a clear message that child-rearing or home-making should not somehow be considered less valuable but indeed equal to money-earning (Silbaugh, 1996).

The relevance of adverse conduct or fault on financial provision to spouses upon divorce

Current English law shows that fault or adverse conduct is still relevant to the allocation of financial provision in divorce and ancillary relief proceedings, and must be considered under s. 25(2)(g) of the Matrimonial Causes Act 1973, but usually only where the conduct is extreme (personal violence towards a spouse, gross behaviour such as hiring a person to kill a spouse, child abuse within the family, treating a spouse in a particularly degrading manner, for example imprisoning him in a caravan while the wife stays in the family home with her young lover). However if both spouses have engaged in equally disgusting behaviour, the court might disregard the conduct altogether in making the financial award post-divorce (see *Leadbeater* [1985] FLR 789).

As the House of Lords made clear in *Miller* [2006] UKHL 24, conduct is only to be taken into account in exceptional cases where it satisfies the criteria under the Matrimonial Causes Act 1973; that is, where it would be 'inequitable to disregard' it and where it can be clearly seen that one party is more to blame than the other.

In the United States, the position in the early twenty-first century is that a majority of jurisdictions has held that fault is only a relevant consideration in the court's distribution of property where it has an economic impact on the marriage. Of the 49 jurisdictions which permit the trial court to divide marital property equitably, 27 do not permit consideration of fault that has no economic impact. For fault to be considered, it has either to have directly affected the amount of property available for allocation in the wake of the divorce, or it was conduct which constituted an extreme form of harm and damage. Otherwise, a victimized spouse would still receive prima facie half of the marital property upon divorce (see Part II, Chapter Two on United States law, for references which support these points).

Comparative perspectives on marital property regimes in European law

A fundamental difference in approach between English common law and most of continental Europe may be noted, namely that there is no system of property regimes as such under English law. Hence in English law, since 1882, under the Married Women's Property Act of that year, married women have acquired no particular proprietary rights on marriage and are governed by a 'separate property' rule, that is, both parties retain their individual, separate rights to property when they marry. Hence, unless there is a specific written agreement to the contrary, if a married woman brings no personal wealth to the marriage or acquires any after it, she would acquire no property rights purely by virtue of her marriage. In contrast, under the Napoleonic Code of 1804, France adopted a matrimonial property regime whereby there was community of moveable property brought to the marriage and community of any property of any nature acquired after the marriage. Of course, the parties have the option to enter into a different regime under a prenuptial agreement but the party found to be 'at fault' for the divorce who is also a donee will not be able to enforce such an agreement; the same applies if he is the applicant to a separation divorce. Germany has a deferred community property regime, also called the community of gains, whereby there is separate ownership of property by the couple during the marriage but, as soon as the couple divorces, any surplus which one partner might have earned during the marriage will be halved and paid to the other partner.

United States

The early American immigrants took with them English law and English family law traditions which meant that they retained the English common law legal method. This is built on the centrality of case law as the key source of law, supported and supplemented by legislation. However, although the common law approach remains in cases, courts, administrative procedures and principles, the influence and impact of the American written Constitution has led to a different focus in the application of their laws. Four themes may be highlighted: (i) the distribution of marital property at divorce; (ii) changes in the economic consequences of divorce; (iii) convergence of community property and the common law system; and (iv) the acceptance of premarital/prenuptial agreements.

Distribution of marital property at divorce

Several States have diverged from the classic English common law approach to the distribution of property upon divorce. A key difference has been the adoption of community property or deferred community property which is usually associated with the Franco-German matrimonial systems. However, as far as couples whose assets far exceed their reasonable needs, if they approach a court in England for an order for property division and spousal maintenance, the impact of cases such as *White v White* (2000) means that the English courts have created a deferred community property system for some cases. Their approach in these 'big money' cases is to try to make financial awards in accordance with a 'yardstick of equality' and 'fairness' and this could mean a 50/50 split (see Cretney (2003) p. 249).

Changes in the economic consequences of divorce and marital property

Oldham notes: '[I]n the last few decades, it became accepted in all states that a divorce court has the power to divide some or all of the spouses' property, and this routinely occurs in divorces today if the parties have property to divide. Before that time, there was no express statutory authority for equitable distribution of the parties' property' (Oldham, 2008, 427). This did not mean that legal authority did not exist in any non-community property States before a few decades ago. On the contrary, between 1939 and 1948 a number of States displayed enthusiasm for a community property system so long as it provided tax advantages for married couples. These were repealed when the tax advantages were no longer available (Oldham, 2008, p. 428). In the late nineteenth and early twentieth centuries, a wealth of case law reveals that a number of States had adopted statutes that gave divorce courts the power to divide property. Nevertheless, it was not until the 1970s and 1980s that a majority of non-community property States enacted equitable distribution statutes (Oldham, 2008, p. 428 and see the many cases and statutes cited therein under fn. 68).

Convergence of community property and common law systems

Fifty years ago, many common law States did not expressly permit property division at divorce. As of 2008, all States accept some version of a deferred community or community property system (Oldham, 2008, p. 429). Hence, the majority of States allow only certain property to be divided (frequently all acquisitions during marriage other than gifts or inheritances) and a minority permit all property to be divided. In a few community property States, marital property has to be divided equally but all other States permit an equitable division of property (Oldham, 2008, p. 429).

Acceptance of premarital/prenuptial agreements

Now that premarital agreements have become acceptable in the United States, it has been possible for the rights of the economically vulnerable spouse upon divorce to be reduced through contract or even eliminated in some States. Hence, if there is no prenuptial agreement, it has become generally accepted that most property accumulated during marriage will be divided approximately equally between the spouses at divorce (Oldham, 2008, p. 446). If there are minor children, all States have established a formula for calculating the presumptive amount of child support (Oldham, 2008, pp. 446–7). In a related development, and in contrast with child support practice, in almost all States, the spousal support rules now give the United States courts considerable discretion (Oldham, 2008, p. 447). This echoes the English approach where the relevant statute (Matrimonial Causes Act 1973) gives the courts a very wide discretion in deciding spousal maintenance and property division upon divorce. However, the English judiciary have not shown any enthusiasm until very recently about recognizing prenuptial agreements, although this may well change in the future. A landmark ruling by the English Court of Appeal in July 2009 suggests that England should not be out of step with other countries and that in future prenuptial agreements should be regarded as binding unless there is a reason not to do so (see 'The Radmacher Case', *The Times*, 3 July 2009). The case will probably go on appeal.

Other common law jurisdictions

Australia has a separate property regime, thus marriage per se has no effect on the spousal property rights. As under English law, however, upon separation the courts have a wide statutory discretion to alter the property rights of the parties.

New Zealand has introduced via statute an equal division of matrimonial property (subject to exceptions, including a right to contract out of the relevant statute), in the Matrimonial Property Act 1976. Hence a deferred community or deferred participation scheme exists with regard to property like gifts, bequests and property owned before marriage.

DOMESTIC VIOLENCE

Overview

Greater protection for women from domestic violence has been noticeable in the last three decades but progress has been neither uniform nor speedy for a variety of reasons. These range from doctrinal (the unity principle whereby husband and wife were one, and that one was the husband); to cultural (law enforcement agencies regarded violence within the family as a private matter and the state and the law should not intrude into a private sphere of activity); to intrinsically negative (because the victims of such violence are unwilling to report such incidents, and even if they do will retract their testimony or change their minds about testifying against the perpetrators of such behaviour).

England and Wales

English law on domestic violence has developed in a piecemeal fashion. In the 1970s, legal remedies were based on the type of court in which a complainant brought their case. Thus, the cheaper magistrates' courts had a limited range of remedies under the relevant statute, whereas the statute regulating actions in the more expensive High Court and county courts was able to provide more effective remedies – at least in the sense that conduct such as pestering and molestation, which fell short of physical violence, could still be addressed by legal action. The problem of the private/public divide continued to cast a shadow and it has been only relatively recently (in the 1990s) that the police have been given more sensitive guidelines about how to deal with complaints about domestic violence and not be inhibited from taking action because of any notion that alleged violence taking place between domestic partners is a private matter best left to be sorted behind closed doors. Eventually, the two main statutes were supplemented by another statute which permitted the eviction (albeit temporary) of a spouse from a matrimonial home if there had been evidence of conduct amounting to physical and other forms of serious violence. The current law was expanded further in 2007 and now includes stalking and other forms of harassment and the main criterion which guides the courts is a balance of harm test.

There appear to be conflicting reports regarding the effectiveness of the latest domestic violence law in Britain towards the end of the first decade of the twenty-first century. *The Times* ('Women at risk failed by domestic violence law', April 14, 2008) reported that thousands of women continue to be at risk of assault because the new laws have backfired. Victims are reluctant to obtain a court order, since this might give their partners a criminal record and up to five years' imprisonment. However, the Crown Prosecution Service has denied the claim by a judge (reported in the same *Times* article) that non-molestation orders have fallen by between 25 per cent and 30 per cent. The Crown Prosecution Service claims that the number of cases and the conviction rate has been higher than in previous years.

Europe

Both France and Germany have several statutory measures to deal with domestic violence. France recognizes domestic violence as a crime and treats the violence committed by a husband or partner as an aggravating factor to the offence. Marital rape is recognized as a crime, and French law may order the eviction of a violent spouse and remove the right of the victim to continue to reside in the family home. The German Penal Code prescribes severe penalties for crimes of violence against human beings and this includes crimes of marital and domestic violence, yet domestic violence is still not treated as a crime prosecuted by private indictment, thus the police and state authorities are obliged to institute criminal proceedings whenever they are informed that an incident of violence has occurred. There is also a statute which provides for the use of video in criminal proceedings to protect the victim from the stressful procedure of direct testimony and from having contact with the offender. All 16 German district police forces have their own domestic violence regulations but apparently differ in their willingness to implement these regulations.

In 2005, a new law was implemented which introduced the Platzverweiz, a court or police order which places an injunction, exclusion, displacement or banning order on the perpetrator but only for a short period of time.

Asia and Africa

Even a jurisdiction like Japan, a traditionally male-dominated society, which, under feudal laws, allowed a husband to hit his wife as a form of discipline and required her to accept this as a form of obedience, has now recognized domestic violence as a serious problem and has passed the Prevention of Spousal Violence and Protection of Victims Law in 2001. This law contains restraining orders and protection orders similar to those laws which exist in the United States. Under this law, spouses are included among those protected against physical harm or bodily injury. The term 'spouse' may include male or female and includes unmarried partners and former spouses in cases where violence is inflicted both before and after a separation. An amendment to the law in 2004 has widened 'violence' to include not only physical violence but also psychological and sexual violence. However, the protection order applies only to physical violence.

The South African Domestic Violence Act 1998 defines domestic violence to include not only physical abuse but also sexual abuse, emotional, verbal and psychological abuse, economic abuse, intimidation, harassment, stalking and damage to property. The 1998 Act also provides that the hearings must be held in camera and a perpetrator can be sentenced for up to five years in prison.

United States

United States laws provide a variety of measures to deal with domestic violence. There are the typical protection orders, restraining orders and a panic button electronic device which, when pressed, sends a high priority message to the police, being geared to victims at high risk of domestic violence. Schneider's survey of United States law on domestic violence in the last 50 years (see Schneider, 2008, discussed in detail in Part IV, pp. 313–14) emphasizes the intractable nature of the problem. This echoes the problems faced in other jurisdictions such as Britain, where there are difficulties arising from using criminal sanctions as the central method of dealing with the problem, and the sobering finding that some women victims remain passive in the face of such violence and will not be persuaded to report the violence, to avoid criminalizing their partners.

Australia

All Australian jurisdictions have introduced legislation to provide protection to victims of domestic violence. The detail of the legislation varies from State to State but they all provide for a court order to be made on a balance of probabilities to protect the victim from further violence. Breach of orders has been made a criminal offence enabling the police to arrest without a warrant any persons who have contravened a protection order. A wide range of behaviour is covered under the legislation. A major problem which bedevils Australian women victims is that the laws only seem to protect women who are financially able, residing in urban settings and belonging to dominant cultural groups, whereas women from culturally diverse backgrounds, Indigenous women and women living in rural and remote environments are the least protected (see Stubbs, 1994).

Other jurisdictions

The Russian Federation experienced severe socioeconomic disruption and a high divorce rate in the wake of the disintegration of the former Soviet Union, the effects of which were felt in the 1990s. Spousal homicide, with more than half of the victims being women, has been a particularly worrying phenomenon. In 1996 this galvanized the Russian Federation into enacting a new family policy by decree of the President. This led to the formulation of a Code which recognized and sought to protect against violence in the family. The Code emphasized assisting families in their difficulties and aimed to expand the system of social support for families, especially women and children. This resulted in a significant growth in facilities and shelters. The Russian Federation's 1994 Code of Civil Law, 1996 Code of Criminal Law and 1997 Code of Criminal Procedure all address protection against violence in the family.

CHILDREN

The best interests of the child standard

Global overview

Glendon reminds us that the traditional relationship between parent and child was 'organised around a model of a married mother and father whose legal authority over the child was virtually exclusive … [and] one of the most salient trends in family law has been the acceptance of new ideas about parenthood, with parenthood increasingly detached from marriage and biology, and with parental authority modified by growing recognition of children's rights' (Glendon, 2006, p. 14).

In cases involving disputes and competing claims over children, the basic guideline remains the furtherance of the 'best interests of the child' a term that has been used by various courts and in legislation around the world, usually in the context of custody, guardianship and contact or access cases in Western legal systems. It is also used in other legal systems, even hybrid ones such as South Africa, where the term appeared in 1948 in *Fletcher v Fletcher* (1948) 1 SA 130 (A), where the South Africa courts said that the best interests of the child was the main consideration where a custody order was made after divorce. The best interests test is now the yardstick used in every matter affecting the child (see Part II, Chapter Four on African and Asian family law). Glendon's survey suggests that the standard has been applied with 'increasing uncertainty in the manner of applying that standard' (Glendon, 2006, p. 15). For instance, in custody disputes between biological parents, the trend is to emphasize the importance for the child of a continuing relationship with both parents, 'regardless of whether the parents are married, divorced or unmarried to each other' (Glendon, 2006, p. 15). Glendon sees this as part of the tendency to 'reconceptualize' the rights involved as rights of the child rather than the parents. Such an approach can be seen in international cases (involving European Convention of Human Rights provisions) such as *Johansen v Norway* (1996) 23 EHRR 33, to which Glendon refers. In *Johansen* the European Court of Human Rights referred to the need to strike 'a fair balance' between the interests of the parents and the child and declared that in carrying out this balancing exercise, the court will attach particular importance to the best interests of the child which, depending on their nature and seriousness, may override those of the parent.

The best interests guideline has been interpreted in various jurisdictions 'to permit and in some places, even to presumptively mandate, joint parenting after divorce, with both parents having equal decision-making power' (Glendon, 2006, p. 15). In some civil law jurisdictions, for example Belgium and Hungary, joint custody is presumptively granted to the parents, provided they lived together, regardless of their marital status. On the other hand, joint custody would have to be requested by the parents if they wished a court to grant it, as in Austria and Germany. In France, there is a general rule that joint exercise of parental authority is the norm even after divorce and the judge may only assign its exercise to one parent if the welfare of the child requires this (Civil Code, art. 372, as amended by the Law of 8 January 1993).

The notion of parents continuing their rights over their children even after a separation or divorce is also followed in common law countries and is the philosophy behind the Children Act 1989 (UK) where a separation or divorce of the parents will not affect the retention of parental responsibility by both parents per se. However the court can make a ruling that the child should reside with one of the parents upon the application of that parent or if they believe that the welfare of the child requires such a ruling. In practical terms, the form of joint residence order used in England and Wales has been found to be impractical, and in the majority of cases mothers will remain the primary physical custodian of young children.

Another trend noted by Glendon is the 'widespread revision' of child custody laws to permit grandparents, and even non-relatives, to petition for access or contact ('visitation') rights (Glendon, 2006, p. 15). This has led to legal systems recognizing concepts such as de facto or psychological parenthood. In Australia, under s. 60(2)(b) of the Family Law Act, as amended in 1995, 'children have a right of contact, on a regular basis, with both of their parents and with other people significant to their care, welfare and development'. In 2000, in *Troxel v Granville* 530 US 57 (2000), the United States Supreme Court affirmed the importance of permitting fit parents to decide what is in their child's best interest in a case where grandparents had applied for access (or visitation) rights against the wishes of their daughter-in-law, the children's widowed mother.

The welfare principle v art. 8 of the European Convention on Human Rights

As we saw in Part V, on the impact of the European Human Rights Convention on family law, and on English family law in particular, there is potential conflict or incompatibility between art. 8 of the Convention and the principle that the welfare of the child should be the paramount consideration in all cases involving the child's upbringing or welfare. Several academic commentators have weighed in on this issue, and they highlight the various interpretational difficulties which the wording of the article creates. Article 8 encourages parents to view any grievances they have with the state over their child's upbringing from an adult standpoint which causes adults and the courts to lose sight of the fact that it is the children's rights which need proper assessment and deliberation. It is only when children themselves are the applicants that the courts find it essential to consider the children's position as fully fledged rights-holders (Fortin, 1999, 2006). Hence, when younger children are involved, arguments relating to the children's interests are only part of a discussion which focuses on how infringement of adults' rights may be justified (Fortin, 2006, p. 326). Bainham argues that in many areas of the law involving children, little attempt has been made to articulate children's rights as rights (Bainham, 2002). In essence, Fortin submits that the English family courts have not been meeting the demands of the Convention, and that a reinterpretation of the paramountcy principle under the Children Act 1989 should be undertaken, as well as a radically different approach to evidence relating to children's best interests (Fortin, 2006, p. 299). Harris-Short also points out that her survey of the relevant case law suggests there is a marked failure in many of the post-implementation Convention cases to engage with the Convention arguments in any sustained manner because, while art. 8(1) requires independent consideration of the rights of the child's parents, the 'paramountcy principle' under the United Kingdom Children Act requires that, in matters relating to the upbringing of a child, the child's welfare must be the court's only consideration (Harris-Short, 2005, p. 353). Hence the standard approach taken by the English courts in cases where the child's upbringing is directly in issue, is to give detailed consideration to the welfare test and the child's best interests, and then at the end of the judgment to turn somewhat dismissively to art.8 and conclude that it has no material effect on the decision which was based on considerations of welfare (Harris-Short, 2005, p. 359).

The mature minor and recognition of children's rights

A noteworthy development in the last 25 years of Anglo-American jurisprudence has been the partial emancipation of the more mature child, in that the older child who is considered to possess a sufficient level of understanding will have his or her views taken into account in various circumstances. This sort of older child is called the 'Gillick competent' child (after the name of a leading English case, Gillick v West Norfolk and Wisbech Area Health Authority [1986] 1 FLR 229) and referred to as the 'mature minor' in United States law. The one limitation is that in English law, at least, even though the child might be considered Gillick competent, this will not result in the English courts giving that child a 'right' to take his or her own life, as illustrated in a series of cases in English law (see for example Re W [1992] 4 All ER 627 and Re M [1999] 2 FLR 1097). English law has also moved towards giving the older, mature child the right to be heard or to have legal representation in proceedings which have an impact on their interests and their future upbringing (see for example Re S [1993] 2 FLR 437; Re H [1993] 2 FLR 552, where the court emphasized that on the question of whether the child was old enough to have his request for a replacement of his guardian ad litem granted, the real issue was not the child's age but her understanding; and whether the child would be able to give instructions in the light of the evidence that would be produced in court, respectively).

Justice Munby, in a lecture delivered in 2005, also poses several challenges and highlights some pressing issues. First of all, in relation to children, he sees the need to develop a proper jurisprudence of children's rights and to work out the implications of the emerging concept of the teenage child's autonomy. Second, he believes there is a need to rethink the meaning of welfare (in the context of children) and to re-examine the extent to which best interests are most appropriately met by the application of old-fashioned paternalism. Allied to this is the need to re-examine whether the principle that the child's interests are paramount is really compatible with the European Convention.

Right of adoptive children to gain access to information about birth parents

Another development has been the right given to adoptive children to gain access to information about the identity or the relevant medical characteristics of their birth parents. One standard method is for all parties to agree to an open adoption where all parties agree to waive confidentiality from the outset. The other method is to establish centres where adoptive children and birth parents can leave information at any time to facilitate contact if both parties are prepared to do so. An instructive case comes from France where the birth parent's interest in privacy continues to be protected. In *Odievre v France* (2003) ECHR No. 42326/98, the European Court of Justice held that France did not violate the adopted child's right to family life or equality by denying him access to his birth records. The crucial finding was that the child's right had to be balanced against the natural mother's rights and since French law allows women to give birth anonymously, the mother was entitled to exercise her right to do so in this instance. The court even agreed that the law rendered the applicant permanently unable to access such a right in these circumstances.

International Recognition of Children's Rights – the United Nations Convention on the Rights of the Child

Glendon observes that a major influence on the law pertaining to parents and children has been the advance of the concept of children's rights, which led to widespread, global recognition of the United Nations Convention on the Rights of the Child of 1989 (Glendon, 2006, p. 16). The provisions of that international treaty restate and reinforce existing child protection measures and have been widely accepted. However, the more controversial provisions of the Convention were those which give children rights which they may even assert against their parents, such as freedom to express oneself and to receive information; freedom of thought, conscience and religion; freedom of association; and protection of privacy and correspondence. Under art. 5 of the Convention, the role of the parents is to serve as guides 'in a manner consistent with the evolving capacities of the child'.

Concluding perspectives on child custody

Elrod and Dale conclude their survey of the last 50 years of child custody law in the United States with comments equally applicable to child custody disputes in most jurisdictions that use the best interests standard. They note that the future will present a challenge to reform family law so as to minimize the divisive custody battles and to develop the legal processes and procedures that will help children and families through divorce and separation but this does not mean scrapping the best interests approach. In their view, it means there 'must be a concerted effort among multiple professionals to keep developing models to help families ... whatever paradigm shift occurs, whatever direction the pendulum swings, and whatever the prevailing scientific and societal views of children and families that we choose to embrace, if it does not reduce conflict, it will not be in the best interests of children' (Elrod and Dale, 2008, p. 418). Reducing conflict and promoting the best interests of children remains the never-ending quest for most mediators, counsellors, judges and any legislators who seek to promote and improve the welfare of children for whom they are responsible.

European perspectives and harmonization of family law

In April 2007, European Union justice ministers announced that they had agreed a new European Union regulation on jurisdiction and applicable law in matrimonial proceedings, called Rome III. The present position is that every member state applies its own rules as to which law is applicable to a divorce where the spouses are of different nationality or where the couple lives abroad. Hence, a German-Dutch couple who lived in Germany is allowed to be divorced in Germany under German law. However, if the Dutch spouse petitioned for divorce in the Netherlands, Dutch law could be applied which could lead to a different outcome. The European Commission says that the new regulation would avoid this uncertainty by providing uniform rules for determining the law applicable to divorces with an international dimension. Subject to some limitations, it would give spouses the right to choose both the court with jurisdiction in a member state, as well as the applicable law. Hence, a French court may be chosen by a couple to be the forum for a divorce in relation to which Spanish law is applied. From a British perspective, the United Kingdom government has the right to opt out of proposals relating to European civil and family justice and has exercised that right with regard to Rome III. However, the United Kingdom government has also said that it intends to remain involved in the negotiations as it retains the right to opt-in once the regulation has been drafted.

It was also announced by European Union ministers that they have agreed to take measures to improve existing arrangements for the cross-border recovery of maintenance orders made within the European Union. Apparently ministers have agreed on the guiding principles to govern future negotiations seeking to arrive at the formulation of a regulation which would enable maintenance decisions made by courts of any member state to be automatically enforceable in all other member states. Council President and Federal Minister of Justice Brigitte Zypries announced that a central authority will be set up to support European Union citizens entitled to maintenance to recover any arrears (*Family Law Bulletin*, May 2007).

International Human Rights and family law

The United Nations Universal Declaration of Human Rights

The United Nations Universal Declaration of Human Rights 1948 declared in art. 16, para. 3: 'The family is the natural and fundamental group unit of society and is entitled to protection by society and the State.'

Other international conventions

Other human rights instruments make a similar declaration to that of the United Nations Declaration, for example the International Covenant on Civil and Political Rights of 1996 (art. 23, para. 1), the International Convention on Economic, Social and Cultural Rights of 1996 (art. 10, para. 1) and the Charter of Fundamental Rights of the European Union of 2000 (art. 33, para. 1). However, the supranational instrument that has had the most influence on the family law of nation states has been the European Convention on Human Rights of 1950 as interpreted by the European Court of Human Rights in Strasbourg (see Part V on the European Convention).

The United Nations Convention on the Rights of the Child states in its art. 3: 'In all actions concerning children, whether undertaken by public or private social welfare institutions, courts of law, administrative authorities, or legislative bodies, *the best interest of the child shall be a primary consideration*' (emphasis added). This Convention has been described as 'the most rapidly and universally accepted human rights document of [the 20th] century' (Bennett Woodhouse, 1999, p. 815). Bennett Woodhouse sees this Convention as 'striking evidence of a major twentieth-century revolution' in how children's law is conceptualized (Bennett Woodhouse, 1999, p. 815).

The European Convention on Human Rights

As we saw in Part Five, on human rights and family law, another significant development in English family law has been the incorporation of the European Convention on Human Rights into English law by the bringing into force of the Human Rights Act 1998 on 2 October, 2000. English judges have adapted to their new role as the guardians of the European Convention. It is a matter of some debate whether they have been wholly enthusiastic in acting as enforcers of the rights under the European Convention where there has been a potential conflict with the welfare principle. We explored these issues and the case law in considerable detail in Part V on the Human Rights Act, hence suffice to say that judges have not always indicated that art. 8 rights are relevant in their approach to the enforcement of Convention rights alongside the domestic law relating to children, except where the child has been the direct applicant in a case. Indeed, several British academics believe that the English judiciary has demonstrated resistance to the European Convention rights in disputes involving children. It would also appear that the European Court is currently facing a huge backlog of Convention-related applications and runs the danger of being overwhelmed by its case load (see Part V).

Of course, the European Human Rights Convention has also influenced and impacted on other countries in Europe, and the European Court has been said to have derived a 'whole code of family law' from art. 8 of the Convention (*Marckx v Belgium* (A/31) (1979) 2 EHRR 330). The three articles dealing with family law are art. 8 (giving the right to protection of family life), art. 12 (dealing with the right to marry within fairly precise boundaries) and art. 14 (prohibiting discrimination). As we saw in Part V on the impact of the European Human Rights Convention on family law, the European Court has had to develop its jurisprudence on protecting family rights under the Convention on a case-by-case basis, as the three articles dealing with this protection have not always been wide enough in scope to provide such protection. The European Convention has therefore utilized the 'consensus or the "common European standard" among the Contracting States' (Antokolskaia, 2007, p. 242) and invoked the doctrine of the margin of appreciation to strike a balance between extending the protection of family rights and exercising judicial restraint.

Concluding perspectives

Convergence and divergence trends in family law

In her survey of three decades of family law, Glendon notes both convergence and divergence trends in family law in general. As far as convergence trends are concerned, by the late twentieth century, 'broad similarities had appeared in the family law systems of the liberal democracies of the West and a comparative approach was routinely being employed by law reformers and scholars in most countries' (see Glendon, 2006, p. 7). These trends 'merely formalized and systematized transforming trends that had long been diffuse and partially realised in the laws of Western liberal democracies [and] have not proceeded at the same pace everywhere, and have taken different forms in different places' (Glendon, 2006, p. 7). Nevertheless, her survey reveals that 'almost all the world's legal systems have now been affected by the advance of human rights ideas in general, and women's equality in particular' (Glendon, 2006, p. 7).

On the other hand, diversity persists in family law and Glendon cautions that despite the broad convergence trends noted above, divergence should also be noted, since 'significant national and regional differences persist in family law, sometimes manifesting themselves through different legal norms, sometimes through differing judicial interpretations of similar legal norms, and sometimes through differing levels of official supervision of private arrangements' (Glendon, 2006, p. 7).

On the future of legal marriage in the United States in forthcoming years, Ann Estin observed in 2008 that in the past decade in the United States, 'marriage has been both pushed and pulled, urged and denied, extended and withheld' but argues that Americans still place a high value on marriage and that demographers estimate that 90 per cent of them will marry at some point in their lives (citing Goldstein and Kenney, 2001). She argues that 'the shape of marriage has changed significantly over fifty years, but the fundamental importance of marriage has not. Marriage still matters to families and to society' (Estin, 2008, pp. 252, 350). There seems little doubt that although marriage has decreased in popularity, partly offset by the spectacular rise in cohabitation, it remains a 'cultural icon of commitment' (Regan, 1999, p. 661) and for a variety of reasons, should continue to be supported. Regan also argues that provided it retains the social validation necessary to sustain its credibility, marriage could serve as an institution 'that helps to forge character by providing occasions to cultivate traits of fidelity and forbearance' (Regan, 1999, p. 661). Morrison also supports retaining the institution of marriage, and seems quite forthright in declaring: 'Marriage is good for society and unquestionably good for children' (Morrison, 2002, p. 79). These represent the contemporary views of some of the leading academics in the United States, who make it clear where their sympathies lie, but it is obviously pertinent to remember that the United States is certainly 'pro-family' (particularly for the traditional paradigm) in its public pronouncements.

Comparative law perspectives – sources of law and law reform

It is perhaps apt to remind ourselves that while civil law jurisdictions (which are based on Roman law) have a tradition of codifying their laws in comprehensive and authoritative codes, organized to suit different fields of law and social interaction, common law jurisdictions have only recently adopted the practice of responding to a perceived social, commercial or political problem by passing a statute. The judiciary has historically dealt with such problems as they present themselves, in court, as a result of a dispute between parties or because of a prosecution by the state against organizations or individuals seen to pose a threat to public order, safety or morals. The point that is being made is that it is more likely that a civil law country would attempt to solve their social and other problems by passing a new or amending law whereas a common law country, until relatively recently, would not have done so.

Convergence or divergence in family law?

As far as the debate on convergence is concerned, the preceding survey has indicated that in a range of jurisdictions in common law and civil law legal systems, as well as in hybrid systems such as South Africa and Japan, marriage has undergone radical changes, as has divorce, with no-fault divorce being introduced either to replace fault-based divorce or to co-exist with fault-based grounds; and divorce replacing death as the endpoint of marriage (Pinsof). A unifying or universal ground for divorce appears to be the notion of 'irretrievable breakdown' but, as we have seen, a multitude of interpretations and variations lie beneath that seemingly straightfor-ward concept or statutory guideline (see the analysis by Antokolskaia, 2007).

In England, there has been a gradual movement towards the equalization of spouses which has been replicated in other Western regions, such as France and Germany and in the United States, Australia and New Zealand. This has not been total by any means but there has been considerable progress made towards greater equality. There has also been a movement towards the equalization of property rights for spouses, particularly in the context of post-divorce financial provision by the courts and a greater judicial recognition of the need to ensure that one party does not suffer a greater detriment in the allocation of property and matrimonial assets post-divorce. Perhaps even more notable is the equalization of spouses' rights in legal systems such as Russia, where their family laws strive to maintain such parity and have done for several decades. However, as Arlette Gautier reports, having analysed various sources from legal codes, case studies and 40 reports to the Commission to Eliminate Discrimination against Women, in 2003, 83 countries had egalitarian marriage rights, 38 admitted the husband as the head of the family and 57 maintained the obligatory obedience of the wife. Hence, she concludes that legal equality has progressed in Europe and America and it is still an objective in half the other countries (Gautier, 2005, p. 47). The codes included Western, Islamic and Chinese codes.

All available statistics from the jurisdictions we have examined suggest that mar-riage as an institution appears to be in decline but it is by no means certain whether it will become extinct in the next few decades. On the other hand, cohabitation has seen a spectacular rise in common law and civil law jurisdictions and with the destigmatization of children born outside marriage there has been a marked increase in such births, with figures starting from 25 per cent upwards being the proportion of non-marital births. There has also been a huge rise in the number of single-parent families, the majority of whom are female.

Another feature which appears to be a global phenomenon is the growing legal recognition of the right of same-sex couples to enter into a legally sanctioned relationship; called civil unions, domestic partnerships, registered partnerships, life partnerships (Germany) and pacs (France). However, only a few jurisdictions have allowed same-sex marriage, which has been a bone of contention for some same-sex couples. It is arguably simplistic and superficial to say that all these laws indicate convergence of family laws per se, as there are several crucial differences from jurisdiction to jurisdiction, even, or perhaps particularly, within an area such as Western Europe (see Bradley, 2005), not least between the different kinds of registered or legally recognized domestic partnerships in that region. Undoubtedly, political, social and cultural differences remain but it is arguable that cohabitational relationships outside marriage, both opposite-sex and same-sex, have moved from being a moral issue to a question of justice (see Barlow *et al.*, 2005).

Domestic violence has been addressed by a number of common law and civil law jurisdictions, and the resulting laws have made progress in providing better protection for victims of such violence in a variety of situations – from stalking to more serious assaults – and this exhibits common elements in both common law and civil law jurisdictions. However, the inherent and endemic problem remains which is the difficulty of persuading victims to testify against the perpetrators of violence. This to a certain extent has been brought about by criminalizing violence committed in the home. A particular cause for concern has been the claims of alleged violence against immigrant communities and ethnic minorities in countries as far apart as France and New Zealand.

The best interests standard and the legal transplant issue

As far as children are concerned, all societies have, in one form or another, mutatis mutandis, adopted the best interest standard as a criterion or guideline in resolving disputes over children or making decisions pertaining to their welfare and upbringing, often as a pragmatic response to the case at hand.

The topic of legal transplants in family law has been explored elsewhere (see de Cruz, 2001). Drawing on that article and its editorial introduction by Harding and Orucu, it may be reiterated that the pragmatic approach works well in family law, as this produces principles which have been adapted to reflect the changing social, religious and economic conditions of the host country. Furthermore, as court decisions assume greater authority both in the common law and civil law jurisdictions, similarities will be created by transplants, irrespective of legislative intervention. There is also the impact of international conventions, which have been discussed in this and other chapters, which emphasize the best interests standard. The greater the number of jurisdictions which adopt these conventions, the more such a standard will be common currency. In short, the best interests test is increasingly used in several jurisdictions and has transcended the common law/civil law divide, indicating that such transmigration can become embedded in very different environments. Thus, my preliminary research suggests that in France, Germany, Sweden, the United States, England and Wales, Australia, New Zealand, the Far East, Sri Lanka and India, the best interests test is used as a guiding principle and must serve, prima facie, as an example of a successful legal transplant in family law. My study of this concept, which has to be regarded as arguably superficial because of the wide field of reference, nevertheless indicates that several historical, religious and political factors, all receptive to the best interests principle, have often managed to override the established values such as patriarchal dominance (see de Cruz, 2002; Harding and Orucu, 2002, p. 101) and the guideline/criterion has managed to supersede local interests and traditions previously supported by social legitimacy in many jurisdictions, stretching from India to Indiana, Sri Lanka to New Zealand. The key requirement for a successful transplant in a host country is a suitably receptive environment. In regions where this has been present, the process of transplantation has embedded successfully, but it needs to be remembered that the particular mentalité of a country, its culture and its traditions will often mean that the particular concept will have to be interpreted, applied and, if necessary, adapted in accordance with the prevailing customs, norms and philosophies of that country. This has been the case in Asian jurisdictions such as Singapore, India and Hong Kong. Of course, the fact that Western colonization has taken place in all these regions has been a powerful influence in securing a meaningful transplantation of foreign concepts. On the other hand, in those regions steeped in their indigenous culture, religion and traditions, where a strongly patriarchal society is deeply ingrained, combined with a lack of exposure or resistance to Westernization, no foreign or imposed law which supports the autonomy of women or children will find it easy to take root. This is the case with certain African and Oriental jurisdictions.

Challenges for family law in the twenty-first century

Pinsof argues:

> '[A] new system of laws needs to be created that recognises the appropriate rights and responsibilities of partners, their families of origin, and their offspring in all of the four major pair-bond structures (married, divorced, unmarried, cohabiting, unmarried co-parents), their major permutations, and gay-lesbian marriage. This system must transcend the dichotomous marriage versus everything-else model by legally recognising and appropriately protecting nonmarital cohabiting, nonmarital childbearing, and childrearing, as well as marriage.'
>
> (Pinsof, 2002, p. 152)

This illustrates the sort of challenge that faces all developed societies in the twenty-first century.

In her masterly overview of three decades of global legal and social change, which we discussed in Part I, Mary Ann Glendon poses several challenges which face family law in the twenty-first century. There are several questions which she argues were not given a great deal of attention in the years when their activity was most intense: 'What ideas about marriage, family life, and human flourishing are being promoted in each legal system? What issues have been treated as important and which have been excluded or obscured from view? What kinds of state regulation most benefit families and family members and what kinds undermine their capacity to help themselves?' (Glendon, 2006, p. 24).

Glendon further highlights the difficulties which arise in trying to resolve the various dilemmas which societies face in the twenty-first century. Resolving these problems involves

'finding a just balance among competing goods. Not the least of the problems is many of the developments that have weakened family ties are unintended consequences of freedoms that modern men and women prize. Yet no society has found a complete substitute for the voluntary provision of care, services and support furnished by family members for their dependants'.

She continues:

'The challenges are formidable: How can society take account of children's needs (and the preferences of most mothers) without perpetuating women's subordination? How can society respond to the needs of persons in broken or dysfunctional families while strengthening, or at least not undermining, the stable families upon which every society depends for the socialisation of its future work force and citizenry?'

(Glendon, 2006, p. 25)

The somewhat sobering global landscape which she describes from the outset of her review is that in affluent and impoverished countries alike, there are 'unresolved problems arising from the diminished capacity of both family and state to furnish care for the very young, the frail elderly and other dependants' (Glendon, 2006, p. 3).

To all these challenges may be added the fact that in both the East and West, the proportion of people who live well into their sixties and beyond has risen quite markedly. In Britain, it has been estimated that if the population of the over seventies continues to grown at its current rate, there would be a need for 20 per cent more housing and accommodation for them, with all the implications for social care and supportive social services which this would entail. This raises the further challenge of providing what used to be classed as 'elderly' people, but who are now living several years longer, with a respectable quality of life through adequate housing, social care and employment. A current issue that has arisen in Britain is whether people should be allowed to continue in paid employment beyond the current retirement age of 65 where they appear to be physically and mentally capable of doing so. This matter is likely to require determination not just by the government of the day but possibly in the courts, as well. Providing the best possible care for the increasing proportion of the elderly population, whether in legislation, social care or health provision may be one of the most demanding challenges for family law in the years to come. The manner in which societies deal with this challenge will be a measure not just of the quality and comprehensiveness of their social policy but ultimately a touchstone of their humanity, which may set the tone for their family law for the next few decades of the twenty-first century.

Concluding observations

Our comparative survey has shown that all jurisdictions, irrespective of their cultural traditions or their heritage, have gradually come to terms with radical transformations in the nature of the family, given greater equality to women in the family and the workplace, manifested widespread acceptance of divorce and given increasing legal recognition to the rights of unmarried cohabitants, whether opposite-sex or same-sex and sought to apply the best interests standard to resolve problems relating to their children. The big questions remain: Should we continue to support the institution of marriage? If so, how? What is the best way of ensuring justice and fairness for unmarried cohabitants in situations involving unequal bargaining power or exploitation? Is legislation the best solution for dealing with cohabitants' property rights? Should the law begin to allow adults to have more latitude in making their own arrangements with regard to maintenance, child support and financial settlements?

In the early twenty-first century, the story of family law across the ages, in several different jurisdictions, particularly in Western or Westernized jurisdictions, appears to have started as a morality play and has evolved into a modern soap opera where nothing lasts forever and some people expect every aspiration to be achieved and every problem to be resolved within a relatively short period of time. Yet all progressive and mature societies should be slow to discard the values, institutions and ideals which have sustained modern civilizations for several centuries, while being prepared to undertake modernization of certain laws if they are patently oppressive, discriminatory or harmful.

Marriage has never been under greater threat as an institution but there is nothing in our comparative study to suggest that social policy should not continue to support it for a variety of reasons: first, because it offers an unequivocal method of demonstrating a serious, long-lasting commitment and its basic expectations and obligations (at least, to love and honour each other, in sickness and in health) are generally well-known and widely accepted; second, because it remains a cultural and public symbol of commitment and may serve to be an institution that 'forges character by cultivating traits of fidelity and forbearance' (Regan, 1999); and third, because it is generally seen as better for children, if at all possible, to have two married parents – not least to share the responsibilities of childcaring and to provide a more balanced view of attitudes to life. Social policy should also encourage fathers to play an active role in the family, and, if absent or non-residential, to continue to provide financial support, which should be strictly enforced. Finally, the welfare, nurturing and protection of children particularly at the earlier stages of their childhood should continue to be a high priority in all societies. The virtually universal acceptance of the best interests of the child standard, despite its inherent indeterminacy, shows the widespread acceptance in all jurisdictions across the world of prioritizing the needs of children whenever there are disputes over their welfare and upbringing.

Judges, governments and legislators in all modern (democratic) societies will need to decide in the years ahead which values and ideals they wish to engender, to cope with the many moral and pragmatic dilemmas and challenges which we have highlighted in this chapter. In the light of the present global economic crisis, even more turbulent and uncertain times may well lie ahead for many families across the world. Family law in all jurisdictions may well need to play a decisive and positive role by continuing to protect the most vulnerable members of society and, by upholding core values of fairness and equality of treatment, to ensure that future generations will not inherit a society that is morally bankrupt and culturally bereft but one that cares for all its members.

Further reading

Antokolskaia, M 'Convergence and Divergence of Divorce Laws in Europe' (2006) 18 CFLQ 307.

Antokolskaia, M 'Family Law: Moving with the Times?' in Orucu and Nelken (eds) *Comparative Law – A Handbook*, 2007, Hart, Ch. 11.

Bainham, A 'Men and Women Behaving Badly: Is Fault Dead in English Family Law?' in Dewar and Parker (eds) *Family Law: Processes, Practices, Pressures*, 2003, Hart, pp. 523ff.

Barlow, A and James, G 'Regulating Marriage and Cohabitation in 21st Century Britain' (2004) 67 Mod LR 143.

Barlow, A, Duncan, S, James, G and Park, A *Cohabitation, Marriage and the Law. Social Change and Legal Reform in the 21st Century*, 2005, Hart.

Blair, DM and Weiner, MH *Family Law in the World Community Cases, Materials and Problems in Comparative and International Family Law*, 2003, Carolina Academic Press.

Boele-Woelki, K 'What Comparative Family Law Should Entail' (2008) 4 Utrecht LR 1.

Collier, R 'Fathers 4 Justice, Law and the New Politics of Fatherhood' (2005) 17 CFLQ 511.

Cretney, SM *Law, Law Reform and the Family*, 1998, Oxford UP.

Cretney, SM (ed) *Essays for the New Millennium*, 2000, Jordan.

Cretney, SM *Family Law in the Twentieth Century – A History*, 2003, Oxford UP.

Cretney, SM *Same-Sex Relationships*, 2006, Oxford UP.

de Cruz, P 'Legal Transplants: Principles and Pragmatism in Comparative Family Law' in Harding and Orucu (eds) *Comparative Law in the 21st Century*, 2002, Kluwer Academic, pp. 101ff.

Dewar, J 'Family Law and its Discontents' (2000) 14 Int Jnl of Law, Policy and the Family 59.

Dewar, J and Parker, S *Family Law – Processes, Practices, Pressures*, 2003, Hart.

Douglas, G, Pearce, J and Woodward, H 'Cohabitants, Property and the Law' (2009) 72 Mod LR 24.

Fineman, MA *The Neutered Mother, The Sexual Family, and Other Twentieth Century Tragedies*, 1995, Routledge Press.

Garrison, M 'The Decline of Formal Marriage: Inevitable or Reversible?' (2007) 41 Fam LQ 491.

Glendon, MA 'Family Law in a Time of Turbulence' in Chloros *et al.* (eds) *International*

Encyclopedia of Comparative Law, 2006, Mohr and Martinus Nijhoff, Vol. IV, pp. 1–27.

Goldstein, JR and Kenney, CT 'Marriage Delayed or Marriage Foregone? New Cohort Forecasts of First marriage for US Women' (2001) 66 Am Soc Rev 506.

Goody, J *The Family in European History*, 1999, Blackwell.

Hahlo, HR and Kahn, E *The South African Legal System and its Background*, 2nd ed., 1973, Juta & Co.

Herring, J 'Why Financial Orders on Divorce Should be Unfair' (2005) 19 Int Jnl of Law, Policy and the Family 218.

Hitchings, E 'Everyday Cases in the Post-White Era' [2008] Fam Law 873.

Hughes, D, Davis, M and Jacklin, L 'Come Live with Me and be my Love': A Consideration of the 2007 Law Commission Proposals on Cohabitation Breakdown' (2008) 72 *The Conveyancer* 197.

Krause, HD 'Marriage for the New Millennium: Heterosexual, Same Sex – Or Not At All? (2000) 34 Fam LQ 271.

Krause, HD 'Comparative Family Law – Past Traditions Battle Future Trends and Vice Versa', in Reiman and Zimmerman (eds) *The Oxford Handbook of Comparative Law*, 2008, Oxford UP, Ch. 34, pp. 1099–1129.

Lowe, N 'National Report for England and Wales' in Boele-Woelki, Braat and Sumner (eds) *European Family Law in Action*, Vol. I *Grounds for Divorce*, 2003, Intersentia.

Mason, MA, Skolnick, A and Sugarman, SD (eds) *All Our Families*, 2003, Oxford UP.

McGlynn, C 'The Europeanisation of Family Law' (2001) 17 CFLQ 35.

Morrison, DR 'A Century of the American Family' in Katz, Eekeelaar and Maclean (eds) *Cross Currents*, 2000, Oxford UP, p. 57.

Morrissey, S 'The New Neighbours. Domestic Relations Law Struggles to Catch Up with Domestic Life' (2002) 88 *American Bar Association* 37.

Munby, Justice 'Families Old and New – The Family and Article 8' (2005) 17 CFLQ 487.

Oldham, JT 'Changes in the Economic Consequences of Divorce' (2008) 42 Fam LQ 419.

Phillips, R *Untying the Knot*, 1991, Cambridge UP.

Pinsof, A (ed) *Marriage in the Twentieth Century – Trends, Research, Therapy and Perspectives* (2002) 41 *Family Process* (Special Issue).

Polikoff, N 'Ending Marriage as We Know It' (2004) 32 Hofstra LR 201.

Probert, R and Barlow, A 'Displacing Marriage – Diversification and Harmonisation within Europe' (2000) 12 CFLQ 153.

Regan, M 'Marriage at the Millenium' (1999) 33 Fam LQ 647.

Rheinstein, M and Glendon, MA 'Interspousal Relations' in Glendon (ed) *International Encyclopedia of Comparative Law*, 1980, Mohr and Martinus-Nijhoff, Vol. IV.

Scott, ES 'A World without Marriage' (2007) 41 Fam LQ 537.

Shaw, C and Haskey, J 'New Estimates and Projections of the Population Cohabiting in England and Wales' in *Population Trends 95*, The Stationery Office, 1997.

Sugarman, SD 'What is a "Family"? Conflicting Messages from Our Public Programs' (2008) 42 Fam LQ 231.

Summers, RW and Hoffman, AM *Domestic Violence – A Global View*, 2002, Greenwood Press.

Swindells, H 'Crossing the Rubicon – Family Law post The Human Rights Act 1998' in Cretney (ed) *Family Law: Essays for the New Millennium*, 2000, Jordon, pp. 55ff.

Vaver, PF 'Family Law – Divorce without Fault' in Elkind (ed) *The Impact of American Law on English and Commonwealth Law*, 1978, West Publishing Co.

Verschraegen, B 'Divorce' in *International Encyclopaedia of Comparative Law*, 2004, Mohr and Martinus Nijhoff, Vol. IV, Ch. 5.

Xanthaki, H 'Legal Transplants in Legislation: Defusing the Trap' (2008) 57 ICLQ 659.

Index

Aboriginal and Torres Strait Islander Australians 131, 296–7, 315
abortion 112, 160, 233, 250, 361, 363–5, 373
Act on Settlements between Offenders and Victims in Criminal Law (Germany) 299
Act to Protect Witnesses in Questioning in Criminal Proceedings and to Improve Victim Protection 1998 (Germany) 299
Administration of Estates Act 1925 (UK) 242
adoption 31, 165, 168–9, 174, 226, 390
Adoption Act 1976 (UK) 291
Adoption and Children Act 2002 (UK) 240, 291
Adoption Matters Amendment Act 1998 (South Africa) 169
adultery: and child custody 97; and divorce 22, 25, 29, 31, 42, 44–5, 67, 78, 122–4, 136, 180, 190–1, 193, 367, 378; evolution of law 8; fabricating evidence of 79
adverse conduct 28–32, 53, 381
African Charter 166–7, 199
African law 149–51, 161, 198
Alabama 87
Alaska 87, 91
alcohol abuse see drunkenness
alimony 29, 31, 86–8, 108, 203, 209, 212, 214–16, 276, 360
Ancient Rome 12–13, 372–3
Andorra 280
appreciation, margin of 324
apprehended violence orders 297
Argentina 280, 374
Arizona 87, 91–2
Arkansas 87, 90
artificial insemination 82–5, 136, 213, 361, 363–4, 368

Asylum and Immigration Act 2004 (UK) 324–5
Australia: court structure of 120, 134; federation of 115; powers of Commonwealth government 114; responsibilities of States and Territories 121
Australian Capital Territory 257
Austria 14, 17, 26–7, 340–1, 344, 388

Baden-Wurtenburg 300
Bangladesh 21, 185
Basic Law (Germany) 274
Basic Principles of Marriage and Family Law 1968 (Russia) 205
Basutoland see Lesotho
battered child syndrome 106, 310
Bechuanaland see Botswana
Beijing Platform 308
Belfast Agreement 1998, 321
Belgium: divorce in 26–7; marital equality in 17; and unmarried mothers 346
best interests principle 53; application of 100–1; checklist 131, 146; compared between jurisdictions 132, 146; criticism of 101; and ECHR 342–5, 349, 351–2, 388–90; in Hong Kong 181; in India 185–6; in international conventions 396–7; in Singapore 196; in South Africa 166–9, 387; transplantation of 12
bigamy 42, 64, 158, 190, 227, 271, 325
Bill of Rights (South Africa) 174
Bill of Rights Act 1990 (NZ) 144
birth: rates 115–17, 308, 367; registration of 61, 213, 216–17
birth control 10, 30, 45, 78, 116–17, 160, 250, 361, 363–4, 373

Black Administration Act (South Africa) 173
Botswana 159
Brazil 17, 280, 362, 374
brideprice 154–9, 163, 198, 305, 374
Britain, aging population of 398
Buddhism 21, 197

California 79, 84–6, 91–2, 98–9, 104, 213, 251, 253–4, 280, 377
Canada 135, 199, 264, 266, 281, 337–8, 362, 375, 378
canon law 6–7, 13, 27, 41, 44, 63, 203
care proceedings 31
Catholic Church 14, 27, 41, 45, 56, 63, 155, 314, 372, 374, 376
Charter of Fundamental Rights (EU) 392
Charter of Rights and Freedoms (Canada) 338
child abuse 53, 104, 106–7, 129, 288, 292, 305, 381
child-betrothal 156, 198
Child Care Act 1983 (South Africa) 168–9
child custody: abolition of term in UK and Australia 131; in Africa 155; in Belgium 388; and best interests principle 55, 70; in Europe 71–2, 340–1; in France 388; in Germany 388; in Hong Kong 181–2; in India 186; and irretrievable breakdown 90; in Japan 228; joint 62, 71, 99–100, 110, 279, 388; and non-parents 388; in NZ 143; in South Africa 167, 169; and spousal abuse 103; in United States 96–9, 101–3, 110–11, 391
child protection 104–7, 121, 128
child-rearing 6, 53, 99, 380
child support: amount of 62–3, 110, 383; in Australia 128, 133; liability for 30; as prerequisite to divorce 24; responsibility for 61, 360; in Russia 211–12; and sexual relations 8–9; in UK 133–4
Child Support (Assessment) Act 1989 (Aus) 121, 128, 133
Child Support Act 1991 (UK) 134
children: definition of 219; abandonment of 186; adult 63, 217, 233, 303, 339; in Australian law 128–31; best interests of see best interests principle; born outside marriage 20, 34, 216–17, 368–9, 395; contact with 30–1; convergence of laws on 72–3, 79; custody of see child custody; of de facto couples 279;

disabled 67, 214–15; and divorce 47–8, 52, 61–3, 70–1, 388; and domestic violence 28–9; and ECHR 326–7; in English law 53–6, 132, 220, 389–90; equality of 208; extra-marital 168; and family life 331–2; in German law 70; illegitimate 61, 70, 174, 215, 233; illegitimate 61, 70, 174, 215, 233; in India 185–6; in Japanese law 233; legitimacy of 4, 61, 70, 79, 174, 189, 197, 215, 224, 226, 233; in Nigerian law 172–3; in NZ law 143–7; parental responsibility for 9, 55–6, 85, 108, 129–30, 169, 306, 346, 388; property of 54; relevant 28, 291–2, 294; removal from parents 331, 349–53; rights of 79, 103, 129, 131, 167–8, 170, 218–21, 321, 343, 387, 389–90; in Russian law 208, 218–21; in Singapore 196–7; in South African law 166–7, 174–5; in US law 96, 98, 132
Children Act 1989 (UK) 5, 30, 53–5, 61, 73, 98, 128, 130, 132, 144, 181, 196, 220, 291–2, 343, 345, 349–50, 388–9
Children and Young Persons Act 1933 (UK) 30
China: influence on Japanese law 223; People's Republic of (PRC) 176–9, 182; Republic of (ROC) 178
Christianity 149, 151, 197, 372
Civil Code (California) 98, 255
Civil Code 1804 (France) 5, 57–8, 60–1, 381
Civil Code 1894 (France) 269, 271, 388
Civil Code 1898 (Japan) 223, 225
Civil Code 1947 (Japan) 225–7, 230, 233
Civil Code 1994 (Russia) 207, 387
Civil Code 1995 (Russia) 204, 207, 310
civil law, in Russia 202
civil law systems 5, 17–18, 56, 92, 202, 223, 239, 256, 300, 359, 368, 394
Civil Partnership Act 2004 (UK) 7, 265–7, 273, 337–8
civil partnerships see civil unions
civil rights 135, 203, 311, 313, 375
civil unions: and definition of family 4; in England and Wales 265–7, 362; in France see pacs (civil pact of solidarity); in Germany 265, 274–6, 362, 395; in New Zealand 264, 269; and same-sex couples 81, 264, 267, 372; in Scandanavia 281; and siblings 247; in

South Africa 162, 173; in United States 267–8
Civil Unions Act 2006 (South Africa) 162, 164, 173
Code of Criminal Procedure (Germany) 299
Code of Criminal Procedure 1997 (Russia) 310, 387
Code of Law governing Marriage, The Family and Guardianship 1926 (Russia) see Family Code 1926 (Russia)
Code on Marriage and Family 1969 (Russia) see Family Code 1969 (Russia)
cohabitation: and family life 330–1; and marriage 66, 189; outside marriage see de facto couples; and paternity 216; qualifying contribution 249
Cohabitees Act 1987 (Sweden) 239
Cohabitees Act 2003 (Sweden) 276–7, 279
collusion 42–4, 79, 123
colonization 11, 151–2, 198, 397
common law: in America 14–15; and de facto couples 255–6; of Germany 63; and marital property 91–2, 109; sources of 5; in South Africa 167–8
common law marriages see marriage, common law
common law systems 91, 109, 137, 151, 295, 382–3, 388, 394
Commonwealth of Independent States 202
community fund 17–18
community property: deferred 69–70, 94, 109, 137, 141–2, 379–80, 382–4; in English law 52; in French law 60–1; in Netherlands 17; origin of 17; in Russian law 209–10; in United States 91–3, 109, 383
companies 139, 340; convergence of divorce laws 71–2 see also divorce laws
comparative law methodology 32–5
concubinage 22, 70, 177–9, 182, 188–9, 198, 252, 374
Connecticut 87, 267, 280
contact orders 55, 220
contraception see birth control
contrat de marriage 18
Convention on the Elimination of all Forms of Discrimination against Women 321
corporal punishment 199, 321
Costa Rica 362
Crime Act 1994 (USA) 311

Criminal Code (France) 300
Criminal Code 1996 (Russia) 310, 387
Croatia 280
cruelty 42, 57, 59, 78–9, 87, 89, 122, 124, 136, 190, 192, 359, 367
curatorship 230–1
customary law: in African tradition 150–1, 153, 155, 158–9, 161, 163, 172–3, 199, 374; Chinese 177–8; coexistence with Western-style law 21; and colonization of America 14; in India 185; marriage under see marriage, customary; in Singapore 190; in South Africa 162–3, 174
Czech Republic 26–7, 264, 280

de facto couples: definition of 239, 248, 250, 258, 262, 271; in Africa 174; in Australia 120–1, 125, 257–9; breakup of 241–2; and civil law 256; and death 242; and domestic violence 293; and ECHR 328; in England and Wales 240–1, 243–9, 256; in France 269, 273; in Hong Kong 178, 182; legal recognition of 7, 174, 239–40, 396, 399; in Netherlands 281; in New Zealand 137–9, 142, 260–4; and non-molestation orders 291; in Norway 279; prevalence of 365, 368–9; property of 137, 260; reform of law on 281–2, 371–2; in Russia 204–5, 209, 213; in Sweden 276–9; in United States 81, 249–55, 361
De Facto Relationships Act 1984 see Property (Relationships) Act 1984 (NSW)
De Facto Relationships Act 1991 (NT) 257–8
De Facto Relationships Act 1996 (South Australia) 257–8
deferred community see community property, deferred
Denmark 9, 26–7, 264, 269, 280, 342
depravity 191
desertion 31, 42–3, 57, 59, 78, 87, 89–90, 122, 124, 136, 180, 190, 192–3, 266, 367
disappearances 206–7
District of Columbia 267, 280
divorce: administrative 26, 43; in Africa 155, 157, 159, 185; in Australia 122–4, 134, 146; and child custody 71; conduct upon 29–30, 35; costs of 120; on demand 27, 204;

divorce (*continued*)
distribution of property on 51–3, 60–1, 86, 92–6, 109, 382; in England and Wales 377; and fairness 380; financial consequences of 29, 361, 382; in France 378; grounds for 22–3, 114, 123, 136; in Hong Kong 179–80; in India 184–5; initiated by women 119; in Japan 226, 228; in Morocco 170; of Muslims 193; by mutual consent 23–6, 28, 58, 60, 63, 67–8, 71, 184, 228; in New Zealand 136–7; no-fault 23–5, 27, 31–2, 80, 87–90, 94, 98, 120, 123, 134, 208, 374–8; overview of 359–60; prevalence of 20, 366, 395; in Protestant tradition 14, 376; right to 326, 347; in Russia 203–7, 378; and separation 24–6, 29, 42, 60, 123–4, 136, 180; in Singapore 190, 193–4; social attitudes to 399; in South Africa 165–6; undefended 8, 43–4; in United States 377–8
Divorce Act 1975 (France) 60
Divorce Act 1979 (South Africa) 165
Divorce Act 2004 (France) 60
Divorce and Matrimonial Causes Act 1867 (NZ) 136
divorce laws: in Australia 122; convergence of 71–2, 383; in England 28, 41–6, 90, 378, 381; fault/no-fault dichotomy 27, 80, 88, 374–7; in France 56–63; in Germany 63–70; harmonization of 27, 71–2, 383; historical background of 21–2; in Hong Kong 180, 182; in India 186, 378; and irretrievable breakdown 25; modernization of 71; in Russia 208–9; in Singapore 189, 191–2, 199; in South Africa 378; in United States 78–80, 86–9, 108, 374
divorce petitions 44, 124, 191, 193, 199, 378
divorce rates: in Africa 157; in Australia 117, 122; in Germany 65; in Japan 226; in Russia 207, 309, 386; in Singapore 192–3; in South Africa 166; in UK 46–8; in USA 81, 88, 250
Divorce Reform Act 1925 (UK) 54
Divorce Reform Act 1969 (Eng) 29, 43, 180
Divorce Reform Law 1975 (France) 56
doctrine of unity *see* marriage, unity theory of
domestic partnerships *see* de facto couples

Domestic Proceedings and Magistrates' Court Act 1978 (UK) 290, 323
domestic relationship, definition of 306
Domestic Relationships Act 1994 (ACT) 257
domestic violence: definition of 288; allegations of 133; in Australia 295–8, 315, 386; and children 103; and divorce 59, 67, 87; in England and Wales 288–95, 314, 384–5; in France 300–1, 315, 385; in Germany 298–300, 314, 385; growing emphasis on 119, 396; in Italy 314; in Japan 301–4, 385–6; legal consequences of 28–9; and marital property 32, 95; perceptions of 287, 289–90; reasonable apprehension of 132–3; in Russia 308–10, 314, 386–7; and shared parenting 129, 132; in South Africa 305–8, 315, 386; in United States 310–15, 386
Domestic Violence, Crime and Victims Act 2004 (UK) 29, 291, 293–5
Domestic Violence Act 1998 (South Africa) 306, 308, 386
Domestic Violence and Matrimonial Proceedings Act 1976 (UK) 290
drug abuse 67, 175, 215, 297, 350
drunkenness 104, 215, 296–7, 305, 308

economic abuse 306, 386
economic disparity *see* marriage, economic disparity between partners
Egypt 14, 150
elder abuse 288
embryo transplantation 361, 363
emotional abuse 288, 296
Equal Employment Opportunity Act (Japan) 235
equality, presumption of 246
equitable distribution *see* divorce, distribution of property on
European Convention on Human Rights (ECHR): and abortion 365; and children 147, 340, 348–51; and civil partnerships 272; and damages 352–4; and de facto couples 247; and discrimination 341–2; effect on family law 392–3; establishment of 322; family provisions of 326–8, 330, 332; and immigration 338–9; and right to marry 324–6; and same-sex couples 333–4, 337; and transsexuality 334–6; volume of applications 354–5

European Court of Human Rights 247,
322–4, 328, 332, 335, 338, 343, 351,
353–5, 387, 392
European Union 34, 280, 391–2
exclusion orders 290, 299

family: African 152, 154, 156, 160–1;
American 75, 80–1, 102; in Ancient
Rome 12–13; in Australia 114–19;
diversity of 359; European 34–5, 372–4;
extended 3, 119, 152, 171, 175, 197–8,
224–5, 234, 374; ideology of 203, 208,
345; in Japan 235; Maori 140; nuclear 3,
76, 79–80, 115–17, 119, 152, 164, 225,
227, 366, 373; reunification of 351; and
same-sex relationships 164; in Singapore
197–8; in South Africa 173–4, 176;
transformation of 366, 368, 399
family chattels 140–1
Family Code (California) 84, 92
Family Code 1918 (Russia) 203–4, 207, 215
Family Code 1926 (Russia) 204, 210, 216
Family Code 1969 (Russia) 205, 216
Family Code 1995 (Russia) 202, 205,
207–14, 216–20, 222
Family Court of Australia 120–1, 134
Family Court of Japan 228–9, 231–2, 235
Family Court of Western Australia 121
Family Courts Act 1984 (India) 184
family law: definition of 3–4; in Asia
176; in Australia 114, 119–20, 129–30,
134, 145; in China 176–7; and ECHR
323–6, 354; in England and Wales
370–1; and best interests principle 12,
53, 100–1, 132, 146; and comparative
methodological principles 32–5; evolution
of 15–16, 234; and family behaviour 20;
future of 397–400; in Germany 274; great
debates in 359; harmonization of 280,
376, 391–5; history of 4–5, 190; in Hong
Kong 182; and Human Rights Act 1998,
344–6; in India 374; Islamic 188; in Japan
223–5, 227, 234–5; in mediaeval Europe
13; in modern Europe 56, 372–3; in New
Zealand 146; in Nigeria 171; Oriental
and Occidental 21; reforms 189, 200,
225, 360; and reproductive technology
82–3, 363; in Russia 205, 207, 209, 211,
214, 221–2; and sexual relations 6–8;
in Singapore 187–8, 374; and social
change 369–70; sources of 5–6, 394; in
South Africa 166, 174; statization of 14;
transplantation of 11; in United States 24,
75–6, 81–2, 107–8; universalization of
14–15
Family Law Act (California) 252
Family Law Act 1975 (Aus) 120–6,
128–32, 134, 388
Family Law Act 1986 (UK) 267, 337
Family Law Act 1996 (UK) 8, 44, 241,
291–3, 377
Family Law Act 2004 (NZ) 144
Family Law Amendment (Shared Parental
Responsibility) Act 2006 (Aus) 130–2,
146
family life: changes in 15, 20; and ECHR
327–30, 338–40, 347–8, 365; and
religion 12
family norms 4, 211
family privacy 76, 314
family property 9, 13, 19, 188
Family Protection Act 1955 (NZ) 137
Family Register, Japan 225, 230, 232–3
family violence *see* domestic violence
family violence orders 129, 132
Family Violence Prevention and Services
Act 1984 (USA) 311
Fatal Accidents Act 1975 (UK) 242
fathers: biological 10, 155, 172, 216; non-
residential 8, 218, 399; unmarried 241,
346–7, 369
fault: in adoption and care proceedings 31;
and child custody 98; and child support
8, 30; and divorce 23–9, 31–2, 41, 44–5,
59–60, 87, 122–3, 184, 189–90, 192–3,
378, 381–2, 395; in family law 146, 374;
and financial provision 31–2, 53; and
property distribution 94–5
Federal Law on Basic Guarantees of
the Rights of the Child in the Russian
Federation 1998, 219, 221
Federal Magistrates Court (Aus) 121–2
female-headed households 10
feminists *see* women's movement
financial misbehaviour 30
Finland 27, 265, 269, 280, 331, 340, 348
First Right to Marriage Reform Act 1976
(Germany) 298
Florida 87, 250–1
foster care 106–7
France, aging population of 226
Fundamentals of Russian Federation
Legislation on Citizen's Health 1993,
213

gender: equality 98, 101–2, 153, 203,
210–11, 214, 225, 302, 304, 308, 375,
399; inequalities 301, 314; and marriage
7; reassignment of 332, 334–5, 337;
stereotypes 97
Gender Recognition Act 2004 (UK) 332,
337
general aid 232
Georgia 87
Germany, division of 64–5
Ghana 159
globalization 16, 367
grandparents 55, 63, 131, 176, 198, 227,
233, 275, 331, 348, 388
guardianship: of adults 229–34; in
Australia 114; in civil law 5; in
European law 15, 61–2, 72; in New
Zealand 143; in South Africa 169
Guardianship Act 1968 (NZ) 143, 145
Guardianship and Wards Act 1890 (India) 185
Guardianship Law (Japan) 230
Guardianship of Infants Act 1925 (UK) 54
Guardianship of Minors Act 1925 (UK) 54
Guardianship Ordinance (HK) 181

Hague Convention on Private International
Law 107
Hague Convention on the Civil Aspects of
International Child Abduction 128
harassment, criminal 292
Hawaii 267, 280
Hindu Marriage Act 1955 (India) 183–5
Hinduism 14, 21–2, 183, 187, 190
HIV/AIDS 32, 95, 170, 175, 184, 270
hojo see general aid
homemaker services *see* housekeeping
homogamy 34
Hong Kong 176–82, 199, 374
hosa see curatorship
housekeeping 53, 69
housewives 117–18, 204, 215, 227, 229, 375
Housing (Homeless Persons) Act 1977
(UK) 290
Housing Act 1985 (UK) 242
Housing Act 1996 (UK) 291–2
Human Fertilisation and Embryology Act
1990 (UK) 83, 85, 213
human rights: debate around 321–2; and
Human Rights law in English courts
336–40; and family law 166; and
globalization 16; in Japan 302; law of
322; in New Zealand 259; and social
issues 119–20; and welfare principle
in English courts 336–40 *see also* best
interests principle
Human Rights Act 1993 (NZ) 259, 268
Human Rights Act 1998 (UK) 267, 321–3,
327, 332–3, 336, 342–5, 348, 352,
354–5, 393
Human Rights Commission Act 1977 (NZ)
259
Hungary 26–7, 388
husbands: abuse of 313; marital powers of
174, 187, 199, 289, 374
hybrid legal systems 5, 11, 223, 287, 359,
365, 387, 395

Iceland 26, 280
Idaho 87, 91–2
Illegitimacy Act 1969 (Germany) 70
Illinois 87, 102, 104
immigrant communities 15, 301, 303, 315,
339, 382, 396
immigration law 177, 179, 304, 324–5,
330, 338–9, 347
in-vitro fertilization 83–4, 213, 217, 329,
361, 363, 371
incest 190
India, legal systems in 183–4
Indiana 9, 87, 397
Indigenous Australians *see* Aboriginal and
Torres Strait Islander Australians
individualism 140, 156, 198, 224
infanticide 185–7
inheritance: in Ancient Rome 13; and civil
unions 275; and de facto couples 242,
255, 260; in Hong Kong 177–8; in Japan
226; in South Africa 163; and unmarried
parents 346
Inheritance Act 1975 (UK) 242
injustice, serious 138–9, 259, 261, 268
insanity 24, 43, 57, 64, 122, 136, 192, 367
intestacy 82
irretrievable breakdown: in America 89;
in England 43, 90; establishment of
24–6, 31, 179, 266; factors causing 22;
in Germany 64, 66, 71; in Indian law
184–6; in Ireland 23; in Russia 204–5; in
Singapore 191–2; in South Africa 165
Islam 14, 16, 21–2, 24, 149–51, 183, 187,
190–1, 301
Islamic law 14, 24, 150, 189–91
Israel 4, 6, 280–1, 362
Italy 17, 26, 314, 340, 355

IVF *see* in-vitro fertilization
iye see family, extended

Japan: demographic changes in 226–7,
    229; legal system of 223; value system
    of 224
Joint Household Act 2002 (Norway) 279
Judaism 190, 197
just satisfaction 352–4

Kansas 87
Kentucky 84, 87
Kenya 149, 158–9
koseki see Family Register, Japan

Latvia 338–9
Law of Domestic Relations 3
Law on Guardianship by Agreement 1999
    (Japan) 232
Law Reform (Married Women and
    Tortfeasors) Act 1935 (UK) 50
Law Reform (Testamentary Promises) Act
    1949 (UK) 138
legal transplants 11–12, 148, 175, 199,
    396–7 *see also* best interests principle
Lesotho 159
Libya 150
Life Partnership Act 2001 (Germany) 274
Life Partnership Law (Revision) Act 2004
    (Germany) 276
lobola 305
Louisiana 65, 87, 91–2
Luxembourg 280

Maine 87, 267, 280
maintenance: calculation of 68; collection
    of 8–9; and de facto couples 241, 259;
    of parents 197, 233, 374; spousal 52,
    96, 110, 120–1, 123, 125, 127, 166,
    195–6, 214–15, 253, 323, 360, 375, 380,
    382–3
Maintenance of Parents Act 1995
    (Singapore) 197–8, 374
Malawi 158–9
Maori 140
marital misconduct 25, 29, 88, 377
marital property: definition of 125; in
    Africa 174; allocation of 29, 95, 360,
    382; in Australia 125–7, 146, 384; in
    civil law 18; convergence of systems
    72; in England and Wales 50–1, 72,
    379–81; in France 381–2; in Germany

69, 382; historical context of 49–50; in
    Hong Kong 180–1; identification of 93;
    in New Zealand 137–42, 384; reserved
    19; in Russia 204, 210–11; in Singapore
    194–6; and social class 15; in South
    Africa 17, 163–4; systems of 17–19,
    60–1, 72, 91–2, 163, 174, 379; in United
    States 32–3, 90–1, 94, 109, 381–3; and
    women's equality 16–17, 366
marriage: definition of 153, 332; in Africa
    153–7, 162, 198; African customary
    153–4, 162; age of 301; alternatives to
    79; in Ancient Rome 13; arranged 34,
    198, 374; in Australia 117; between
    dead and living 171–2; ceremonies
    of 7, 20, 76, 152, 157, 189, 207, 209,
    335; child 185–7; childless 10; civil
    47, 76, 163, 173, 203–4, 227, 268,
    338, 360–2; common law 77, 174;
    common law definition of 7, 165, 337;
    in communist ideology 20; contracts 19,
    154, 210–11, 287; of convenience 325;
    customary 153–5, 157–9, 162–3, 174,
    177; dissolution of 5, 42–3, 122, 124,
    374; downgrading of 360–1; early 193;
    economic disparity between partners
    138, 141–2, 260; equality of spouses 17,
    208, 395; and fidelity 8; in France 269;
    future of 361–3, 399; indissolubility of
    4, 22, 27, 41, 57–8; individualization
    of 15; informal 204, 240; interracial
    77–8; in Ireland 48–9; in Japan 227;
    legal definitions of 3; length of 48; in
    mediaeval Europe 13; in Morocco 170;
    polygamous *see* polygamy; rape within
    289, 299, 301, 385; rejection of 371;
    religious 174, 183, 204; right to 184,
    324–6, 332, 334; roles in 118; in Russia
    205–6, 209; secularization of 14, 20,
    119; separation from sex 9; in Singapore
    190; social attitudes to 329; social
    purposes of 6, 363; in South Africa
    162; transformation of 365–8; trends in
    European law 19–20; in UK law 256,
    336; in United States 76–7, 108, 394;
    unity theory of 17, 49, 91, 289; void
    138, 260; woman-to-woman 155, 171–2
Marriage Act 1823 (England) 199
Marriage Act 1961 (Aus) 121
Marriage Act 1961 (South Africa) 162, 164
marriage rates 46–7, 119, 269, 273, 308,
    361, 368–9

Marriage Reform Ordinance 1971 (Hong Kong) 177
Married Women's Property Act 1835 (US) 16, 90
Married Women's Property Act 1870 (UK) 49
Married Women's Property Act 1882 (UK) 49–50, 381
Married Women's Property Act 1964 (UK) 323
Maryland 78, 87, 267
Massachusetts 78, 85, 87, 104, 267, 312, 362
maternal dyad 10
maternal preference principle 143
Matrimonial and Family Proceedings Act 1984 (UK) 43, 180
Matrimonial Causes (Amendment) Ordinance 1995 (HK) 180
Matrimonial Causes Act 1857 (UK) 42, 114, 190
Matrimonial Causes Act 1937 (UK) 89, 189
Matrimonial Causes Act 1959 (Aus) 122–3
Matrimonial Causes Act 1970 (Nigeria) 172
Matrimonial Causes Act 1973 (UK) 5, 29–30, 45, 51, 53, 60, 71, 90, 95, 110, 180, 182, 195, 240, 248, 266, 323, 332, 335, 337, 377, 381, 383
matrimonial home 28, 46, 50–1, 59, 195–6, 241, 384
Matrimonial Homes Act (UK) 290
matrimonial offences 26, 29, 31, 42–3, 192
Matrimonial Proceedings Act 1963 (NZ) 136
Matrimonial Proceedings and Property Ordinance (HK) 180
Matrimonial Property Act 1976 (NZ) see Property (Relationships) Act 1976 (NZ)
Matrimonial Property Act 1984 (South Australia) 174
mental illness 165, 220
Mexico 280
Michigan 87, 251
misconduct 31–2, 64–5, 95, 192
Mississippi 87, 90, 250–1
Missouri 87
molestation 289, 291–2, 384; and domestic violence in England and Wales 291–2
monogamy 77, 158, 373
Morocco 170, 301

mothers: legal 83–5, 213; unmarried 217, 346, 361
murder 29, 67, 96, 136, 300, 304–5, 309, 386
Muslims see Islam
Muslims Ordinance 1957 (Singapore) 189

Nationality Law (Japan) 227
Native Americans 250
Natural Fathers of Children Born out of Wedlock Act 1997 (South Africa) 168–9
Nebraska 365
Nevada 87, 91–2
New Hampshire 82, 87, 268
New Jersey 83, 87, 268, 280
New Mexico 87, 91–2, 281
New South Wales 114–15, 122, 257–8, 297
New York 78–9, 95, 281
New Zealand, constitution of 135–6
Nigeria 158–9, 171, 173
non-molestation orders 28, 291–5, 385
North Carolina 32, 95, 250–1
North Dakota 87, 250–1
Northern Ireland 321, 323
Northern Ireland Act 1998 (UK) 321
Northern Territory 257
Norway 26, 269, 279–81, 331, 344, 351

occupation orders 7, 28, 138, 241, 291–4
Offences Against the Person Act 1861 (UK) 291
Ohio 87
Oklahoma 87
Oregon 267

pacs (civil pact of solidarity) 265, 270–3, 281, 283, 362, 395
pair-bonding paradigm 369
Pakistan 6, 21, 34, 185
palimony 251–3
panic buttons 311–12, 315, 386
parent-child relationship 3, 86, 101, 152
parentage 9, 30, 61–3, 84, 121
parental authority 62–3, 218, 235, 387–8
parental consent 31, 77, 159, 219, 265
Parental Kidnapping Prevention Act 1980 (US) 107
parental responsibility see children, parental responsibility for

parental rights: in Australian constitution 114; and de facto couples 241; and ECHR 339, 346; extension of 102; in Japan 226; in Russia 217–18; in South Africa 167, 169; and surrogacy 84
parenting, shared 129
parenting orders 120–1, 129–31, 134
parenting plans 101–3, 110, 131, 146
paternal authority 185, 187
paternity: in English law 217; recognition of 330; in Russian law 215–17
Penal Code (Germany) 298–9, 385
Pennsylvania 87
Platzverweis 300, 385
polygamy 21, 77, 152–5, 158, 160–2, 178, 188, 305
Portugal 17, 26–7, 280
postcard divorces 207, 378
pregnancy 9, 209, 213–14, 363, 365
prenuptial agreements 61, 70, 72, 110, 199, 382–3
Prevention of Spousal Violence and Protection of Victims Law 2001 (Japan) 302–3, 385
primary caretaker rule 98–9
private law 5, 13, 15, 344
Probate Code (California) 255
prohibited steps orders 55, 220
Promotion of Equality and Unfair Discrimination Act 2000 (South Africa) 163
Property (Relationships) Act 1976 (NZ) 137–9, 260–2, 264, 268–9, 384
Property (Relationships) Act 1984 (NSW) 257–9, 261, 268
Property (Relationships) Amendment Act 2001 (NZ) 137–8, 260, 268
Property Law Act 1958 (Victoria) 257
Property Law Act 1974 (Qld) 257
proportionality 324–5, 344, 346
prostitution 253, 263
Protection from Harrassment Act 1997 (UK) 288, 291–3
Protection from Violence Act 2000 (Germany) 298–300
protection orders 220, 292, 297–8, 302–3, 307, 311–12, 315, 350, 385–6
public law 6, 344, 348
Puerto Rico 91

qualifying contribution 249
Queensland 115, 120, 122, 257, 296

rape 8, 42, 136, 289, 299–301, 306, 336
Recognition of Customary Marriages Act 1998 (South Africa) 162–3
relationship property 138–9, 141, 260
Relationships Act 2003 (Tasmania) 257
remarriages 10, 21–2, 27, 46–7, 165, 361
Rent Act 1977 (UK) 8, 242, 333–4
reproductive technologies 81, 85, 363–4
residence orders 32, 55–6, 90, 131, 133, 220, 388
restraining orders 293, 297, 299, 302, 312, 315, 385–6
Rhode Island 87, 281
Roman-Dutch law 161, 167, 186–7
Roman law 4–5, 394
Romania 340–1, 355
Russia: and ECHR 355; in Imperial period 210; in Soviet period 5–6, 64, 202, 206, 309
Russian Constitution 1993, 205, 207, 221

same-sex couples: and adoption 165, 168, 174; in Australia 121, 257, 268; debates on 361; dissolution of 102; in English law 333–4; in France 270–3; legal recognition of 264, 281, 362, 366, 368, 370, 395–6; lesbian 264, 268; in Netherlands 281, 337; in New Zealand 261, 264, 268; and reproduction 81; in Russia 209–10; social attitudes towards 329, 371; in United States 267–8; and marriage *see* same-sex marriage
same-sex marriage: in Belgium 281, 337, 375; debate on 363; in France 272, 281; movement for 256; in Netherlands 375; in South Africa 162, 164–5, 173, 281, 374; in UK 265–7, 281, 336–8; in United States 362
Scotland 25–7, 89, 249, 265–6, 282
Second Charter of Justice 1826 (Singapore) 187, 199
separate property 18–19, 50, 69, 72, 91–3, 125, 137, 141, 146, 210, 384
separation orders 366
Serial mating 10
sex: premarital 9–10; within marriage 6–7, 45
sex equality *see* gender equality
Sexual Offences Act 2003 (UK) 291
sexualities 7–9, 118
Shariah law *see* Islamic law
Sierra Leone 159

significant harm test 292
single parent families 10, 81, 119, 226–7, 309, 359, 395
slavery 77, 90, 104, 250, 289
Slovenia 280
social law 6, 148
Social Security Act (US) 105–6
socialist countries 5, 17, 223, 375, 378
Societies for the Prevention of Cruelty to Children (SPCCs) 105–6
South Africa: African law in 150; court system in 161, 166; Constitution of 164–5, 167, 175
South Australia 115, 257–8
South Carolina 78, 87, 97
South Dakota 87
Soviet Union see Russia, in Soviet period
Spain 6, 27, 80, 92, 244, 280–1, 337, 375, 391
Special Marriage Act 1954 (India) 183
Special Procedure 8, 43–4, 124
specific issue orders 55
spousal abuse see domestic violence
spousal homicide see murder
spousal maintenance see maintenance, spousal
spouses, equality of see marriage, equality of spouses
Sri Lanka 186–7, 396–7
stalking 288, 293, 298, 306, 311, 313–14, 385–6, 396
Statute of Frauds (California) 255
Straits Settlements Divorce Ordinance 1910 (Singapore) 190
superannuation 125
surrogacy 82–6, 174, 211–13, 361, 363–4
Surrogacy Arrangements Act 1985 (UK) 83, 85, 364
Swaziland 156, 159
Sweden 23, 27, 226, 239, 269, 276, 279–80, 396
Switzerland 17, 24, 26, 280

Tanzania 159
taonga 140–1
Tasmania 115, 120, 257, 280
tender years doctrine 97
Tennessee 87, 310
Texas 87, 91–2, 251
torts 13, 313

transsexuality 7, 321, 332, 334–7
trusts: constructive 137, 242–3, 246, 252–3; family 139, 142
Turkey 14, 161, 355

Uganda 158
Ukraine 355
Uniform Marital Property Act 1983 (US) 93–4
Uniform Marriage and Divorce Act 1981 (US) 95, 100, 132
Uniform Parentage Act 1973 (US) 84, 364
United Nations Convention on the Rights of the Child 103, 128, 167, 175, 186, 207, 218–19, 321, 390
United States, Fourteenth Amendment to Constitution 77–8, 91, 98, 102
Universal Declaration of Human Rights 227, 322, 392
unreasonable behaviour 31, 45–6, 48, 90, 193, 266
Utah 77, 87

Vermont 87, 268, 280
Victims of Crime Act (USA) 311
Victoria 115, 122, 257
Virginia 76–8, 87, 250–1

Washington State 91–2, 100, 267
welfare legislation 15, 229
welfare principle see best interests principle
West Virginia 87, 250
Western Australia 115, 120–2, 280
widows and widowers 21, 138, 142, 157, 161, 177, 188, 253
Wisconsin 91–2, 94
women: and poverty 52, 380; rights of 15–16, 49, 54, 79, 90–1, 153, 160, 170, 204, 227, 366; status of in Africa 157, 160–1, 163, 173, 305; stereotypes of 116, 133
Women's Charter 1961 (Singapore) 189–92, 194, 196
women's movement 54, 58, 101, 120, 160, 296, 363
Wyoming 87

Zambia 159